T3-BOD-423

Library of
Davidson College

MAN
IN THE
UNIVERSE

Creation Motivation
Technology & History

MATTHEW J. KUST

1981
PLUTARCH PRESS
ALEXANDRIA, VIRGINIA

909
K97m

MAN IN THE UNIVERSE, copyright © 1981 by Matthew J. Kust. All rights reserved. Printed in the United States of America. No part of this book may be reproduced, stored in a retrieval system or transmitted in any form by any means, electronic, mechanical photocopying, recording or otherwise, including media depiction or presentation, without prior written permission of the publisher, except in cases of a limited number of brief quotations in books, articles or reviews. For information, address Plutarch Press, P.O. Box 5151, Alexandria, Virginia 22305

Library of Congress Cataloging in Publication Data

Kust, Matthew J.
  Man in the Universe.

  Includes index.
  1. Civilization—History. 2. Technology and Civilization. 3. Human evolution.

I. Title.

CB69.K87   909   81-50890
                             AACR2   81-7711

Distributed by: Advent Books Inc., 141 East 44th Street, New York, N.Y. 10017

ISBN: 0-89891-004-8

Dedicated to Montie
My Steadfast Helpmeet

Of the gods we believe, and of men we know, that by a necessary law of their nature they rule whenever they can. And it is not as if we were the first to make this law, or act upon it when made; we found it existing before us, and shall leave it to exist for ever after us; all we do is to make use of it, knowing that you and everybody else, having the same power as we have, would do the same as we do.

—Thucydides

Contents

Religious Cosmology—Christian, Hindu. The Universe—formation, galaxies, solar system, duration. The Earth—composition, continents, water, atmosphere, hydrologic cycle, precarious balance for life. Matter and Energy—$E = MC^2$, kinds of energy, conservation of energy, life as manifestation of energy.

The Primordial Sea—fermentation, photosynthesis, duality of life. The Invertebrates, trilobites. Transition to Land—fishes, amphibians, The Reptiles—dinosaurs, the egg, extinction. The Mammals—the womb, social behavior. Reproduction—bi-sexual replication, DNA, Darwin's "natural selection", gene mutation, man's interference with natural selection, evolution of bisexual reproduction. Universality of Life—chance and necessity, inevitability of rational being, living organism as energy engine. Life Outside Earth.

Emergence of Man—primate order, hominids. Homo Erectus—ice ages, life on the tundra. Neanderthal. Cro-Magnon—advent of agriculture. Motivation of Man—survival, intra-specie dominance. Social Organization—the hunt *cum* home, pair bonding, the hunting territory, exogamy. Man at the Dawn of History.

Role of Technology—cumulative, exponential development. Maximization of Muscular Power—Stone tools (Oldawan, Achulean, Levallois,

Mousterian and Magdalenian techniques), early missiles (spear thrower, bow and arrow), metallurgy (copper, bronze, iron). Utilization of Animal Power—invention of agriculture, domestication of animals, importance of the horse in history, slow realization of horsepower (stirrup, horse-collar, horseshoe), slavery (ancient, Graeco-Roman, colonial, Chinese, Indian).

Elemental Energy—watermill, windmill, sailing ship. Chemical Energy—coal, petroleum and gas, steam and internal combustion engines, steel and aluminum. Electrical Energy—generator, electric motor, vacuum light bulb, heat appliances. Nuclear Energy—fission and fusion reactors. Future Sources of Energy—nuclear, solar, geothermal and elemental energy. Science and Mathematics—Arabic numerals, decimal system, the zero, algebra, geometry and higher mathematics, mechanical calculators, electronic computers.

Battle of Kadesh (1296 B.C.)—Egyptian and Hittite imperialism, three-man chariots of Hittites, decline Egyptian suzerianty in Near East. Battle of Carrhae (53 B.C.)—Roman imperialism in Near East, Parthian mounted archers, defeat and decapitation of Crassus, defeat of Mark Anthony at Praaspa, evolution of missile warfare. Battle of Hastings (1066 A.D.)—mounted shock combat, feudalism, the Normans, knights versus axemen. Battles of Tabasco, Tlaxcala, Tenochtitlan (1519-1521 A.D.)—discovery of Western hemisphere in 1492, Spanish conquest of Mexico, horses and canon, construction of navy by Cortez, conquest of Peru, North America. Battle of Surigao Strait and Hiroshima (1944-45 A.D.)—radar controlled naval gunfire, atom bomb, American technological superiority. Other episodes—Philistine superiority over Israelites, chariots and iron weapons (1200-1000 B.C.). Archimedes' defense of Syracuse against Romans (212 B.C.). Mongol conquests, horsemen and gunpowder (13th century). Ch'in conquest of China during Period of Warring States (481–256 B. C.), mounted warriors and iron weapons. Mauryan empire in India (300 B.C.), iron technology.

Struggle over surplus production—fertile land, slaves, gold and silver, invention of money, mismanagement of money, gold drain to Asia during Roman times, the Crusades. European plunder of gold and silver in Americas, continuance of bullion flow to Asia, European colonial rule in Asia, reversal of bullion flow (to Europe) during Industrial Revolution, European technological superiority and world dominance.

entertainment—Roman circuses, gladiators, actors, Indian mass amusements, Western ballgames, movies, television, chess, cards.

Tokugawa), Mongol invasions (kamikaze), Portuguese, St. Francis Xavier, Christian persecution, Exclusion Orders, Western intrusion, Meiji Restoration, Imperialism, defeat by Americans.

Conclusions—Technological development and genetical programming of man militate toward destruction. Knowledge and understanding of universe and man's rightful role therein as means of salvation.

Introduction

There has been a phenomenal accumulation of knowledge the past generation or so that enables man to better understand his history. This amassment of knowledge in science, anthropology and archeology has diminished the worth of the orthodox historical approach to the comprehension of man's role on earth. No meaningful approach to a deliberation on man's reason for existence, it would seem, can be made without the integration of this new knowledge into the history of man.

Most recorded history to date has been a chronology of man's activities on earth or of some national or regional sector thereof. While such record is interesting, even meaningful to some extent, it does little to enlighten humanity on it's *raison d' etre*. It is a super-structure without a foundation. The five thousand years of recorded history is only a short span in the period of two or more million years of man's existence on earth. It is but a fleeting moment in the 3.5 billion year evolution of life on this planet. In geologic time, thus, the five millennia of recorded history is hardly measurable. A study of the history of man, it would seem, should not and cannot be confined to this short time span.

Recorded history has also been rendered less meaningful by compartmentalization. It is the history of a nation, of a continent, of an era. Not of man, not of humanity. Toynbee deplored this past approach and conducted his study on the basis of whole civilizations. He postulated that civilizations grow and die as social bodies and sought a possible reason for this historical observation in man's propensity and behavior.

Societies and civilizations, groupings of peoples in time and space, flourish and pass away, but the human race continues. It has for a million or more years. And it may for another million or more. But the history of humanity still remains to be written.

That human societies wax and wane can hardly be gainsaid. There is historical evidence. It is only recently that the fascinating Hittite Empire, fleetingly alluded to in the Bible, has become known. The Scythian civilization, for years considered to be a figment of Herodotus's imagination, has now come to light. And there is being added much archeological evidence. Noteworthy, in this respect, are the vanished Neolithic societies of Catal Huyuk, Jericho and others.

But it will require reaching back in time beyond the 5000 years of recorded history to acquire more understanding of the human phenomena. It may even profit understanding to delve into the very essence of life on earth itself and into the fundamental forces of the universe.

Equally important is the necessity to free the mind of man of accumulated psuedo-knowledge. Prior to the development of the advanced knowledge mentioned at the outset man was unable to explain rationally the physical— and even psychic-phenomena around him. One can hardly imagine the frightfulness of a bolt of lightening and the ensuing roll of thunder to early man whose intellect was already well advanced but who was not yet possessed of the meteorological knowledge to understand it. The moon with its recurring golden splendor must have awed and puzzled by its confusing remoteness and propinquity. Even more terrifying to man must have been the realization that his life was terminal. No other form of life on earth possesses this realization and it must be assumed that man did not gain this knowledge until, perhaps, 95 per cent of his evolution to date had transpired. Early man's life doubtless always met untimely death in the battle for survival in a hostile and yet uncontrolled environment.

In this early milieu, when man's intellectual development outpaced his knowledge of his reason and place on earth, he can only be excused for resort to psuedo-knowledge for a rationalization of his being. How else could he have maintained his sanity. He ascribed supernatural origin and being to the natural phenomena he did not understand. There were Gods of Thunder, Gods of Light, Gods of Darkness and so on. His fear of death was mitigated by the idea of immortality. And as intellectual development progressed, still outpacing the accumulation of knowledge, man created the unitary diety, doubtless, to instill some order in the undisciplined pantheons of the day.

The Judeo-Christian-Islamic creation of the One God will no doubt, go down in human history at some future date as the greatest mental— circuitousness of all time. In this intellectual *tour de force* man has conjured up a God in his own image and then attributed to him all of the creative powers of the universe, including the creation of Man himself—in the image of God. Notably excluded or treated with insouciance was the rest of life on earth. And even a large portion of the rest of human life. But in spite of its intellectual circuitry this portion of the psuedo-knowledge by which man has lived, and perhaps retained his sanity, has served its purpose in the development of man.

This spurious knowledge now shackles the mind of man and has set back the advancement of human thought by thousands of years. And it is not going to be easy to free man of this enslavement. While scientific knowledge has now proved that lightening and thunder result from the elemental forces of the universe and not from a God of Thunder it is far more difficult to demonstrate the non-existence of a unitary God for this involves an impossible feat of logic—proving a negative. But this, or something like it, will be necessary if man is to achieve a new understanding of his reason for existence based upon the latest advancement of human knowledge.

It should be noted, before passing on, that some other sectors of humanity should find it easier to advance to the new rationality because of their resort to a psuedo-knowledge more compatible with ultimate reality. The Hindu-Buddhist religion and culture, which actually embraces more of humanity than the Judeo-Christian-Islamic faiths, has intuitively or otherwise developed a psuedo-knowledge far more in harmony with the revelations of modern knowledge. The Hindu theology does not segregate human life from other life on earth. In fact, in the ingenious doctrine of the transmigration of the soul human and animal life is interchangeable. This even contains a certain degree of scientific plausibility. The concept of Brahma, who is the Ultimate God as distinguished from the one God, embraces all the fundamental forces of the universe, including all of the life therein. Again, a concept far more compatible with the ultimate reality now being revealed by advancing knowledge. But like all the other spurious knowledge that has sustained man in the past it too must be foresaken for a new rationality based upon the newly derived knowledge.

In this respect one can only find Toynbee deficient and wanting. After a brilliant and engaging analysis of the rise and fall of civilizations, Toynbee offers merely psuedo-knowledge in his return to Christianity for the salvation and advancement of mankind. This is no longer adequate. Mankind must achieve a new rationality based on the most advanced knowledge for it's salvation. Otherwise, there will be no salvation.

Far more perceptive in this regard is the biologist-philosopher and Nobel prize winner Jacques Monod, who has contributed greatly to the scientific knowledge of the nature and origin of life on earth. In his book *Chance and Necessity*, he deplores the psuedo-knowledge of Western civilization and advocates a new rationality based on objective scientific knowledge. In his words:

> No society before ours was ever rent by contradictions so agonizing. In both primitive and classical cultures the animist tradition saw knowledge and values stemming from the same source. For the first time in history a civilization is trying to shape itself while clinging desperately to the animist tradition to justify its values, and at the same time abandoning it as the source of knowledge, or *truth*. For their moral bases the "liberal" societies of the West still teach—or pay lip service to—a disgusting farrago of Judeo-Christian religiosity, scientific progressism, belief in the "natural" rights of man, and utilitarian pragmatism. The Marxist societies still

profess the materialist and dialectical religion of history; on the face of it a more solid moral framework than the liberal societies boast, but perhaps more vulnerable by virtue of the very rigidity that has made its strength up until now. However this may be, all these systems rooted in animism exist at odds with objective knowledge, face away from truth, and are strangers and fundamentally *hostile* to science, which they are pleased to make use of but for which they do not otherwise care. The divorce rate is so great, the lie so flagrant, that it afflicts and rends the conscience of anyone provided with some element of culture, a little intelligence, and spurred by that moral questioning which is the source of all creativity. It is an affliction, that is to say, for all those among mankind who bear or will come to bear the responsibility for the way in which society and culture shall evolve.

Equally penetrating in this connection is the wisdom of Einstein, who found his "religious" experience by contemplating the mysteries of the universe, and the existence of life in it. He wrote in the *New York Times* on November 9, 1930:

> ... there is found a third level of religious experience . . .I will call it the cosmic religious sense. . . . which recognizes neither dogma nor God made in man's image . . . . A God who rewards and punishes is. . . unthinkable. . . . I assert that the cosmic religious experience is the strongest and the noblest driving force behind scientific research. . . . a deep faith in the rationality of the structure of the world. . . . The ethical behavior of man is better based on sympathy, education and social relationships and requires no support from religion.

An attempt will be made in this analysis of history to interpret and reevaluate the story of man on the basis of the revelations of the most advanced knowledge. Volume I will set forth the thesis and discuss generally the facts of history and prehistory within its context. Volume II will consist of a series of Notes on important aspects of the thesis. The importance of the horse in the history of man is not generally appreciated. The horse was the first most effective extension of the power of man through the use of energy outside himself. It increased tremendously man's ability to dominate his environment, other men and things in general. Empires were created, nations were conquered, and cathedrals were built through the facility of the horse. The invention of the horse collar for more effective use of the horse power in agriculture in 10th century France, perhaps more than anything else, made the beautiful Gothic Cathedrals of Europe possible. Without the horse collar there may not have been a Chartres! But one must add, that without the stirrup there may not have been as much slaughter in war during medieval times either. So it goes!

There will be other similar Notes on Money, Slavery, Energy and the like. Volume II will be open ended with Notes added periodically as time and research permit.

Thesis

The view of history to be propounded here is predicated on the fact that man is merely a part of the fundamental energy of the universe. He is, to be sure, a most unique part thereof as, after several million years of evolution, he has achieved a high degree of rationality so that he now possesses the capacity to contemplate the whole. No other universal force, possesses this faculty. If there is life on other planets, for instance, a moon of Jupiter, it is doubtless of a lesser order of evolution and without the power to reason. And it is only open to speculation whether there is rational life outside this solar system so no account can be taken of it in any study of the existence of man.

It is now reasonably well understood that life on earth evolved out of the interaction of inorganic matter and the basic energy of the universe. Life is, therefore a manifestation of this fundamental energy. All forms of life on earth until the evolution of man could only exert their own muscular energy for survival. The strong of body, the fleet of foot or wing, those with special evolutionary attributes such as teeth, claws, armor and the like were able to defend or attack accordingly for survival. Man, however, through an extraordinary gift of nature—the power to reason—was able to draw upon energy outside himself. He was able to extend the power of his hand, so to speak, through the rational capacity of his brain. In due course of time he was able to dominate all other forms of life on earth and adjust to the environment for unchallenged survival. And when he felt secure against other forms of life and the master of his environment he began to direct the external energy at his command against his fellow man. When and why this occurred will be dealt with later but it does not really matter for it has been man's capacity and propensity, certainly during the span of recorded history and doubtless many millennia earlier. Men organized in tribes, states or nations which could marshall superior force would dominate other societies of men.

Technology, therefore, is the key to the understanding of history. Man's unique capacity to augment and marshall energy outside himself through tools and machines is the central fact of his life. Moreover technological innovation is cumulative. It has escalated from the stone hand axe a few million years ago to the nuclear bomb today. But as man's command over more energy grew through technological innovation so did human strife. That is why so much of history is an account of war. There has been a war in the human community every three years during the span of recorded history! History does not record how many humans lost their lives in war. But it is known that more than 40 million lives were lost through war during the generation after the start of World War II, which attests to the fact of technological accumulation and man's undiminished propensity to use that technology against his own kind.

Man's proclivity to direct the energy at his command against his fellow man would appear to be a natural function of his manifestation of energy. Like other forms of life on earth man is structured genetically to fulfill the law of survival of the fittest. Life's genetical programming for survival embodies a two fold expression. The first is interspecial, exerted against other forms of life (by carnivores mainly) for food supply. Man owes his development to this motivating factor. Today it is no longer a problem for him as he derives his meat supply from animal husbandry. The second is intra-special dominance that forms the basis of the hierarchial societies of mankind. The dominance instinct was structured into the evolutionary process for the propagation of the genes of the specie best suited for its survival. The instinct to dominate is no longer necessary for man as he is now supreme on earth. But the propensity to dominate others continues to motivate man and his history has been largely a story of men dominating other men and societies of men ruling other societies.

Man has not only developed the capacity to utilize energy external to himself, he has, in addition, learned to accumulate and store this external energy for future use. This quest for stored energy, or wealth, has been a chief cause of strife among men and has to date known no bounds.

The story of man is not all war. He has probably spent as much time in peace as he has at war. But how well he lived in peace has been equally dependent on his technology. The first law of survival is food. How well he ate and how much time he had to devote to the effort of food supply depended on his technology. For, perhaps, ninety-five per cent of his existence to date man was wholly occupied with this function. His technology had not progressed to the degree where he was able to store energy for future need. It was only after the discovery and development of agriculture and animal husbandry (dated about 8000 years ago) that man produced a surplus of energy beyond his current need.

The production of this surplus energy to be stored for future use freed mankind for other pursuits, the primary one being the development of new technology for greater command over the basic energy of the universe. This process obeys a hyperbolic curve. There has been more technological accumulation, reckoned certainly in terms of increasing command over energy, the past 100 years than the entire preceding million years or more of man's existence. And it is not unreasonable to expect this technological accumulation to continue until man is able to harness directly the ultimate source of all energy, the sun, and its counterpart the nuclear energy of inorganic matter on earth.

The leisure afforded man by technological innovation has, of course, not been devoted entirely to the creation of more technology. Man has used much of it for the enjoyment of life. It should be noted hastily that this has been possible only recently (say the last 10,000 years) in the history of man. For millions of years he was in the grip of the law of survival that little or no time was available for enjoyment. And how much joy and happiness there is in life today may well be open to question. Perhaps there is great truth in Thoreau's dictum that "The mass of men lead lives of quiet desperation."

Nonetheless, technology has given more leisure and man has used that leisure to create things of beauty. Music, painting, sculpture, architecture, textiles, cuisine and other pleasures to his senses. But these are merely the by-products, or corollary benefits, of technological innovation the main purpose of which is to fulfill his primary function as a manifestation of the fundamental energy of the universe.

A word, before concluding, on religion. Man has probably expended more energy on temples, monuments, graves and other efforts relating to his religious beliefs than on any other pursuit except war. Why? The answer can also be found in the law of survival. Obviously nothing in nature dictates or warrants it. But as man's rationality outpaced his wisdom and understanding of the universe and life in it he resorted to psuedo-knowledge to explain certain phenomena about his life. And nothing, perhaps, terrified him more than the realization that his life was terminal, that death was certain. He conjured up a life after death to mitigate the fear and unacceptability of death.

To assure his life after death—the safe passage of his soul into heaven, paradise or the like—man propitiated his God or Gods, provided for the appropriate burial of his body and made various related arrangements. An aberration related to the basic law of survival. Here too it should be noted that those men who had the greatest command over stored energy or wealth were able to provide best for themselves in this respect.

In war or in peace, therefore, the story of man has been found in his technology. Technology gave him command over energy outside himself. He has used this tremendous power to dominate all other life on earth, his environment and finally his fellow man. His technological capacity also afforded him the time and energy to build cultures and civilizations, that is, the finer and enjoyable aspects of his life on earth. Man's technology, his ability to utilize energy outside himself, is then the fundamental factor of his history.

Some may find this thesis unacceptable. They may feel it demotes and denigrates man. Particularly those conditioned to view man as a creature of devine origin and the universe as his special usufruct. It is respectfully submitted that this is not true. The natural scheme of things is far more beautiful and inspiring than anything conjured up by religion. To paraphrase Francois Muriac "What this Professor says is far more incredible than what we poor Christians believe." No person of intellect and culture can contemplate the complex and orderly structure of the universe, the miracle of the evolution of life and the super miracle of the derivation of a rational being out of this milieu without spiritual effect that renders pale by comparison any religious experience. Nature's wisdom pales into insignificance the grandest designs of the Gods of man. And in the universal scheme of things man is still Nature's noble artifact.

I
The Universe

When and how did it all begin. It would appear that it was not by an act of divine creation on Sunday, October 23, 4004 B. C. at precisely 9 A. M. as per Bishop Ussher's annotation in 1650 A. D. to the King James version of the Bible. Yet Western man, until quite recently, lived by this dogma for some three centuries. And the vast majority of people in this sector of mankind still live out their brief sojourn on earth knowing and understanding little else.

On the other hand, Hindu cosmology intuitively comes nearer to the conclusions of modern astronomy. Hindu religious lore views the existence of the universe as cyclic. Brahma, the creator, recreates the universe every 8.64 billion years. This is called the Kalpa, a day and a night in the existence of Brahma. This cycle repeats itself 3600 times (360 times a year for 100 years) before Brahma dies and everything becomes chaos again. Thereafter a new Brahma is born and the cycles repeat themselves. There are also epochs within these cycles representing eras of existence. Although the time involved is at variance with modern knowledge the Hindus, at least, reckoned the existence of the universe in billions of years, as is now known to be the case.

Astronomers, however, estimate the universe originated about 15 billion years ago. The earth is 4.5 billion years old. Unlike the astronomers, geologists can be more certain with respect to the age of the earth as they possess relatively accurate means of measurement of the earth's age through the use of radioactive elements. These elements have a reliable and measurable loss of radioactivity. It is reckoned in terms of half-lives, based on the number of years that the element loses one half of its radioactivity. Thus by comparing the ratio of the radioactive atoms to ordinary atoms of the element or the resultant atoms after loss of radioactivity the age of the rock, fossil or other material containing the element can be determined. Carbon 14 is the element most frequently used in this connection because of the importance of carbon in all living things. But it has a half-life of only 5,730 years. Thus, while a most useful tool for archeologists and anthropologists, it is not adequate for the geologist.

Fortunately there are other elements with longer and more adequate half-lives. Potassium decays into argon with a half-life of 1.3 billion years; uranium into lead with a half-life of 2.25 billion years; thorium into lead and rubidrium into strontium with half-lives of 14 billion and 60 billion years respectively. Geologists have found old rocks on earth approximately 3.6 billion years old with these measuring devices. But the earth came into existence in a gaseous and fluid state much earlier. Through similar measurement of meteorite fragments, originating at the same time as the earth, geologists now generally agree that the earth evolved some 4.5 billion years ago. Recent measurements on moon rocks also tend to confirm this conclusion.

It is now believed—and reasonably well supported by empirical knowledge—that present existence began with a tremendous cosmic explosion, of a thermonuclear type, about 15 billion years ago which hurled cosmic debris into space. This cosmic debris was thereafter aggregated into huge swirling clouds of gas by the force of gravity known as the galaxies. But the gravitational process also operated within the galaxies to form stars like the sun. Each star in turn acquired its own system of planets, satellites, asteroids, meteorites and comets. Some of these planets captured portions of the coalescing cosmic debris as satellites—like the earth's moon—by the same force of gravity. In fact, this neat and regular arrangement of matter carries through the whole universe down to the tiny atom.

The primeaval explosion still possesses an outward thrust. The galaxies continue flying outward and away from each other. This is referred to as the theory of the expanding universe. The forces of gravity which held the original mass together have not yet been able to overcome the energy imparted to the cosmic debris by the explosion of the mass. It is believed that this will transpire, however, in another 30 billion years or so when the galaxies will reverse their flight into space and start to return toward a common center under the force of gravity. The entire cycle will embrace a period of some 80 billion years or so! As all this coalescing matter is concentrated ever more by the force of gravity extreme temperatures will again be generated inside the mass to set off another mammoth explosion and the 80 billion year cycle will start anew. A new universe will be born!

There is at this time, by no means general agreement on the theory. While the foregoing was the prevailing view among astrophysicists until 1970 many now feel there is insufficient evidence of any slowing of the outward thrust of the galaxies. Further understanding of the universe must await a better view into space, which can only take place at some non-terrestrial site unobstructed by the earth's atmosphere. It is doubtful, however, that more precise knowledge of the universe will effect appreciably man's life on earth.

There is still much the astronomers and astrophysicists do not understand about the universal scheme of things. But there is also much that they have been able to observe, verify and understand. It was only in the 16th century that Nicholas Copernicus, a brilliant Polish lawyer and astronomer, began to disabuse the mind of Western man that the sun revolved around the earth. The ancient Greeks, Hindus and others reached this conclusion much earlier. In fact, most Europeans at that time still thought the world was flat. A few decades earlier Columbus had difficulty recruiting sailors for a trip to reach India westward across the Atlantic as many feared they would fall off the edge of the world somewhere out in the ocean.

Little progress, however, could be made until Galileo in 1609 developed the telescope. Though Galileo's telescope represented a huge step forward centuries passed before the skies could be penetrated by very powerful instruments such as the 100 inch telescope on Mount Wilson and the 200 inch pyrex disc on Palomar Mountain. The latter was placed into operation only in 1947. These giant telescopes coupled with modern photography permitted a leap forward in the understanding of the universe. Further technological progress in this respect for deeper penetration into the universe does not seem possible because of the blurring obstruction of the earth's atmosphere. But the placing of equally powerful telescopic equipment on the moon or a satellite station where the view is free of an atmosphere can be the next leap forward in further study and understanding of the universe. This too will doubtless come to pass. Then too, other astro-tools not dependent upon light may be developed for deeper study from the earth. Much progress is already being achieved by radio telescopes and specialized electronic equipment. But nothing will perhaps substitute for an atmosphere-free view with a powerful telescope.

There are millions of galaxies in the universe still thrusting outward from the center of the primeval thermonuclear explosion. Each galaxy is a disc type swirl of cosmic debris out of which stars, like our solar system, are being constantly formed. The galaxies resemble a Fourth of July pinwheel flinging out long spiral streamers of interstellar dust and gas as they rotate around a hub or center. The Milky Way, to which our solar system belongs, is 100,000 light years wide and 25,000 light years thick. A light year is the distance traveled by light in one year. This translates to almost 6 trillion miles! And the Milky Way is not the largest galaxy but most are smaller. Though most galaxies assume this spiral disc characteristic some do not show much spiral movement. And a few, about 3 percent, are in an irregular shape in which no new stars are forming. Their energy appears to be mostly spent.

The galaxies can and do collide in their outward thrust into space. Such cosmic accidents must be truly fearsome spectacles, second, perhaps, only to the primeaval explosion. Fortunately for man the Milky Way exists rather isolated in space. The nearest sizeable galaxy, the notable Andromeda, is some 2.7 million light years away. Andromeda is one of the three galaxies visible with the naked eye even though it is a quintillion miles from earth. Its sighting and identification was first recorded in 964 A. D. by the Persian astronomer Al Sufi. The other two are small but closer galaxies known as the Magellanic Clouds, named after Ferdinand Magellan the first man to circumnavigate the earth in the early 16th century. These galaxies can be seen only in the southern hemisphere and were first sighted by Portuguese sea captains in the 16th century.

Stars form and die within the galaxies. Their life cycle is reasonably predictable but not precisely definable. Stars are not all alike because of their accidental genesis. They differ in size and burning rate. As already alluded to, gravitational forces inside the swirling galaxy, particularly in the dust and gas streamers, concentrate the cosmic debris until the atoms form a critical mass for the start of a thermonuclear reaction. For a time there is a struggle between the outward thrust of the released nuclear energy and the inner pull of gravity until a stability is achieved for a sustained nuclear fire. The star continues to burn its nuclear fuel for billions of years until an imbalance transpires from the concentration of heavy by-products of the nuclear fire, such as heavy helium ash, settling inside the core causing an eventual explosion or collapse which step by step leads to the death of the star—a dampening, so to say, of the nuclear fire. The nuclear physics involved in the explosion or collapse and death of a star is extremely complex with parts yet not fully understood and it need not detain us here.

The amount of mass concentrated by the gravitational forces at work in the galaxy and the mix of elements in the mass determine the intensity and duration of the star. The hottest and smallest are blue stars, the slower burning and biggest are red stars, with the yellow stars in between. These are not watertight categories as the stars range in between in varying shades of blue-white, red-yellow and the like. The sun is a medium yellow star. The life span of these stars range from a few to over a hundred billion years. The suns' life expectancy is 10 billion years.

Most stars eventually collapse but a few of the large ones explode toward the end of their life span. This phenomena is misnamed nova and supernova as it was first thought to be the birth of a star rather than its death throes. Supernovas occur only once every few centuries in any one galaxy. But since there are billions of galaxies astronomers observe and record several supernovae each year.

Supernovas have occured in the Milky Way in 1604, 1572 and 1054 A. D. The last, the first recorded by man, was noted for posterity by Chinese astronomers. This explosion occurred in the Crab Nebula where astronomers today observe the dying remains of the exploded star. Small stellar explosions are called novae. They are far more frequent but much less forceful.

More normal is the collapse of a star. In its decline a star first bloats enormously in size causing its surface to cool. Its color changes from the normal yellow, white or blue first to orange and then to red. Although red signifies it is burning cooler, enormous heat is given off at this stage because of its immensely greater size. This tremendous loss of heat eventually cools the star and it shrinks into dwarfdom. The last days of the star are passed as a white dwarf. Eventually the white star burns out leaving a black cinder behind. All energy is now spent. Our sun today is in mid passage in its life span and is expected to peter away in 5 billion years.

Even the exploding star—supernova—eventually collapses as not all of its matter is thrown off in the burst. But they do so with a difference. A supernova either throws off or leaves behind a concentrated ball of neutrons about 10 miles in diameter, rotating to a thousand times per second and pouring out radiant energy, particularly in the X-ray range, at an incredible rate. The powerful magnetic field generated by the neutron star channels the radiant energy emitted into narrow beams which hit the earth with the pulsating regularity of the rotating star. Hence, they are also called pulsars. Pulsars eventually slow down and become inert as their energy dissipates.

The Crab pulsar was the first identified in 1968. It is a leftover of the supernova noted by Chinese astronomers in 1054 A. D. Since 1968 more than a hundred pulsars have been discovered. The physics connected with a neutron star or pulsar is staggering to the mind of man. The enormous forces of gravity have concentrated the matter in a pulsar so that a teaspoon of the neutron star material would weigh a billion tons! Matter of such density if dropped from a man's hand (say) in the middle of the United States would pass through the earth and emerge on the other side. If the matter of the earth could be reduced to an equivalent density found in a pulsar the earth would shrink to a sphere only 328 feet in diameter!

The latest discovery in cosmic phenomena is the black hole. It is something even denser than the pulsar. The gravitational forces are so great that no energy can escape it. It cannot be seen or heard by astronomical instruments. Whence its designation as a black hole. But that does not mean nothing is there. In a way, it is the ultimate manifestation of Einstein's theory $E = MC^2$. A black hole is pure M. Astronomers believe that a black hole is the final stage in the collapse of a large star. Only a large massive star could produce the necessary material for the generation of the gravitational forces required to overcome all the energy in the residual matter of the dying star.

A black hole can only be detected indirectly. A black hole by its nature will attract and submerge into its vortex any cosmic matter that comes within its enormous gravitational pull. Hence, if it comes near another star it will draw off matter and energy from it. As the captured gases spiral into the vortex intense heat is generated causing the emission of much radiant energy in the form of X-rays. Hence, the presence of enormous X-ray emissions in the vicinity of a star is an indication of a black hole. Astronomers have now observed such phenomena in Cygnus X-1.

It may be that there is a black hole—an ultimate black hole—in the universe which will eventually suck into its vortex all the spent matter of the burned out galaxies. If the expanding universe theory proves valid there will have to be found the source of the tremendous gravitational forces required to attract all the matter in the universe, after its energy is spent, back to its original source. This is going to prove a monumental challenge to astronomers and astrophysicists.

This cosmic process apparented our solar system. The sun is one of the billion stars in the Milky Way galaxy. It is situated about 30,000 light years from the hub of the galaxy. Its nearest neighbor is 4 light years away—about 24 trillion miles. The sun was born about 5 billion years ago after the Milky Way was formed.

It was formed out of an amorphous cloud of dust and gas like that still being formed. Astronomers are able to observe the process of formation now and can be more certain on how our solar system evolved. While the Milky Way is thought to have consisted of pure hydrogen in its beginning, other elements were created by the birth and death of the earliest stars so that after 5 billion years or so the interstellar clouds could truly be labeled *dust* and gas. Restructuring the atom from its simple form in hydrogen and helium to an ever more complex arrangement of protons and electrons up through the iron element could transpire only in the immense heat generated by a dying star. Restructuring it beyond the iron element could transpire only in the even higher heat generated by an exploding star or supernova.

Eddies in the cloud started to aggregate this interstellar dust and gas around centers of gravity which eventually organized the cloud into a flat revolving disc with a growing center and concentric circles of streaming cosmic debris. The center was destined to become the sun and the concentric streams of dust and gas, eventually themselves swirling into concentrated centers of their own, were destined to become the planets. The heaviest concentration (99.6 percent) of the interstellar dust and gas was in the sun. This consisted of pure hydrogen, an atom most susceptible to nuclear fusion. The heavier elements tended to rotate further away from the center and eventually formed the planets. Thermonuclear reaction set in as the hydrogen in the center increased in temperature under the impact of gravity. The solar furnace grew hotter and hotter from red to orange to yellow where it reached stability for sustained nuclear reaction. The radiant energy of the sun drove off the gases surrounding the inner planets—Mercury, Venus, Earth and Mars—which promoted their solidification around the heavier elements—iron and other mineral rocks. In the asteroid belt the mineral elements failed to solidify for some unknown reason and they circle the sun as separate lumps of matter. Outside the asteroid belt where the sun's radiant energy is weaker the planets retained their gases and stabilized as larger and lighter planets. Saturn is so light it would float on water. Some of the planets captured satellites in their gravitational fields, but none as large as the earth's moon. Jupiter and Saturn have 22 satellites between them. Finally there are the eccentric comets which do not fall into the single plane circular orbit pattern of the planets and asteroids but follow elliptical orbits around the sun taking them to the outer limits of the solar system. Comets consist of frozen gases and grit whose streaming tails ignite while circling the sun. There are some 100 billion of them, any one of which could collide with the earth or other planets and perhaps did in the past in their erratic traverse through the solar system.

The sun, like any star, is destined to die. While astrophysicists cannot be sure precisely when this will occur, as they have no means at this time to measure the amount of hydrogen still left in the solar furnace, they are generally in agreement the death throes will set in about 5 billion years from now. Since the sun is a medium sized star it can be expected to burn for 10 billion years before its stability is overcome by a heavy accumulation of helium ash in its core. When this occurs the sun will bloat into an enormous red ball which will cover three-fourths of the sky on earth. It's heat will be so intense it will melt everything and extinguish all life on earth. After some two billion years the sun will start to shrink into a white dwarf and exist in this ever cooling stage for billions of years. Then, with all it's energy spent, it will turn into a cinder in space. During this stage the earth will be covered with ice as all it's water will be in a frozen state.

The earth is the most fortunate of the planets. It is comfortably spaced where the radiant energy strikes with moderation. Just hot enough to dissipate the poisonous gases that embrace the outer planets and just cool enough to permit a solid state of it's surface. And, the first essential of life— water—is able to exist in its useful state. It resides in what has come to be termed the "life belt" of a star, that is, for life as it is known on earth.

Before turning to an understanding of the earth, a pause must be made for an admiration of the universe. The awesome energy manifesting itself in a cosmic structure of logical development can only strike man, a puny manifestation of this universal energy, with subject reverence. Even the occasional asymmetry adds to its logic. One can only empathize with Einstein—that the contemplation of the mysteries of the universe is the greatest spiritual experience available to man.

At this time, if one can be forgiven the resort to levity, it may be appropo to note a cartoon that appeared in the April 26, 1974 issue of the *Wall Street Journal*. The cartoon depicts a scene inside a Palomar type observatory with an astronomer addressing his assistant who is having a midnight snack while scanning the sky through the powerful telescope. The astronomer says "It just doesn't seem right for you to contemplate the universe and eat a baloney sandwich at the same time."

Further reference to Hindu cosmology might be in order again before leaving the subject of the universe. If the theory of the expanding universe proves to be the ultimate truth, as it appears it will at this stage of learning about it, one's mind cannot fail to be titillated by how closely this correlates with the Hindu view of the creation of the world. In the *Matsya Purana*

Vishnu (an incarnation of Brahma) is described as the lord of the Whirlpool that sucks back all that it has once produced and is the Death of the Universe. The ancient Hindus believed the universe passes through recurring cycles for all eternity. There is no finite beginning nor will there be a finite end. Moreover, there are cycles within cycles in the universe. The shortest is 8.64 billion years, the Kalpa, or day and night in the life of Brahma. Actually this is not too far off on the expected life of the solar system. The largest cycle, the 100 year life of Brahma, is 311,040 billion years (8.6 billion × 360 days × 100 years). This is, to be sure, considerably longer than the expected 80 billion year life of the universe. But there is an intermediate cycle—a year in the life of Brahma—of about 3000 billion years.

Man cannot be certain in his present stage of incomplete knowledge that there are not other or that there have not been previous universes in space and that, as a group, they obey a greater cycle. Already astronomers seem to be observing remote cosmic phenomena that might be outside this universe or leftover from a previous universe. Britain's Jodrell Bank Observatory spotted a pulsar in 1970 which is believed to be 45 billion years old. This universe is thought to be only 15 billion! If the longer age of JP-1953 proves out it would have to belong to another older universe. It would be a phenomenal feat of human intellectuality if the ancient Hindus intuitively deduced an even greater cosmos than the one now thought to exist.

It is not, however, surprising that the Hindus should have thought in such grand concepts. They comprise, doubtless, one of the most intelligent sectors of mankind. It is not generally recognized that modern science owes a heavy debt to the mathematical genius of the Hindus. It was the Hindus who founded the mathematics on which modern science depends with the invention of the decimal system, the concept of zero, and the so-called Arab numerals. Western man mistakenly attributes this mathematical genius to the Arabs. The Arabs themselves referred to mathematics as *hindisat* (the Indian art). The Arabs merely conveyed this higher mathematics to Western Asia and Europe. More on this later.

The mathematics of the Graeco-Roman world was hopelessly inadequate and cumbersome for any scientific advance. Imagine trying to write one trillion in Roman numerals. Hence, early Mediterranean civilizations had to think small. On the other hand, the minds of the Hindus were unfettered by underdeveloped mathematics. They were able to comprehend, intuitively to be sure, a universe of grand design, more compatible with the universe modern knowledge now reveals to man.

THE EARTH

The earth is a small planet revolving about a medium sized star, of which there are billions in each galaxy, situated in a moderate sized galaxy, of which there also are billions, in an immense universe of which there may be more than one. That is man's home in the universal scheme of things. It is needful, therefore, to understand it well. Yet man's technology finds it easier to look into the far limits of space than to plumb the inner depths of the earth.

The earth is a beautiful spectacle from outer space. Colored satellite photographs show a many splendored sphere of verdant green vegetation, azure blue waters and billowy white puffs of clouds floating above. These colors represent the essentials of life on earth.

The heavier elements of the nascent solar system were captured by the gravity center that was to be the earth. After the nuclear furnace in the sun ignited, most of the lighter elements were driven off by the radiant energy of the sun, leaving the earth with a wide mix of the 92 elements. As it solidified the friction of the shrinking process and the heat resulting from the decaying radioactive elements raised the temperature of the earth a point where, geologists believe, the entire mass was molten. As this solidifying process diminished the earth began to cool and form an upper crust of solid matter. The core of the earth still remains molten with a temperature between 4000°–8000° F.

The earth is the heaviest planet in the solar system. But it is not of even density throughout its sphere. The core, which is 2175 miles thick, is composed of molten iron and nickle. Next is the mantle, some 1800 miles in depth, its composition is still poorly understood. The mantle is in a molten or plastic state. Atop this mantle floats the crust only a few miles thick. It is mostly solid rock, but of lesser density than the mantle.

The temperature of the crust increases greatly with depth. Two miles down it exceeds the boiling point of water. If water percolates to this depth it issues forth to the surface in the form of geysers, as seen in the Yellowstone National Park and elsewhere. This may one day be a potent source of heat energy for man. Geothermal electric power plants are already in operation on an experimental basis.

The rock in the earth's crust is of three types; igneous, sedimentary and metamorphic. Igneous rocks originated from molten rock called magma issuing to the earth's surface from volcanoes and fissures in the earth's crust. As it cooled it assumed various forms from smooth basalt to grainy granite. Sedimentary rocks were formed from sand and clay washed into lakes or ocean floors where they hardened under pressure into a soft rock like sandstone, limestone, shale or dolomite. It is in these rocks that fossils of early life are found. When these soft rocks became subject to even greater pressure and heat as they were imbedded deeper in the earth's crust they underwent further recomposition into harder rocks. Sandstone changed to quartzite, limestone into marble and so forth. Slate, schist and gneiss are other common metamorphic rocks.

Rock is not hospitable to life. Erosion and weathering however, converts it into soil in which plants thrive and form the essential link to solar energy for life on earth. Soil is rock broken down into fine particles in the form of sand and clay. In the beginning the source could only be igneous rock. Later of course, it could by any of the three basic rocks of the earth's crust. The agents of erosion are the wind and rain. The hydrologic cycle is the primary process for this purpose. As water is evaporated from the oceans, lakes and other places by the sun and dropped in the form of rain and snow on the continents, its flow back to the seas constantly erodes small particles from the rocks of the earth's crust and deposits these particles in the valleys of the land and the continental shelves of the oceans. These ground or soil deposits vary from place to place and accumulate most readily in the valleys between mountain ridges of the earth's crust. They form the fertile river valleys which became the bread baskets of the earth. In some of these valleys or plains the soil is very thick. The alluvium in the Gangetic Plain, for example, is some 2000 feet deep!

The rocks (and soil) of the earth's crust are primarily mixtures of 8 of the 92 elements; oxygen 47 per cent, silicon 28 per cent, aluminum 8 per cent, iron 5 per cent, and sodium, calcium, potassium and magnesium constituting the balance of less than 4 per cent each. The oxygen-silicon compounds predominate, but these 8 elements combine chemically to form nearly 2000 minerals in the earth's crust.

The earth's crust floats on top of a liquid and plastic sphere which increases in heat with depth until it reaches temperatures near 6000° F at it's center. This internal heat is conducted to the surface where it maintains a temperature of 68° F, a condition compatible with life on earth. Yet there appears to be no danger of the internal heat melting the surface, as the crust acts as a good insulator to contain the heat. At the same time the inside of the earth appears to be cooling off as radioactivity diminishes relieving the possibility of the onset of nuclear reaction inside the sphere.

But as the earth cools it creates other problems and difficulties. The crust folds and wrinkles like a drying prune. The result is earthquakes, eruptions of magma through fissures in the crust and, most important, a rearrangement of the continents and oceans.

Three hundred and fifty years ago Sir Frances Bacon called critical attention to the jig-saw puzzle fit of Africa and South America along their Atlantic coastlines. Since then it had puzzled many scientists but it was not until the 1920's that a German meteorologist named Alfred Wegener came forth with the theory of continental drift to explain this curious phenomena. He postulated the existence of a single continent eons ago which he called Pangaea sitting in a single ocean named Panthalassa on the earth's surface. Eventually as the earth cooled and shrunk Pangaea cracked and began separating to form the Atlantic ocean between the parting continent. At first he was ridiculed, as so often happens in cases of genuine genius, but soon plant and animal fossil evidence tended to support such bygone separation of the land masses. Notable in this connection were the Rudists (invertebrates extinct for 100 million years or so) which have been found in such unconnected areas as the Caribbean, the Pyrrenes and the Himalayas.

Greater confirmation of the theory resulted from the American Navy's program to map the ocean floors after World War II. The U. S. Navy found a steep Mid-Atlantic ridge and continental shelves beneath the Atlantic coastlines which fit together, even more precisely than the coastlines of Africa and South America, all the way from Iceland to the tips of the two continents. The ridge, moreover, is capped by a long slit emitting heat and lava from the inner depths of the earth. Recent confirmation was given to the theory by the rise of the new island of Surtsey off the coast of Iceland. Formerly skeptical geologists began to subscribe to the drifting or floating continents and it is now the generally accepted view of the earth's surface.

The continents are the lighter portion of the earth which floated to the top and solidified like a cork on top of the plastic mantle. At first the crust formed an undivided continent, but as the earth continued to cool and shrink the solid continent cracked and started to shift apart on the plastic mantle. These cracks are beneath the oceans and girdle the earth in curved ridges. The pattern has been likened to the seams of a baseball. Heat and lava or molten magma issues forth from these ridges as the earth continues to shrink and the once solid crust keeps spreading on the plastic mantle. The spreading is very slow only about one inch a year. The bottom of the crust is by no means smooth as it shifts slowly on the mantle. The mountainous areas of the continents go down into the mantle as much as they rise above the surface, much as a floating object on water, so that the bottom of the crust is undulated, like its surface, as it shifts over the mantle.

Earthquakes are also the result of this movement of the crust on the mantle. As the erupting ridges push the continents apart the shifting crust has to go somewhere. This caused faults to develop in the earth's crust with one edge sliding under the other. The most prominent is the San Andreas fault which runs along the Pacific coast line of South and North America. In this collision one edge or plate of the crust is pushed down into the mantle where it melts, while the other plate is pushed up higher toward the surface to form mountains such as the Andes. This collision of the plates of the crust causes periodic earthquakes along the San Andreas fault. Volcanoes of molten magma also erupt along these faults. There are a half dozen or so of these crustal plates with overlapping edges or faults. Most of them have continents on their surfaces. Another major fault runs above the Mediterranean across the Mid-East, beneath the Himalayas to Indonesia in the Far East. The Himalayas have been pushed nearly six miles above sea level by the plate on which the subcontinent of India rides.

It would appear then that the composition of the earth will be hospitable to man for some time to come. It possesses just enough internal heat to permit water to remain on its surface in a liquid state—a very essential requirement for life. There would appear to be no danger of overheating through increased radio-activity or nuclear reaction to melt the crust. On the contrary the earth seems to be cooling instead, causing further cracking and shifting of the surface. This causes regional problems to man's habitation but nothing of a cataclysmic nature is expected. The continents drift apart ever so imperceptibly but, beyond adding a mile to a transatlantic voyage from time to time, causes man no difficulty. Man is able to rely quite confidently on the stability of the earth's composition for a long life on his planet.

Equally important for life on earth is the atmosphere. Plants would not thrive without it's carbon dioxide. Nor would there be any soil for them without the hydrologic cycle of the atmosphere. Animals cannot exist without plants. Moreover, animals need the oxygen in the air for their life process. And human existence would not be possible without the ozone layer of the upper atmosphere to absorb the lethal ultra-violet rays of the sun.

The atmosphere is much more complex than generally thought. It is composed of several layers. The first extending 5 to 10 miles up is called the troposphere. It is a mixture of air, water vapor and dust particles. This is the life zone. Its density permits flight by birds, insects and even man through the triumph of his technology. Air is a mixture of nitrogen 78 per cent, oxygen 21 per cent, argon 0.9 per cent, carbon dioxide 0.03 per cent, with half a dozen or so other gases comprising the balance. It has the capacity to attract and hold evaporated water. The troposphere is where weather, so vital and important to life, manifests itself.

The stratosphere occupies the next 10 to 15 miles. It has a lower sulphate level and an upper ozone level. Ozone is heavy oxygen—each molecule contains three atoms of oxygen. It is formed when an electrical charge or ultra-violet rays act upon ordinary oxygen. Its order is often noticeable near electric generators or ultra violet-lights. Its importance in the upper atmosphere cannot be overexaggerated for it serves as a screen of the sun's ultra-violet rays which would destroy life on earth if permitted to pass unchecked through the atmosphere.

The neosphere, next in ascendancy, occupies another 10 to 15 miles. Its service to man is to incinerate most of the meteors approaching the earth from outer space. The ionosphere which lays in the atmosphere between 50 and 350 miles up is important to man as it reflects certain radio waves back to earth, making short-wave radio communication possible. It also acts as a trap for sub-atomic particles from the sun. Finally, there is the exosphere, about 200 miles thick, of rarified air tapering off to nothingness after 600 miles above the surface of the earth. In addition to its function as a protective screen against the sun's lethal particles and rays the atmosphere also provides a blanket of insulation to keep the heat generated by the earth and absorbed from the sun from escaping the surface.

If one were to single out a substance on earth on which almost everything depends, without which there could be no life, it would be water. Water is colorless, tasteless and odorless. But it is ubiquitous. It is everywhere. It covers nearly three-fourths of the earth's surface in the form of oceans, lakes, rivers, ice caps, and glaciers. There are some 326 million cubic miles of it. All but 3 per cent is in the oceans! Of this small fraction 2 per cent is frozen in ice caps and glaciers, leaving less than 1 per cent to recharge the lakes, rivers and soil of the earth. But this appears to be quite sufficient for the life process.

There is much obscurity on the origin of water on earth. It was doubtless present in most of the interstellar cloud from which the solar system formed but after the sun's nuclear furnace ignited it was too hot near the sun and too cold far from the sun for water to exist in liquid form. The earth is situated in the midst of the 75 million mile zone where water can exist in all its forms— liquid, vapor and ice. This is the so-called life zone of a star. Water on Venus, situated on the inner rim of this zone, can exist only as vapor as the surface temperature on the planet is about 1000° F. Small amounts of vapor and ice particles have also been detected on Mars. There can be only speculation on the situation when the earth was molten and hot in its early stages. Most of the water must have existed as vapor. If the earth lost any water it was later replenished from within as the earth cooled and solidified. It would appear that once the earth cooled and stabilized it has retained all its water ever since. It has been merely recycled.

Water possesses two characteristics without which there would be no life. It evaporates readily into the atmosphere and it floats in its solid state. The latter feature is important for otherwise all the water on earth would freeze into solid ice and become unavailable for the life process. As the water of the oceans, lakes and rivers begins to freeze the ice rises to the surface and acts as an insulation for the water beneath keeping it from freezing. This thin layer of ice melts when the weather warms up. If the ice sank to the bottom the opposite would result and the body of water would freeze solid. It would insulate the water from the warmth of the earth in turn. The temperature balance on earth would not be able to melt the ice and it would remain frozen solid forever.

The propensity of water to evaporate is equally important as, otherwise, all the water would end up in the oceans leaving the continents lifeless. Instead, water constantly evaporates into the atmosphere which transports it and deposits it on the land in the form of rain. This is known as the hydrologic cycle. Only a small amount of the earth's water is involved in the hydrologic cycle at any given time—less than one per cent—but over the ages most of the water of the earth participates. All of this water is precipitated from the atmosphere every 12 days. As soon as it falls on the land as rain, snow or hail it starts its journey back to the sea under the force of gravity. Much of it in rivers but most of it underground via acquifers—

porous soil strata like sand, gravel or conglomerate. These acquifiers normally parallel the rivers flowing to the sea so that a river, as it has been said, flows 10 per cent above ground and 90 per cent underground. This forms the so-called river valleys of the world. It is not without historical significance that the earliest civilizations were situated astride these fertile river valleys constantly nourished with life-giving water by the hydrologic cycle. The Egyptian civilization was founded on the Nile, the Sumerian, Babylonian, Assyrian and others on the Euphrates-Tigris doab, the Indian on the Indus and Ganges and the Chinese on the Yellow and Yangtze rivers. Not only was agriculture based on surface irrigation from the river, but shallow wells tapped the underground part of the river as the water flowed to the sea.

Even though the hydrologic cycle precipitates the same amount of water every 12 days the rain or snow is not evenly distributed over the land mass. Some areas, the deserts, receive little or none, while other areas, the tropics, receive an overabundance of rain. The temperate zones, where the bread-baskets of the world are situated, too are not favored regularly and evenly by the cycle. Slight variations in the jet streams, temperatures and even ocean currents cause the precipitation to come in floods and droughts. It is still mainly chance outside the control of man.

The hydrologic cycle performs, as already mentioned yet another life supporting function. It breaks down the rock into soil. This near magical substance water has still another unique quality. It is an almost universal solvent. As it precipitates from the atmosphere and as it wends its way back to the sea it dissolves countless minerals, salts and other matter. This enables it to erode the rock it encounters on its way to the sea. And as the particles erode they are in turn dissolved or suspended and carried by the water to be deposited in the valleys and deltas of the earth to form fertile land for plants.

The hydrologic cycle is powered by the sun. A tremendous amount of heat is required for water to evaporate. This heat energy comes from the sun. At the same time the sun's heat causes the atmosphere to move and circulate from place to place. The earth's rotation also contributes to this movement. In general, the greatest evaporation occurs above the oceans and as the vapor laden atmosphere moves over the higher elevated land masses the cooler air encountered causes a precipitation of the vapor on the land. It should be noted, that the transportation of the water to the higher elevation of the land invests it with much potential energy. Man has since time immemorial used this potential energy in various forms of water power. Modern technology now enables man to divest the water of this energy in the facile form of hydroelectric power.

The weather is a complex subject. Suffice it to say that the hydrologic cycle constitutes the heart of it. The energy involved is enormous and uncontrollable by man. Perhaps it will always remain so. The total amount of energy released by a thunderstorm is equivalent to that of a large atomic bomb. Fortunately it is widely distributed. The devastation caused by a hurricane or tornado is awesome. Yet they have only regional impact on the life of man and do not threaten his existence.

The weather cycle has, however, proved erratic. This could recur and threaten or gravely restrict life on earth. The glacial cycle is the result of only a 4° F. or so variation in the mean temperature of the surface of the earth! About a million years ago the Pleistocene, or ice age, set in which caused some 30 per cent of the continents to become covered with glaciers thousands of feet thick. At present only about 10 per cent is so covered. At least four glacial cycles have been detected. The fourth glacier began about 60,000 years ago and has been retreating now for about 10,000 years.

The last glacial period, known as Wurm, covered Canada and great portions of the United States. Sites of great cities such as Boston, New York, Chicago, Cleveland and St. Louis were beneath ice. The British Isles, Scandanavia, large portions of France, Germany and Russia were similarly under ice. The summer temperature of Europe and North America did not rise above 50° F. Winter temperatures, of course, were far below freezing. Summer temperatures in areas eventually covered by ice did not rise above freezing as the glacier approached. The preceding glacier, called Riss was even more severe. It lasted about 75,000 years from about 200 to 125,000 years ago. Most of Europe was again covered with ice. So was North America, but at this time, as well as during the Wurm Glacier, there was no human life on this continent. Riss was the first glacier to try the endurance of homo sapiens. The earlier glaciers existed during the time of homo erectus, but this earlier man apparently migrated to more hospitable areas. When the Riss glacier set in homo sapiens were well established in Europe and decided to stay. Early homo sapiens and neanderthal man's ingenuity was tested to the utmost in the struggle to survive under these conditions. There is a school of thought that his success in this challenge contributed greatly to an evolutionary leap forward in the growth of man's intelligence.

The glaciers exposed more of the continents to human habitation for they lowered the sea level by 500 feet or so. Parts of the shallow continental shelves became habitable land. As the glaciers melted, of course the water locked up in the ice caps returned to the sea and flooded these areas again. In fact the fabled flood of the Old Testament and other West Asian lore some 5000 years ago may have been the reflooding of the Persian Gulf as the water level rose in the Arabian Sea and broke through the narrow strait of Hormuz.

The cause of the glaciers is something of an enigma to geologists. Why did the recurring cycle begin only a million years or so ago, particularly, when all evidence indicates that the Tertiary period that preceded the Pleistocene epoch was a warm period. Finally, geologists ask whether the cycle is one that can be expected to repeat itself in the future. That question can only be answered with any degree of certainty after the cause of past glaciers is known. There is, it should be noted here, evidence of ice ages earlier than the Pleistocene epoch, even as far back as the pre-Cambrian era, but they are not as clearly verified or understood as the recent glaciers. But there is now a scientific tool for determining the temperatures of the oceans from the composition of the shells of ancient invertebrates dating back 500 million years. Results of this exercise indicate that the water temperature of the oceans varied as much as 10° F. from time to time. It must, therefore, be concluded that glaciers are a much older phenomena than the Pleistocene epoch.

There are, to be sure, several theories, some astronomical, others geological. One astronomical explanation is that the earth's axis shifts every 26,000 years. While this has the effect of narrowing the temperate zones its periodicity does not appear to coincide with the glacial cycle. The more accepted astronomical theory is based on changes in the earth's elliptical course around the sun which lowers the mean annual temperature a few degrees. This might be sufficient to upset the delicate balance of the hydrologic cycle. But here too, though much better, the periodicities do not appear to square off. Still another astronomical theory holds that periodic variations in the heat received from the sun cause the glacial cycle. While this sounds very plausible there is yet no scientific proof.

A geological theory given considerable support postulates a substantial elevation of the continents, particularly their mountains, which occurred toward the end of the Tertiary period. The earth apparently cooled and shrank greatly at this time causing the crustal plates to shift and slide under each other. The Rocky Mountains and others arose at this time. Furthermore the entire continents are believed to have risen a few thousand feet. This resulted in more snow and less thawing at the higher elevation. Unfortunately the theory might explain the first glacier but not their recurrence thereafter. In fact, the glaciers themselves cause changes in the elevation of the continents. Scandanavia has risen 1000 feet since the retreat of the last glacier. But it is hard to believe that this effect of the glaciers could cause the glaciers themselves.

Another geologic theory is predicated on shifts in ocean currents resulting from the movement of the crustal plates. It is believed that the Pacific and Atlantic oceans were once connected by a depression of the Isthmus of Panama eliminating the warming effect of the gulf stream on North Atlantic waters. This too does not appear to explain the recurring nature of the glaciers.

Finally there is the stark fact that the glaciers have recurred at least four times in the Pleistocene age with some degree of regularity. It would seem to follow that another glacier might ensue in the next 50 to 100,000 years.

Such a spectacle would be horrendous. The present world is already trending toward overpopulation. Any reduction in the land area for the production of food, and even decent living space, could prove intolerable for life on earth. Fortunately such recurrence of a glacier would be slow and measurable in advance so that the technological ingenuity of man would have a chance to cope with it. Perhaps, the advance of the glacier could even be checked by such relatively easy steps as painting the ice black to absorb more of the sun's heat to melt it.

The foregoing sets forth, if anything, the precarious balance of forces on earth and in the universe for the continuation of man's life. As will be seen in the next chapter man owes his existence to pure chance. Pure chance may also terminate it. But there is also now the real possibility that man may inadvertently or irrationally terminate his existence through his awesome power of using energy outside himself. It is, therefore, in order to pause to examine some of these possibilities of chance and irrationality that will or could bring about the demise of man.

First the imperatives. Astronomers know with reasonable certainty from their study of other stars that the sun will start its dying cycle 5 billion years or so from now. It will grow huge and much more hot so that the temperature on earth will rise to 1000° F. All the water will be evaporated and suspended in the atmosphere as a thick cloud. Metals like lead, zinc, tin and others will be in a molten state. More of the lethal rays of the sun may penetrate to earth. Assuming man still exists as a specie at that time he will either have to migrate to a more hospitable part of the solar system, like Titan, a satellite of Saturn, or a planet in the life zone of a neighboring star. The latter would be a formidable technological feat as the nearest star Alpha Centauri is 4 light years away (or 24 billion miles!). Quite obviously only small colonies could participate in such cosmic emigration. On the other hand man's technology might be so advanced that adequate defenses against the sun's heat and rays might be developed.

After two billion years this situation will change dramatically to the other extreme. The sun will spend its energy and start to cool. After reflooding the earth the water will freeze into a permanent ice cap covering the earth. Should man have survived the earlier hot epoch through technological superfeat he will now have to direct his technological prowess in another direction. Again it may be possible for he could produce the necessary energy through thermonuclear power from matter on earth. There is, for instance, plenty of hydrogen in the water on earth for the purpose. In fact, it is entirely foreseeable that man could perpetuate his life on earth far beyond the limitations imposed by the normal life cycle of the stars of the universe. But it would be a life far different from that he has so far known here on earth.

Much can however happen before this ultimate cosmic cataclysm. There could be an intergalaxial or interstellar collision. Such cosmic accidents have and do occur. But as already stated both the Milky Way galaxy and the sun within it are favorably situated in the universe to minimize such cosmic accident. There also could be a strike by a huge comet or meteorite which would, perhaps not destroy the earth but change its axis or its solar orbit which in turn could upset the delicately balanced weather, hydrologic or other cycles upon which human life depends. There is no way to assess the probability of such cosmic occurrence except to note that it could happen.

The threat of another glacier has already been discussed. But there is an obverse side of this coin. If the temperature of the surface of the earth should become warmer (say) by 10° F. or so, the remaining ice caps would melt and raise the sea level by 300 feet. Much of the coastal areas where most of the people live today would become uninhabitable. The food growing areas would diminish. A similar plight as that described earlier in connection with another glacier would beset man. Furthermore, if this should be coupled with a cessation of the cooling and shrinking of the earth so that the elevation of the crustal plates no longer continues, erosion over the eons will flatten the continents and all or most of the crust will be covered with water. Again man's technological ingenuity might be able to cope with it by constructing huge and massive dikes to keep the water off the continents or develop some way of life upon the water.

Man could also inadvertently destroy the delicate balance of his environment. He has only recently entered upon the industrial age wherein he has learned to use chemical and even nuclear energy beyond his complete comprehension. Only very recently has he come to realize that he could pollute the atmosphere or water supply and destroy their life giving or protecting benefits. If the protective layer of ozone in the stratosphere for instance is destroyed (as it could be by freon released from aerosol containers, refrigerators and the like) permitting excessive lethal ultra violet rays to penetrate to earth all life would be exterminated. Too much release of carbon dioxide (some is, of course, necessary for the life cycle) into the atmosphere from internal combustion engines, thermal stations, chemical plants and other sources increases the insulating effect of the atmosphere and the surface heat of the earth. This could interfere with the glacial cycle for good or ill as already discussed. Industrial pollution of potable water could also have deleterious effect on life as only a limited amount of the earth's abundant water supply is available in the hydrologic cycle. It would seem, though, that man should be able to bridle his greed in order to avert such man made calamities.

Far more disturbing, of course, is man's irrationality coupled with his increasing command over energy. The use of this energy against his fellow men could maim or destroy the human race. But this is getting ahead of the story which will be developed in succeeding chapters.

The foregoing discussion of the precarious balance of conditions on earth and in the universe for man's continued existence is not to be viewed as an exercise in science fiction or the prediction of armageddon. Its purpose is to set forth the awesome forces of nature by whose sufferance man exists on earth. Anyone who has ever had the misfortune to be caught on a small boat off the New England coast in a howling Northeaster comes away with an appreciation of the insignificance of man in the face of elemental forces of the universe. If man can remain both humble and confident in the face of these realities he will find himself in a better frame of mind for working out his ultimate salvation in the universal scheme of things.

MATTER AND ENERGY

Matter and energy are everything. There is nothing else. They embrace everything from the immensity of the universe to the minuteness of the atom. The atom is the basic unit of matter. The ancient Greeks surmised the existence of an ultimate unit of substance. They called it an atom, derived from atomos, meaning indivisible. Centuries later Isaac Newton speculated on an ultimate unit of matter and John Dalton, early in the 19th century, deduced that every element was composed of such fundamental units. But it was only recently—through the work of Ernest Rutherford in England and Niels Bohr of Denmark in the 20th century—that the nature of the atom came to be reasonably well understood.

The atom exists in the same form everywhere in the universe whether it resides in a man's fingertip, a piece of radioactive uranium or in the core of the white hot sun. It may startle one to realize that all the atoms in his body originated in the cosmic dust and gas of the universe. These same atoms doubtless passed through the life cycle of some bygone star. The atom is in fact, a miniature solar system consisting of a nucleus of protons, neutrons and a score or so of other particles held together by nuclear force (called mesons) with electrons in orbit around the nucleus. The electrons may number one to over one hundred. They orbit in certain spherical shells around the nucleus. The number of electrons and their orbital positions determine the different elements of matter. The simplest and most basic is hydrogen with one electron. Uranium has 92 electrons.

The atom is not "solid". In fact, it is mostly space. If the nucleus of the hydrogen atom is viewed as being the size of a golf ball its electron would be orbiting one mile away! But because electrons orbit the nucleus of an atom at the unimaginally incredible speed of some quadrillion times per second the entire structure takes on the properties of substance. Yet, it has been stated that if all the space could be squeezed out of the atoms in the Washington Monument it would form a solid no bigger than the tip of a finger! Contemplation of this sort befuddles the imagination.

If man cannot see it, or feel it, and can only postulate it, how can he be sure of the structure and behavior of the atom. The answer, of course, is that he could not otherwise have made the nuclear bombs, generated nuclear power and derived the many other results from releasing the energy locked up in the atom.

Despite this phenomenal success with nuclear energy physicists still ponder and differ on the precise nature of the atom as they probe deeper into its enigmatic nucleus. A score or more different particles have been identified. Each particle has an anti-particle like the electron and positron. They annihilate if and when they collide. The basic particles are now thought to be "quarks" interrelated by electronic and gravitational forces. Tremendous effort and resources are being expended at Fermiland, a Cathedral for Physics, near Chicago and the Center for High Energy Research at Cern, Switzerland where scores of scientists are at work on probing the nature of the atom. It might yet be concluded that the atom consists of pure energy contained by some cohesive nuclear force to give it the substance and characteristics of matter. This would not be inconsistent with Einstein's universal equation $E = MC^2$. Matter may be just another state of energy.

Atoms do not usually exist by themselves. They form chemical bonds into molecules. Water, the most abundant, and essential substance, is composed of two atoms of hydrogen and one atom of oxygen—H_2O. Molecules form further aggregates bound together chemically and/or physically, such as minerals, plants, animals and the like. It is in these aggregate forms that matter is seen, felt and otherwise known to man.

Matter exists in four states—solid, liquid, gas and plasma. The different states depend upon the amount of heat energy ingested by the matter. Water is normally a liquid. Reduction of heat causes it to freeze into a solid. Addition of heat causes it to evaporate as steam, a gaseous state. The fourth state plasma does not normally exist on earth. It is super-super heated substance with temperatures in excess of 100,000° F. The only example on earth is the state of matter inside a hydrogen bomb explosion. The best example, of course, is the sun which, like any other star, is a white ball of plasma.

But matter is essentially energy at rest. The entire substance of an atom can be converted into energy. This incredible insight into the nature of things is due to the prescience of Albert Einstein the foremost scientific genius of mankind to date. He encapsuled it in his famous equation $E = MC^2$. Matter is converted into energy equal to its mass times the square of the speed of light—light being the ultimate and basic form of energy. This process in its fullest is transpiring in the sun and the stars and in various lesser degrees throughout the universe.

Energy manifests itself in many different ways. The main kinds of energy may be listed as follows: light, heat, chemical, mechanical, electrical and nuclear.

Light is the ultimate and most essential form of energy. Its primary source is the sun and stars. But it can also be generated by chemical and electrical energy on earth. Radiant energy also includes x-rays, radio waves, infrared and ultraviolet rays and others. These too can be produced on earth from radioactive and other matter. Light and the related rays and waves consist of the smallest particles in motion. The speed of light is 186 million miles per second.

Electrical energy is based upon the electron. An atom is normally electrically neutral, that is, the positive charge in the nucleus is balanced by the negative charge of its electrons. But when electrons escape from their orbit they will be attracted by atoms with missing electrons. The force of this attraction is electrical energy which manifests itself as electric currents, electomagnetism and other electronic phenomena.

Heat is predicated on molecular activity. The faster the movement of the molecules in matter the greater its heat. This molecular activity can be transmitted to other matter by conduction, radiation and conveyance.

Nuclear energy results from the fission of an atom or the fusion of two atoms releasing energy from the nucleus of the atom or atoms. The energy released is in the form of heat, light and various rays and waves.

Chemical energy derives from the molecular breakup or rearrangement of matter. The molecular reconstitution sometimes requires heat or a catalyst to initiate it. The energy is released in the form of heat, light, electricity and mechanical energy. Fire is the best example of chemical energy releasing heat and light.

Mechanical energy is simply an object in motion. The motion is usually generated by other forms of energy. The chemical energy of the internal combustion engine is transferred into mechanical energy of a car or truck through its impact on the pistons, crankshaft, gears, connecting rods and wheels. But the earliest manifestation of mechanical energy on earth, with the exception perhaps of a rolling stone down a mountainside or water flowing to the sea, is the muscular action of animals and other life on earth. Animals release chemical energy from food and convert it to muscular power of their bodies. The analogy to an internal combustion engine is striking!

In the past generation or so man has extended his control over sources of universal energy almost beyond belief. He is now on the verge of using directly solar energy and the nuclear energy of the atom. The promise of success with the former is better than the latter. To be sure, man already utilizes nuclear energy to generate electricity, but this is not a direct use of nuclear power. It is merely utilizing a by-product, the heat energy derived from a nuclear reaction. The electricity produced does not differ from that generated by heat derived, for example, from the burning of coal. The direct utilization of nuclear power, however, poses some almost insurmountable problems. First and foremost, there is no substance on earth that could contain the plasma resulting from atomic fusion which can sustain itself only at a temperature of 180 million degrees! Equally difficult is the disposal of the radioactive wastes resulting from the release of nuclear energy, which is harmful, and could be fatal, to the existence of man. But even in this difficult area there has already been a modicum of success in containing plasma by magnetism without any metal to hold it. It is still a formidable task to transfer this method from the laboratory into practical use.

All these forms of energy are interchangeable and usually are by man for practical use. For example, the mechanical energy of a hydroelectric power plant is transformed into electrical energy by the generator and the electrical energy is transformed into the mechanical energy of an electric motor—compressor in a refrigerator, the heat energy of a toaster or the light energy of an electric bulb. In this transformation none of the energy is destroyed. This is known as the Law of Conservation of Energy. To be sure, some of the energy may escape into the atmosphere and is not tranferred into mechanical energy for man's use. Some kinds of energy, on the other hand can be used by man only indirectly. The abundance of light energy emanating from the sun can be utilized directly only by plants which convert it back to matter. But man can utilize this matter as food for release of chemical energy to be transformed into muscular power. The interchangeability of energy is at times difficult to comprehend but always wondrous to behold.

Energy is and can be stored for future use. Much of it is stored by nature. This is commonly referred to as potential energy or latent energy. Kinetic energy is the term applied to an object in motion. Thus a rock perched on a hill has potential energy created by the force of gravity. This is transformed to kinetic energy when the stone rolls down the hillside. The best use man has made of such potential energy resulting from the force of gravity is the hydroelectric power plant. Far more important an example of potential energy, which man has used so advantageously for the rapid technological advance of the past century or so, is the fossil fuels—coal, petroleum and natural gas. This store of energy originated with plants and animals, which millions of years ago converted solar energy into plant and animal matter. Due to the climate and geologic conditions of the times much of this organic matter was submerged into murky swamps where it decomposed chemically into hydrocarbons and was preserved in the earth's crust for future use as fuel. This, unfortunately appears to have been a non-recurring process making fossil fuels a wasting asset which will soon be exhausted by man.

More germaine, however, is the latent energy of food which sustains man as a manifestation of energy on earth. Plants convert the energy of the sun into food for mammals and other life on earth. Some of these mammals are in turn used for food by others. Omnivores like man use both plants and animals for food. The energy of plants—and animals to a lesser extent—is stored by man for future use. Granaries have been a part of man's history for millennia. And it is not without reason that it has been said throughout history that an army marches on its stomach.

Assuming science is right—and there appears no rational reason to doubt it—that existence consists of nothing but matter and energy, where does that leave man. He can only be a part of this universal scheme of things. Man is, therefore, nothing more than a manifestation of the fundamental energy of the universe. His substance or being is composed of atoms and molecules (85 per cent is water) arranged in a structure that functions as a converter of chemical energy into mechanical energy of his body and the electrical energy of his brain. It is the latter function that, of course, distinguishes man from other life on earth. Were it not for his power to reason man's history on earth would not differ from that of the extinct dinosaurs. But it is this conflict between the irrational and the rational power of man that has made his history so perplexing and frustrating. And at this time in his evolution man is still seeking his salvation from this conflict which could prematurely terminate his existence on earth.

II
Life on Earth

Life on earth doubtless evolved three or four billion years ago, but there is little or no evidence of it until the Cambrian period. The time span reaching back 500 to 600 million years is divided into eras, epochs and periods known as the geologic time chart. There are three broad eras called Paleozoic, Mesozoic and Cenozoic, Greek terms for early, middle and recent life. Each era of life is further subdivided into Cambrian, the first in the Paleozoic, followed by Ordivician, Silurian, Devonian, Mississippian, Pennsylvanian and Permian. The Paleozoic lasted some 340 million years and is the age of the invertebrates. The Mesozoic is subdivided into three periods, the Triassic, Jurassic and Cretaceous. It is the age of the dinosaurs. The Mesozoic era lasted about 160 million years. The recent era, the Cenozoic or the age of the mammals, is subdivided into the Tertiary and Quaternary periods, which in turn are broken down into epochs. The present one, the Quaternary begins two to three million years ago. This is the age of man. The Pleistocene epoch, sometimes called the ice age, lasted until about 10,000 years ago. The present epoch is the Holocene, and is the time of civilized or modern man. A geologic time chart is set forth on the opposite page for ready guidance on the evolution of life on earth.

About 3.5 billion years ago, as previously noted, the new planet earth stabilized out of interstellar dust and gas and formed a solid crust. There was, at first, a single flat and arid continent surrounded by an immense sea of liquid water. Above was a poisonous atmosphere of hydrogen, ammonia and methane. There was as yet no breathable oxygen needed for higher forms of life. But the vital hydrologic cycle was already at work. The water of the sea was being repeatedly washed over the single continent forming soil from rock and transporting much of it into the sea. Lightning and thunder permeated the atmosphere. Deadly ultra violet rays penetrated to earth as there was yet no ozone level above to absorb them. As the earth cooled and shrank hot magma kept oozing to the surface through cracks and fissures in the crust. All this was constantly showered by the radiant energy of the sun creating a warm tropical like climate on earth.

MAJOR STRATIGRAPHIC AND TIME DIVISIONS IN USE BY THE U.S. GEOLOGICAL SURVEY

Era or Erathem	System or Period	Series or Epoch	Estimated ages of time boundaries in millions of years
Cenozoic	Quaternary	Holocene	
		Pleistocene	
			2–3
	Tertiary	Pliocene	
			12
		Miocene	
			26
		Oligocene	
			37–38
		Eocene	
			53–54
		Paleocene	
			65
Mesozoic	Cretaceous	Upper (Late) / Lower (Early)	
			136
	Jurassic	Upper (Late) / Middle (Middle) / Lower (Early)	
			190–195
	Triassic	Upper (Late) / Middle (Middle) / Lower (Early)	
			225
Paleozoic	Permian	Upper (Late) / Lower (Early)	
			280
	Carboniferous Systems — Pennsylvanian	Upper (Late) / Middle (Middle) / Lower (Early)	
	Carboniferous Systems — Mississippian	Upper (Late) / Lower (Early)	
			345
	Devonian	Upper (Late) / Middle (Middle) / Lower (Early)	
			395
	Silurian	Upper (Late) / Middle (Middle) / Lower (Early)	
			430–440
	Ordovician	Upper (Late) / Middle (Middle) / Lower (Early)	
			500
	Cambrian	Upper (Late) / Middle (Middle) / Lower (Early)	
			570
Precambrian		Informal subdivisions such as upper, middle, and lower, or upper and lower, or younger and older may be used locally.	
			3,600+

THE PRIMORDIAL SEA

Life as it evolved later could not exist in this milieu. But the essentials for such life—the elements carbon, hydrogen, oxygen, nitrogen, phosporous and sulphur—were present in the poisonous and other compounds of the atmosphere, the earth and the sea. All that was needed was some form of energy to rearrange them into the organic materials of life. And the radiant energy of the sun and the electricity in lightening filled the need. Most likely it was a bolt of lightening resulting from the hydrologic cycle—doubtless billions of lightening strokes—in the primordial sea which proved to be the catalyst.

The result was the formation of amino acids, the essential proteins of life, and nucleic acids, which includes DNA the hereditary factor of reproduction. For millions of years life on earth consisted of little more than these elemental organic materials. Gradually they formed more complex, though still simple forms, like modern viruses, fungi and bacteria living by the process of fermentation. There was yet no free oxygen to breathe. They fed on each other and the organic materials of the primordial sea. The seas of this period have been described as an organic soup. It was, in fact, a dead end for life as a means to the vital energy of the sun had not yet been established. But the very process of fermentation was to make possible further evolution of life.

Fermentation produces carbon dioxide as a by-product like the bubbles emanating from beer or champagne. A new form of life containing chlorophyll, a substance capable of utilizing directly the energy of the sun was now possible. Photosynthesis, which converts carbon dioxide, water and sunlight into sugar evolved. Plant life based upon carbohydrates and not dependent upon the organic materials of the sea came into being. This first plant life also resided in the sea in simple form such as algae.

Photosynthesis produces an important by product—atmospheric oxygen. While free oxygen in gaseous form destroyed many of the fermenting organisms, those that survived formed a new way of life based upon oxygen and organic material, eventually leading to animal life. It took, however, another billion years of photosynthesis before enough oxygen was produced to give this new form of life scope for rapid development.

The foregoing analysis is no longer learned speculation on the origin of life as the natural process has been duplicated in the laboratory. In 1953 S. L. Miller, a graduate student at the University of Chicago, constructed an apparatus for circulating steam through a mixture of ammonia, methane and hydrogen (contained in the earth's atmosphere several billion years ago) and subjected the mixture to a high energy electrical charge. The mixture was then condensed and the cycle repeated. After a week the water became turbid and red containing a wide mix of amino acids. Since 1953 other similar experiments were conducted varying the components of the mix with the result that every major constituent of living organisms have now been synthesized.

Whether this life originating process is still transpiring in nature is an interesting thought. It would, of course, have to occur in the sea or, other body of water. But in view of the predatory nature of life in the sea, such newly forming organic material would be promptly used up as food by the more advanced life forms already there at this time.

Conditions were now set for the evolution of life on a dual and interdependent basis. The nexus to the ultimate source of energy, the sun, was plant life based upon the process of photosynthesis. Photosynthesis requires carbon dioxide, a by-product of animal life. Animal life, in turn, depends upon oxygen, a by-product of photosynthesis and the plants themselves for food. After these two life processes stabilized, some two billion years ago, they marched hand in hand, so to say, developing progressively more intricate forms of plant and animal life reaching ultimately the complex and even beautiful forms known on earth today. This evolution was slow at first with ever accelerating complexity. There is little fossil evidence of this primordial life for another 1.5 billion years—until the so-called pre-Cambrian age—because these animals were shell-less and spineless. The first shell-bearing animals, or invertebrates, evolved only during the Cambrian period some 500–600 million years ago. Plants, too, were soft without fibre and trunk. Both disintegrated in the sea without a trace. Fossil fuel from plants is a latter day phenomena. The only exception, perhaps is the stromatolites dating back a billion years. They were formed by algae which trapped bits of sediment to form huge cones on the ocean floor, some as high as 50 feet.

After pre-Cambrian times the fossil record is quite good. Paleontologists have been able to trace the evolution of life reasonably well from this record in the rocks during the past 600 million years. The fossils are found primarily in sedimentary rock. Never in igneous formations. Sometimes in metamorphic. During the past half billion years or so plant and animal life would sink into the sand and clay bottoms of shallow swampy seas and lakes where its decomposition would be prevented by the submersion (in some cases a replica was produced by mineral substitution). Meanwhile the sand and clay would solidify into sedimentary rock entrapping the shell or skeleton for posterity, to be uncovered later by a breakup of the rock.

THE INVERTEBRATES

The soft bodied organisms of pre-Cambrian times began to develop protective mineral shells and outer skeletons in order to survive in the predatory environment of the sea. One can easily imagine the carnage that must have transpired in the primordial sea as life evolved more complex and diverse organisms whose survival depended upon other organisms as food for the manifestation of energy. Resort to armor must have been the need of the day as, indeed, it has been advantageous ever since. Those few that evolution blessed with a shell or similar armor survived best and, called invertebrates (not because of the shell but due to the lack of spine), dominated life during the Cambrian, Ordivician, Silurian and even the Devonian periods—a span of some 250 million years.

The now extinct, almost beautiful, Trilobite was the dominant form of life during the Cambrian period. An estimated 60 per cent of Cambrian period fossils are Trilobites! The Trilobite can be likened unto a cross between a Maryland crab and tropical lobster. Its head consisted of a hard shell followed by a segmented carapaced body and tail appropriately ornamented with external appendages and antennae. This external skeleton had to be molted from time to time, as with todays crabs and lobsters, to permit growth and development. Trilobite fossils are found in all sizes up to a foot or so in length. The finest collection of Trilobite fossils, perhaps, is found in the Museum at Prague, Czechoslovakia. There are hundreds of them many exceeding six inches in length. Many are embedded in shale—beautiful black specimens. The others in light and brown sandstone. This collection was assembled during the railroad building period of the 19th century when deep cuts were made through the highlands of Bohemia. Such cuts into the earth always provide the best opportunities for the collection of fossil specimens. The Trilobites apparently were primarily mud eaters, crawling along the sea bottoms sifting organic material out of the sand and clay sediment. It is also thought they subsisted on the algae in the seas. They were extinct by the end of the Paleozoic era, some 250 million years ago.

Another 30 per cent of Cambrian life consisted of brachiopods, a clam like hard shelled invertebrate. While the brachiopods are not extinct their prominance has dwindled in the sea. The remaining 10 per cent consisted of cephalopods, molluscs, bivalves and others not all of which possessed armor for survival.

Life started to spread gradually to the land during the Silurian period some 400 million years ago. By then the hydrologic cycle had created a considerable amount of soil. Plant life in the sea had generated an abundance of free oxygen in the atmosphere. Plants found the greater availability of sun light on the land a large advantage to their life process of photosynthesis. And the animals of the sea found the greater abundance of food on land equally favorable. Hence, the thrust of the evolution of life onto the land at this time.

To be sure, the transition could not be and was not sharp. By Silurian times the fossil record notes the development of fishes, the first vertebrates. The origin of vertebrates is still not clearly known. At first the fish were jawless dependent, largely, on swiftness of movement and some armor for survival. Later they developed jaws and teeth to become the terrors of the sea. Armor was shed for mobility, jaws and teeth. The shark dates back to the Devonian period, sometimes called the age of fishes.

The Devonian period was also a time of unusual shrinking and buckling of the earth's crust that thrust up mountains and rearranged the seas leaving large muddy areas rich in organic material exposed to air and sun. Plants found these conditions ideal for development. And the fish found the new source of food attractive and the mobility in the swampy mud not too unlike the waters of the sea. Gradually they developed into amphibians, their fins became half-legs, living in and out of the water at the same time. A new form of life evolved which would lead eventually to mammals and man. The amphibians developed legs for mobility on land and lungs to utilize the free oxygen of the air.

Formidable obstacles plagued the transition of life to land in the reproductive area. In the sea male and female of the specie deposited their gametes in the water which protected them from premature death by drying and where mobility and propinquity promoted their connection. The amphibians, like their modern counterparts the frogs, returned to the water for reproduction. The newly born, like the tadpole, spent their infancy in the water until their legs and lungs matured for life on land. The great leap forward toward self sufficiency on land came only later with the reptiles, the successors of the amphibians, who evolved the egg for reproductive purposes. The reptilian male would deposit his gametes inside the female's body who in turn would encase them, along with her gametes, in a leathery egg containing nourishment and fluid to promote fertilization and new life. The egg was laid in the warm sand of the beach where the heat from the sun fostered the incubation and hatching of the new life. A similar problem confronted plants which were also dependent on water as a medium to facilitate reproduction. Suffice it to note here that plants developed the flower and the seed for reproduction on land. This was, indeed, a gift of nature to man for the earth would be a less beautiful place without the flowers.

THE REPTILES

The transition to life on land by the amphibians was furthered by the reptiles. The reptiles not only evolved a self sufficient reproductive process on land but developed legs underneath their bodies for better locomotion on the ground. The amphibians could only waddle; the reptiles could walk—and run—some up to 30 miles per hour. This transition began in the Pennsylvanian period. By the end of the Paleozoic era, the Permian period, some 225 million years ago animal life was half amphibian and half reptilian.

The Mesozoic era (in particular the Jurassic period) was the age of the reptiles, that spanned the time period 225 to 65 million years ago. About 250 species have been exhumed from the fossil record, ranging from the enormous brachiosauras standing 80 feet from head to tail and weighing 55 tons to the small psittacosauras of 5 feet and 50 pounds. The dominant

Davidson College Library

reptiles were the dinosaurs. The word was coined from ancient Greek and means "terrible lizzards". The most prominent dinosaurs were the huge sauropods 70–90 feet in length weighing 30–50 tons. The diplodocus and brontosaurus are the most familiar. Their elephantine bodies with long neck and tail are well known to school children and museum goers. They were vegetarians. The theropods, the meat-eaters, were the terrors on the reptilian scene. They walked on their hind legs. Their fore legs were short, and more arm and claw like, for facilitating the huge jaws with sharp teeth in tearing the flesh of other reptiles on which they fed. Allosaurus, 50 feet in length weighing 8 tons, was the brute of the early Mezoic era. He was surpassed in ferocity during the Cretaceous period by tyrannosaurus, 50 feet in length weighing 10 tons. Tyrannus rex, as he is often referred to, had a large head and jaws with rows of sharp six inch teeth. There were also smaller carnivores like deinonychus, 8 feet long weighing 100 pounds, whose agility enabled it to mount the less mobile sauropods and tear mouthfuls of flesh from their neck and back. A third group consisted of the ornithischians, a diverse group of domed, horned and armored dinosaurs. They too were vegetarians and not as vicious as the theropods. Their lethal accoutrements were used mostly for defense against tyrannus rex and his kind. Stegosaurus, for instance, had two rows of segmented bony plates running on each side of his spine from his head to his tail and four enormous spikes on the end of his tail. A full swing of the spiked tail could deliver a lethal blow to allosaurus or tyrannosaurus.

The reptilian scene must have been one of constant carnage and scavenging. The sauropods had to consume enormous quantities of plants and foliage in order to energize their huge tonnages. One can easily imagine a herd of brontosauruses ravaging an acre or so of shrub and forest in an afternoon leaving it looking like the aftermath of a forest fire. These huge vegetarians could strip small branches and bark from the trunks of the soft conifers of the Mesozoic era. But in order to digest this roughage, since it had no teeth to chew it up, the dinosaur had to keep smooth oval or rounded stones in it's stomach, like it's cousins the birds who require small pebbles to facilitate digestion. Such rounded stones have been found with the fossil remains.

As they grazed in the lush and tropical forest the sauropods had to be constantly aware of impending attack by the vicious theropods. Their powerful tail was their only defense, but a solid hit would send allosaurus reeling often with a broken foot or ribs. But allosaurus had to succeed to survive and when he felled a 50 tonner there was more meat available than he could devour, albeit his bites comprised hundreds of pounds of flesh at a time. When he left the carcass, sated for the time being, the scavengers moved in to complete the feast—the flying or gliding reptiles from the air, the lesser reptiles on the land, and, not to go unnoticed at this early date, the furry little pantothere, the earliest mammal. But more on it later.

These huge dinosaurs found refuge in the shallow waters for their relaxation and rest. They did not dare sleep on land. There they would submerge their massive bodies leaving only the small head partially afloat to breath. Unlike the elephant of today they had no difficulty navigating the muddy bottoms of the lagoons and estuaries for they could contract their flat feet to the circumference of their forelegs and pull them out of the mud like a reed.

The female sauropod also left herself vulnerable when she had to lay her eggs in the sand on the beach. She probably received no protection from the male even though coupling was necessary for fertilization of the eggs. Pair bonding developed only later with the mammals. In fact, once the female deposited her eggs in the sand her job was finsihed. The young had to make their own way into the protective waters to survive and many, doubtless, lost their lives on the way to safety. Many a female doubtless, also lost her life during the vulnerable position when her body was semi-submerged in the sand while laying the eggs and while occupied covering them in the sand with her tail and nose. Left uncovered, the eggs would have been eaten by other small reptiles and the newly emerging mammals. At that, one can be sure, many a dinosaur egg ended up as food instead of a newly born.

The birds are also reptiles and, somehow, managed to survive the demise of the dinosaurs. But little is known about their origin and development during the Mesozoic era as their fossil record is rare. The first flying vertebrates were gliders rather than true flyers. Pterosaur had a wing span of 20 feet structured of a leathery sheath, not feathers, and a long sharp beak for picking up fish near the surface as he glided over the water. Later jurassic birds were also larger than todays species, but had already developed feathered wings and bodies.

Mention is also in order of lesser reptiles that too managed to survive. The water reptiles, alligators and crocodiles, are much the same today as during Mesozoic times. Their amphibian way of life must have been an advantage against other reptile predators and during the cataclysm. Turtles are virtually the same throughout, their survival due doubtless to an impregnable armor. The lizards and their successors down the line, the snakes, also managed to survive. Poisonous fangs and secluded habitation were the snakes big advantage.

There is no clear evidence in the fossil record on the rather abrupt demise of the dinosaurs at the end of the Mesozoic era about 70 million years ago. Several theories are extant. An interesting one is that the reptiles werc vulnerable in the reproductive area. The emerging mammals, it is postulated, ate their eggs and this aborted the reproduction of the huge reptiles. The abruptness of their demise in the fossil record uncovered to date would seem to belie this theory, plausible as it may sound. A more credible theory is that their abrupt disappearance was due to some catastrophe in the universe that caused a colder climate on earth. It should be recalled that the reptiles evolved, developed and prospered in a warm semi-tropical climate that prevailed during the Mesozoic era. They had a very poor body temperature control system limiting greatly their range of temperature tolerance. Had they been able to survive beyond the Mesozoic era they would have doubtless succumbed to, or been considerably diminished by, the cold temperatures of the Pliestocene epoch when glacial cycles prevailed. Certainly not in their great habitats which are now the states of Wyoming and Colorado. During the ice age this area was on the threshold of the glaciers. But there is no geologic evidence of any glacier at the end of the Mesozoic era. Moreover, the effect of a glacial cycle would not have been abrupt and some of the dinosaurs should have survived in the tropical zones.

More likely would be the occurrence of a super nova, that is, an exploding star, close enough to the solar system to blow away into space part of the earth's atmosphere. If such a cosmic blast had sheared away the ozone shield all life on earth would have come to an end. Not merely the dinosaurs. We know of course, that it has not, so it had to be an explosion of a lower order. But such a lesser blast could have diminished the insulating protection of the upper atmosphere so that the temperature, particularly at night, dropped beyond the narrow tolerance level of the big reptiles and they quickly died off. The lesser and surviving reptiles could have avoided the catastrophe in the protective warmth of the water, in the case of alligators and crocodiles, the blanket effect of the feathers of the birds or on or in the warm ground, in the case of the lizards and snakes. Hence, the super nova theory has much to be said in its favor. It would of course, have had to be an exploding star within a 100 light years of the earth to have such an effect.

It may also be questioned how abrupt the end really was. The demise may have occured over a period of several million years and yet appear abrupt in the fossil record. The little mammals could have eaten a lot of dinosaur eggs in a few million years. Perhaps in the end the epitaph on the grave of the dinosaurs will read that they evolved by the egg and perished by the egg.

The real cause or causes (there may have been a configuration of them) of the demise of the dinosaurs is bound to occupy the minds and the efforts of paleontologists for years, but because of their apparent abrupt end they are frequently considered nature's grand failures. They have even become the subjects of man's humor. One may well question whether this attitude is justified. The dinosaurs were the dominant form of life on earth for some 130 million years! Man's record is only about 3 million, with no assurance he will continue to be the dominant form of life on earth for another 100 million years or so. To be sure, they had a small brain, but, otherwise they were magnificent physical specimens. Not only huge but extremely intricate muscular power mechanisms. Their spines and sinews were structured much like modern construction cranes. It has been mistakenly believed at first that these huge animals only dragged their long tails behind them. To the contrary, not only were they able to carry them aloft but whip them from side to side with a force that would send tryannus rex reeling. No doubt they possessed muscular energy and power unmatched before or after in the evolution of life on earth. That they vanished through some evolutionary deficiency (the vulnerability of their reproductive process) or overwhelming universal phenomena should not detract from their prominence in the history of life on earth. All forms of life will end sooner or later. Even man in all his superiority may meet untimely extinction in the face of some overwhelming force of the universe.

THE MAMMALS

The mammals evolved from the reptiles. There is fossil evidence of mammal-like reptiles as early as the Permian period. As before, when the amphibians and reptiles lived contemporaneously there was coexistence between the reptiles and early mammals. Their main differentation again was in the reproductive area. The mammals evolved a system where the fertilized egg was retained in the female body until the new life was ready for birth. In addition the female developed mammilary glands and appendages to feed the new life for a short period after birth until it could fend for itself. The yolk of the reptilian egg was dispensed with in favor of sustenance directly from the mother's blood stream while the embryo developed inside the uterus. The fluid required for the reproductive process was provided by the placenta in the uterus.

The significance of this evolutionary development can hardly be exaggerated. Not only was better protection of the emergent life provided by the placental method of reproduction over the external egg but it provided the first step towards social life. The female-infant bond ensued. This in turn led to pair-bonding of male and female in many mammal species. And while there were doubtless additional factors involved, the family led to more complex social organization, particularly among *homo sapiens*, the most evolved mammal to date.

Quite obviously such a major evolutionary development, as with the egg before, transpired over millions of years and there were hybrid transitory forms of life some of which have survived to date. There were the marsupials, which started the embryonic life inside the female body but gave a premature birth to the new life. The birth cycle was completed inside an abdominal pouch on the mother's body where it was sustained by a mammilary system until it was mature enough to live independently. Today's familiar representatives of this reproductive system are the kangaroo and the opossum. There were also the menotremes which laid eggs, but suckled the newly hatched with mammilary glands and nipples. Surviving examples today are the platypus and spiny anteater. These hybrid mammals owe their survival perhaps, to the special geologic history of Australia where most of them are found.

A superior reproductive system, to be sure, is not the only advantage for survival developed by the mammals. Equally important was bodily temperature control, based upon warm blood with a regulator located in a bigger brain, hair for bodily insulation and sweat glands for bodily cooling. If the theory that the dinosaurs succumbed to an undue temperature change proves out, the newly emerging mammals were not to be done in by any such environmental change.

Then too, there were improvements in the body, not so much in strength but in agility. The structure of the body was upgraded for greater and faster mobility. The forelegs began to evolve into hands, so that some mammals could live in the trees for greater safety. The structure of the teeth changed to facilitate the digestive process and convert the body into a more efficient energy engine. In addition to long sharp teeth for biting and tearing, as with the reptiles, molars along with salivary glands in the mouth evolved for chewing and pre-digesting the food before it entered the stomach.

And finally a larger brain started to evolve to coordinate this more intricate animal structure and mechanism. This is, of course, the main path to man as will be discussed in the next chapter.

This latest animal, the mammal, with its superior body and emerging intellect began to dominate life on earth, after the reptiles, during the Cenozoic era, the past 70 million years or so. The fossil record reveals some 2600 mammal genera, about half of which are already extinct, grouped further into 28 different orders. Most notable are the primates (man, apes, monkeys), carnivora (dogs, cats, wolves), ungulates (horses, cows, sheep), and rodentia (squirrels, gophers, rats). Like the reptiles, mammals too are herbivorous, carniverous and omniverous, with the largest number comprising herbivors. Also, they have adapted to life on land, sea and in the air. The bats are flying mammals, whales, dolphins and porpoises live in the sea. Seals are at home on both land and in the sea. By far the largest number live on land, in keeping with the evolutionary trend of transition of life onto land.

BIRDS AND INSECTS

The direct line of evolution of life to man is traced from the sea through the fishes, amphibians, reptiles and mammals. But two side lines deserve mention. They are the birds and the insects. Far less is known about the evolution of both as they have left a meager fossil record. Largely because of their predominantly airborne habitat and fragile bodies, they left little of themselves in the sedimentary formations. The best, though inadequate record of the insects is in ancient amber, the fossilized sap of the conifers. Whole insects are sometimes found entrapped and preserved in this medium.

Birds derived from reptiles during the Jurassic epoch. They reproduce by the egg; but they are warm blooded and insulated with feathers, which are mammilian features. There is fossil evidence of large gliding reptiles with membraned, not feathered, wings and bodies. There had to obviously be a transitional airborne reptile but so far little evidence has been found in the rocks. But we know that these airborne reptiles with certain mammilian features not only survived but have proliferated grandly and beautifully.

Insects are invertebrates who made the transition to land during the Mesozoic era about 300 million years ago. Instead of lungs they developed *trachea*, tiny tubes and holes in their body shells, for the intake of atmospheric oxygen. This respiratory system, together with an external skeleton, has limited the size they could attain. Hence, insects have remained the tiniest animals even though the most numerous. More than 700,000 species are known.

The insects serve an important function for the continuance of life on earth. The plants depend upon them for fertilization of the flower for their propagation. Man has realized this interrelation, perhaps since the dawn of agriculture. There is, for example, the interesting story in the Bible where Joseph ingratiates himself with the Pharoah by introducing a beehive into the royal orchard and thereby multiplying the fruit of the trees.

Science-fiction often times postulates the take over of the earth by the insects in view of their staggering reproductive rate and, in some cases, their capacity for social organization. This would appear to be a needless scare. The insects due to their inability to achieve any size are vulnerable to predators. The almost equally abundant birds can be depended upon for containing their numbers. Moreover, man now possesses the technology to destroy chemically, biologically or otherwise any such development. Man has more to fear from reaping the whirlwind—the chemical pollution of the environment.

Nonetheless this spectre is real, particularly in the case of the social insects, the bees, ants, termites and others. The ants in the jungles of Africa and South America are capable of laying desolate the land over which they direct an organized march. Locusts, too, can demolish acres of vegetation in one of their aerial swoops.

There is an interesting school of thought which holds that the social behavior of these insects is merely an extension of the basic organization of life itself. The evolution of life is nothing more than the increasingly complex organization of single cells into a single organism each cell performing a congenitally assigned function within the plant or animal. Man consists of about 60 trillion cells each performing it's fixed function in the body and brain. Insects were limited in this ever increasing cellular organization and growth because of their external skeletons and limited respiratory capacity, so they were forced to resort to social organization of their individual selves to be able to exert greater social energy and power for survival. Instead of intercellular communication via the brain they developed an inter-sensory system based upon the sense of smell. These chemical signals are called pheromones. Though still poorly understood this system of communication is able to organize into one social unit a score of more millions of ants so that their combined power is that of a large animal. Moreover, these insect social organizations contain a modicum of intellectual capacity as they conduct animal husbandry and agriculture to sustain the group. Ants herd, tend and milk aphids for a secretion called honeydew. This phenomena is readily observable in any orchard where the ants keep the aphids on the trees much to the annoyance and detriment of the fruit grower. In addition, the ants cultivate fungus gardens cutting up the leaves of fruit trees for the purpose. Ants have however, to date been only seed gatherers, not having mastered the art of cereal culture.

The foregoing theory holds further that the social instinct of the insects is the same evolutionary phenomena that underlies the social instinct and organization of the higher mammals, particularly man. It is predicated on the ancient wisdom that "divided we fall; united we stand". It is a manifestation of the basic survival instinct of life. Until the advent of the mammals there is scant evidence of cooperation among individual life for survival. It is believed, however, from a study of some dinosaur footprint fossils in Texas that the giant reptiles moved in herds for group defense. The insects are an exception to the rule. The social instinct and organization of man will be considered subsequently.

REPRODUCTION

The foregoing discussion emphasized heavily the reproduction of life. It may be in order to ask why life was structured by Nature to be terminal rather than perpetual. A very good reason is that an unrenewing and unchanging organism would have possessed no adaptability to environmental change. Such organism would have been doomed.

Simple organisms in the beginnings of life and even today reproduce a-sexually. They simply split in two, each half an exact replica of the parent. This is the process of cell multiplication in any living organism and constitutes the process of organic growth. Simple organisms consisting of a limited number of cells follow this method in reproduction by simply subdividing all their cells between two new organisms. Such basic cellular reproduction is called *mitosis*. But such reproduction does not possess the flexibility for maximum adaptation to environmental change. Something more was needed for continued evolution. That came with bi-sexual reproduction.

Cellular growth and reproduction came to be controlled by the genes, the hereditary factors of life. Genes are made up of a nucleic acid called DNA (deoxyribonucleic acid) and are situated in the nucleus of the cell. The genes are contained inside paired chromosomes. Each chromosome may contain thousands of genes. In organic growth and a-sexual reproduction the paired chromosomes are divided for the formation of the two new cells.

As living organisms evolved more complex structures the process of mitosis was adequate and necessary for organic growth but inadequate for reproduction. An elephant has 6 quadrillion cells. Mitosis would require splitting each one of these cells to reproduce so complex an organism. Nature designed instead, a more facile system of sexual reproduction for the purpose known as *meiosis*. And it built into the system the facility of mixing the genes of two organisms to maximize the development of favorable features for environmental adaptability.

Sexual reproduction confines renewal of life to special cells called *gametes* (such as the sperm and ova) which are produced only in the sex organs of the body. When the cells of the organism divide in the sexual organs half the chromosomes of the original cell are passed on to each of the two new cells. Each of the two, however, reproduce themselves exactly to make four cells. These four cells, or gametes, each contain half the number of chromosomes necessary for the final or complete organism. The new organism can only be formed by joining with the gametes of another organism of the same specie. The two gametes form cells with a full complement of chromosomes, but in the process the genes of the organisms are mixed at random.

Bisexual reproduction of the species instilled life with the supreme facility of adapting to a changing environment for survival which resulted in great variation in the forms of life on earth as was seen earlier. Life became increasingly more complex over the eons, to assure its survival, until it culminated in a creature with the immense power to reason. Man today has structured within him the two systems of cellular reproduction discussed above. Meiosis determines the genetic composition of his cells. This structure is different in every individual for it derives from a random mix of the genes of the two parent cells. Each individual life is, in other words, the result of a throw of the genetic dice. And the combinations are nearly unlimited. It has been calculated that for man there are 10^{1000} possible genetic combinations! But once the genetic structure of the new life is fixed by fertilization, or joining, of the gametes the organic growth of the new life proceeds by the process of mitosis whereby the multiplying cells are exact genetic replicas of the original cells. The genetic structure is fixed for the new individual.

Another very important factor effects the reproductive process. The genes are not immutable. They can and are changed by radiation or chemical reaction. Such change can be good or bad. In the latter case where it weakens the features for survival the individuals die and the bad genetic effect of radiation or chemical reaction disappears with it. Where the mutation produces a favorable gene such gene will eventually spread through the population and improve the survival of the specie. New species owe their genesis to the process of gene mutation. Yet such profound genetic mutation is a rare occurrence in nature.

It would seem clear that the development of favorable features for adaptability is a very slow process. It must necessarily span many generations. Generations, of course pass quickly in small fast multiplying animals like bacteria and insects. In the case of the complex mammals the generations pass slowly. But environmental change too is normally ever so imperceptible. Hence, the two go hand in hand. The process of meiosis is not adequate to cope with a sudden and substantial environmental change, such as must have occurred on earth and/or in the universe 70 million years ago which brought about the quick demise of the dinosaurs. And the possibility of another sudden dramatic change in the terrestial environment still confronts life on earth today.

Life's adaptation to a changing environment is called the process of "natural selection". Mankind owes a debt to Charles Darwin for this bit of seminal insight. Darwin started life studying theology, but soon shifted his interest and life's work from the supernatural to the natural. Fifty years earlier Jean Baptiste de Lamark postulated the theory of the evolution of life. It was then called transformism. Underlying the thinking was the thought that the forms of life were not fixed and immutable but subject to constant change. Darwin set out to prove it. Most everyone is familiar with his voyage on the *H. M. S. Beagle* to the Galapagos and East Indies where he observed and gathered information to support the thesis. The result was his well known publication in 1859, *The Origin of the Species*, with the subtitle "by means of natural selection". It was only after Darwin's work was coupled with that of a Moravian monk named Gregor Mendel who unraveled the genetic code that the theory of natural selection came to be fully understood. Curiously though the two men, both 19th century contemporaries, worked independently and their respective work was unknown to the other.

The process of natural selection can best be illustrated by the following example: If a colony of moths of the same specie half of which are white and the other half brown are let loose in the forest they would over the generations most likely end up as a colony of brown moths. The white moths would succumb more readily to predators because they are more visible in the green and brown forest. The brown genes would eventually dominate the specie because the brown color is an advantageous feature for survival in the dark forest. Such phenomena has now been actually observed and recorded in nature.

Certain moths in the Manchester area of England were predominantly speckled, black and white, to blend into the lichen-covered tree trunks. This made them less visible to the birds. After Manchester industrialized, starting about 1850, the pollution from the factories gradually poisoned the light colored lichen and the tree trunks darkened. The birds could now see the speckled moths and began decreasing their numbers. There was, however, a dark grey mutant in the moth population that comprised only about 1 per cent of their number in 1848. But by 1898 the dark grey moths comprised 99 per cent of the population and the speckled moth 1 per cent! This amazing conversion occurred because of the change in the color of the tree trunks. Dark grey was now the favorable feature for survival and the moths with such genes soon dominated the specie. It should be hastily added that such profound adaptability could not occur over a short span of 50 years in the more complex organisms like mammals and reptiles whose generations pass far more slowly. It should also be pointed out that paleo-biologists have noted a faster rate of change, or adaptability, as life evolved more complex organisms. Mammals have adapted more quickly than reptiles and so on back in time. If so, this would appear to bode well for the future of life on earth, except for the fact that man is interfering with the process of natural selection.

Man has now introduced into the life process unnatural selection. He did so just about 10,000 years ago with animal husbandry and agriculture. The science of eugenics is based on reproduction of the species in order to develop features favorable to man's needs and not favorable to the survival of the species. The two may not, and pretty surely are not, in most cases the same. It is believed by some, for instance, that wild animals bred in zoos may in time be deprived of some of their inbred qualities to survive in the jungle once again. But far more disturbing is man's interference with the process of natural selection for his own survival. Ever since man has come to dominate life on earth, particularly in the recent past, when his technological advance has given him a sense of security, he has enabled the weak not only to survive but to reproduce. This may not have stemmed from pure altruism. It may, in fact, derive from man's instinct for survival. It may well be questioned whether this is good for the future of the human race. It is quite obviously an interference with Nature's law and a challenge of Nature's infinite wisdom. But this is too complex and unknown a subject for hard and fast conclusions. There is yet no visible effect but then a few thousand years is only a minute in geologic time. Man must, however, be mindful of the subject in working out his salvation on earth.

After Nature structured bisexual reproduction for perpetuation and survival of life, there still remained the problem of the most facile way for the joining or mating of the gametes. The primary requirement was providing a watery medium for the mating as the gametes perish—as does all life—without water. While life remained in the water male and female of the specie simply issued their gametes in close proximity into the sea and left it up to chance to achieve the connection. But with the transition of life on to the land a serious problem arose in this respect. At first the amphibians returned to the seas, lakes and rivers for reproduction. Another obstacle in the transition period was the fast flowing water in the rivers, estuaries and tidal basins where the transitory life began to concentrate. The chances of connection of the gametes was reduced. At this time a tremendous evolutionary step occurred when reptiles developed the external egg which confined the gametes in a protective shell together with the nutrition and water needed for the fertilization and development of the new life. Concomitantly, male and female of the specie had to develop the respective faculties and instincts for fertilization of the egg while it was being formed inside the female's body. How this new attribute of life evolved cannot be derived from the fossil record and will, perhaps, always remain a matter for speculation and conjecture.

The external shelled egg, however, was found wanting in many respects. Its chief inadequacy was its vulnerability to predators. Another dificiency was the absense of protection and sustenance of the newly born. Birds have, however, solved some of these problems with the nest. The mammals, however, evolved placental reproduction, together with a mammilary system to succor the newly born, to overcome the deficiencies of the egg. Fertilization and development of the new life remained inside the female body where it was better protected from predators. Placental reproduction too has deficiencies. It is unduly burdensome and painful for the female of the specie. The pain of birth has increased as mammals developed greater intelligence requiring a larger head to protect the ever enlarging brain. In the case of man with his big brain and head to accommodate it birth has become painful and difficult for the female. Whether or how evolution will cope with this problem cannot be known at this time. But it is entirely possible that man may through technological innovation solve or alleviate the problem by fertilization, incubation and birth in the laboratory. The implication of such man made interference with nature can only be dimly perceived at this time so it can only be given passing mention and left open for further contemplation.

UNIVERSALITY OF LIFE

Jacques Monod, the Belgian biologist-philosopher, 1965 Noble Prize winner, who contributed significantly to man's understanding of the hereditary and reproductive factors of life, entitled his book *Le Hasard et la Necessite*—(Chance and Necessity). Monod derived his title from Democritus who wrote "Everything existing in the Universe is the fruit of chance and necessity".

To paraphrase Monod's thesis: Life is the result of pure chance. A stroke of lightening in the primordial sea; a gene mutation by the radiant energy of the sun. But once the genetic pattern of a living organism is fixed by chance it must develop and reproduce accordingly. The only variance Nature permits is through the genetic mix of bisexual reproduction to facilitate adaptability for survival. But this is merely an exception to the rule.

This would appear to be the universal rule of life on earth equally applicable to the lowest and the highest organism. From the protozoa to man. But that any particular form of life evolved is accidental. The evolutionary process could just as well have skipped the dinosaurs or man himself. Yet there would appear to be a built in imperative for the ultimate evolution of some form of rational life because of the operation of the law of survival of the fittest and the genetic mix of bisexual reproduction for adaptability to environmental change. Organisms have to grow more complex for maximum adaptability. Cellular complexity requires a highly developed sensory and nervous system to coordinate the illions of cells in higher forms of life such as the primates. This in turn calls for a central control mechanism like the brain. And eventually a superbrain like that possessed by man capable of rational thought. It would seem, therefore, that where ever evolution of life operates in the universe the end product, if and when achieved, should be a being with the power to reason.

Life is also structured the same in all living organisms. Amino acids for organic growth and nucleic acids for reproduction and control of organic growth. The variance is merely in the number of cells and their distribution and function in the living organism. In large animals the number of cells runs into the trillions and quadrillions, all precisely organized and regulated accordingly to the genetic code of the individual life. A large organism is a marvel of cellular organization. It becomes immediately obvious that cellular growth must (Monod's Necessity) follow a fixed pattern for otherwise the new living organism would become a riotus and monstrous structure unable to survive. Everyone is, of course, familiar with death of a living organism through cancer, which results from riotus cellular growth in a part of the body when the genetic regulator fails to function properly.

The living organism is an energy engine, again, from the lowest to the highest form of life. Food is taken into the body where it is transferred into chemical energy for transmission to the muscles of the body for locomotion in search of food for the continued survival of the organism. This manifestation of energy continues until the animal meets untimely death or the energy machine wears out and expires. But before it expires it reproduces itself according to the universal rule already discussed.

Even the physical structure of an animal, especially the vertebrates, seem to fall into a universal pattern. There is a fore and aft orientation around the alimentary canal keeled to a spine. The brain which controls the organism is appropriately fore where also are located most of the sensory faculties (eyes, ears, nose, et al) for piloting the organism. Food is taken in the forward end through the mouth converted to energy inside the body and the wastes discharged aft. This is the basic structure of animal life with only minor variations. In other words, animal life is organized along the alimentary canal.

Finally there is the structural symmetry of the animal. The left side of the spinal column is the same as the right. Legs, arms, sensory features come in pairs. There are no three legged animals. Man has, however, designed and constructed three wheeled vehicles. Such symmetry seems to be confined to external features. Internal organs are not usually paired. The genital organs too are an exception. But even these exceptions hold true for all or most animal structure. And this too holds true for most animals.

LIFE OUTSIDE EARTH

It may be in order to pause, before proceeding to the evolution of man, to contemplate the possibilities of extra terrestrial life. As already noted life as known on earth can exist only in the so-called life zone of a stellar system. But it is estimated by astronomers that there may be, in our galaxy alone, some 10^{11} planets in the life-zone of the billions of stars in the Milky Way that could support some form of life. Surely, then, it is not inconceivable that life exists elsewhere than on earth.

It is one thing, however, to conclude that extra terrestial life may exist but still another to assume it is in the likeness of man. For that matter, even that it is a form of rational life. On the other hand it could also be super intelligent life beyond the ken of man on earth. To quote Professor David L. Clark of the University of Wisconsin "Because of the uniqueness of environment, genetics and time, it appears unlikely that man's equivilents at least in recognizable form could exist elsewhere. . ." Professor Carl Sagan of Cornell believes that "If we started all over again, even the same physical conditions, and just let random factors operate, we would never get anything remotely resembling human beings". That is why reports of voyagers from outer space where the extra terrestrial creatures are depicted as beautiful upright versions of man on earth can only be suspect.

The time factor alluded to by Dr. Clark is important. Let us imagine for a moment that super intelligent creatures from another stellar system reached earth 100 million years ago, they could only report to their fellow creatures back home that they found life consisting of enormous and ferocious creatures without any intelligence and that it was no place to colonize. A half billion years ago they would have reported that there was a low form of life in the sea and that the land was barren and inhospitable to intelligent life. And so it would be with man, given the necessary technology, if he set out to explore for extra terrestrial life in the universe.

Extra terrestrial life can therefore only remain a titillating speculation at this time. Man has, perhaps, nothing to fear from such speculation today as was the case in 1600 A. D. when the Dominican monk Giordano Bruno was burned at the stake for suggesting the possibilities of extra terrestrial life. Man does not possess at this time the technology for any such exploration. Man may, some day, achieve such technology. The nearest star, however, is thousands of years travel time away from earth! The only present possibility is radio communication with such life. But that assumes solving each other's codes. A formidable task indeed.

There is still the remote possibility of other life in the solar system. Venus, Mars, Jupiter and Saturn (or one of their moons) could have some kind of elementary life. And this could prove useful to fill the gap in man's knowledge of life before the fossil record. If life on Mars proved to be at an evolutionary stage life on earth was 3 billion years or so ago it could shed much knowledge on the evolution of life on earth. Such exploration is within man's technological capacity and could be achieved before the end of the 20th century. Initial satellite probes for life on Mars to date have proved unpromising.

Life is a manifestation of the energy of the universe. But it need not be based on the carbon principle of life on earth. There could be other sources and means of utilizing the energy of the universe. It is remotely possible life could have evolved on a silicon-hydrogen principle. At this time man is developing machines (computers) capable of performing complex mathematical and information processing exercises that are based on silicon transistors. Hence, extra terrestrial life could have evolved differently from that here in earth. This thought gives still another dimension on what kind of life could or may exist on another stellar system.

III
Evolution of Man

Man has been described as the greatest success of biological evolution to date. His attributes are several and significant. First and foremost is his highly developed brain, which gives him the power to reason; an attribute possessed by no other form of life on earth. Next in importance are his dextrous hands. The hand of man possesses a mechanical virtuosity still unsurpassed by his technological innovation. Less important, but extremely significant, are man's upright posture, vocal mechanism, stereoscopic and color vision and the other keen senses of hearing, smell, touch and taste.

The human body in its prime, undiminished by dissipation, abuse and the ravages of age, is a thing of beauty. No one could possibly deny that after viewing it at its best in a classical ballet like Swan Lake or in the Hindu dance the Bharatanatyam, two art forms of man designed to exalt the human body, But one must give pause for thought that this may, after all, be only a subjective deduction of man himself. Perhaps a diplodocus considered another diplodocus a thing of beauty too. Then also, there are other animals that man would consider things of beauty—a thoroughbred race horse, some purebred dogs and many of the wild creatures.

But these attributes of man did not arise overnight. His basic structure and organization can be traced, first to the invertebrates, which developed an organism oriented around the central alimentary canal. Next the fishes, which developed the spinal column and internal skeleton to house and protect the alimentary canal. To these developments a half a billion years or so ago man owes his fore and aft orientation and eventually his upright posture. His legs and arms are traceable back to the fins of the fish, which matured into the waddling limbs of the amphibians and the strong under body legs of the dinosaurs. And when man's early mammilary ancestors took to the trees the fore limbs developed into true grasping and dextrous hands with a thumb opposing the fingers. Stereoscopic vision followed to enable this early ancestor to navigate safely in the trees with depth perception for leaping from limb to limb. A superior brain was needed to complement the dextrous hands and stereoscopic vision for the agility and cunning required by life in the trees. To his early mammal ancestors man is also indebted for his body temperature control mechanisms. All these developments culminated in the primates, the life genera from which man most recently ascended.

In technical terms man belongs to the chordata phylum. A phylum is a division of life of which there are nineteen. The chordates include fishes, amphibians, reptiles, birds and mammals. Each of these classes of chordates break down to orders such as carnivora, rodentia and primates. Man belongs to the primate order.

The grasping hand and stereoscopic vision, a marked advantage of the primates, originated with the prosimians (pre-monkeys) in early Cenozoic times some 60 million years ago. Prosimians were small cat sized creatures with long tails. They were tree dwellers. A descendant, the lemur, exists today in Madagascar which was separated from Africa since early Cenozoic times. The tarsiers in the Philippines, Borneo and Sumatra and lorises in India, Africa and other parts of Asia are also prosimians.

About mid Cenozoic times—some 30 million years ago—the monkeys of the suborder anthropoidea evolved with longer arms, more dextrous hands and larger heads to protect an enlarging brain. They were followed shortly by the emergence of the hominoidea which includes the apes and man. The hominoids apparently evolved from the old world monkeys in Africa, having been separated from the new world monkeys by their non contiguous habitats. The latter do not appear to have evolved further.

During the Miocene epoch—about 15 million years ago—the apes and man started to go their separate ways with man and his ancestors forming the family hominidae. A common ancestor of the apes and man was probably dryopithecus, also called pro-counsul, an enlarged monkey-ape who attained the upright posture and had already shed his tail. Dryopithecus had many ape-like, even man-like features but his brain was still monkey-sized. The apes and men had now begun to foresake the trees but not for good. Present day apes still retain their arboreal habitat. The gibbon and orangutan spend most of their time in the trees, whereas the chimpanzee and gorilla have all but forsaken them.

The story of the parting of the apes and hominids is not yet clearly known. The fossil record still has many gaps. After dryopithecus comes ramapithecus, known to date only through a half dozen jaw fragments found in India and Africa. His name derives from the Hindu god Rama. Pithecus derives from the Greek word pitecas (ape). Ramapithecus is considered a direct ancestor of man and a descendant of dryopithecus. But until his skeleton, or parts thereof, are found it will not be known whether he had already attained an upright posture. His teeth however, are man-like.

A word at this point about teeth. It is always a source of wonder to laymen how much a paleo-anthropologist can determine from fossilized teeth. In the first place teeth, (usually with accompanying jaw fragments) are most frequently found in the fossil record because they are the hardest and most imperishable parts of the human body. Perhaps, anthropologists, therefore, had to become adept at interpreting their meaning. The set of the teeth, the size of the bicuspids, number of cusps, the folds of the molars and other dental features have become important clues to the identification of fossil finds. Much more important, but less readily available of course are the skull, limb and pelvic bones. They reflect intelligence and posture, two dominant features of man. Dating of the fossil finds is no longer an insurmountable problem with radio-active techniques. Although differences and arguments still ensue over the age of new fossil finds within the fraternity, paleo-anthropology has become a reasonably reliable science.

After ramapithecus comes australopithecus who emerged about 2.5 million years ago. A skull was first found in South Africa in 1924 by Professor Raymond Dart of the University of Witwatersrand. Other skull and body bones were found soon after. These later finds revealed a larger creature about the size of a gorilla weighing about 150 pounds. The other was chimpanzee-sized, weighing between 80–100 pounds. Both species were ground dwellers with upright, though slightly stooped, postures. The limb bones were like that of modern man. But the size of the brain was no more than a third of man today, averaging about 500 cubic centimeters. The smaller was called australopithecus africanus, the larger, australopithecus robustus. They were men in every respect but size and intellect.

HOMO ERECTUS

Next in line is homo erectus, who emerged 1.3 million years ago or so. Java Man, found in 1891, and Peking Man who lived about 500,000 years ago are examples of homo erectus. His body was very much like modern man but his brain volume averaging about 1000 cc was much smaller. He had a protruding brow and is sometimes called "beetle-browed". Homo erectus spread throughout the world from his place of origin in East Africa.

Much of the knowledge on man's origin in East Africa is owed to Louis and Mary Leakey who spent their lifetimes—some 30 years—digging for fossils of animals and man at Olduvai Gorge in Tanzania. There they found teeth, skulls and bones and stone tools of australopithecus and homo erectus. The Leakeys' work added immense knowledge and at the same time generated controversy on the lineage of man. They found specimens of both australopithecus africanus and robustus, naming the former homo habilis (handy man) and the latter zinjanthropus boisei. The Leakeys were able to date habilis with some certainty at 1.75 million years ago due to the favorable geological situation in Olduvai. Habilis was found to be a tool user. Boisei was a vegetarian. The two apparently coexisted some two million years ago.

Habilis was extremely gracile and man-like so that Leakey felt he could be labeled homo. It was thought he was an advanced africanus. His brain capacity though was only about 657 cc whereas 700 cc is generally considered as the dividing line between man and his ape like ancestors. Yet his brain capacity was greater than the 500 cc or so of australopithecus. Habilis could, therefore, be a link between australopithecus africanus and homo erectus. Robustus and boisei were probably outside the line of ascent of man.

Olduvai gorge is at the southern end of the Great Rift of Africa, a 4000 mile north-south gash down the east side of Africa beginning with the Red Sea cutting inland across Ethiopia, Kenya and Tanzania. An international team of paleoanthropologists launched an expedition in 1967 into the Ethiopian segment of the Great Rift where the escarpments expose volcanic ash layers dating back 4 million years, 2 million years older than those at Olduvai gorge. At the same time the Leakey's son, Richard, worked the Rift near Lake Rudolph in northern Kenya. These efforts yielded valuable hominid fossil finds of both habilis and boisei. Richard Leakey's find, believed to be homo habilis, goes back 2.6 million years. The international team dates it's homo finds on the Hardar river in northern Ethiopia back 3.5 million years. These latest finds create doubt that homo habilis is descended from australopithecus africanus. They may have been contemporaries with their common ancestor still remaining to be discovered.

There are, to say the least, some unfilled gaps during the period 15 million to a million years ago when homo erectus dominated the scene. About the only hominid fossil evidence during the first two thirds of this period is ramapithecus, which can at best be labeled meager knowledge. The east African finds are now in a confused state. It may yet turn out that australopithecus is not a direct ancestor of man—simply a cousin—and that a common ancestor still remains to be found. But what is known is sufficient knowledge of man's origin to understand his place in the evolution of life on earth. To sum up then. Hominids separated from the apes about 15 million years ago. There evolved several kinds by 5 million years ago. One eventually attained greater intelligence, who is called homo, and gradually dominated and exterminated the others.

A million years or so ago homo erectus was supreme on the scene. He found his way to all parts of the old world. Man did not come to the Americas, however, until 30,000 years or so ago. As he extended his life into the northern regions of Europe and Asia he encountered some trying conditions for survival for this was the time of the Pleistocene ice age. But by then erectus had become an adept tool user and had developed the organized hunt for his meat supply. Man had now become primarily carnivorous. Robustus, the vegetarian vanished somewhere about a million years ago. This adaptation of the carnivore way of life is generally thought to have been the making of homo sapiens or modern man. Early man had to rely on intellect to overcome his physical inadequacies as a hunter of animals stronger and swifter than he. He (like the ants) had to organize the hunt for greater group power in his struggle to survive. This required communication. Communication required more and more intellect. All these needs aided and abeted the growth of the brain. Those with the superior intellect genes survived better the risks of the hunt, dominated the individuals organized for and around the hunt including cohabitation with the greatest number and superior females of the group. Man rode the intellect genes in the evolutionary process to domination of life on earth.

It is interesting to speculate how and why man became a meat eater. Primates are primarily vegetarians. They do eat insects and other small animals and their mammal ancestors were insectivores. But when they took to the arboreal life they lived mostly off the fruit of the trees. Primates, however, will take readily to a meat diet as has been demonstrated in zoos and laboratories. When early man began to evolve he was doubtless still a vegetarian. Australopithecus robustus remained a vegetarian. Food on the ground was, perhaps, more scarce than in the trees so man's ancestors were forced to eat what may have been available. They probably took to meat, at first, as scavengers in the wake of the carnivores. Later they may have, through group action, wrested game killed by the carnivores as do the jackals and coyotes to this day. And as their fondness for meat increased—somewhere along the line they realized it was more nourishing per weight than vegetarian food—they began to kill small game. Eventually, they graduated to the hunt for large animals.

At this time Nature blessed man's ancestors with another advantage. They began to shed their primate hair in favor of sweat glands. Perspiration cools the naked body. A distinct advantage under the hot African sun. Concomitantly man's metabolism increased and he could indulge in longer bursts of energy. This served him well in stalking large animals who would tire before him and become vulnerable to the kill. Although sweating gave man an advantage in the hunt some biologists consider it a mixed blessing. The loss of water and sodium makes man more susceptible to exhaustion.

Homo erectus also developed the use of fire. How this came about is likewise lost in obscurity, but a bit of conjecture can reproduce a likely scenario. Fire occurs in nature normally and regularly from volcanoes, lightening and spontaneous combustion. There are about 10,000 forest fires started by lightening each year. There is no reason to believe it was any different a million years ago. Most animals fear fire but homo erectus was intelligent enough to overcome this fear and realize its advantages in keeping him warm and, after some time perhaps, in cooking his meat. The latter probably came about by accident, something like that described humorously by Charles Lamb in a Dessertation upon Roast Pig. Homo erectus may have dropped a piece of meat in or placed his kill near the fire and found that the roasted meat tasted good. And though he may not have known that roasting increases the nutritive value of the meat he found it succored him better. Ultimately cooked meat was to have cosmetic effect as man no longer required massive jaws for chewing raw food and his facial features became more gracile and attractive.

Homo erectus, among his other achievements, acquired and developed speech and language. It was, doubtless, very rudimentary and may have even begun to develop before his time. Two things are known to be necessary for speech. The first is brain capacity. It is found in the study of human babies that speech only begins after the brain reaches 750 cc in size (about one year in modern man). Erectus had attained such intellect with a brain size average of about 1000 cc. Equally important is the development of a pharnyx and the related physical vocal features of the mouth and throat (position and mobility of the tongue, nasal cavity, position and capacity of the larnyx). This machinery of speech is only embryonically developed in the apes who also lack the brain capacity for speech development. Attempts to teach apes speech have met with failure.

How well it was developed by homo erectus is not known and open to controversy. Some interesting experiments were conducted by Dr. Philip Lieberman, a linguist, at the University of Connecticut and Dr. Edmund S. Crelin, an anatomist, at the Yale medical school based on the skull anatomy of Neanderthal man and they concluded that he, living some 40–100,000 years ago, had not yet developed the physical features of the vocal apparatus needed to make the complicated sounds of modern speech.

The speech and language of erectus obviously was not that of modern man. This great attribute of human evolution was millions of years in the making. When erectus first achieved a workable language will probably never be precisely known. He spanned a million years so that the development was probably continuous with a fairly good speech and language in hand by the end of the period. It is thought that this great development too was in response to the challenge of the hunt and societal organization it begot. Good communication between members of the hunting group increased its efficiency and diminished the risks involved. The imperatives of the hunt obviously demanded constantly better communication. And over the eons this cross fertilization resulted in human speech and language.

Language enabled erectus to think and communicate in concepts. He was no longer confined to dealing with material things by sight and hand. It was the start of man's cultural evolution. Homo erectus was about to evolve into homo sapiens. This was another "leap forward"—if one may be forgiven the use of such anomolous term for the infinitesimally slow pace of biological evolution—in the development of man as the average brain capacity of 1500 cc of homo sapiens is 50 per cent greater than erectus. It should be emphasized once again that this great enlargement of man's brain was a slow process transpiring, perhaps, over a half a million years or more. But by about 250,000 years ago, homo erectus graduated to homo sapiens.

A quarter of a million years ago was a time of geologic turmoil on earth. It was the period of the great ice age. Homo erectus, however, was not greatly effected by the glaciers as he stayed away from them retreating to his habitat in the savannas of Africa and Asia. But as the ice receded around 250,000 years ago all of Europe, including Great Britain, enjoyed a warm even tropical climate and erectus, becoming sapiens, moved into Europe in numbers. His stone tool technology (more on this later) advanced significantly. In fact, it is this great advance in his tool making that has caused anthropologists to graduate man to the stage of homo sapiens. There is unfortunately little fossil evidence to go by.

NEANDERTHAL

But then came Riss, one of the most horrendous glaciers, which spanned the period 200 to 125,000 years ago. The temperature in England, once nearly tropical, did not go above freezing in midsummer! Early homo sapiens had to retreat before its advance. This was, of course, merely part of his nomadic life, but now he became almost entirely dependent on meat for his food supply. Vegetation on the tundra was scarce and mostly non-digestible for man, consisting of lichens and shrubs. Animals, however, such as the reindeer, could thrive on it. An ecological bond of sorts arose between man and reindeer such as still exists today in Lapland. The hunt became a matter of life and death, for early homo sapiens survival depended upon it for food, clothing and other requisites. It has already been mentioned how the imperatives of the hunt brought the superior intellect genes to the fore and it was during the period of the Riss that man's brain capacity evolved to its present level. By the end of the Riss glacier homo sapiens, now as Neanderthal, had evolved an intellect and physical prowess to about his highest and present level. There would appear to be little or no growth in intellectual capacity the past 100,000 years for some still non-understandable reason. Growth in knowledge has, of course, progressed tremendously as it is cumulative and transmissible to succeeding generations. Each generation can and has added to the store of knowledge, particularly during the past generation or two.

Most of the foregoing anthropological knowledge and theory has been derived from the stone, bone and other tools and artifacts left by early homo sapiens. There is still a dearth of human fossils during this period. In fact, there is more fossil record of homo erectus. The famous Peking and Java men, dating back a half million years or so are erectus men. Only two fossils exist that are thought to represent early homo sapiens—the skulls found in Swanscombe, England and Steinheim, Germany dated back 250,000 years. In 1971 the De Lumleys, Henry and Marie-Antoinette, husband and wife, of the University of Marseilles found a cave in the Pyrenees where early homo sapiens lived at the time of the onset of the Riss, about 200,000 years ago. Only one crushed skull of a 20 year old was found, but the cave contained many tools and artifacts. The fossil record uncovered to date does not pick up again until the Neanderthal period 100,000 to 40,000 years ago.

The first remains of Neanderthal man were found in 1856 in a limestone quarry in the Neander Valley—called Neanderthal in old German—near Dusseldorf, Germany. Much of the skeleton was destroyed because the workers did not know what it was. Only the skullcap, ribs, some limb bones and part of the pelvis were saved. There followed years of controversy—and even ridicule—over the find before it was properly identified and placed in the ancestry of man. During the past century numerous Neanderthal skeletons were found in Europe and the Mid East. A particularly notable site is the Shanidar cave in Iraqi Kurdistan where nine Neanderthal skeletons were found.

Neanderthal man has been much maligned. In the past he was generally portrayed as stooped, hairy, and brutish. His emergence in 1856 occurred at a most impropitious time. Darwin's evolution theory was challenging conventional wisdom on the origin of man and the Establishment tried to ridicule the theory out of existence. Darwin was caricatured in cartoons with the body of an ape. Speculation on the physiognomy of Neanderthal was doubtless affected by the tenor of the time.

For a long time Neanderthal was not even considered in the line of ascent to modern man. In part, this was due to his abrupt disappearance in the fossil record some 40,000 years ago. But he is now considered to be a true homo sapiens in direct line to modern man. There is even evidence he may have been more cultured than originally thought. In one of the burial spots in Shanidar cave flowers were found near the skeleton, a token of familial love and sensitivity in the burial. Also there is evidence that the maimed, doubtless the victims in the hunt, were cared for in the cave rather than left to die in the field.

Neanderthal too survived a glacier—the Wurm—which covered most of Europe from 75,000 to 10,000 years ago. Perhaps the Wurm was not as severe as the Riss, but it too must have proved a difficult challenge to Neanderthal. Although anthropologists do not believe there was any appreciable growth in man's brain capacity during the Wurm glacial period there is yet no convincing explanation why this should be so. The fossil record would appear to be too thin for hard conclusions. Also, the brain capacities are reckoned in broad ranges—1100–2200 cc for modern man. The mean could shift considerably in such ranges. The conclusion, moreover, seems belied by man's great advance in tool making about 50,000 years ago when Neanderthal developed the Mousterian flake-trimming technique and a great variety of specialized tools. On the other hand, Harvard biologist Ernst Mayr believes that societal changes in the hunting group arrested the process of natural selection. The group grew large, facile communications enabled the less intelligent to learn from the brightest the survival techniques of the hunt, and access to females was more free and democratic for all members. At this stage of knowledge there is still inconclusive proof that man's intellectual capacity did not increase during Neanderthal time. Perhaps now that Neanderthal is viewed more favorably different conclusions may be derived.

CRO-MAGNON

Neanderthal man vanished about 40,000 years ago, to be replaced by Cro-Magnon man who is considered a modern man, homo sapiens sapiens. The name Cro-Magnon is derived from a rock shelter near the village of Les Eyzies in the Dordogne region of southwest France where the first remains of modern man were found in 1868. That Neanderthal vanished may be inaccurate but so it was thought at first. And in the insouciant view of Neanderthal he was facilely considered an aberrant. It was concluded that the more modern Cro-Magnon man did him in, except that no one could explain where Cro-Magnon came from to accomplish such feat. It is now thought, however, that Cro-Magnon descended from Neanderthal. What bothered anthropologists was how brutish Neanderthal could beget handsome Cro-Magnon. They were plagued, as is often the case, by an unfortunate gap of 15,000 years in the fossil record. The most recent Neanderthal remains from La Chapelle-aux Saints are dated 40,000 years ago, and the oldest Cro-Magnon skeleton found in Czechoslovakia, is dated 26,000 years ago. But even 15,000 years it would seem could not effect such a change. They overlooked, however, the fact that there is a broad range of features in any given species. There are modern men walking the streets of New York City today, some dressed in Brooks Brothers suits, who possess features like those allegedly of Neanderthal man. Hence, it is now believed that if the fossil record were profuse it would show an imperceptable shift from the brutish to the handsome norm in the ascent from Neanderthal to Cro-Magnon man. At any rate, it is now the prevailing view that Cro-Magnon descended from Neanderthal. There may be, however, a plausible explanation for the belief that Cro-Magnon exterminated Neanderthal. The ascent of Neanderthal to Cro-Magnon could have taken place first in the Mid-East. Fossil finds in Israel and Lebanon would tend to confirm it. Cro-Magnon then with his superior technology invaded Europe and conquered (and assimilated) his backward Neanderthal cousins. This would be in keeping with human recorded history.

Cro-Magnon man was still a hunter. In fact, the Wurm glacier was at its maximum when he started to evolve. His life was, as before, organized around the hunt. His tools advanced greatly. He invented the bone needle and began to sew animal skins into form fitting clothes. He brought mankind to the dawn of agriculture around 10,000 years ago. By then the Wurm was in full retreat and the stage was set for the flowering of man on earth.

Cro-Magnon became the earth's first artist. There are the cave paintings at Altamira, Spain with pigments intact after 20,000 years! And the venus figurines found scattered widely over Europe. These voluptuous nude female statuettes were, doubtless, fertility symbols. Lastly, are the many hand carved ivories—antler and stone pieces—including even the handles of every day tools.

These artistic remains attest not only the developing cultural bent of men but more leisure for such non-productive effort. It was man's advancing technology at work. Cro-Magnon invented several tools to improve the hunt, most noteworthy, the spear thrower. This was a simple rod about a foot long crooked and recessed at one end to fit the end of the spear. The leverage enabled him to throw the spear three times the speed possible by hand. This weapon was more lethal and he could kill animals from greater distances. Other devices like the snare and fishhook facilitated the supply of meat and fur. Furs and hides were now used by Cro-Magnon for shelter and dress. Fossil remains of postholes at the archeological sites bears it out.

The retreating glacier also served to augment the food supply. Vegetation in profusion and variety reestablished itself on the vacated land and Cro-Magnon began gathering the fruit, nuts and seeds of the plants. In the division of labor of the hunting group this task doubtless, fell to the women. This inevitably led to agriculture and the demise of the hunt as the main sustenance of man.

This transformation of the life of man from the hunt to agriculture and animal husbandry is perhaps the greatest single event in the story of man. Equally important though may be the industrial revolution of the past 200 years. These events are technological developments, not biological evolution which determined man's progress until recently over the eons. By the time man reached the advent of agriculture he had already arrested the process of natural selection and his evolution henceforth was technological and cultural. He has not, unfortunately been very successful in conducting this technological and cultural evolution on a rational basis. Millions of years of biological evolution has left him with instincts and motivations, designed by Nature for his survival, which he has not been able to control. It is in order next to examine the motivations of man in order to understand his history.

MOTIVATION OF MAN

The evolution of life on earth, set forth above, culminating in the creation of man, a being with the power to reason, begs the query—what motivates the life of man. Men of reason would not make war. Wars bring only pyrrhic victories, albeit that there may be short term gains to nations and ephemeral glories to men. There is more in the biblical adage "He who lives by the sword dies by the sword" than meets the eye. There must, therefore, be factors in the genetical structure of man that cause him to act in a manner that his intellect tells him is inimical to his specie.

As we have seen, Nature, in its infinite wisdom, programmed life genetically for the survival of the species. Any damage these aggressive forces of survival could wreak on others were checked by the limited amount of energy each form of life had at its command. But when these evolutionary forces brought forth a form of life with great intellect, which could use this intellect through technological innovation to command more and more energy outside itself the danger that this awesome command of external energy would be directed by the irrational, instead of the rational, was created. It is one thing when a man has merely his hands to vent his aggression against another and quite a different situation when he has a gun. Recorded history has been, largely, the sad story of the irrational forces in man directing his increasing command over external energy. But this is getting ahead of the story. Let us pause to discuss these irrational motivations of man.

These motivations fall into two categories. Those directed inter-specially and those directed intra-specie. It is the latter that are most germaine to the history of man. The basic motivation, of course, is the survival instinct. All forms of life are both aggressive and defensive with respect to other species in this regard. The carnivores are structured genetically for aggression against other animals for their food supply. Had Nature evolved all animal life to subsist off plants there would have been no need for this inter-special aggression. But it should be recalled that the earliest form of life was carnivorous. Herbivores came later only after plant life evolved. At any rate, this inter-special aggressiveness is manifested without any anger or hate feelings by predators. Photos of lions attacking ungulates reveal a benign facial expression during the kill.

The reaction of the victim, however, is considerably different. Fear dominates its reaction. The first impulse is to flee, particularly by those which are fleet of foot. When escape is not possible the victim will usually become violent, to the point of desperation against hopeless odds. And at times super feats are achieved. The expression "fought like a cornered rat" is used to describe this reaction.

Man has at this stage of evolution mastered all other life on earth through his technology so that the inter-special struggle for survival is no longer a significant motivating factor in his life. In fact, he has even foresaken the hunt, which dominated the greater part of his existence to date, in favor of domesticated animals for his meat supply. There remain only the ecological problems in man's relation to other animals on earth. Hence, inter-special matters need not detain us further.

Man's intra-specie behavior is, however, another matter. In this important area man is a very mixed up creature. The confusion emanates from both his biological and cultural development. It would appear from studies of animal behavior—the more evolved the specie the more so—that animals are genetically structured for intra-special domination. There is the pecking order of fowls, the pride of the lions and others. But more pertinent, intra-special domination is a pronounced characteristic of the primates, the order of life to which man belongs.

Life in a primate group—gorillas, chimpanzees, macaques, languars, baboons and others—is stratified and structured. Every member, particularly on the male side, knows his place. Status brings both privilege and responsibility. The top member or members of the hierarchy are expected to defend the group or subordinates with their lives if necessary. They are responsible for order in the group which requires occasional physical violence against a subordinate or female member. Above all they are protectors of the young and their mothers. It has been noted that infant care becomes more important for survival as the specie grows more complex. The rigidity of the order varies somewhat from specie to specie. The baboons are extremely rigid. The chimpanzees more relaxed and friendly.

The dominant males are entitled to the best of everything. The best food, their choice of sleeping spot, the best and longest grooming from females and subordinates. And more significant copulation with the best and greatest number of females. In some cases, like the baboons, exclusive possession of a female in estrus. Chimpanzees, however, are more democratic with respect to females in heat giving all males access in the order of hierarchial status.

This sex privilege of the dominant male is thought to be a chief reason for the genetically structured dominance behavior of the primates and other societal animals. In the purely biological realm dominance is based upon the superior qualities of the individual. He is usually bigger, stronger and wiser. Dominance is based on merit. Dominance, with its sex privilege, was designed by Nature for maximum perpetuation of the superior genes of the specie.

Pair bonding is not a normal feature of primate life. There appears to be some pair bonding tendency, however, among baboons and gorillas. It is more common, however, among carnivores. Man may have been influenced by them when he assumed the carnivore way of life. Among the primates the female in heat makes herself available to any male. In the case of the baboons the dominant male does not assert his privilege in the beginning of estrus and the female can only attract the subordinate males. But the dominant male takes exclusive possession of the female of his choice at the height of estrus when she is ovulating and ready to be bred. Inferior females are usually ignored by him. This is calculated to promote the best possible genetic evolution of the specie. At the same time the subordinate males are not frustrated in their sexual drive which promotes the affinity of the group.

Among the females there too is a hierarchial structure, though less rigid because females are subordinate to males among the primates. Then too, most of their lives are preoccupied with borning and rearing the young. This disability does not necessarily require inferiority as some animal groups like the hyenas are female dominated. In the case of females in the primate group dominance is also based on merit. In exercising their sex privilege the dominant males will usually choose the dominant females as sexual partners.

Dominance is necessary to maintain order and discipline in the group. An undisciplined group is ineffective. As the primates took to the ground in search of food leadership and discipline became more important in their encounters with the large carnivores. When baboons move on the ground the leader exercises strict command. He will halt the group, which remains motionless, while he reconnoiters a thicket for possibilities of predators before permitting any member to enter it in search of food. If he senses the presence of predators he orders the group to detour around the thicket. Such order became essential for survival when the defenseless primates took to the ground habituated by the physically superior carnivores.

Dominance in the primate groups appears to be based upon individual superiority. Greater strength, greater wisdom due to extraordinary intellect, a confidence and courage exuded by the individual aware of his superior qualities and like factors. The dominance-subservience relationship evolves within the group as the individuals grow and develop. It is, however, backed by aggression or threat of aggression. Violence flares up occasionally between challenger and challenged for position. It also seems important for the dominant male or males (some primate groups are led by a senate of two or more dominant males) to assert their dominance. This has become highly ritualized. When the dominant baboon male, through stern look, baring teeth or other display of aggression asserts himself with a subordinate male (or female) the latter, by way of obescience, upends himself in an invitation for copulation. The superior male proceeds to mount the subservient male and engages in a few mock copulatory strokes. This ritual serves to reassert the dominance of the superior male and it has to be repeated constantly by the superior male with subordinates, particularly with those challenging his position. When the superior male fails to assert himself successfully in this ritual he loses his position of dominance.

Hereditary factors are important. The male offspring of a sexual union of eminent individuals is more likely to be born with superior qualities. But in addition he is reared in more advantageous surroundings coming under the protection of a paramount female and her dominant male consort. He soon acquires the attitude and feeling of superiority. If he was also lucky in the throw of the genetic dice so that he is able to back his superior attitude with favorable biological features he is quickly on his way to becoming a dominant male in his group.

There is every reason to believe that man is genetically structured like his primate cousins. Everyday observation reveals man's propensity to dominate his fellow man. But in man this biological instinct has been wrested out of its genetic context and frought with danger because of man's ability to command energy on his behalf through his technological prowess. When man decided to become a carnivore he was ill equipped for this way of life. Nature had fitted him out to be a vegetarian. He had neither the fangs, jaws or paws nor the speed to catch and kill large animals. But Nature did provide him with great intellect to make tools to offset this biological deficiency and he eventually became the foremost predator of the animal world. But herein began man's confusion with respect to the instinct to dominate.

In the case of the true carnivores which Nature endowed with lethal attributes for killing other animals Nature also built in checks upon their intraspecial aggression. A lion will aggress against another male in the pride asserting his dominance but will usually stop short of lethal violence because of a built in genetical factor against intra-special killing. Such genetical structuring was necessary in animals with lethal powers if dominance motivation was to be used for maximum genetical evolution of the specie. This built in genetical check is also observed in herbivores equipped biologically with lethal features for defence or other purposes. Reindeers, for example, will engage in horn locking contests over the possession of females in estrus but will not carry the fight to the extreme of thrusting the sharp antlers into the soft underbelly of the opponent.

This genetically structured check on lethal intra-special aggression in manifesting the instinct to dominate has apparently not been structured or has been weakly structured into primates. That is so because there would appear to be less need for such genetic check. Primates are vegetarians and not biologically equipped with lethal appendages. They can only bite severely but not fatally. If a fight developed out of the instinct to dominate it could at best end in a bloody mess but seldom death.

When man attained power outside himself through his technology he became equipped with lethal weapons. To be sure he developed the weapons for the hunt but the hand axe could also serve to crush the skull of his fellow man or the sharp spear to stop his heart. He was now a converted carnivore with lethal power to kill large animals including his own kind. But genetically he was still a primate with a poorly developed check mechanism on intra-special aggression in the manifestation of his instinct to dominate. He had, therefore, to do the next best thing which was to develop cultural checks on his intra-special aggression. Herein came into play the societal features of the hunt that man was forced to organize for his survival as a carnivore.

It should be noted here that any form of life is genetically structured with several and many instincts. Some take over in certain situations, they aid and abet each other, they check each other, as discussed above, in a constant interplay directing the behavior of the animal. There is a "great parliament of instincts" as Nobel prize winning ethologist Konrad Lorenz refers to the situation. And it would appear that it was the very basic instinct for survival that dictated certain societal or cultural checks on man's intra-special aggression.

Emerging man realized that his survival as a carnivore required intra-special cooperation. In concert with others he could hunt more effectively and defend himself better. The herding of animals for defense is well known to ethologists. Predators, even the big cats, will desist from attacking animals herded in a group. Their tactic is to separate one from the group or attack a straggler. The primates utilize group living for increased safety. There is every reason to believe that man is genetically structured with the same survival instinct.

But group defense is an occasional matter to meet a specific survival situation. Man needed continual cooperation for his food supply, once he chose to rely on meat which required extraordinary effort. He was forced to depend more on group action than the primates who remained vegetarians. This eventually resulted in a social organization based upon both primate and carnivore behavior and predicated upon both biological instincts and cultural mores.

SOCIAL ORGANIZATION OF MAN

The primates, we know, are societal animals. But so are many carni-vores—the lions, wolves, prairie dogs and others. And everyone is familiar with the insect societies—the ants, termites and bees. It has already been mentioned in the preceding chapter that there is an interesting theory that holds that the affinity of individuals of a species for survival is merely an extension of the unity of the cells of a complex organism each performing an assigned function in the organization of that specific form of life. One ant is nothing but an ant colony has the energy of a large animal. The ant colony is motivated by instincts and so, it would seem, that genetic programming is the basis of the societies of the higher animals.

The societal instincts, however, differ in the species. The primate group does not usually have a home base. It has a territory but seldom a home. Carnivores behave differently. They too have a hunting territory but also a home base where the group habitates. The lion pride is the best example.

When early man descended from the trees he, doubtless, lived in a primate society such as that of the apes today. The group moved in its territory in search of food, climbed the nearest tree or trees to rest or sleep in safety from the predators and conducted a structured life based on the dominance instinct. But as he adopted the carnivore way of life he began to emulate carnivore habits. In fact, a home base became even more important to man than the carnivores as the hunt became his primary way of life. The main reason for this was man's developing brain that, above all else, made the carnivore way of life possible for him. To protect the delicate brain man's head had to grow larger and larger as his intellect increased. To borne the human infant only when it could be relatively self sufficient in a few days after birth, like do the lower animals, would have required an enlarged pelvic region in the human female that would have been incompatible with early man's developing upright posture. Nature, it would appear, therefore, compromised by programming a premature birth with prolonged infancy of the new born child. This had two profound effects on man's emerging social organization as a carnivore. The human female became more preoccupied with child rearing and could not join the hunt. In the pride of the lions the female, in fact, does most of the hunting and so it is with the hyenas. But in the human society the hunt was exclusively a male responsibility. The second effect was the need of a base or home where the human female and the unduly helpless children could remain in safety while the males (sometimes away for days) roamed the group's territory in search of game. This, perhaps, led to the first division of labor in the human society for the women, in order to contribute to the food supply, took to gathering vegetarian food—seeds, nuts, roots, fruit and the like—around the home base. Man was always an omnivore despite his preference for meat. It was only in certain situations such as life on the forbidding tundra during the ice age that he was wholly dependent on meat for food.

Pair bonding is also believed to have evolved out of the hunt *cum* home base way of life. To be sure, pair bonding is not peculiar to man. Birds and some carnivores mate by couples, but it is seldom the close, intimate and lifelong relationship evolved by man. Primates do not pair bond. An integral part of human pair bonding is the sexual availability at all times of the female to the male. Man is the only form of life that does not obey the estrus cycle. This development is doubtless a factor of his superior intelligence. How and why this feature of the human society evolved remains open to speculation but there are some discernible compelling reasons for it. More on this later.

Primates are subject to the estrus cycle. When in its command the female will accept any male. But in the structured primate society the dominant male has and usually exercises his privilege of sexual possession or priority to the female in estrus. This must have been the type of society from which man emerged but doubtless found unsuitable for his new way of life. The hunt separated males and females during the day and often for several days at a time. Furthermore, the dominant males needed the cooperation of the subordinate and young males in the hunt and could not treat them with insouciance upon return to the home base, as does the head baboon, by taking exclusive possession of a female in estrus. Moreover, the males doubtless returned with heightened sexual drives from the hunt with its challenge of physical danger and strain. Anthropologists believe that pair bonding and sexual opportunity within the bond at all times evolved as the solution to the situation. This became the bedrock of the human society forever after. It will be seen in the discussion subsequently on the rise and fall of human societies that a very important factor in the fall of a civilization is the weakening or breakdown of pair bonding between male and female. A high divorce rate is a leading indicator of a society in disintegration. As Juvenal, the Roman satirist, said "A woman who marries often does not marry at all". In other words, there can be no sound pair bonding in a society where divorce is free and rampant. Such society loses its cohesion and foundation.

While pair bonding is, doubtless, an instinct where it is found to exist in other forms of life, it would appear, to be a cultural development in the human society. During most of man's existence built around the hunt it was adhered to faithfully as it was advantageous even necessary for survival. Any disruptive factor had be ameliorated or eliminated in the hunting group constantly struggling for food. Every member of the group was acutely aware of its survival value. He needed no compulsion to abide by this necessary feature of the early human society. But after man forsook the hunt for agriculture, and eventually urbanized his life, this feature of the human society had to be backed by legal sanctions lest the less intelligent, the weak and the irresponsible undermine the bedrock of man's social organization.

The essential counterpart to the home base was the hunting territory. Most of the higher animals have structured within them a territorial instinct. It is a factor of the survival instinct designed for the equitable distribution of the food supply intra-specie. There is, on the other hand, no territorial conflict inter-specie. In fact cohabitation of a territory by different species is often mutually beneficial. Primates and ungulates move together so as to benefit from their respectively keener senses of sight and smell for joint defense against predators.

The primates, in particular, are highly territorial. In the trees it operates both horizontally and vertically. The howler and colabus monkeys, for instance, spend their lives in the tree tops. On the ground the territory is necessarily horizontal and larger. Vegetarians need less territory. Carnivores require a much larger range for their hunt. It has been observed that a baboon group of 40 commands a territory of only 15 square miles. But a band of 20 African bushmen require a hunting area of 440 square miles.

The territorial instinct is an essential feature of man's genetic makeup. It was basic to his food supply. A hunting group will defend it vigorously against other humans. Prior to the dawn of agriculture it can be imagined that human hunting groups of two score or more were spaced out in 500 square mile or so territories in the habitable areas of the world. When such area proved insufficient to feed the group it had two choices; to poach upon the territory of it's neighbors or migrate to some unclaimed area. Both were doubtless resorted to. The latter propelled man over the entire face of the world. The former probably resulted in many a bloody fracas.

This scene is not so remote in time. When the Europeans began to appropriate the hinterland of the North American continent they encountered precisely such human societies. Trampling upon the sacred hunting grounds of the Indians resulted in many a loss of scalp. But equally or more important was the observation of wars over hunting grounds. Some interesting lore has crept into American history and literature from this manifestation of the territorial instinct. There is, for example, the Indian brave's desire to be transported to the happy hunting ground after death. Then too, there is the quaint and charming custom of smoking the peace pipe after the resolution, bloody or otherwise, of a territorial conflict. The ritual was obviously designed to assuage the humiliation of the defeated chief. The humbling gesture of the victor sharing the same pipe with the vanquished, together with the sedative effect of nicotine, had the result of quieting aggressive instincts and salvaging bruised egos.

It must have become obvious to early man that bloody encounters over territories had to be amelioriated or eliminated for mutual benefit. He must have sought out escape mechanisms like the negotiated peace *cum* pipe smoking ceremony of the American Indians. Anthropologists believe that the practice of exogamy derived at least, in part, from such need. Exogamy, of course, has a tremendous genetic virtue as it broadens the combinations and permutations in the throw of the genetic dice, but this early man could not have been expected to understand. It must, therefore, have had some other felt advantage. Intermarriage between and among the hunting groups created a kinship that served to ameliorate bloody conflicts between them over territories. It also provided a channel of communication for the exchange of knowledge on hunting techniques and technological innovation. Thus a cultural development also served a biological function in the evolution of man.

There is an interesting bit of Asian history as recently as the 16th century. A. D. that bears out the virtue of exogamy in ameliorating human conflict. When Akbar, the Turko-Mongol, launched his conquest of Hindusthan he was unable to subdue by force the fierce Rajput warriors of Rajasthan. He decided instead to offer marriage to a Rajput princess and to make her the queen of India. He consolidated the move by making her brother the general of his army and another Rajput his minister of finance. In addition he married his son and eventual successor Jahangir to a Rajput princess. Jahangir's son and successor Shahjahan was therefore, three-fourths Rajput even though he remained a Muslim. He was, however, a most tolerant Muslim unlike most of his coreligionists. Needless to say Rajput Hindus and the Moghul Muslims lived in peace for two centuries because of Akbar's wise policy of intermarriage between them.

The territorial imperative—defense or offense—has been an important factor in most human conflict. After the hunt was forsaken for agriculture, which brought forth urbanization, the hunting groups or tribes, grew into city-states, then kingdoms and now nations with ever increasing membership. But the territorial instinct has remained.

MAN AT THE DAWN OF RECORDED HISTORY

An attempt may now be made to sum up man's basic motivations and behavior. As a primate man is genetically programmed for intra-special dominance and the manifestation of a territorial imperative. The latter tendency was augmented when man decided to adopt the carnivore way of life. The home base, more important to him than either the carnivores or primates, became a central factor of his territorial imperative.

Nature did not, however, program these instincts for homicide. On the contrary, it structured check instincts on intra-special aggression in the carnivores biologically equipped with lethal powers. In the primates such check instincts are weaker as primates are not equipped with teeth, jaws or paws that can readily kill other animals or their own kind. Thus Nature could rely upon a certain balance or lack of power in the case of primates.

Unfortunately, man has upset this intricate balance designed within him by Nature with his technology which enabled him to command energy beyond that bestowed upon him biologically. But the same intellect that produced his technology also made man realize he could not use this power with impunity against his fellow man without destroying his kind. He proceeded to create cultural checks on his intra-special aggression to make up for the lack of genetic checks such as Nature provided the carnivores. Cultural checks depend upon intellect and reason. They are not the reflex actions as are the biological instincts. The risk that the biological instincts would break through or prevail over the cultural always remained with man and still does today.

Furthermore, with technological progress resulting in the creation of wealth, the dominance instinct has resulted in ludicrous enormities throughout history. The dominance instinct begat greed—an insatiable desire for the personal accumulation of the wealth created by the society. To be sure, while the dominant baboon enjoys first call on the food, sex, grooming and other pleasureable amenities within the group he does not accumulate them beyond his immediate needs, Wealth, earned or ill-gotten, bestowed status in the human social hierarchy. Men became status seekers. Besides wealth, official title and organizational position were sought by any means, honorable or dishonorable. Possessions like the big house on the hill, a cadillac or rolls-royce, jewels and furs and other accoutrements were sought as indicia of status. The story of man is checkered with intra-special violence and immorality resulting from the perversion of the dominance instinct programmed within him genetically. Only occasionally did status coincide with merit as Nature designed it for the survival of the species. This aspect of man's behavior will be dealt with further in Chapter VIII on Wealth, Power and Revolution.

The same power of reason that produced man's technology and brought great amounts of energy under his command also enabled him to understand that social checks and balances had to be created to prevent deadly violence within the human race. Man was able to build these checks upon the bedrock of cooperation for survival dictated by the hunt. This led to friendship between man and man growing out of the shared experience and dangers of the chase. A man whose life was saved by another in the hunt remembered the favor the rest of his life. The time spent at night around the fire in conviviality and warmth, appetites sated after a successful kill, must have served to further the bond of friendship. Pair bonding between male and female resulted in the most intimate and lasting affinity possible for humans.

Customs and usages evolved out of these bonds of cooperation and friendship that welded the societies of early man together which provided the necessary checks and balances on the lethal confrontation of his biological instincts with the growing power resulting from his technological innovation. To be sure, the elemental genetic instincts broke through the cultural checks frequently resulting in internicene injury or death. A neanderthal fossil uncovered at Mount Carmel in Israel bore the evidence of a fatal spear wound. The point of the spear passed through the top of the man's thigh bone and hip bone socket ending up inside his pelvic cavity. In general, however, it can be assumed that the face to face encounters required by the still rudimentary technology of the time facilitated the force of the cultural checks, designed by early man, on his biological instincts. But the clash between the biological and cultural motivations became greater as man's technology accumulated and as social relations became less personal with the growth of bigger societies resulting from the passage to agricultural and industrial civilizations. The dominance instinct was designed by Nature for defeat not murder. But rituals of defeat and subservience are difficult to manifest when the lethal blow is delivered over long distance. By the same token homicide is more readily acceptable and less repugnant if it can be done remotely.

This then is the creature the process of evolution brought forth upon this earth. Like all forms of life man is basically motivated by certain genetically structured instincts, which developed and can change only imperceptibly over the eons. But unlike the other forms of life he has the power to reason. Through his intellect he has formulated a body of usages, customs, and eventually, laws to regulate his intra-specie behavior. But in the interplay of his biological instincts and his cultural checks upon them the latter have failed too often to prevail. Unfortunately, his gift of intellect has enabled him to command ever increasing amounts of energy outside himself which gives him enormous lethal power over his fellow man. The deadly results of this unhappy interplay of biological, cultural and technological forces seems to be growing out of control. The result has been a rather dismal history of man.

IV
Technological Innovation and Accumulation—Pre-Industrialization

Evolution blessed man with a nimble brain and clever hands. These unusual attributes enabled him to develop and accumulate technology for command over energy beyond that conferred upon him through biological inheritance. The development of this technology was slow—very slow in the beginning because of man's limited brain capacity. Australopithecus africanous, 2.5 million years ago, had a brain capacity of only 500 cc. Homo erectus a million years ago, still had a brain capacity of only 1000 cc. It was only about 250,000 years ago that man's brain capacity reached 1500 cc and, perhaps, not until the time of neanderthal did it reach its present capacity as high as 2200 cc in some individuals. Throughout this evolutionary period it can be said that the hand of man kept outreaching the capacity of his brain. The hand, by necessity, was responding to the demands and imperatives of the hunt. Man needed tools to extend the power of his hand for survival against animals stronger and fleeter than him. But technological development was necessarily slow until man developed his maximum intellectual capacity.

There is yet another reason for the slow growth of technology. Technology is built upon the technology of the past. The wheel had to precede the gear. The fundamental knowledge had to be developed first as a precondition for the more complex technology that followed.

The accumulation of technology also depends upon the facility of transmission of the knowledge from man to man and from generation to generation. Until the development of speech, at first, and of writing later early man was handicapped in his technological accumulation. Anthropologists are puzzled by the fact that there was so little technological progress during the long tenure, nearly a million years, of homo erectus. Anthropologist Grover Kranz thinks that it was primarily the fact that erectus had not developed biologically the speech mechanism for facile communication of knowledge to others that was responsible for this lag. Experiments show that a child cannot speak until it is a year or so old when its brain capacity is 750 cc, about half its adult size. Since erectus had an adult capacity of only 1000 cc he was unable to speak until much later in his life than a child today.

At the same time his life expectancy was less than 30 years. Thus he had a few short years in which to develop and disseminate technical knowledge. Communication of technical knowledge to his fellow man is equally important to the growth and accumulation of technology. In this manner more minds are able to work with it, synthesize it and add to it.

As technology spread and accumulated it seemed to acquire a life or momentum of its own. It begot, almost automatically, a more complex technology. William Fielding Ogburn points out in his *Social Change* that new inventions and technical ideas are conceived by men working independently in different parts of the world at the same time. In other words when technological accumulation reaches a certain level it calls for the next step to a higher level. The individual who creates the new invention is virtually a handmaid in the process. It has already been discussed that Darwin and Mendel conceived the theory of hereditary evolution (different aspects of it, to be sure) unaware of each other's work or existence. Ogburn made a systematic.study of new inventions and ideas and sets forth some striking examples to support his thesis. He lists nearly 150 ideas, discoveries and inventions conceived by two or more persons working independently, sometimes continents apart. Some noteworthy examples include the following: Logarithms by Burgi in 1620 and Napier-Briggs in 1614. Calculus by Newton in 1671 and Leibnitz in 1676. The law of inverse squares by Newton in 1666 and Halley in 1684. Discovery of oxygen by Scheele in 1774 and Priestly in 1774. Invention of the telegraph by Henry in 1831, Morse, Cooke-Wheatstone and Steinheil in 1837. The sewing machine by Thimmonier in 1830, Hunt in 1840 and Howe in 1846. The reaper by Hussey in 1833 and McCormick in 1834. The use of the internal combustion engine in automobiles by Otto in 1876, Daimler in 1885 and Selden in 1879.

The technology of man has had and still appears to have a hyperbolic development and accumulation. For a million years or two man's tools show only slight improvement. Neanderthal developed some 60–70 different tools. Cro-magnon over 100. In modern times the exponential nature of technological development is obvious to everyone. There has been more technological development in the last 200 years than occurred throughout man's preceding history. And there has probably been more during the past generation than the preceding 200 years!

Such hyperbolic accumulation of technology with its ever increasing command over energy by man has created a crisis of monumental proportions for the survival of mankind. It hardly needs mentioning again that man now has command over the fundamental energy of the universe to an extent he can destroy himself if not all life on earth.

Technological accumulation has not followed a steady and consistent progression. Like most human activity there have been periods of great creativity followed by plateaus of consolidation. The most notable periods of technological creativity were the founding of agriculture about 8000 years ago in the Near East and the Industrial Revolution, concentrated mainly in England, during the century 1750–1850. Actually it will be noted that the latter technological leap forward of man cannot be narrowed to so short a period nor to one people, but it can be said it flowered at that time and place. In fact, the momentum of the Industrial Revolution is still in progress. Whether mankind will again lapse into a period of consolidation remains to be seen. This might indeed be in the best interests of man as it would afford him time to develop better cultural checks on his biological instincts that at the moment cannot be trusted with the awesome power of his technology.

Finally it should be noted that technological creativity has not been possessed by mankind equally and in general at any given time. Different societies at various times possessed technological superiority. And invariably the people with the superior technology were able to and usually did dominate the others. This is not surprising in view of man's biological instinct to dominate his fellow man. The most notable example of recent times is England. Britannia ruled the waves—and dominated the world— during the 19th century because of the technological superiority acquired in the Industrial Revolution. It lost it's dominance to the Americans in the 20th century. In a broader sense of course, it was western civilization particularly its north European and American sector, which dominated the world with its superiority in technology during recent history. But this supremacy is now seriously challenged by the Russians and Chinese. And so it has been throughout recorded history and doubtless during pre-history.

It is also interesting to note that the dissemination of advanced technology cannot be restricted or curtailed. The new technology is eventually acquired by others. At times it may require stealth. The British prohibited the export of models or designs of the spinning and weaving machines they developed during the 18th century. The Americans tried to build them without success. The breakthrough came when Samuel Slater was persuaded to emigrate to the colony by attractive monetary offers for models of the new machines. Slater memorized the details of Arkwright's frames and left surreptitiously for America. In partnership with William Almy and Moses Brown he built from memory and experience the first mechanized textile mill in Providence, Rhode Island in 1793. Slater's mill was soon duplicated by others so that some 50 mechanized textile mills were in operation in America by 1800. England was unable to preserve its monopoly in the advanced textile technology. It was, however, a different story in India. But more on that later.

Even more striking is a recent episode involving nuclear missile technology. Striking, in that it comprises an irony of the cold war that gripped the world during the mid 20th century. China owes its success in the achievement of the nuclear missiles, in large measure, to the technical knowledge and experience acquired in America by Dr. Tsien Hsue-shen. Dr. Tsien came to America from China in 1934 on a scholarship. He received degrees from the Massachusettes Institute of Technology and the California Institute of Technology, the country's leading engineering schools. Thereafter he was Goddard Professor of jet propulsion at Cal Tech and did research work for the U. S. Navy on missiles. In 1950 when Americans were in the grip of irrational McCarthyism Dr. Tsien was accused by the American government of being a communist and planning to send secret documents to communist China. After he was sentenced to be deported the government concluded the charges concerning the secret documents were without foundation and tried to prevent Dr. Tsien from leaving because of his technological knowledge. By this time Dr. Tsien was thoroughly disaffected with America and left for China in 1955 where the communist government placed him in charge of their missiles program. In 1966 China launched its first guided missile with a nuclear warhead on a test target.

So it appears, that no peoples can preserve its technological superiority for long without constant creativity on the frontiers of technological innovation. There can be no resting on the oars lest superiority is lost and with it the ability to dominate other people of the earth.

STAGES OF TECHNOLOGICAL DEVELOPMENT

Man's technological development can be divided roughly into five or so stages.

1. Maximization of muscular power
2. Utilization of animal power
3. Utilization of elemental energy
4. Development of chemical energy
5. Development of nuclear energy

Each stage succeeds the other with a shorter time span and gives man an accelerated command over energy in the exponential manner noted above.

MUSCULAR POWER

In the beginning man was only able to augment his muscular power through the development of tools. "Man is a tool using animal" said Benjamin Franklin. In this respect he is virtually unique. There are a few examples of very elementary tool use by other forms of life, but they contribute only minimally to the muscular power of the animal, bird or insect. The burrowing wasp for instance, grasps a small pebble with its mouth to tamp sown soil over its nest of eggs. A darwin finch uses a cactus spine to pick insects out of tree bark. A sea otter uses a rock as an anvil on which to crack shellfish. Even the primates do not use tools much beyond this degree. Chimpanzees will use a stick to poke into ant and termite mounds and eat the insects adhering to the stick. They also hurl stones and sticks. Baboons will roll rocks downhill for defense. Tool using is, therefore, unique even among the more complex forms of life. And took making is virtually unknown.

It must be presumed then that when early man descended from the trees to adopt a carnivore way of life on the ground his capability did not extend beyond the throwing and other rudimentary use of sticks and stones. Unfortunately all anthropology has to go by in tracing man's development as a tool user and maker are the remains of his stone tools. It stands to reason that man has always used wood, and doubtless more so in the beginning, for his early tools. But wood is perishable. A stick to dig for roots and insects must have been an early tool. So was a club to kill small game. A pointed stick (an early spear) was perhaps one of the first tools fashioned by man for the hunt. The first spear or lance fossil made of yew-wood dated back some 400,000 years was found preserved in a bog in Claxton-on-the-sea, Essex, England. By that time erectus was proficient in the use of fire and the pointed tip was fire hardened. Tempering wood with heat for hardness appears to be a bit of sophisticated technical knowledge for that time.

Man must have used stones from the beginning of his life as a hunter. He could hurl them to wound animals. He could pound animals to death with a hefty stone in his hand. Eventually he realized that stones broken or chipped found in a river bed were more effective both in the hunt and for the cutting and tenderizing of the meat. After this it was merely a small step to sharpening of stones by chipping an edge of a stone with another stone. These early stones with chipped edges are hard to distinguish from stones chipped and broken naturally in river beds by the flow of water and other natural forces. Only a trained anthropologist is able to distinguish them.

The Leakeys date these earliest man made stone tools excavated at Olduvai, and called pebble tools or choppers, to the period 1.25–1.75 million years ago. This method of tool making is called the Oldowan industry. The pebble tool or chopper had an irregular cutting edge as only a few flakes were removed from each side. They were used, presumably, for skinning animals and for chopping the meat into pieces small enough to chew.

About a quarter million years ago there was a notable improvement in stone tools. The stones were flaked more profusely creating at least two regular serrated edges. This is called the Achulean industry. But as can be noted from the time reference homo erectus made little progress in tool making during his million years of life. It was only during the Mindel-Riss interglacial period when homo erectus was graduating to homo sapiens that a substantial improvement in stone tool making appears in the fossil record.

Most museum goers are familiar with the Achulean hand axe. It is roughly an isosceles triangle in shape, tapering to a slender tip. The base is slightly bulbous to fit into the palm of the hand. The two sides are chipped to form sharp cutting edges. The two sides usually come to a sharp point opposite the bulbous end. Its width is normally 2–3 times its thickness. Some of these

Achulean axes are as long as 18 inches. They obviously could not have been designed for use in the hand. Anthropologists think these large axes may have been used in traps designed to deliver a heavy blow on the head to the entrapped animal. On the other hand they could have been held by both hands to deliver a heavier blow. Most of the Achulean axes found to date are of a size that fits snugly into the palm of the hand, about 6–8 inches long and 3–4 inches wide.

The Achulean tools were produced by a more delicate and refined chipping or flaking method. Instead of using a hammerstone as in the Oldowan industry early man used a hard wood dowel or bone to strike or push the flakes off the core. Certain rocks like flint, quartzite or chert were particularly amenable to such delicate treatment and most of the sharp tools of this time were made of flint.

The flakes that were struck off the core proved useful as other tools. This must have been true from the very beginning as the flake had an even sharper edge than the matrix from which it was struck. These sharp flakes could be used as scrapers (of animal skins), knives (to cut meat and sharpen wooden tools), chisels and other small tools. As flint became the primary stone for tools these flakes proved even more useful because of the tendency of flint to break up into thin sharp blades. Some of these flakes were inches long with razor sharp edges that provided extremely effective knives and tips for spears.

About 150–100,000 years ago the emphasis shifted to these flake tools. A new method of tool making, called the Levallois technique, evolved for the production of flakes. Instead of a by-product of a core tool the flake was now the main product. A cylindrical core slightly tapered toward one end was first prepared in the same manner as the production of a core tool. When the core had a rough bellpepper shape sharp slender flakes were chipped off by light blows on the edge of the broader end of the core. This was continued around the core, like peeling an artichoke, until a small center remained. As many as 50 flakes could be produced from such a core. To be sure, this required a thorough analysis and understanding of the grain propensity of the core. But early man had acquired by this time a good understanding of his raw material. These flakes were then further shaped into knives, scrapers, chisels, burins, fishhooks, spear tips and arrow heads.

There were in final analysis only two basic methods of tool making during the stone age. The core method and the flake technique. In neolithic times, after the advent of agriculture, man developed the stone polishing technique which, together with the development of metals, superseded the stone age technology. Polished stone tools, particularly stone axes, continued to be used into the 20th century.

Neanderthal techniques produce some three score or more tools. His tool kit still contained the rougher Achulean hand axe and other core tools, but more and more of them were the refined flake tools. The making of these tools is called the Mousterian technique and the time referred to as the Mousterian culture, some 45,000 years ago.

Cro-magnon refined the technique further by preparing longer cores from 5 to 12 iniches long and striking off long thin flakes called blades only a fraction of an inch thick. Blades are flakes that are at least two times as long as they are wide. These blades were sharp and ready for use as knives when struck off the core but were usually worked further into a variety of tools. Cro-magnon made over 100 different stone tools. They required more chipping to achieve many more types of special purpose tools. One of these was the burin, a sort of chisel used to shape and cut ivory, bone and antlers into other tools or ornaments. Until the invention of the burin early man was unable to work materials like bone and ivory into fine tools and artifacts. The burin was used for instance, to cut a narrow strip out of a bone to be shaped into a sewing needle. A hole was bored into one end for the eye by another flake tool called a perforator. The bone strip was then rounded into the shape of a needle by the burin. Needles were important to Cro-Magnon and Neanderthal for making clothes from skins and furs to meet the challenge of the ice age. It must be presumed early man made the earlier needles of wood, but bone needles were obviously stronger and smoother.

A puzzling artifact of Cro-Magnon is a baton made of deer antlers. It consisted of a section of the antlers about 8 to 10 inches long with a half inch or so hole in the triangular end where two forking tines are cut off. No one is quite sure of its use. It is thought it might have been a scepter of the leader and it has, therefore, been called the *baton de commandment*. It could also have been an art piece. At this time early man had acquired more leisure and he was creating things of beauty. Another find that would fall into this category is a finely chipped "laurel leaf" blade discovered in France which is 11 inches long and less than a half inch thick. It seems too delicate and refined to have been used as an implement. It reflects, if anything, the virtuosity of the stone age artisan.

Cro-Magnon's techniques have been found to vary during his time from 40,000 to 10,000 B. C. Anthropologists divide them into five periods— Perigordian, Aurignacian, Solutrean, Magdalenian and Azilian. The Magdalenian from 15,000–10,000 B. C. is the high point in Cro-Magnon technology. This preceded by a few thousand years the dawn of agriculture.

Cro-Magnon's stone technology represents not only greater diversity and refinement of stone tools, but a more efficient use of raw material. Flint was not readily available everywhere. As man spread over the earth his source of flint grew more remote. Perhaps some sort of trade had already developed by Cro-magnon's time. At any rate, a more efficient use of the available flint became necessary as tool techniques and use increased with population growth. Cor-Magnon was able to convert a pound of flint with the Magdalenian technique, of striking long thin blades, into 40 feet of cutting edge. The Mousterian flake technique of Neanderthal yielded only 40 inches per pound. The Achulean method of core chipping gave homo erectus only six or so inches of cutting edge!

These figures bear out again, in a way, the hyperbolic character of technological development. For two million years or so early man's technology developed ever so slowly. Then it seemed to explode during Neanderthal's and particularly Cro-Magnon's time. And so it shall be seen, man's technological accumulation has maintained this characteristic growth to date.

Cro-Magnon's technology was not confined to stone tools. He used a wide variety of raw materials such as wood, bone, ivory and antlers for a vast array of tools and artifacts. In addition to more powerful weapons to kill animals he made scrapers, cutters, burins, perforators, needles and the like for the production of comfortable clothing, shelter and even luxuries like jewelry and art pieces. Warm well sewn and durable clothes were essential for both Neanderthal and Cro-Magnon to survive during glacial times. We are living today in a warm period. Most of the time during the past 75,000 years the weather ranged from cool to very cold. Twenty thousand years ago the mean temperature of France was probably around 10° F! Clothing and shelter were, therefore, important matters of survival for Cro-Magnon. It must be presumed that he had to clothe himself in the fashion of the Eskimo in the Arctic temperature today.

A noteworthy invention of Cro-Magnon was the spear thrower. It is a rod of wood, bone or antler a foot or two long with a hooked end. The hooked end is notched or recessed to hold the end of a spear. The spear thrower engaged the end of the spear behind his shoulder and the spear was positioned at eye level for aim as it was thrust forward with a snap of the arm at the target. This device enabled Cro-Magnon to throw the spear with considerable leverage. The velocity of the spear was increased three-fold or so with the spear thrower. Man could now hunt at greater distance from his prey which not only increased his efficiency but decreased the danger of being gored by the animal. Experiments with such a spear thrower demonstrate that a seven foot spear could be thrown 150 yards, twice the distance thrown by the unaided arm. A deer could be felled at distances up to 100 feet. Man could now hunt alone instead of in a group as it was no longer necessary to surround the prey in order to spear it. Fewer hunters got killed or hurt. Cro-Magnon were enabled to live a longer and healthier life.

The earliest find of a bone spear thrower dates back 14,000 years. It was found in a cave at La Placard, France. Some 70, made of antler, were found near Lake Constance, but not many are found as most were probably made of wood. American Indians used them. The Aztecs called it an atlatl. Australian aborigines still use the spear thrower today. They call it a womera.

The technological advance of the spear thrower should not be overlooked. It is perhaps, man's first employment of the law of mechanics to extend the power of his hand. He had doubtless used the lever to move large stones or other purpose, but the spear thrower is a far more sophisticated use of mechanics.

From the spear thrower to the bow and arrow was the next logical step forward. It is, of course, a monumental step as it represents man's earliest attempt to concentrate energy toward an objective. Unfortunately anthropologists are unable to determine with any degree of definiteness the time and place of the invention of the bow and arrow. The bow, of course was made of perishable wood and sinew or gut. So was the arrow except for the head. Stone tipped arrow shafts have been found in Germany which are thought to be about 10,000 years old. A couple of bows have been found in bogs in Denmark which date back some 8000 years.

But it is believed Cro-Magnon used the bow and arrow much earlier. The first clear representation in cave art of a bow and arrow has been found in North Africa, believed to fall within the period 30,000–15,000 B. C. The Sahara was verdant grassland at this time. It probably entered Europe by way of the Iberian peninsula which was a land bridge during the lowered sea level of the Wurm glacial period. There is also evidence of the bow in the Near East about the same period. Whether it spread there from Africa or was invented independently and contemporaneously remains unclear. At any rate, the bow and arrow spread to Europe from one of these places. In fact, the bow and arrow spread to all parts of the world except Australia. The aborigines of Australia know only the spear thrower even today.

The bow and arrow had great advantages in the hunt. It was, of course, more lethal as the hunter could invest the arrow with greater energy. This increased his distance, accuracy and killing power. Equally important, man could now launch his lethal missile from a hidden or camouflaged position adding immeasurably to his stealth in stalking animals.

By the same token, of course, man acquired a superior weapon for use against his fellow man. It may be presumed that at this time territorial disputes tended to arise as population increased with advancing technology creating pressure on the hunting areas. A band of 50 living by the hunt needs some 500–1000 acres for survival. It would have been easy for such band with bows and arrows to subdue another without them even if armed with spear throwers.

Henry Fairfield Osborn who wrote and compiled an authoritative treatise entitled *Men of the Old Stone Age* a generation or so ago, much of which, to be sure, has now been superseded by increased anthropological knowledge accumulated thereafter, postulates an intriguing scenario in this respect:

> From this scanty evidence we may infer that the new race competed for a time with the Neanderthals before they dispossessed them of their principal stations and drove them out of the country or killed them in battle. The Neanderthals, no doubt,

fought with wooden weapons and with stone-headed dart and spear, but there is no evidence that they possessed the bow and arrow. There is, on the contrary, some possibility that the newly arriving Cro-Magnon race may have been familiar with the bow and arrow, for a barbed arrow or spear head appears in drawings of later stage Cro-Magnon history, the so-called Madgalenian. It is thus possible, though very far from being demonstrated, that when the Cro-Magnons entered western Europe, at the dawn of the Upper Paleolithic, they were armed with weapons which, with their superior intelligence and physique, would have given them a very great advantage in contests with the Neanderthals

It must be recalled Osborn wrote his beautifully illustrated book at a time when conventional anthropological wisdom had handsome Cro-Magnon annihilating brutish Neanderthal. One need merely amend Osborn's scenario slightly for greater speculative credence today by having Cro-Magnon from the Near East, more technologically advanced, invading Europe where a more backward Cro-Magnon, or still Neanderthal, was subjected but not annihilated, and eventually assimilated into an advanced Cro-Magnon culture. Such scenario would be more in keeping with recorded history where one sector of the human race subjected and dominated another constantly because of superior technology.

The next step was to metals for tools and weapons. Stone continued to be used throughout—even into the 20th century—for tools. Flint actually provided a sharper cutting edge, but it had the disadvantage of being brittle so that it shattered easily. Metals, of course, were more durable. And as weapons of war they were more dependable for they were less likely to break at a critical moment.

There would not appear to be much technological advance during Mesolithic times. Pottery was, perhaps, being developed at this time. Some finds in Japan date back to 10,000 B. C. The polishing of stone may have started. The Neolithic period (circa 9000–6000 B. C.) that followed, however, was a time of great technological advance. Agriculture was started. And the use of metals began.

The earliest find to date of man's use of copper is in a cave in the Zagros mountains of northeastern Iraq. It is dated back to about 9500 B. C. The next find is dated much later around 7200 B. C. in Cayonu Tepesi in Turkey consisting of three pins (one hooked) and a tapered reamer. After this nearly a thousand years go by without any archeological evidence of copper but then around 6500–5000 B. C. discoveries became numerous all over the Near East.

It would seem logical that this area yield the earliest evidence of man's use of copper as it abounds with copper in its pure state. It was found in branched shapes, called aborescent copper, thin laminated sheets and in solid chunks of purple black matter. The native copper could be hammered into ornaments or tools. Apparently early man was in no hurry to use copper for tools as the oldest finds consist of ornaments, jewelry or light useful things like pins. But this is understandable for he had stone which provided him with adequate tools. It was only after the development of agriculture which created surplus production or wealth over which men could fight that man felt the need of more reliable and durable weapons.

Equally important, doubtless, was the limited supply of native copper. The general use of copper for tools and weapons necessarily had to await man's discovery of extracting copper from ore. How this occured can only be surmised. That the discovery occurred through the accidental melting of copper ore in his cooking fire has pretty much been ruled out because the usual temperature in a hearth does not reach a high enough degree (1300°– 1500° F) to smelt copper oxide ore. A temperature upwards of 2000° F is needed to liquify copper thoroughly. A more logical guess is that the discovery was made by the potter in his kiln. The early potter probably used copper oxides to provide a blue colored glaze on his clay. This may have left bits of smelted copper in his kiln which would doubtless have puzzled him at first but in due time led to a deduction the copper was smelted from the copper oxide powder. Once this was realized the smelting of copper from the ore in a kiln became the primary operation. The kiln had an additional feature needed to smelt copper, not available in an open fire, for it limited the amount of oxygen and provided the correct smelting atmosphere. By 3000 B. C. kilns were widely used for the smelting of copper ore.

The valley of Timna in the Negev desert, referred to in the Old Testament, was one of the first copper mining and smelting sites. Copper production at Timna probably dates back to 4000 B. C. In the beginning it was rudimentary. Malachite copper ore was gathered in the river beds, pounded and crushed to gravel like aggregate. The smelter was a circular stone clay lined fireplace sunk into the ground. It was loaded with crushed malachite copper ore and charcoal made of acacia wood. Oxygen was fed into the fire by mouth through tubes made of rolled strips of hide fitted with heat resistant ceramic ends. After the furnace reached a temperature in excess of 1500° F the mix was left to cool. The copper pellets were imbedded in the slag which had to be broken up to free the pure copper.

During the ensuing millennia the copper production was organized by the Egyptians into an efficient large scale operation to supply the markets of their empire. By 1200 B. C. an efficient furnace was developed which could attain temperatures of 2000° F. Oxygen in regulated amounts was fed into the furnace with bellows made of goatskins. It was built on the edge of a depression so that the slag could be run off while in a molten stage leaving a disc of pure copper in the furnace-well below the slag tap hole. At 2000° F the furnace could liquify the copper so that it separated and sank below the molten slag. This method of smelting copper with improvements has been used ever since.

The Timna valley cliffs were rich in malachite and it was easily removed from the soft sandstone matrix. A man could easily mine enough malachite in a day to yield 8 pounds of copper. And the furnaces were kept going on a 24 hour basis. The mines produced great quantities of copper for the people of Egypt and the Near East around 1200 B. C.

About 100 miles to the north was the village of Abu Matar where some of the copper was cast into tools and weapons—axe heads, chisels, spear tips, swords and other useful objects. The molds were carved in blocks of stones where the melted copper shrunk as it cooled and was easily removed. Imperfections and rough edges were smoothed out on a stone anvil with stone hammers.

Once the art of smelting was achieved it was easily applied to other ores, those that could be reduced at temperatures around 2000° F. Iron smelts at 3650° F, hence it still awaited further technological development. But tin and lead, the metals that formed bronze and brass with copper smelted at the lower temperature.

How the technique of alloying metals was discovered is also lost in obscurity. Then too, tin ores were not indigenous to the Near East where copper was developed. Later, of course, around 2000 B. C. or so trade had developed so that tin was imported by the Near East empires from Bohemia, Spain and even far away Britain. But as far back as 3000 B. C. objects of bronze were found in the tombs of Near East rulers. Some archeologists believe, therefore, that the Zagros mountains in early times contained tin as well as copper ores. In fact, further north in the Caucasian highlands, from where the Sumerians imported copper, there is an abundance of tin ore. It is also surmised that the alloying of copper and tin may have originated here by accidental mixing of malachite and cassiterite (a common ore of tin) in the kiln. Copper ore is seldom pure containing impurities such as arsenic, nickel, lead, bismuth, antimony and others. In fact, the earliest copper smiths found that their copper varied from place to place and some perspicacious metal smith may have deduced that a copper-tin mixture produced a superior metal. Earliest bronzes are copper-arsenic mixes, perhaps originating naturally. At any rate, with the development of bronze the age of metals was ushered into the life of man.

The bronze age, it would appear, began in the Near East where Sumerian kings were buried nearly 5000 years ago with an abundance of worldly goods (and human sacrifice) to assure them of a good life in the hereafter among which were many bronze artifacts. But the metal technology spread in due course of time to other parts of the world.

The Harappan civilization of the Indus valley which spanned the period 2500–1500 B. C. worked bronze with great skill. The Harappans hammered tools and weapons from flat pieces of bronze, riveted and soldered joints of the metal and produced bronze castings even by the advanced lost-wax method. There is no evidence of the use of iron, however, by the Harappans.

It is not clear whether the Indus valley civilization developed the metal technology by itself or whether the technology was transmitted to it from the Near East. There is evidence of trade between Sumeria and the Indus valley at this early date. It may have been by way of the Persian Gulf or the Khyber pass from Afghanistan. There is evidence of a bronze working center at Mundigar around 2500 B. C. in the Baluchistan hills of eastern Persia. The metal working art could have been transmitted to Harappa and Mohenjo-daro, the two cities of the Indus civilization, from Mundigar via the Khyber pass.

Even more obscure and puzzling is the emergence of the bronze age in China. There is no archeological evidence of bronze until the Shang dynasty (circa 1500–1000 B. C.) when it springs full bloom on the China scene. Beautiful and complex pieces were found in 1928 in the ancient burial city of An-yang. Although the Chinese did not appear to know the lost-wax method of molding they employed complex multipart molds soldered together with imperceptable seams.

It is equally obscure how and when Chinese metal technology developed. Since it would appear to be extant in the Near East millennia earlier there was a predeliction to presume it was transmitted to China from there, either by Sumerian or other metal smiths wandering to China or the obverse, Chinese travellers venturing southwest across the Gobi desert. The recent discovery in northern Thailand of bronze technology over 5000 years old leads to the conclusion it came to China originally from the south instead. But the sophisticated and complex bronze work of the Shang dynasty (circa 1500–1000 B. C.) tends to cause one to strongly suspect that the Chinese themselves developed most of their own bronze metallurgy. Evidence has been found of a neolithic culture 500 miles west of An-yang with highly developed pottery. A kiln was found capable of generating 2000° F of heat or more. These early potters used oxides for color. Hence, there is every reason to surmise that they evolved their own metallurgy. Unfortunately Chinese archeology is underdeveloped. Ancestral graves are sacred and revered. To be sure, Shang bronzes have been purloined from graves by irreverant robbers for centuries, but archeological work has been hampered by ancestral veneration. An-yang was not worked until 1928. Thus more digging into the past may yet develop more knowledge on the origin of bronze metallurgy in China.

Archeological evidence indicates the Chinese possessed the capability to smelt iron in their highly developed pottery furnaces which could attain temperatures of 3500° F or more. In fact it would appear that the Chinese were the first people to make cast iron. They approached iron as if it were bronze. Yet there is no evidence of widespread use of iron until China's Period of the Warring States, when the country was embroiled in wars among its states leading to the collapse of the Chou dynasty. The great demand for weapons could only be satisfied by a more plentiful metal. Both wrought and cast iron objects suddenly appear on the China scene, as did bronze a millennia or so earlier, in great variety and workmanship. During the Warring States Period (circa 481–256 B. C.) iron displaced bronze as the dominant metal for both weapons of war and agricultural implements.

There was another noteworthy bronze working center in Bohemia centered at Unetice, a village near Prague, around 1500 B. C. This was a time of considerable turmoil in Europe with waves of migration and warfare over territory. The Beaker people (so called after a bell-shaped clay cup found in their graves), who preceded the Uneticians did not appear to have a highly developed metal industry. The Uneticians, however, who succeeded around 1800 B. C. did. They exploited the abundant copper and tin resources of the Carpathian mountains. The fact that Bohemia was situated on the trade crossroads of Europe doubtless facilitated the development of a bronze industry. Traffic from the Near East to the West via the Danube and from the Mediterranean to the Baltic through the Brenner Pass crossed Unetician territory. Unetician bronze objects have been found from Wessex, England to the Near East. The Uneticians also have the technological distinction of inventing the safety pin.

Bronze technology made the Uneticians rich. They built fortified villages. Much of the metal was used for weapons of war as this was a time of strife in Europe, but unlike the Chinese the Uneticians also extended the use of bronze to agriculture. Thus while Chinese peasants were harvesting grain with stone sickles during the Shang dynasty the Europeans were using sickles made of bronze. Bronze torques used for neck and wrist wear were another common handicraft of Unetician smiths.

It is believed that the Uneticians—as well as other bronze centers of Europe such as Spain and Cyprus—acquired the metal working technology from the Near East. By 2000 B. C. trade routes extended all over Europe from Western Asia. It should be noted the early metal smiths were itinerant workers. They gravitated to areas where the metal ores were found. This was, obviously, a matter of economics as it was easier to move the technician to the raw materials than the other way around. The smith produced the metal at the ore site reducing the need for transporation to that of refined metal. Needless to say, the early metal smiths were elite members of their societies. In the Unetice societies they were exempt from agricultural work. But in other societies, due to the dirty nature of the work, the smiths were not always accorded the status commensurate with their technological prowess.

Gold and silver were much sought for metals even before copper. Found in its natural state gold was worked as early, if not earlier than Neolithic times. But since both play a minor role in the technology of man the development of these metals need not detain us further here. The role of gold, however, as a store of wealth over which man has fought for millennia will be discussed in considerable detail later.

The paramount metal of man is, and has been since antiquity, iron. Its origin is equally, if not more, obscure. It would appear though that it was the invention of the Indo-Europeans, a vigorous and technologically superior peoples that erupted out of the Caucasian area upon the old and sedentary civilizations of south and west Asia and upon the nascent civilizations of Europe during the early part of the second millennia B. C. They thrust as far East as the Indian subcontinent where they overcame the old Harappan civilization. The amalgamation of the two cultures brought forth the Hindu civilization, one of the eminent human cultures. In Iran, the result was the Persian empire. In Anatolia the Hittite empire arose. In Europe they generated the Graeco-Roman and eventually the European civilization of modern times. There were also some eccentric historical results. For instance the Hyksos, who seemed to appear from nowhere, suddenly imposed their rule over the Near East and even the Egyptian empire for a century or two (circa 1686–1567 B. C.). The Hyksos are now generally thought to be Indo-Europeans. These invasions lasted for centuries. At first they were directed at the Semitic, Dravidian, Egyptian and other peoples.

The Indo-Europeans owed their prowess primarily to the domestication of the horse and the invention of the war chariot. One can imagine what terror they must have struck in the minds and hearts of the foot bound armies of the sedentary empires with these new war machines. Even the Bible (II Kings VII, paragraph 6) refers to the terror struck in the hearts of the Syrians by the prospect of such attack. The pounding of the hoofs, the neighing of the horses, the rumble of the chariot wheels, the streaming arrows and spears, the slashing of swords from the charioteers as the vehicles sped by must have frightened the foot soldier into immobility. Even if the foot bound soldier was able to bring down a horse with his spear or sword the carnage inflicted on the defenders by the dying writhing animal and splintering chariot was doubtless greater than the loss to the invaders. There is little wonder that the old civilizations of the time succumbed easily in the face of such overwhelming military superiority.

Though less clear it is believed that the invading Indo-Europeans also possessed iron weapons. Perhaps not the earliest waves, but certainly by 1500 B. C. After the Hittites imposed their hegemony over Anatolia (modern Turkey) and its diverse peoples the early part of the second millennium B. C. they started to exploit the rich iron resources of the area, and during the period 1400–1200 B. C. held a virtual monopoly on the manufacture of smelted iron. There is an interesting letter from the Pharoah begging the Hittite King (Hatti Prince as he is referred to in ancient Egyptian historical documents) for some iron. The Hittite king refused. It should be recalled that toward the end of the second millennium B. C. the Hittite and Egyptian empires were the giants of the day vying for dominance of the Near East.

Another interesting Hittite letter written by King Hattusilis III (circa 1275–1250 B. C.) responding to a request from an Assyrian king for "good" iron states that such iron will be sent later as this was "a bad time for producing iron". Meanwhile he writes "I am dispatching an iron dagger blade to you. . ." It was doubtless a token of good faith. Why it was a "bad time for producing iron" is unclear. Perhaps it was harvest time and highest priority had to be given to the food crops. After all, even the indomitable Hittites could not eat iron!

It is not certain whether the Hittites owed their monopoly to superior technology or a good indigenous supply of iron ore plus, of course, ample wood for charcoal. But such raw materials existed elsewhere—iron is the most abundant metal on earth—so it is not unreasonable to conclude the Hittites possessed superior technology. That in turn begs the question whether they developed the superior technology or imported it from the Indo-European heartland in the Caucasian region.

In part this obscurity may be due to the complex nature of iron technology that probably took centuries to develop. The smelting of iron and working it into a good metal represents a tremendous advance in the technology of man. Unlike the non-ferrous metals where smelting results in a refined metal ready for casting and working, the smelting of iron ore produces a spongy mass or bloom that must be kept hot while it is hammered repeatedly to produce wrought iron. But wrought iron is soft and malleable. While useful in many respects it does not keep a sharp cutting edge. In order to toughen it, wrought iron has to be carburized to transform it into cast iron or steel. Wrought iron contains little or no carbon, steel has between 0.15 to 1.5 per cent and cast iron 1.5 to 5 per cent. This carburization process is believed to have originated in the Armenian mountains. Professor Forbes of Amsterdam attributes the invention of steel making to the Chalybes who were subjects of the Hittite kings. It consisted of constant reheating of the wrought iron in hot charcoal (from whence the iron absorbed carbon), hammering and quenching with water until the desired quality of iron or steel was attained.

It is immediately realized that the production of "good" iron required better furnaces, the development of tongs, hammers and anvils to handle the hot blooms and bars of wrought iron, the development of new techniques for infusing carbon into the iron and the learning of the art of tempering by repeated heating and quenching of the wrought iron. Then too, there was the matter of slagging the gangue from the iron ore with various fluxes, most commonly lime. This varied with the type of impurities contained in the ore. All this had to be developed by intuition and experience as the scientific understanding of properties of iron were not to be had by man for another three thousand years. It would not be surprising if the acquisition and perfection of such complex technology by man took several centuries.

After 1200 B. C. iron makng technology spread to other parts of the world. Perhaps the destruction of the Hittite empire broke the monopoly on iron technology. The subject Chalybean smiths could now wander abroad seeking new raw materials and clients. Evidence of iron smelting is found in Egypt, Iran, Greece and other places around 1000 B. C. or shortly after. One of the most important sites was Hasanlu in northeastern Iran. Situated on the crossroads of the east-west-south trade routes it thrived on iron trade with many countries. Its smiths apparently knew the art of carburizing iron into steel. Hasanlu, at its height in the 9th century B. C. was soon sacked by invaders but the iron works and iron artifacts were buried in the process enabling modern archeologists to reconstruct its life.

Iron making technology spread to Europe the early part of the first millennium B. C. It was centered at Hallstatt, Austria and produced good iron for the people of Europe. The Hallstatt people grew wealthy on iron production. The oldest known iron-smelting furnaces, dated around 500 B. C. were found at Hittenberg in the Austrian Alps. The furnaces were arranged in pairs. One was probably used for smelting. The other for reheating the bloom or wrought iron for hammering and tempering. It is a puzzle of archeological work in this area that no iron working furnaces have been found in Anatolia or the Near East dating back to the second millennium B. C. The Hallstatt people transmitted the technology to Britain which is rich in iron ore, where a flourishing iron industry developed after 500 B. C. By 100 B. C. British smiths were laminating strips of iron for more effective tires for chariot wheels, hoops for barrels and tools. When Julius Ceasar invaded Gaul and Britain he was impressed with the quality of celtic chariots and their iron industry in general. The British used iron for many agricultural and domestic purposes—axes, knives, razors, plowshares, andirons, chains and others.

The evolution of iron making in China has already been discussed. In India iron technology appears early in the first millennium B. C. The Harappans did not possess it. And it is not clear if the Indo-Europeans had iron when they came to the subcontinent around 1500 B. C. Probably not. The first mention of iron—referred to as black bronze—is found in the later Vedas (circa 1000–500 B. C.). Manu (circa 300–200 B. C.) refers to iron as if it were in common use—even cooking utensils. It would seem that by the time of the Mauryan empire, founded in 300 B. C. iron was in common use in India. There is even speculation the Mauryas, whose capital was at Patiliputra, the site of modern Patna, in Bihar state where rich iron ore deposits are found, may have risen to power because of their iron weapons.

Thereafter the Hindus developed into the greatest iron makers of antiquity. The "seric" steel the Romans imported from Abyssinia was not from China as the name implies but, in fact, the famous Wootz steel from Hyderabad. Presumably the Abyssinian merchants hid the fact from the Romans to protect their source of supply. The same Wootz steel was later imported by the Arabs and Turks for manufacture of the famous Damascus swords. Muslim sultans boasted their swords were so sharp they could cut a silk handkerchief floating through the air.

While Europe and the Mediterranean area lapsed into disorganization and decline after the fall of the Roman empire during the first few centuries of the Christian era iron production continued to improve in India. The best evidence of it is the famous iron pillar of Meharauli in New Delhi. It was produced about 400 A. D. as a memorial to Chandra Gupta II and originally erected on a hill near Ambala in the Punjab. This uncommon pillar is nearly 24 feet high, with a diameter averaging 15 inches and it weighs nearly 6 tons. It is not a casting but was built by welding together discs of forged iron. But most remarkable is the fact that after 1500 years it shows no sign of rusting. The freedom from corrosion is attributable to the purity of the wrought iron used in its construction. An analysis has been made of the pillar which indicated it was 99.72 per cent pure iron, the rest being small amounts of carbon, sulfur and phosphorous. This is high grade iron even by todays standards.

Further developments in metallurgy were not to be made anywhere in the world for another thousand years or so until the middle of the present millennium. This later development will be taken up with the discussion of industrialization. In fact, there was considerable retrogression in iron making. This is understandable for the metal smiths of antiquity were pragmatists not yet scientists. They made good iron by feel, intuition and experience, which had to be passed on by way of apprenticeship. In times of great social upheavals like the fall of the Roman empire or the muslim invasions of India much of the art got lost.

UTILIZATION OF ANIMAL POWER

In his quest for command of more energy man soon brought under his control the muscular power of other life on earth—animal and man power. This was associated intimately with the development of agriculture, which some feel is the greatest socio-economic revolution of the history of man. When man changed his way of life from that of a hunter-gatherer to a food producer his entire history on earth took a dramatic turn. This agricultural technology enabled him, for the first time, to produce a surplus which could be stored as wealth for future use. The social implications of this develop-ment will be discussed in some detial in Chapter VIII on Wealth, Power and Revolution, but suffice it to say now that the production of a surplus freed man from a day to day and hand to mouth existence and enabled him to devote more time to a multitude of other activites—including warfare over the surplus—that now constitutes his history. Agriculture also fixed his habitat on or near the land where his crops grew and his animals foraged. Greater and ever greater social organizations of man replaced the small intimate hunting groups. First villages and then cities. This aggravated seriously the conflict in man between his biologic instincts and cultural controls. But more on this in Chapter VIII. In this Chapter we are concerned with the development of agriculture as it extended man's command over energy.

Agriculture has two broad aspects, the growing of crops and the domestication of animals. It is not clear which came first nor does it really matter. The earliest evidence of crops is found in the Near East where wild wheat and barley grew. The wild grains were gathered at first and people began to settle where they grew abundantly. Once grains played a substantial role in the diet it was, perhaps, natural for man to assist nature in promoting their growth by cultivation. Here it may be noted that since food gathering to supplement the hunt was relegated to women that the invention of the cultivation of crops was probably an invention of the woman of the human race. Anyway, its nice to think that is the case if for no other reason than to deflate the machismo of the male of the specie.

The earliest evidence of cultivation of wheat and barley was found at Jarmo in the Zagros mountain region of Iraq dating back to 7000 B. C. or so. Black carbonized wheat kernels have been found in the remains of the dwellings at Jarmo. They have been dated fairly accurately by the carbon-14 method. From such origin wheat and barley cultivation spread throughout the Near East, paticularly the so-called fertile crescent a strip of rich bottom land that straddles the Tigris-Euphrates doab from the Persian Gulf up into Turkey and down the eastern shore of the Mediterranean to the Sinai. Wheat and barley were cultivated in the Nile valley around 5000 B. C. and by 3000 B. C. both the Egyptians and the Sumerians conducted a flourishing production of cereals with a complex system of irrigation.

Particularly noteworthy in this respect is the neolithic town of Catal Huyuk in Anatolia which flourished as early as 7000 B. C. Traces of the cultivation of barley, wheat, and other crops and the bones of domesticated animals—goats and sheep—are found among its ruins during the ensuing millennia. Although the people worshipped the auroch, a ferocious wild ox of the time, there is no evidence they had domesticated it. Copper and lead trinkets date back to 6500 B. C. There is evidence of smelting (a lump of slag) at a level dated around 5800 B. C. Woven cloth found in connection with burials also dates back to this time. Catal Huyuk is one of the oldest cities—another is Jericho in Palestine—uncovered to date which reveals a substantial population subsisting with a modicum of affluence on agriculture.

Agriculture spread or evolved independently everywhere by 3000 B. C. The Indus valley civilization (circa 2500–1500 B. C.) cultivated wheat, barley, peas and sesame. Cotton was first grown in India. So was sugar cane though, perhaps not by the Harappans. Goats, sheep, cows and other animals were domesticated, but not the horse. The same situation prevailed in China around 3000 B. C. The Chinese favored millets. So did the people of ancient Europe. Rice is thought to have originated in north west Indo-China and spread from there to the rest of Asia.

Again it is not clear how much of the agriculture technology was transmitted and how much developed independently. It would appear that cereal growing was transmitted to Egypt and Europe from the Near East. Whether it was transmitted to India and China or was developed independently by the Chinese and Indians has not been determined. Cotton and sugar were developed in India and spread to the Near East and Europe. Alexander the Great is credited with bringing cotton, which he called "vegetable wool", to Europe after his invasion of the Punjab in 326 B. C. Rice spread everywhere from Indo-China, where it was founded, as a foodgrain. Here too even at an early stage in technological accumulation Ogburn's law of simultaneous and independent invention appears to have operated. And if it needs further proof, it is supplied by the independent development of agriculture in the Americas.

Agriculture was invented in Central America long before 3000 B. C. The Mayas grew maize (corn), beans, pumpkins, tomatoes, and pimento. The Incas added the potato (white and sweet), peanuts, avocado, gourds and other crops. None of these crops were known in the old world until the Americas were discovered. Nor did the American Indians know the cereals and other crops of Europe and Asia. Domestic animals were virtually non-existent in early American agriculture. The Incas raised the guinea pig for food and the llama, alpaca and vicuna for pack animals and wool. Other Indians do not appear to have had any animals for meat or power. Milk products were unknown. The diets of the Incas, Mayas and Aztecs were largely vegetarian. The north American Indians with some notable exceptions (the Mississippi culture), on the other hand, lived mostly by the hunt. Agriculture was minor and subsidiary. It is noteworthy that cotton was discovered and cultivated independently by the early peoples of Peru around 3000 B. C. about the same time it was developed in India.

More important to this study was man's domestication of animals. To be sure, plant food fueled more effectively man's own muscular and electrical energy but it did not extend his command of energy outside himself. Even the domestication of animals, particularly in the beginning, served the same purpose that it too assured man a ready and steady supply of meat. But it had one significant advantage over the hunt in that it enabled man to store his meat supply—on the hoof, not in a can or freezer yet—for future use. In other words the creation of another source of surplus. Later when man learned to milk animals it gave him a further source of food.

Sheep and goats were domesticated first, around 8000 B. C. in the Near East. Pigs too around 7000 B. C. in Anatolia although they were never great favorites in the Near East. Pigs were developed later by Chinese and Europeans in the more temperate climates. Pork was dangerous because of trichinae particularly in hot climates. Also pigs are not milked. Milk made sheep and goats such favorites. In addition they yield wool, fur and hides for clothes. But these animals could not be used for power.

The cow came later (circa 6500 B. C.) as it was a more difficult animal to tame. It was domesticated in Anatolia and Greece. But once domesticated it was a much more useful animal as it could be hitched to the plow, cart and later various rotary motion machines. Some peoples, like the Hindus, revered the cow for it's good to man. The neolithic society of Catal Huyuk (circa 7000 B. C.) worshipped the bull, but this may have been more out of fear of bovines than greatfulness as in the case of the Hindus.

The cow is a clumsy plodding animal that could not increase man's command over external energy in any substantial way. This role was destined to be filled by the horse. It should be noted, though, that the water buffalo remains the main source of agricultural power even today throughout most of Asia. The Indians also use the Brahmin bull to pull the plow and cart. But even in Europe and America the ox continued to be used well into the 19th century.

The onager, or wild ass, was the first equine to be domesticated around 3000 B. C. in the Near East. The Sumerians used the onager to draw carts and chariots. These "chariots" were rough and heavy vehicles with solid wooden wheels. They were still not the fast war chariots of the Hittites and other Indo-European people already mentioned earlier. In order to harness the onager the ox yoke had to be supplemented by a breast strap made of hide to keep the yoke from slipping down the onager's neck. This unfortunately tended to choke the onager which restricted the load it could haul. In fact, the long delayed invention of the horse collar (circa 10th century in France; earlier in China) deferred by three thousand years the replacement of the ox by the horse for agriculture and heavy transport. Although the horse is four times as strong as an ox, yoking (and choking) the horse like an ox prevented the horse from exerting much more power than the ox. And since it costs considerably more to feed a horse it was uneconomic to replace the ox with the horse for agriculture for three millennia after its domestication.

The wild horse roamed the steppes of Eurasia. It was in the Black-Caspian sea area where the Indo-Europeans first domesticated it around 3000 B. C. Wild horses roamed all over Europe during Paleolithic times and were hunted by early man for food. The most notable fossil remains of such hunts have been found in Torralba and Ambrona, Spain, dating back 300–400,000 years ago. Homo erectus apparently frightened them with fire or otherwise to run over a cliff in panic and fall to death or serious injury whence they would be dispatched with a spear thrust. This was, perhaps, the only way erectus with his still backward stone technology could hunt these swift and powerful animals. The horse actually originated in the Americas some 50 million years ago (a tiny 15 inch creature but the progenitor of todays' horse) and through geological vicissitude ended up in the Eurasian land mass. The horse only returned to the Americas with the conquistadors in the 16th century A. D.

It required four major inventions that spanned some three millennia before man was able to command the full power of the horse for transport, agriculture and warfare. They were, the chariot, the saddle with stirrup, the horse-shoe and the horse collar. And as is so often the way of man the requirements of war got priority over those of peace. The war chariot and the saddle *cum* stirrup came first; the horse collar and shoe last.

The horse and the war chariot burst upon the Near East as an effective war machine almost suddenly during the forepart of the second millennium B. C. While most archeologists accept the domestication of the horse by the Indo-Europeans some find it difficult to accept that the light spoke-wheeled chariot could have been invented by the "barbarians" of the day. Such invention would belong more appropriately to the highly civilized Egyptians or Babylonians. But the Indo-Europeans may have not have been so backward technologically as the doubters think. It should be recalled that at around this time they were developing the complex iron technology which was far advanced to the metallurgy of Egypt and Mesopotamia. Anyway, history and archeology seem to indicate that by 1500 B. C. the Indo-Europeans were terrorizing the old cultures of the day with horses and war chariots. The technology spread fast. The Hyksos introduced the horse and chariot to the Egyptians. The Assyrians, doubtless, copied the Hittites of Anatolia and the Hurrians of northwest Mesopotamia. The first treatise on the raising and training of horses was written by a Hurrian. It is dated back to 1350 B. C. The Hurrians were Indo-European people who became subjects of the Hittites in 1366 B. C. Their kings bore Indian names, and their land was called Mitanni. It was situated in northern Syria.

The treatise consists of some 1000 lines and is written in the Hittite language. The man who authored the tract refers to himself as "Kikul of the land of Mitanni". The book abounds in sanskrit terms. The reasonable conclusion of this archeological find is that the Hittites employed Hurrians to learn horsemanship. It also supports the thesis that the domestication of the horse belongs to the Indo-Europeans.

Ceram, the Hittologist writes "At some time during this period (middle of the second millennium B. C.) in some place among the Hittites, Hurrians, Kassites (the Indo-Europeans that captured Babylon), and the barbarian Hyksos, horse training, the art of riding, and a special form of two-wheeled chariot had been perfected. The *light battle chariot* had become a new weapon of war. . . the future of civilization in the Near East, and therefore the future of the world, had been revolutionized by the new invention."

There is evidence of the horse and war chariot in Persia around 2000 B. C. The Aryan conquest of India around 1500 B. C. was probably facilitated by the war chariot, though there is no actual evidence of it, as it would be in line with the events of the time. The first evidence of the war chariot in China is dated around 1300 B. C.

The bit for control of the horse appears, except in China, almost from the start. Even the earliest ones are made of metal. The Egyptians used the jointed bit as early as 1200 B. C. Onagers and oxen were controlled by a ring in the nose. Such ring would doubtless have ripped the nostrils of so spirited an animal as a horse.

The romance between man and horse started almost immediately. Nothing attests this better than the affectionate and admiring renditions on the Greek vase, the Egyptian monument or the Assyrian bas relief depicting the horse, with its dilated nostrils, arched neck and prancing feet as a thing of beauty and energy. The Hittites, Egyptians, Assyrians, Greeks and others of this period were charioteers. Though they also rode astride the horse other peoples were destined to develop this phase of horsemanship. When this developed the affinity between man and horse grew even closer.

Mounted horsemanship was developed by the peoples of the Eurasian steppes—from Hungary to Manchuria. They are called the Scythians, Sarmatians, Yueh-Chi and Hsuing-nu. Herodotus first visited the Scythians in the 5th century B. C. on the Black Sea and described their ways, their love of horses and their superb horsemanship. But centuries earlier the Scythians were already invading Anatolia and the Near East as fierce marauders on horseback. They allied themselves with the Assyrians against the Cimmerians, Medes and other peoples of Western Asia and the Near East. They were the undisputed rulers north of the Black Sea from Hungary to the Caucasus. The Sarmatians ruled to the east above the Caspian Sea. Beyond the Aral Sea was the domain of the Yueh-Chi. The Yueh-Chi invaded India during the first century B. C. and ruled in the northwest until about 200 A. D. Mongolia was the realm of the Hsuing-nu. The Chinese built the Great Wall (completed 214 B. C.) against them. They were the predecessors of the Mongols who ruled from China to Europe around 1200 A. D.

These people owed their prowess to horsemanship. Man appears to have mounted the horse only after he first learned to hitch him to the chariot. There may be two reasons for this sequence. When the wild horse was first domesticated he was a much smaller animal. It was only after centuries of breeding, grain feeding and care that the horse grew in size so that he could carry a man with ease. The pony sized horse was well adapted for the light chariot where speed not strength was of the essence. Depictions of the horse around 1000 B. C. show it as a pony sized animal. There is, for example, a lion hunting scene on a 9th century relief showing the Assyrian king Ashurnasirpal slaying lions with a bow and arrow from a chariot drawn by three horses. The lions are nearly the same size as the horses. This could, of course, be artistic license but similar impressions are derived from other representations of chariot horses. Even Scythian portrayals show a smaller horse with the riders feet nearly touching the ground.

It is—a second reason—one thing to harness a horse but quite another to mount it. A horse is instinctively wary of predators pouncing on it's back (this is a biologic feature millions of years old). It must have taken courage and time for man to learn how to overcome this obstacle. Even when a horse is trained he remains tempermental and occasionally uncontrollable. Herodotus relates in Book IV the following interesting episode:

> There was one very strange thing which greatly aided the Persians, and was of equal disservice to the Scyths, in these assaults on the Persian camp. This was the braying of the asses and the appearance of the mules. For, as I observed before, the land of the Scythians produces neither ass nor mule, and contains no single specimen of either animal, by reason of the cold. So, when the asses brayed, they frightened the Scythian cavalry; and often, in the middle of a charge, the horses, hearing the noise made by the asses, would take fright and wheel around, pricking up their ears, and showing astonishment. This was owing to their having never heard the noise, or seen the form, of the animal before: and it was not without some little influence on the progress of the war.

Cavalries have also been known to stampede in the face of elephants and camels. Alexander the Great encountered some difficulty in this respect when he invaded India and his horses were frightened by the war elephants of the Indian army.

The first horsemen rode bareback. Even the Scythians rode on rudimentary saddles. These were simply blankets or felt pads designed, perhaps, only to keep the rider from getting wet from the sweat of the horse and slipping off his back. They rode without stirrups with feet dangling and knees clamped to the side of the horse. The modern saddle with stirrups was not to appear for two thousand years. But even after the stirrup was used in Europe the Mongols still rode their horses bareback.

The first horseman, therefore, gained mobility not might from the mounting of the horse. Many a warrior, doubtless, slipped off his horse in the heat of battle when he lost his balance swinging his spear or sword or shooting his arrow. He was still not locked into his mount by the contoured saddle and the stirrup as the medieval knight of Europe.

After man developed the chariot and learned to ride mounted on the horse—the first mastered by 1500 B. C., the latter by 500 B. C.—equine technology remained on this plateau for two thousand years. It even fell out of favor with the Greeks and Romans who dominated the Mediterranean area for over a millennium. The Romans resorted to slavery for agricultural power. Mining and minor industry was also conducted with slaves. Slaves were abundant and cheap. It cost less to have two slaves turn a quern than a donkey. The lack of an effective harness made animal power more costly than manpower for agriculture and industry.

It is more difficult, however, to understand the low priority the Greeks and Romans placed on cavalry in warfare. Perhaps the terrain in Greece was nonconducive to the mounted warrior. Greek military power relied on the hoplite—heavy armed infantryman. But the Macedonians used cavalry to support their famous phalanx. Alexander the Great relied primarily on cavalry for his conquests. In India he defeated with his mobile and effective horsemen the huge army and elephant corps of the Indian king Porus. Alexander's love for his horse Bucephalus (who died in this battle) is one of the great man-horse romances of history.

Rome relied on its legions, except for a brief emphasis on cavalry to checkmate the Carthagenian heavy cavalry. But after the defeat of Carthage the cavalry was relegated to secondary importance. The Romans were masters of seige warfare. More emphasis was again placed on the cavalry to protect the "limes" of the Empire as the barbarians were usually mounted and the legions needed greater mobility to pursue these frontier raiders. Each legion on the Rhine or Danube had 120 horsemen to 480 infantrymen. The eastern empire, however, reverted to cavalry and it became the principal military power of Byzantine.

The maximum use of horsepower awaited the invention of the stirrup, the horseshoe and the horsecollar. A small stirrup to fit the big toe appears in India around 100 B. C. This is characteristic of the Indians who are accustomed to anchoring sandals to the foot with a round loop for the big toe. But such stirrup was not adaptable to cold climates requiring heavy shodding of the feet. The big toe stirrup reached China, apparently with the spread of Buddhism from India throughout Asia at this time. The Chinese reshaped it to a full foot stirrup around 400 A. D. The Persians either got the invention from China or India or developed it themselves and by about 700 A. D. it was in widespread use in western Asia. The Arabs appropriated the idea from the Persians who they conquered and converted to Mohammedanism around this time.

Neither art or archeology provide clear evidence how the stirrup got to Europe. It could have come from central Asia via the mounted nomads (the Huns at this time) invading Europe. It could also have been learned from the muslims who were penetrating into Europe during the 8th century A. D. At any rate, Charles Martel (715–741 A. D.) took the stirrup and founded upon it a new type of military warfare.

Combat was now based on horsepower not merely horse speed and mobility. Man and horse were one, welded together by the saddle and stirrup. This new warfare—shock combat—called for new weapons. The Carolingian wing-spear with a heavy stock and a cross-piece behind the blade was invented to prevent too deep a penetration into the body of the enemy—man or horse—so that it could be easily withdrawn and not lost. Shields and armour were redesigned and so on. The cross-bow, an import from China, came into use against the mounted warrior. It served as the anti-tank weapon of the middle ages.

Furthermore, the entire structure of society underwent a profound change to accommodate the new type of mounted horsemen. Feudalism was born. Charles Martel and his sons needed the new horse mounted warriors to consolidate and expand Frankish power. Maintaining a mounted warrior was expensive. Horses needed pasture and grain. Feudalism was devised to give each knight a land area—with the necessary manpower tied to the land—to maintain a fixed number of mounted and armed military units for the kings command.

The middle ages witnessed a revolution in agriculture based on horsepower. It is too easily lost sight of today that until very recently agriculture comprised the employment of 90 per cent of mankind. Food by the very nature of man must have first priority and it was not until the advent of mechanized and chemicalized agriculture of modern times that the vast majority of mankind was freed of the necessity to produce food and fibre. In America where agricultural productivity has been brought to the highest point it comes as a shock to realize that as late as 1920 the American farmer could produce enough food and fibre for only seven persons including himself and his family. But by 1978 he could subsist 60! The world average is still only 5. Yet even today in most of the world outside the highly industrialized countries the vast majority are employed in agriculture because of low food and fibre production.

The physical, economic and social conditions in Europe around 1000 A. D. called for a revolution in agriculture. First, the soil of northern Europe required more working. It consisted of heavy and moist sod that had to be cut, turned over and broken up. The mould board plow was invented for the purpose. The origin of the mould plow is somewhat obscure. The Slavs were the first Europeans to use it by the late 6th century A. D. Whether the Slavs developed it or got it from Asia is not clear. In any event the new plow was carried West so that by the time of Charlemagne (742–814 A. D.) it was in widespread use throughout northern Europe.

In the lighter and drier soils of the Near East and India the scratch plow was and still is preferred in order to conserve moisture. The soil required less breaking up. All that was needed to work the scratch plow was one or two oxen. The mould board plow called for a brace of six or eight oxen. There was thus more need to turn to the more powerful horse for agricultural power in Europe.

Feudalism cried out for more agricultural production with greater reliance on the horse. More and better horses were needed for military purposes. This meant agriculture had to produce the food to feed them. Unlike the oxen, which could subsist off grass and straw, the horse required grain. Oats which originated in the Near East but was largely ignored there became a major crop in Europe to feed horses. And oats required cultivation. As the medieval knight took on more and more armor agriculture was required to breed and feed a larger horse which could carry a man plus all that iron. This had a favorable feedback as a bigger and stronger horse could furnish more power for cultivation. From this need eventually evolved the powerful Percherons, Belgians and Clydesdales of Europe.

Two inventions were required before the maximum power of the horse could be utilized for plowing and cultivation. The horse had to be harnessed in a manner that would not choke him. The draw had to be placed on his shoulders instead of his breast and neck. The answer was the horse collar with traces, appropriately padded and supported by the harness, hitched to the load. This enabled a horse to pull 4–5 times the weight he could pull with the yoke-breast strap harness. The earliest evidence of the use of a horse collar in Europe dates to the 9th century. By the 10th century the horse collar was in general use in Europe.

The horse had also to be shod lest his hooves break or disintegrate under heavy loads. In the moist soil of northern Europe the horse's hoof became soft and sensitive. The iron horseshoe nailed to the hoof appears in Europe toward the end of the 9th century. There is evidence of nailed horseshoes in the graves of Siberian nomads dating back to the early 9th century. They were also used in the Byzantine empire around this time. By 1000–1100 A. D. the horseshoe was used widely in Europe for both military and agricultural purposes.

The horse collar and nailed iron shoe were in general use in Europe by the end of the 11th century. Agricultural productivity increased greatly. Land transport became more efficient benefiting both agriculture and the reemerging commerce of medieval Europe. This freed more people for the arts and finer pursuits of life. Gothic cathedrals were built all over Europe out of religious zeal and gratefulness for the new prosperity. The foundations of western civilization were laid at this time in Europe.

Coinciding happily with these needs and developments was the resurgence of iron production in Europe. During the centuries after the fall of Rome (476 A. D.) the mines of France, Germany and other parts of Europe fell into disuse. The Celts made good use of iron during Roman times. Julius Caesar admired the iron rims on their chariots and wagons. Apparently the iron was not of "steel" quality as it is reported the Celts had to stop fighting in the heat of battle to straighten their swords. These old mines were opened and worked again by Carolingian times to meet the demands of feudal warfare and agriculture. Peter the Venerable, Prior of Domene in the Dauphine, prepared a text on underground ore mining in Breda valley around 1120 A. D. which sets forth the methods of preventing cave-ins, shoring the shafts with timber, breaking up and lifting ore, lighting the shafts with candles and other matters. The metal smith became, once again, an important member of the feudal society.

The stirrup, collar and the iron nailed shoe finally, after three thousand years, enabled man to command the full energy of the horse. That however, exhausted the potential of animal power for man and in the centuries to come he would have to develop mechanical and chemical power to extend his control over more external energy. To be sure, there were some other animals man domesticated but none superseded or even matched the horse.

Elephants were used in warfare and industry. Even today elephants are used in Burma and Thailand and south India to work and haul teak logs from rugged forests. It was domesticated in India around 2000 B. C. Elephants do not breed in captivity so it is necessary to capture wild specimens to maintain their number. Elephants were used in warfare, perhaps to frighten the enemy more than as efficient engines of war. When Alexander met Porus in India the Indian elephant corps of 200 beasts proved one of the biggest challenges he encountered on his world conquest. They frightened his horses. By adroit tactics Alexander maneuvered his cavalry around the elephants and struck the Indian army from the rear. Pyrrhus used elephants to trample the Roman infantry in the Battle of Heraclea in 280 B. C. Hannibal employed elephants (even marching them across the Alps) to invade Rome in 219 B. C. He lost most of his 37 elephants in the alpine snow.

The camel is another animal used by man. It was domesticated about 3000 B. C. (the dromedary in Saudi Arabia; the bactrian in southern Russia). The camel is a good work animal. It is used to pull a plow, cart and various rotary machines in India and western Asia. The persian wheel is often powered by a camel. The persian wheel is a water lifting device consisting of a conveyor belt with buckets which scoop up water in a shallow well twenty or so feet deep and bring it to the surface. The conveyor belt is powered on the surface by a shaft pulled by a draught animal in a rotary motion around the well head. The shaft and conveyer are appropriately geared for transmission of the animal power. The persian wheel is best adapted for lifting water in river valleys where the water table is within 10–20 feet of the surface.

The camel has been a most useful pack animal for transport across desert terrain because of its ability to go without water for long periods—camels have been known to go 30 days without drinking. They can also survive longer than other animals without feeding. In addition to transportation and power camels supply meat and milk. They have been and still are of great economic importance to the Arabs and peoples of central Asia.

Camels have also been used in warfare, mostly by the Arabs. The camel's affinity for desert living enabled the Arabs to raid the settled civilizations and to retreat into their desert sanctuaries. The Arabs used the desert as a retreat like the Europeans used the sea to facilitate their imperial conquests. The camel was their vehicle for the purpose.

Elsewhere in the world other animals have been used. In the western hemisphere the Incas used the llama and alpaca as pack animals. There is no evidence they used them for agricultural or military purposes. The horse came into widespread used by the north American Indians only after it was brought to this hemisphere by the Europeans. In fact, the easy conquest of the Incas and Aztecs by the Europeans is attributable largely to the military advantage of possessing the horse. Unlike the situation in the old world the men of the Americas did not use animals to any significant extent to increase their command over external energy.

The other major use of animal power by man was the enslavement of his fellow man. Slavery comprises one of the sorriest aspects of the history of man. It appears on the human scene with the advent of agriculture when human labor was substituted for hunting prowess as the primary source of food supply. The hunting group had no incentive to enslave other men. It would have been uneconomic—an extra mouth to feed—and dangerous to arm an erstwhile enemy for participation in the hunt. The hunting groups had achieved a social organization in harmony with biologic necessity. The males, stronger and swifter but, above all else, freed by nature of the biological burden of gestating and rearing the young, assuring the meat supply. The females preoccupied perhaps, three-fourths of the time with the perpetuation of the specie used the remainder of their time gathering vegetarian food to supplement the meat supply. There was obviously no room for slaves in such socio-economic order and enemies of the group were slain instead of enslaved in any territorial disputes. There is little or no slavery among the remaining aborigines who still live by the hunt. The hunting group (by which man has lived for millions of years except for the last ten thousand or so) achieved a brotherhood and democratic way of life man has been trying to recapture ever since without any great success. To be sure, there was dominance based on merit.

The agriculture revolution changed the situation. This new technology for the first time, enabled man to produce more food than he needed from day to day. Equally important it was food he could store—cereals and meat on the hoof. Man could now produce a surplus over that which he needed to live. This surplus unfortunately could also be appropriated by the dominant individuals. It can be likened to the grabbing of the biggest and sweetest orange by the dominant baboon. Once man realized the economic value of slavery it fitted handily into the newly emerging social order based upon a perverted dominance instinct. In ancient Rome, Greek mathematicians, philosophers and other intelligensia were enslaved by the pedestrian Roman, doubtless, more for ego gratification than economic worth.

Prehistory leaves little or no evidence of slavery, but it is a going institution of man from the start of recorded history some 5000 years ago. The Sumerians developed complex laws and regulations on slavery including ransom and manumission. The main source of slaves, as it always has been during antiquity, was war and later piracy. But already in Sumer there was enslavement for unpaid debt, perhaps, the second most frequent source of slavery.

The Amorites who took over from the Sumerians in Mesopotamia around 2000 B. C., augmented the institution of slavery. Hammurabi's code abounds with provisions on slavery. A runaway slave could be executed. So could a person helping a slave escape. The master could not kill his slave. And so on.

The Assyrians who ruled Mesopotamia during the first millennium B. C. were a warring people prone to enslave their victims. Ashurnasirpal III (884–859 B. C.) records that in one expedition he returned with 15,000 subjects together with the ruler's sister, the daughters of the rich nobles, 5000 sheep, 2000 cattle and 460 horses. The king, nobles and army officers were put to death in a bloody massacre to teach other subject peoples not to revolt.

Slavery was also resorted to in Egypt, but to a lesser extent. This was due in large measure to the system of land tenure that bound the mass of peasants to the land. Their lot differed little from the slave who worked the land in Mesopotamia as they too were not allowed to keep the surplus they produced. Technically they were free, owned their own house and could not be sold. But they could not leave the land assigned to them. Outside this peasantry there were the slaves obtained in war or voluntary bondage that did household and other menial services. They did not constitute a large number in the society.

Egypt's notoriety in connection with slavery is due to the story of the Israelites. The Israelites were a nomadic tribe in the Palestine and Negev desert area that sought refuge in the lower Nile delta around 1600 B. C. This was common practice of such nomadic semites when drought, insects and the vicissitudes of climate made life intolerable in the desert areas. Their descent into Egypt coincided with Hyksos rule over Egypt so that their presence for a hundred years or more in the rich delta was unmolested by the foreign rulers of Egypt. Ordinarily the Egyptians demanded bondage for such presence in the Nile valley by the nomads of the desert. And when Hyksos rule was overthrown the Israelites were placed in bondage and made to perform menial tasks—the making of bricks according to the Bible. There is no mention of the Israelites or Moses in the historical records of Egypt making the Bible the only source of information on this episode that was destined to effect profoundly the history of a large sector of humanity.

Thousands of slaves—prisoners of war, foreigners settling in the delta like the Israelites and others—were forced to work on the vast construction projects of the Pharoahs Seti I, Ramses II and others. It is stated in the old Testament that "they built for Pharoah treasure cities, Pithom and Ramses". In Old Kingdom days the Pharoahs built the pyramids by levying a corvee on the Egyptian peasantry when their labor was not required to till the soil and harvest the crops. Under the imperialistic New Kingdom (1567–

1085 B. C.) Ramses II and other Pharoahs had a large supply of slaves for construction projects.

The story of bondage and the escape from bondage of the Israelites as reported in Exodus sheds considerable light on the institution of slavery in ancient times. It reveals that peoples living on the verge of starvation in marginal or submarginal agricultural lands were willing to trade freedom for bondage to people controlling the fertile areas so that they would have freedom from starvation. Why then did they foresake the hunt for agriculture. For precisely the same reason, for as population grew it was not possible to subsist the greater numbers on the game in the ever diminishing territory controlled by the hunting group. Man's struggle to survive, until the last century or two, has always been to secure enough food to live. The hunt was actually never given up. Men have always hunted and fished, into modern times, to supplement agriculture. Agriculture had to be invented by man for his continued growth and command of the earth. But once invented it provided a means, by appropriation of the surplus production, for strong individuals to master the weak through the institution of slavery.

Another impression from this historical episode is that slavery was not seriously questioned, let alone challenged, as a way of life. Moses encountered considerable resistance to the flight from bondage. Several times it appears in Exodus that the children of Israel upbraided him for leading them from the economic security they enjoyed in bondage in Egypt. First, when they were trapped before the Red Sea (believed now to be a misstranslation—the crossing took place instead at the Sea of Reeds in the Nile delta) they said unto Moses "Let us alone, that we may serve the Egyptians. For it has been better for us to serve the Egyptians, than that we should die in the wilderness." And later when Moses sent scouts to Canaan "to spy out the land" and they returned to report that the Promised Land was occupied and settled by the Amorites, Amalekites, Hittites and others he had a near revolt on his hands. "Let us make a captain, and let us return to Egypt" they said to one another!

Even more significant is the attention accorded slavery in the Mosaic Code. There is, first, no commandment that "thou shalt not enslave thy fellow man". The Tenth Commandment forbids a man from coveting his neighbor's man or maid servant. In the "judgements" that Moses set before the people the first attention is given to slavery, by placing limitations on the enslavement of a fellow Hebrew. Such servant is to be freed "for nothing" after six years. But if his master gave him a wife during his servitude, and she bore him children, such wife and children belonged to the master. Should he wish to remain with his family he would have to serve his master forever. A man is to be punished if he kills his servant; otherwise, it seems, he could "smite" him with impunity "for he is his money". However, if he puts out his eye or knocks out his tooth the servant is to go free.

It may be deduced from the commandments and judgements that Hebrews could enslave non-Hebrews without restriction. From time to time, the Bible reveals the prophets and the rabbis tried to alleviate the plight of the enslaved but they were not too successful as it was so deeply ingrained in the socio-economic structure of the agricultural societies of ancient times. In Jeremiah it is reported that king Zedekiah decreed that all Hebrew slaves shall be freed, "but afterward they . . . brought them into subjection" again. For this breach of covenant says Jeremiah the Lord punished the Israelites by defeat and enslavement by the king of Babylon.

Toward the end of the first millennium B. C. there were movements among the Israelites for the abolition of slavery. The Essenes, a non-violent revolutionary group, living in communal brotherhood, not only rejected slavery among themselves but purchased freedom for slaves outside their group. They believed slavery violated a law of nature which created all men as brethern. Jesus Christ was believed to have been an Essene or, at least, in communication with them. Philo of Alexandria reports on still another group of Hebrews living in exile in Egypt, near Alexandria, the Therapeutae, who rejected slavery. They believed that "nature has borne all men to be free". These were unfortunately small voices crying in the wilderness of a world more slave than free.

Slavery reached its height during Graeco-Roman times. The Iliad and Odyssey speak freely of slaves. One of Odysseus swineherders, Eumaeus, was captured by the Phoenicians as a boy and sold into slavery. The Phoenecians, the foremost traders of this period and the founders of Carthage, made a wholesale business of slavery. A voyager in those days ran a fifty-fifty chance of ending up a slave far away from home. The foundation of the Greek economy was slavery. Slaves did all the menial work so that the Greek citizen could pursue the political, intellectual and artistic interests of life. They worked the households, the fields, the workshops, the mines, the ships and everything that required muscular power. The silver mines of Laurium were worked entirely by slaves. Large slave owners would contract with the state for the right to work the mines on a royalty basis. The slaves were their capital like earthmovers, cranes, trucks and the like are the capital of modern day contractors. It was the mines of Laurium that made Athens rich and financed her imperialism. When the Greeks colonized the Medeterranean area they usually enslaved the people living on the land they took. In their wars of conquest the Greeks acquired many slaves. In addition, persons unable to pay their debts and poor people selling their children to fend off starvation added to the slave rolls. At the height of its glory classical Greece consisted of a high proportion of slaves. In 431 B. C. historians estimate the city of Athens (including the port of Piraeus) had a population consisting of 60,000 citizens, 25,000 metics (foreigners) and 70,000 slaves! It was only the citizens who enjoyed the benefits of Greek democracy; the metics and slaves were outside the pale of political life in Athens.

It is difficult for us 2500 years later to understand how the Greeks reconciled slavery with democracy. Many of the Greek intellectuals questioned and some rejected slavery as contrary to the law of nature. The epicureans, cynics, stoics and other philosophical schools condemmed slavery. Alcidamas wrote "God created us all free; nature makes no slaves." But the giants of Greek philosophy rationalized the institution of slavery. Plato embraced it. He even incorporated it into *The Republic*. But it was Aristotle who undertook to rationalize the meaning of slavery in human life and history. In his *Politics* he writes:

> We may therefore say that wherever there is the same wide discrepancy between two sets of human beings as there is between mind and body or between man and beast, then the inferior of the two sets, those whose condition is such that their function is the use of their bodies and nothing better can be expected of them, those, I say, are slaves by nature. It is better for them, just as in the analogous cases mentioned, to be thus ruled and subject.
>
> The slave by 'nature' then is he that can and therefore does belong to another, and he that participates in the reasoning faculty so far as to understand but not so as to possess it. For the other animals serve their owner not by exercise of reason but passively. The use, too, of slaves hardly differs at all from that of domestic animals; from both we derive that which is essential for our bodily needs. It is then part of nature's intention to make the bodies of free men to differ from those of slaves, the latter strong enough for the necessary menial tasks, the former erect and useless for that kind of work, but well suited for the life of a citizen of a state, a life divided between war and peace. But though that may have been nature's intention, the opposite often happen. We see men who have the right kind of bodily physique for a free man but not the mind, others who have the right mind but not the body. This much is clear: suppose that there were men whose bodily physique alone showed the same superiority as is shown by the superhuman size of statues of gods, then all would agree that the rest of mankind would deserve to be their slaves. And if this is true in relation to physical superiority, the distinction would be even legitimately made in respect of superiority of mind. But it is much more difficult to see quality of mind than it is to see quality of body. It is clear then that by nature some are free, others slaves, and that for these it is both right and expedient that they should serve as slaves.

As if not quite self convinced by his argument on the naturalness of slavery Aristotle proceeds to argue that, in any event, it is legal to enslave prisoners of war as they are part of the spoils of victory. But here too he seems troubled by the force of his argument.

Slavery did not seem to bother the conscience of the plutocratic Romans. It became the national policy of imperial Rome. In conquest after conquest down through first century B. C. Rome subjected half the people of Europe and the Mediterranean area to slavery. Piracy was rampant at this time and served to add to the slave rolls of the empire. It was only when piracy began to interfere with the Roman ships carrying the spoils of war and products of the empire home that the Romans decided to do something about it. Pompey was given a free hand against the pirates in 66 B. C. and he cleared them, once for all, out of the Mediterranean. Some 10,000 pirates were killed; 400 of their ships taken and 120 of their fortresses destroyed. By the first century B. C. the slave foundation of the Roman society was established. There is no reliable census on the ratio of citizens to slaves in Rome. In the first century A. D. Gibbon states that at least half the population was slave.

All economic life was based on slavery. The latifundias, workshops, mines, markets and ships were worked by slaves. The smaller freeholder of land was displaced by the large holders who worked the land with slaves. These erstwhile farmer-citizens became a flotsam of unemployed on the streets of Rome. In order to keep such a potential revolutionary force at bay the Caesars had to feed them. First a wheat subsidy, then free bread, eventually rations of pork, olive oil, salt and other food products. Their idleness had to be diverted with free entertainment—chariot races, gladitorial contests. Slaves were now so cheap they could be sacrificed for amusement.

Slaves conducted trade and commerce, as it was considered beneath the dignity of a Roman citizen to participate in the market place. This, however, began to change after the first century B. C. Crassus (circa 115–53 B. C.) owned various productive enterprises.

The worst condition of slaves was in the mines, galleys and in the arena. The mines and quarries were worked by slaves and criminals, largely through slave contractors. There were gold and silver mines in Spain, Gaul and Dacia; copper mines in Portugal and Cyprus; tin and lead mines in Britain and other mines and quarries all over the empire. Hundreds of slaves chained to their oars powered the ships of Rome. And as an ultimate degradation slaves and criminals were trained to kill each other as gladiators for the amusement of the Romans. Howard Fast's *Spartacus* sets forth graphically the harsh lot of the Roman slave in the mines, galleys and arenas of the Roman world.

There is, to be sure, an obverse side where the lot of the Roman slave was tolerable and to some degree enjoyable. Slave ownership, after all, was an economic matter. Masters could not treat them unmindful of destroying their investment. Most trained them in some skill or craft so that they could be productive. Such training proved useful to the slave in case of manumission.

They had to feed and clothe them reasonably well in order to maximize their muscular power. Social clubs and cooperative societies for slaves were licensed by the state. At the annual Saturnalia feast slave and master exchanged positions for a day of mutual conviviality. In the great Roman households the slaves lived on or near the property but, to be sure, in the least desirable quarters.

Roman law gave the slave no rights. He owned no property. He was permitted no marital status. All his children were illegitimate. He had no standing in the courts. His owner could deal with him as he sought fit, including death. Runaway slaves were crucified when caught. During the mid and late centuries of the empire sentiment began to ameliorate a bit. Laws were enacted against harsh treatment. Roman philosophers started to question the morality of slavery. Seneca taught that all men were created equal and it was against nature to enslave a fellow man. Epictetus was also scornful of slavery.

Manumission, however, appeared to be easier in Rome than elsewhere. A master could free his slave by letter or by word before witnesses. Many freed their slaves on their deathbed, as if to clear their conscience. Such freedom did not confer Roman citizenship; that could only be done by the state. A slave could also purchase his freedom. As the empire matured freedom was made easier and easier to secure.

The wonder is that there were not more slave revolts in a society where slaves outnumbered masters. Romans dreaded the prospect. The Romans had a proverb that "every slave is an enemy we harbor." Yet the only serious revolt of note is that by Spartacus in 73 B. C. Prior thereto there were lesser revolts around the empire mainly in Sicily. They were dealt with summarily and without alarm. But the revolt of Spartacus shook the Roman world.

It arose out of the most degrading aspects of Roman slavery. Spartacus, a man from Thrace, was a gladiator-trainee in the academy at Capua. He and his fellow trainees—vigorous and strong Germans, Gauls and others who made good fighters, broke out of the school. They had nothing to lose as they were destined to die in the arena anyway. They garrisoned on Mount Vesuvius and delivered defeat to the Roman soldiers over a period of some four years. Spartacus attracted other runaway slaves so that at the height of the revolt he had an army of 120,000 including a cavalry. Terror gripped Rome and the Senate had to assign Crassus and Pompey, the two top generals of the legions, to quell the revolt. Dissension in the ranks of the slaves advanced their downfall. Crixis, the Gaul, split off part of the army to plunder Italy and was defeated first. Crassus and Pompey finally annihilated the rest of the army of Spartacus in the south but they did not capture Spartacus. No one knows what became of him. Either he was cut to pieces in battle or he escaped. Some 6000 of the recaptured slaves were crucified on crosses lining the Appian way from Rome to Capua!

If the gladiators who were skilled with weapons could not carry off a successful revolt how could the mass of slaves, unarmed and untrained in arms, hope to succeed. The state had control of the military technology and the wealth to employ it against the slaves. Moreover, the more facile way to freedom was manumission which the Romans appear to have made possible and feasible. So each slave had to work out his salvation for himself. At any rate, the empire survived for centuries half free and half slave, although some historians attribute the fall of Rome to the institution of slavery.

Christianity at best tended to ameliorate not abolish slavery. Both the western and eastern churches tolerated it, employed it themselves and even engaged in the slave trade. Thousands of Slavs (whence the term slave derives in the English language) and Saracens were employed in the monastaries of Europe. The Byzantine empire abounded with slaves. They had virtually no protection under the law and their only escape from cruelty was the sanctuary of the monastary. The Muslim world too was built upon slavery and later when it was dominated by the turks, the Ottoman empire devised one of the most efficient systems of slave bureaucrats, the Janissaries, to administer the empire for centuries. The Ottoman turks recruited some of the brightest boys around 10–12 years old from their subject peoples in southeastern Europe and western Asia, trained them long and specially for administration and then placed them in responsible posts in the empire. They were not allowed to marry and have families, they were accorded elite priviliges and granted favors to insure their loyalty to the emperor. In a way, it may be said they were modeled after the guardians Plato devised for optimum human rule. Their counterparts, the Mamelukes in Egypt, however, revolted in what constituted, along with Spartacus, one of the few serious revolts of slaves in history. The Mamelukes, however, succeeded and ruled Egypt for three centuries (1250–1517 A. D.).

Two factors tempered the institution of slavery in Europe the forepart of the present millennium. The development of feudalism which favored serfdom to slavery for agricultural labor and the emergence of some restrictions on slavery by the Church. In the 13th century the Church decreed that Christians could not enslave Christians. Jews were forbidden to have Christian slaves. The Church also encouraged Christian masters to free their slaves for heavenly reward.

Slavery and serfdom existed side by side in medieval Europe. Slaves did the menial work such as household chores, handicrafts and the like. Serfdom, as in ancient Egypt, was doubtless more tolerable but the serf was not a free man. Yet his life was tied to a piece of land and that satisfied his territorial instinct for greater tranquility in life.

The Childrens Crusade of 1212 A. D. is a sad and poignant episode of slavery in medieval times. Stephen of Cloyes, a religiously inspired French shepherd boy, organized a crusade of his peers to try to free the holy land from the Saracens. He led them to the port of Marseilles where they fell into the hands of Venetian slave traders who sold them into slavery in Egypt. The Church, either out of impotence or indifference, appears to have done nothing about it.

European slavery assumed one of its nastiest aspects during the period of colonialism. After the discovery, exploration and conquest of the western hemisphere the Europeans suddenly acquired vast areas of agricultural land for cultivation. They were unsuccessful in enslaving the American Indians so they turned to the black African for the necessary labor. It should be noted that the Europeans did not create the black slave market. It flourished for centuries in Africa below the Sahara, but largely for a limited muslim demand for slaves for north Africa and the Middle East. The Europeans turned to this ready market for their agricultural labor needs in the new world. By the 18th century the plantations—sugar, cotton, tobacco, indigo, cocao and others—of the Americas were manned by negro slaves. The nasty aspect of European colonial slavery was its racial overtone. The word negro—although it merely means black in Portuguese—took on a degrading approbrium. Until this time slavery was devoid of any racial connotation. It was so ubiquitous. Romans may have preferred the Gauls, Germans and Greeks because of their aryan affinity but people were not enslaved on account of race or color.

Slavery was universal until recent times. Every society practiced it. It may have varied in intensity and cruelty with different people and in differing socio-economic structures. But everywhere man enslaved his fellow man to perform the hard and menial tasks of the predominantly agricultural societies prior to industrialization. This discussion has dwelt primarily on the situation in civilizations flourishing in the Mediterranean area of the world, but societies outside this area engaged in slavery with virtually the same intensity and purpose.

Chinese history is replete with reference to slavery. After the rise of the Chinese empire with the Han dynasty following the Period of the Warring States thousands of prisoners of the civil wars became slaves. Another source was the border skirmishes with the Hsuing-nu, the mounted raiders from the Gobi desert. Political prisoners comprised still another source. Men were sold into slavery for debt. Poor families sold their children to fend off starvation. There are a score or more reports of widespread selling of children into slavery during droughts, famine and other economic calamities. Slaves were also imported from Java. It was the same sources as in other societies.

The slaves performed about the same functions as elsewhere. Artisans—potters, weavers, musicians—were attached to the households and estates of the nobles, as were horse-herds, grooms and outriders for carriages. The unskilled were worked to death clearing the jungles for more agricultural land. Perhaps, somewhat unique was the demand for female slaves as entertainers (much like the Japanese geishas), courtesans, and concubines.

Concubinage, a spurious polygamy, formed an integral part of the Chinese culture.

Slavery was also well established in the Hindu society, although slaves were much less numerous than in the Graeco-Roman civilization. In fact, Megasthenes the Greek Ambassador to India in the third century B. C. reported there were no slaves in India. Slavery in the Hindu society was milder and Megasthenes was unable to see it clearly in the caste system of the country. The *Mahabarata* states that the vanquished in a war became the victor's slaves. A man might lose his freedom for crime or debt. A man could sell himself into slavery. Children of slaves were slaves. All these types of slavery are recognized in the Smrtis, the law books of the Hindus. The *Arthasastra*, an ancient text on law and administration, contains many regulations on slavery. Sales of children into slavery were forbidden except in dire emergency. A promise to sell oneself or his children into slavery made in dire emergency was not enforceable in law. Slaves could own property and earn money in their spare time. Caste did not exempt a person from becoming a slave, but a high caste slave could not be forced to perform lower caste or defiling work. Slave girls were protected against rape by their master. In such event the master was required to set her free. And if the master got a slave girl pregnant, even with her consent, he was required to set her and the child free. Some law books forbad corporeal punishment of a slave; others restricted beatings only on the back. A master was admonished not to stint on the food he furnished his slave "who does the dirty work for him." A master was also required to look after his slave in old age.

Slaves performed the same kind of work in ancient India as they did elsewhere. They were usually domestic servants. They worked the land and mines. Agriculture did not, however become dependent on slavery. There was no counterpart of the Roman latifundia. The farm worker, unskilled laborer and craftsman were usually free men. As in Rome slaves often rose to responsible positions, as king's top counselors. There are, to be sure, numerous references to cruelty to slaves in India, but on the whole it would appear the lot of slaves in the Hindu society was less harsh than elsewhere. That is, perhaps, the reason Megasthenes reported as he did.

The old civilizations of the Americas also engaged in slavery. The soldier historian Bernal Diaz del Castillo with Cortez in Mexico records that he saw in the Aztec markets "Indian slaves, both men and women, and they brought them along tied to long poles with collars around their necks." The Aztec code was quite explicit on slavery. Prisoners of war were destined for sacrifice to the war god Huitzilopatchli. Slaves, therefore, were largely criminals, debtors and those voluntarily assuming slavery or sold by parents for reasons of poverty. In the latter case parents could substitute children so that the whole family could share the burden. The contract of enslavement was explicit and usually mild. The services to be rendered were limited with precision. The slave was allowed to have his own family, hold property and even own other slaves. His children were free. No one could be born into slavery in Mexico. In this important aspect Aztec slavery differed from that elsewhere. Slaves were seldom sold or traded, but unruly and vicious slaves were sold or transferred to the priests for sacrifice. The Incas, on the other hand do not appear to have enslaved the people they conquered on their land but subjected them to their iron will and central rule from Cuzco. If they refused to submit they were summarily liquidated. It was in effect, a form of slavery in situ.

Slavery still exists into modern times. It has been rendered obsolete and/or abolished in the advanced industrialized societies. There are vestigial remains of socio-economic slavery in Africa and western Asia. As late as 1975 stories issued out of Africa that the once proud Tuaregs of Timbuktu were selling their daughters into slavery. The Tuaregs who lived on the edge of the Sahara for 1500 years or so as camel mounted raiders of the sedentary populations on the rim of the desert, themselves keepers of slaves, have encountered hard times after seven years of drought in mid-Africa. They now, like their ancient counterparts, are forced to sell their children into slavery in order to avoid starvation.

There is also the controversial subject of penal servitude, particularly that involving political prisoners. Such involuntary servitude does not, however, involve the technological development of man, the subject of this discussion.

V
Technological Innovation and Accumulation—Industrialization

The machine finally abolished slavery by making it technologically obsolete. Agricultural labor is being displaced by the tractor. Construction work by the earthmover and crane. A powered rotary ditch digger can do twenty man-days of work in an hour. Hard menial work has been or soon will be done by machines not slaves or even wage earners. Industrialization will eventually, and already has in the highly developed countries, eliminate the use of all animal power. The horse and mule population of the United States declined from a high of 27 million in 1915 to a low of 3 million by 1960. Today there is still considerable reliance on animal power—and to some extent even on slavery—in the underindustrialized countries of Asia, Africa and Latin America. But even in these countries the days of muscular power are numbered.

Industrialization begot a new system for the distribution of the national product. It was the wage system, the job, employment and various other names by which it goes. Basically the change was from status to contract. A person was no longer made to produce as a slave, serf, bondsman or servant. He worked on a job for wages or salary. How much it changed his economic situation is arguable, but it did change his socio-political position in that he was a free man. The plight of English women working on all fours pulling carts in the coal mines of Wales for pennies in the 19th century, so poignantly decried by Karl Marx, did not obviously differ much from the Roman slave working in the gold and copper mines of Spain. Her social and political freedom was rendered quite valueless by her penury. The only compulsion to work under the job system—and it is a powerful compulsion—is to avoid starvation.

The accelerating pace of technological accumulation, however, is fast rendering the job system obsolete as a means for the distribution of the national product in a highly industrialized society. The fully automated factory that will provide few if any jobs is at hand. And as national production becomes more and more automated it will not be possible to distribute the product on the basis of employment as there will not be sufficient jobs to employ the entire population. Yet there is at this time no social engineering, or even much advanced thinking, on this problem. The only noteworthy treatise is the *Capitalist Manifesto* by Mortimer Adler and Louis Kelso in which they advocate universal private ownership of the productive facilities so that everyone's basic livelihood would derive from profit on investment rather than employment. To date the idea has been virtually ignored. Communism or socialism, it would appear to have no solution for this problem, even though the productive facilities are owned by the state. Yet the industrialized countries face social and political crises of monumental proportions because the job system of distribution of wealth has been rendered obsolete by rapidly advancing technological development.

ELEMENTAL ENERGY

A first step in the direction of industrialization was the harnessing of the elemental energy of the earth—the flowing water and the wind. To command this source of energy man invented the water-mill, the wind mill and the sailing ship.

Although there is evidence of water mills at the turn of the Christian era their widespread use did not develop before the beginning of the present millennium. By the 13th century A. D. all industry was powered by the gravitational flow of water. There were flour mills, saw mills, fulling mills, tanning mills and countless other mills. On a tributary of the Seine at Rouen there were 2 mills in the 10th century, 5 in the 12th, 10 in the 13th and 12 about 1300 A. D.! In the district of Aube water mills multiplied from 14 in the 11th century to nearly 200 by the start of the 13th century.

It is puzzling why water power was not fully exploited during Graeco-Roman times as the principle was well known to man at that time. Perhaps, it was impeded by the cheap manpower provided by slavery. Others feel that the rivers of Greece and Italy did not provide the necessary abundant flow of water the year round to power the mills.

Another reason may be that the mills used in the Near East, Greece and elsewhere were inefficient and not a great improvement on man and animal power. Needless to say, one of the earliest needs for power was the rotary quern for grinding wheat or barley into flour. To turn the quern without gears dictated a horizontal water wheel which was very ineffective in utilizing the flow of the stream. Its energy output was not much greater than that of a donkey or two slaves, the conventional means of powering the quern during Roman times. It was only after the invention of the Vitruvian mill in the 1st century B. C. which could derive 5–6 times the power from the same stream that a real incentive arose for a conversion from muscular to water power for the grinding of corn. The Vitruvian mill had a vertical water wheel, either undershot or overshot, which transmitted the power through gears to a horizontal mill stone. Although Pollio Vitruvius, an eminent Roman architect and engineer, invented the vertical water wheel in the first century before Christ it was not seriously utilized for some 400 years! One of the earliest examples of the use of water power is the Roman flour factory at Barbegal, near Arles, France. It was built in the early part of the 4th century A. D. alongside the old aqueduct of Saint Remy (built 63–12 B. C.) to utilize the water carried by this water main. Two sets of eight overshot wheels were built down a slope to utilize the water flow of the aqueduct to power eight mill stones each of which could grind 15–20 kg. of grain per hour. The entire mill could produce 28 tons of flour per day. Since that could feed a population of 80,000 and Arles had only 10,000 residents it is presumed the mill was used as a source of flour for Rome or for the Roman legions stationed in Gaul. A similar flour mill has been found by archeologists in Prety, near Tournus, Burgundy that supplied the legions of northern Gaul.

The Vitruvian water mill continued to be used until it was superseded by the turbine. There were technological improvements in the gears. But wooden gears continued in use until the 19th century for the power utilized was never so great as to require metal gears. There was also improvement in the control of the water for the mill. Mill ponds or reservoirs were constructed for storage and controlled release of the water to the wheel. The mill race and chute for proper flow of the water under or over the wheel was designed, for maximum impact on the wheel. The overshot wheel was usually favored.

Tide mills were used but not to any great extent. There was one at the mouth of the Adour, France in the 12th century. Tide mills were used in Venice at this time. Dover harbour had a tide mill at the time of the Norman conquest.

The use of the vertical wheel was widespread in China too after 1300 though there is no clear evidence of its earlier use. Particularly noteworthy is a depiction as early as 1313 of a spinning mill powered by an undershot waterwheel. But the use of water power for operating bellows for iron making goes back to the first century. A few centuries later the water powered trip hammer was used in the metallurgical industry. It is believed that the bellows and trip hammer were operated by the horizontal water wheel which was always favored in the east. Yet a trip hammer requires considerable power and the Chinese may have used a vertical wheel for this purpose. The Chinese were familiar with a vertical wheel from the use of the noira, a water lifting devise, as early as 100–200 A. D. The earliest use of water power for bellows and the trip hammer in Europe dates to the 16th century. For some unknown reason, the use of water power outside the metallurgical industry in China was slow. Perhaps it was a technological frame of mind wedded to the horizontal wheel.

The noira, believed to have been invented in India but highly developed by the Chinese, is a huge vertical wheel (up to 50 feet in diameter) with bamboo buckets attached to its circumference for lifting the water from the stream. While some are powered by man or animals, most are fitted with paddles which turn the wheel in running water. The noira is still widely used for irrigation in China today.

The origin of the noira is difficult to date. Joseph Needham concludes tentatively that it was probably invented in India, reached the Graeco-Roman world during the first century before Christ and China in the second century A. D. There is some speculation Vitruvius may have derived the idea for the vertical wheel from the noira.

Next to water power in importance was wind power. The origin of the windmill is unclear. Some believe it originated in Persia and found its way to Europe through Russia and Scandinavia. Others think it was brought to Europe by the Muslims via Morocco and Spain. Then too the European windmill, from the beginning, was a more substantial and formidable machine than the lightweight and often flimsy windmills of the Mediterranean area and the East.

The earliest record of a windmill in Europe is the reference to one in a gift of land around 1180 A. D. to the Abbey of St. Sauvere de Vicomte in Normandy. During the 13th century numerous references are found. Shortly after, the windmill became a prime-mover of northern Europe from eastern England through the low countries to Russia. It is often mistakenly believed that the windmill was invented to reclaim and drain the low countries. Actually the evidence is that the windmill, as its counterpart the watermill, was first used to grind flour. Usually the flour mill consisted of two decks of single or double millstones geared to the central shaft. Such disposition of the millstones enabled the miller to use both decks in a strong wind and only one in a weak wind. In the 15th century the Dutch invented the *wipmolen* or hollow post-mill for pumping water to drain the polders and the windmill came into widespread use in Holland for reclaiming the Zuider Zee. In 1592 the first wind saw-mill was built at Uitgiest, Holland by Cornelis Cornelisz. It was mounted on a raft so it could be easily warped to bring the sails into the wind. The logs were transported to the barge in the water.

The windmill is in effect an inverted Vitruvian water mill. The power is transmitted down from the sails instead of up from the water. The vertically rotating vanes are geared to the horizontally rotating central shaft and machines. The essential element of the windmill is an understanding of the aerodynamics of the vanes for the extraction of maximum power from the wind.

The earliest European windmills were post mills. Both the housing and the sails were mounted on a strong post so that the mill could be rotated into the wind. Later as the mills grew bigger a turret was constructed on top of the millhouse to which the sails were mounted. In this type of windmill only the turret had to be rotated to keep the sails pointed into the wind. Winches were devised and added to lighten the task of rotating the post mills or turrets.

The Dutch became in due course the foremost millwrights of Europe. It is recorded that a Dutchman built a mill at Cologne in 1392 and another at Speyer that year. By 1600 they dotted the whole of Holland with *wipmolen* for their famous drainage system. It is reported that around 1800 there were 12,000 windmills in Holland.

The windmill was unknown to the Greeks and Romans. The Persians write of windmills as early as the 7th century A. D. It appears to have originated in the province of Seistan which is described by the Arab geographer Al-Masudi (947 A. D.) as a "land of wind and sand". He goes on to state that the inhabitants use the wind to turn mills to pump water from wells to irrigate the gardens. Also to grind corn. A later historian reports the use of windmills in Afghanistan, where a strong north wind blows, for pumping water and grinding corn. From Persia and Afghanistan the windmill spread to India and China where it was used to pump water, grind corn and crush sugar cane. The windmill also became the source of power for the irrigation works of Egypt and the Near East. The windmills of the East, however, were of lighter construction than the heavy Dutch mills of Europe. A mill house was not always used. In China the sails were often mounted and geared to an irrigation pump and operated in an open field.

The windmills of the East were and still are entirely different from that of Europe. The European windmill is, in effect, a reverse propellar operating on the screw principle. The Persian and Chinese windmills operate horizontally, attached directly to a vertical drive shaft. No gears are necessary to change the rotary motion.

The Persian windmill normally has four vanes, usually made of wood fixed at 90° positions on a square wooden drive shaft. The vanes are housed at the top of a square millhouse with an opening (approximately half of the side) at the right side of each wall to admit the wind. Such openings permit operation of the mill irrespective of the direction of the wind. Unlike the European mill it need never be turned into the wind. If it is desired to have the shaft turn in the opposite direction the openings are constructed at the left side of each wall. The quern or other machinery is installed and housed below the floor where the vanes operate. Where the wind is dependably from one direction as it is in Seistan or Afghanistan it is merely necessary to install a wall or baffle shielding the left side of the vanes from the wind.

The Chinese who, it is believed, got the idea of the windmill from Persia, converted it, as is their wont, to their own technological frame of mind. They simply adapted the lug sail from the junk to the horizontal windmill. Eight or so long rectangular sails are fixed and rigged on a cylindrical frame in a manner whereby the sails luff when coming into the wind and are automatically set by the sheets as they rotate into position to receive the full force of the wind. The Chinese windmill will also operate regardless of the direction of the wind. Moreover, it does not need the housing and wall openings of the Persian mill. The Chinese horizontal mills can be seen standing freely in the open fields operating irrigation pumps, sugar mills and other machinery without any housing of any kind.

There is an interesting speculation that the horizontal windmills of the East owe their origin to the wind operated Buddhist prayer wheels of Tibet. Tibetan monks employed a four cup anemometer to turn their prayer wheels. But the Tibetans did not take up Buddhism until the 8th century which would appear to be a century later than the first windmills were thought to be seen in the province of Seistan. On the other hand, Buddhism reached Central Asia from India as early as the second century B. C. and Buddhist monks elsewhere may have employed the device.

The windmill depends even more on the vagaries of the weather than the watermill. In places like northern Europe where the winds are strong and steady it was a very effective source of power. In the heartland of India, however, where the wind is either violent or non existent the windmill has had limited usage.

During the period 1600–1800 numerous refinements were made to both the watermill and windmill to make them more effective power mechanisms. The design, maintenance and repair of these ever increasing complex machines were done by the carpenter and the millwright, as the structure, including the shafts and gears, was made entirely of wood. By the 18th century these carpenter-mechanics acquired a pretty thorough pragmatic understanding of mechanics and were ready to graduate to the status of machinists in the age of steam. Noteworthy in this respect was John Smeaton of England (1724–92). He introduced the cast iron shaft to overcome the problem of rotting of the nose of the wind-shaft on the old wooden windmills. Later he mounted the sails on the cast iron hub fixed to the nose of the windshaft. This permitted an increase in the number and length of the sail arms.

Subsequently iron was introduced into the gears leading to cycloidal gearing. Iron was used also to make the shuttered sails. The East Anglia postmills became the best designed and efficient mills in Europe. The English were already displaying the mechanical genius that was destined to usher in the Industrial Revolution in the 18th century.

Smeaton also invented instruments to measure the horsepower and effectiveness of water mills and windmills. He concluded that overshot wheels gave greater horsepower (about twice the output under same conditions) than undershot wheels. The breast shot wheel was designed as a compromise where due to physical conditions it was not possible to take full advantage of the overshot wheel. Eighteenth century waterwheels had an output of 5–10 horsepower. Water wheels were hitched in series when more energy was required. Such as the Marley machine built for Louis XIV by carpenter Rennequin in 1682 with a capacity of 124 horsepower. Its actual

output, however, was only about 75 horsepower because of faulty maintenance. The typical Dutch windmill too had a capacity of around 10
horsepower.

The windmill and watermill continued to develop as the main source of
power in pre-industrial Europe when the steam engine began to displace
them. But they continued to overlap with steam and the internal combustion
engine right up to modern times. The steel light framed windmill to pump
water for irrigation and general agricultural uses dotted the prairies of
America until the 20th century.

Wind and water power have some interesting aspects. It is virtually free
power. The water or windmill is of cheap and durable construction that lasts
decades. It is available to anyone; it cannot be monopolized. It does not
pollute the atmosphere. The mills are picturesque. Unfortunately, it is
limited in potential and was soon bypassed by man in his unquenchable
thirst for more energy.

There is an amusing oft quoted poem that bears repeating at this point
written by one Antipater of Thessalonica around the 1st century B. C.:

> Women who toil at the querns, cease now your grinding;
> Sleep late though the crowing of cocks announces the dawn.
> Your task is now for the nymphs, by command of Demeter,
> And leaping down on the top of the wheel, they turn it,
> Axle and whirling spokes together revolving and causing
> The heavy and hollow Nisyrian stones to grind above.
> So shall we taste the joys of the golden age
> And feast on Demeter's gifts without ransom of labour.

The wind was used to power the ship. How man learned to navigate the
waters need not detain us unduly. From the floating log to the dug out and
the raft, from the frame boat covered with skin or wood, man in due time,
graduated to the more formidable vessels that could navigate the sea.

The earliest evidence of the sail is in the Nile valley. The ancient
Egyptians were indeed twice blessed people. Not only did the Nile fructify
their agriculture with rich soil and abundant water it provided a most central
thoroughfare for the empire. Just as dependably as the Nile flowed north the
wind blew south! The Egyptians very early, perhaps around 3000 B. C.,
learned to put up a sail to run upstream and to return by the current. This
peculiar situation dictated a somewhat unique design of the early Egyptian
boat with the mast stepped forward for a large rectangular sail to maximize
running before the wind. Earlier boats made of reeds or papyrus had a bipod
mast lashed to the forward sides as the papyrus raft was too infirm to step a
single pole mast amidships. Egyptians were plagued in their ship construction by want of good indigenous wood. It was not long before they began
importing the cedar from Lebanon for their boats. In fact, this may have
been the way Phoenicians learned about the sail.

The Mediterranean invited seafaring. Another thrust in boat development came from the Greeks. The Greeks and Minoans used dugouts on which they gradually built sides to increase their size. This evolved into the keel boat that was capable of coping with the rough open sea.

Drawing on these two influences the Phoenicians developed the first effective cargo vessel powered primarily by the wind. It was a tubby vessel usually 2–3 times as long as it was wide. It ranged from 30 to 80 feet in length. The bow and stern were built high with two oar-rudders affixed to each side of the stern. The planks were covered with pitch to make them watertight. It must be for this reason that Homer refers to the Phoenician craft as "black ships" in the Odyssey. The mast was stepped slightly ahead of amidships. The large rectangular sail hung from a yard arm which was controlled by a line at each end running to the stern deck. The sail was furled to the yard arm by six or more lines, called brails, in the manner of an Austrian shade.

The Phoenician ship could not tack into the wind. Its single sail permitted the ship to sail only abaft or abreast of the wind. The Phoenicians, however, knew the Mediterranean so well that they could sail its waters facilely despite this limitation. They had to wait out calms and unfavorable winds, but then time was of less importance in those days. In fact, they eventually ventured outside the Mediterranean to Britain, the Azores and even around Africa (circa 600 B. C.).

In the last millennium before Christ all or most trade moved by sail. Naval warfare, however, depended on oar-powered vessels. The sail ship could not go windward at this time, hence it possessed no maneuverability for warfare. The state could and was willing to defray the expense of manpower in exchange for greater maneuverability of the oar-powered boat for warfare. Trade, on the other hand, for economic reasons opted for the less expensive albeit slower and less maneuverable sail boat.

The Phoenicians were equally instrumental in developing the oar-powered warship. Their colony Carthage had around 500–300 B. C. the finest naval fleet in the Mediterranean. The Carthaginians had complete control of the western part of the sea. At the other end the Greeks were the foremost naval power at this time. The Persians too built a fleet, employing the Phoenicians whom they ruled, for their plan to invade Greece. The Persian fleet was annihilated by the Greeks in the fierce battle of Salamis in 480 B. C.

The common warship of 300 B. C. was the trireme. It had three banks of oars on each side. In order to employ more manpower the warship had to be longer or the oars had to be banked. The latter was obviously better as the boat could be kept shorter and more maneuverable. Another method was to put more men on each oar, which had the disadvantage of requiring longer oars more vulnerable in battle. But ships of this period were built with as many as five men on an oar. Archeology does not reveal, nor is there a clear record of precisely how the many oars were deployed and coordinated in the operation of the ship. Needless to say the triremes and other warships of the day were rowed largely by slaves. The galley slave was, perhaps, along with the mine slave the most oppressed human being in the history of man.

The Romans, proverbial landlubbers, had to become sailors to defeat Carthage. They built a fleet based upon a wrecked Carthaginian vessel that washed ashore in Italy and eventually destroyed the Carthaginian fleet. But the real credit goes to some Roman genius who invented the corvus, a wooden gangway about 25 feet long with a long sharp iron spike which was dropped on the deck of the Carthaginian ship holding it fast alongside while the Roman soldiers boarded the enemy ship to dispatch its sailors in hand to hand combat. What the Romans did, in effect, was to convert naval to land warfare and it won the day.

Naval technology remained on a plateau for two thousand years in the Mediterranean area after the invention of the sail cargo vessel and the oar-powered war ship. There were, to be sure, some changes in design. Sails were added to the warships so that the oarsmen could rest if the wind was favorable as the ship sailed from place to place. In battle only the oars were used. The Mediterranean war-galley around 1500 A. D. was still a trireme about 120 feet long, 15 feet wide and with 100–150 oarsmen pulling 3 banks of oars. The alternative to the trireme was a single bank of oars with each oar pulled by several men. As many as eight men on an oar were used. A single mast forward carried a lateen (triangular) sail. The trading-galley had 3 masts with lateen sails. Oars were provided only for emergencies, channels and docking. The full rigged ship still awaited development after 1400 A. D.

There were, of course, developments in sail ships outside the Mediterranean area. Most noteworthy in this respect is China which has contributed, perhaps, more significantly to naval technology than any other civilization with the invention of the compass, watertight compartment and the central balanced rudder. The earliest Chinese vessels were the keelless wedge-shaped sampans designed for river and coastal traffic. They are still in use today. The sail ship of the Chinese, however, was the junk. It was an enlarged sampan with a high riding aftercastle, three or so masts with battened sails and a post rudder set in a well in the stern. Marco Polo was filled with wonder in describing the junks. Chinese merchant ships had 50–60 cabins, some luxurious for the head merchants. There was nothing akin in the 13th century Europe. The battened sails could be furled by dropping the halyard. The bottom of the sail would fold with the battens like a venetian blind. The Chinese were able to sail to windward. Watertight compartments increased the safety of their ships.

During the Ming dynasty (1368–1634 A. D.) the imperial navy ranged the Pacific and Indian ocean with 3100 warships, 400 armed transports and 250 merchant ships (called treasure ships) to trade with and to collect tribute from 70 states under Chinese suzerianty. After the Ming dynasty succumbed to Manchu domination the development of naval technology was halted. The junk was no match for the European ships and cannon of the 18th and 19th centuries.

Chinese naval technology was considerably advanced over that of the Mediterranean area until the development of the full rigged ship by the Europeans. It started from the premise of the flat bottomed hull—like the Egyptians. The junk has no keel, stem-post or stern-post. But almost from the beginning the Chinese used bulkheads giving great strength to the hulls of their ships. As early as the 2nd century A. D. they used watertight compartments to make their ships unsinkable. Watertight bulkheads also permitted the Chinese to use free-flooding self-bailing compartments fore and aft which served to counteract the pitch of the vessel in rough seas. Joseph Needham postulates an interesting theory that the Chinese came naturally to this type of hull construction because of their use of bamboo, which Nature structured with watertight compartments. Watertight compartments were not known in the West until the 18th century. In 1787 Benjamin Franklin recommended them "after the Chinese fashion" for ships carrying mail across the Atlantic. Sir Samuel Bentham, brother of the famed Jeremy Bentham, constructed ships for the Admiralty with watertight bulkheads "contributing to strength, and securing the ships against floundering, as practiced by the Chinese of the present day."

Equally noteworthy, the Chinese were able to sail to windward as early as the 2nd century A. D. This was accomplished with fore and aft lug sails made of woven bamboo mats or cloth with bamboo battens. The sails were rigged on multiple masts which were sometimes staggered thwartwise to prevent the fore sails from taking the wind from the after sails. Multiple sheets, each leading to a bamboo batten, were employed for more efficient setting of the sail. The battened cloth sails are sometimes gathered at the luff edge making the lug sails look like giant fans. Smaller junks sometimes used a sprit sail. Junks so rigged could sail 45° into the wind. The later European full rigged ship could not sail much closer than 60°. Modern racing yachts can do 35°.

It is also worthy of note that the Chinese never resorted to a widespread use of the multi-oared warships like the Mediterranean peoples. The degrading spectacle of the galley slave was never part of the Chinese scene. The Chinese were of course, familiar with oars. They frequently had to resort to them in the calm China sea and in maneuvering channels. They rowed standing enabling them to use shorter oars. They also propelled small craft by feathering the oar astern. One reason cited for this lesser use of oars is an earlier capability as early as the 2nd century to sail into the wind. Also there may have been less need of warships than in the contending Mediterranean area as Chinese imperialism was never seriously challenged from the sea.

The Arab dhow is also noteworthy though it never became a formidable ship. The dhow is and was mainly a merchant ship designed for the peculiar monsoon weather of the Indian ocean and Arabian sea. The dhows ran south on the northeast monsoon during October–May and returned by the southwest monsoon on the African trade run. Very little is known of Arab ship building and navigation. It seems they borrowed the compass and the centered rudder from the Chinese centuries before the Europeans. It is believed the dhow originated in Abyssinia and first navigated the Red Sea. The co-called lateen (latin) sail was always the rigging of the dhow. In fact, it is believed the Europeans copied the lateen sail from the dhow. Arab merchantmen adapted and developed the dhow after the 7th century and made regular trips from the Persian Gulf to China, Malacca and India. The trips were apparently hazardous. An old Arab proverb states "arriving in China without losing one's life enroute is already a miracle; returning safe and sound is unheard of." Running the monsoon and the pirates in the Indian ocean was obviously a multiple danger.

The dhow, moreover, was a rough and uncomfortable boat. It was, in effect, a large skiff with one or two masts each carrying a large lateen sail. The bigger ones carried a jib. They could sail to windward. The lateen sail enabled the dhow to sail 45° into the wind. The Arabs did not, when tacking, come about into the wind. The sailors let go of the sheet, then would haul the yard upright to the short mast, shift its foot to the other side and reset the sheet. Meanwhile the helmsman would change course appropriately for the opposite tack. Such a tack would be frowned upon by a modern sailor from the west, but the dhow sailors execute it with aplomb. The dhow sails cannot be reefed. The sailors replace it with a smaller sail in a high wind. The dhow it is seen, must be constantly rerigged underway. Needless to say, the Arabs did not develop any effective naval warfare with the dhow.

The Hindus never developed any effective warfare either. In fact, they were not seafaring people. The Hindus, however, colonized southeast Asia during the first millennium after Christ. This thrust was carried out by the Pallavas (300–900 A. D.) and the Cholas (850–1267 A. D.) of south India. As it so often is the case with Indian history there is little or no evidence of the type of ship used by them for the colonization of Indonesia and Indo-China. There is some evidence the Hindus used the sprit sail for going windward as early as the 2nd century A. D. There is evidence also that the Indonesians used the canted rectangular sail. Thus it may be concluded the Hindus and their southeast Asian colonists knew how to sail into the wind shortly after the beginning of the 1st millennium A. D.

There was heavy trade between India and the Romans, Arabs and other Mediterranean people. But most of the sought after Indian spices, steel and textiles and other goods moved in foreign bottoms. The Indians felt no need to transport their wares abroad.

The highest development of the sail ship was destined to occur in the West during the period 1300–1850 A. D. It was part of the growing mechanical ingenuity of the Europeans that set the stage for the Industrial Revolution.

The full-rigged ship—deep-hulled, heavily keeled with commodious holds and extremely seaworthy—provided a better gun platform and more efficient ocean transport, so it began to replace the oar-powered galley of medieval times. Gunpowder reached Europe from China during the 14th century and by the 16th century European gunsmiths were producing formidable canon. The heavy canon could not be mounted effectively on the fragile galleys. The canon also dictated a different type of naval warfare, the objective of which was to destroy the enemy ship from a distance. The ramming and boarding type of naval warfare for which the galley was designed was made obsolete by the canon. But the two types of naval warfare overlapped for a century or so.

The last battle of note fought with the oar-powered galley was the Battle of Lepanto in 1571. The Pope sanctioned an attack on the Ottoman Turks, who were interfering with Venetian trade in the eastern Mediterranean, by the Holy League—Venice, Genoa, Spain, and the Vatican and others. The encounter took place in the Gulf of Parras of the Greek coast between 400 Christian and Turkish galleys. After four hours of ramming, boarding and churning of the sea with thousands of oars the Turks were thoroughly defeated escaping with only 40 of their 250 galleys. The Christians sank 80 and captured 130 Turkish vessels. Especially noteworthy were the six Venetian galleasses (canon bearing three masted lateen sail ships) towed on the periphery of the battle which delivered shattering broadsides into the Turkish galleys, a harbinger of things to come.

Seventeen years later in 1588 the English destroyed the Spanish Armada mainly with heavy canon bombardment. There was no ramming or boarding. Even firearms did not come into play. Broadside tactics dominated naval warfare thereafter. These two battles coterminus in time are set forth in juxtaposition to demonstrate a sharp change in naval warfare that dictated the development of a new type of vessel, the full rigged sailing ship. The ship was too heavy for rowing. Greater power could be derived only from the wind. Moreover the maneuverability for close range warfare provided by oars was no longer needed for bombardment. It should also be noted that it represents a dramatic shift of technological prowess from the Mediterranean area and the Mideast to Europe.

The full rigged ship had two sources of development. The earliest in Spain and Portugal; the other in northern Europe. Henry the Navigator was sending small two or three masted caravals with lateen sails down the coast of Africa the fore part of the 15th century. These little caravals appeared to be rigged much like the Arab dhows. But this is understandable in view of Muslim occupation and influence on the Iberian peninsula.

The square sail was added by the end of the century to the foremast of the larger ships. The square sail was more suitable for ocean going and European sailors were learning how to set it to sail to windward. By 1492 Columbus had ships with square sails for his famous crossing of the Atlantic.

In fact the *Nina*, which started the voyage as a caraval, was rerigged with square sails in the Canary islands.

The French, Dutch and English, drawing heavily on Portuguese and Spanish naval architecture, began building larger ships called carracks. In 1512 Henry VIII's ship the *Regent* of 1000 tons, carried 151 iron and 29 brass guns, and was manned with 400 soldiers and 300 marines. It was lost in a battle off Brest with the French ship Cordeliere. The French ship caught fire and both ships were destroyed.

Henry replaced the *Regent* with the *Great Carrack* of 1500 tons, popularly known as the Great Harry. It was rebuilt in 1545 as a smaller ship of 1000 tons. A mania for bigness had developed at this time but the big ships were unmanageable. In addition the Royal Navy by 1546 had twenty ships from 60–1000 tons, fifteen galeasses from 140–450 tons, ten pinnaces from 15 to 80 tons and thirteen oared barges.

The finest warship of the 16th century was the galleon. It was invented by the Portuguese but soon adopted by the English. It's keel to beam ratio was increased to three instead of the earlier two or two and a half. It was thus a slimmer ship. Its aftercastle still rode high. Its silhouette looked like a high heeled platform shoe. The galleon was rigged with four masts each carrying one to three square sails. In addition there were mizzen and bonnet sails. The galleons were fast and maneuverable. They were not well suited for merchant ships as cargo space was reduced.

The Europeans used these formidable ships to conquer the world during the 16th and 17th century. The English East India Company set sail in 1600 with four merchant ships of 300 and 600 tons measure. They were three masted with a sprit sail-top mast at the end of the bowsprit. The Europeans, with these superior ships, were able to challenge so formidable a power as the Mughal empire of India. On land their small forces would have been annihilated by the Indian nabobs, but they had the great advantage of being able to retreat to the sanctuary of their ships at sea. The Mughal empire had no navy. The Europeans used the sanctuary of the sea to attack land powers immensely greater than their puny numbers in order to achieve their objectives. Albuquerque's hit and run attack on Indian ports gave the Portuguese domination of the Indian ocean during the 16th century. In due time Europeans achieved global empire. They used the sea like the Arabs used the desert to defeat the Persian empire a millennium or so earlier. The Arab vehicle for the purpose was the camel, often referred to as the ship of the desert.

During the 17th and 18th centuries the galleon type ship was improved. Much of the impetus came from the East India Companies of England, Holland and France who needed faster and more efficient cargo carriers for their Far East trade. Length to beam ratios increased. The fore and aft castles were lowered. Headrooms in the cabins below decks were increased. Hulls were strengthened with heavier planks. Iron and copper were introduced in various places to increase strength and prevent barnacles. Gear was improved. Greater use was made of deadeyes, capstans and ratlines. The sail plan was improved for better aerodynamics and windpower. The big ships had four masts each with one or more retangular sails capable of close hauling for sailing to windward. Lateen sails were used fore and aft. Top and bonnet sails were used with the square sails. Smaller ships had three masts with similar subsidiary sails. These ships on the India run were not only more efficient but things of beauty under sail.

The 19th century witnessed the highest evolution of the sailing ship. It was the clipper ship, the queen of the sea around 1850. Unfortunately the sail ship reached its peak at a time when the age of steam and steel was ready to preempt the oceans with greater horsepower and speed. Hence, the clipper had but a brief day in the sun.

But what a day it was. Its sleek hull with a cloud of sail aloft made the clipper the most beautiful machine ever designed and built by the hand of man. Two hundred or more feet long, masts reaching for the wind two hundred or so feet into the sky and 10,000 and more yards of canvas billowing aloft white as the clouds. As many as five masts, each with as many as five square sails stacked two hundred feet high, with lateen jibs, moonrakers, flying kites and other subsidiary sails, made the sail structure look like a flying cloud. In fact, one of the famous clippers was named just that.

The clippers could do 12 to 15 knots with aplomb. The biggest ever built (by the Germans who had overtaken the English and Americans by the late 19th century), the *Preussen's* could do 17 knots. Her 60,000 feet of canvas could generate 6000 horsepower. The *Preussen's* premature demise in her eighth year in 1910 when struck by a British steamer in the English channel was a sad episode in windjammer history. The clippers were not efficient cargo vessels for the hull had to be narrowed, the poop and foc'stle eliminated and other sacrifice of space in favor of speed. They could, therefore, subsist economically only on the more lucrative type of transportation. Americans used them in the gold rush days to transport prospectors from the east coast to California around Cape Horn. The *Flying Cloud* made the run from New York to San Francisco in 89 days in 1854. She lost two topmasts off Valparaiso but the captain pressed on without them still at 12 knots. The American skippers seldom doused sail unlike their more cautious British counterparts. The Yankee clipper was also widely used in the China trade. Not only was expensive cargo like opium involved, but the clipper was needed to outrun pirates and the authorities in the smuggling nature of much of the trade. The Navigation Acts of the British forbade trade by others in certain areas of the world. These Acts were repealed in 1849.

The Americans also devised the so-called packet service across the Atlantic. Unlike their predecessors the ships sailed on schedule whether or not fully booked. The runs were fast—a fortnight or so. Fare was about

$200, wine included. At first the packets got the rich tourists and business-men, but in the end, when the cunards (steam and steel ships) took over this lucrative trade, they carried mostly emigrants to America.

The clipper was an American invention. Hence, the designation, the Yankee clipper. But the British were quick to adopt the clipper for their Far East trade, particularly for the transport of tea to Europe and America. The clippers were particularly effective in sailing the light winds of the China sea.

One of the most romantic events in sailing ship history was the race in 1866 between the *Ariel* and the *Taeping*, two British tea clippers, from Foochow to London. The prize was £ 100 to the winner's captain. Also a freight bonus of 10 shillings a ton for the first tea landed on the London docks. Crowds lined the white cliffs as the two clippers sailed neck to neck through the straits of Dover. They were picked up by tugs for the run up the Thames and the *Taeping*, drawing less water, arrived first by twenty minutes, 99 days and 15,000 miles out of Foochow! The *Ariel* logged 14 knots at times with all canvas flying.

Captain McKennon of the *Taeping* very graciously acknowledged a tie and shared the prize with Captain Keay of the *Ariel*. The two captains in jovial fellowship repaired to the Ship and Turtle Tavern for ale to calm their jagged nerves and swap tales of the voyage. It was clipper racing at its best.

These two clippers were not large. They were around 700 tons and only three masted, but heavily canvassed for the light winds of the China sea. They were designed for one purpose—to fill English tea cups as inexpensive-ly as possible. Their sleek hulls made them wet ships in constant danger of pooping, that is, their sterns going awash when running before a high wind in a heavy sea. In fact, the Ariel was believed to have pooped when it was lost at sea in 1872 on a voyage to Sidney.

Western domination of the world owes much to the development of the sailing ship. The clippers were the plumes in the cap of British imperialism. There were in the main the more rugged galleon type merchant ships (Indiamen) of the Far East trade. And behind them all was the Royal Navy, which depended on the full-rigged wooden vessels well into the 19th century. The Battle of Trafalgar in 1805 was fought with ships of wood and sail. So was the War of 1812 out of which the American Navy was born. Steam ships did not take over until the latter half of the 19th century.

For a thousand years and more man harnessed the energy of the water and the wind, the byproducts of the hydrologic cycle powered by the radiant energy of the sun. And in the process he became a mechanic. By the 18th century he found these sources of energy wanting in his innate drive to command more external energy. He had by then developed the pragmatic knowledge and mechanical ingenuity to reach deeper into the fundamental energy sources of the universe. He was now ready to go into the chemistry of matter to release and harness more energy for his command.

It should not go unnoticed that a profound historical shift in the development and accumulation of technology transpired with the exploitation of the elemental energy of the earth. As was or should have been noted until this time technological creativity resided in the East—western Asia, India and China. Now the center of technological creativity shifted west to Europe. It has remained there to date.

CHEMICAL ENERGY

The year 1750 is generally regarded as the beginning of industrialization. It would be myopic, however, to view it as the birth of the machine. The water mill and windmill were machines. What is, therefore, really meant by industrialization is that a new and greater source of energy was brought under the command of man to power his machines, the flour mills, saw mills, textile factories and the like. The most significant thing about this technological breakthrough is that for the first time man began to look inside matter for his increased source of energy. He found a way to harness the increased molecular action generated by the oxidation of carbon.

The chemical reaction was nothing new. Homo erectus discovered fire a half million or more years ago. But until 1750 man was only able to use this heat energy to warm himself, cook his food, fire his kilns, smelt his metals and a few other uses. He did not yet achieve the technical ability to convert the heat energy of fire to mechanical energy to power his machines.

The invention through which this was first achieved was the steam engine. Through the conversion of water to steam and back again to water, by the addition and subtraction of heat energy, the steam engine was able to harness the forces of expansion and contraction into reciprocating *cum* rotary motion to power the machines of man. But before tracing the development of the steam engine let us pause and examine the fundamental source of the heat or chemical energy on which the steam engine was based.

When man's technological development was ready for this new source of energy, he found that Nature had furnished him an abundance of raw material for the purpose. It was the fossil fuels mentioned and discussed in Chapter II. They were available to man in three forms—coal, petroleum and gas. The first hundred years of the Industrial Revolution exploited only the first.

Most of the coal of the earth was formed by geologic conditions not too well understood during the Carboniferous period (345–280 million years ago). Plant life had evolved abundantly by this geologic period. The earth was still wet and swampy. Volcanoes and mountain forming were extremely active during this and the succeeding Permian periods. Vast quantities of vegetation sank into the swamps. Much of it was compressed in the earth by crustal upheavals and shifting. The decomposing vegetation was buried and formed into deposits of almost pure carbon. Twenty feet of vegetation was required to form a foot thickness of coal. This process kept repeating itself for millions of years. Time and geologic pressure transformed the vegetation into coal. The result was the creation of a great store of energy for man's use millions of years later.

Coal deposits are found in sedimentary rock of all geologic ages from the Devonian to the Pleistocene and the process of coal formation is occurring even today in the peat bogs of Ireland, Virginia and North Carolina. But from the peat bog to a coal seam depends upon a configuration of geologic conditions unlikely to recur that were most prevalent during the Carboniferous and Permian periods. Thus the formation of fossil fuels is a non-recurring phenomena and when man exhausts their present supply he will have to seek other sources for continuation of his increasing command over the energy of the universe. We shall see, of course, before this chapter ends, that man is already on his way to the utilization of other sources of energy locked up in matter.

Coal deposits exist almost everywhere on earth, but some places have greater concentrations. Britain was so blessed. Coal mining in Britain antedates the steam engine by centuries. Coal was dug at Newcastle as early as the 13th century. By 1750 it was widely used instead of wood or charcoal by brewers, glassmakers, brick makers, smelters, smiths and others. In fact, coal mining itself begot the steam engine for which it provided the energy. As the British coal industry exhausted the surface and near surface seams its shafts and galleries had to go deeper into the ground. When they went below the water table the galleries flooded with water. At first, the miners used man and animal powered pumps to keep the galleries dry but as the galleries went deper and deeper muscular power became insufficient for the job.

The steam engine, also called the fire engine in the beginning, came to the rescue. Again, as with other inventions, the steam engine was known to the Greeks. The translation of Hero's *Pneumatics*, which set forth the principles of a steam engine, in 1575 brought the idea of Europe. But it remained, more or less, a scientific toy. As the pressing need for more power to pump water out of the mines grew Europeans began thinking about the use of steam for the purpose. Thomas Savery of England and Denis Papin of France first publicized the idea of a steam drawn pump in 1712. Newcomen's contribution was the use of separate boiler for providing the steam. Newcomen's engine was extremely inefficient but it did pump water from the mines. His engine depended, largely, upon the weight of the pump rod and piston to draw steam into the engine cylinder where it was condensed by injecting a spray of water. This produced a vacuum in the cylinder and atmospheric pressure thrust the piston up on its power stroke. These early steam engines were sometimes called atmospheric engines as it was the pressure of the atmosphere that provided the power, albeit that it was the condensation of the steam that created the necessary vaccum for the purpose. John Smeaton also designed and built such atmospheric engines which were an improvement on Newcomens. He nearly doubled the efficiency of this early engine. The big deficiency of the atomospheric engine was the great heat loss involved in cooling the cylinders directly with the injection of water. By 1725, though, the Newcomen engine was used widely not only for pumping mines but for lifting water to operate water wheels.

James Watt, generally regarded as the inventor of the steam engine, made the improvements and innovations that enabled man to derive maximum power from the use of steam. At first he continued Newcomen's and Smeaton's work on steam pumps. He realized that the cooling of the cylinder with a water spray reduced its efficiency, so he devised the separate condenser off the cylinder for the purpose. In addition, he insulated the cylinder with wood to keep it hot. Finally, he introduced steam behind the piston on its downward stroke to substitute for water as a seal between piston and cylinder and to assist atmospheric pressure in the power stroke.

Watt's major innovation was to adapt the steam engine for rotary motion. At about the same time he invented the double acting engine with power behind each stroke of the piston and the governor to maintain an even rotary speed under varying loads. He introduced oil to seal and lubricate the piston. In addition he made several improvements in the valves, connecting rods, gears and other parts of his complex and more efficient engine. By 1786 the engine he made for the Albion flour mill produced 50 horsepower. In the next twenty years the firm of Boulton and Watt installed 84 engines in cotton mills, 17 in breweries, 18 in canal-works and 9 in worsted mills.

Although Watt took out a patent for an engine worked by steam pressure his greatly improved engine was still essentially a vacuum-engine, because he continued to work with low pressure steam. He was greatly opposed to the use of high pressure steam because of the danger involved. High pressure steam required improved boilers. In the early 19th century Richard Trevithick in England and Oliver Evans in America developed the use of high pressure steam engines and the steam engine became the major source of industrial power during most of the century.

Watts and his contemporaries were plagued with inadequate machine shops and mechanics to produce the precision parts required by their steam engines. Tolerances between piston and cylinder could not be brought down to less than half an inch. The demand for precise fittings and parts spurred the ironworks, aided now by the steam engine, to produce improved metal production. John Wilkinson, a British ironmaster, made and patented in 1774 an improved boring machine for making canon which was also able to bore accurate cylinders for engines.

The steam engine called for improved metallurgy. No longer was industry able to rely on wooden gears and other moving parts. Steam power required sturdier machines. Again, England led the way.

Coke was substituted for charcoal in smelting iron. The effective use of coke was made possible by Smeaton's blowing-cylinders and Watt's steam engine which made possible the increased blast of air required for burning coke in the furnaces. Coke had many advantages. It was cheaper. England was exhausting its wood supply but had plenty of coal. It was harder and less friable so that the smelting furnaces could be stacked more heavily without collapsing the charge and blocking the air passages in the mix for good oxidation. It also had some disadvantages. It produced iron with high carbon and sulphur content. Coke smelters produced pig iron not wrought iron. It was not malleable. But ironmakers learned to make it malleable by the process of puddling. Puddling consists of remelting and stirring the molten pig iron in a reverbatory furnace until atmospheric oxygen reduces the carbon content. Later air was blasted into the mixture to hasten the process. The resulting decarburized iron became malleable like the wrought iron produced with charcoal. Other impurities like sulphur and phosphorous were also reduced.

This idea also led to the Bessemer process of making steel. By simply regulating the extent of decarburization in blasting the melted pig iron with air steel (with 0.15 to 1.5 per cent carbon) was made. After 1850 the Bessemer process, improved and perfected, replaced the more expensive and laborious crucible process and steel began to replace wrought iron as the leading industrial metal.

There is an interesting, even tragic human story involved. William Kelley, an American, actually conceived the idea in 1847 before Henry Bessemer of England but due to ridicule and other factors moved too slowly for a patent. Bessemer got the initial U. S. patent as Kelley did not apply until 1857. But when Bessemer applied for renewal Kelley was able to prove prior invention and was awarded the patent in 1857—the same year he was declared bankrupt!

Curiously though the rest of Europe and America did not rush to coke for smelting iron, perhaps because they still had plenty of wood. This was particularly true in the United States where wood was being cleared from the land with abandon for agricultural purposes. But the future had to be with coal.

The greatest English innovation was the blast furnace. James Beaumont Neilson conceived the idea, in 1828, that forcing hot instead of cold air into the smelter would increase its efficiency. The furnace worked hotter and thereby could carry a bigger charge. Three times as much iron could be produced with the same fuel when a blast of hot air at 600° F was used. Neilson's invention vastly increased the output of iron.

A generation later the Siemens brothers, German natives residing and working in England, adopted the hot air blast idea to steel making. Their open hearth furnace, patented in 1861, displaced the Bessemer converter. This made possible larger and more efficient furnaces. Towards the close of the 19th century this process dominated steel making.

Technological innovation in working the iron and steel kept pace. Steam powered forges displaced the water-driven hammers. Rolling mills improved. Greater power made cold rolling possible. Bar mills, slitting mills, tube mills, and other machines for finishing the metal were invented. Finally special alloy steels—chromium, tungsten, manganese and nickle were developed for special qualities of hardness, sharpness and other needs. Samuel Sheffield introduced his renowned tungsten alloy steel in 1871 which was so hard and sharp it could cut mild steel at 150 feet per minute. These alloy steels made possible the machine tools of modern industry.

At the beginning of the 20th century the modern iron and steel industry based on pig iron production in blast furnaces, fueled by coke, and steel making in open hearth furnaces and the Bessemer converter was well founded. England led the way before 1800. Iron production rose from 17,000 tons in 1740 to 2,100,000 tons in 1850. The technology spread to Europe by mid century and was taken up with vigor in America around 1850. Prior to the Civil War (1861–64) the United States produced a modest 500,000 tons of iron and steel; by 1900 it produced 13 million tons of pig iron and 9 million tons of rolled steel products! The iron and steel technology spread soon to other parts of the world. The first coke furnaces were erected in Russia in 1870. In 1875 the first coke furnace was built in India by the Bengal Ironworks Company which was not very successful. It was only in 1903 when Jamshedji Tata, the parsee industrialist of Bombay, erected, with American technical assistance, the modern steel plant at Jamshedpur in the state of Bihar (which abounds in 60 per cent iron ore) that modern steel making was established in the land of superior iron of antiquity. The first modern iron-works was built in China in 1893 and in Japan in 1897.

An innovation in metallurgy during this period worthy of mention is the smelting and refining of aluminum, the metal that made possible aircraft development in the 20th century. The extraction of aluminum had to await the development of electric power as the refining of aluminum depends upon electrolysis.

The French were foremost in the pioneering stage. Laboratory experiments with aluminum salts began in the 18th century. It was not until 1845 that Henri St. Claire Deville developed the process for producing pure aluminum. Deville's process was highly uneconomic. Two advanced processes, however, were patented in 1888 and 1889 that founded the modern aluminum industry. The first was the preparation of aluminum oxide (alumina) from bauxite developed by Karl Joseph Bayer of Austria. The second was the electrolytic reduction of alumina to pure aluminum which was simultaneously developed by Charles M. Hall in the United States and Paul L. T. Heroult of France. The Hall process was used in America while the Heroult process was used in Europe.

The rise of aluminum progressed slowly until the advent of the aircraft industry which needed a light metal. The greatly increased need of both commercial and military airplanes around mid-20th century gave the aluminum industry a tremendous boost. But even then the aluminum produced and used is less than 5 per cent of iron and steel.

The iron and steel technology made possible the next innovation for increased power development, the internal combustion engine. Instead of using water as the medium for converting heat energy into mechanical energy the internal combustion engine used air. A liquid fuel was required. It was provided by petroleum, another important fossil fuel.

Petroleum, like coal, was known to men of antiquity. Seepages of petroleum in Mesopotamia and parts of Europe were used for caulking ships, paving roads, lubrication and medicinal purposes for thousands of years. The Chinese even drilled for petroleum with percussion bits and bamboo tubes before the Christian era. But the difficulties of extracting petroleum from the earth and its limited use until the technological breakthrough of the Industrial Revolution left this important source of energy unutilized until the last century or so.

The geology of petroleum is less well understood than that of coal. Petroleum occurs in formations of almost every geologic period but is most prevalent in the Tertiary period sediments (3 to 65 million years ago). Many of the American oil deposits, however, date back to the earlier Cretaceous, Carboniferous and Ordovician periods. Animal or plant life, or both, was mired in the mud of marine waters and embedded in sedimentary formations of sandstone, shale or limestone. Salt water caused the decomposition to take a liquid form. Furthermore, the decomposing animal and/or plant matter was entrapped in domed or curved cavities created by folding, faulting or upward dipping of the formations where over the eons it separated into three components, gas above, petroleum beneath, both floating on a bed of water. Utilization of the gas and petroleum required the tapping of these domes with wells. The gas would rise by pressure, as would some of the petroleum. But the petroleum had normally to be pumped to the surface. At first, petroleum deposits were found by pragmatism and luck, but soon geologists were employed to locate the most likely areas. Finding the domes or curved formations was and is still a matter of sinking exploratory wells. The record shows, however, that exploratory drilling without benefit of geology results in one successful well out of 30 drilled, whereas the ratio rises to one out of 7 when wells are drilled at sites selected by a geologist.

Economic impetus was given to the exploitation of petroleum by the invention in 1783 of the flat woven wick oil lamp for lighting. Whale oil was used first in the lamps, but it was too expensive to compete with gas lighting. The distillation of kerosene by Abraham Gesner, a London physician with a penchant for geology, in 1853 provided such inexpensive fuel. Gesner and his partner, Thomas Cockrane, the Earl of Dundonald, organized the Asphalt Mining and Kerosene Comapny to exploit Gesner's patents on kerosene. They worked with natural asphalt from Trinidad. An analogous company was established in America. By 1856 the demand for kerosene was growing rapidly. As Gesner predicted it displaced whale oil and made "possible a long lasting holiday. . . for the finny monsters of the sea."

This led to the first successful oil well drilled by Colonel E. A. Drake at Titusville, Pennsylvania. After going down 69.5 feet the well began to flow oil on August 27, 1859. In 1861 the first refinery to process the oil was established. The industry grew rapidly all over the United States. By 1870 there were more than 2000 wells; in 1902 almost 119,000; in 1954 about 500,000! Overproduction overtook the industry from the outset. Within three years after Colonel Drake's first well the price dropped from 20 dollars to 10 cents a barrel. Europe, west and north, had no easily accessible reserves of oil. But petroleum was found in the Ukraine, Rumania and the Black Sea area. These fields were all well developed the latter part of the 19th century. Man suddenly had at his disposal a new and cheap source of energy. All that was needed was an engine to convert it to mechanical energy.

The idea of an internal combustion engine dates back to the latter part of the 17th century. Christian Huygens of Holland devised an engine for burning gunpowder. The idea was to create a vacuum in the cylinder when the gases cooled relying on atmosphere pressure for the power stroke. Denis Papin of France experimented further along this line. It was only in 1859, however, that Etienne Lenoir of France designed an engine that ran on a mixture of gas and air. Lenoir's engine was modeled after the double acting steam engine, the gas and air merely took the place of steam with the mixture ignited by an electric spark at the appropriate moment in the cycle of the piston.

The internal combustion engine varies in principle from the steam engine. Both depend upon the release of chemical energy stored in fossil fuels by oxidation or burning. In the steam engine this chemical reaction takes place outside the cylinder in a separate furnace and boiler. The steam is transported to the cylinder through pipes and valves where the steam pressure transmits its energy unto the piston. In the internal combustion engine all this transpires inside the cylinder. In the four cycle engine (there are also two cycle engines), sometimes referred to as the Otto cycle after its designer N. A. Otto of Germany, the first downward stroke intakes a mixture of gasoline and air from the carburetor. The next up stroke compresses the mixture (in a ratio of 7:1 or so) at which point it is ignited by an electric spark (a hot rod is sometimes used for ignition) at the timely moment. As the mixture burns the gases expand and exert pressure on the downward power stroke. The fourth up stroke exhausts the spent gases. The flywheel powers the cycle through the three non-power strokes. The reciprocating motion is converted to rotary motion through the crank shaft. The number of cylinders varies up to 8, appropriately synchronized and connected to the crank shaft.

The auto ignition or diesel engine operates on the same principle except that the fuel mixture is ignited by the heat of the compressed air into which the fuel is injected. To attain the necessary heat for self ignition the compression ratio has to be high. Diesel engine ratios go as high as 12–20 to 1. This requires a more ruggedly constructed engine. The injector which replaces both the carburetor and spark plug, has to be powerful in order to inject the fuel into the highly compressed air. The fuel injection is timed so that burning and expansion of the gases commences at the start of the third stroke, a downward one, for maximum power transmission to the piston. The diesel engine can burn a cruder cheaper oil which lowers its operating cost. But it is more expensive to build.

The earliest internal combustion engines operated on gas. The gasoline or petro engine was patented by Gottlieb Daimler of Wurtemburg in 1885 after he perfected the surface carburetor to properly vaporize and mix the gasoline and air before intake into the cylinder. At the same time Karl Benz of Mannhiem was designing his first motor vehicle to operate on petrol. These two names have been linked and foremost in the development of the automobile ever since. Meanwhile, following closely in their wake was Rudolph Diesel, another German engineer, who invented the auto ignition engine, thereafter bearing his name, in 1892. The diesel engine had the best thermal efficiency of all the other steam, gas and petrol engines of that date, because it operated over a greater heat range than the others.

Both types of petroleum engines presented a number of difficult mechanical problems. The synchronization of the strokes and proper connection to the crankshaft posed engineering difficulties. The design of an effective carburetor and fuel injector was not easy. The governors had to be extra effective as the engines ran at high speeds. The cylinder, piston, valves and other parts had to be machined precisely. But by the end of the 19th century European and American mechanics were well skilled for these technological tasks.

The two types of engines were more complementary than competitive. The lighter higher speed petrol engine was more suitable for automobiles, small boats, pumps and the like. The heavier diesel was more appropriate for factories, locomotives, ships, tractors, construction equipment and such where power but not speed was required. By 1900 the internal combustion engine was supplanting the steam engine as the prime mover.

But steam was not to be ousted yet. The invention of the turbine came to its rescue. The principle of the turbine was first employed for water power early in the 19th century and is used exclusively today in hydroelectric projects. Around 1800 Richard Trevithick toyed with the idea of directing a jet of steam against a small water wheel type device but it did not use the steam efficiently. In 1884 Charles Parsons of England perfected the turbine as an effective engine. Parsons realized that the steam pressure should be released gradually through a series of stages inside the turbine to get maximum thermal efficiency. Each stage had a set of curved blades or vanes on the rotor which was turned by the velocity of the steam under pressure as it rushed past the blades. The principle advantage of the turbine is that it converts the heat directly into rotary motion eliminating the complex mechanism of transforming reciprocating to rotary motion.

Parsons invented the steam turbine with the end in view of generating electricity. It resulted in the birth of the thermo-electric power station that has been the chief source of electric power ever since. C. H. Parsons & Company founded in 1889 has been a leading electric power equipment manufacturer to date. George Westinghouse, founder of Westinghouse Electric Company, acquired the rights to manufacture the Parsons turbine in the United States in 1895. Both made additional improvements. Major developments were also made by others, the most noteworthy being, C. G. P. Laval in Sweden, A. C. E. Rateau in France and C. G. Curtis in America.

In the mid 20th century the turbine principle was specially adopted for flight within the atmosphere as the turbojet engine. The first turbojet plane was flown in Germany in 1939. England and the United States developed it independently during the war in 1941. In the turbojet the blades suck air and compress it into the combustion chamber, where the fuel (naptha or kerosene) is injected. The mixture builds up tremendous pressure as it burns. The burning gases are ejected with high velocity which gives the airplane the power thrust. Where greater thrust is required an after combustion chamber is used for additional fuel injection. The turbojet dispenses with the propeller and other moving parts. Greater thrust can be imparted to the airplane than with propellers.

The ramjet engine even dispenses with the turbo-compressor depending upon its speed through the atmosphere for the air supply. It has a diffuser, a cone shaped funnel, for compressing the air before it enters the combustion chamber. The ramjet cannot function at slow speeds. A launching device is required. It is, therefore, not feasible for use in commercial and even most military air transportation. The ramjet engine is used mainly for rockets, missiles and some types of military aircraft.

The rocket engine has brought the use of chemical energy to its highest development. A fuel and oxidizer are brought together to generate heat in the form of hot exhaust gas. The fuel may be in liquid or solid form. The basic elements are usually hydrogen or carbon, with increasing use of lithium, beryllium, manganese and aluminum. The most frequently used liquid rocket fuels are kerosene, alcohol, ammonia derivatives. The American spacecraft program uses hydrogen as a fuel. The oxidizer elements are usually oxygen and flourine, in such forms as liquid oxygen, nitric acid, and nitrogen tetroxide. When solid fuels and oxidizers are required they are generally a rubberized heavy hydrocarbon and percholate of nitrate. In this highly specialized field where economy is not a factor man is no longer dependent upon carbon from fossil fuels as the source of chemical energy.

ELECTRICAL ENERGY

Electricity is not a new source of energy. It is a different form of energy, however, as man has with electricity harnessed a basic force inside the atom. In Chapter I it was discussed that electrons will flow from atoms possessed of an excess of electrons to atoms that are deprived of their normal number. Hence, if such excesses and deficiencies in electrons in matter can be induced externally a tremendous force can be generated. Man's invention of the generator or dynamo accomplished such purpose. The generator has to be worked mechanically, however, with a prime mover such as a water or steam turbine or internal combustion engine. Electricity is, therefore, a conversion of mechanical power derived from the chemical or elemental energy discussed above.

Why then would man convert mechanical energy to electrical and back to mechanical energy again through an electric motor, particularly, since there is some loss of energy, albeit that electric generators and motors are extremely efficient. The prime mover utilizing the basic source of energy can be situated for convenience and/or economy near the source of the fossil fuel, water power (here there is no choice) or for other economic or environmental reasons at a site removed from the place of use. Moreover, the electrical energy is divisible so that it can be used in places far from each other and for different purposes. For instance the same hydroelectric or thermo-electric plant can power motors in factories, light the streets of cities and energize the numerous appliances found in modern houses. Finally the ultimate users of the energy are freed of the noise and chemical pollution emanating from the prime movers, particularly those using the fossil fuels. Electricity, therefore, owes its widespread use to its convenience and facility of distribution and use.

Michael Faraday discovered the principle of electromagnetic induction in the forepart of the 19th century. It was set forth in a paper he read before the Royal Society of Arts in London on November 24, 1831. Faraday was a scientist and after announcing his monumental discovery he left the practical development of his principle to others.

The principal of electromagnetic induction is simply that the passage of an electric current through a conductor sets up a magnetic field. When the conductor is coiled around a piece of iron it temporarily magnetizes the iron. And if the iron is hammered the magnetism becomes permanent. Furthermore, the obverse is also true, that is, if you rotate a coil of wire inside a magnetic field it will generate the flow of electricity in the coil. Faraday, also postulated "transformer" action—essential to the distribution of electrical energy—that the flow of current in a coil of wire will induce a flow of current in another coil.

From these basic principles it was deduced that the rotation of a coil of wire inside a magnetic field, or vice versa, the rotation of the magnet around the coil, generated the flow of electricity in the coil of wire. Generators of both types were constructed in the beginning. Hippolite Pixii exhibited the first generator in Paris in 1832. It had a revolving magnet and a stationary coil. A rotating coil in a fixed magnet was constructed by Saxton in 1833 and this type of generator went into production by E. M. Clarke, who was a manufacturer of scientific instruments, in the 1830's. A commutator was added to the armature to convert the raw alternating current to direct current. This proved to be largely unnecessary and today 95 per cent of electricity is used in its basic alternating current state. The direct current detour arose probably more out of poor understanding of electricity than necessity, but the misdirection plagued the electricity systems of large cities like London, New York and others well into the 20th century.

These early pioneer generators using permanent magnets were used largely for laboratory purposes and lighthouse illumination. Curiously, there was also a great belief during these early days in the therapeutic value of electricity and the faithful subjected themselves to mild shocks for health objectives.

It remained, however, until the development of the electromagnetic field before the generation of electricity became efficient and widespread. The principle of the electromagnetic generator was to have the prime mover turn the coil *and* supply the electricity to create the magnetic field. The key to the process was the residual magnetism left in the iron of the magnetic coil, which started a trickle of electricity to flow when the coil armature started to rotate. Eventually the flow of electricity would build up to the maximum for which the generator was designed. This was known as the self excited field. It dispensed with the permanent magnet which limited the efficiency and capacity of the generator.

The principle of the electromagnetic generator was first noted in a British patent secured by Soren Hjorth of Denmark in 1855. In 1863 Henry Wilde received the original patent for the electromagnetic generator and his firm of Wilde & Company of Manchester started to produce them in great numbers. Meanwhile W. E. Von Siemens did pioneering work on the electromagnetic generator in connection with his development of the telegraph, but he failed to patent his ideas. Others, like S. A. Varley and Charles Wheatstone contributed to its development. The term dynamo-electric came to be used instead of "self excited", so that generators have also come to be called dynamos. Improvements continued to be made, particularly on the armature, by such men as Zenobe Theophile Gramme, a native of Belgium, Emil Burgin of Basel and the Siemen interests in Germany. In America Thomas

Edison pioneered in electricity and started the manufacture of direct current generators in 1880. By the end of the 19th century electric power production and distribution was well developed.

End use machinery, equipment and appliances were developed *pari passu* with the effective generation of electricity. The greatest use was motive power for factories, farms, shops and households. The electric motor is merely a generator in reverse. Electricity creates a magnetic field in a coil of wire wound around an armature. At the same time another magnetic field is created in coils surrounding the armature. The respective magnetic poles are synchronized to attract and repel so as to impart rotary motion to the armature. In a direct current motor the armature is required to have a commutator to reverse the direction of the current and change the magnetic field at the appropriate time to keep the armature rotating.

During the latter 19th century when alternating current came into widespread use the alternating current motor was invented in 1888 by Nikola Tesla in America. Tesla's motors were manufactured by Westinghouse. The A. C. motor needs no commutator. It depends instead upon the alternating current to change the magnetic field. The motor is designed to synchronize with these changes for the necessary forces of attraction and repulsion. Both D. C. and A. C. motors continue to be used as they possess different advantages, but by far most motors are the alternating current type.

Next in importance in the use of electricity is illumination. The earliest attempt was the arc light but it could not produce a steady light. Incandescent metallic filaments, however, were short lived as they oxidized in open air. It was only after the filament was enclosed in a vacuum tube or bulb that a sustained electric light was effective.

Two men conceived and developed the idea independently and concurrently. Joseph Swan made incandescent filaments of strips of carbonized paper as early as 1848, but did not perfect the vacuum bulb for it until 1878. Thomas Edison accomplished it in 1879 and promptly patented it in England as well as in America. Swan was reluctant to patent his electric bulb as he thought the basic idea—a carbon filament glowing in an evacuated glass bulb—was not patentable. By the time he moved he was foreclosed by the Edison patents. In 1905 tungsten was substituted for carbon as the filament and has been used ever since.

Heat elements constitute another important use of electricity. A modern household is filled with such appliances ranging from electric stoves, toasters, water heaters and room heaters. But modern industry also uses electric heat. Aluminum is smelted with electricity. Electric furnaces are even used to produce steel. The telegraph, telephone, radio and the modern electronics industry are operated by electricity. Electricity permeates modern life in the factories, on the farms and in the homes of the industrialized countries.

NUCLEAR ENERGY

Nuclear energy is a new source of energy. Man in the 20th century started to bring under his command the fundamental and ultimate energy of the universe. It is the energy contained in the nucleus of the atom, the basic unit of matter. For a century or so earlier, man tinkered on the periphery of this basic source of energy with his mastery of electricity. The invention of the electromagnetic generator enabled him to pry the electron loose from the atom and harness the force of attraction of the electron back to the atom. But prying loose the weakly held electron was far easier than releasing the energy in the cohesive nucleus of the atom. Moreover, harnessing the energy of the electron tapped only a fraction of one per cent of the total energy of the atom.

Tapping this basic energy required either fission or fusion of the atom or atoms. The former splits an atom (uranium, plutonium, thorium to date) to release some of the energy in its nucleus. The latter fuses two atoms (hydrogen) to create a new atom (helium) whereby some of the energy inside their nuclei is released. The scientific knowledge required for this technological innovation started to accumulate at the turn of the 20th century. After Albert Einstein developed his equivilance theory, wherein he postulated that matter was convertible to energy and vice versa, he set forth his deduction in his now renowned mathematical equation $E = MC^2$. Further work on releasing this basic energy, however, had to await a better understanding of the structure of basic matter, the atom. This came in 1911 when Ernest Rutherford deduced from experiments conducted in the Cavendish laboratory at Cambridge University that the atom was like a minature solar system with a massive nucleus around which electrons revolved. Further work by Rutherford and Chadwick in England, Walter Boeth and Hans Becker in Germany and the Curies in France led to a better understanding of the nucleus of the atom. The proton and neutron were identified. In 1939 Otto Hahn and Fritz Strassmann bombarded uranium with neutrons and found that some of the atoms split into lighter elements. At the same time some of the mass was converted into energy in the fission of the atoms. Also new neutrons were freed in the process, which could split more of the uranium atoms. Unfortunately the neutrons could not be controlled and most were lost. A means had to be found to control these neutrons and make the process of fission self sustaining through a "chain reaction".

At this stage World War II broke out and many of the European scientists, some of them refugees from the Nazis, feared Germany would be the first to develop the atom bomb. Out of this concern emanated the famous letter to President Roosevelt from Albert Einstein advocating that the United States undertake to produce the nuclear bomb. President Roosevelt acted promptly by setting up the Manhattan Project in a squash court at Stagg Field at the University of Chicago. The project was headed by Enrico Fermi of Italy. He was assisted by 39 scientists. Fermi decided to embed the uranium in graphite as carbon did not absorb the free neutrons. The neutrons were simply bounced back into the uranium which increased their chances of splitting more atoms. To guard against a runaway nuclear reaction ending in an explosion of energy Fermi inserted cadmium rods into the uranium to absorb excess neutrons. The cadmium rods were simply pushed in or pulled out of the "pile" to slow or speed the reaction. In 1942 Fermi was able to report that a self-sustaining nuclear reaction had been achieved.

It took another three years to perfect the nuclear reaction for the atom bomb. In 1945 two of the bombs were dropped on Japan and it promptly surrendered to the United States to end the war in the Pacific. The Japanese could not continue the war in the face of such overwhelming American technological superiority.

After the war nuclear energy was adapted for peacetime use. The heat of the nuclear reaction was used to produce steam to generate electricity. The first large scale atomic power plant in the United States for the generation of electricity was built in 1957 at Shippingport (near Pittsburgh) in Pennsylvania. But for the nuclear furnace the rest of the power plant is the familiar steam turbine and generator. The initial reactor core consisted of 165 pounds of enriched uranium surrounded by 14 tons of uranium oxide. The latter slowly converts into plutonium which sustains the reactor for the long run. The reactor is housed in a carbon steel vessel. Water under pressure is pumped through the reactor where it is heated to 550° F and through a heat exchanger which heats the water that produces the steam for the turbo-generator. The plant produces 100,000 kilowatts, enough electricity for 400,000 people. Shippingport was a joint effort by the American government, Westinghouse and the Duquesne Light Company. Admiral Hyman Rickover was involved in the project. He was already promoting the development of nuclear power for submarines. The U. S. Navy launched its first nuclear powered submarine, the *Nautilus* on January 21, 1954. On its maiden voyage it traveled 62,500 miles without refueling. Two million gallons of diesel oil would have been required by a non-nuclear submarine for such mileage.

Pressurized-water reactors like the one at Shippingport are the most common. There are other types. The water-boiling reactor produces the steam inside the reactor. Gases like carbon-dioxide and helium are used to transport the heat from the reactor to the boiler. Liquid metals, like graphite or beryllium oxide, and a uranium solution or slurry have also been used for the purpose.

Two problems have impeded nuclear power development. In the beginning economic feasibility was lacking. That has now been overcome by technological improvement and the rise in the cost of fossil fuels. More difficult is the problem of disposing of the nuclear wastes and dangers connected with the fission reactors. But nuclear power based on fission is now a feasible and economical source of energy.

FUTURE SOURCES OF ENERGY

As man moves into the last quarter of the 20th century it is becoming obvious that his ever growing demands for more energy has assumed a major crisis. Merely maintaining the level of energy use attained in 1975 for the projected population growth over the next century or so will exhaust not only the unreplenishable reserves of fossil fuels but also the fissionable nuclear fuels by the year 2050. Man has, therefore less than a century to find new sources of energy.

Not only will the old sources of energy be exhausted but the demand for more energy will grow because of man's burgeoning technology. High grade ores are being used up and greater energy will be needed to extract metals from lower grade ores. More fertilizer and power will be needed by agriculture to produce food for the larger population. Disposing of the wastes and effluence of such increased consumption of food and raw materials will require great amounts of energy to render these wastes harmless and recycle them into useful raw materials. Where will this energy be found. It is reasonable to conclude though that man has now accumulated sufficient basic technology to meet this monumental challenge.

Most promising, obviously, is to continue on the path of harnessing the fundamental energy of the universe as it is inexhaustible. But this will require bringing under control nuclear fusion reaction involving the more stable elements—hydrogen (deuterium and tritium) and lithium. The present nuclear power plants operate at the other end of the element scale with unstable atoms more readily susceptible to fission or splitting. Uranium and thorium, however, are limited in supply, like the fossil fuels, and will also be exhausted within a century by man. But here too, there is a ray of hope. It is the "breeder" reactor. Breeder reactors are based on the fission principle but designed to produce more nuclear fuel like plutonium than they burn while in the very process of consuming the natural fissionable material. The American government is conducting a large research program to perfect the breeder reactor and, in the short run, it holds great promise as an energy source. Unfortunately nuclear power based on the fission principle is both dangerous and the wastes are poisonous to life on earth. Disposal of these wastes is and will continue as a formidable if not insurmountable problem.

Scientists believe, therefore, that the best hope for energy in the future will be nuclear power based on the fusion principle. Nuclear fusion is relatively free of polluting and poisonous wastes. But more important its raw material, mainly hydrogen, is inexhaustible. The technological problems, however, in the practical use and control of nuclear fusion are almost insurmountable. Yet there is hope.

The main reason is that nuclear fusion occurs at temperatures unheard of on earth and unmanageable by man's technological achievements to date. Nuclear fusion requires temperatures over 100,000,000° F to sustain itself! Everything turns to plasma, the fourth state of matter, at that temperature. While the sun is in a state of plasma, matter in that state is unknown on earth except in the rare instances of high voltage lightening or now inside a thermonuclear explosion. None of man's metal vessels or other techniques can cope with plasma. Moreover, until quite recently scientists did not understand the properties of plasma to ponder ways of containing it. In the past decade or so they have invented the "magnetic bottle" which has great promise for the handling of matter in a plasma state.

Nuclear fusion reaction has until now been achieved only for destructive purposes. This is, of course, the hydrogen bomb which was first exploded by the United States at Eniwetok in 1952. The necessary temperature (180,000,000° F) to initiate fusion in the hydrogen bomb was produced by the explosion of a fission type plutonium bomb. In other words, an atomic bomb was used to trigger a hydrogen bomb. In a bomb, of course, there is no interest in controlling the explosion so the problem of containing the intense heat does not arise. It is another matter when the energy is desired for constructive purposes.

Hydrogen bombs are known as thermonuclear devices because of the intense heat involved. Unlike elements on the higher end of the scale hydrogen atoms are very stable and have a propensity to repel instead of attracting for fusion. It requires extremely high temperatures to change this propensity and cause them to fuse. But when they fuse they form an unstable combination which almost instantly explodes, emiting a free neutron, to form helium. Electrons, protons and other particles are also released. It is this explosion which creates the heat energy man can one day hopefully harness for his needs.

The harness scientists are presently developing is the "magnetic bottle". It is a doughnut-shaped machine that the Russians have christened the "Tokomak". In the plasma state, to which hydrogen would have to be heated for a sustained nuclear fusion reaction, the electrons are ripped out of orbit which results in a gas like state of separately moving electrically charged nuclei and electrons. But as soon as plasma cools by striking air or metal it becomes a gas or solid. Hence, the problem for scientists was to prevent such cooling. They came up with the idea this might be possible with electromagnetism which would repel the electrically charged particles and keep them contained within the plasma body. After twenty years of research and experimentation, and overcoming most difficult problems, the scientists finally achieved a "magnetic bottle" for containing and controlling plasma. But the plasma they have contained so far is not hot enough to initiate fusion. Until 1978 the Russian scientists, led by Dr. Lev. A. Artsimovich were more successful than their American counterparts. But in July, 1978 the Tokomak at Princeton University achieved temperatures of 60 million degrees Celsius thereby assuming a commanding lead over the Russians. The Russian tokomak at the Kurchatov Institute at Moscow has reached temperatures of only 13 million degrees. The Americans still have far to go to attain a tokomak capable of containing a self sustaining fusion reaction believed to require a 100 million degrees Fahrenheit temperature.

There remains one more difficult problem before a controllable fusion reactor can be achieved. It is heating the plasma to sufficiently high temperatures (over 100 million ° F) to initiate and sustain fusion reaction. Attempts to achieve the high temperatures is being made with lasers. A laser beam is a coherence of powerful light rays that generates intense heat. The laser beam would be focussed on a mixture of deuterium and tritium, two isotopes of hydrogen, the most likely fuel for a fusion reactor. The resulting plasma would be contained in a magnetic bottle. But if and when this is achieved there is yet no assurance that the magnetic bottle will contain such high temperature plasma.

As in the fission reactor the heat from fusion reaction would be used to produce steam for the generation of electricity. The medium to conduct the heat would pose a problem. At the moment, it is believed liquid lithium, heated by the plasma, could be used for the purpose. The hot lithium would be circulated from the fusion reactor through the boiler of the thermal power plant. Serious thought is also being given to by-passing the turbo-generator through capture and control of the electrons and protons emanating from the nuclear fusion reaction for direct electrical transmission. A method to accomplish it is being studied at the Lawrence Radiation Laboratory, Livermore, California whereby the electrons and protons would be leaked from the reactor into a long fanshaped chamber containing an array of electrodes to attract the electrically charged particles and direct them into high tension transmission lines.

Thus it is seen, in late 20th century that man is on the threshold of harnessing the ultimate energy of the universe. If he succeeds, and one can now be sanguine on the outcome, man will have created miniature solar furnaces of his own here on earth. Man would truly be playing "God" as the saying goes even though that phrase may be antithetical to the central theme of this study of history.

Man can and should, however, make better use of the energy of the sun, the solar furnace provided him by the universal scheme of things and to which he owes his existence, before and while he is preparing to create solar furnaces of his own on planet earth. Experiments with solar energy are now being conducted with increasing intent and pace. But there are several difficult problems. One is how to bridge the night. Another is the obstacle of the clouds. Solar heating appears very feasible as ways can be devised to store the heat of the day for the night. Solar cookers using reflector discs to concentrate sunlight can develop temperatures up to 350°, hot enough to boil a quart of water in 15 minutes, have been produced but they are unreliable and dependent on a sunny day. Two factories were started in India in 1946 to manufacture such solar cookers for the poor of India who are reduced to using cow-dung and faggots as cooking fuels. The factories failed because the promoters of what appeared like a good idea (India has plenty of sunny days) overlooked the fact that the poor of India prepared their main meal of the day at sundown. It would seem though that a solar energy program could be developed to provide some of the energy needs of man despite its shortcomings as the source is quite inexhaustible. Ammonia could be liquified for refrigeration by sunlight. Radios are powered in the satellite program by the sun. Sunlight also activates the flow of electricity between special alloys.

Elemental energy can once again be exploited to the utmost. Waterpower has and is being fully developed for hydro-electric power. The wind could be used again to operate small generators for rural use. More promising, however, for substantial electric power generation is the surge of the tides. In the Bay of Fundy in Nova Scotia, the tide rises and falls 18 feet twice a day moving two billion tons of water each time. This enormous flow of water is now being harnessed for the generation of electric power. Unlike solar energy the rise and fall of the tide is very dependable. Bays and channels exist almost everywhere for the construction of tidal powered electric plants.

The heat of the earth is another great source of energy. Geothermal electric power plants date back to 1904 when Italian engineers brought under control the steam issuing out of the ground at Lardarello in Tuscany. The steam is produced from water seeping into volcanic fissures. It reaches temperatures of 350° F or more. Geothermal power, however, can be produced anywhere on earth by simply drilling a dry well or set of wells deep enough into the ground and circulating water to this depth where the heat of the earth turns it into steam. The steam is then brought to the surface to power turbo-generators. The earth's temperature increases 10° F for every 60 feet of depth. Hence, a well drilled 10,000 feet down would encounter temperatures of 250° F or so, hot enough to produce steam. The temperatures below the surface vary from place to place depending upon the proximity of volcanic fissures and other magma seepages so that higher temperatures could be encountered at such places with lesser depths. Geologists would be able to find such places to enable power companies to exploit more economically the heat energy in the depths of the earth. Geothermal energy holds great promise for it is available everywhere and it is, for all practical purposes, inexhaustible.

It would appear that man has several sources of energy to bring under his command and he possesses the necessary scientific knowledge and technology to do so. He must, of course, pursue the ultimate goal of bringing under his control the fundamental energy of the universe through the development of an effective nuclear fusion reactor that can be the source of inexhaustible energy. But until he achieves this technological breakthrough he can exploit the more readily available sources of geothermal, solar, elemental and nuclear fission energies.

SCIENCE AND MATHEMATICS

The Industrial Revolution was ushered into history by practical men. John Smeaton, Thomas Newcomen, James Watt and the others were clever mechanics. Science and mathematics were of little consequence to them. But industrialization would have been stunted right from the start had not science and mathematics been developed as an important helpmeet for technological innovation.

Man has toyed with numbers, surveyed fields and even scanned the heavens since time immemorial, certainly since the invention of agriculture, as rudimentary geometry and astronomy were important for the cultivation of the land. But higher mathematics were unimportant to technological innovation until the last two centuries or so. Today there could be little or no technological development without it. That did not, however, detain man from indulging in abstract mathematical thinking much earlier as a sheer exercise of his intellectuality.

It would appear that the mathematical genius of mankind resided in the first instance with the Hindus. Unfortunately, the vagueness of their history makes it difficult to date the precise age of Indian mathematical creativity. But this much is generally agreed upon. The Indian mind conceived the so-called Arabic numerals, the concept of zero and the decimal system (or place value notation based on the power of 10) without which there could have been no higher mathematics. Indian mathematics was assimilated by the Muslims in the 8th century during the golden days of Islam when the scintillating Abbasid empire ruled Western Asia to the frontiers of India. In fact, many Arabs settled in the Sind as early as 712 A. D. where they lived peacefully for centuries. In 771 A. D. the *Siddhantas*—the foremost Indian texts on mathematics and astronomy—compiled by Brahmagupta (588–660 A. D.) found their way to Baghdad and the caliph Al-Mansur had them translated by Al Fazari into arabic. In the *Brahma Siddhanta* Brahmagupta discusses positive and negative numbers, indeterminate equations of the first and second degree, square and cube roots, cyclic quadrilaterals, right angled triangles, measurement of solids and other higher mathematical problems. The great Persian mathematician and astronomer Al-Khwarizmi (780–850 A. D.) compiled a comprehensive scientific text in which he refers to mathematics as *Ilm Hind* (the Indian science). A treatise of his was translated into latin as *Algoritimi de Numero Indorum* (Al Kwarizimi on the Numerals of the Indians) in the 12th century which continued to be used as the principal text in European universities for several centuries. In due time algorithim (European corruption of Al-Khwarizmi) meant an arithmetic based on the decimal system.

There was an even earlier Indian text called the *Aryabhatiya* compiled by Aryahbata at the early age of 23 in the year of 499 A. D. His text included algebra, geometry, astronomy and physics. He used the decimal system in both his mathematical and astronomical computations. He covered algebraic identities, indeterminate equations and progression. In geometry he carried out the value of *pi* to 3.1416. The Greeks never went so far. Such computation was not achieved in Europe until the 15th century. By then the Hindus carried *pi* to nine figures. Aryabhata was also first to compile a table of sines for each degree of the triangle. Another text around this time, the *Surya Sutras* sets forth sines, cosines and other aspects of trigonometry.

Much of western mathematical terminology issues from sanskrit and/or arabic. The word cipher for zero derives from the arabic *sifr* which in turn comes from the sanskrit word *sunya*, meaning empty. The trigonometric term sine derives from the arabic *jayb* which originated with the sanskrit word *jiva*. The word algebra, as is generally known, comes from the arabic *al jabr*.

At the time the Muslims transmitted (and developed further through such men as Omar Khayyam) the Indian mathematics to Europe the western Mediterranean area was a mathematical void. The Romans had no genius for mathematics. Moreover, their system of numerals (the counting of marks) made higher mathematics virtually impossible. Greek numerals based on alphabetical notation were not much better. But the Greeks had a penchant and genius for geometry and even algebra. It started with Pythagoras (582–507 B. C.) and culminated with Euclid (circa 300 B. C.) in his famous text the *Elements*. But here too can be detected an Indian genesis.

Pythagoras was born at Samos at a time when the Persians ruled western Asia from Ionia (which included Samos) to the Indus river in India. It is recorded that Pythagoras traveled extensively over the breadth of the Persian empire and studied with the Brahmins of India. That his entire life was profoundly affected by Indian thought and religion is reflected in his philosophy and the Pythagorean cult he founded. He preached reincarnation and advocated release from successive rebirths through abstention and rejection of human desires in order to attain reabsorbtion into the greater whole, ideas similar to nirvana and the concept of the all encompassing Brahma of the Indians. Due to their beliefs Phythagoras and his followers eschewed the eating of flesh, became vegetarians and shared their worldly goods in common. In their intellectual life they pursued mathematics with love and vengeance and became renowned for the Pythagorean theorem and other geometric ideas.

There is evidence the Pythagorean theorem was known to the Indians centuries before the Pythagoreans expounded it in the Greek world. The Brahmins of India took to geometry early in connection with the construction of sacrificial alters in the open fields. The Pythagorean theorem is already set forth in the *Sulva Sutras*, a geometric text thought to have been written around the 8th century B. C. It is, therefore, not unreasonable to conclude that Pythagoras imbibed the geometry of the Hindus along with their religious thought upon which he based his philosophy.

A question immediately arises as to why Pythagoras did not bring back from India the concept of zero with its related negative numbers and the decimal system of numeration. The answer probably is that the Hindus had not yet developed these mathematical innovations by the 5th century B. C. The earliest evidence of the zero appears only about 200 B. C. in a book on prosody, the *Chandahsutra*, by Pingala. The so-called Arabic numerals are first recorded on the Rock Edicts of Ashoka around 250 B. C. The date of origin of the decimal system in India is unknown.

There appears to be much confusion about the origin of the concept of zero. It is often stated that the zero symbol was used in Mesopotamia as early as 300 B. C. But the Mesopotamians used the zero merely as a demarcation between numerals, The Mayas, on the other hand appeared to employ a true concept of zero in their numerals, but their independent development of it had no impact on the mainstream of mathematical growth. Evidence of the zero has also been found in Cambodia and Sumatra dating to 638 A. D., but this is doubtless the result of Indian colonialism in the area.

The early civilizations of the Mediterranean area had only rudimentary mathematics. The Egyptians did not progress much beyond addition and substraction despite their colossal engineering feats in connection with the pyramids. The Sumerians and later Babylonians, however, progressed further even indulging in elementary algebra. They developed a sexagesimal system based on the number 60 the remnants of which still survive today in 60 minutes, 60 degrees and the like. Apparently, through a prodigious feat of intuition, the ancient Sumerians sensed the rhythm of the universe in the number 60 and predicated their arithmetic upon it.

After the fall of Rome Greek geometry and algebra continued only in the eastern empire and there merely in a moribund state where it too was resuscitated by the Muslims during the days of the Abbasid empire. Euclid's *Elements*, Ptolemy's *Mathematical Composition*, Aristotle's *Physics* and countless other Greek scientific works were translated into arabic during the 9th century for eventual repassage to Europe.

This mathematical genesis was destined to flower into the higher mathematics of the Europeans to facilitate the greatest technological development of man to date. Descartes (1596–1650) adopted algebra to curves. Logarithms were next developed by Burgi in 1620 at Prague and Napier in 1614 at Edinburgh working independently of each other. Napier's priority was finally adjudicated in 1914! Calculus also was developed independently by Newton in 1671 and Liebnitz in 1676. Equally noteworthy is the fact that 500 years earlier the Indian mathematician Bhashara (1114–1178) discovered differential calculus but it was never transmitted to Europe, for the scholarship and facile communications of the Muslims that prevailed several centuries earlier no longer existed. Moreover the Indians never applied their higher mathematics to technological innovation probably because they came under enervating foreign rule soon thereafter.

The Chinese too were creative in mathematics. It appears, however, that their innovations did not flow into the mainstream of mathematical development set forth above. Numerals written in characters appear as early as 300 B. C. They had a place value system of sorts two thousand years ago. But development of a true place-value numeration and the concept of zero did not occur until the Sung period (960–1279 A. D.) when the advanced system was adopted from India with the coming of Buddhism to China. Algebra and trigonometry were likewise learned from the Indians. The Chinese had developed geometry on their own quite early and by 250 A. D. arrived at a value of *pi* as 3.14. The complex script of the Chinese was a handicap to its mathematicians. For example, algebraic equations were set forth in tabular form. The Chinese did not know the equal (=) sign until late.

Mechanical calculators were used by man from early times. The Chinese had a system of counting-rods as early as 500 B. C. The invention of the abacus is lost in obscurity. Herodotus mentions it in use in Egypt during the 5th century before Christ. Both the Greeks and Romans used it. The Hindus had the abacus as early as 200 B. C. In the western mind it is associated with the Chinese, but the abacus was not in use in China until about 1500 A. D. although there are some vague references to "ball-arithmetic" dating back a thousand years earlier that may have been some kind of abacus. The abacus came to be known in Europe only in the 11th or 12th centuries. Today the abacus is still widely used in Asia even though it is now the age of calculators and computers. There was an interesting contest during the American occupation of Japan in 1946 between a champion Japanese abacus operator and a U. S. army payroll clerk with a desk calculator. The Japanese expert beat the calculator in everything but multiplication. The abacus would of course be no match for a modern computer.

Before discussing computers mention must be made of other calculating devices. The slide rule based on logarithms was invented by Edmund Gunter in 1620. This was followed by the adding machine developed in 1640 by William Oguhtred but not really perfected until 1820 by Charles Xavier Thomas in London. These calculating machines operated mechanically and were powered by hand, later by electricity.

The technological leap in mechanical computation was calculation and information processing by electronics. But it took over a century to develop. Mathematics professor Charles Babbage at Cambridge University built an automatic computer in 1812 which he called a difference engine. Its purpose was to compute mathematical functions of an independent variable of x that would be useful in navigation, astronomy and the like. Babbage next planned a more capable computer which he called an analytical engine that could store numbers as well. British scientist Lord Kelvin (William Thomson) experimented with an automatic analog computer in 1879. Nothing much came of these early efforts due mainly to insufficient technology at the time.

The effort was taken up by the Americans in the 20th century. In 1930 an attempt to construct an automatic analog computer at the Massachusetts Institute of Technology under the supervision of Dr. Vannevar Bush was successful. The MIT group called it a differential analyzer. It was still a mechanical device although powered by electric motors.

World War II gave a tremendous boost to the development of electronics for military purposes. The U. S. Navy developed radar controlled gunfire that was instrumental in the defeat of the Japanese navy. More on this later. After the war this new technology became available for peace time use. In 1946 the ENIAC (Electronic Numeric Integrator and Calculator) was developed by the engineers headed by Dr. John W. Mauchy at the University of Pennsylvania. Its multiplier could carry out as many as 500 multiplications per second. ENIAC contained some 18,000 vacuum tubes that had to be contained in a large room.

In 1961 IBM constructed an improved computer for the Atomic Energy Commission laboratory at Los Almos, New Mexico which could perform additions in 1.5 microseconds, multiplications in 2.7 microseconds and division in 10 microseconds. It had a memory bank of about 98,000 registers of 14 decimal digits each. It could solve problems for which mathematical methods were known but too large and complex for human facility. The computer used transistors and integrated circuits.

It was the transistor that revolutionized computer technology. It is now possible to make a silicon chip microcomputer the size of a little finger to perform all of the computations performed by ENIAC! Moreover the cost of the microcomputers is less than $100.

Computers can perform difficult mathematical computations like square and cube roots, trigonometric functions, differential equations and other problems with a speed ten billion times faster than the human brain. This amplifies greatly man's capacity for analytical thought. But it should be quickly added that computers can do only what man programs into them.

The general sciences—astronomy, physics, chemistry, geology and others—on which technological innovation relies have grown *pari passu* with the development of mathematics upon which in varying degrees they depend. Further technological accumulation would no longer be possible without science and mathematics.

VI
Technological Superiority—
Historical Episodes

Technological superiority normally begets dominance in production, trade and war. Technological superiority, as will be discussed later, also makes possible greater and better enjoyment of life through increased food production and better cuisine, more leisure for the arts and the like. But nowhere has superior technology been more telling than in the conflict between man and man for dominance on earth.

This must have been true from the very beginning, though we have clear evidence of it only since the time of recorded history. When men came into conflict with other men during the stone age those with better hand axes, spears and other stone tools had an advantage in the conflict. Later the sling and dart gave further advantage for man could now deliver hurt or death from a distance. The spear thrower of Cro-Magnon augmented this capacity even more. Finally the bow and arrow made possible the mortal manifestation of energy against another human being far more effective. This much we know for the use of the bow and arrow spills over into recorded history and there is ample evidence of its advantage in warfare.

The development of metals provided another source of advantage in warfare. Flint knives and spears could kill as well but they shattered easily and were not as reliable in battle as bronze. Iron proved the ultimate metal of warfare because of its hardness, sharpness and availability. As iron became more plentiful man fashioned it into the formidable sword of antiquity. In his *Conquest of Civilization* Breasted says of the sword:

> It was the Danubian craftsmen who produced a sword with enough weight in the blade to make it a striking weapon. The striking sword, which might be brought down upon the foe like the blow of the axe, was far more formidable than the thrusting sword which, as it was received from Egypt, was only an elongated dagger. The possession of this heavy striking sword gave Europe an enormous military advantage over the Near East and was yet to alter the course of History.

The role of the horse in human warfare has already been alluded to. For three thousand years and more the effective use of the mobility and energy of the horse has been decisive in battle. Only during the last century or so has man turned from the horse to chemical energy as his main engine of war. Industrialization made possible the mechanized warfare of the 20th century. But the most striking example of technological superiority as the decisive factor in human warfare was the use of the atom bomb in 1945 by the Americans against the Japanese in World War II.

Technological superiority was, of course, only temporary as the advanced technology was soon acquired by others. Where both sides in a conflict possessed the same technology other factors went into the equation for victory. Better organization, leadership and strategy, territorial and physical advantage, overextension and the like would then tip the balance. But superior technology, supported by sufficient wealth to manifest it fully and effectively would usually overcome these other factors.

It is in order next, after these preliminary remarks, to sketch briefly some historical episodes wherein superior technology was decisive in human warfare and domination.

THE BATTLE OF KADESH—1296 B. C.

The first striking example on the pages of history of technological superiority in warfare was the horse and chariot of the Indo-Europeans some 3500 years or so ago. Its earliest appearance is associated with the kings and nobles of Mitanni, in what is now northern Syria, who, bearing Indian names, and worshipping some of the same aryan Gods as the Indians, burst forth across the frontiers of the Hittites into Anatolia and into the fertile crescent with their new and terrible engines of war crushing the infantry of the kingdoms in the area as if they were made of paper maché. The Hurrians, as the people of Mitanni were called, came from the grasslands of the north where the horse was first domesticated by man. They settled astride the caravan route across the Euphrates and around 1500 B. C. controlled this vital area. They held the Assyrians as subject people and kept the Hittites at bay. These horsemen from the north were a formidable military power at this time in the Middle East.

The most notable historical event of this period is the conquest of the Egyptians with the horse and chariot by a far ranging contingent of Indo-Europeans. These people are known as Hyksos who imposed foreign rule upon the Egyptians in the lower regions of the Nile (circa 1786–1567 B. C.)

Very little is known of the Hyksos. Earlier historians believed them to be a semitic group. The latest deliberations fix them as Indo-Europeans and their possession of the horse and chariot would tend to support this view. Perhaps they were a splinter and adventurous group from Mitanni. But it is also possible they could have been semites from the fertile crescent who acquired the technology from the Indo-Europeans.

It is interesting too that about this time (second millennium B. C.) the aryans invaded and conquered the Harappans of south Asia. Even greater obscurity surrounds this historical event. But it would not fall into the category of wild speculation to conclude that there occurred here a conquest similar to that of the Hyksos in Egypt. E. L. Basham, a noted English historian on India, concludes ". . . it is probable that the fall of this great civilization was an episode in the movement of charioteering people which altered the face of the whole civilized world in the 2nd millennium B. C." The Harappan civilization at this time was as highly developed and formidable as Egypt or the societies of western Asia. Yet it was overwhelmed by what must have been a small group of aryans issuing into the Punjab through the Khyber pass. The aryans doubtless came with horses and chariots. The Harappans did not have the horse. It is noteworthy that the lords of Mitanni had the same names (and language) as the aryans conquering India.

But back to the Mediterranean area. The only historical source to date on the Hyksos are the Egyptians. The haughty Egyptians refer to them derisively as "shepherd kings or foreign chieftans". But it is obvious that if such insignificant people could conquer so advanced and powerful a civilization as Egypt they must have possessed great military superiority. Moreover, the Egyptians acknowledge that they acquired the horse and chariot from the Hyksos. Hence, the strong inference that the Hyksos were adventurous Hurrians, or some other indo-European people, who had mastered the horse and invented the war chariot. The Egyptians at this time, wealthy though they were, possessed only the ordinary technology of war. They fought without armor, lugged unmanageable shields and wielded small battle axes and rudimentary bows. The Hyksos had body armor, scimitars and daggers, powerful bows made of wood and horn and, above all, horse drawn chariots. But within a century or two the Egyptians mastered the horse and chariot and expelled the Hyksos from Egypt. Meanwhile the Hittites also mastered the horse and chariot, subjected the Hurrians (circa 1366 B. C.) and extended their empire into the fertile crescent. The stage was set for a major clash between these two imperialistic giants of the second millennium B. C. and it came in the Battle of Kadesh on the Orontes river (in modern Lebanon) in 1296 B. C.

After the ouster of Hyksos rule the old civilization of Egypt, which dates back to 3000 B. C., had a resurgence. The Pharoahs of the New Kingdom, Thutmose III, Seti I and Ramses II of the 18th and 19th dynasties (1567–1085 B. C.) built a powerful military establishment based upon the new technology transmitted to Egypt by the Hyksos. The wealth and political organization of the Egyptians enabled them to utilize the new technology to the utmost. Egypt had an army of charioteers second to none. Thutmose III conquered Palestine and Syria extending the Egyptian empire right up to the kingdom of Mitanni on the Euphrates. In 1450 B. C. the empire extended from the Euphrates in the north to Napata (modern Sudan) in the south.

A similar development was transpiring in Anatolia. Seventeen centuries before the Christian era a sector of the erupting Indo-European peoples settled in Anatolia and established their capital at Hattusa. They were the Hittites. They are generally regarded as the people who developed the smelting of iron. They also had the horse and chariot, which they either brought with them from the north or acquired from their cousins and neighbors the Hurrians of Mitanni. By mid-millennium the Hittites were wealthy enough and possessed of the most advanced technology to start empire building. Around 1600 B. C. Mursili I sacked Babylon. A power struggle over succession to the throne and other internal disorder set back empire building for about two centuries. The Hurrians were powerful at this time and kept the Hittites in check. But Suppiluliuma I (circa 1374–1355 B. C.) extended the empire into Syria and to the Tigris in the east, including the kingdom of Mitanni.

The two empires were now eye to eye in Syria and a clash between them was inevitable. For a time Egypt had turned inward, away from empire building, under Akhenaton (1379–1362 B. C.) who concentrated all his effort on reform of the polytheistic religion of Egypt. The rest of his successors of the 18th dynasty were also nonimperialistic. But by the end of the 13th century a strong ruler Ramses II (1379–1362 B. C.) came to the throne and he set out to resurrect the Egyptian empire in the Near East. Meanwhile Suppiluliuma was succeeded, first by his son Mursili II, and then a grandson Muwatalli (1306–1282 B. C.), both strong monarchs, who established firm Hittite rule in Syria. The battle of Kadesh occurred in the spring of 1296 B. C. It is the first battle in history that is recorded. Unfortunately the record is by the Egyptians and terribly biased, but a critical analysis, together with collateral historical facts, enable a rather reliable reconstruction of what actually transpired. No Hittite record has yet been found though their historical records are quite abundant in other respects. What actually occurred appears as follows. Reacting to appeals from present and former client states in Palestine and Syria against Hittite rule Ramses II set out with an army of 20,000 men in four divisions—the Amon, Re, Ptah and Sutekh— to attack the Hittites. The precise objective of Ramses II is not clear. Presumably he hoped to destroy the Hittite army. He must also have sought to regain territories in Syria formerly brought under Egyptian rule by Thutmose III. Ramses campaign was hailed by some of the subject nations chafing under Hittite rule and he was even able to get Bentesina, king of Amurru (modern Lebanon), to defect and ally himself with the Egyptians. This gave Ramses a great advantage as he had friendly ground for his march up the Mediterranean coast.

Muwatalli, with an equal force of 20,000 men, awaited the Egyptian army at the walled city of Kadesh on the Orontes river. About half his force was equipped with the Hittite three-man chariot consisting of the charioteer and two soldiers armed with spears and bows and arrows. He had 3500 of these chariots. They were the most advanced and effective war machines of the day. The Egyptians had only a two man chariot. The assault power of the Hittites was vastly superior.

Ramses II committed a couple of errors right from the start. First, his spies were unable to secure reliable information on the location of the Hittite army. Ramses relied, therefore, on two bedouins who reported to him that Muwatalli fled north with his army, in fear of Ramses, to Aleppo. Who these informers were is unclear. They may have been planted by the Hittites to deceive Ramses. But only a supreme egotist like Ramses would proceed on such intelligence.

His second mistake was to string out his army. Ramses with his Amon corps proceeded ahead and confidently made camp to the northwest of Kadesh. The Hittite army was to the southeast and screened from view by the walls of the city. Ramses was completely unaware of its propinquity. As Re corps was approaching the city from the southeast Muwatalli crossed the Orontes and pounced upon them. His swift and powerful chariots scattered and almost annihilated Re corps. The remnants of Re corps finally caught up with Ramses and Amon corps, pursued hotly by the Hittite chariots, catching them unprepared and throwing the entire Amon corps into panic and flight. Hittite chariots had Ramses completely encircled and at the mercy of the Hittite army.

By all odds that should have ended the matter. At this point two things occurred that rescued Ramses. First the Hittite army degenerated into a mob and began looting and fighting over the spoils found in the Egyptian camp. The abandoned tools, weapons and provisions, oxen and onagers, the tents and wagons of Ramses camp proved too much for their loose discipline. Second, a contingent of Egyptian or Canaanite troops appeared, as if from nowhere, and started to attack the Hittites. They were not from Ptah or Sutekh corps which were still far to the south unaware of the battle. It is believed they were reinforcements which landed on the Mediterranean shore and marched to join the army of Ramses. The Hittites broke away and retired behind the walls of Kadesh. Ramses retreated back to Egypt. Egyptian imperialism was not resumed in the Near East until 930 B. C. when Egypt invaded Palestine and plundered the Temple of Solomon.

Ramses II returned to Egypt for a long rule of 67 years during which span of time he constructed some of the finest monuments by which the Egyptian civilization came to be known and judged by posterity. There was Luxor, Karnak, Abydas and Abu-Simbel. They abound with commemorative freizes and narratives of Ramses' exploits, prominent among them, his ''glorious victory'' over the king of Hatti at Kadesh. There is also a poem written on papyrus by a bard of the court. It is the work of a propaganda minister or officials such as has seldom been matched thereafter. It cannot, however, stand the light of critical reading.

The theme of the narrative is how Ramses snatched victory from the jaws of defeat. The defeat is amply recorded in its "admissions against interest" but the victory is related in unbelievable phantasy. After confirming that the Hittites decimated Re corps and panicked Amon corps the Pharaonic chronicler portrays Ramses standing alone encircled by 2500 Hittite chariots lamenting "my foot soldiers and my charioteers have abandoned me to the enemy, and none of them held fast to fight against them." In desperation he appeals to his God Amon for help. "What are these Asiatics to you Amon? These wretches who know nothing of God" he implores. Amon responds by investing Ramses with supernatural power. "He was like a bull with sharp horns" sings the royal bard, . . . "the mighty lion . . . the jackal who in a moment traverses the circuit of the earth . . . the divine, splendid falcon." Seized with God-like power Ramses, with his loyal charioteer Menna, proceeds single handed, arrows flying to the right, spear thrusts to the left, to destroy the Hittite army. "Behold 2500 chariots surround me, and now they lie hacked to pieces before my steeds. Not one of the foe could lift his hand to fight" says Ramses.

Thus having disposed of 7500 men and 5000 horses and 2500 chariots in one fell swoop he looks around to see where Muwatalli might be hiding "the wretched prince of Hatti, however, stood in the center of his own army, and for fear of His Majesty he did not come forth into the fighting." So, still possessed of his extraordinary energy, Ramses proceeds to annihilate the remaining 1000 chariots of the Hittites. There is no account, curiously, of the capture or slaying of Muwatalli, who by now stood before him stripped of his 3500 chariots. "Never before has one man alone, without foot soldiers and chariots, defeated hundreds of thousands" concludes the Pharoah's propagandist.

What boggles the mind 3300 years later is why the ancient Egyptians believed this tale and permitted their leaders to desecrate their national monuments with such patent nonsense. A critical reader of this chronicle of the Battle of Kadesh by Ramses' propagandists in the 20th century can only conclude the Pharoah suffered a humiliating defeat in his encounter with the Hittites. Collateral facts corroborate this conclusion. First, the Egyptians never set foot on Hittite territory. At Kadesh they were still 375 miles from Hattusa, the Hittite capital. In fact, the defacto boundary between the two empires after the battle was considerably south of Kadesh, below Damascus on the Nahrel Kelb river. This is hardly consistent with an Egyptian victory. Bentesina pledged his allegiance, once again, to Muwatalli after the battle. This too does not comport with an Egyptian victory. Muwatalli obviously survived the battle as it is recorded he signed a treaty of friendship with Ramses.

After the Battle of Kadesh peace reigned for nearly a century between the two empires. Egypt stayed out of the Near East and the Hittites did not extend their rule beyond Damascus. In fact, the Hittites, under Muwatalli's successor Hattusili, and Egypt signed an elaborate non-aggression pact in the "twenty-first year" of Ramses rule. It was inscribed on a silver plaque. It is interesting to note that the preamble describes the two monarchs as equals. Thereafter the peaceful relation between the two countries was further augmented by the marriage of a daughter of Hattusili to Ramses. Not only was this unusual in Egyptian practice but she was made the chief wife of the Pharoah.

The central fact of this conflict is the superior war chariot of the Hittites. To analogize, it was as if an army equipped with World War II tanks encountered another using World War I tanks. The Egyptians, even allowing for the human factor, did not have a chance against the Hittite charioteers. It is not surprising that the Hittites were able to decimate one fourth of Ramses army in one lightening charge and the news thereof panic another fourth, leaving the Pharoah encircled by 2500 chariots—three to a chariot—as his chronicler states. It would have been neater for history had Muwatalli retained control of his winning army and finished the battle conclusively by slaying or capturing Ramses. But historical events are seldom neat; they tend, instead to be messy. Though the battle may have ended in confusion the lesson of the role of superior technology comes through the haze clear and persuasive.

That this was a historic battle can hardly be doubted. After it Egyptian suzerainty receded from the Near East. But the Hittites seemed uninterested in filling the vacuum. And a century later the Hittite empire was destroyed by the "sea people" as they are referred to in Egyptian history. The Egyptians too, after Ramses, went into decline. The result was that the Near East was without great power influence for several centuries thereafter.

In the two millennia before Christ the Near East appears to have been a somewhat unique part of the world. No great indigenous peoples or power resided in the area. It was peopled by nomads barely subsisting in the largely forbidding land. But geography placed it astride the trade routes of the time. Cities sprang up along these routes to service the caravans and in turn derive economic subsistance from them. The nomads were constantly threatening the cities, who would appeal to their overlords, the Pharoahs of Egypt, for assistance to keep the nomads at bay. The Egyptians were of course, vitally interested in protecting the caravans and keeping the trade routes free and clear of danger from these marauding tribes. A sort of shepherd-city dweller historical dialectic prevailed that shaped the destiny of the area. Most of these nomads and people of the cities were semites. There were the Amorites, Akhadians, Aramaeans, Ammonites, Edomites, Moabites—and Israelites. The Israelites left the area somewhere around the middle of the second millennium for Egypt and ended up as slaves of the Pharoahs.

Around 1225 B. C. Moses led them out of bondage back to Canaan, but when the Israelites arrived in the Promised Land they found it inhabited by the ·Ammonites, Moabites, Edomites and other semitic tribes who had remained there during the Israelite's absence. The Israelites were forced to fight for the Promised Land and over the next two centuries or so wrested most of it from the other semitic tribes.

The interesting thought is whether the situation might have developed otherwise had the Hittites not checked Egyptian power in the area so that the long established cities, as was their custom for centuries, could have appealed for help from the Pharoahs against the zealous and aggressive Israelites. In such case, the Israel nation may never have emerged and the Judeo-Christian religion that has played so important a role in the history of man may have withered away as a belief of "one" of a large number of semitic tribes in this forbidding area of the earth.

BATTLE OF CARRHAE—53 B. C.

During the last century before Christ the Romans had reached the extent of their empire. Caesar conquered Gaul in the West and Lucullus and Pompey planted the Roman eagles solidly in the Near East. Carthage was destroyed and the Greeks subjected during the preceding century, making Rome (after Pompey eliminated the pirates in 66 B. C.) the master of the Mediterranean. In the west the Romans were stopped by the Germans on the Rhine but this was not of great concern as there was little beyond the Rhine of interest to the empire builders. The East, however, was different. Beyond the Euphrates laid India and China. Alexander the Great, the idol of the Graeco-Roman world, got as far as India in his world conquest and every Roman wished to equal or outdo him. Moreover, the Romans wanted the gold and wares of the Far East. The women of Rome demanded silk from China and muslins from India which were brought by caravans over the Old Silk Road at great expense to the Romans. China and India wanted only gold for their goods as they considered the manufactures of the Graeco-Roman world inferior to theirs. Pliny estimated the annual loss of gold at 100 million sesterces and complained "so dearly do we pay for luxury and our women."

After his campaign in Spain and elimination of the pirates in the Mediterranean Pompey went east in 65 B. C. to take over command from Lucullus, the brilliant general who extended Roman power in Asia Minor and the Near East. Pompey finally defeated Mithradates, the king of Pontus in Asia Minor and, his ally and son in law, Tigranes of Armenia in 63 B. C. Having secured Roman rule in Asia Minor and Armenia Pompey directed his attention to Syria to the south. He deposed Antiochus the Asiatic, a Seleucid confirmed in power by Lucullus, to establish direct Roman rule. In order to fortify the boundries of the Roman government in Syria Pompey found it necessary to confront the Parthians. The Parthian king Phraates, who allied himself with the Romans against Mithradates and Tigranes, felt betrayed when Pompey wanted to extend the frontier of Syria beyond the Euphrates in violation of the treaty between them. But neither Pompey or Phraates pushed the matter into war at this time and the desert area between the Euphrates and Tigris in Mesopotamia became an ill-defined and uneasy boundary between Roman Syria and Parthia. A Roman unit was established in the walled city of Carrhae on the east side of the Euphrates which was an important way station on the caravan route to China.

This *modus vivendi* continued for a decade. During this time the political situation in Rome deteriorated. The Republic was in disintegration. Defacto power was in the hands of a triumvirate composed of Pompey, Caesar and Crassus, who vied with each other for ultimate power. Both Pompey and Caesar had already distinguished themselves on the battlefield. Crassus had only the defeat of Spartacus on his record. He craved greater distinction in his quest for supreme power and what could be better than to follow in the footsteps of the great Alexander. Unfortunately, Crassus was not the soldier of the stature of Pompey or Caesar. But he was a tremendously rich man deriving his wealth from real estate in Rome and a multitude of commercial and manufacturing enterprises all over Italy. Caesar was heavily in financial debt to Crassus and consented to the expedition. Crassus' love of gold and riches was legendary. All this propelled him into a purblind ambition to break through the Parthian defenses and to march on to glory and gold, in the footsteps of Alexander, to India and, perhaps, even to China.

Had Crassus been less blinded by greed and a better soldier his sixth sense would have warned him of the danger and even folly of his enterprise. Lucullus and Pompey approached the Parthians with considerable diffidence, sensing, good soldiers that they were, that the Parthians fought differently than the Romans. Mommsen, commenting upon Lucullus' seige of Tigranocerta in Armenia in 69 B. C., states "The exhaustless shower of arrows which the garrison poured upon the Roman army, and the setting of fire to the besieging machines by means of naptha, initiated the Romans into the new dangers of Iranian warfare."

But who were the Parthians? Historians seem unable to make up their minds whether to consider them true Persians or not, albeit they occupied the same ground as the empires of Cyrus, Darius and Xerxes. For instance, it is considered un-Persian that the Parthians moved the capital from Persepolis in the south to Ctesiphon to the north on the left bank of the Tigris. The Parthians were indigenous people pursuing a nomadic life in the eastern provinces (where Khorosan province is situated today) since time immemorial. They had also a close affinity with the Scythians to the north. They may even have been Scythians who migrated into the eastern provinces of Persia. The Parthians probably owed their military prowess to this affinity and intercourse with the Scythians. They were superb horsemen! Moreover, the Persians, Parthians and the Scythians were all indo-Europeans.

After Alexander conquered Persia he established Greek rule through the Seleucids. But in a century or so Greek rule grew weak and the Parthians in the east began to erode the area under Seleucid control. By the second century A. D. the Parthians extended their rule as far as the Euphrates. At the time of Mithradates I (171–138 A. D.) Parthian rule extended from India to Syria and even Asia Minor. It was in Asia Minor and Armenia where Roman and Parthian conflict first arose and in these areas the Romans prevailed. The rough and mountainous terrain of Armenia and Anatolia was unfavorable to Parthian cavalry. Moreover, Parthia proper was never enthusiastically behind Mitradates and Tigranes in these battles. In fact, Phraates later allied himself with the Romans against the Armenians in return for the Euphrates as a boundary with Syria. Hence, Parthian arms had not yet been pitted against the Romans in full extent.

It was now 54 B. C. Crassus was already 60. His greed for gold was world renouned. His lust for power was only second to his love for gold. He arrived in Syria early in the year but was in no hurry to march against the Parthians. He first took time to despoil the temples of Syria and Jerusalem of their treasures. He also devoted the year to reconnaissance and campaign planning and here he promptly made two mistakes. First he relied on the intelligence of Abgarus the Arab who allied himself with the Romans and attached his bedouin army to the legions of Crassus. Abgarus turned out to be a source of great misinformation. He reported to Crassus that the Parthians were evacuating the western provinces. He said the Parthian army was in flight and recommended hot pursuit across the Mesopotamian desert. Now Crassus had two choices in his march to the Parthian capital of Ctesiphon. He could cross the Euphrates and march along its left bank to Seleucia on the opposite side of the Tigris from the capital where the two rivers were only a few miles apart. This would have been a much longer march. The shortest route was across the desert along the route of the caravans to China and India. Against wiser counsel (his lieutenant Gaius Cassius was against the desert crossing) Crassus opted for the latter relying instead on the foolish, perhaps, deceitful advice of Abgarus. Crassus had by now assumed his victory over the Parthians and already imagined himself the conqueror of India with its great store of gold. He was going to rectify, in one fell swoop, the adverse balance of payments over the years in Roman trade with India. Finally in May 53 B. C. the army of Crassus—seven legions, 4000 cavalry and 4000 archers and slingers—some 40,000 strong crossed the Euphrates and headed across the desert toward Carrhae. For days they marched and plodded across the hot desert without spotting the Parthians. When they came to the first tributary of the Euphrates, the Balissus, mounted scouts of the Parthians were observed on the other side. Crassus dispatched Abgarus and his arabs to reconnoitre. Abgarus failed to return. Crassus proceeded with the march but when the Romans crossed the Balissus they heard the sudden thunder of the Parthian kettle drums signaling the charge of the Parthian heavy cavalry. It was now June 6, 53 B. C. and the two armies locked in battle in the Mesopotamian desert some 30 miles south of Carrhae. The Roman archers and slingers were useless against the superior bows of the Parthians which could dispatch arrows effectively over 500 yards. The rounded stones and arrows of the Romans could not negotiate anywhere near the distance. When these auxiliaries were destroyed the Parthian mounted archers concentrated on the Roman infantry. As the legions closed ranks in a dense square 12 cohorts to a side, which under any other circumstance would have created a formidable military formation, the Roman infantry became even more vulnerable to Parthian arrows. The legionnaires could not touch the Parthians with their swords and spears while the Parthian bows hurled steel tipped arrows at the mass of Roman infantry with such force from 500 paces that the arrows penetrated their shields as if made of paper maché.

The Romans hoped in vain that the Parthian cavalry would deplete their arrow supply but these hopes were dashed when they saw the camel train of the Parthians loaded with arrows. The bowyers of Parthia must have been busy for months making arrows for the army. The Parthians kept outflanking the Roman legions but instead of closing the circle around them they suddenly broke off the attack and fled. Publius Crassus, the brave and impetuous son of the commander who distinguished himself under Caesar in Gaul, followed in hot pursuit with a division of cavalry and infantry 6000 strong. But when some considerable distance separated Publius from the main Roman army the Parthians, as was their tactic, suddenly wheeled and annihilated the entire division with their bows and arrows. Only about 500 were taken prisoners. Publius caused himself to be stabbed by his shield bearer so he would not fall hostage to the Parthians. It was now nightfall and the Parthians, unaccustomed to fighting at night, broke off the battle shouting to Crassus that they would let him bemoan the loss of his son through the night and return to finish the battle on the morrow. The Romans, of course, did not wait for the morning.

By now Crassus was bereft of his judgement and ability to command. The army wished to replace Crassus with Cassius. After a brief retreat behind the walls of Carrhae, where they found refuge from the Parthian arrows, the remnants of the Roman army moved in the direction of Armenia. They were overtaken by Surenas, the Parthian general, who began to make overtures of peace. A personal conference was arranged between the two commanders. Surenas, mindful of the betrayal of Pompey, demanded a treaty in writing making the Euphrates the boundary between the two empires. Then in a gesture of friendliness Surenas presented a beautiful steed to Crassus as a present from the Parthian king Orodes. Octavius, the other Roman lieutenant general, however, misconstrued the gesture when Parthian soldiers attempted to place Crassus on the horse as an attempt to capture the Roman commander. Though disarmed Octavius wrested a sword from a Parthian and .stabbed the groom. The conference degenerated into bedlam and bloodshed; the Roman officers were put to death; and the Roman army made captive. Crassus promoted his death in the melee in order to avoid the indignity of capture. Gaius Cassius managed to escape similar demise with a squadron of soldiers and returned to Syria where he and others could relate the history of the death of Crassus and the defeat of the Roman legions by the Parthians. About half the Roman army was lost, another 10,000 were captives of the Parthians and sent to the eastern provinces as slaves and only some 10,000 managed to return to Syria.

The Parthian view of the battle is not recorded. Like many other Asians the Parthians were poor historians. Much of what occurred is therefore lost in obscurity. There is, for instance, the true role of Abgarus the Arab. When the Battle of Carrhae commenced Abgarus and his bedouins were on the side of the Parthian army. He either deceived Crassus and even led him into the Parthian trap or when defeat and annihilation were imminent defected to the Parthians to save himself. Only the Parthians knew. There is also the true disposition of the severed head of Crassus. A version, related by Mommsen, states that the head arrived in Ctesiphon while king Orodes, at a marriage feast for his son Pacorus, was watching a group of Greek players acting out Euripides' play *The Bacchae*. The actor playing the part of Agave exchanged the head of Crassus for the mock head of Pentheus he was carrying on his staff and thus completed the play to the amusement of Orodes and his court. A real Greek tragedy! Oriental lore also has it that Orodes, knowing of Crassus love of gold, had his mouth filled with molten gold in mockery of his lust for the metal. Whether it is true or not it makes a good story—that the greed of man should be sated in a manner when the dominance instinct that begot the greed could no longer quicken to its satisfaction.

In 33 B. C. Marc Anthony decided to pick up the fallen banners of Crassus and march to Ctesiphon and onward to India. Another Phraates was now king of the Parthians. He strangled his father Orodes to take the throne. Orodes was then eighty! One wonders why it was necessary. Anthony decided not to cross the Mesopotamian desert. He planned instead to cross the Euphrates river higher up, traverse the Armenian hills into Media, capture its capital of Praaspa and march south from there across the hills and valleys of Parthia to Ctesiphon. The mounted Parthian archers were ready for him. The Parthians were, however, greatly outnumbered being able to muster only 40,000 cavalry against the Roman army of 100,000 or more, which included 40,000 horsemen to match the Parthian cavalry. This gave the Parthians all the more reason to keep a distance.

Almost from the start things went badly for the campaign. For some reason Marc Anthony was in great haste and his baggage train, including his siege equipment, was outdistanced by the main body of legionnaires. This left an important segment of his army vulnerable to the Parthian arrows. Plutarch states Marc Anthony's haste was prompted by his desire to return to Cleopatra, whose charm beclouded his judgement.

At the first crossing of the Euphrates the Parthians destroyed much of the Roman river pontoon bridge assemblage together with valuable engineers. The baggage train then moved up the river where it could be forded and started for Praaspa across Armenia. There were 300 wagons, an eighty foot ram and other siege equipment escorted by two legions, including 2000 slingers and a small contingent of cavalry. The Parthian mounted archers dispatched the entire column from a safe distance and set fire to the wagons and siege equipment. It was a massacre not a battle. Anthony lost 10,000 of his men in this battle.

This left Marc Anthony preparing a siege of Praaspa without the usual gear for such assault. At great labor he had his legions build a mount of ground to scale the walls. But the Parthian horsemen were soon upon him and he ordered a retreat. The Parthian cavalry harrassed him all the way back, with archers behind every bush and in every wadi, mounted bowmen descending upon the legions in force in every open space, until a third of the legions was destroyed. Marc Anthony was lucky to survive the ill conceived campaign. The Romans did not challenge the Parthians for a century or more drawing their lines in the East on the Euphrates. Plutarch states however, that Anthony entertained the idea of invading Parthia again but he realized he would have to equate or outmatch the Parthian mounted archers. He proposed an alliance with the king of Media, who had a falling out with king Phraates, to supply the necessary cavalry to checkmate the Parthian army. The plan never materialized as Anthony was dissuaded in his purpose by Cleopatra.

In the retrospect of history what transpired at Carrhae and Praaspa was basically the clash of two types of warfare—the sword against the missile. The latter was obviously superior. It could deliver death from a distance. In the words of Mommsen: "Here, where the Roman weapons of close combat and the Roman system of concentration yielded for the first time before the weapons of more distant warfare and the system of deploying, was initiated that military revolution which only reached its completion with the introduction of firearms."

The Parthians did not, of course, invent the bow and arrow nor did they domesticate the horse. Even the deployment of the weapon from horseback was not their invention. That belongs to the Scythians, their cousins once removed. Herodotus describes such tactics by the Scythians as they lured Darius deep into their territory and then wheeled on him when he was most vulnerable in an open filed. Archers, mounted and on foot, were part of all the armies of antiquity but they were always auxiliaries—the main part of the army invariably consisted of hoplites, legionnaires and other soldiers with the sword. Overwhelmingly these armies were men of the sword whether mounted or on foot.

The Romans brought combat with the sword to its height and built with it a great empire. They wedded to the sword their genius for order and discipline. Campaigns were a matter of rigid order in contrast to the disorganized warfare conducted by the Parthians. For instance, when the legions bivouacked for the night they constructed a stockade wall with a deep moat around it to thwart a surprise night attack. It involved tremendous effort for what seemed like a fleeting use. But the importance of it was demonstrated when the cohorts of Rome—not as well disciplined as the legions—failed to do so in their initial campaign against Spartacus only to succumb to massacre in their unprotected camp one night at the hands of the rebellious slaves.

Along with the perfection of sword combat the Romans became masters at siege warfare. Their mobile multi-storied assault towers 70 or more feet high their 80 foot mobile battering rams—a heavy timber fitted with an iron head often shaped like a rams head—and a wide assortment of catapults rendered every city wall vulnerable to their attack. Once the Roman army breached or broke through a wall the superior Roman swordsmen finished the job of delivering death and defeat to the city's inhabitants. The invention of the corvus, already mentioned, enabled the Romans to convert naval to land warfare. Once the spiked gangplank locked the enemy ship to the Roman galley and the Roman swordsmen scrambled across it on to the enemy ship to engage its crew and soldiers in hand to hand combat the battle differed little to that on land.

All of this might was of no avail against an enemy capable of delivering death from a fast moving horse at 500 paces. How the Parthians evolved this new type of warfare is not clear. They do appear to be the first nation of substance that predicated their warfare entirely on the mounted archer. To be sure, we know from Herodotus that the Scythians centuries earlier fought exclusively from horseback though they were nowhere as effective archers. Cavalry was now known for centuries but the effective combination of the mounted man and the bow seems to have been perfected by the Parthians. The legions always had an auxiliary of cavalry but its use was secondary, largely to round up the enemy so the legions could concentrate on it in hand to hand combat.

The major factor in the picture was, of course, the Parthian bow. It was superior to anything found in the Mediterranean area. The bow was brought to its highest development at this time in the East. The Chinese, in particular, were master bowyers. The caravan route led through Persia and provided a facile line of communication and trade for the advanced techniques and materials for the production of superior bows and arrows. Chinese bowyers may even have plied their craft in Parthia either as slaves or itinerant craftsmen.

The bow of the East was made of a composite of wood, horn and sinew. Well seasoned maplewood was favored for its elasticity and capacity to absorb glue. The black horn of the water buffalo of India and south east Asia was used for the best bows. Glues to weld the laminated composite bow into one instrument were made of animal sinews and fish heads. A superb bow took years of carving, glueing, heating, drying and shaping. The reverse bow was set in an opposite curvature of its strung position, which required a year or more of drying and setting in this position. The bow strings too were carefully constructed. The best were made of many strands of raw silk interlaced and welded with fish glue. This is astonishing for silk from China during Roman times cost around $800 per pound!

A Parthain bow made by a master bowyer from the best materials could deliver an arrow with deadly accuracy over 500 yards or more. Such bows took several years to construct and only the nobles could afford them. The normal bow of the Parthian horsemen could obviously not have been of such quality nor was such bow needed to prevail over the enemy armed primarily with a sword or spear.

The arrows were steel tipped in order to penetrate the shields and armor of the enemy. The shaft was made of stout wood. The feathers to assure accurate flight came from a multitude of birds with differing favorites among the bowyers. These stout steel tipped arrows could penetrate bronze shields and steel armor one or two inches thick with ease. One arrow, in particular, deserves special mention. It was a three-bladed steel head arrow, designed to cut arteries of men or animals for speedy death. It was used primarily in the hunt of ferocious animals like the lion and tiger. But a highly skilled Parthian bowman with a superb bow could hit a man's throat, cut his jugular, and cause swift and final death.

The bowyers in Parthia were, *ipso facto*, treated as an elite group. It is believed many foreigners, particularly Chinese, came to Parthia to ply their trade. Though the record is meagre it seems obvious that the manufacture of bows and arrows was a major industry in a country whose military prowess was based upon the mounted archer.

It is a source of some wonderment why the Graeco-Roman world did not place more emphasis on the mounted archer in its warfare. The horse was successfully mounted by man centuries earlier in Scythia and was ridden all over the Mediterranean world. But Greek and Roman warfare remained predicated on the foot soldier. The Graeco-Roman world remained wedded to the sword, which it invented and developed into a foremost weapon of war. But it could not have been cultural inertia alone. For one thing, the rugged terrain of Europe, Greece in particular, was not conducive to cavalry so that its great attribute of mobility was considerably diminished. Equally important may have been the high economic cost of maintaining a horse. The Mediterranean area did not possess the vast grasslands of the Caucasian area for the inexpensive breeding and rearing of horses. About the only

Graeco-Roman peoples who used the cavalry effectively were the Macedonians. Had Alexander not made the cavalry an equal arm with the infantry in his campaign against the Persians he would not likely have broken through to India. But after him, the Romans, once again, reverted to infantry as the main body of their army. To be sure, they used cavalry but only in an auxiliary and secondary role.

Similarly too the Greeks and Romans knew and used missiles, including the bow and arrow. The Greeks invented and the Romans used and developed further a wide assortment of ballista or catapults to hurl stones, darts and arrows. They were an integral part of their siege warfare. But the ballista were mostly immobile and short range. Why the lack of emphasis on the bow and arrow (obviously very mobile) is another of those inexplicable historical facts. An important reason, however, may be the wet and humid climate of Europe and the Mediterranean area. Moisture softens the glues and renders the wood and horn flaccid in a composite bow diminishing substantially its power and accuracy. The Graeco-Roman peoples may, therefore, have found the bow less effective and unreliable and dismissed it as a weapon for further use and development. The Parthians and other people of the East lived in dry or drier atmospheres. Moreover, the Parthians were solicitious towards their bows in this respect being always mindful of their dryness. They kept them unstrung except in emergencies and while in use and could be found constantly drying them in the sun.

Anyway, whatever the reasons, the Parthians were the people that wedded the mobility of the horse with the long range lethal power of the eastern bow and stopped the imperial thrust of the wealthiest and mightest power of the day. Otherwise, they had very little else going for them. They were a disorganized society loosely held together by a king constantly in danger of regicide. Their wealth could not match that of Rome. The Parthian army had little discipline. To be sure, they possessed some advantages. They fought in the desert and open spaces which was conducive to their kind of warfare. They sat astride the caravan route to the east from which they profited financially and technologically. And the Romans were overextended in any conflict beyond the Euphrates. Yet the Parthian rule in Persia lasted four centuries! Almost as long as the rule of Rome over the Mediterranean area. In so far as the record of the rise and fall of human societies goes that is not an insignificant accomplishment. It is difficult to ascribe it to anything else except their prowess in war with the mounted archer.

It may seem to some that too much attention has been given to the conflict of the Romans and Parthians over the crossing of the Euphrates. It is believed, however, that the Battle of Carrhae represents as well as any episode in the history of man the importance of technological superiority in the determination of human conflict. One can only agree with Mommsen that Carrhae stands as a milestone in the development of human warfare, that of superiority of missile warfare. Missile warfare, thereafter graduated to fire-arms, cannon, bombs and, today, to the nuclear missile.

But there are further lessons in the Battles of Carrhae and Praaspa and these will be developed in subsequent chapters. Roman power was overextended in Parthia—a mistake committed by nations throughout history. Superior technology is effective only where it is supported by adequate wealth—mainly a productive economy. The Persian economy kept the Parthian cavalry amply supplied with good horses and arrows. The vicissitudes of history also played their part. Alexander may not have reached India had not the Persian empire of Darius been in decline and disintegration by 325 B. C. Crassus, on the other hand, encountered a Persian empire reinvigorated with new blood of the virile Parthians. Had he encountered instead a weak Persian empire he might have gone down in history, like his Macedonian idol, as Crassus the Great instead of Crassus the Decapitated.

BATTLE OF HASTINGS—1066 A. D.

A most important event in medieval times was the Norman conquest of England. It started a sequence of events that spanned most of the second millennium of the Christian era and led eventually to the.domination of the world by the English speaking peoples. At the risk of oversimplification it can be said that this important event was facilitated by the invention and effective use of the stirrup which made mounted shock combat possible. It fostered a new and improved type of warfare that prevailed in the Battle of Hastings in 1066 A. D. and brought Norman rule to England.

The evolution of feudalism based upon the mounted armored knight has already been discussed, in part, in Chapter IV. It was a Frankish development. Its founder was Charles Martel (715–741 A. D.). He realized the value of the stirrup in mounted warfare which could lock the power of the horse into a man's thrust with the spear or sword and deliver a blow to the enemy such as had not been possible theretofore. The stirrup was not a European invention. It was conceived by the Indians and developed by the Chinese. How it came to Europe is not clear. But by the eighth century it was known to the Franks.

What Charles Martel realized was its potential for shock combat and for this the Carolingians invented two accessories to create the new war machine. The first was the Carolingian wing spear, a long stout spear with a cross-piece behind the blade. Without the cross piece the power of the horse would have caused the spear to penetrate the enemy—horse or man—so deeply the horseman would have been unable to withdraw it for the continued battle. Moreover the risk of being unhorsed by his irretractable spear would have been great. The second was the kite shield, an elongated shield flat or rounded on top and pointed at the bottom, designed to protect the left side and leg of the knight. Eventually the horseman was carapaced in iron so that mounted he was unrecognizable except by his heralded shield and flying pennon. In time the armor became so heavy the knight had to be hoisted on his mount with block and tackle. The horse too was armored so that the mounted knight of medievel times was the heavy tank of the day.

This new war machine was expensive. It was not possible in the eighth century for the king to finance the cost by taxation. The economy was 95 per cent or so agricultural and wealth was held primarily in land. Charles Martel conceived the idea of endowing his warriors with land in exchange for the maintenance of a fixed number of knights commensurate with the value of the grant. Much of the land at the time was owned by the Church. So Charles Martel seized large tracts from the Church to endow his new warriors. His successors Pepin and Charlemagne continued the practice and by the ninth century the feudal system was well established in France. The Carolingians with their new found military power, predicated mainly on mounted shock combat, became the foremost power in western Europe.

In the ninth century the Vikings invaded the British Isles, western Europe and even Russia. These people from Scandanavia owed their prowess to their seafaring and were able to terrorize the empires of the day for two centuries or so. One group, probably from Norway, under Rolf the Viking (also called Rollo) established themselves in Normandy. Rollo was recognized by Charles the Simple, king of France in 911 A. D., by a grant of land in the valley of the lower Seine. Rollo, and his followers, converted to Christianity and soon integrated themselves into the customs and manners of the French society. By the first half of the eleventh century the Normans were the foremost warriors of France, establishing an empire on southern Italy and Sicily and venturing into the Near East on pilgrimages to the Holy Land.

Such are the antecedents of William the Conqueror. He was the bastard son of Robert I, the sixth duke of Normandy. The story goes that young Robert, not yet 20, was charmed in 1027 by the beauty and grace of a young maid, then 17, named Herleve of the town of Falaise when he spied her dancing in the street (another version has it while washing clothes in a stream). He forthwith appropriated her for his bed. From this connection issued William, the conqueror to be, in 1028. Her father's name is thought to have been Fulbert and he was a tanner. The story should delight any student of evolution and primate behavior as it appears to fit Nature's law of selectivity. Scandanavian genes mixed with those of Gaul to produce a genius. William certainly turned out to be just that.

This remarkable maid of Gaul subsequently married Herluin, Vicomte of Conteville, and bore him two sons. One was Odo the famous bishop of Bayeux and later the Earl of Kent; the other Robert, Count of Mortain, a large landowner in England after the conquest. It was her misfortune, however, to die before William's famous victory at Hastings.

William's father Robert died in 1035 in Asia Minor while returning from a pilgrimage to Jerusalem. William thus became the Duke of Normandy while a child of seven. His illegitimacy plagued his early years. He had often to fight for his inheritance. Throughout, William had the support of the king of France. Together they finally routed the conspirators against William at the Battle of Vales Dunes in 1047. An interesting feature of this battle is that it was fought on both sides entirely by cavalry!

William was a master of the new mounted shock combat. The Normans became the foremost knights of Christendom and their fame spread all the way to the Holy Land. They were on the lookout at this time for new adventures.

Across the channel the situation in England was in some disarray. Canute, who imposed Danish rule upon the Saxons in 1016 died in 1035. Canute's death ended the Viking rule. Up to 1042 the throne was passed among his sons until Godwin of Wessex took matters into his own hand and placed Edward the Confessor of the Saxon line on the English throne.

Edward lived in exile in Normandy during Canute's reign where he became more French than English. He was very religious. Though formally married to Godwin's beautiful daughter there was no issue of the marriage. Norman influence infiltrated the court and church in England which Godwin did his utmost to disuade. Norman influence made its impact on England years before the conquest. Godwin was driven into exile in 1051 by the Normans at court but he and his son Harold, backed by force, prevailed upon Edward for a restoration of their estates. Godwin died in 1053 and Harold succeeded him as earl of Wessex and became, once again influential at court.

Succession to the English crown became a matter of great concern at this time in view of Edward's want of heirs. During Godwin's exile William visited Edward and claimed Edward promised to recommend him as his successor. William feared Edward might designate Harold instead who now wielded great influence at court. William was Edward's cousin (Edward's mother Emma was his grandfather's sister) whereas Harold was related merely through the marriage of his sister to Edward.

In 1064 Harold was shipwrecked by high winds on the French coast and captured by the count of Ponthieu who ransomed him to William. They became great friends (they are shown hunting together on the Bayeux tapestry), William knighted Harold and received Harold's promise under sacred oath (upon St. Edmund's bones) to support him as successor to the English crown. In return William promised to make Harold earl of the whole province of Wessex and marry him to his daughter. Feeling secure in Harold's oath William liberated him to return to England where Harold resumed his close association with Edward.

This is the Norman version of Harold's oath as depicted on the renouned Bayeux tapestry. The Saxons questioned the validity of Harold's promise.

Harold doubtless made the promise. Had he not taken the oath he might not have lived to tell about it. Moreover, the bargain was not without merit for Harold. After all his claim to the throne was weaker than Williams. Unfortunately for William the arrangement did not have the approval of the Witan, the constitutional body that had to approve succession to the English crown.

Edward the Confessor died in January, 1066, recommending Harold as his successor. The Witan approved. Harold was crowned king with solemn rites at Westminster Abbey which Edward had just built. The church of Rome, however, withheld its blessing on the grounds that Harold violated his oath to William. The sanctity of oaths was the very essence of feudalism and the church was reluctant to tamper with the social order of the times.

A "hairy star" or comet, later identified as Halley's comet, flashed across the skies at the time of the coronation which was interpreted by William and his followers as a heavenly omen that Harold's takeover of the English crown was a sacrilege. They could hardly realize in their state of inadequate knowledge that it was probably the same comet that appeared at the time of Christ's birth which Christians, including the Normans, considered a heavenly herald of the Nativity. With better public relations Harold might have turned the event to his benefit. At any rate, it would not have mattered for the issue was to be resolved by strength of arms.

Harold's coronation prompted two invasions. The first from Norway by king Harold Hardrada who claimed succession through the Viking line. He was joined by Harold's rebellious brother Tostig. So, as William planned his invasion he could not be sure which Harold he would encounter.

William planned well. Above all he was mindful of securing his home base since he was about to depart with his knights across the channel. He fortified his left, years earlier, by subjecting Brittany and Maine. His right he compromised by his earlier marriage to Matilda of Flanders in 1053. He secured the sanction of the king of France. He had the blessing of the Pope. Finally, he felt, he had an omen from Heaven through his self-serving interpretation of the appearance of Halley's comet.

He was able to attract many adventurous knights to augment his Norman vassals. Brittany provided a substantial number. There were Normans from south Italy, knights from Flanders, France and Spain. All were attracted by Williams' fame as a warrior and the promise of land in England. They were a force of some 7000 strong. William had 600 ships built for the crossing. By late summer he had his force and fleet ready at St. Valrey, at the mouth of the Somme, ready for the invasion. But things did not go well at the start. For six weeks the wind blew unfavorably. His sailors knew not how to tack into the wind. The assemblage was growing uneasy. William had to resort to extraordinary tactics. He had the bones of St. Edmund carried up and down the coast with great pomp and circumstance. The wind changed! William gave orders to sail.

Meanwhile Harold was forced, first to deal with the invasion from Norway in the north. He defeated Hardrada and Tostig in a glorious victory at Stamford bridge near York in Northumbria on September 25, 1066. Hardrada is reported to have said of Harold "he sat firmly in his stirrups." This was, however a battle of infantry. An interesting feature of this conflict is the fact that Harold's housecarls, who were vikings, distinguished themselves in the English victory. This battle ended for all time the Viking threat to England.

The channel crossing also did not go well for William. His ship was faster and soon outran the rest of the fleet. Consternation set in. With customary bravado and insouciance William calmly breakfasted (including wine) with his staff and the fleet soon caught up. Calm prevailed as the fleet came safely to anchor in Pevensey Bay on September 28. William disembarked, stumbled and fell flat on his face. His followers thought this might be a bad omen. Recovering his composure he said with great presence of mind "I have taken England with both my hands." or words too that effect.

No opposition appeared. Harold was rushing down from York. The local fyrd or militia had given up on the Normans after weeks of watchfulness. A fortnight of preparations ensued before the start of the march on London. Meanwhile Harold reassembled an army, filling the depletions from the Battle of Stamford bridge and marched toward the south coast. His army, consisting almost solely of infantry, is thought to have outnumbered the Normans. On October 13, Harold reached a summit—the hill of Senlac—lying north of Hastings from which he could block the road to London. The Battle Abbey now stands on this summit.

He massed his men closely with locked shields on three sides of the rise with the north side protected by a steep slope. In the center of the square stood Harold and his brothers. It was a formidable position, one most difficult to approach with mounted troops. Harold felt confident. He had great faith in his axe-men. Furthermore, he had just had a great victory at Stamford bridge.

William first sent his infantry and archers against the English. The infantry could not dent the massed and shielded phalanx. The archers had difficulty in hitting their targets as they were forced to shoot up-hill. Many of their arrows glanced off the shields of the Saxons or went over their heads.

Meanwhile his cavalry stood in readiness with the Normans in the middle, the Bretons on the left and a miscellany of adventurers on the right. William was at the head of his Normans with a holy talisman around his neck and the papal banner above his head. At first the cavalry could not penetrate the solid English formation. Furious fighting took place on the periphery. It is believed Harold's brothers fell in these skirmishes. At this point the left wing of William's army took flight and a section of Harold's army, tasting victory, broke the ranks in hot pursuit. William rallied his Normans and cut them to pieces. There followed two feigned retreats by the Normans with the Saxons again in pursuit, thus breaking up the English ranks. Once the English dispersed they were at the mercy of the mounted warriors.

William next ordered his archers to lob their arrows from above into the English ranks. One of the arrows hit Harold in the eye. When the Saxons saw their stricken leader they panicked and ran down the hill where they were confronted by the Norman knights. The flight became general and the battle turned into a slaughter. The wounded Harold was apparently dismembered by the sword wielding horsemen so that it was almost impossible to piece together his body for burial.

Many of Harold's army hid in the woods from where they harrassed the Normans. William camped the night on the hill among the slaughtered. He distinguished himself in the battle. Three times he was unhorsed. At one time near panic reigned in the Norman ranks when rumor spread he had been killed. William doffed his helmet so all could see and thus rallied his troops.

William proceeded to London where he was crowned king of England on Christmas day 1066 at Westminster. He quickly consolidated his power south of the Humber river. But in Northumbria he had to deal with the powerful Saxon lords, Edwin and Morcar, who refused to recognize him. Eventually he subdued all of the Saxon chiefs and placed his followers on their lands as vassals of a feudalized England. Norman influence spread everywhere and onto everything, language, law, manners, architecture and other aspects of life.

In retrospect the outcome at Hastings was predictable. The Saxons had many advantages. They outnumbered the enemy; had a commanding position on the hill of Senlac, were defending their homeland, had in Harold a great commander and were flushed with their victory at Stamford bridge. But the Normans had the superior military technology. It was the case of the Norman knight against the Saxon axe-man. It was eleventh versus seventh century warfare. It was not that the English did not know the stirrup. But unlike the Carolingians they did not know its potential and never put it to effective use in warfare. For that they paid a heavy price of extinction in history.

The Normans, profiting by propinquity, learned the technology and social order of feudalism well from the Franks. This was not the first or the last time the channel proved to be a formidable barrier in history. In fact, the Normans became the foremost knights of the eleventh century. William, in particular, was a great warrior. There is some obscurity about his leadership at Hastings. Most historians conclude that the first retreat of his left wing was the result of panic, not design, though they accept that the next two feigned retreats were premeditated. It is entirely possible the Normans were familiar with feigned retreat in cavalry warfare from their experience in Sicily and the Holy Land. Feigned retreat was familiar practice in the East for more than a thousand years. The Scythians, the first horsemen, used it against the Persians. The Parthians resorted to it against the Romans in the Battle of Carrhae a thousand years before Hastings. Not only were the Saxons closely massed but they were on top of a hill. Feigned retreat was precisely the order of the day in such situation.

But battles are notoriously messy. Men panic. Primates are biologically structured to flee from danger to their lives. That is why man had to devise the cult of bravery and cowardice for his conflicts for domination. Thus William's warriors of his left wing may have panicked and fled when the going was rough. Anyway, William's superb generalship turned it to his advantage and it was the beginning of the breakup of the Saxon ranks so that his Norman knights could exercise their military advantage in the battle.

For five centuries or so the medieval knight dominated the conflicts of man in Europe. Greek mythology conjured up the Centaur; medievel technology gave the Centaur incarnation with the invention of the stirrup. The stirrup made man and horse one; the result was the mounted armored knight, the most effective war machine of the time.

BATTLES OF TABASCO, TLAXCALA, TENOCHTITLAN 1519–21 A. D.

By the middle of the present millennium two technological innovations occurred which were to determine one of the most dramatic episodes of the domination of man by man in the history of the earth to date. It was the complete subjection, near annihilation, of the societies of the western hemisphere by the men of Europe. The civilizations of the western hemisphere had no communication with those of the Euro-Asian continent because the technological development of man up to that time was not sufficiently advanced to bridge the two oceans that separated them. Consequently, there was not the normal transmission of technology that transpired regularly between the societies of the great Euro-Asian land mass constantly narrowing the technological gap between the most and least creative among them. The result was that when the two made contact the civilizations of the western hemisphere lagged their fellowmen in the rest of the world by a millennium or more in technological development. The outcome of the contact, when it came, was disastrous for them.

The two technological innovations were interdependent. The first was the development of the full rigged deep keeled ship that could tack into the wind and serve as a sturdy platform for the newly developed cannon. The second was gunpowder which could impart greater energy to a missile than theretofore possible and deliver death and destruction from a considerable distance. The harnessing of the wind for navigation has already been discussed in Chapter V. Gunpowder was a Chinese invention and was transmitted to Europe in the 14th century.

Saltpeter (potassium nitrate) was mixed with sulphur to create an explosive chemical composition in China before 1200 A. D. But the Chinese used it mainly for ceremonial and amusement purposes in the form of firecrackers. Some use was made of it in warfare in the form of bamboo mortars and grenades. It was doubltess transmitted to Europe by the Mongols where it was quickly developed into a major weapon of war. By 1325 cannon was in use in Europe. Shortly thereafter handguns or firearms were invented. Europe was deficient in the production of saltpeter and had to depend upon imports from India. This impeded, at first, the development of cannon and firearms, but by the 15th century they were in full use.

Gunpowder did not, however, revolutionize warfare immediately. It was only one of the means of warfare. In fact, the highest development of the crossbow, another Chinese invention, occurred only after the introduction of gunpowder. Mounted shock combat was not foresaken either and lasted well into the 17th century. Thus, in the 1500's, European warfare consisted of a great variety of weaponry from the mounted cavalier to the cross-bow to the gun and cannon.

In 1942 Columbus discovered the western hemisphere sailing three of the new ships, for the first time, across the mid-Atlantic. He was the first European of record to make contact with this unknown sector of humanity whom he mistakenly called Indians thinking he had circumnavigated the world and landed in India. In fact, it took the Europeans years to realize there was a considerable land mass between Europe and India across the ocean to the west. In the next two decades the Spaniards developed a substantial colonial empire called Hispaniola in the Caribbean area with its capital in Santo Domingo. Cuba, the biggest island in the area, was quite heavily settled, with ranches, plantations and mines, by the second decade of the 16th century and the stage was set for a thrust onto the mainland.

The first contact with the mainland was made by Cordoba in 1517. He sailed past the Yucatan peninsula with three ships, 110 men, as far as Champoton. He returned with tales of fierce warriors, pyramids and gold. It fired the imagination of the men of Hispaniola. Valasquez, the governor of Cuba, fitted out an expedition under Grijalva who explored the gulf in 1518. At Champoton Grijalva had to fight a large army of Indians but at Tabasco he was warmly received. He returned with more imaginative and titillating reports—and 20,000 pesos worth of gold! Cuba was now afire with enthusiasm for a greater expedition and the man destined to lead it was Hernando Cortés.

In 1519 Cortés had already been in Hispaniola for 14 years. He left Spain in 1504 in his 19th year, having dropped his study of law for the life of an adventurer in the New World. In his early 30's, now a rich owner of plantations and mines in Cuba, he was married to Catalina Juarez making him a brother in law of Governor Valesquez. He was twice elected mayor of Santiago. He was by this time thoroughly conversant with the effervescent politics of Cuba and was able to manipulate the situation to have himself designated to head the expedition. The fact that he staked his wealth on the venture carried great weight. Velasquez, however, did not trust him and it took a bit of maneuvering to prevent the governor from withholding the commission. Velasquez would have like to head the expedition himself but he was too fat for the physical vigor required and too miserly to stake his fortune on the undertaking.

Cortés sailed on February 10, 1519. He had 11 ships of 70–100 tons, 509 soldiers, about 100 sailors and, most important, 16 horses and mares. His weapons consisted of 32 cross-bows, 13 muskets, 4 falconets (small cannon), a few heavy brass guns and a great store of powder and balls. The cavaliers and soldiers had armor and steel lances and swords. Also included were 200 Carib Indians, several negroes and some Indian women.

Among his soldiers was one Bernal Diaz del Castillo who in his later years was to chronicle the expedition of Cortés. He had already accompanied Cordoba and Grijalva on the earlier excursions. Bernal Diaz's account engagingly written, together with that of Francisco Lopez de Gomara, who was never in the New World let alone on the expedition but was Cortés's chaplain and secretary in Spain, comprise the main sources on this historical episode. Both are now translated into English. William H. Prescott, the near blind American lawyer, relied primarily on Bernal Diaz and Gomara for his comprehensive and authoratative *Conquest of Mexico* published in 1856. It remains the prime historical account of the fascinating event.

The Cortés expedition mustered on the island of Cozumel on the east coast of Yucatan, rounded Cape Catoche and headed for Tabasco where they expected a friendly reception as Grijalva had got the year before. Instead they were met with arrows and javelins even before they anchored at the mouth of the Tabasco river. The next day, March 14, 1519, Cortés fought his first battle on the plain near the city.

Twelve thousand warriors surrounded the Spaniards. Point blank cannon fire was leveled at the massed warriors and as they fell back the Spaniards pursued them with swords. At this point Cortés entered the battle with his cavalry of 14 horsemen which frightened and panicked the Indians. He had been detained by some swampy terrain. Bernal Diaz reports they thought that horse and man were one, never having seen a horse before. Soon 800 Indians lay dead, thousands of the stricken were carried away by the warriors and the remainder fled in terror. Cortés had won easily his first big battle at Tabasco with the Indians.

The Battle of Tabasco was not only the first but perhaps a most significant one in the entire campaign. First, it demonstrated to the Spaniards that with cannon and horses they could readily defeat large contingents of Indian warriors. More important, however, was the impact of the defeat on the Indians. Cortés was not yet in the realm of the Aztecs but still in the land of the ancient Mayas over whom the Aztecs now exercised hegemony. The

Aztecs had a system of communication whereby artists would depict a scene on cloth—a pictograph—and transmit it to the capital in a few days time. The Spaniards were somewhat aware of the Aztec pictograph from previous contacts even before they knew of the Aztecs. Thus reports of the defeat were well on their way to Mexico including, to be sure, depiction of the mounted Spanish warrior. When Cortés demanded tribute in gold from the defeated Tabascans he was told that most gold was to be found in Mexico. He and his followers were now growing dimly aware of a vast empire further inland and determined to find it.

Two more important developments transpired at Tabasco. When Cortés assembled the defeated caciques (local chiefs or lords) after the battle he decided on a demonstration to impress them, once again, with the prowess of Spanish arms. He stationed one of the mares which had just foaled in a thicket behind the site where the caciques would be assembled and he positioned a loaded falconet to the side of the site. At a signal, after the caciques were before him, he had a soldier set off the charge resulting in a thunderous roar and belching of sulphurous smoke from the cannon. The caciques were paralyzed with fright. Then a big virile stallion was brought before the caciques. When the stallion got the scent of the mare hidden behind the caciques he began to snort and paw the ground furiously creating even greater fright among the assembled chiefs. One can be sure that pictographs of the scene were on their way to Mexico very soon. Whether Cortés understood at this time the scope of the impact of the demonstration it was nonetheless a superb bit of psychological warfare.

The other development was the acquisition of a very competent interpreter without which the expedition would have been sorely handicapped. As part of the spoils of battle the Tabascans gave Cortés 20 Indian maidens, among them was the beautiful and brilliant girl Marina (her Christian name after baptism) who spoke the Aztec and Maya languages. Earlier Cortés, while mustering at Cozumel, ransomed a Spaniard named Auguilar who had been enslaved by the Indians on Yucatan when he was shipwrecked on the penninsula nine years earlier. He had while so enslaved learned the language of the Mayas. Through Auguilar and Marina, Cortés could now communicate with the Aztecs.

Marina was of royal blood. Her mother sold her into slavery while still a child when she wished to remarry after her father's death. Marina was more than an interpreter. She very quickly learned Spanish, became an important advisor on the Aztecs, uncovered several of their treacheries and accompanied Cortés through thick and thin of every battle. She was also a companion of his bed and bore him a son who later became a person of standing in Spain. The Aztecs were unable to pronounce r's, so they called her Malina. Since Cortés could communicate only through her he was called Malinche, meaning Marina's lord or master.

Regarding Indian women, Cortés' commission provided that he was to prohibit marriage or other cohabitation with them, mainly because they were not Christians. Cortés solved the problem by baptising them. This took care of the issue of sex that always preoccupied armies on foreign expeditions.

Cortés proceeded up the gulf and established a settlement at Vera Cruz from where he planned to explore the interior. There an embassy from the capital awaited him.

Who were the Aztecs. They had just extended their power over the area now covered by Mexico, Guatemala and the Yucatan penninsula. Their origin is obscure but they are believed to have been a nomadic tribe from the north that settled in the Mexican valley around the 10th century. They mixed not only genes but culture with the people residing there and adopted much of their religion and mythology. Pertinent to our story is the God/man Quetzalcoatl who was the messiah of Aztec religious orthodoxy. Quetzalcoatl ruled the Aztecs during their golden age and then left, or was driven away by the priests, to the east across the gulf to some land beyond the sea from where he was to return with his sons to rule once again over the Aztecs. Quetzalcoatl was described by the oracles as tall, fair skinned and heavily bearded and wearing a helmet much like the knights of Europe. The description fitted the Spaniards. The chief deity of the Aztecs, however, was Huitzilopotchli, the war god, who was constantly propitiated by human sacrifice, preferably enemy warriors captured in war. There were many other gods in the Aztec pantheon of no great importance to our story.

The Aztecs were well organized, had a prosperous agriculture, a highly developed culture and cuisine, and capable of great artistry with precious metals, gems and feathers. They possessed fairly good knowledge of astronomy, chronology and mathematics. They were even familiar with the concept of zero. Technologically, however, they were extremely deficient. They had no knowledge of the hard metals. They possessed no mechanical skills—they did not even use the wheel. They had no domesticated animals for power. Their navigational skill did not extend beyond the canoe. In warfare they fought only with spears tipped with obsidian or copper. They used stone slings and bows and arrows. Their bows were not, however, of the calibre of the laminated wood and horn bows of the East. They had a rather fearsome war club studded with serrated obsidian. Also a long spear tipped with copper that Cortés found useful for his purposes.

The myth of Quetzalcoatl added considerably to the success of the expedition. Many Indians were convinced Cortés and his Spaniards were the sons of Quetzalcoatl returning to Mexico to rule over them. But as is probably the case of all messiahs there was no universal recognition or acclaim of Cortés as Quetzalcoatl. The old caciques, as we shall see, were more convinced than the young warriors. Though there is no record of it the priests were doubtless the prime rejectors as their power might be undermined by the return of Quetzalcoatl, particularly, when the pretender was propagandizing a new religion that worshipped only a wooden cross and the image of a woman with a child. Montezuma in his dual role as king and priest could not be sure so he waffled and procrastinated.

Cortés was propitiated with gold but Montezuma would not invite him to his capital at Tenochtitlan. It seems Montezuma hoped Cortés would leave the country when satisfied with plenty of gold and thus relieve him of the difficult decision of recognizing or disavowing Cortés as the son of Quetzalcoatl. Had Cortés been less purblind about his own religion and appreciated better the myth of Quetzalcoatl he could have proclaimed himself the Aztec messiah and the conquest of Mexico might have been attained without a struggle. Then after a few years of consolidation of power against the entrenched priesthood he could have converted the Aztecs to Christianity with ease.

After consolidating his position on the coast with the establishment of the Vera Cruz settlement and winning as allies the nearby Cempoallans Cortés set out for Tenochtitlan. By now Cortés discovered another weakness of the Aztecs; that they were hated by their subject peoples and many were ready to revolt. Cortés hoped he could also win as allies the Tlaxcalans who the Aztecs could not subdue and whose territory he would cross on his way to Tenochtitlan.

Many of his men did not want to undertake the hazardous expedition. They learned they would have to cross deserts, traverse mountains and pass through lands of possibly hostile Indians. They were in favor of returning to Cuba as, by now, they had acquired a considerable store of gold. Cortés then took a desperate step and destroyed his ships so the men would have no way of leaving Mexico. But before he did so he presciently removed and stored at Vera Cruz all of the ships sails, fittings, hardware and other materials. This was to prove important, as we shall see, in the final Battle of Tenochtitlan. This step also freed the 100 sailors for duty on land. Leaving 200 soldiers or so to garrison Vera Cruz Cortés departed with about 400 men, 15 horses, 7 pieces of artillery and a number of firearms and crossbows. He had also 1300 Indian warriors and 1000 Indian porters to drag the guns and carry the baggage.

The Tlaxcalans unfortunately proved extremely hostile. They were led by Xicotencatl, a young cacique who remained unconvinced that the Spaniards were the sons of Quetzalcoatl. He was anxious to prove that they were mere mortals and not gods. The first encounter was with about 6000 warriors who were quickly put to flight by artillery, muskets and cross bows. The major Battle of Tlaxcala came a few days later on September 5, 1519 when Cortés resumed his march to Tenochtitlan. They routed again some 6000 warriors who first obstructed the march and when they emerged from a ravine into a large open field about 6 miles long they saw arrayed before them Xicotencatl with an army of some 40,000 warriors. This, of course, was a mistake on the part of the young cacique, inexperienced as he necessarily was in European warfare, for such open field was most advantageous terrain for cavalry and artillery. The artillery mowed them down mercilessly in this open massed formation. Under the Indian military code the killed and wounded had to be carried from the field of battle—doubtless born out of the nefarious practice that captives in war were sacrificed to the war god—and soon most of the Tlaxcalan warriors were engaged in carrying away their casualties. Here the Spanish horsemen inflicted additional damage with their steel swords as they found their enemy in this compromising position. But the Tlaxcalans fought bravely and ferociously. A peculiar incident occurred in the midst of battle. The Tlaxcalans ganged up on one of the horses and severed its head. Then they dragged the dead horse behind their line, cut it to pieces and sent the pieces for exhibition around the country. Apparently this was done to demonstrate to the people that the horses of the invaders were mortal and not supernatural beings. It was probably an inspiration of the young cacique who refused to believe Cortés was the Indian messiah. It did deprive Cortés, nonetheless, of a valuable horse and reduced his cavalry to 14.

Xicotencatl made one more assault—this time at night. The Indians did not normally fight at night but the priests advised it on the premise that the Spaniards prowess was not effective in the dark. Cortés learned about it in advance through his spies and the assault resulted in another disaster for the young cacique.

Xicotencatl finally capitulated and the Spaniards were welcomed into the capital city of Tlaxcala. The old caciques, Maxima, the head man, and Xicotencatl's father were differently disposed toward Cortés—they apparently accepted him as Quetzalcoatl. In fact, both became Christians within a year. This proved a major breakthrough for the missionary aspect of the expedition. The Tlaxcalans now became steadfast allies of the Spaniards. It was natural for them as the Aztecs were their historical enemies. They proved immensely valuable to Cortés in his final assault on Tenochtitlan two years later. But in the interim the young Xicotencatl was to give Cortés more trouble.

Montezuma's hope that the fierce Tlaxcalans would do away with the Spaniards were not only dashed but the two were now allies. At the ancient city of Cholula he prepared a trap for the invaders. He had the Cholulans invite them into the city where these allies, with the help of his Mexican warriors, would annihilate them. But Marina uncovered the plot and Cortés nearly demolished the ancient city with cannon. The Spaniards killed countless Cholulans.

Cortés now had to traverse the mountains and he chose a route between the twin volcanoes of Iztaccihuatl and Popocatepetl. These peaks rise some 9000 feet above the plain that itself was about 8000 feet above sea level. A party of Spaniards scaled Popocatepetl, considered the war god's haven, without dire consequences once again impressing the Indians with their fearlessness. As they came out of the mountains Montezuma again tried to divert them onto a route where his Mexicans laid in ambush. But through the good intelligence provided by his Indian allies Cortés avoided the trap. Montezuma was apparently now convinced that Cortés was indeed possessed of powers of divination.

He was finally of the mind to invite Cortés into the capital and sent him a message to that effect. He sent his nephew Cacama, the cacique of Texcoco, a city on the other side of the lake from the capital, to meet Cortés as he approached Lake Chalco. The Spaniards for the first time saw the fabulous cities built on water that they had been hearing of.

Tenochtitlan, the capital, was built on an island situated in the southwest end of a crescent shaped Lake Texcoco. At the southern end it connected with Lake Chalco and in the north with Lake Zumpango. A dike five miles long was constructed a mile or so east of the capital to control the water during periods of heavy rains.

Tenochtitlan was connected with the mainland by three main causeways. To the west the Tacuba causeway, the shortest, was about two miles long. The Tepeyac causeway, to the north, was a bit longer. The one to the south, the Iztapalapan causeway, ran due west for two miles to the suburb of Xoloc and then turned north for three miles to Tenochtitlan. These causeways were about 15 feet wide intersected by many canals, with bridges, in the central city. The inner city had both streets and canals as thoroughfares. The three causeways comprised the main streets intersecting the main square where stood the palaces and the great temple (called Teocalli). To the northwest from the main square stood the market place of Tlatelolco which was to prove the site of the demise of the Aztecs. The Spaniards had never seen anything like it. It must have been the most impregnable fortress in the world.

This time, however, the Spaniards did not have to fight for it. They were met instead by Montezuma himself as they reached the outskirts of Tenochtitlan along the Iztapalapan causeway and escorted to the palace of Axayacatl in the main square across from the great Teocalli. This palace was in a large walled compound where Cortés could lodge his Spaniards, the horses and his Indian allies. It was now November 8, 1519. That evening the Spaniards celebrated with a cannon bombardment that reverberated through the streets of the capital.

Montezuma's behavior throughout is an enigma. He constantly vacillated between the warrior and the priest within him. But Cortés singleness of purpose, his ability to anticipate events, particularly Montezuma's treacheries, and those awful horses and cannon apparently tipped his thinking favorably toward Cortés. He must have been opposed strongly by the priests and many of the young warriors under their influence. But history does not record the Aztec version of the conquest nor the private thinking of their emperor. There can be little doubt that in his welcoming speech Montezuma acknowledges Cortés as Quetzalcoatl or the son of Quetzalcoatl. Montezuma, of course, may have been deceitful again. He did however, like and admire Cortés.

Cortés was uneasy about his situation. He fortified the Axayacatl palace and compound with his artillery and firearms and kept his men under constant vigilence. But he realized that he was in a trap. The Mexicans could deny him food and water and his army would perish.

He now decided upon a desperate move of making Montezuma his prisoner and, in this respect, Montezuma played into his hands. He instigated a revolt against the Spaniards at Vera Cruz. When Cortés learned of it he requested Montezuma to summon the cacique from the coast who assaulted the Spaniards and he asked him, under threat of force, to place himself and his court under Cortés in the palace of Axayacatl. Surprisingly Montezuma complied and when the cacique was brought before Cortés he was adjudged guilty and ordered burned at the stake in orthodox Spanish inquisition manner. But before he died he disclosed he was acting under orders from Montezuma. Cortés then placed Montezuma in chains for this complicity. This ruthless and insousciant action on the part of Cortés greatly offended the Aztecs and compromised Montezuma without the possibility of redemption with his people. They viewed the burning at the stake as a vile act of inhumanity and vowed, overlooking their own barbarity, to sacrifice Cortés and his men to Huitzilopotchli by cutting out their hearts on the sacrificial stone. A revolt of sorts was nipped in the bud by Cortés, with Montezuma's help, ending up in the imprisonment of its leader Cacama and several other caciques.

At this point Montezuma declared himself and the Aztecs vassals of emperor Charles of Spain, whom he recognized as Quetzalcoatl and Cortés as his son or representative. He turned over all the gold in his palace and ordered his subjects to do likewise. He refused, however, to convert to Christianity. Cortés felt he had now to attack the priests and he even forced them to set up a cross and alter in the great Teocalli. This was unwise to say the least. Attacking a peoples religion is like kicking them in the solar plexis; the more so, the more primitive and uncivilized they may be. The priests must now have really exercised every influence they had with their people against the Spaniards.

Trouble arose for Cortés from another quarter. Before his march to Mexico Cortés saved one of the ships and dispatched it with plenty of gold directly to Spain in an attempt to derive his authority straight from the crown. Valesquez was enraged by this circumvention of his commission and sent Narvaez with a force of 800 men, 80 horses, 80 arquebuses (large muskets fired from a bipod), 30 cross-bows—a formidable army—to arrest Cortés and bring him back to Cuba in irons. Cortés quickly left Tenochtitlan leaving Alvarado in charge with 100 men and instructions not to let Montezuma and the five caciques to escape the palace. Cortés outwitted the arrogant but feckless Narvaez and took over his army. Narvaez was imprisoned at Vera Cruz.

Real trouble, meanwhile, was brewing in the capital. The crisis was precipitated by an unprovoked massacre on a harvest festival and dance in the great square in which many of the Aztec elite including some caciques were killed. Six Spaniards also lost their lives. Alvarado claimed he had it on good intelligence that the dance was a prelude to a sneak attack on the Axayacatl compound and he had to act to avert the attack. He was probably right as the Aztecs were already mustering for an assault.

Cortés promptly started back to the capital. At Tlaxcala he learned that the Aztecs had his garrison under siege and had shut off their food and water. He now had an even greater force and found no challenge on the causeway in his march to the square. Cortés was furious with Montezuma for failing to order his people to reopen the markets and supply his forces with food. Montezuma pleaded he could do nothing as a prisoner but suggested he release his brother Cuitlahua, one of the imprisoned caciques, the lord of Iztalpalapan who would be able to arrange the food and water supply. Cortés agreed. But this was a mistake for Cuitlahua merely led the assault against the Spaniards. Cortés had at this time the biggest force of his entire expedition—1250 Spaniards, nearly 100 horses, 8000 Tlaxcalans and plenty of gunpowder. He had no difficulty defending the compound even though the walls were breached and buildings fired. As the Aztecs poured through the breaches they were mowed down by artillery and muskets. Cortés counterattacked in the streets but his infantry and cavalry were mercilessly attacked from the house tops and from canoes in the canals. In these straits the cavalry was at a great disadvantage. Cortés even built mobile engines of war to protect his arquebusiers and crossbowmen while they moved down the streets to clear the housetops of warriors. Thousands upon thousands of Indians were killed. But Cortés realized this could get him nowhere. He ordered Montezuma to try to call off the attack. Montezuma complied but pleaded it would do no good. When he mounted the wall the fighting stopped and four caciques came forward to talk. The parley was interrupted with a sudden barrage of stones and arrows. One of the stones hit Montezuma in the head and he died three days later. His death removed a powerful factor operating for the Spaniards. They were now on their own.

Cortés knew that his position had become untenable. He was in a trap. While he could hold off the Aztecs with superior weapons they could deny him food and water. He decided therefore, on a retreat along the Tacuba causeway. It turned out to be something of a disaster. He opted for a night retreat which proved to be a mistake for the Aztecs, as was not their usual practice, decided to fight at night this time. Furthermore, the Spaniards would not leave their store of gold behind, which now amounted to 700,000 pesos worth (about 125 million dollars at todays value of $500 an ounce) and weighed some 8 tons! It required 8 horses and 80 Tlaxcalan porters to carry it.

The Aztecs cut the causeway and attacked the retreating column mercilessly with bows and arrows, slings and spears from canoes. All the gold, artillery and great numbers of Spaniards, Tlaxcalans, horses and supplies were lost in the water and on the causeway. The Spaniards called it the *Noche Triste*—the sorrowful night. It was June 30, 1520. They had by then been camped in the Axayacatl compound for nearly 8 months.

When Cortés finally reached Tacuba he found he had lost some 600 Spaniards, over 2000 Tlaxcalans, 45 horses (he now had only 23 left) and most of his artillery and firearms. Fortunately the invaluable and indomitable Dona Marina survived the disaster. The caciques, held prisoners, including Cacama, the lord of Texcoco, perished in the retreat.

Cortés hastily set out for Tlaxcala around Lake Zumpango and as the Spaniards approached the city of Otumba they ran into an Aztec army of 200,000 warriors massed on a plain outside the city under the new Aztec emperor Cuitlahua, Montezuma's brother. This was a fatal mistake on the part of the new emperor. While deprived of their artillery the Spaniards still had around two dozen horses. Unlike the Tlaxcalans the Aztecs had no idea of the power of mounted shock combat. On the causeways of the capital the cavalry was rendered useless by the narrow ground and slippery pavement. The Spanish horsemen cut the Aztec warriors to pieces. Some 20,000 were killed by charge after charge of the cavaliers. The Spanish infantry which still had their steel swords and could outbattle the Indian warriors followed closely in the devastation. In a bold and masterly stroke Cortés supported by two cavaliers, charged through the mass of Indians and thrust his spear into the Aztec commander. The Aztec army disintegrated thereafter and fled. Cortés was free of harassment on the rest of his march to Tlaxcala. The Battle of Otumba was fought on July 8, 1520.

The Tlaxcalans, fortunately, welcomed the Spaniards and commiserated with them on the disasterous defeat in Tenochtitlan. The young Xicotencatl, however, favored turning against the Spaniards now that their fortunes were low. The old caciques overruled him. The older Xicotencatl said the Aztecs could not be trusted and added "the gods abhor perfidy. And were not their guests the very beings whose coming had been so long predicted by the oracles."

Cortés was permitted to recuperate and rethink his expedition in Tlaxcala. He refused to be dissuaded by his men to abandon the conquest and opted for an assault on the capital as soon as he could regroup and resupply. Here the breaks were to go his way again. A ship sent by Velasquez to Vera Cruz fell into his hands. Also three ships from Jamaica that came to establish a colony. And a ship arrived from the Canaries loaded with arms and military supplies. All this provided Cortés with 150 men, 20 horses and plenty of arms and ammunition. Also on their expedition into the mountains the

Spaniards found sulphur. The deserts had plenty of natural nitrates. They could thus manufacture their own gunpowder.

But Cortés knew by now he could not conduct a successful assault without commanding the waters of Lake Texcoco. The causeways had to be freed of the effective attack by the Aztecs from canoes. Moreover, he could also blockade the city and cut off its food supply by controlling traffic on the lake. He decided therefore, to build a navy! He had among his men a first rate arkwright Martin Lopez and he had stored at Vera Cruz the necessary sails, fittings and supplies that he salvaged from his original ships. He set out to build 13 brigantines with the help of the Tlaxcalans. His plan was to build them in Tlaxcala, then disassemble the wooden components and fittings, carry them by porters 20 leagues (about 50 miles) over the mountains, reassemble them and launch them on Lake Texcoco! A really daring plan, but without which he probably could not conquer the Aztecs. Lopez had already constructed two similar vessels while they were in the capital. Montezuma called them "water houses". Cortés was apprehensive about the possible trap he was in and thought the vessels could be used for evacuation across the lake. The Aztecs, however, burned the ships when they beseiged Alvarado in the palace compound while Cortés was on the coast dealing with the Narvaez threat.

The brigantines were ready by December 1520. Cortés was able to muster 600 Spaniards, 40 horses, 9 cannon and 80 arquebuses and cross bows. He had plenty of gunpowder and balls. In addition he now had nearly 150,000 Indian warriors armed with bows and arrows, long spears and obsidian studded clubs. It was a greater force than he had when he first entered Tenochtitlan.

The Aztecs had a new emperor, who was destined to be their last, named Guatemozin (also Guatemoc, Guatemuza and various other translations). He was a fierce young warrior of 25 married to Montezuma's beautiful daughter. His spies kept him informed on the Spaniards and he was ready for their assault.

Cortés left Tlaxcala on Christmas day 1520. He planned first to neutralize, ally or otherwise secure all the cities around the lakes and to center his activities at Texcoco, across the lake from the capital. He knew he would have 4 months or so for the purpose as it would take that long to reassemble and launch the brigantines. The plan would also keep his soldiers occupied and in training for the assault on Tenochtitlan.

Several favorable developments occurred during this period. First the capture of Texcoco proved easy. The cacique Coanaco fled to the capital and the city was deserted. Cortés installed Cacama's brother Ixtlilxochitl as the lord of Texcoco. This young cacique had an interesting birthright. When he was born the priests advised he be put to death as the stars foretold he would ally himself with their enemies when he grew up. But the old cacique replied that the time was at hand when the sons of Quetzalcoatl were to return and if the Almighty selected his son to cooperate with them "his will would be done." Be that as it may, Ixtlilxochitl proved a great ally of the Spaniards. Not so, however, the young cacique from Tlaxcala Xicoten-catl. He deserted to the Aztecs in the mistaken belief Cortés could not win. Cortés recaptured him and, after consulting with his father who agreed it was treasonable behavior, executed him by hanging. It removed a thorn in the side of his otherwise invaluable alliance of the Tlaxcalans.

While the brigantines were being reassembled 3 vessels arrived at Vera Cruz from Hispaniola to reinforce Cortés. This added 200 men, 70–80 horses and plenty of arms and ammunition. After augmenting the garrison at Vera Cruz Cortés had 818 men, 87 horses, three large cannon, 15 lighter ones, 118 arquebuses and cross bows and adequate supplies of powder, shot and balls for the attack. Cortés however, considered the 13 brigantines the primary factor in the assault for as he states in his third letter to emperor Charles V "I was very anxious that our first encounter should be a victorious one and should be made in such a way that they should be deeply impressed with fear of the launches, *for the launches were the key of the whole war*, and it was on the water where the decision would come" (italics added).

It is somewhat difficult from the historical record to get an exact description of the vessels. They are variously referred to as brigantines, sloops or launches. No weight or dimensions are to be found. But in order to launch them the canal, which took 8000 Indians two months to excavate, on which they were floated from the city of Texcoco to the lake was 12 feet wide and 12 feet deep. It may be concluded from this that the vessels had a draft of about 10 feet and a beam of about 10–12 feet. Such a beam and draft would probably call for an overall length of 35–40 feet. A vessel of these demensions built of heavy timber would displace several tons of water. It could generate considerable power underway at 5–7 knots. From 16th–17th century Spanish paintings and engravings the vessels are depicted as small caravals (they even had poops) with a single mast and a lateen sail. They were equipped with twelve long oars for power when there was no wind.

Bernal Diaz informs us that Cortés placed 12 cross bowmen, musketeers, an artillery man, 12 oarsmen and a captain on each vessel. He adds "Cortés also divided among them all the boat guns and falconets we possessed and the powder he thought they would need." To accommodate such a comple-ment of men and guns required at least a boat of the size deduced above. At any rate, it was far superior to the canoe of the Aztecs.

Cortés' plan of attack called for an approach along the three main causeways and he divided his forces accordingly. Sandoval was to come along the Tepeyac causeway from the north; Alvarado on the Tacuba causeway from the south, and Cortés along the Iztalpalapan causeway from the south. The brigantines were to support them by clearing the canoes from the vicinity of the causeways. But before Cortés gave orders for the march he wanted to impress the Aztecs with the lethal power of his little navy.

As the fleet came into the southern part of the lake a signal was given by Guatemozin from a high rock in the water to launch his canoes to meet the Spaniards. The lake was becalmed at the time and the brigantines had to be rowed. Cortés thought it best to row away from the canoes. Suddenly a strong breeze swept across their poops and Cortés ordered the ships to come about into the wind. The breeze freshened and the brigantines were well underway when they crashed into the Aztec fleet of canoes capsizing them by the score. The water was full of thrashing drowning Indians. To add to their discomfiture the musketeers and crossbowmen showered them with balls and arrows. Thousands perished in the encounter. Cortés achieved his objective. He instilled a high regard of the Aztecs for his brigantines and he won control of the lake. He then assigned 3 or 4 of the vessels to each causeway to support the forces approaching Tenochtitlan along them. It is no wonder that the timely breeze convinced Cortés and his men that God was, indeed, on the side of the Spaniards.

The victory was not to be easy. It would take two months! The Aztecs fought bravely, fully committed to death, in the defense of their capital. Each foot of the causeway had to be contested. The cavalry was not too helpful but the brigantines, by keeping the canoes at bay, proved invaluable. The Aztecs were everywhere—perhaps 100,000 warriors—on the house-tops, bridges and canals from where they directed their stones and arrows. If the Spaniards approached too fast they found the causeways cut behind them. Both Alvarado and Cortés found themselves so trapped. Cortés finally ordered a wholesale destruction of all the buildings along the causeways and the use of the debris to fill gaps and otherwise augment the causeways.

Cortés got another break during the assault. A vessel of Ponce de Leon mistakenly put into Vera Cruz laden with arms, ammunition and stores. It was seized and its cargo promptly forwarded to Mexico.

Toward the end of July the Aztecs were cornered in the northwest section of the island between the Tacuba and Tepeyac causeways. They were without water as Cortés cut the acqueducts early in the assault. Food was denied them as the brigantines imposed a complete blockade of the city. The Aztecs were reduced to eating rats and roots and drinking brackish water. Thousands were dying of malnutrition and disease. But they fought on defiant as ever. The priests kept sacrificing the captured Spaniards in full view of the attackers from the tops of their pyramided temples in the customary gruesome manner of cutting out their hearts while holding them supine on the sacrificial stone. This both enraged and scared the Spaniards who could only mumble "there but for the grace of God am I."

Cortés made a final devastating attack from both the causeways and the brigantines leveling the quarter where the Aztecs made their last stand. Guatemozin tried to escape in a canoe but was captured by one of the brigantines. He was later hanged. It was only on August 13, 1521, two months after the start, that the attack on the capital came to its final end.

Tenochtitlan was completely leveled. Only about 50,000 of its population of some 300,000 were alive.

Cortés decided to rebuild rather than abandon the capital. This was doubless a wise move in view of the Aztec refusal to acknowledge defeat. A Cathedral was built where the great Teocalli formerly stood. The alter replaced the sacrificial stone. The palaces were replaced by great stone manor houses of the new Spanish nobility. Mexico henceforth became a Latin and Christian state.

The Aztecs fought with great courage and dedication. They had religious zeal and faith in their gods. They loved their country and had plenty of nationalistic fervor. And they teemed with machismo. So, they were not inferior to the Spaniards. They had but one deficiency—they were technologically inferior to the men from Europe. They were at least a thousand years behind in this respect.

In fact, the Aztecs had a fortress the likes of which has probably not been erected by men before or after. Their capital was built on water and accessible only by three causeways two to three miles long! Had it been otherwise; had Cortés been able to engage the Aztecs on an open field—all 100,000 warriors—he could have defeated them in a day—perhaps two—with his cavalry and artillery. The Battle of Otumba bears out this conclusion, as do the Battles of Tabasco and Tlaxcala.

It could be argued that had the Spaniards been unable to achieve an alliance with the Tlaxcalans and other subject peoples of the Aztecs they could not have overwhelmed them. It should be immediately noted that this valuable alliance was the result of their great victory in the Battle of Tlaxcala made possible by cavalry and artillery. It might be contended that the victory of Cortés resulted from the myth of Quetzalcoatl. But Cortés pretty much negated this favorable factor with his purblind Christianity. His missionary zeal had constantly to be checked and slowed by Father Olmeda. Had he not attacked the Aztec religion so frontally he might have subdued the Aztecs more readily. But hardly anyone can fault Cortés in this respect, as the gruesome human sacrifice *cum* cannibalism, which was the bed rock of the Aztec religion, was abhorrent and repellent to a civilized man. It cannot be gainsaid therefore, that it was the technological superiority of the Spaniards that made the conquest of Mexico possible.

The story of the conquest is almost unbelievable. That the Spaniards, never more than 1200 men with never more than 100 horses and 100 muskets and cross bows and less than a score of cannon could conquer a nation of millions with a virtually impregnable fortress for a capital strains credulity. No novelist could have conjured up a more complex and fascinating plot.

A similar and equally incredulous story transpired a decade or so later in the conquest of Peru. It was, however, more sordid. The conquistador in this episode was Francisco Pizarro. Unlike Cortés he was of lowly antecedents. An illegitimate child of poor parentage he grew up as a swineherd. He could not read or write. Yet he attained knighthood and, prior to his assassination in 1541, was the undisputed master of an Andean empire stretching from Ecuador to Chile. It too was a feat attributable mainly to the superior technology of the conquerors.

Pizarro had only 180 men, 27 horses and some cannon, arquebuses and cross bows. He too was favored with a messiah myth of "white men with beards" coming to rule the Incas. Moreover his campaign came at a time the Incas were involved in a civil war of succession. Pizarro captured Atahuallpa the Inca (in emulation of Cortés) who offered to fill the 17 by 22 foot room in which he was imprisoned as high as he could reach with gold artifacts and two adjoining smaller rooms with silver ornaments in a like manner. After collecting some 15 tons of gold and 130 tons of silver for the Spaniards Pizarro had Atahaullpa garroted. At Cuzco, the Inca capital, the Spaniards plundered a like amount of gold and silver. But the greatest asset was the discovery of Potosi, doubtless the most bountiful silver mine of history, some 600 miles southeast of Cuzco. More on the fabulous Potosi in Chapter VII. The conquest of Peru is as fascinating, though less palatable, as that of Mexico but in the interest of brevity it will not be detailed here.

The messiah myths of both peoples doubtless facilitated the Spanish conquests. But it was the energy and power manifested by their superior technology that gave these myths reality to the Indians. One can be sure that had the Spaniards come barehanded their white faces and beards would have proved insufficient to dominate these powerful empires.

In North America the same thing happened, but here the process of domination took centuries, not a few years. The quest was for land not gold, as there was no gold. The Indians were less developed cuturally and lived in small scattered tribes. There were no great empires like the Mayas, Aztecs and Incas of central and south America. There was, however, a highly developed society on the Mississippi river called Cahokia (near east St. Louis) that flourished between 900-1000 A. D. But it had vanished by the time of the advent of the Europeans. A well developed society, the Pueblo, also existed in the southwest. There were no great battles but countless skirmishes in which many Europeans were killed. But it was the gun against the bow and arrow so that the outcome was a foregone conclusion. The Indians did not give up the land readily and the settlers had to be constantly armed. The result was such anomalies as the early Virginians attending church services with a musket by their sides. The vestiges of this early conflict with the Indians may be the reason the Americans are such gun toting people today. During the 19th century, after the Indians acquired the horse and firearms, some serious battles were fought with the U. S. army. The most famous, is, perhaps, the Battle of Little Bighorn, which was fought in southern Montana on June 25–26, 1876. In a surprise attack General Custer and 264 of his men were killed by Sioux Indians who refused to stay on their reservation. But as in the case of the Aztecs and Incas, the north American Indians were doomed because of their inferior technology.

The north Europeans who conquered the north American continent were differently motivated than the Spanish and Portuguese. The latter enslaved the Indian and made him work the land for them on large estates and plantations. The north European eliminated the Indians from the land he coveted and worked it himself. Consequently north America was always a labor shortage economy causing the north American to invent and develop machines to do the work. This major difference in colonial policy is, perhaps the primary reason the north Americans industrialized so rapidly in the 19th century while central and south America remained underindustrialized.

How many Indians lost their lives in the European takeover of their homelands is not definitely known. Estimates of population in the western hemisphere before the European advent vary considerably with the figures of 15–20 million most readily agreed upon. About one million were in north America, 7 million in Mexico and central America and 10 million in south America. These figures may be too low as allowance should be made for the uneasy consciences of the demographers, decendents of the European conquerors, making the estimates. By the early 17th century only about 2 million Indians remained in Mexico. In 1910 there were only 220,000 Indians in the United States. The Incas too were believed to have been reduced to half or so by the Spanish conquest. Some prefer to refer to the European domination of the Indians as genocide. While the Indians remain, particularly in central and south America, as a depressed people in the substrata of the American societies their past cultures have been virtually obliterated. If it is not genocide it is certainly (if one can be permitted to coin a word) sociocide.

BATTLE OF SURIGAO STRAIT AND HIROSHIMA, 1944–45 A. D.

In the ensuing centuries man's technological development grew hyperbolically. Cortés' little gun platforms, the brigantines, grew into the 50,000 ton dreadnaughts of the 20th century capable of supporting many cannon with 16″ calibre, firing armor piercing high explosive shells at targets 20 miles away or more. On land, motorized armored vehicles and tanks replaced the horse. Missiles with terrifying energy could now be delivered over extremely long distance. War between men became more devastating and destructive than ever. More than 50 million lives were lost in the decade or so preceding mid-20th century. But as always technological superiority was the chief ingredient for victory.

The capacity to manifest the superior technology became ever more important as the means of warfare became more complex and costly. A nation had to possess the wealth, now called industrial capacity, to produce sufficient amounts of the superior armaments in order to prevail over other nations. This of course, has always been true. When the production of wealth was primarily agriculture Charles Martel had to use land grants to support his new type of warfare, the mounted warrior. As technology became more intricate a nation had to develop industrial capacity to support the new mechanized warfare.

Nowhere has this tenet been better manifested than in the recent conflict between Japan and the United States. Japan was first defeated in the Pacific by the superior naval technology and industrial might of the Americans. The *coup de grace* was later administered at Hiroshima when the United States dropped the first atom bomb on that city. This constituted a monumental technological breakthrough for mankind in it's command over the fundamental energy of the universe.

The war started with Japan's attack on the American navy at Pearl Harbor on December 7, 1941. President Roosevelt called it an "act that would live in infamy." It is more likely to go down in history as the greatest miscalculation of power of all times. Japan had at that time an industrial structure based on an annual steel production capacity of 4 million tons. The United States industrial might was based on 80 million tons of steel production! Moreover Japan had to import all or most of the iron ore and petroleum needed to support its meagre industrial capacity which, as will be seen later, made its strength extremely vulnerable to the enemy.

At the start of the war the technological superiority of the Americans was not readily visible. The United States had for two decades allocated very little of its wealth to armaments. The Japanese had meanwhile acquired the latest technology from Europe and America with which they built a first rate navy. They had under construction in 1941 two of the largest battleships in the world—the Yamato and Musashi—displacing 68,000 tons and carrying nine 18″ guns. These dreadnaughts could do 27 knots. They had modern carriers and well trained pilots. Realizing or sensing that perhaps they lacked strength in depth they decided to knock out the American navy in one swift surprise attack. The attack on Pearl Harbor sank or crippled most of the American battleships, but the aircraft carriers were at sea at the time and thus averted similar fate. The attack, however, did set back the American counter-attack by a couple of years.

Japan followed Pearl Harbor with quick and successful thrusts in the south Pacific, conquering the Philippines, Indonesia, Singapore, Malaysia, Thailand and Burma. The new Japanese empire was called the Asia co-prosperity sphere. Japan needed desperately the resources of this area, particularly the petroleum of Borneo, Java and the Philippines.

The crippled American navy undertook to check the Japanese thrust toward New Guinea, and possibly Australia, during 1942–43 and several important naval engagements occurred in Melanesia. At this time Japan had a technological advantage in a superior torpedo driven by oxygen giving it greater speed and range. American torpedoes were still propelled by compressed air. The Japanese torpedoes had a range of 22,000 yards at 49 knots and 44,000 yards at 36 knots! In the Savo island battle they provided the margin for victory. In the north Pacific the weakened American navy was able to prevent the Japanese navy from taking Midway. Midway was the haven for the American carriers that were used to bomb Tokyo. The attack was made on June 4, 1942. Both fleets were involved *en masse*. The Americans had radar detection by now and they had their planes in the air before the Japanese fleet struck.

During 1942–43 the Americans directed their technology and industry with undivided attention toward war and soon perfected radar, first for detection and later for fire control. Radar is a contraction for radio detecting and ranging. American and European naval scientists were experimenting with radar already in the mid 1930's. In the late summer of 1933 Dr. Rudolf Kuhnhold of Germany achieved a radar echo return from a small surface vessel eight miles out at sea. In December, 1934 U. S. naval research teams achieved a 3 mile return from an aircraft. The U. S. navy was able to build upon this early research when the war commenced and it was given ample funds for radar development. Shortly after Pearl Harbor the navy was being fitted with radar detection for both surface and aerial purposes.

This was a stunning and demoralizing blow to the Japanese sailors. They always had supreme confidence in their prowess in night combat. They felt they could detect enemy ships first and launch their superior torpedoes for the decisive blow before the enemy was aware of their presence. Now they were detected even on the clearest night while it was still impossible for them to view the enemy with their best optical instruments. And worse yet, they were not even immune in zero visibility. They were now at the mercy of the enemy's radar.

Already in 1943 the advantage of radar was decisive in many instances. On August 6, 1943, for example, Rear Admiral Sugiura was convoying a proposed landing of 900 Japanese soldiers together with supplies on Kolombangara in the Solomon islands with four destroyers. It was 2330 and a black night. Visibility was only about two miles—an otherwise ideal situation for the landing. The convoy was detected with radar by four American destroyers which launched their torpedoes before the Japanese sailors were aware of them. Three of the Japanese destroyers were sunk. Only the Shigure, last in line, escaped. We will hear of this ship again in the Battle of Surigao Strait. Fifteen hundred or more Japanese sailors and soldiers were floundering in the sea too far from land to swim ashore. When the Americans offered them life lines they defiantly rejected the rescue going down to death instead singing the Hymn of the Dead which ends with the words "I shall have no regrets, having died for the Emperor."

In World War II the carriers gained ascendancy over the battleships and cruisers as the major striking arm of the navy. The dreadnaughts were still important but this was their last war. Naval aircraft had wider range and more effective means of delivering bombs and torpedoes on target. By 1944 the American navy also attained superiority in the air. The Americans were able to build airplanes faster. Their planes and carriers had the advantage of radar. Equally important, the Americans were able to train pilots better. In the beginning of the war the Japanese pilots were well trained and their planes good. But each successive wave of new pilots was less well trained. The reason was the lack of aviation gasoline. Japan had to import gasoline from Borneo and Java. American submarines were becoming more effective in interfering with these long sea lines. Consequently, the limited supply of gasoline had to be allocated first to operations and next to training of pilots. Japanese pilots got only 100 hours of flight training in contrast to the 500 hours of their American counterparts before going into battle. The loss of aircraft rose commensurately. During the period April 1943 to April 1944 Japan built 9952 aircraft of which 6334 were lost!

After the Battle of the Philippine Sea during June 19–20, 1944, the Japanese navy was virtually without air support. The Americans were preparing to retake Guam at this time when the Japanese navy offered battle with its full complement of carriers. Japan lost 424 aircraft; the Americans lost only 126. The poor training of the Japanese pilots was decisive. In addition Japan lost 2 carriers 1 light cruiser and 2 tankers. The battleship and remaining carriers were heavily damaged and returned to Japan for repairs. The battleship and cruisers were finally equipped with radar for detection. The Japanese naval officers were overjoyed for they knew that they could no longer depend upon airplanes for reconnaissance in view of the American air superiority.

The naval war was now moving to a climax. The Americans were hedgehopping from one strategic island to another on their way to Tokyo. The Philippines were next on the schedule. Japan realized that if the Americans recaptured the Philippines it was the end of the Asia coprosperity sphere—and ultimate defeat in the war. The Americans had to be stopped here.

The plan devised—called SHO (victory)—was both ingenious and admirable. The navy would launch a 3 pronged assault designed to annihilate General MacArthur's amphibious fleet in San Pedro bay of Leyte gulf. This would be coordinated with a Japanese army attack on General MacArthur's forces on Leyte—having no possibility of escape once the amphibious fleet was destroyed—with the objective of capturing the General and demanding the surrender of the Americans!

The vital role of the imperial navy was to be carried out as follows: two task forces, one approaching from the south through Surigao strait, called the southern force, and the other from the north through San Bernardino strait, called the center force, were to converge on Leyte gulf in a pincer movement and destroy the American amphibious force anchored in San Pedro bay. To free these task forces of attack by the American third fleet a northern force consisting mainly of the remaining Japanese carriers was to approach from the north, to the east of Luzon, to decoy Admiral Halsey away from Leyte gulf. This would leave only Admiral Kinkaid's seventh fleet, which consisted of old battleships, cruisers, escort carriers and destroyers to defend Leyte gulf. The Japanese admirals thought they could cope with this part of the U. S. navy and still carry out their main purpose, that is, the destruction of MacArthur's amphibious force. MacArthur landed on Leyte on October 20, 1944. Sho plan called for the assault two days later. It was, however, two days late.

Few Americans realize that the plan came perilously close to success. The decoy of the third fleet was highly successful. The old ships of the seventh fleet however, were equipped with fire control radar enabling them to engage the Japanese ships long before they had any idea the American ships were nearby. This the Japanese admirals did or could not know.

On October 24, 1944 Admiral Nishimura was headed for Surigao strait and scheduled to arrive in Leyte gulf at 0430 on October 25. He was in the van of the southern force with the battleships Yamashiro and Fuso, the heavy cruiser Mogami and four destroyers sometimes referred to as force C. The battleships mounted twelve inch guns and could make 24 knots. They were a match for the old American battleships except in fire control. Admiral Shima followed by some 40 miles with the heavy cruisers Nachi and Ashgira, the light cruiser Abukuma and four destroyers. Nishimura's force C was first sighted by airplanes from the carrier Enterprise at 0905 on October 24 in the Sulu sea.

Admiral Oldendorf received orders from Admiral Kinkaid at 1513 to prepare for night action. He formed his battle line consisting of 6 battle-ships—West Virginia, Tennessee, California, Maryland, Mississippi and Pennsylvania—at the northern entrance to Surigao strait. This position placed the dreadnaughts at cruising speed athwart the passage into Leyte gulf where a part of General MacArthur's amphibious fleet was anchored. Another line, consisting of four heavy cruisers and four light cruisers, was formed six miles ahead of the battleships. It was a naval officers dream of a T formation. In fact, it was a doubly crossed T. The West Virginia, Tennessee and California were equipped with the latest Mark 8 fire control radar; the other three with Mark 3 radar fire control equipment. The cruisers too had radar controlled guns.

The ships were, however, improperly supplied with ammunition as they were preparing for the bombardment of Yak when they were reordered to stand by for the Philippine invasion with major naval engagement in the offing. They had too small a proportion of armor piercing (AP) shells to high capacity (HC) ammunition intended for shore bombardment. Though not as good, the HC ammunition was, nonetheless, effective against enemy vessels. But in deference to the situation Admiral Oldendorf ordered his battleships to open fire only at 26,000 yards (approximately 15 miles) and cruisers at 15,000 yards (approximately 9 miles). At this range the firing could be more effective. The Japanese ships had no radar controlled guns. They had by now radar detection but it was inferior to that on the American ships.

Before Nishimura came within this range he was to be harassed first by PT boats and later destroyers as he steamed up the narrow straits. The PT boats had a dual purpose. First to report from time to time on the position of the Japanese task force and second a nuisance to Nishimura which he dealt with capably. Not so, however, was he able to cope with the destroyers which did a heroic job of damaging the Japanese ships, including a good torpedo hit by the destroyer Melvin on the old battleship Fuso, which caught fire, blew up and sank at 0338. The destroyer Yamagumo was also hit and sunk at 0319. But the Yamashiro and Mogami and the other destroyers while receiving hits, pushed on steadily for Leyte gulf unaware of the trap into which they were moving.

The PT boats kept up their scouting and harassment from 2250 to 0300. The destroyers made contact when Nishimura's group was some 30 miles from battle line. It was around 0200. There followed a furious battle with the American destroyers for an hour or so which slowed the movement of the task force. At 0323 radar screens on the battleships registered the Japanese ships. They were then about 20 miles away. When the Yamashiro came within 15 miles of battle line the radar controlled guns began firing from the battleships and cruisers. It was now 0351.

The night was pitch black, punctuated only by the exchange of fire with the destroyers. The Japanese ships, having no radar fire control, were discharging their guns only on targets made visible by the fires and searchlights. At this juncture all hell broke loose as hundreds of shells—6 to 16 inch began to rain upon the Yamashiro and her escorting ships. Captain Smoot who witnessed the holocaust from his destroyer reported "The devastating accuracy of this gunfire was the most beautiful sight I have ever witnessed. The arched line of tracers in the darkness looked like a continual stream of lighted railroad cars going over a hill. No target could be observed at first; then shortly there would be fires and explosions, and another ship would be accounted for."

At 0359 the Yamashiro veered sharply to the left anxious no doubt to retire from the hell fire confronting it. At 0409 the Mississippi administered the *coup de grace* with a hit at 19,790 yards (approximately 11.5 miles). The Yamashiro capsized and sank at 0419 on its course south away from the fire. Admiral Nishimura, as did all hands, went down with the ship. No one was left to tell the story from the receiving end of this devastating radar controlled fire.

Admiral Oldendorf halted the firing at 0409 when he received reports from his destroyers that the radar was picking them up as targets. This enabled the crippled Mogami and the destroyer Shigure to turn about and retreat south. At this point Admiral Shima caught up with force C. In the confusion his heavy cruiser Nachi collided with the crippled Mogami. When Shima saw that the Fuso and Yamashiro had been destroyed he promptly retreated from Surigao strait with the Mogami and Shigure limping behind. When daylight broke American aircraft finished the destruction of the Mogami with a torpedo hit. Only the Shigure of Admiral Nishimura's seven ships remained alive, though crippled, after the Battle of Surigao Strait.

It was now the morning of October 25th and there ensued what must be one of the biggest snafus (navy jargon meaning "situation normal all fouled up" or words to that effect) in U. S. history. It was a combination of bad judgement, wrong assumptions, tardy and misunderstood communications and, in large measure, a divided command. The seventh fleet was under the command of General MacArthur. The third fleet only was under Admiral Nimitz, the Chief of Naval Operations. The seventh fleet was composed of old ships designed to protect General MacArthur's amphibious operations. All the new ships and carriers, intended for offensive purposes, were part of the third fleet. The divided command was loosely coordinated in Washington. But MacArthur was generally a law unto himself so that there was no unified command in the area of operation. In fact, Admiral Halsey writes in his book "If we had been under the same command, with a single system of operational control and intelligence, the Battle of Leyte Gulf might have been fought differently to a different result. It is folly to cry over spilled milk, but it is vital for the navy never to expose itself again to the perils of a divided command in the same area."

If it is any consolation, however, the Japanese navy was anything but a model of operational efficiency. The three forces had the worse possible communications. Admirals Nishimura and Shima did not seem to be in contact with each other. The latter did not know the former was under attack. Their first contact was when the Nachi collided with the Mogami. At one time in the battle off Samar Admiral Kurita thought he was firing upon Admiral Ozawa. And so on. But back to the fighting.

Admiral Kurita encountered rough going in the Sibuyan sea on his approach to San Bernardino strait during daylight on October 24th. Admiral Kurita's center force consisted of the two new battleships Yamato and Musashi, three old battleships, ten heavy cruisers, two light cruisers and nineteen destroyers. A truly formidable force. He lost three of the cruisers on his passage from Singapore to the Philippines in a highly successful attack by the American submarines Darter and Dace. In the Sibuyan sea American planes from carriers swarmed like flies over center force. Some 259 sorties in all were made against Kurita. They zeroed on the new battleship Musashi and sank it, scoring one of the most brilliant strikes in the Pacific war. The Musashi took 19 torpedoes and 17 bombs before she sank. The Yamato and Nagato each took two bomb hits and the cruiser Myoko had her shafts damaged by torpedoes and had to return to Brunei (Borneo) for repairs.

Admiral Kurita had no air support. The naval air arm had been knocked out in June in the Battle of the Philippine Sea. Moreover, what was left of it was being used by Admiral Ozawa to decoy the third fleet away from Leyte gulf. And the land based planes on Luzon chose to strike the American carriers instead of providing cover for center force. These land based planes did score a notable success in sinking the American carrier Princeton.

When the attack broke off at 1400 center force seemed to be turning back—actually it was only milling around to minimize the attack. At 1714 Kurita resumed course but there was no hope now of arriving in Leyte gulf at 0430 in the morning. Meanwhile, the American pilots (as is usually the case) made exaggerated reports of the damage they inflicted. It was at this stage that Admiral Halsey committed his first error of judgment. He took these reports at face value and concluded "that center force had been so seriously damaged in the Sibuyan sea that it could no longer be considered a serious menace to seventh fleet" in his dispatch to General MacArthur and Admiral Nimitz. Actually, he should have known better as the lesson of the Battle of Sibuyan Sea is that air attacks by themselves, even under the extremely favorable conditions of this one, cannot knock out a fleet of battleships and heavy cruisers. In fact, center force was still 75 per cent intact, in spite of the brilliant attacks by the submarines and aircraft. The sinking of the Musashi by air attack was something of a miracle.

Moreover, Admiral Halsey appeared obsessed with the Japanese carriers. "Where the hell are those goddam carriers" he and his staff kept asking each other. The carriers still not fully repaired (expected to be ready only in November) with pilots so poorly trained they could not be entrusted to fly the aircraft aboard, slipped out of Japanese waters undetected by American submarines standing watch for them. It seems the submarines got tired of waiting (as did king Harold's fyrds at Hastings) and left before Admiral Ozawa weighed anchor. This suited Ozawa well as he did not want to be detected this early in his decoy venture. Later, however, when he wanted to be detected he sent out without success reconnaissance aircraft. Most failed to return because of the incompetence of the pilots. For these reasons Admiral Halsey had difficulty finding "those goddam carriers." He finally found the northern force at 1730 on October 24 off the northeastern tip of Luzon. Halsey promptly took off for the north. But before he did so he designated a task force 34 consisting of four fast battleships (including the New Jersey), two heavy cruisers, three light cruisers and fourteen destroyers to be spun off from task force 38 to meet Admiral Kurita in case he came out of San Bernardino strait. It was not possible to send American ships into Sibuyan sea as it was mined and only the Japanese had charts of the safe channels. But in the end he ordered the entire task force 38 to go after the northern force. Task force 38 consisted of six new battleships, five big carriers, five light carriers, two heavy cruisers, six light cruisers and forty-one destroyers. Admiral Ozawa's task force consisted of one big carrier, three light carriers, two converted battleships (after decks made into flight decks) with three light cruisers and eight destroyers for escort. It was 65 American ships against 17 Japanese ships considerably lighter in every respect. The Japanese carriers had only 166 aircraft. Most of these had been sent out on reconnaissance and were either lost or landed on Luzon. It was an overkill, like swatting a fly with a sledge hammer. Needless to say the northern force was annihilated.

But its sacrifice was highly successful as it lured the entire third fleet north so that when Admiral Kurita issued out of San Bernardino strait after midnight on October 25th Admiral Halsey was 300 miles away. All he encountered was Admiral Sprague's sixteen small carrier escorts which were patrolling off Leyte. Admiral Kurita, however, mistook the CVE's for the big carriers of the third fleet. The "baby flattops" fought bravely and ferociously, made plenty of smoke screen which confused and baffled the Japanese Admiral. An outcry arose over the navy communications lines for task force 34 but it was off in northern Luzon with the third fleet indulging in the overkill of the northern force. Not even a destroyer was left on watch at the eastern end of San Bernardino strait for the possible emergence of center force! But fortunately for the Americans Admiral Kurita decided to give up the fight and retreated back through San Bernardino strait. Why he did so defies understanding. For one thing he thought he was encountering the third fleet. For another, news had reached him of the annihilation of force C in Surigao strait a few hours earlier. Kurita probably concluded there was little to be gained in closing the upper claw of the pincer when the lower claw was shorn off. His ships, particularly the destroyers were low on fuel by this time. Anyway, he decided to retire and save the heart of the Japanese navy to fight another day.

The controversy over this American *snafu* has been raging ever since. Aside from the fact that this merely adds another chapter to a long history of bungling by generals and admirals since the dawn of history it really made no difference in the outcome of the war. The victory in Leyte gulf had already occurred at 0351 to 0409 in Surigao strait when Sho plan was demolished by the destruction of force C. To be sure, had task force 34 been at the eastern entrance of San Bernardino strait it would have doubtless destroyed center force in the same fashion as force C was destroyed for its battleships too were equipped with radar fire control. Moreover, had Admiral Kurita pushed on to Leyte gulf, as he was capable of doing, it is most likely he too would have been destroyed at that point as Admiral Oldendorf was still there with his battleships which, though low on armor piercing ammunition, still possessed the "magic" of radar fire control.

The Yamato had another day. It was a sad one though. After Leyte gulf the Japanese launched the kamikaze attacks. The word means "divine wind" and derives from the destruction of the Mongol fleet by a typhoon when the Mongols tried to invade Japan in the 13th century. The Japanese believed the Goddess Ise sent the destructive wind to save the Japanese from foreign domination. Religious sanction aside, the kamikaze attacks were an act of desperation by the Japanese whose naval surface and air dominance was now destroyed. About the only effective maneuver left to the poorly trained Japanese pilots was to fly their aircraft with bombs attached onto the decks of the American ships. This act of desperation however, cost the American navy great loss. The Americans lost 36 ships, 763 aircraft and 368 ships were damaged. The price to the Japanese was the loss of 7800 aircraft!

After the Philippines the Americans invaded Okinawa. It was the spring of 1945. The damage suffered by the Yamato in Leyte gulf was now repaired. The Japanese decided to send her to relieve the situation in Okinawa. She left on April 6, 1945 with just enough fuel for a one way trip. The officers and men knew, though they did not articulate it, that it was her last trip. She never made it to Okinawa. The next morning at 1220 American planes swarmed over the Yamato and her escort consisting of the light cruiser Yahagi and seven destroyers. Six torpedoes and five bombs knocked out her guns and caused a 40° list. Shortly after 1400 the Yamato sank with all hands. As she sank a spontaneous cry was heard repeated three times "Long live the Emperor." The destruction of the Yamato was the end of the imperial navy.

In final analysis the naval victory in Leyte gulf belonged to the American scientists and electronics engineers, the bungling of the admirals to the contrary notwithstanding. This conclusion does not derogate from the feats of heroism and courage displayed in the various battles by the American officers and sailors, for the effective use of superior technology still depends upon the human mind and hand. But by the same token also its ineffective use is the result of human frailty.

While the imperial navy of Japan was being overwhelmed by American superior electronic technology and industrial might another technological development was underway that was to lead to the final surrender of Japan in the war. It was the atom bomb dropped on Hiroshima on August 6, 1945.

The development of the atom bomb was already discussed in Chapter V. After Enrico Fermi and his bevy of scientists achieved the first self sustaining nuclear chain reaction on December 2, 1942 in a squash court at the University of Chicago the Americans were still faced with the formidable problem of fashioning this new form of energy into a weapon of war. It was to take another three years to accomplish, involving the labor of 500,000 men and women at a cost of two billion dollars—a mighty technological and industrial effort.

The first problem was the production of the fissionable material in sufficient quantity. A large gaseous diffusion plant was constructed at Oak Ridge, Tennessee to separate U-235 from U-238. The uranium isotope U-235 was the fissionable material needed for the bomb. At the same time another plant was constructed at Hanford, Washington, on the Columbia river, to produce plutonium from U-238. The man made plutonium was also highly fissionable. The two approaches were undertaken in case one failed. Both proved successful. The production of fissionable material was the so-called Manhatten project as it was directed by the Manhatten District of the Corps of Engineers under General Leslie Groves.

Meanwhile at Los Almos, New Mexico scientists and engineers under the direction of Dr. J. Robert Oppenheimer began work on the bomb itself. The main problem was to achieve a critical mass at the desired moment of explosion while transporting the fissionable material up to that point safely and without mishap. TNT charges were placed behind wedges of uranium or plutonium placed in a circle which, when exploded, pushed the wedges toward the center of the bomb to form a critical mass for the self sustaining nuclear explosion. Until ignited the bomb could be safely transported to its destination as the wedges of fissionable material by themselves did not form a critical mass.

A workable bomb was exploded on July 16, 1945 before dawn on the desert at Almogordo, New Mexico. A blinding flash illuminated the desert followed by a great mushroom-like cloud billowing on top of a great column of smoke. There followed a thunderous roar, trembling of the earth and a wave of intense heat. Its destructive power could be only guessed as the bomb was first exploded over the desert.

President Truman was now faced with a momentous decision. His counsel was divided. Some thought Japan would not surrender until after a bloody invasion costing, perhaps, a million American lives and several times that in Japanese lives. On July 26, 1945 President Truman and Prime Minister Atlee called upon Japan to surrender or face "the devastation of the Japanese homeland." There was no response.

On the morning of August 6, 1945 a single plutonium bomb was dropped on Hiroshima killing 68,000 of its residents. An equal number were injured. By afternoon many who escaped unharmed began to die of radiation. The bomb, equivalent to an explosion of 20,000 tons of TNT, demolished 80 per cent of the city. At the epicenter the temperatures generated were in the millions of degrees. Factories, hospitals, schools and homes disappeared. Buildings more than a mile from the epicenter were partially destroyed or badly damaged. It was a man made destruction such as had never been effected.

Yet Japan did not surrender. On August 9, 1945 another bomb made of U-235 material was exploded over Nagasaki with similar destruction. Some 38,000 residents were killed. The emperor finally overrode the objections of his generals and admirals and Japan surrendered on August 14,1945.

The European sector of World War II involved no similar technological gap. The outcome was determined by the combined overwhelming industrial might of the Allies. The Nazis, like Napoleon before them, committed the fatal mistake repeated throughout history of overextension of their power in Russia where they lost 13 of their divisions. The Germans did not possess the industrial might to fight a war on two fronts. The Americans, to be sure, were developing a superior technology and had the European war not ended before the atom bomb was perfected it would most likely have been used against the Germans to end the war.

OTHER EPISODES

The five historical episodes set forth above where technological superiority was the determinative factor were selected for detailed discussion because their outcome had a profound effect on the history of man. They were historic battles. There were, of course, countless lesser conflicts where superior technology was determinative. It seems appropriate, therefore, to mention and discuss briefly some of the other interesting historical episodes before terminating this chapter.

When Moses reorganized the Israelites and led them out of bondage in Egypt to the Promised Land in the Near East around 1225 B. C. he found the land settled and occupied by others. These were mostly Semitic tribes with technology no better than that of the Israelites. Some of the Canaanites on the western plains did have horses and chariots as noted in the Song of Deborah. Over the centuries from 1200 to 1050 B. C. the Israelites overcame many of these tribes and took their land. But on the coast they encountered an Indo-European people, the Philistines, who possessed iron weapons and horse drawn chariots. The Israelites could not defeat them and wrest from them the rich coastal areas of Palestine. That this was considered part of the Promised Land is clear in the Book of Joshua. The Israelites had every intention to take it.

The Philistines were a part of the so-called "sea people" who burst upon the Near East presumably from the Aegean sea area. They overran and succeeded the Hittites in Anatolia and invaded Egypt where they were finally repulsed by Ramses III in 1188 B. C. A contingent of these peoples settled along the Mediterranean coast and came to be known as the Philistines. The name Palestine derives from them. They came equipped with the advanced technology of the Indo-European peoples, the smelting of iron, domestication of the horse and with bow and arrow. Unfortunately, like so many Indo-European people they left no historical record and all that is known of them is derived from the history of their enemies the Egyptians and the Israelites, whose accounts must necessarily be taken with circumspect. Admissions against interest, as usual, is the best evidence in such cases.

The first military encounter came when the Israelites pushed out of the mountains into the Plain of Sharon (coastal area near modern Tel Aviv). This was an unfortunate site of battle for the Israelites who, as far as can be determined, had only bronze for weapons as a flat terrain is most advantageous for chariot warfare. The Israelites were slaughtered *en masse*. The Bible says 4000 Israelites were "smitten". Many more were enslaved. The Israelites tried again. This time they carried into battle the Ark of the Covenant to assure that God would be on their side. The priest Eli agreed with considerable reluctance and designated his two sons to carry the Ark from Shiloh to the site of battle. An even greater slaughter resulted. God was unable to overcome Israel's deficiency in technology. Some 30,000 Israelites fell! The Ark was captured by the Philistines. Eli's two sons were killed and when Eli heard the news he collapsed and died.

Apparently the Ark caused a plague to befall the Philistines so they returned it to the Israelites. When it was returned the plague broke out among the Israelites. "Fifty thousand three score and ten were "smitten" at Bethshemesh where the Ark was returned.

The Israelites retreated into the rugged terrain of central Canaan where the Philistines could not pursue them with their chariots. In the gorges, ravines, caves and mountains the fighting was reduced to hand to hand combat in which the resolute Israelites were able to stand their ground.

The Israelites, loosely joined by tribes heretofore, decided now to appoint a king to defend them against the Philistines. But Saul, their first king, (circa 1020–1004) suffered many defeats at the hands of the Philistines in the forbidding terrain of central Canaan. The Israelites also scored some notable victories, but it seems, the encounters were merely with Philistine outposts and not the main army. The Philistines had iron spears, swords and armor which provided the margin of victory. It was in one of these battles that David slew Goliath, who was probably not ten feet tall as the Bible asserts, with a sling shot. In a way, the story of David and Goliath is an early example in history of the superiority of a missile over the sword. It has been the evolution of human warfare ever since.

David became a national hero. Saul feared he would take the throne from him, so he set out to kill David. David promptly defected to the Philistines, it would seem, with two purposes in mind. The first was for safety from Saul. The second was to learn the secrets of the superior warfare of the Philistines. The Philistines welcomed him and even made him the lord of one of their cities in the south, Ziglag. David fought many battles for them but none against the Israelites.

The Philistines were now preparing an attack on Saul from the north through the valley of Esdraelon. They mustered thirty thousand chariots, six thousand horsemen and "peoples as the sand which is on the sea shore in multitude." The Philistine king Achish wanted David to join them in the attack but his generals prevailed upon him to excuse David as they did not trust him. David was, of course greatly relieved and retired with his followers to Ziglag. The Philistines slaughtered the Israelites on the western slope at Mount Gilboa (rising from the plain of Jezreel) killing Saul's three sons, including Jonathan the great friend of David. Saul was severely wounded by a Philistine arrow and committed suicide to avert capture alive. Saul had consulted a witch before the battle to bring back the prophet Samuel from the dead for consultation but the seance had no favorable effect on the outcome.

David became king of Israel around 1000 B. C. after a long and bitter struggle with the heirs and supporters of Saul. He consolidated and extended the kingdom and finally repulsed the Philistines. The Bible does not report any battles or victories, but it is reasonable to presume that while fraternizing with the Philistines David learned their technology of war and adopted it for his use. In the Book of Samuel it is stated that the Philistines guarded their iron smelting technology as top secret denying it to the Israelites. But by David's time the iron smelting technology was no doubt transmitted to the Israelites. Similarly, with respect to the horse, for we know that Solomon was a great horseman. In Chronicles it is stated that "Soloman had four thousand stalls for horses and chariots and twelve thousand horsemen." David apparently did not adopt the horse and chariot but then it was not very useful in his hilly domain. On the other hand, the Philistines may have declined as a power on their own for by this time they had existed as a powerful nation for 200 years which is about as long as most societies last. It should be noted that while the Israelites ousted the Philistines from central Canaan they never occupied their land on the coast.

Archimedes was the greatest scientist of antiquity. He lived circa 287–212 B. C. in the Greek city of Syracuse. He is, perhaps, best known for Archimedes principle, a method of measuring specific gravity. There is the familiar story related by Vitruvius. He states that Archimedes conceived the principle when immersed in a public bath. He was pondering how he could test whether the king's goldsmith alloyed the gold crown with silver and kept the displaced gold. The displacement of water by his body triggered the idea. Suddenly he ran into the street naked crying "Eureka! Eureka! I have found it!"

Unlike his predecessors and colleagues he was a master of applied science. Among other things he invented the so-called Archimedian screw to lift water from mines and for irrigation, the block and tackle and numerous ballista. He understood the laws of mechanics and, in fact, wrote a treatise entitled the *Elements of Mechanics*. It was in this connection that he made his impact on the history of warfare.

Archimedes lived in one of those unfortunate times in history. The Greek civilization to which he belonged was in decline and decay. Its culture had, however, radiated all around the Mediterranean area and some of the Greek colonies possessed at this time more power than the mother country. Syracuse was such an outpost of the Greek civilization. But it was now caught between two powers vying for supremacy in the western Mediterranean—Carthage and Rome.

King Hieron, to whom he may have been related, commissioned Archimedes to use his scientific ideas to develop engines of war. Though they were not used while Hieron lived they became useful later when the Romans beseiged Syracuse. In the second Punic War (218–201 B. C.) Syracuse allied itself with the Carthaginians. The Romans sent one of their best generals Marcus Claudius Marcellus to conquer Syracuse. Syracuse was a walled city right up to its beautiful harbor. It was situated in a bay 3 miles long and a half mile wide.

Marcellus came first by sea. He was met by huge flying stones from catapaults set up behind the walls. As the Roman ships came close to the walls they were picked up by giant cranes with hooks and capsized. Other ballista consisting of cranks and pulleys dropped heavy stones or lead weights on the ships to sink them. Bowmen harassed the Roman sailors with arrows shot through apertures constructed in the walls from where they could work their bows shielded from the Romans. And when the Roman fleet retreated and anchored in the bay, so that Marcellus could reconnoiter the baffling situation, Archimedes set the Roman fleet afire with solar mirrors directed from the walls!

Repulsed at sea Marcellus decided to approach the city by land. But here too Archimedes had the walls fortified with ballista. The Roman soldiers refused to advance against the flying stones. The Romans who thought they would capture Syracuse in a matter of days gave up the siege after eight months. One man—a man of science—was able to keep at bay a powerful Roman navy and army for nearly a year!

The Romans, of course, took Syracuse eventually. They were too powerful. Marcellus blockaded Syracuse by land and sea for three years. When the citizens were starved and weakened the Romans breached the walls and captured the city in 212 B. C. Marcellus gave orders that Archimedes was not to be injured. During the sack of the city of Roman soldier came upon Archimedes, now 75, working on a mathematical problem. Archimedes pleaded for time to finish the problem before surrendering to the Roman. The latter stabbed the old scientist. Marcellus mourned and erected a memorial for Archimedes, in accordance with Archimedes wish, consisting of a sphere within a cylinder on which were engraved the equations for the relationship of their volumes and areas. Archimedes considered the discovery of this mathematical principle the greatest achievement of his life. While quartered in Sicily in 75 B. C. more than a century later Cicero reported hc found the memorial covered with vines and thorns but still in the form of the sphere and cylinder.

Genghis Khan and his heirs forged an empire that stretched from the Pacific to the Danube in the 13th century A. D. That it did not extend to the Atlantic resulted from a mere fortuity. Their military prowess like that of their predecessors, the Hsiung-nu against whom the Chinese built the Great Wall in the second century B. C., rested upon the mounted warrior with the laminated eastern bow. But it is not generally recognized that the Mongols also employed some of the most advanced technology of the time in their military conquests.

To be sure they did not create the technology but adopted it from the Chinese. It has already been pointed out that the Chinese invented gunpowder but did not readily adapt it for military use. The Mongols, however, were quicker to realize its military potential though they never really developed it into their major means of warfare.

In his thrust westward Genghis Khan had to confront the powerful Muhammad of Khwarizm who had established a formidable Muslim empire in central Asia centering on Samarkand but extending from Persia into India. Muhammad tried to avert the conflict by proffering an alliance and trade treaty but when Genghis Khan replied he would be happy to have him as a vassal Muhammad was insulted. When he murdered two of Genghis Khan's ambassadors war was commenced in 1215 A. D.

Muhammad mustered 300,000 men. Genghis Khan had only about half that number but they were equipped with the latest military technology acquired from the Chinese. Ballista that could hurl 300 pound stones, flame-throwers and even cannon. The Mongols also had a closely woven heavy silk vest, another Chinese invention, that could not easily be pierced by arrows. Muhammad was defeated and Genghis Khan annexed most of western Asia to his empire. Yen-lu-Chu-Tsai, who accompanied Genghis on this campaign left a very interesting account of the numerous battles and cities conquered together with many beautiful poems about Samarkand and Bokhara.

Genghis Khan died in 1227 and was succeeded by his third son Ogadai. In 1237 Batu Khan, a grandson of Genghis, invaded Europe. Reports of the carnage visited upon the Russians by his golden horde stagger the mind. No fortified city could withstand their siege machines. Sir Bernard Pares, the noted British authority on Russia, states that Batu Khan used a crude form of artillery in these sieges.

As the golden horde pushed into Hungary in 1241 word arrived that Ogadai had died. Batu terminated the invasion to return to Karakorum for the selection of a new leader. The golden horde never returned to Europe. But for this fortuitous event the golden horde might have penetrated all the way to the Atlantic. The Mongols had the military superiority to do so.

Kublai Khan who succeeded to the Mongol throne in 1246 turned his attention toward China. After 19 years of war he succeeded in conquering the Sung dynasty in southern China. Later he extended Mongol hegemony over Burma, Thailand and Indo-China. In 1284 Kublai Khan invaded Japan and got caught in a typhoon. The invasion ended in disaster. The irony of the conquest of China is that the Mongols used Chinese technology against them. Wolfram Eberhard, the American authority on China, states "during the many years of war against the Sung dynasty in south China the Mongols already made use of small cannon in laying siege to towns.''

Iron weapons have played a decisive role in history on many occasions. It was not that iron made a better weapon than bronze but once its technology was mastered iron could be produced in greater abundance and less expensively. This enabled those with the iron technology to arm more men for conflict. The Hittites were the first to have this advantage though Ceram discounts it in favor of the horse and chariot as their great technological advantage in war. We have just noted that iron weapons gave the Philistines technological superiority over the Israelites. There are scores of other instances where iron weapons were determinative in history.

The conquest of north central Italy (between the Tiber and Arno rivers) by the Etruscans about 750 B. C. is attributable to their metallurgical skill. Their origin is obscure. They are believed to have come from Anatolia during the great migrations of the so-called ''sea peoples'' around 1000 B. C. Their technological expertise enabled them easily to subject the Villanovans that resided in the area. During the 6th century the Etruscans operated one of the biggest iron works of that age at Fufluna (near modern Piombino). The iron ore came from the offshore island of Elbe. Archeologists have uncovered mountains of slag heaps from which it has been deduced that annual production at Fufluna was from 10,000 to 12,000 tons for some 400 years! Iron became one of the Etruscan's main exports.

The Dorian conquest of Greece around 1100 B. C. is likewise attributable to the Dorian supremacy with iron weaponry. The Dorians issued out of central Europe where the Hallstat culture based on iron was situated. Scholars differ whether the Dorians swept or filtered into Greece, but they overwhelmed the Mycenaeans whose civilization was still based on bronze. The Dorians were unlettered, rough and war like leaving their most profound impact as the Spartans. Their domination of some other parts of Greece, notably Attica, was not so thorough. In Peloponnesia the Dorians enslaved the Mycenaeans and made them helots (serfs).

The horse was the source of supremacy in war for three thousand years. The Indo-Europeans, in particular, made use of the horse to dominate other people. The Hurrian domination of Assyria from 1750–1350 B. C. was based upon their development and military use of the horse and chariot. The rise of the Scythians to power around 700 B. C. was based on their abilities as the first mounted horsemen. The Medes and Persians built an empire with the mounted horseman. Riding on the horse spread from one end of the Eurasian steppes to the other during the beginning of the first millennium before the Christian era though it is generally believed it originated with the Scythians and other Indo-Europeans in the west. It spread eastward to the Yueh-chi, who were a mix of Indo-Europeans and Mongolian races in central Asia and to the Hsuing-nu, a Euro-Mongolian race in Mongolia. The acquisition of this technology by the Hsuing-nu had a profound effect on the history of

China. Erection of the Great Wall against these mounted warriors proved to be largely an exercise in futility in this respect (Owen Lattimore asserts the Wall had another purpose and that was to keep the Chinese peasant from escaping his bondage to the land). It was not until the Chinese invented the cross bow which was powerful enough to fell the nomadic horsemen that China, under the great Han emperor Wu (140–86 B. C.), was able to stop the Hsuing-nu—for a while at least.

Toward the end of the Shang dynasty (circa 1600–1028 B. C.) the Chinese used the horse and chariot which was probably introduced from western Asia. When the succeeding Chou dynasty broke up around 481 B. C. China entered the era (481–256 B. C.) known as the Period of the Contending States with 14 (composed of the previously 1000 feudal fiefs) states vying for supremacy. It was the northern states that won out as they had better cavalry. They had closer contact with the Hsuing-nu who raised and traded the horses for food and textiles with the Chinese. During the early part of this period (around 300 B. C.) the state of Chao (present day Shansi) was supreme because of its powerful army based on mounted horsemen. In the end the state of Ch'in, its neighbor to the west (present Shensi) won out, largely too, because of its supremacy with cavalry due to a better access to a supply of horses from Mongolia. Iron also played its part during this period. It has already been discussed in Chapter IV that the Chinese developed the iron technology at an early time independently of its innovation in the Near East. By 500 B. C. iron making was well known in China. And the northern states, particularly Chao and Ch'in had access to the best deposits of iron ore in the country.

Finally some surmise on the role of iron in the history of India. Unfortunately, due to the propensity of the Hindus to ignore their antecedents, the history of India is very obscure. We do know from other sources though, that India was one of the foremost producers of first rate iron and steel during antiquity. Around 500 B. C. the tribes of India were consolidated into four strong and warring nations. Preeminent among them was the Magadhan kingdom with its capital at Pataliputra, the site of modern Patna, in Bihar state which contains even today the best iron ore deposits in India. By 350 B. C. the Magadhan empire was extended over the entire gangetic plain by such strong rulers as Bimbisara, Ajatasatra and Mahapedma Nanda. Chandragupta Maurya defeated the Nandas around 300 B. C. and extended his rule from Pataliputra into the Punjab and over the rest of India to form the first Indian empire. It is believed that the knowledge of iron technology was instrumental in this early empire building in India.

VII
Production, Plunder and Trade

We have been tracing heretofore the biological and technological evolution of man. In the last chapter certain historic battles that effected profoundly the history of man were discussed to demonstrate that those people with technological superiority impose their will upon others. From time to time it has already been mentioned that it was not the superior technology alone that made the difference but the "effective" use of the superior technology that was equally important.

The paramount factor in the effective use of technology is the wealth of the society. In modern times it is not only important to have superior military aircraft and missiles but a nation must be able to produce thousands of them. Three thousand years ago it was as basic as having the largest granaries. Today it is industrial capacity not merely agricultural productivity.

Wealth is generally acquired through production, plunder and trade. In the first instance wealth can only derive from the surplus production of man. But after the surplus is produced it can be appropriated by others through plunder or trade. Herein again comes into play the dominance instinct of man. As in the case of the dominant baboon who appropriates the best orange or banana so it is in the case of man where the dominant men and societies appropriate the surplus made possible by the technological development of man. History is largely an account of this struggle over the surplus within and between the societies of man in revolution, war and trade. This struggle has been over both the productive facilities and the stored surplus in the form of grain and cattle, precious metals, implements and weapons.

This quest for wealth started in a serious way only with the discovery and invention of agriculture. Wealth is the surplus productivity of man susceptible to storage that is not needed for day to day survival. While man lived by the hunt he could not store the perishable meat. Moreover, he was probably able to provide only the food required from day to day. Man was also a food gatherer in parts of the world where the climate permitted, so it is entirely possible he may have started to store some of the non perishable roots, nuts and wild grains. Yet that is not the case of normal primate behavior. At any rate, this hardly constituted a surplus that can be called wealth.

The institution of agriculture as the main source of livelihood by man advanced him technologically to a position where he could now produce surplus food. The surplus cereals were stored in granaries and the surplus meat was stored in the flocks and herds of fowl and animals. Archeological sites of bygone capitals or citadels seldom fail to include a granary as one of the chief buildings. The granaries of ancient Egypt are proverbial. And the central image of biblical times is the herd of sheep and goats.

As man's technology progressed the store of metals, tools, weapons, implements and other wares was added to the food surplus. This emerging technology brought forth a number of productive facilities ranging from the simple potter's kiln to the rather complex copper smelting facilities at Timma in the Sinai. But throughout most of man's history the primary factor of production has been land. It is only in the last two centuries or so that the main factors of production have shifted away from land to industry and, even today, most countries still derive more than half their production from agriculture.

The earliest struggles of man were over fertile land. The first possessers of the fertile river valley areas had constantly to defend their territory against invaders from the less fertile highlands. Some had geographic advantages such as the ancient Egyptians whose fertile valley was surrounded by deserts and sea. The fertile crescent, on the other hand, was easily accessible and the history of that territory is one of successive invasions. Similarly, the history of north China is constant invasion by the nomads from the northwest into the fertile Yellow river basin.

India enjoyed the protection of some of the most formidable mountain barriers in the world so it had the advantage of long periods of respite from foreign invasion. After the Aryan conquest about 1500 B. C. there is no record of foreign intervention until Alexander the Great penetrated the Hindu Kush in 326 B. C. Thereafter, India suffered constant invasions through the Khyber Pass by the peoples of central Asia coveting the riches of the fertile Indus and Gangetic plains. The ultimate invasion came by sea, however, when the Europeans dominated India into modern times for three centuries. But more on this later in this chapter.

The story of the Bible is largely a struggle for fertile land. At a propitious moment in history when the Hyksos captured the Nile delta (circa 1600 B. C.) the nomadic Israelites from the Near East took advantage of the situation made possible by the temporary foreign domination of the Egyptians and settled in the fertile Nile delta. When the Egyptians regained control over the delta they enslaved the Israelites and made them brick makers and construction workers. Moses marshalled the Israelites around the concept of the Promised Land and led them out of slavery from Egypt. But when they arrived in Canaan the Israelites found the Promised Land settled and occupied by others. It took centuries of war and conquest before the Israelites got control of Canaan. At that, the Israelites were never able to dominate the coastal areas of Palestine because of the resistance of the Philistines.

After fertile land was acquired it required men to work it. In most cases the conquerors retained the people already settled on the land in some kind of servile status. The main or chief by-product of war in ancient times was captives to enslave for the hard and menial productive work of the dominant society. As already mentioned and to be seen again the near inhuman labor in the mines during ancient times was done by slaves.

In due time gold became a primary store of wealth and spoil of war. In fact, during pre-Christian times most metals were in short supply and of great value to men. Metals constituted a store of wealth over which men and nations warred constantly. By Graeco-Roman times men had generally settled on gold and silver as precious metals and based their money on them, particularly for facilitating trade with other countries. The role of gold in the struggles of mankind is almost unbelievable but it gripped the minds and hearts of men for millennia well into modern times.

Land, slaves and gold have during most of man's recorded history been the main objects of his drive for domination. In the beginning the spoils of war were quite basic. The Assyrian king Ashurnasirpal III (circa 884–859 B. C.), as already noted in Chapter IV, records that he returned from one expedition with 1500 captives, 500 sheep, 200 cattle and 460 horses. The captives, as was the accepted custom of the day, were enslaved. But 800 years later when Crassus marched against the Parthians he had uppermost in mind the gold of Persia and India!

Concurrently, or not long after men began to plunder each other's surplus production, they resorted to the less violent practice of exchanging their surplus goods. But it did not take man long to learn to exploit his advantages in trade. An early example was metallurgy. If a peoples were lucky to sit astride good ore and also possessed advanced metallurgical skills to work it they could become wealthy through trading on these advantages. An early example was the Uneticians of Bohemia. Around 1500 B. C. the Uneticians produced some of the finest bronze in the ancient world. They traded the bronze and bronze artifacts as far west as the British isles and via the Danube to the Near East. The Unetician safety pin, which they invented, and other artifacts have been found in these far flung areas. This favorable trade transformed the farming villages of the Uneticians into fortified highly organized towns. Their trade in bronze was centralized, inventories of bronze were kept and foreign commerce regulated. Unetician farmers were using bronze sickles while farmers elsewhere were still using stone cutting tools. The metal smiths were the elite of this early metal working society.

Similar examples are found in history in the case of iron and other metals. Exploiting technological superiority or other advantages in foreign trade to produce wealth for the dominant society has continued throughout history. The most recent example is the low price western oil companies were able to pay the underdeveloped countries for crude oil for years because they possessed the necessary technology to bring the oil out of the earth and process it into marketable petroleum products above the ground. At mid-20th century Kuwait received only 8 cents a barrel for its crude oil from the western companies. Consequently, Americans were able until recently to get gasoline for their automobiles for 20 cents a gallon. Their European counterparts benefited even more from this great trade advantage.

In the beginning trade was conducted through barter. Homer leaves us a graphic picture in the Iliad of such trade. The Achaeans were now assembled before Troy preparing for the great assault. They slaughtered oxen for their supper. Homer then related "Many ships had come from Lemnos. . . freighted with wine . . . From this supply the Achaeans bought their wine, some with bronze, some with iron, some with hides, some with whole heifers and some again with captives." Whereas this is clearly an example of barter it already contains the embryo of money. The captain of the ship from Lemnos obviously did not accept these goods for his wine because he wanted to consume them. He knew he could return to Lemnos and exchange them for more wine or other goods which he could again sell at a profit abroad. In fact cows were one of the earliest mediums of exchange in the ancient world. In the agricultural economies of the time a cow had general acceptability. When a wheat farmer traded his wheat with a herdsman for a cow it was barter. But if the wheat farmer already had his own herd of cows, but still took the cow for his wheat because he could trade the cow with the metalsmith for a plow the cow became a medium of exchange. And so money evolved. Cows were for centuries a medium of exchange, a measure of wealth, a reference for the price of goods—all attributes of money.

Money had to evolve with the technological advance of man, otherwise it would have been impossible for men to exchange the surplus production of their technological development. The division of labor begot by technological development derogated from the self sufficiency of an individual and he required some means to exchange his production with others to satisfy all his needs. It would serve no purpose to detail the various items that have served men as money around the world but eventually man settled on the precious metals—gold and silver—and at times the not so precious metals like copper and iron. Metals, especially gold and silver, possessed the qualities of portability, divisibility, imperishability, homogeneity and above all, general acceptability. Gold enabled a Near East merchant to exchange his sheep and goats for bars of gold, carry them across the Gobi desert and frozen tundra of Mongolia to China to exchange them for silk. Without a medium of exchange like gold the Old Silk Road of antiquity would have never have seen the light of day.

While the invention of money was essential as a handmaiden of man's technological development, mankind has much cause to rue the day money was introduced into human affairs. Next to war and religious bigotry nothing in the affairs of men has caused so much grief and suffering. Money requires careful management, but from the beginning to the present day man's experience with money has been its mismanagement. The result has been recurring inflation a chief cause of the decline and destruction of the societies of man.

Money in the modern sense did not evolve until the invention of coinage of the precious metals with each coin bearing a stated value. It is generally agreed that coinage was invented by the Lydians about the middle of the millennium before the Christian era. Herodotus, the first historian, credits the Lydians as "the first of all nations we know of that introduced the act of coining gold and silver." These Lydian coins were made of electrum, an amalgamation of gold and silver, which left them vulnerable to easy debasement. Also, the coins were struck by merchants and not the Lydian government. Later Croesus (circa 560–540 B. C.) took over the coinage and abandoned electrum in favor of separate gold and silver coins that could not be easily debased.

The Greeks, at the same time or shortly after, also developed coinage. Whatever the time factor it was the Greeks who developed fully and effectively the first monetary coinage of man. Greek coins were made of silver.

While bars of gold, silver or other metal could serve as well as coins as a medium of exchange the traders were faced with the uncertainty of the weight and fineness of the bars. Coins eliminated these problems by having the value of the metal stated on their face. This, of course, created another problem for the coins could be debased. In fact, in times of dire financial crisis people usually refused to take anything but the raw basic metal.

The Greeks favored silver because they had at Laurium the finest silver mine in antiquity. Laurium was situated in the tip of the penninsula of Attica. Laurium made Athens great and sustained its imperial power for years. At first the silver from Laurium gave Athens a great trade advantage. The Athenians had money acceptable to everyone for its foreign trade. This wealth enabled Athens to buy slaves and start industries to produce goods to sell abroad. It no longer had to rely on its poor soil for food as it could import cereals from the Bosphorous. Attica was converted to specialized agriculture based on the olive and the grape. This produced wine and oil for export.

The excess silver produced at Laurium was stored in the temples for future emergencies. It seems the Greek felt that the additional factor of sacrilege would deter robbers. And such emergency was to come soon in the form of Persian imperialism. Xerxes launched an invasion of Greece in 480 B. C. He had the finest fleet Persian wealth could command. At this time the Persians ruled the Phoenicians who possessed the most advanced naval technology of the day. But the Greeks, greatly outnumbered, also possessed the advanced naval technology and plenty of reserves of silver in their temples to assemble an equivalent fleet. The outcome favored the Greeks. They destroyed the Persian fleet at Salamis and Xerxes was forced to retire from Europe in 479 B. C. To be sure, Xerxes fell victim to the folly that destroyed many imperialists before and after his day by overextending his power far from home, but the Greeks owed their victory to superior naval technology and the wealth to manifest it effectively against the Persians.

Thereafter Athens became a great imperial power but her days of glory did not last long. Like most nations Athens exhausted its wealth in war and senseless imperialistic ventures. In this case it was the misadventure in Syracuse. Thereafter the Spartans succeeded the Athenians as the dominant state in classical Greece.

Athens, nonetheless, managed its money much better than the Romans. The Greeks realized that the acceptability of their coins abroad rested on their purity. Their coins were normally 98 per cent silver, which is better than sterling. Their monetary unit was the drachma. The purchasing power of the drachma at the start of the 5th century B. C. was a bushel of grain. The Athenian owl—a coin with the image of the owl of Athena—was readily and generally accepted throughout the Mediterranean area during the 5th century before Christ. The Athenians resisted depreciation of the drachma for years but in the end they succumbed as is the way with all dominant societies. War and foreign adventures are the greatest engines of inflation. War compels nations to debase their money. And so in the end it was the case with Athens.

The mines of Laurium were worked with slaves. The government owned the minerals and leased the right to work them to private contractors for an initial payment of a talent ($6000) and a royalty of one-twenty fourth of the silver produced. The operators worked the mines with their own slaves or hired them from other slave owners. Nicias, who led the Athenian forces to defeat at Syracuse, is said to have made $175 a day by leasing 1000 slaves to the mine operators at Laurium.

The working conditions at Laurium were inhuman. There were some 20,000 slaves working 10 hour days on their knees, their stomachs and their backs in galleries three feet high and two feet wide. The broken ore had to be passed from hand to hand out of the galleries as they were not wide enough for two men to pass each other. Great profits were reaped by the slave owners, operators and the Athenian government for 100 years or more. The annual royalties of the government amounted to 100 talents ($600,000). The exhaustion of the mines in the 4th century B. C. was an important factor in the decline of Athenian power and glory.

After the invention of money by the Greeks and the basing of the money on the precious metals the destinies of men and nations revolved for centuries around the quest for the precious metals. To gain power to dominate other peoples nations pursued the acquisition of gold and silver through plunder and trade. Millions of humans were virtually consumed in bringing the gold and silver out of the ground. These slaves too were prized as spoils of war. This continued well into the present time when industrialization changed the order of things to the more basic materials required by a highly technological production. It is in order, therefore, to sketch briefly this history.

The Phoenicians arose as traders at about the same time as the Greeks. They concentrated on the western Mediterranean where they founded Carthage. Around 300 B. C. Carthage was the wealthiest city on the Mediterranean. The development of coinage by the Greeks was quickly adopted by the Carthaginians and they had the precious metals for the purpose. Centuries earlier the Phoenicians had captured the gold, silver, tin and copper mines of Spain and traded the metals all over the Mediterranean area. During the 4th century before Christ the Punic stater, made of gold, was readily acceptable in Carthaginian trade around the Mediterranean.

The Carthaginians too dissipated their wealth in debilitating imperialism. For centuries they fought the Greek colonies in the western Mediterranean. But Carthage exhausted itself in its invasion of Italy. The Romans repulsed Hannibal in 216 B. C. and eventually destroyed Carthage in 146 B. C.

It is to be noted that the Romans realized the value of precious metals and seized the mines of Spain during the first Punic war (264–241 B. C.). Carthage gave first priority to the reconquest of the mines in 237 B. C. In 207 B. C. Scipio recaptured Spain and the mines were thereafter worked for the benefit of Rome.

Until the last two centuries before the Christian era Rome was primarily agricultural. The Punic wars gave the Romans a taste for conquest and domination. The Roman farmer made a good soldier. He was strong, courageous and amenable to stern discipline. The result was the famous Roman legion. The legions were supported by the ingenuity of the Roman engineer. It has already been mentioned that the invention of the corvus enabled Rome to defeat the Carthaginian navy which until then dominated the western Mediterranean. This tactic enabled the Romans to destroy the Carthaginian fleet in their first encounter off the coast of Sicily in 256 B. C. Roman engineers went on subsequently to design and construct some of the most effective siege machines known in antiquity to facilitate the foreign conquests of the legions.

These conquests were expensive, but for two centuries or so the plunder more than compensated Rome for the effort. Slaves and precious metals poured into Rome. By the end of the Republic Rome controlled the gold and silver mines of Spain, Gaul, Dacia, Thrace and Nubia. Needless to say these mines were worked with slaves captured in the wars of conquest or purchased from pirates.

At the beginning of the Christian era a phenomena was in full force which was to play an important role in the history of man for some two thousand years. It was the drain of wealth—gold and silver—to Asia. The gold drain actually started centuries earlier but it was in full force by the time of the Roman era. At this time the Asians possessed superior technology for the production of desirable goods highly prized by the Romans and others. The Greeks and Phoenicians were mainly traders. The Romans farmers. Technological superiority did not shift from Asia to Europe until the last quarter of the second millennium after Christ. Until then the people of the Mediterranean area sought the superior manufacturers of the East.

China produced silk, paper, drugs, cinnamon bark and other desirable products. Silk was traded pound for pound—for gold. India produced muslin, dyes, steel, gems, ivory, spices and the like. The cotton of India was so fine that a piece of muslin 39 inches wide and 6 yards long (a sari) could be pulled through a finger ring! Pearls, precious stones, perfume and rugs came from Persia and Arabia. Mid East merchants transported these products from China and India in costly caravans. Each city along the route exacted tolls and other charges. Much of the gold stayed with these middlemen. The silk was dyed and woven into cloth in Syria for reexport to Rome. There was also glass from Tyre and Sidon. And linen from Egypt. All these products and services had to be paid for in gold or silver as the Asians would accept nothing else for these goods. The Mediterranean area produced mainly food but in this respect the Asians were self sufficient. Actually, Rome, after ruining its agriculture, became even dependent on Egypt for wheat.

During the period of conquest the Romans became rich on the spoils of war. Precocious and rapacious Romans became multi-millionaires. Crassus acquired a net worth of 170 sesterces ($100 million). Among other properties he owned a gold mine in Spain. He is reported to have said that no Roman should consider himself rich unless he could raise, equip and maintain his own army. This insatiable greed for gold, of course, led to his misadventure against the Parthians.

Crassus knew where more gold was to be found. His keen sense about gold made him aware of the gold drain to the East. A century or so later knowledgeable Romans were acutely aware of the gold drain to India, China and other parts of Asia. Pliny (23–79 A. D.) estimated the gold drain at 100 million sesterces ($60 million) to India and Arabia alone. As early as 22 A. D. Tiberias wrote "How are we to deal with the peculiar articles of female vanity, and, in particular with the rage for jewels and precious trinkets, which drains the Empire of its wealth." History records that the dissolute life of imperial Rome continued and with it the drain of wealth to the East.

This loss of the precious metals caused the Romans to grossly mismanage their money which begat the inevitable inflation that flows from monetary irresponsibility. Some historians ascribe the fall of Rome to this mismanagement of money. Whereas inflation is usually a factor in the decline of most societies, it is probably an oversimplification to ascribe the fall of Rome to the debasement of its currency. There were many causes of which the loss of its wealth (the reason for its money mismanagement) was no doubt very important.

Rome's original coin was the as. It consisted of a pound of copper in the form of a rod one foot long. This was reduced to two ounces by 241, one ounce by 202 and a half ounce by 87 B. C. In A. D. 60 it was a quarter ounce! When the Romans launched their imperialism two centuries before Christ they began to coin silver, called the denarius. For centuries they kept the denarius at its original value but by 100 A. D. it too was subject to debasement. Nero lowered the silver content to 90 percent, Trajan to 85, Aurelius to 75, Commodus to 70, and Severus to 50. The aureus, a gold coin, which was first minted by the generals during the last days of the Republic to pay for their soldiers and continued by the Caesars, originally contained one fortieth of a pound of gold. Nero reduced it to one forty-fifth. Caracalla to one fiftieth, Dioletian to one-sixtieth and Constantine to one seventy-second. The denarius was repudiated by the government under Diocletian (284–305 A. D.) which signaled the bankruptcy of the western portion of the empire.

Constantine subsequently established his rule in Constantinople (330 A. D.) which was the beginning of the Byzantine empire. Most of the wealth was now in this part of the empire. The Byzantine empire employed it to dominate the eastern Mediterranean area for about 8 centuries.

The Byzantine empire was more productive than Rome. For example, it established its own silk industry. Legend has it that two Nestorian monks from central Asia, or some Persians, smuggled the eggs of the moth in a hollow cane out of China. Presumably they, or someone else must also have brought to Byzantium the technology of silk growing, reeling and twisting into yarn. But, as already discussed in Chapter VI, human technology cannot be kept secret. In 552 A. D. Justinian made the silk industry a state monopoly.

The Byzantines also invented Greek fire. The invention is attributed to one Kallinikus during the 7th century. The chemical formula was kept a strict secret, but it was a concoction of naptha, nitrate, sulphur and carbon. It was sprayed ignited upon an enemy ship or other object much like the flame thrower used by modern armies. It was also flung from a catapault in solid form timed to ignite on its target. This technological advantage enabled Constantinople to maintain the strongest navy in the Mediterranean for centuries. It was an important factor in the impregnable fortifications of the city.

Constantine set out immediately to restore integrity to the currency. A new coin called the solidus or bezant was minted consisting of one-sixth of an ounce of gold. Its value was maintained for centuries, but by 1000 A. D. it too was debased by the eastern emperors and it degenerated to the lowly and almost worthless sou.

In the west the Caesars in Rome could no longer maintain the frontiers. They lacked the money for the purpose. The Goths, Franks, Germans and other peoples took over Europe and it reverted to an agricultural, mostly non-monetary society. The monastary and the manor became the chief economic units. They were self sufficient independent entities. What trade existed was mostly on a barter basis. There was very little bullion or specie left in Europe for monetary trade.

Finally, the rise of Muslim power served further to isolate Europe from the East. In the 7th century the Arabs captured Sicily and Spain thereby gaining complete control of the Mediterranean. European trade with the East dwindled to a trickle. Moreover, the Arabs raided the coastal cities of Italy and France for what little wealth still remained.

But as Muslim power in the Mediterranean waned and as Constantinople was by-passed in trade the European cities, particularly in Italy, began to reverse the flow of wealth. Venice, Genoa, Pisa and Amalfi built formidable navies. Unfortunately they had little to trade, but they capitalized on the slave trade. The Muslims, now ruling Egypt, were eager to have these slaves. Gold and silver began to move back to Europe. Genoa minted the silver grosso. Venice followed with the gold florin. These coins came to be widely accepted in Mediterranean trade after 1000 A. D.

At this stage a curious phenomena arose that was to have profound historical repercussions. It was the Crusades. Christianity easily and readily converted the Germanic tribes that took over from the Romans in Europe. These "barbarians", having no philosophy or science of their own, took to Christianity with a fervor. Will Durant refers to this period in European history as the Age of Faith. Christianity's holy places—Jerusalem and other places mentioned in the Bible—were, however, in Asia and under the rule of non Christians. It was destined that these men of great faith would one day set out to recapture these holy places for their God. The clergy had no difficulty in whipping up the fervor of the Europeans for this venture, for they could promise everything. A man could not lose. If he died on the way to the Holy Land he would go straight to Heaven; if he succeeded in wresting Jerusalem for the Church he would be doubly rewarded in Heaven. The early Crusades were pitiful affairs from the military standpoint, but as so frequently is the case the political situation in the Near East with various Muslim factions (the Turks and Arabs and Arab sects) at odds with each other, and Constantinople becoming more and more isolated, this rag-tag army from Europe was able to capture Jerusalem in 1099 A. D.

It is the fourth Crusade (1202–1204 A. D.), however, which is of primary importance to the topic of this chapter. While the Italians participated in the earlier Crusades by providing naval transport and assisting in the assaults, for which they received trading rights in the port cities (Tyre, Acre, Jaffa) of the eastern Mediterranean, they always had their eye on gold more than God. The Venetians, finally, subverted the fourth Crusade into a raid on Constantinople and plundered the Byzantine empire of much gold, silver, gems and other wealth. It rectified in some measure the flow of wealth from west to east.

The third Crusade (1187–1192 A. D.), perhaps the most romantic of them all, did not accomplish much except to wrest free access for Christian pilgrims to Jerusalem. The Muslims were reunited once again under a strong leader, Saladin, and in control of the Holy Land. The leadership of the third Crusade was shared by the kings of England, France and Germany. In the end the leadership devolved upon Richard the Lion Hearted. His exploits have given rise to many legends making this crusade the most colorful in history. But the Popes remained unsatisfied as the Muslims still retained control of the Holy Land.

Pope Innocent kept agitating for another assault on the Holy Land and the shrewd Venetians came up with a plan. They proposed to furnish naval transport for 4500 knights and horses, 9000 squires, 20,000 infantry, and nine months supplies for prepayment of 85,000 marks of silver ($35 million). Venice would, in addition, provide 50 war galleys on condition half the spoils of conquest would go to Venice.

The Doge Henry Dandolo, now 95 and perhaps the greatest man Venice ever produced, was to lead the expedition. The knights and soldiers were mainly French. Although Innocent had in mind an assault on the Holy Land from Egypt the wily Dandolo had no intentions of attacking Egypt with which Venice now enjoyed a lucrative trade. He had in mind instead, first, an attack on Zara, an Adriatic city that had defected from Venice to Hungary and, finally, Constantinople itself. But Innocent decreed that there was to be no attack on Christian cities. Undeterred by the Pope's stricture and threats of excommunication Dandolo assaulted both Zara and Constantinople and plundered them for their wealth. In Constantinople the Venetians knew where the treasure was hidden from years of trading with the Byzantines. Great quantities of gold, silver, gems, silk and ermine were taken. The Venetian share is not known but the share of the French is estimated as 400,000 marks of silver ($160 million). Thousands of art masterpieces were stolen. Among them were the four bronze horses that now grace the Piazza di San Marco in Venice. Venice was now master of the Mediterranean and it had the wealth to muster the finest navy of the day for the purpose.

Far more important than the wealth that was transferred to Europe by the Crusades may be the technological knowledge gained by the Europeans in these contacts with Asia. Silk and glass technology was mastered by the Italians and French. Europeans learned of the compass and other navigational instruments developed by the Chinese. They may even have learned of gunpowder in these contacts. New plants, crops and trees were transplanted to Europe—rice, sesame, lemons, melons, peaches, apricots, cherries, dates, shallot and scallions. The windmill and the lateen sail became familiar to them. Some of these techniques and ideas had already been filtering into Europe from the Arabs through Sicily and Spain but now their dissemination became widespread. They fired the imaginations and enthusiasm of the Europeans. The development of the heavy windmill and the fully rigged keeled ship to harness the power of the wind were the outgrowth of this westward movement of the techniques of the East. As was discussed in Chapter V the windmill was perhaps the greatest catalyst for the development of the mechanical genius of the north Europeans which eventually ushered in the Industrial Revolution. The fully rigged ship was, on the other hand, the machine that facilitated the domination of the world by the Europeans after the 16th century. The Crusades were certainly instrumental in this shift of technological superiority from Asia to Europe during the latter half of the present millennium.

At the same time the Crusades also stimulated the desire for the good living and luxuries enjoyed by the Muslims. Silks, muslins, tapestries, rugs, gems, dyes, scents, pepper, ginger, cloves and cinnamon, virtually unknown around 1000 A. D. in Europe, were in great demand in the 13th century. This required bullion and specie and the precious metals continued to drain to the East.

But Europe was now to acquire a new source of gold and silver through its discovery and conquest of the Americas. In part, the discovery was due to the taste developed by the Europeans for the fine textiles and spices of Asia. Europeans were anxious to free themselves of dependence on the caravans which were being constantly interrupted by war or other calamaties in central Asia and the Near East. They yearned for a sea route to India and China. They had by this time developed a substantial sea going vessel in the full rigged deep hulled ship and were ready for such adventure.

They did achieve their objective in reaching India and China by sea but they got an unexpected bonus in discovering new lands and civilizations with plenty of gold and silver to plunder. The establishment of a sea route to India and the Far East, quite obviously doomed Venice as a power for Europe no longer was dependent on the caravans and Mediterranean trade for the products it wanted from Asia.

The fore part of the 16th century saw an unprecedented flow of gold and silver to Europe, mostly through Spain. The plunder of the Aztecs and Incas for gold and silver has already been detailed in the last chapter. Gold was not used for money in these Indian societies so it did not hold the same value to them as it did to the Europeans. Gold was used mostly for religious purposes and for art and adornment by the caciques and other members of the elite. This variance in values resulted in what must be one of the most curious trades in history. Bernal Diaz mentions, time and again, in his narrative that the Spaniards traded glass beads for gold with the Indians. The Indians, unfamiliar with glass technology found the multicolored glass beads beautiful and desirable. Since gold was not as highly esteemed as in Europe and Asia they were willing to trade it for the glass beads. In the European scale of values this was a good deal as glass was abundant and easy to produce. But such peaceful acquisition of the gold accumulated in the Americas was too slow. So the Spaniards set out to take it by force since they had the power to do so.

The plunder of the gold, substantial as it may have been, was obviously a non recurring event. Since it was placer gold it was accumulated slowly over time. The sustained flow of precious metals to Europe from the Americas was from the famous silver mines of Potosi located high in the Andes in Bolivia. Pizarro and his men became aware of these mines early in their quests and by the middle of the 16th century the Spaniards worked them fully. As was usually the case in these times the mines were worked with forced labor of the Indians. The Spaniards frequently had near revolts on their hands from the unwilling miners. The most serious was an insurrection in 1780 headed by Tupac Amaru.

In today's values several billion dollars worth of silver was shipped to Europe from Potosi. When Drake raided the Isthmus of Panama across which the Spaniards transported the silver he captured a mule train of 190 mules each loaded with 300 pounds of silver! But the scope of the operation can also be read in the magnitude of the human involvement. In 1651 Potosi had a population of 160,000 and was the largest city in the Americas until the 18th century. After the silver was exhausted Potosi became famous for its tin mines of modern times.

The history of Potosi still remains to be written. There is apparently much material in the libraries and archives of Bolivia and Spain awaiting research. But what is known reveals a boom town like that of other silver mines such as Virginia City in the United States during the 19th century, only that it lasted for nearly three centuries! The Incas apparently knew of Potosi a century or more before the Spaniards came. Legend has it that the Inca Huayana Capac halted mining at Potosi when he heard a tremendous noise and mysterious voice commanding him "to take no silver from this hill. It is destined for others." The Spaniards were undeterred—perhaps they were the "others" for whom the silver was intended—and started mining Potosi in 1545. There ensued at once the greatest mining boom in history. Twenty five years later a census of Potosi by Viceroy Francisco de Toledo showed a population of 120,000! In 1650, a hundred years later, while the colonists in Massachusetts and Virginia were concerned about surviving the next winter, Potosi had a population of 160,000 drowning in wealth. "As rich as Potosi" used to be the saying in 16th century Europe when describing an extremely rich person or other object of fabulous wealth.

Potosi was a typical mining town. Gambling and fighting flourished. Around 1700 there were 14 dance halls, 36 gambling houses and one theatre with an admission charge of 50 pesos. There were some 700–800 gamblers and 120 prostitutes. Most renowned was the courtesan Dona Clara whose home and salon were fitted out with the luxuries of Europe and Asia. Women were scarce in Potosi as most could not abide the cold climate where the summer temperature did not go above 70° F. There was much fighting over the favors of the few who came to the city.

The mining was done by forced labor, known as the mita. The Indians were assigned to units called repartimientos, and a certain portion of each group was required to work in the mines for a fixed period of the year. The miners, who were usually Spaniards or creoles, worked the Indians assigned to the mines. The mita was opposed by the church. There was always a shortage of labor. A quaint custom arose that permitted anyone to work the mines during weekends and holidays and keep the silver to themselves. There is no record of the silver so extracted as it did not pay the royal fifth. No one really knows how much silver came out of Potosi. Production figures compiled by Lamberto de Sierra, treasurer of Potosi, in June 16, 1784 show that the crown received 151,722,647 pesos and the miners 850,513,893 pesos of silver during the period 1556–1783. But this was only the silver on which the royal fifth was collected.

The cerro, or mountain of Potosi, was first worked from the top by the Spaniards where the ore was almost pure silver and could easily be smelted. By 1556 the good ore was exhausted and more complex technology was required to work the poorer quality ore. The ore had to be crushed, thirty-two lakes were eventually built to impound the summer rains for water power for the grinding mills. In 1626 one of the dams burst and destroyed a large part of the city. The greatest technological achievement was the use of mercury to extract the silver from the ore. At first the mercury came from nearby Huancavelica but eventually it had to be imported from Europe and China.

The refined silver was cast in cylindrical ingots that were loaded on llamas for transport over the Andes to Lima and other coastal cities. From there the ingots were shipped to Panama and transported across the Isthmus by mule trains. The treasure ships carried the silver on its final leg of the voyage to Spain. It was already mentioned that Sir Francis Drake raided these mule trains in the 1570's. The alternate route down the Plata river to Buenos Aires was never developed because of hostile Indians along the 1500 mile route.

By 1800 Potosi was exhausted. The Spaniards had other silver mines in Mexico but none yielded the silver that did Potosi. So symbolic of Spanish rule was Potosi that Simon Bolivar made it the terminal point of his revolution against Spanish rule. When he reached it on October 5, 1825 Potosi was a mere shadow of its former resplendence. Bolivar spent seven weeks of triumphant celebration of independence in the city. On October 26 Bolivar, accompanied by General Jose Antonio Sucre, climbed the cerro and delivered a triumph oration, "We came victorious from the Atlantic coast.

In fifteen years of continuous and terrific strife, we have destroyed the edifice that tyranny erected during three centuries of usurpation and uninterrupted violence. . . Standing here on this silver mountain of Potosi, whose rich veins were Spain's treasury for three hundred years, I must declare my belief that this material wealth is as nothing compared with the glory of bearing the ensign of freedom from the shores of the Orinoco to plant it on the summit of a mountain which is the admiration and envy of the world.''

The Spaniards and Portuguese were the first Europeans to employ the new technology—the full rigged ship and firearms—to dominate the Americas and trade with India and the Far East. In dividing the world between them for conquest and trade Pope Alexander VI in his famous Papal Bull of 1494 awarded the Americas to Spain. The Indian civilizations in the Americas were so backward technologically that it was easy for the Spaniards to overwhelm and plunder them of their gold and silver. They also appropriated their land, which in the long run, proved to be a far better source of wealth. The Portuguese, on the other hand, in the territory awarded them by the Pope found no such backward societies, albeit they had more wealth than the American Indians, so they had to resort to trade. India was ruled by the powerful Mughals, but the Portuguese had the advantage of sea power. They could only capture and establish coastal trading posts and when the Muslims threatened to destroy them they would simply retreat to sea in their ships. The tactic, however, proved successful and Alburquerque founded the Portuguese colony of Goa in 1510 from whence Portuguese naval power dominated the west coast of India. Diu, Daman, Salsette, Bassain, Charil and Bombay were other coastal settlements. Attempts at colonization failed because of the persecution by the Deccan Muslims and the greater attraction and propinquity of Brazil for the purpose. Similar trading settlements were established by the Portuguese at Macao to trade with China and Timor to trade with Indonesia. The Far East trade was monopolized by the Portuguese for most of the 16th century.

The north Europeans, particularly the English, arrived on this scene a century or so late. The Spaniards and Portuguese had already established their positions. So they resorted to piracy to obtain their share of the spoils. The English were not great seafarers at the start of the 16th century, but as the population increased and as the yoemen were ousted from the land they began to take to the sea as adventurers. Some indulged in piracy in the North Sea. Others began to raid the low countries in resentment of Spanish imperialism so close to England. By the latter half of the century the English had mastered both the construction of formidable sailing ships and seamanship to challenge the Spanish Armada in 1588 and defeat it, to be sure, with considerable assistance from the weather and good fortune. They could now prey on the Spanish silver fleet and raid the rich Spanish colonies in the West Indies with impunity. The raids on the Spanish and Portuguese however, started decades earlier. The first Englishmen of note who preyed on Spanish shipping was Francis Drake. Equally notable was John Hawkins, who was actually more of a slaver than a pirate. After a raid on Lima and other west coast cities, where he captured a Spanish treasure ship, Drake returned to England in 1580 with 2.5 million pounds of silver and other treasures. The English crown took an equivocal position on these adventures. Elizabeth was pleased with the wealth they brought to England, but did not wish to break openly with Philip of Spain over them. But after the attack by the Spanish Armada in which Hawkins distinguished himself, Elizabeth knighted both Hawkins and Drake. A century or so later Charles II knighted the buccaneer Henry Morgan who sacked Panama in 1671 and made him governor of Jamaica. The line between piracy and state policy was very thin in England in those days. In 1597 Drake and Hawkins launched an expedition to wrest the West Indies from Spain. This audacious scheme ended in disaster as Spain was still too formidable a power to succumb to a couple of English adventurers. Both men lost their lives. Hawkins died off Puerto Rico and Drake, of dysentary, off Portobelo.

The other source of wealth for the English was the slave trade. The Spanish needed slaves to work the land they acquired in the Americas. Since Africa fell to the Portuguese in the Papal Bull of Alexander VI the negro slave trade was their perogative. In due time the English began to poach on this lucrative business. Sir John Hawkins was the most famous slave trader of the times. He plundered Portuguese slave ships and conducted raids in Africa for the slaves and peddled them off the Spanish Main. Much gold and silver was gained thereby for England by these slavers.

Moreover the English were not prepared to let the Portuguese monopolize the trade with India. In 1600 Elizabeth chartered the East India Company which founded its first Indian factory at Surat (near Bombay). Madras was established in 1639. Calcutta was founded later in 1698. In 1668 the company acquired Bombay. Bombay was given to Charles II by the Portuguese as part of the dowry of Cathrin of Braganza. Charles did not quite know what to do with it so he transferred it to the company for an annual rent of £10! This small episode is cited here to show the insouciance of the Europeans in their newly emerging dominance over India. These three ports became from then on, the centers of English economic penetration of India under the East India Company and came to be called the presidencies of Bombay, Madras and Calcutta. Even today they remain principal cities of India.

The French came last. *The Campagne des Indes Orientals* was formed in 1664. They established their trade centers at Surat, Pondicherry, and Chandernager (near Calcutta). In due time Pondicherry became the main French city in India. Bitter rivalry ensued thereafter between the Europeans for commercial primacy in India. The Dutch were the first to retire from the fray choosing instead to concentrate on their trade with Indonesia. The

Portuguese did not extend their operations beyond the west coast centraliz-ing their presence in Goa.

This left the French and English to struggle for supremacy in India. The French had a very able man in Joseph Francis Dupleix, who was the governor of Pondicherry when the French and English went to war over the Austrian succession in 1740–45. The war spilled over into India and the two mercantile companies, although they tried to remain neutral, found them-selves at war in the Carnatic, the east coast area of the peninsula. They started to vie for support from the Indian princes and in this struggle the French lost out. A young clerk of the company by the name of Robert Clive distinguished himself in the Carnatic wars and gave the English dominance in this part of India.

The final defeat of the French was to transpire, however, in Bengal. The English until now maintained a policy of refraining from taking any territory in India except their small trading centers. In 1698 the company was granted the zamindari (revenue rights) of three Bengal villages, one of which was Kalekata, where Calcutta was established. In addition the Mughal emperor, ordered the Nawab of Bengal to issue a *firman* commuting the company's custom duties to an annual payment of Rs. 3000.

But difficulties with the Nawab of Bengal continued. When the war broke out again in Europe between the French and English in 1756 the English fortified Calcutta fearing an attack by the French from Chandernagar which was up river from Calcutta. The Nawab, a young, violent and suspicious man named Surajah Dawlah, who had just succeeded to the throne, misinterpreted it as a military move against him and he attacked Calcutta in 1756. The assault resulted in the notorious Black Hole of Calcutta, wherein 146 English prisoners were confined in a room 10 × 15 feet in 100° temperature for a night and all but 23 perished. The company sent Clive to retrieve the English cause. Clive recovered Calcutta in January 1757 and, forthwith decided to depose the Nawab. The Nawab was unpopular with his own people. The Hindus hated him. And he made an enemy of Mir Jaffar an important Mughal official at the court. Clive marched against the Nawab with the support of these Indian elements and defeated him at Plassey on June 23, 1757. Mir Jaffar was installed in his place. Thereafter the Nawab of Bengal was in effect an English puppet. The French were now completely outmaneuvered. They were allowed to keep their trading centers but their influence was destroyed.

The Battle of Plassey is generally regarded as the beginning of British rule in India. As with the pirates two centuries earlier the British government took a benign attitude, pleased with the results but pleading it was the action of a private company and not the British government. It enabled Winston Churchill, the old imperialist, to write later "To call this process 'imperialist expansion' is nonsense, if by that is meant deliberate acquisition of political power. Of India it has been said that the British empire was acquired in a fit of absence of mind.'' That did not prevent Churchill from saying years later, when he was Prime Minister "I have not become the King's first Minister in order to preside over the liquidation of the British Empire" in answer to India's struggle for independence.

In line with the history of the world for the past two millennia the plunder of the Americas for its precious metals and gems and the new sea trade with India and the Far East resulted once again, in a drain of the newly acquired wealth to Asia. The flow of gold and silver to Europe during the 16th and 17th centuries, first, stimulated business in Europe. It generated also the greatest inflation in this millennium until that of modern times. Spain enjoyed a brief period of imperialism extending its rule over the low countries. In due time, however, the gold and silver flowed East along the new sea routes to pay for the textiles, spices and luxury goods the Europeans desired from Asia. From 1711 to 1720 the annual export of bullion by the East India Company averaged £ 434,000. Like their predecessors the Romans the English started to debase their currency to make the vanishing bullion stretch. In 1760 the shilling had lost one-sixth, and sixpence one-quarter of its original weight in silver, while the crown piece had almost disappeared. By mid-18th century much of the bullion plundered from the Americas had drained to the East and Europe was again desperately short of bullion and specie. It was at this time that the English gained control of India and a new source of wealth became available to them. The hoards of gold, silver and precious gems in India were fabulous. In a devastating raid on Delhi in 1739 Nadir Shah of Persia stole the famous Peacock Throne of the Mughal emperors. This was a solid gold and jewel encrusted masterpiece. Valuable artifacts like this of precious metal and stones were common in India. Moreover, every peasant woman had her 22 carat gold or solid silver ankle, wrist or neck band which represented the family's wealth. When multiplied by 50 million women that represented a large amount of bullion. Much of the gold and silver was still in its original European coinage. When the Nawab conducted Clive through his vaults he saw among the piles of precious metals, gems and artifacts, bezant and florin coins.

How much of this store of precious metals and gems the English plundered (they used more palatable terms) is not known. It was not only the leaders like Clive who enriched themselves but every lowly clerk of the company participated in the aggrandizement. All this wealth eventually found its way to England to fructify its economy.

There is reason to believe that Clive was quite restrained in his enrichment in India. At his trial for impeachment, where he was acquitted, he pleaded "Am I not rather deserving of praise for moderation which marked my proceedings. Consider the situation in which the victory at Plassey had placed me. A great prince was dependent on my pleasure; an opulant city lay at my mercy; its richest bankers bid against each other for my smiles; I walked through vaults which were thrown open to me alone, piled on either hand with gold and jewels Mr. Chairman, at this moment I stand astonished at my own moderation.'' This evoked a unanimous resolution from the House of Commons that "Robert Clive rendered great and meritorious service to his country.'' All this wealth and glory however, did not bring peace to Clive for he committed suicide a few years later.

His administration in India after Plassey shows he had the interests of the company at heart as much as his own. After his victory at Plassey Clive requested the Mughal emperor in Delhi to appoint the company the Diwan of Bengal, Bihar and Orissa, perhaps, the richest region in India. Under Mughal organization finance was separated from general administration. The Diwan collected the revenues and after making due provision for provincial administration, remitted a certain amount to the emperor in Delhi and retained the remainder for his services as tax collector. Clive's report to the board of directors dated September 30, 1765 estimated the annual profit from the Diwani as £ 1,650,000! The company reassessed the land revenue in the famous Permanent Settlement of 1793 which appropriated from one-third to one-half of the output of the land in revenue. As the company extended its rule over Oudh (north India), Madras (south India) and the territories wrested from the Marathas in the Bombay area additional land revenues flowed into its treasury.

Most of the surplus revenue was used to purchase Indian goods for export from india. The Indian people were made to pay for the goods the English imported from India! Bullion no longer flowed into the country for its manufacturers. During the period 1766–69 the company's exports amounted to £ 5,686,375. From these basic figures alone it would appear that some £ 75 million were drained from India by the company alone during the period 1765–1813 when the British government changed the policy requiring that the land revenue be used in India.

Finally there was the financial strategem known as the home charges, whereby the Indian people were made to pay for their own conquest, government and the extension of the British empire in Asia. When the revenues of the company proved insufficient, the deficit was accumulated as a debt by the company to the British government. The home charges included the salaries and pensions of the English serving in India as administrators or soldiers. The administration of Indian affairs in London was debited to the home charges. After 1833 when the trading privileges of the company were terminated, and it continued as an administrative body for British rule in India, dividends of 10.5 per cent to the company's shareholders were added to the home charges to be paid out of Indian revenues. The Indian revenues of the company were usually insufficient to meet the home charges and by the time the company was terminated, after the mutiny in 1859, the deficit in the home charges stood at £ 69 million. When the company was liquidated, the Indian people were required to assume this debt to England and repay the shareholders their capital investment in the company. Romesh Dutt, the Indian economist and historian who has detailed the economic drain by the English from India in his *Economic History of India* wrote that "the empire was thus transferred from the Company to the Crown, but the Indian people paid the purchase price."

The home charges and the debt they generated continued after the mutiny. At the outset, when the British government took over direct rule over India in 1859, £ 40 million was added to the debt as Englands cost of suppressing the mutiny. By 1900 the Indian debt stood at £ 244 million. In 1900–1901, states Romesh Dutt, the home charges came to £ 17.5 million. The £ 17 million remitted as home charges was spent in England for (1) interest on the Indian debt, (2) interest on railways and (3) civil and military charges.

English historians justified the economic drain on several grounds. The main rationalization was that Indians were merely paying for the government the English provided. It is, however, one thing for a people to pay taxes for government by its own people where the revenues are spent within the country to promote consumption and investment and quite another for the money to be sent abroad to do the same for another country. No matter how the English tried to rationalize the matter it does not change the fact that the payments were a tribute from India to England as has been the custom since antiquity by a subservient nation to a dominant power.

The British government of India, however, was first rate. The Indian Civil Service was competent, uncorruptible and objective. Phillip Woodruff, one of these men who was prematurely retired after Independence in 1947, likened the ICS administration to Plato's guardians. As the ICS was opened to Indians several decades earlier they comprised about half the corps at the time of independence and formed the nucleus of the newly independent Indian government to establish a competent and stable democratic administration. This, at least, was a *quid pro quo* for the wealth drain.

How much wealth was transferred from India to England after 1757 is not precisely known. Montgomery Martin writes in his book *Eastern India* published in 1838:

> This annual drain of £ 3,000,000 on British India amounted in thirty years, at 12 per cent (the usual rate in India) compound interest, to the enormous sum of £ 723,997,917 sterling; or, at a low rate, as £ 2,000,000 for fifty years to £ 8,400,000,000 sterling! So constant and accumulating a drain even on England would soon impoverish her; how severe then must be its effects on India, where the wages of a labourer is from twopence to threepence a day?

> For a half a century we have gone on draining from two to three and sometimes four million pounds sterling a year from India, which

has been remitted to Great Britian to meet the deficiencies of commercial speculations, to pay the interest of debts, to support the home establishment, and to invest on Englands soil the accumulated wealth of those whose lives have been spent in Hindustan. I do not think it possible for human ingenuity to avert entirely the evil effects of a continued drain of three or four million pounds a year from a distant country like India, and which is never returned to it in any shape.

That the accumulated drain was substantial is evident. That much wealth still remained in India is also clear. But the balance of trade from thereon was favorable to England.

The timeliness of this transfer of wealth was most propitious for it coincided with the emergence of the Industrial Revolution. By 1786 Watts had produced an efficient steam engine of 50 horsepower. Prior to this time improved textile machines were invented and awaiting the new source of power to energize them. There was Arkwright's spinning machine in 1769. Hargrave's spinning jenny in 1764 and Compton's spinning mule in 1779. Cartwright perfected the power loom by 1792. Other inventions for carding, combing, drawing and finishing cotton, wool and flax were developed. They were powered by water in the beginning but from 1790 onward steam power took over rapidly.

All these machines and the steam engines to operate them required substantial capital investment. The wealth flowing into England from India provided much of the necessary finance. The new industries, however, were uncompetitive in the world markets in both cost of production (in part due to the large amount of capital needed) and in quality. The new machines could not produce cotton cloth of the fineness of Indian muslin. But England now had political control over the situation and imposed protective duties, up to 70–80 per cent, on Indian cloth, to protect the new mills at Manchester and Paisley. James Mill and Horace Haymen Wilson in their *History of British India* published in 1844 wrote:

It is also a melancholy instance of the wrong done to India by the country on which she has become dependent. It as stated in evidence (in 1813) that the cotton and silk goods of India up to the period could be sold for a profit in the British market at a price from 50 to 60 per cent lower than those fabricated in England. It consequently became necessary to protect the latter by duties of 70 to 80 percent, on their value or by positive prohibition. Had this not been the case, had not such prohibitory duties and decrees existed, the mills of Paisley and Manchester would have been stopped in their outset, and could scarcely have been again set in motion, even by the power of steam. They were created by the sacrifice of the Indian manufacture. Had India been independent, she would have retaliated, would have imposed prohibitive duties upon British goods, and would have thus preserved her own productive industry from annihilation. This act of self-defense was not permitted her; she was at the mercy of the stranger. British goods were forced upon her without paying any duty, and the foreign manufacturer employed the arm of political injustice to keep down and ultimately strangle a competitor with whom he could not have contended on equal terms.

The traditional weaving industry for which India was renowned for ages was ruined by the second decade of the 19th century. The Indians were now forced to purchase the inferior cottons of the English power looms. The fine Indian muslins prized by the ladies of Athens, Rome, Constantinople, Venice and other ancient capitals were now to vanish forever from the earth. The new textile technology eventally made cotton goods, though of lower quality, cheaper than those produced by human labor. Sir Perceval Griffiths, another prematurely retired Indian civil servant, sums up the situation in his book *The British Impact on India* as follows:

> Early in the nineteenth century substantial reductions were made in the British import duties on Indian piece goods—the duty on muslin was reduced from $27^1/_3$ per cent to 10 per cent and that on calicoes from $71^2/_3$ per cent to 10 per cent. These reductions to a level too low to be protective did not help Indian exports, and by 1830 Indian exports of cotton goods to Britain had dwindled to a negligible figure. *The simple fact was that in the new conditions of the textile world Indian cloth goods had ceased to be competitive.* (Italics added)

By 1830 England became the foremost industrialized country in the world. Her capital intensive industries were efficient mass producers able to outcompete all others. At this time British economic policy changed to free trade to the great detriment of India. Thus, while America, France, Germany and other underindustrialized countries at the time were pursuing vigorous protectionist policies to offset England's competitive advantage India, as part of the British empire, was required to pursue a policy of free trade. Nothing could have been better calculated to keep India from developing a textile industry based on the new technology to replace its ruined weaving industry.

India eventually developed a cotton industry based on power spinning and weaving. The American civil war (1860–64) provided the opportunity. The war curtailed American supplies of cotton to England and other European countries which gave a good market to India for its cotton grown in Gujerat. This brought some £ 75 million to the merchants of Bombay who invested it in textile machinery (ironically purchased from England) to start fifteen new mills during the period 1870–75. These new Indian industrialists clamored for protective duties which the British government constantly denied. The Indian struggle for protective duties was not won until the 1920's when British hold on India was weakening in the independence movement.

Thus for 150 years or more the British drained millions of pound sterling annually from India through outright plunder, at first, and thereafter collecting Indian revenues to pay English administrators and soldiers, purchase Indian goods for export to England and pay for the overhead in London to rule India and the extension of its empire in Asia. Finally, through self serving economic policy the British preserved India as a captive market for its manufacturers which garnered additional profits for the English. In the cold view of history this can only be called plunder by a dominant nation of the wealth of a subservient nation, palatable connotations to the contrary notwithstanding. That this constant flow of wealth or capital, to employ a more modern economic term, to England helped to make it the foremost industrial power of the 19th century cannot be gainsaid.

Dutch colonialism in Indonesia and French colonialism in Indochina were similar. The economic drain was doubtless less since these countries were not as wealthy as India. China, however, was different as it was never dominated by a single European country. For one thing, China was the most remote and more difficult to reach by sea. Then too, it was ruled by the powerful Manchu dynasty (1644–1911 A. D.) during the period of European expansion and domination of Asia in contrast to the Mughal empire in India which was in disintegration by mid 18th century. By the end of the 19th century a *modus vivendi* was reached among the European nations whereby they agreed all could trade with the Chinese without any one of them being supreme.

China never possessed the accumulated wealth of India, despite its fame for silk. By the time the gold and silver reached the end of the caravan in China much of it had already been appropriated by the middlemen poised between the Mediterranean and the Pacific. But in the 18th century China provided still another product the Europeans desired. It was tea. Silver began to flow to China in considerable quantities from Europe for silk and tea at this time. The Chinese did not want European goods and this posed a problem for the English and other Europeans.

The English and the Americans to a lesser extent found the answer in opium. The Chinese people became addicted to the drug which created a good market for it. The English produced opium in India and shipped it to China in exchange for tea. The Chinese ultimately became alarmed by this influx of opium not only for its debilitating effect on its people but by the inordinate enrichment of the Chinese merchants who bought the opium from the English. The government sent Lin Tse-hsu as its commissioner to the port of Canton with authority to deal with the odius situation. In 1839 he prohibited the import of opium and burned chests of the drug found in the

English factories. In 1840 British warships bombarded the south-eastern coast of China. The British entered the Yangtze estuary and threatened Nanking. In 1842 China capitulated. Under the Treaty of Nanking Hongkong was ceded to the British, certain other ports opened for European trade and a war indemnity paid. This was the start of several successive capitulations which eventually gave the European powers and the United States great dominance in China. The opium wars are an example of how amoral dominance among nations has frequently been in history.

European dominance of the world was over by mid-20th century. The English and French dissipated their wealth in two enervating Germanic wars during the forepart of the century. They could no longer afford to maintain their dominance in Asia. Moreover there was little left to exploit as Asia was now in dire poverty. The English lost their technological superiority to the Americans and Russians. They no longer possessed the capital to maintain an efficient industrial capacity.

It bears repeating again that the Industrial Revolution, still only two centuries old, marked a profound change in the history of man. It shifted the center of technological superiority to Europe and with it reversed the ancient drain of wealth to Asia. Two centuries of European dominance drained Asia of most of its wealth creating an inordinate and discriminating poverty in this sector of mankind. The Asians must now seek the advanced technology from the West in order to increase their productivity and alleviate this poverty. Unfortunately they lack the wealth or capital for the purpose. This is recognized by the Europeans, Americans, Russians and others and they have made several attempts through foreign aid programs, international finance agencies and the like to transfer the modern technology and capital to Asia, Africa and Latin America. The Asians and others, however, are required to pay dearly for the capital and modern technology. Most are now hopelessly in debt to the West. It is in effect a new form of dominance by the western nations.

It is not foreseeable at this time that the Asians can rectify the situation by force as did the Europeans a few centuries ago. The accelerative nature of technological development provides a formidable obstacle. As long as the western nations, primarily America and Russia at this time, remain technologically creative, they will continue to dominate the world. The technological creativity of the Europeans (including the Americans and Russians) could, however, peter out—it always has in the case of previous societies— while it is rekindled in Asia (China and India mainly) to an extent where the Asians, once again, become technologically superior. In such event it would be merely a repetition of history for the Asians to appropriate the wealth of the West by force. It is equally not foreseeable that the people of the West would voluntarily redistribute some of their wealth to the Asians to enable them to increase their productivity and alleviate their poverty. That would not be in keeping with the historical record of man to date. It would also not be in harmony with man's biological instinct of domination. But one can and should harbor hope in this respect as it would be a step toward the salvation of man on earth.

History thus records that as soon as man advanced technologically to produce a surplus he had constantly fought over the possession of that surplus. In this chapter we have detailed this struggle as it obtained between nations. There has been an equal strife within nations or states over the distribution of this surplus.

VIII
Wealth, Power and Revolution

Aristotle articulated the principle that the unequal distribution of wealth was the main cause of political instability of a society. He lists seven causes of revolution and places the maldistribution of wealth at the top. And so it has been throughout history, after Aristotle and doubtless prior to his time, ever since man produced a surplus through his technological development.

The last chapter detailed the struggle between nations for the surplus production of mankind. This has occupied a large measure of man's time and energy. Even more effort, however, has been devoted by man to the struggle over the surplus within his society. The situation of the corporate executive in modern times bears this out graphically. For years he studies in schools, colleges and graduate courses in business administration. Thereafter he spends most of the rest of his life in the struggle within a corporate heirarchy for increased salary and other benefits with which to command an increasingly greater share of the national production. His salary and wealth beget status and dominance. The struggle over the surplus production resulting from man's technological development, first within his own society and, second, with other societies has occupied the overwhelming proportion of man's time and energy on earth during the past 10,000 years or so. It is in large measure the warp and woof of history.

Animals do not fight or struggle over a surplus. They produce none. Herbivores spend most of their lives seeking plants to sustain life. If such plant life is insufficient they perish of malnutrition. Carnivores kill other animals regularly from time to time to maintain life. Man lived accordingly for all but 10,000 years or so of his two million or more years of life on earth.

As a hunter and forager man merely satisfied his daily needs. It was only after the invention of agriculture that he produced anything beyond his current needs, which promptly begot the problem of a fair and just distribution of the surplus production. It was only natural that the dominance instinct in man would come into play in sharing the surplus. The dominance instinct was, of course, in sway before man was capable of producing a surplus. In the hunting group the leader had first call on the food supply and the superior females of the group, as is observed in primate behavior today. This primacy was structured by nature into most species in order to assure optimum development of superior traits in the struggle for survival. In the hunting phase of man's existence the dominant male or males tempered their greed as they needed the cooperation of all members of the hunting group for mutual survival. Yet it would be unwarrranted to over stress or over romanticize this degree of cooperation. There is, after all, evidence of violence in the hunting group in the Neanderthal find with a spear thrust in his abdomen. But it stands to reason that the dominant males in early man's hunting groups had to bridle their greed lest they defeat their own good. This degree of cooperation and tempering of the dominance instinct, doubtless, carried over into the early agricultural societies.

By the time of recorded history, some five thousand years ago, the early civilizations, based upon agriculture, had become quite complex. Agriculture was organized on the alluvium and water supply of the river valleys of the earth through control of the flow of water, as in Egypt, or irrigation systems, as in Mesopotamia, China and elsewhere. The ruling elite, or dominant individuals now lived in cities or capitals. These early societies usually depended upon a strong leader, a king or pharoah, which was, doubtless a carryover from the hunting group. He was surrounded by other dominant individuals who derived their position as members of his bureaucracy or as land owners or otherwise. Dominance was predicated on wealth and status. The ruling elite had appropriated most of the surplus enabling them to maintain armed forces against the dominated majority. Relations between rulers and ruled had by now become remote and impersonal. Early recorded history is replete with repressive acts perpetrated against recalcitrant subjects. At the advent of recorded history human societies were all structured heirarchies predicated on the primate dominance instinct.

Despite the fact that the growing impersonal relationships of the expanding societies of man diminished the tempering effect on the ruling elite there were other forces at work that produced an ameliorating influence on the selfishness of the dominant individuals. To deny too severely their subject's participation in the consumption of the surplus was counterproductive. The slave, serf or tennant who produced the surplus had to be reasonably well fed, sheltered and clothed if he was to be a healthy and strong cultivator of the land of the ruling classes. Even under slavery, the most demeaning human status, it was in the owners interest to feed and clothe his slave well lest he dissipate his investment. Acts of cruelty and degradation were perpetrated upon slaves but they were most likely the exception, not the rule. But beyond this the dominated majority was not permitted to share in the distribution of the production and accumulated wealth of the society. This remained true until the Industrial Revolution, which greatly increased production. A greater proportion of the dominated majority had to be permitted a larger share of the national production not only because of the growing social awareness for a more equitable distribution of wealth but because the ruling elite needed a broader market for the more abundant production of its new technology. This begot the middle class that has played so important a role in the industrialized societies of the past two centuries or so. Political and civil liberties are meaningless until there is freedom from want. Democracy cannot flourish until more individuals than belong to the dominant minority are sufficiently secure economically so as to enjoy the political liberties and exercise the privileges afforded by a democratic form of government.

It is not the purpose of this review of history to discourse on political science. Suffice it to say that the struggle over the distribution of wealth differs little with the political organization of the society. The early civilizations were usually ruled by a monarch. This seems natural as man had only just graduated from the hunting group which required a leader for survival. The absolute rule of the dominant baboon observed in the jungle today supports this conclusion. But the monarch was not as absolute in his rule as it is often stated or recorded. He was merely the momentary head of the ruling elite. If he proved too autocratic he was deposed. Moreover, he was frequently deposed by a strong challenger from within the ruling elite as occurs regularly in primate societies except that with the apes the deposition of a leader is never accompanied by murder. Regicide is the commonest of events on the pages of history. One would be hard put to come up with the name of a Byzantine emperor who was not poisoned, beheaded, blinded or otherwise prematurely bereft of his crown. By Graeco-Roman times the political organizations of man began to deversify. Oligarchies and democracies appear occasionally. But the Greek democracies were not true democracies as the slaves and metics, comprising half the population or more, were not enfranchised. True democracies did not appear until after the Industrial Revolution which ameliorated the struggle over the distribution of wealth. The advanced technology produced a greater surplus which could be spread among more people without undue deprivation of the ruling elite. This made possible a more affluent middle class. An enlightened middle class made possible a true democracy. But the struggle over the surplus did not end; it was merely lessened as a democracy provided better means for relieving the pressures of extreme inequities in the distribution of the national production.

Where the inequity in the sharing of the wealth became too great it brought on rebellion or revolution of the dominated majority. But the ruling elite was usually aware of the possibilities of revolution which would deprive them of both their wealth and their status so the political system normally provided means to relieve the revolutionary pressures within the dominated majority. In ancient Rome where the slaves may have comprised half the population the Romans lived in constant fear of slave rebellions. A Roman saying, according to Martial, was that "every slave we own is an enemy we harbor." But the Romans permitted manumission on liberal terms which served to relieve the pressure to revolt. Despite easy manumission there were still some serious slave revolts. The most noteworthy was that of Spartacus in 73 B. C. already mentioned. An equally serious revolt arose in Sicily in 104 B. C. Both were dealt with ruthlessly by the Roman overlords. Most slaves, however, opted for manumission instead of revolution as they realized the Roman legions were too formidable a force to overcome. During the conquests of the two centuries before Christ, slaves were in abundant supply and could be had for a dollar a head. During the golden days of the empire the price of a slave rose to 400 dollars. Such substantial investment militated toward more lenient and fair treatment of the slaves and there is no historical evidence of slave revolts during the centuries after Christ.

The downtrodden masses are not easily stirred to revolt against the dominant minority. In most societies the dominant minority has properly indoctrinated them through religious or philosophical teachings to accept their lot on earth and seek salvation elsewhere. The Hindu caste system is especially noteworthy in this respect. Even when the rebellion is spontaneous it is usually frustrated by the ruling class as we shall see later in this chapter in the discussion of the Chinese Revolution. A successful revolution requires capable leadership. Thus if potential revolutionary leaders in the dominated majority can be compromised the chances of revolution are diminished. Most societies provide an alternative for such potential revolutionaries through the process that Pareto has labeled the "circulation of the elites." Capable and ambitious individuals within the dominated majority are allowed to move up the heirarchial scale and become accepted members of the ruling elite. The age old mandarin system of China is a good example. In an open society like America today the opportunities for such rise in the social heirarchy is open not only in government but in business and the professions. This process has a two fold effect on political stability. First it enables the superior individuals in the dominated majority to obtain a greater share in the distribution of wealth and, equally important, it brings into the dominant minority greater competence for perpetuating itself.

Societies that do not provide for a "circulation of the elites" are doomed to failure. If the throw of the genetic dice is unfavorable the ruling elite loses its competence to rule and is deposed. The Bourbons of France are worthy of note in this respect. History abounds with cases of great empire builders being succeeded by lesser men who lost control of the empire. But the deposition is usually not by the hands of the dominated majority. Herein enters another phenomena that must be noted. There is another circulation *within* the elite that recurs constantly in history. Here it becomes necessary to distinguish between the political elite and the ruling elite. The latter, normally dominate the former. Occasionally a headstrong king, emperor or dictator gets out of hand but such autocrat is shortlived. In a democracy too there are times of crisis, such as the Great Depression of the 1930's, when the elected officials legislate against the best interests of the ruling elite, but even in democracies it is the people of wealth who manage to protect their interests against the majority of voters. In fact, this occasional spurt of legislation that serves to achieve a more equitable distribution of wealth is a relief measure that makes democracies more viable polities less susceptible to violent revolution.

History records countless numbers of these lesser revolutions that merely change the political elite but not the ruling elite, the dominant individuals who control the wealth of a society. They are known by such familiar designations as palace revolts, coups and the like. A true democracy, particularly one with a well developed two party system, provides for such peaceful change of the political elites which are beholden to different factions in the ruling elite.

Societies are organized variously for the struggle over the surplus. China achieved political stability over centuries through a flexible bureaucratic *cum* land-owning system. If a genius was born among the peasants he could rise to the bureaucracy by passing the mandarin examinations. As a mandarin he was enabled to become a landowner. At the same time the landowners were able to maintain their position by training sons, for which they had the means, as mandarins. India achieved political stability over the ages with the caste system which prescribed every man's status in the society in a way which made it acceptable to the dominated majority. More on this later. In the Mediterranean area the distribution of wealth too was based primarily on landownership, but by Graeco-Roman times wealth came to be measured and transferred in money which made the possession of money, from whatever source derived, a means to status and dominance. It is an interesting commentary that the merchant and trader were held in low esteem under the Asian systems whereas trading, banking, and speculation were more acceptable means to wealth in ancient Greece and Rome. Where money was the means to power the circulation of the elites was more facile and served to promote political stability. The Roman empire was a remarkably stable polity. After the fall of Rome Europe reverted again to a system of landownership. The feudal system also was extremely stable for centuries. It resembled in many ways the Hindu caste system whereby every man's status was prescribed and he shared the production of the land accordingly. The monastary provided a means for peasant genius to rise into the dominant minority. The Industrial Revolution made feudalism obsolete, though it was disintegrating earlier, as industry superseded agriculture as the main producer of wealth. Industrialization brought forth an extremely complex society where, once again, wealth was measured and transferred in money. Money-lending and speculation in land and securities were now routes to wealth and dominance.

After the development of agriculture dominance among men was no longer based purely on merit as Nature structured the instinct. Dominance came to be based on wealth, and wealth, particularly in its money form could be got by theft, fraud, speculation, luck and other unearned means. Herein also enters another consideration arising from man's cultural development—that the sharing of the surplus should be on a fair and equitable basis. Merit and justice came to be regarded as the desideratum for the ideal society, but it has never been achieved. Yet most societies are so organized or strive to be insofar as human greed permits. A nation has to produce to be strong and the producers have to be duly rewarded for their production. A dominant elite that fails to adhere to this principle dooms its own future. It will not only fall behind in technological innovation and development but fail to produce the wealth to use the technology effectively. Its national prominence declines and it usually succumbs to foreign domination. A leading indicator of a society in decline and disintegration is whether the salary of a charioteer or entertainer is greater than that of an engineer or scientist.

While societies strive to distribute their wealth on the basis of merit and justice they too often permit nonproducers to share disproportionately in its wealth. This is particularly true of societies that reckon wealth in monetary terms. In ancient Rome too much wealth was appropriated by the money-lenders and speculators. Great fortunes, among others, that of the famous or infamous Crassus, were made out of speculation in land and other real estate. In modern industrial societies even greater fortunes are made by speculation, as the securities of industrial undertakings have now been added to land as equities for trading purposes. Trading in existing equities produces no wealth. Increases in their value is either due to social and economic development or inflation and belong to society as a whole. Distribution of a large share of the national production to speculators, bankers and other non-producers is another leading indicator of a society in disintegration.

Another non-producer is the criminal. There is first the individual criminal who refuses to abide by the rule that an individual can share in the national production only if he, in turn, contributes to it. To be sure, there are some who steal because the socio-economic system denies them an opportunity to contribute to its production. But most criminals turn to robbery, theft, embezzlement, bribery and fraud as a way to share in the surplus without earning it. The extent of crime wanes and waxes and most societies manage to keep it under control, but a large degree of criminal participation is characteristic of a disintegrating society. The war lord period in China during the days of the Republic is a good example.

A more complex phenomena is organized crime. It is in effect a minor rebellion against a society that is usually in disintegration. Organized crime also thrives well in democracies where justice administered under law gives the criminal certain advantages in evading the law and where the criminal is able to bribe the officials, usually in the lower echelon, of the political elite. Several historical examples can be cited. The Thuggees, from whence arose the word thug, of India lived off robbery and murder for centuries until the British exterminated them in 1831–37 while Lord William Bentnick was

Governor-general. The Thuggees were organized along caste lines. Children of Thuggees were destined for the criminal life. They lived by a rigid code. They committed Thuggee (robbery and murder) by stealth and rationalized their criminal activity in the name of the Goddess Kali. Roving the countryside unarmed in gangs of ten to fifty they posed as gentle and courteous citizens. Three thugs were usually assigned to a victim. When the signal was given by the leader two grasped the victims arms and legs and the third strangled him with a noose. All witnesses were murdered, except children who were adopted into the group. The victims were robbed of their valuables. Each Thuggee was followed by a sacrificial feast.

The Hindus never launched an effort to eliminate this nefarious activity in their society. In fact, it is believed many landlords and officials were in conspiracy with these criminal elements. Hsuan Tsang, the Chinese Buddhist pilgrim who visited India during Harsha's rule (606–646 A. D.) was robbed by the Thuggees or a predecessor sect and nearly sacrificed to the Goddess Kali. This was in contrast to an earlier Chinese pilgrim Fa-hsien, who visited India earlier during the second Chandragupta's rule (380–413 A. D.) and reported admiringly on the peace and order that prevailed in India. He traveled widely throughout the country without molestation. By the time of Harsha the second Gupta empire was in disintegration and organized crime flourished. The same situation prevailed when the British established rule over India as by that time the Mughal empire was in a high state of decay. The British who could view the situation more objectively had no compunction about eliminating these criminal sects.

Better known, perhaps, were the Assassins of medievel times (circa 1090–1256 A. D.). The Assassins were founded by one Hassan Ibn Sabbah of the Ismailite sect of Cairo. The Ismailites were shi-ites whereas the Muslim heartland in Persia and Syria was ruled by Sunnis, the dominant Islam orthodoxy, at this time. Although Hassan predicated his organization on religion—nothing, of course was possible in the Muslim world without a religious basis—he was mainly interested in wealth and power. He boasted that with a half dozen or so dedicated and loyal followers he could become master of the world. The method he employed to get such purblind loyalty is fascinating. The recruits, called fidais, were brought to Hassan's mountain fastness and drugged with hashish and/or opium prior to admission. It was normally introduced surreptiously into their wine. When they came out of their stupor they found themselves in what seemed like the Islamic Paradise—a splendid garden with fountains, flowers, wine, food and above all, beautiful girls with whom they were able to dally to their hearts content. After a few days sojourn in this simulated Paradise they were again drugged and removed from the garden. They were then told they had been in Paradise and would be readmitted if they obeyed the Master faithfully for life or if they died fulfilling his orders.

Robed in white with a red girdle, red slippers and carrying a pair of long curved knives they were sent out in groups of three to pounce upon the victim, frequently while he was prostrate in prayer at the mosque. If the first assassin failed to dispatch the victim the other two finished the job in the confusion that ensued. The Assassins also worked in everyday disguises as servants, camel men, water carriers and the like to accomplish the assassinations. The word assassin derives from *hashshasheen*—drinkers of hashish— the name given to the drug addicted followers of Hassan.

The *raison d'etre* of the assassinations was to instill fear in potential victims, who were then promised immunity and protection (which never failed) if they paid the tribute requested of them. The Assassins preyed primarily on commerce and trade—they were mainly interested in a greater share of the wealth—but they were not above political assassination. Their most notable success was the murder in 1091 A. D. of Nizam al-Mulk, the Persian vizier of the Seljuk sultan Malek Shah, who vowed to eliminate the nefarious order. Malek Shah died the following year. Thus deprived of both its political and administrative heads (Nizam al-Mulk was one of the great viziers of history) the Saljuk dynasty fell into disarray and disintegration. No one dared to attack or even critize them. Lesser members were often slain but the Masters remained unassailable. There is a quaint story about a Muslim pundit who cursed the heretics, but relented after an assassin pounced upon him in his study and pricked his belly with his blade. When his disciples asked him why he terminated his crusade against the Assassins he replied "they have arguments that cannot be refuted." Centuries later a ficticious Mafia Don was able to impose his will upon his victim by "making him an offer he could not refuse." More on the Mafia later.

Hassan and his successors found their safety in impregnable mountain fortresses which they bought or took by force. Most notable was Alamut in northern Persia. It was known as the Eagles Nest. Above the entrance gate was written:

> Aided by God
> The Master of the World
> Breaks the Chains of the Law
> Salute to His Name

Another was the Massif in Syria. Legend has it that the great Saladin, terrorized by the Assassins, attacked the Massif unsuccessfully and eventually came to terms with the Master. Richard the Lion Hearted is said to have employed the services of the Master of the Massif to assassinate Conrad of Montferrat during the Third Crusade. The Master of the Massif was referred to by the Crusaders as the Old Man of the Mountain which title had previously been conferred on Hassan at Alamut by the Persians.

From his stronghold Hassan headed an organization stretching from Samarkand to Cairo. The Assassins amassed great wealth and lived in luxury in their mountain strongholds. Hassan was, at the same time, an eminent scholar. He collected art, enjoyed intellectual discourse and was probably an atheist. He doubtless used religion as a means of power. Terror was the source of the Assassin's strength. Hassan ruled from Alamut for thirty-five years. Master succeeded Master thereafter. There is a dazzling account of Alamut in the *Travels of Marco Polo*.

The Assassins held the Muslim society in hostage and it took the Mongols, who at this time held no brief for Islam, to eliminate them. The Mongols were foreigners in the Muslim society so the Assassin's weapon of terror proved to no avail against them. In 1256 Hulagu besieged Alamut, starved the Assassins into submission, captured the Master, one Ala-ud-din, and put him to death. Other members of the organization were pursued and slain as criminal elements of society. The Assassins in Syria were similarly eliminated by the Mameluke rulers within a decade or two. Thereafter the sect continued as a religious faction of Islam. Most notable is the Ismailite community of Western India who acknowledge the Agha Khan as their leader and pay him an annual tribute of one tenth of their income.

The warlords of China were another example of organized crime. They too flourished during a period of weak political rule. The Manchu dynasty which had been declining for a century or so earlier was overthrown in the Revolution of 1911. The Republic that was established in its place was unable to rule effectively. In fact, it was nearly subverted once again by Yuan Shih-kai its first president. Numerous war lords organized small armies from the disaffected in the peasantry and raided their respective areas for food and valuables. During the period 1911–1927 the political situation in China virtually dissolved so that these war lords were in many regions supreme. But as is sometimes otherwise reported they were no friends of the peasants. They exacted a substantial share of their crops, often in conspiracy with the local landlord, so that the peasantry continued to live in penury. They were not revolutionaries attempting to overthrow the ruling elite (the landlords and bureaucrats) but simply parasitic elements extracting a large portion of the surplus production of the peasants. The war lords were never successfully eliminated by the Koumintang. The Communists however, did so after 1948.

America has the notorious Mafia. It emigrated to the United States from Italy where it flourished in southern Italy and Sicily as early as the 19th century. Another criminal society in Italy was the Camora of Naples. Members of the Mafia emigrated to the United States during the forepart of the 20th century and brought with them many of their internicine rivalries. In America they based their operations in the sumptuary law area. Prohibition during the 1920's gave them a great opportunity for illicit wealth. Prostitution, gambling, drugs and other unlawful activities augmented their wealth. During the post World War II period much of the illgotten wealth was reinvested in real estate, hotels and other legitimate operations. Nevada, where gambling is legal, is particularly notable for Mafia interests. There are no statistics on the amount of wealth controlled by the Mafia but that it is substantial cannot be gainsaid.

The Mafia operates in great secrecy and by a rigid code. Democracies are particularly handicapped in this respect as they cannot resort to autocratic force as did the Communists in China, for example, against the war lords. Then too there is reason to believe that both the ruling and political elites assume a benign attitude toward the Mafia. It is difficult to believe, certainly to accept, that the Mafia could not be eliminated by the ruling elite in America if they so desired as the Thuggees in India were eliminated by the British and the war lords in China by the Communists.

The Kennedy brothers, for the first time in American history, made such attempt and two decades after the perplexing assassination of President John F. Kennedy the accumulating evidence begins to point strongly to the conclusion he was murdered by the Mafia. To compound the tragedy it seems that the top law enforcement and intelligence agencies of the United States became unwitting tools of the criminals. During the early years of the Kennedy Administration the Justice Department headed by the President's brother Robert Kennedy stepped up the prosecution of Mafia members from 60 to 130. Moreover, some 2300 more were slated for prosecution. Such onslaught on organized crime threatened to eliminate the Mafia from the American scene. The Mafia struck audaciously at the very heart of American constitutional government trusting that their code of secrecy (omerta) and the murder of crucial witnesses (including the alleged assassin Oswald) would keep its involvement unknown to the American people. The truth may therefore, forever be in doubt. The American free press, a few inquisitive members of Congress and others continued the probe so that two decades after the assassination the full story is beginning to emerge. Needless to add succeeding President's refrained from further prosecution of the Mafia either out of fear, indifference and, perhaps, even implication.

It would doubtless shock most Americans that there is historical precedent for the American tragedy. The Assassins too murdered the renowned Persian vizier Nizam al-Mulk in 1091 A. D. when he launched a drive to eliminate their criminal organization. The Assassins too drew their wealth from Persian commerce through intimidation and investment as does the Mafia through illicit means, legitimate investment and labor union control. In fact through the alleged control of the Teamsters the Mafia holds the American economy in virtual hostage. Like the Mafia the Assassins too resorted to terror as a source of power. Organized crime is not revolutionary. Its members simply desire a greater participation in the wealth of the society without contributing to its production. It may even be tolerated by the ruling elite as a relief mechanism for revolutionary pressures.

Finally in the criminal category is the bribery and corruption of the bureaucracy. This is, perhaps, the most insidious of social behavior. It is known in history since time immemorial. Bureaucracies are part of, or through which, the ruling elite maintains the order of a society. They are at the very nexus of the wealth distribution system. They can direct, redirect and misdirect the distribution of wealth. The perpetrators of the bribe are usually members of commerce, trade and construction activities which the ruling class engages to perform the activities of the state. Bribery and corruption is doubly deleterious because it enlarges the participation in the wealth of a society by a faction that does not contribute to its production. Moreover, it undermines the confidence of the dominated majority in the ruling elite and militates toward political instability.

A further word on bureaucracy (including military personnel) is in order. Such individuals add nothing to the national reproduction of a country, albeit that it can be argued that the maintenance of order within the defence without are important to a society. The debilitating feature of bureaucracy is reached when a society distributes a disproportionate part of the national product to such members. In the growth period of a civilization such functions are usually performed free out of patriotism and loyalty. In the decadent phase they are performed for money and more money. When Rome had to depend upon professional soldiers and foreign mercenaries much wealth was dissipated to maintain the legions. In 167 A. D. Marcus Aurelius was forced to sell jewels, art objects and other valuables from the imperial palaces to maintain legions made up of mercenaries, slaves, brigands and gladiators to resubdue the rebellious German tribes on the Danube. In 1975 the United States was paying out in excess of $50 billion a year in salaries, pensions and perquisites to maintain a largely professional military establishment. Such disproportionate allocation of the national production to a non-producing sector of society militates toward ruinous inflation which usually destroys a society.

It is seen from the foregoing dissertation that societies have a tendency to permit a distribution of wealth to non-producers or other non-meritious individuals. These are usually peripheral sectors of the society, like the bureaucrats, soldiers, moneylenders, speculators and criminals that constitutes at best a minority of the people. While this undermines the productivity of the society it does not usually destroy it. There is another phenomena observed in history that can prove more damaging and that is a distribution of the surplus to the dominated majority over and above its productivity. It is known as welfarism. The Romans referred to it as *panem en circuses*. The Roman dole insinuated itself on the Roman society without anyone paying attention to it until it was too late to arrest its growth.

As early as 123 B. C. wheat was subsidized for the unemployed in Rome. The subsidy grew until wheat was sold to the proletariat for a few cents a bushel. Sulla abolished the subsidy in 82 B. C., but by 78 B. C. it was back again. In 58 B. C. wheat was furnished free. By the time of Caesar the welfare rolls rose to a frightening total of 320,000, one third the population of

Rome. Caesar reduced them to 150,000 by introducing a need test, but the rolls resumed rising after his death. In 2 B. C. Augustus reduced them again from 300,000 to 200,000, but they resumed their climb and the scope of the dole broadened. By 275 A. D. when the empire was in irreversible decay bread had been substituted for wheat. Free pork, olive oil and salt rations were added. Relief was made hereditary.

Free entertainment was added to the welfare in the form of chariot races, gladiator fights and various and numerous spectaculars like the mock naval battle in the Coliseum. The emperors were, in effect, hostages of the proletariat of Rome. Though they did not have the right to vote each Caesar was cognizant of their revolutionary potential and felt it necessary to feed and entertain them to avert revolt. The cost to the state was enormous as wheat had to be imported from Egypt and Rome was desperately short of gold and silver for such purpose. Bread and circuses is generally considered one of the important factors in Rome's decay as too much of its wealth was distributed to the proletariat, a non or under productive majority.

Today the same phenomena can be observed in the industrialized states of Europe and America. While it does not yet appear to have been carried to destructive lengths, with the possible exception of Great Britain, it is a dark spectre on the horizon that deserves pause for thought. Moreover welfarism can prove more deadly to an industrialized society than to a non industrialized society like ancient Rome. Industrialized countries depend ever increasingly on machines and chemical (ultimately nuclear) power for production. This requires savings and capital investment. A disproportionate distribution of the national product to the majority means greater consumption of wealth of the country as lower income groups usually consume *in toto* their income. It is normally the dominant minority, the ruling class, that saves and invests in productive facilities. Thus diverting the surplus distribution away from the dominant minority to the dominated majority has the effect of diminished reinvestment of the national product in new and improved productive facilities made possible by technological innovation and development. Metaphorically speaking, the people begin to eat their seed corn. Carried beyond a certain point it can only stultify the productivity of the society. At this time, as the human community enters the last quarter of the 20th century it appears as if the English have crossed the rubicon in this respect. Too much allocation of the surplus to labor initiated by labor unionism in the post World War I period coupled with too much welfarism during the post World War II period has left the English with an obsolete industrial plant whose products can no longer compete in the world markets. Heavy taxation and undue inflation to finance the welfare programs has deprived the dominant minority of the ability to save and invest in the most advanced technology. Unionism and welfare are undermining Britain's ability for industrial growth, without which the increasingly greater distribution of the national product to labor and to welfarism for the vast majority will not be possible. As in Rome a process of maldistribution of wealth has insinuated itself into the English society that may be irreversible. It presages the decline of the once mighty English of British empire days into an insignificant state.

Enough has now been said to demonstrate the importance of the struggle over the surplus in the history of man. It is predicated upon the dominance instinct of primates. In biological terms for which Nature programmed it the dominance was based on merit. But even in cultural terms the greater distribution of the surplus to the dominant individuals is not without merit. For the good of the whole society the technological innovators must be more highly rewarded for their creativity, for without technological development there is no surplus production for anyone to share. In highly industrialized societies the dominant minority must receive a large enough part of the surplus to enable it to save and invest in the machines and power required for industrialized production. And this is not any different under socialism where the saving and investment is done by the state, which is necessarily controlled by a dominant minority. In Russia, China and other socialist countries it is a small communist party. Unfortunately human societies seldom are able to attain that golden mean where the distribution is fair and operates for the common good, because man is still in the grip of the biological dominance instinct which has graduated to greed in the cultural milieu where technological development produces an increasingly bigger surplus. And when the dominant minority cannot be made to temper its greed and takes more of the surplus than the dominated majority feels is just to compensate them for their creativity and leadership the result in violent revolution that eliminates the ruling elite.

The most violent and thorough revolutions of recent times have been the Chinese Revolution in 1948 and the Russian Revolution in 1917. The Chinese was predicated wholly on the peasants. The Russian was based mainly on a disaffected peasantry. But before detailing the history of these revolutions it is in order to say a word or two about the theory of revolution of Karl Marx. Marx lived (1818–1883) during the early days of the Industrial Revolution and became obsessed with the deplorable plight of the new industrial worker. He was forced to work long hours in unhealthy surroundings for wages on which he could barely subsist. He concluded that the factory owner appropriated too much of the surplus production of the worker. He thought that this created a revolutionary situation that, with proper leadership, could overthrow a capitalistic society wherein the dominant minority— the capitalists—owned the machines and power facilities of industrial production. He advocated socializing the ownership of all industrial factors of production. Marxism differs from prior revolutions only in kind as peasant revolts aim at the ownership of land, the main factor of production in an agricultural society. Marx merely adapted the age old tenets of revolution to the new industrial age.

But a true Marxian revolution has not yet occurred. It has been frustrated mainly by labor unionism which was only in its infancy when Marx died. Unionism has wrested for industrial labor a larger share of the surplus. In addition, operating within the framework of democracy, labor assisted by middle class liberals secured legislation that improved the working conditions of the workers such as abolition of child labor, a more reasonable working day and week, workmen's compensation and a healthier environment.

Marxism may not, however, be obsolete. Highly industrial societies are fast approaching a crisis with respect to a fair and just distribution of wealth. It is the growing inadequacy of the job as a means of distribution of the national product. As technological development approaches its logical end— the fully or nearly fully automated factory—there may not be enough jobs for all the employable members of the society. The result will be a flotsam of unemployed in the volatile cities of the country similar to the proletariat of ancient Rome. They, not the unionized workers, will be the cruel victims of the industrial age. Whether the dominant minority can keep this new proletariat under control with welfare and television remains to be seen. Such strategy contributed substantially to the decline and fall of the Roman empire. On the other hand, this ever increasing proletariat would be susceptible to revolution under capable leadership for the overthrow of the capitalist system.

In fact, the most valid tenet of Marxism may in the end be the idea of a professional revolutionary. His importance in a true revolution which ousts completely the ruling class has already been proven. Ironically, it was in a revolt in China and Russia which were not industrialized societies. But as already stated a Marxist revolution differs only in the factor of production on which it is based.

THE CHINESE REVOLUTION

The landlord-peasant rivalry has dominated the struggle over wealth throughout most of recorded history. This is readily understandable as agriculture has been the main economic pursuit of man until recent times. Even today two-thirds of the people of Asia, Africa and Latin America derive their livelihood from agriculture. It should not, therefore, be surprising to learn that the Chinese Revolution was in the main a peasant revolt.

The Chinese Revolution is one of the most profound revolts in history. It completely overturned the ruling elite. It reorganized the Chinese society. And most important it set out to industrialize the country in order to make the economy more productive.

Peasant revolts are old and frequent in China's history dating back thousands of years. There is an old saying in China that "when all the people sigh there will be a great wind; when all the people stomp their feet there will be an earthquake." The right to revolt against a ruler is the famous "mandate of heaven" political doctrine of the Chinese. When an emperor or dynasty becomes unpopoular with the people it loses the "mandate of heaven" to continue as the ruling power and it may be deposed; peacefully, if possible, by rebellion, if necessary. This doctrine, however, appears to have worked more in favor of the ruling class to change its political head than in favor of the peasants.

None of these revolutions, however, has completely overthrown the ruling elite before the recent one with the possible exception of the revolt in 1368 that ousted Mongol rule. Actually the latter was more an uprising against oppressive foreign domination in which the indigenous Chinese gentry joined. Hence, the Chinese ruling elite was not ousted but reconfirmed once again in its dominant position. Most of the peasant revolts of the past resulted in the overthrow of dynasties, a mere changing of the guard in the ruling elite.

These early peasant rebellions were poorly led. They were either fomented by or usurped by the secret societies that flourished in the countryside. These secret societies seldom had any socio-economic objectives and failed to coordinate with one another when the plight of the peasants was so serious that spontaneous uprisings occurred in different parts of the country. It was only in the 20th century when the Communist party gave the peasant revolt effective leadership that these age old rebellions succeeded in ousting the ruling elite.

The first peasant rebellion of note was that of the Red Eyebrows in 18 A. D. A few years earlier Wang Mang usurped the throne of the decaying Han dynasty. He is sometimes referred to as China's first socialist as he brought under state ownership such activities as slave owning, salt, wine and iron tool production and distributed land to the landless. The plight of the peasants did not improve, however, as Wang Mang taxed them more than the ousted landlords collected in rent. A genuine popular uprising of the peasants, whose distress had now mounted beyond endurance ensued. It was led by the Red Eyebrows, a secret society, whose members painted their eyebrows red. The uprising was joined by the decendents of the Han dynasty who gradually took over the revolution in order to oust the usurper Wang Mang. The result was the restoration of the Han dynasty under Liu Hsiu in 24 A. D. Millions of peasants and gentry died in six years of fighting but the Red Eyebrows failed to oust the ruling elite. The situation of the remaining peasants, however, was ameliorated as the land of the dead became available, their debts were eliminated with the demise of so many landlords and moneylenders and the new government relieved them of some of the onerous taxes.

The Yellow Turban rebellion of 184 A. D. brought about the end of the Han dynasty. Once again the plight of the peasants had become intolerable as in the time of Wang Mang. The Yellow Turbans were defeated by General

Ts'ao Ts'ao who filled his ranks with Hsuing-nus. He then became the dominant force in the decaying Han dynasty. His son was able to force the abdication of the emperor and to found the new Wei dynasty in 220 A. D. In 400 A. D. the Yellow Turbans led another popular uprising. It too was suppressed by Liu Yu of the eastern Chin dynasty.

Another noteworthy peasant uprising, already mentioned, was against the Mongols in the 1350's. Mongol rule impoverished the peasants beyond endurance. In 1329, according to official statistics 7.6 million persons out of a population of 45 million were starving! Sporadic rebellions continued from 1325 onwards, poorly led at the start. They were directed against the rich in general. The Chinese gentry first sided with the Mongols. In 1352 Kuo Tzuh-sing, a beggar's son and Chu Yuan-chang, a peasant's son, assumed leadership of these popular revolts. The White Lotus society also provided support. Kuo died in 1353. Chu succeeded in winning the support of some of the gentry. These landlords diverted Chu from attacks on the rich to ousting foreign domination. In 1368 Chu captured Peking and ended Mongol rule. By this time the Mongol emperors were weak. There were seven Mongol emperors after Kublai Khan each successively lesser men than Kublai.

The Chinese gentry, once again, ruled China. The Ming dynasty that followed (1368–1644) provided one of the most illustrious epochs in Chinese history. Chu Yuan-chang the first Ming emperor—now called Ming Hung Wu—did not however, forget his original purpose. Land was redistributed to poor peasants. Many of the gentry were forced to move to Nanking, the new capital, thus abandoning their land near Peking which freed the peasants in that area. Other social legislation was directed against the rich. As usual the peasants soon dissipated or otherwise lost these benefits and the Mings found themselves faced with rebellion. A great popular uprising originating in the west, in Szechuan, then spreading to the east arose in the early 1500's. The rebellion failed in 1512 when the rebel fleet of boats was destroyed by a typhoon.

The Manchus who succeeded the Ming dynasty in 1644, unlike the Mongols, chose to rule through the Chinese bureaucracy and gentry. The mandarin system was fully matured by now and the early part of Manchu rule was stable. The 19th century, however, witnessed again some of the most violent and widespread peasant rebellions in China's history.

Profound changes in the Chinese society transpired during the 19th century which laid the foundation for the communist revolution of 1949. At the beginning of the 19th century the population of China exceeded 350 million. The population explosion was due to the development of intensive agriculture starting in Ming times and the peaceful rule of the Manchus. This was more than the arable land could comfortably support. Until now there was always relief for the Chinese peasant as he could move to the south and southwest where more land was available. These areas served as a frontier like the west in America and Siberia to Russia during the past century. By the 19th century there was no more additional land left for cultivation. China did not, moreover, have the advanced technology to industrialize and relieve the pressure on the land. China had isolated itself from the rest of the world which foreclosed any facile transmission of the advanced technology from the West. The gentry and business interests, therefore, invested their accumulated wealth in land aggravating further the struggle in the countryside.

Foreign domination from the West was now encroaching upon China. China's resistance was overcome by force in the two Opium Wars of the 19th century (1840–42 and 1858–60) after which the devastating effect of western technology took place. From their *entrepots*, the treaty ports, England, America, France and others flooded China with inexpensive textiles, hardware and other goods that ruined the handicrafts and cottage industries on which the Chinese peasant relied for his margin of security from hunger. Steam navigation deprived the boatmen of much of their business on the rivers. The effect was to thrust more sustenance of life upon the non expandable agriculture, which aggravated the landlord-peasant friction.

The sporadic rebellions of the early 19th century developed between 1850–70 into what is probably the greatest wave of peasant revolts in history. Like previous peasant uprisings in China they failed but millions of peasants, landlords and others lost their lives. In the Taiping rebellion alone it is estimated that 30 million people met with death. Seventy per cent of the population of Anhwei was annihilated. These revolts developed during the period of the Opium Wars which opened China to western influence and domination. The Manchu dynasty was discredited by the humiliating concessional treaties. The opium thrust upon China drained the country of silver and worsened the exchange rate between silver and copper to the great disadvantage of the peasants as taxes had to be paid in silver while farm products sold for copper. The takeover of the treaty ports by the Europeans worsened the employment situation of the Chinese in these cities. Canton was hard hit as the new treaty ports deprived it of some of its former commerce with the West when it was the only port of entry for the Europeans. Several of the leaders of the Taiping rebellion rose from these unemployed.

The Taiping rebellion arose in Kwangsi, a western province near Canton. It was primarily an agrarian revolt. The movement was also anti-Manchu giving it a nationalistic aura. Its leader Hung Hsiu-ch'uan was an educated man from a family of poor peasants, who had not succeeded in gaining admission (he failed the examinations) to the ruling elite. In 1851 he founded his own dynasty, the Celestial Kingdom of Great Peace (Tai-ping Tien-kuo). The Taiping army, swelled by thousands of peasants, marched northeast and captured Nanking in 1853. Hung made it the Taiping capital for eleven years.

As the Taiping armies moved through central China and the Yangtze valley they excited spontaneous peasant uprisings. Unpopular landlords and tax collectors were executed. Land registers and loan documents were burned. Government offices were ransacked. Land was to be farmed in common. Every person over 16, including women, was to be alloted a plot to cultivate. If crop failure occurred in one region other regions would supply food to the famine area. In sum it was to be a communal system of landholding.

Hung pressed on toward Peking but got only as far as Tientsin. The Manchu army which was unable to cope with the revolt, received some timely assistance from Tseng Kuo-fan, a powerful landlord, who recruited an opposing army of peasants from central China against the Taiping. Western aid also contributed to the defeat. Western officials helped train imperial troops and foreign officials, such as C. G. Gordon, commanded a mixed unit of foreign and Chinese troops against the Taiping. Steamships were made available to transport troops. France and England preferred to have the Manchu government survive as they had just wrested from it important concessions. In 1864 Tseng recaptured Nanking for the Manchus ending the rebellion.

Meanwhile another peasant uprising called Nien Fei took palce in Honan and Anhwie provinces of north China. In 1855 the Yellow river changed its course to flow into the sea at Tientsin creating great misery for the peasants in these two provinces. The Nien raided merchant convoys, the homes of rich landlords, government offices, freed prisoners and distributed the goods to the poor. "Kill the rich, save the poor" was their motto. The Nien revolt was not suppressed by the Manchus until 1868. The Nien were believed to be affiliated with the White Lotus society.

In the northwest and Yunan province several Muslim rebellions transpired between 1853–73. While these revolts were religiously inspired they were based upon the peasantry. The rebellions were mainly against the ruling elite of Chinese landlords and officials who exacted greater rents and taxes than in other parts of China.

Some lesser peasant revolts also arose during this time. The Red Band in Szechuan in 1860, the Red Turban in Canton in 1854. There was little coordination among these several rebellions. The Taiping engaged in some campaigns with the Nien, but mostly these revolts were regionally oriented and inspired. The Manchus triumphed in the end and the peasants were quiet during the remaining 30 years of the century. The peasantry had been weakened by defeat and suppression with some areas not recovering for nearly a century. The Chinese gentry was both strengthened and chastised. Powerful landlords like Tseng Kuo-fan gained great power in Peking.

At this time Western domination increased and began penetrating into the countryside with railroads, factories and trade. In the second Opium War England exacted freedom of navigation on the Yangtze river. The Western

nations made Shanghai, situated at the mouth of the river, their main
entrepot in China. The peasants began to feel the impact of the West and
they did not like it. They could only visualize a worsening of their position
because of the presence of these "foreign devils" and blamed the Manchus
for its weakness in resisting European domination. In 1900, the Boxer
rebellion erupted. At first it was aimed at the Manchus and gentry but the
Manchus succeeded in redirecting it against the "foreign devils". When the
Boxers, so named after their custom of engaging in boxing matches for
sport, sacked the foreign legations in Peking, an international force of
Americans and Europeans was sent against them to quell the rebellion. The
western powers blamed the Manchus and exacted the payment of heavy
indemnities. Some of these funds were used during the early part of the
1900's for scholarships for the Chinese in western universities and other
education purposes. The Boxer rebellion was not a true peasant revolt
although peasants were involved. It was aimed mainly against western
domination.

Sporadic minor peasant revolts continued after 1900. Western ideas
continued to make their impact on the young, particularly the western
educated Chinese. They were disappointed by the resistance to western
technology by the Manchus. The dowager empress Tzy Hsi, who dominated
the court, seemed unaware of China's backwardness in modern technology.
She blocked all efforts of others at the court who wished to emulate Japan
which had launched its industrialization before 1900. Even the defeat by
Japan in Korea in 1895, attributable to her modernized army, did not change
her position. These new and enlightened elements organized the Republican
revolution of 1911 against the Manchus.

Although accompanied by widespread peasant unrest and rebellion the
Republican Revolution was made in the cities—Wuchang, Nanking, Chungking, Shanghai and others. Its leader was Sun Yat-sen, a peasant's son,
educated in English schools in Hongkong. He spent considerable time in
America. But the rebels were mostly western educated sons of the gentry.
They succeeded more by default than assault. The dowager empress died in
1908 and left the throne to a two year old heir Pu Yi. The regent dismissed
Yuan Shih-k'ai the only competent general in the Manchu army, who joined
the revolution with his troops and provided a much needed force for the
rebels. The Manchu dynasty abdicated and a Republic was established in its
stead with Yuan Shi-k'ai as President on October 10, 1912.

The Republic proved incapable of effective rule. The mass of Chinese did
not understand democracy as did the few western educated Chinese who
made the revolution. Yuan tried to subvert the new government and found
his own dynasty based, once again, on the gentry as the ruling elite. He died
in 1916 before he could accomplish his purpose. Further attempts were made
in this direction and ended up with the reinstatement of the deposed Manchu
emperor. By now the democratic wing of the Republic had disassociated

itself from the Peking government and set up its own republic in Canton under the Presidency of Sun Yat-sen. The government in Peking kept disintegrating and lapsed into the so-called war lord period wherein numerous generals, usually from the landed gentry, recruited armies from the dispossessed and unemployed and ruled supreme in their area of control. China was for all practical purposes without a government from 1917 to 1927.

The Republic was a lofty edifice without a foundation. The revolution never made contact with the peasantry. Nothing durable could be established without the support or, at least, acquiescence of the peasants who comprised 85 per cent of the people of China. The gentry was too weak to step into the breach despite Yuan's attempt to reinstate it as the ruling class. The gentry still possessed the land but its economic value was greatly diminished. Western economic penetration provided other opportunities for investment in shares of foreign enterprises and banks. Less expensive rice was being imported into China driving farm prices down. Chinese silk was displaced by the superior Japanese silk and rayon from the West. These changes impoverished and weakened the gentry.

Foreign domination reached its worst point during the fore part of the 20th century. Though no European power was able to gain the upper hand and impose colonial rule on China as did the English in India a century and a half earlier the European powers and Japan started to nibble away parts of the country. Japan took Manchuria, Germany the tip of the Shantung Penninsula, Russia outer Mongolia, France Indo-China (though somewhat earlier) over which China exercised suzerainty for centuries and England attempted to wrest Tibet to add to its Asian empire. Greater trade concessions were being constantly exacted. China was by the 1920's for all practical purposes, a colony of the West.

The second revolution of 1927 occurred next. Again it was not a peasant revolt. Sun Yat-sen decided in 1924 that the time was ripe for a march on Peking. He now possessed a formidable army, trained and organized by Russian advisors under the generalship of Chiang Kai-shek, Sun's eventual brother-in-law. The Republican Revolution was now organized under a party called the Koumintang (revolutionary party) founded by Sun. Sun died in 1925 while in Peking trying to reach a compromise with the government and the leadership of the Koumintang devolved on Chiang.

The Koumintang had its right and left wings, the latter dominated by the newly formed (in 1921) Communist party of China. The march north proved eminently successful. Even the peasants were rallied to its support through the diligent work of the communists who promised the peasants land. But Chiang who favored the communists at first and even spent some time in Russia now came under the influence of his wife's family, the Soongs, who had by now become a leading banking family in Shanghai. As the Koumintang marched north it became obvious that there would be a struggle between the right wing and the communists for control of the new government. Chiang opted for the right wing and ousted and executed some of the Russian advisors. This won over the nascent Chinese capitalist class of Shanghai as well as foreign support. Shanghai fell to Chiang without a struggle and he was able to establish a new republic, known as the Nationalist Government, with its capital at Nanking. Chiang also compromised with the gentry by ignoring the land reform plank of the party for expropriating the land for distribution to the peasants promulgated by the communists.

The die was now cast for the ultimate revolution. The communists established themselves in the mountains of Kiangsi in south China and started rebuilding among the peasants. The communists too had an internal ideological split over the proper conduct of the revolution. There were those who thought the revolution should be predicated on the factory worker, assigning to agrarian revolt a secondary role. This was obviously unrealistic as the industrial workers comprised less than one per cent of the population. Chiang had no difficulty in subduing the workers of Shanghai when they rose against him in 1927. After this episode belated advice was forthcoming from Russia (Stalin who always believed this was now the head of the Russian communist party) that the Chinese communist should concentrate on a peasant revolt. Mao Tse-tung, always of this conviction, became the leader of the party.

Chiang feared the communists. He felt, with his alliance of Chinese businessmen, bankers and the gentry, he could compromise the war lords. In a few years he consolidated his government. The western powers gave him their support. He could now concentrate on the communists. He launched a full scale campaign in the 1930's against them in their areas in the south. Mao decided to remove from so vulnerable a base and undertook the now famous Long March of 1934 into the more secure northwest. At Yenan the communists continued to build peasant soviets but more important they established a vigorous cadre training program. The cadres were educated first in Marxist doctrine and then trained to go among the people to stir them into revolt, aid in the reforms and generally to take over the administration of China.

About this time there occurred in Peking the December 9, 1935 incident which soon spread to other cities. The students staged a mass demonstration against Japan's forcible separation of the north China provinces and they were severely dealt with by Chiang Kai-shek. Thoroughly disaffected the students flocked to Yenan in droves and the cadre training program assumed large scale proportions. A handbook of Chinese Communism was compiled shortly thereafter entitled (literally translated) *Reordering the Winds*. It became the bible and standard equipment of every cadre.

By 1936 the civil war lapsed into a stalemate and served only to weaken China for the impending Japanese invasion. Unable to reason Chiang into compromising the debilitating civil war several of his northern generals kidnapped him and held him prisoner in Sian. Chou En-lai acted as mediator in the dispute. Although shrouded in mystery the incident did bring a halt in the civil war and formation of a United Front between the Koumintang and Communists against the coming Japanese invasion.

The Japanese invasion in 1937 provided the Communist party with a grand opportunity for reaching vast millions of Chinese with their program. As the Nationalist army retreated before the invaders deep into the interior to reestablish itself at Chungking the Eighth Route army (designation adopted after formation of United Front) of the communists worked its way behind the Japanese lines and liberated large areas on the great North China plain. Along with liberation they instituted land reforms among the farmers and ingratiated themselves with the people. To the hundred million Chinese living on the North China plain the Eighth Route army became the saviour and it was here where the Chinese Revolution was made.

When the war ended the Eighth Route army held all but the cities in this area and was ready and able to move into them. Chiang Kai-shek however, struck an agreement with the Japanese General Nakamura not to relinquish the cities to the communists. Meanwhile, with American aid Chiang transported his forces from Chungking to take them over from the Japanese.

The communist held countryside, however, was another matter. This could not be won by strategem but would have to be wrested from them, and Chiang set out immediately to do so. This posed a difficult problem for the communists. They knew the Chinese people were sick of war and did not want to get maneuvered into a position of blame for preventing peace in China.

Thus in the beginning the Eighth Route army gave way before the Nationalist army. But as the Koumintang returned with the landlords all of the land reforms were undone and unhuman punishment meted out to the farmers. Eight years back rent was often forcibly collected. This demonstrated dramatically to the people of the North China plain that the Communist party and not the Koumintang was their best friend.

During this time the Communist party participated willingly in all the attempts made by the United States to mediate the civil war but remained adamant on participation in any coalition government. This Chiang stubbornly refused to accept making himself appear against peace to the Chinese people and only bent on exterminating the communists.

Feeling sure it had won the struggle for peace by mid-1946 the Communist party gave the signal for full scale revolution to the bitter end. Land seizure was substituted for land reform again and the process of overturning Chinese society was in full progress.

The key to the Chinese Revolution was the peasant. Whoever won his heart was destined to rule China. In this respect the revolution differed from the Koumintang revolution of 1925–27 which was primarily an urban movement.

At the end of the war the land problem was well nigh intolerable. Strickly speaking China did not have feudalism but its gentry system was far more vicious. Conditions were bad enough when the Chinese farmer living on an average two-thirds of an acre of land was required to turn over fifty per cent of his crops, but they grew much worse under the Koumintang when the rents and taxes deprived him of 65 to 90 per cent of his production. In addition, the landlord was the local government, with virtual power of life and death over the tenant. It was accepted behavior for a landlord to take his pleasure with the tenant's wife or daughter. If the tenant objected he was cast into the dungeon.

Furthermore, the landlords conducted a cruel system of usury. Loans at interest up to 100% were made to desperate farmers for food and seed and collected without mercy. This gave the landlord a further hold on the tenant and also helped him get the land of small independent farmers. Land concentration shot up greatly under the Koumintang.

Confucianism also made the women of China the subjects of men. Under the confucian ethic one man was measured against another by the size of the family he headed. Consequently the woman's role became that of a producer of sons. This made her lot little more than that of a chattel and so she was treated. Women were bartered, sold, prostituted and raped to satisfy man's lust for power and sex. They were forced into marriage from which there was no divorce. The women of China were also ready to rebel against a society that heaped such indignities upon them.

Chinese society was also oppressive to the sons of rural China. Arranged and forced marriages were equally unpalatable to them. The absolute rule of the father was unpleasant. Many chose to join the Eighth Route army and destroy the society they found so extortionate.

By 1946 the peasants, women and youth of China were ripe for revolt. All that was required was leadership which the Communist party furnished with great cunning and wisdom. It was not easy to move the oppressed masses of China because of strong cultural inertia and resignation to Fate. The technique employed by the communists for overcoming this conservatism and bringing about the revolt is extremely interesting.

The Chinese communists had a name for it. It was called "overturning society." Village after village was turned over. More specifically it meant that land was divided, women were emancipated and a rough sort of local self-government established. English correspondent Jack Belden, who worked behind the communist lines leaves us a graphic picture of the anatomy of the revolution in his book *China Shakes the World*.

The technique was as follows: A cadre would go into a village and seek out the most oppressed peasant. After winning his confidence, which sometimes took days because of fear of reprisal, the cadre would induce the peasant to tell him his tale of woe and then proceed to convince him that his miserable lot was not fate but the doing of the landlord. As soon as the peasant confessed his troubles to the cadre he felt a great psychological release and new freedom. He then became a willing helper of the cadre. Other oppressed peasants were soon brought into the group. This was called the Accusation.

When the group grew larger the cadre would organize an open Speak Bitterness meeting in the village where all the peasants were induced to speak their grievances against the landlord. This had the effect of demonstrating to the peasants the solidarity of their cause and it generated the emotional energy needed for the next steps, the Struggle Against and Settlement with the landlord. Such highly aroused passion frequently culminated in savage physical attack upon and murder of the landlord with knives, pitchforks and other farm implements. Most settlements were peaceful, however, with the landlords surrendering to the peasants when it was clear that the situation was hopeless. The Communist party policy was to conduct peaceful settlements, but partisan warfare when once aroused had a propensity to get out of control.

In the settlement the land was divided in accordance with local justice with which the peasants were familiar. In most cases this amounted to little more than sloughing off rents as the land was already divided into small tenements by the landlord. Local self-government was then established in a village and a militia organized to protect the settlement against counterattack by the landlords. When this was done the cadre would leave for another village to start another "overturning" process.

The landlords did not go down entirely without fighting. They organized counter-settlements which were frequently more savage than any of the settlements. Where they were able to reclaim a village, of their own accord or with the aid of the Nationalist army, the reprisals were terrible. Leaders of the settlement and/or their families would be buried alive. All these attempts failed and merely served to add fuel to the revolutionary fire spreading among the people.

By freeing the peasant from the landlord and women from oppressive marital relations the communists were everywhere riding into power in the countryside. There were two other forces to cope with before they could be masters of China, however, the Nationalist army and the large coastal cities. These presented slightly different problems of attack.

Lacking a strong proletariat force in the large cities on which to predicate a revolution from within communist grand strategy, therefore, called for a complete isolation of the cities from the country. This tactic was plausible in China because its agrarian economy was independent of the cities but the cities were almost completely dependent upon the country for their food supply. It proved unnecessary to carry out this plan, however, as we shall see later.

Meanwhile, the Nationalist army was a more immediate and important factor to deal with. At the beginning of the revolution Chiang Kai-shek had a well equipped well trained army of 4,000,000 men. It was in outward appearance the finest army ever assembled on the mainland of Asia. The Eighth Route army of the communists judged by these same standards was insubstantial. How then was it able to route completely so superior a military force. The answer is found in the contrasting morale of the two opposing armies which in a way reflected the opposing forces in the revolution.

The Nationalist soldier, dragged into service against his will and thereafter kicked, beaten, cursed and starved, turned out to be a poor defender of the Koumintang. Cruelty, deception, inefficiency and corruption permeated the Nationalist army from top to bottom. Chiang's soldiers did not know what they were fighting for, did not care to fight or even what happened to them. The soldiers were little more than slaves. It was an army without a soul. Furthermore, it had done no serious fighting for several years reposing in its Chungking retreat and did not know what war meant.

By contrast the Eighth Route army was composed entirely of volunteers. It had no rank and insignia. There was equal food, pay and treatment for all. Much more important, though, its soldiers knew what they were fighting for. It was freedom from hunger and oppression. High moral was generated with the technique of the Speak Bitterness meetings which brought and kept at a high pitch the revolutionary emotions of hatred, love, anger and revenge within the army. Although the Koumintang generals were aware of the effectiveness of this technique they could not borrow it for it would have resulted in revolt in their ranks.

Recognizing fully the situation the communists set out to liquidate Chiang's army by bringing his soldiers from their unhappy state to rebellion and destroying the remainder in combat. When they met Nationalist army units propaganda squads would shout across the lines to the Nationalist soldiers calling them brothers, reminding them of their miserable conditions and promising them land and freedom from conscription if they came over the communist side. This was answered at first with a barrage of fire but gradually desertions began to take place which in many instances included an entire army. Words proved more effective than bullets in this war. In addition similar persuasion was conducted behind the Nationalist lines especially with high ranking officers. The defection among Chiang's generals to the communist side was astounding. Thus by a combination of politics and war the Chinese communists were able to annihilate the armies of Chiang Kai-shek ending up with most of his American military equipment and even the trained personnel to operate it.

Chiang, of course, aided the process by committing almost unbelievable blunders of strategy. He weakened his middle by a perfectly useless campaign against Yenan thereby permitting the communist commander Liu

Po-cheng to cut his forces in two by marching through to the Yangtze. The
Yenan campaign was an attempt to gain a propaganda victory and obtain
more American aid to fight communism. It had no strategic value. This
blunder was followed by his overextension into Manchuria against all better
advice only to have another communist commander Lin Piao destroy seven
of his American equipped armies. The former became the turning point in
the civil war; the latter the beginning of military collapse for Chiang Kai-
shek. Military defeat came in the Battle of Suchow in December, 1948 to
which Chiang again contributed significantly with his military incompetence.

Only the cities were left and these fell to the communists like ripe plums.
They were not won by the communists but instead lost by the Koumintang.
Chiang's despotism and ineptitude alienated two important groups—the
intellectuals and the merchants. Although a great many Chinese intellectuals
were already in the communist ranks providing the dynamic leadership in
the revolution, the rest that remained loyal to the Koumintang were
subjected to a vicious reign of terror consisting of red witch hunts, loyalty
oaths and other gestapo methods. Escape to the communist side began on a
grand scale. Those intellectuals who were able to insulate themselves
against Chiang's terror were finished off by the runaway inflation. When a
professor's monthly pay could buy only two day's food there was no hope
left.

The economic collapse of Koumintang China is perhaps without historical
precedent. During the period June, 1946 to August, 1948 prices rose 1500
fold. The rate of exchange between the Chinese and U. S. dollars shot up
from 2,665 to 8,683,000. Thereafter inflation was so wild it was almost
impossible to calculate it. The value of the paper on which it was printed
eventually proved greater than the monetary worth of the Chinese dollar!

The terrific inflation also alienated the Chinese businessmen. Money was
worthless so everyone rushed to convert savings into goods. When the
merchants refused to sell for the worthless Chinese dollars they were forced
to do so by the police at the point of a gun. The result was economic
ruination of the Chinese merchants and their conversion to support of the
communists.

This, of course, spelled the end of Koumintang. All that was left was the
compradors, the Western affiliated industrialists and bankers, with whom
the communists would not compromise because they represented foreign
domination which the communists were determined to oust from China. The
end of foreign domination in China was demonstrated dramatically to the
world in the *Amethyst* incident, the British gunboat the communists trapped
on the Yangtze river in April, 1949. Even so short a time as ten years before
such a thing would have been unheard of in China.

The Communist Revolution brought to China a new hope. Perhaps for the
first time in two thousand years the Chinese people started looking toward
the future and not to the past. Chinese communism immediately assumed

the aspects of a new religion. It provided a moral cohesiveness which had been absent in China for over 100 years. The new desire was salvation through self-purification and repentence. This was achieved through the Speak Frankness meetings, a public confessional, where men and women acknowledged openly their wrongs against their fellow man and vowed to mend their old ways. This new drive toward a moral code rid China of the old thievery, rape, corruptness and other crimes. A new social organization based on communism developed in China.

A striking feature of the Communist Revolution was its purpose to industrialize the Chinese economy to make it more productive to support a large and burgeoning population. The capital for the technology. machinery and equipment required for industrialization could only be derived from agriculture. The communists could not, therefore, let the peasants retain all the produce of their newly won land. They pursued from the start a policy of taxation, compulsory grain levies and the like to offtake a third or so of the agricultural production for reinvestment in the economic development of the country. Manchuria was already industrialized by the Japanese which formed a nucleus of modern technology. Additional technology was obtained from the Russians. The surplus production exacted from the peasants provided the capital for the machinery and equipment.

The peasants apparently did not resent or object to such heavy taxation. The new ruling elite, the Communist party, did not use the revenue proceeds for luxurious living as the hated gentry; in fact, they dressed in denim like the peasants. The peasants could see that the taxes they paid were being used for productive purposes. A new harmony had developed between the new ruling elite and the dominated majority.

There is a broader meaning and significance to the Chinese Revolution. The center of technological innovation had shifted to Europe during the past few centuries, enabling the Europeans to dominate Asia. They plundered Asia of much of its wealth to facilitate their industrialization. Thereafter they made of Asia a captive market for the goods of their new industries causing further impoverishment of the peasants. This left India, China and other parts of Asia with outmoded economies unable to sustain their increasing population with a decent livelihood. While European domination continued they were dissuaded from industrializing. The struggle over the national product, primarily agricultural, became more violent as populations increased while the ruling elite could not or knew not how to increase economic productivity. Something had to explode as it did in China which, with the same effort, threw off the yoke of foreign domination and launched the industrialization of the economy. The Chinese peasant has always been a hard disciplined worker. He can now be expected to shift this productivity to the new industries. If China can succeed in its industrialization it cannot fail to develop into a great power, once again, in the world. The prescient words of Napoleon may yet come to pass when he said "China! There is a sleeping giant; let him sleep, for when he wakes, he will move the world!"

RUSSIAN REVOLUTION

The Russian Revolution of 1917 was another complete overthrow of a ruling elite. It too was primarily a peasant revolt. It was different however, from the Chinese Revolution in that the new ruling elite neither led the peasants nor truly understood the socio-economic upheaval from which it was to profit with such world shaking impact. Communist theory at that time predicated its revolution on the industrial worker. Russia in 1917 was non-industrialized—unable even to produce adequately modern equipment for its army—with four-fifths of its people deriving their livelihood from agriculture. The industrial proletariat was a tiny minority in this sea of peasants.

In 1917 the Romanovs were thoroughly decadent. The Tsar and his wife were under the influence of the disreputable Rasputin. The war was going badly. Everywhere there was disaffection with the ineffectual rule of Nicholas II.

The Revolution erupted in Petrograd on March 8, 1917 when the police fired on crowds besieging baker's shops for bread after the grain distribution system broke down. Next day Petrograd was in revolt. Factories and schools closed. Everyone was in the streets. Troops from the Petrograd garrison joined the revolt and the Tsar had no effective force to suppress it. The troops dispatched to Petrograd were unable to enter the city. Nicholas abdicated in favor of his brother Michael but the soviet and garrison in Petrograd refused to accept another Romanov as ruler.

A soviet was elected from the factory workers and soldiers. It set up a provisional government. Alexander Kerensky, a socialist revolutionary, eventually became Premier. The provisional government was a polyglot of disparate elements that never really ruled Russia. Lenin and other Bolsheviks conspired to take over the government and before the autumn passed they gained control. The communists seized power in Petrograd on November 7 and in Moscow on November 14, 1917. Moscow was made the capital. A counter revolution arose supported by foreign intervention that kept Russia in civil war until 1920. Admiral Kolchak led a force from Siberia supported by the Czechs and Americans. Dinekin led a force from the south in Crimea of army officers and men who refused to join the Red army. And the British landed at Archangel in the north. All this merely worked to consolidate communist control and the building of the Red army into a formidable force. The counter-revolution collapsed as it had no positive program. Effective communist propaganda won away most of Kolchak's and Dinekin's soldiers. The allies lost interest once the war ended. And the peasants remained aloof for they had their land.

Russia was reduced to utter chaos during the civil war. The communist contributed to the disorder by their ineptness. They tried immediately to impose Marxian theories and brought production to a standstill. The peasants refused to produce more than they consumed which left the country without food. The social and economic breakdown that ensued is set forth poignantly and graphically by Boris Pasternak in his novel *Dr. Zhivago*.

The peasants made their own revolution. Although the Bolsheviks advocated seizure of the estates, and issued directives to that effect, the peasants had already accomplished it long before November 7. As soon as the Tsar abdicated so that the nobility and gentry had no power to protect their interests they were dispossessed of their land. Sir Bernard Pares in his history of Russia writes, "The peasants, often with great brutality, had themselves made a wholesale clearance of the country gentry; many of these were 'smoked out' and no trace of their former estates was left; at last all the land was in peasant hands." Thereafter it took the communists almost two decades before they could bring the peasants under control and organize them into collective farms.

Two incidents bear noting here to demonstrate the gap that existed between the communists and peasants in the early days of the revolution. The peasants always viewed the nobility and gentry as their enemies not the Tzar. In fact, the Tzar was usually considered the peasant's friend. After the Romanov's were deposed and the peasants took over the land, one village sent a message to Petrograd requesting a portrait of the new Tzar "Revolutesia". The communists, on the other hand, in doctrinaire fashion, weighted the peasants vote at one-fifth that of the factory worker in the new soviets. This was subsequently undone after protest from the peasants and a more realistic understanding by the communist of the true nature of the revolution.

Peasant revolts, as in China, were part of the fabric of Russian history. Serfdom originated in the 16th and 17th centuries as a means to keep the peasants on the land. As was true world wide, until population growth foreclosed it, a peasant could always run away if he disliked the way the landlord treated him. There was always plenty of land elsewhere albeit it might be of inferior quality. Inferior land with freedom was better than black land with servitude. The nobility and gentry had difficulties holding peasants to cultivate the fertile black soil of the Don and Volga basins. They decided, consequently, to tie the peasant to the land by force of law and the status was made hereditary. Actually the peasant was made servile to the ruling class, not the land, as the gentry could use the labor of the serf as they sought fit, on other land and other work including mining, household services and other callings. Some of the peasant revolts were over the dehumanizing work in the mines.

Not all the peasants were serfs. About half were organized in communes with private ownership of land around the village. The land was held and tilled in strips as was the custom in medieval Europe. They paid taxes and rent directly to the state. These taxes and levies were equally oppressive.

Prior to the abolition of serfdom there were a number of notable peasant revolts: Bolotnikov (1616–17), Stenka Razin (1670–71), Bulavin (1707–08) and Pugachev (1773–75). They are known by the names of their leaders, who were usually disaffected members of the ruling class. The Pugachev revolt was the most serious. Catherine the Great was hard put to suppress it. Emelian Pugachev was a Don Cossack who fell into disrepute with the ruling elite. He consequently organized a rebellion of disaffected peasants and other elements in the Urals, crossed the Volga and marched on Moscow. The gentry and nobility in Moscow and St. Petersburg were in panic lest the revolt spread to their inumerable household servants in the cities. Pugachev defeated Catherine's generals, at first, capturing town after town on his way to Moscow. Eventually the army overwhelmed him. A famine on the Volga diminished the enthusiasm of the peasants for the revolt which undermined Pugachev's army. He was defeated and brought to Moscow in an iron cage and executed in January, 1775.

Thereafter peasant rebellions subsided but other social and economic factors militated toward the abolition of serfdom. Emerging industrialization, especially a textile industry—for by now the advanced technology was seeping into Russia from western Europe—required a larger pool of free labor. The emancipation of the serfs was ordered by Alexander II in 1861. Freeing the serfs, however, did not serve to alleviate the poverty in the countryside. During the following half century or so, 1861–1905, the peasant population swelled from 50 to 75 million! Despite the fact, that the now free peasants were able to obtain more of the land and by 1916 probably two-thirds of the arable area was in peasant hands, the poverty of the countryside kept increasing. Peasant ownership, for one thing, was very uneven. A class of wealthier peasants, called kulaks was emerging, who worked their land with tenants, hired labor and increasingly, with machinery. At the other end were landless agricultural laborers or peasants with uneconomic holdings. Land hunger remained acute. Peasant unrest was widespread with periodic recurrence of strikes and outbreaks. One such notable outbreak was that of the Red Cocks in 1905 who went about the countryside burning the houses and barns of the gentry.

An incipient agrarian party called the Peasants Union was formed in 1905 and rural deputies of the first two Dumas kept agitating for land reform. Earlier in 1883 the government set up a Peasant's Land Bank to facilitate the purchase or renting of land from the gentry, state and other landowners for the establishment of individual farms.

The land held by the nobility and gentry had declined considerably since 1861. Yet there were over a million families owning some 100 million acres of land in 1917 which the peasants felt rightfully belonged to them. This land was appropriated by the peasants in 1917 and distributed in accordance with local justice.

In the beginning the communists could do little about the peasants. When they tried to take control of the surplus production through taxation, compulsory grain levies and other means the peasants resisted by producing only what they needed. Grain production dropped by half between 1917 and 1921. In 1921 Lenin instituted his famous NEP policy which permitted agriculture, as well as industry, to operate and develop freely in order to reconstruct the Russian economy to is pre-war level of production. By 1926 the communists felt strong enough to bring the peasants under control and launched what is sometimes referred to as the second or Stalinist revolution to collectivize farms. The main target of the collectivization of the farms were the kulaks who had become relatively prosperous individual farmers. They were still small farmers by American standards, owning only around 50 acres of land. The small holders, many of them still farming cooperatively, under the ancient commune system fitted easily into the collective farms. The *raison d'etre* of the collective farm was to industrialize agriculture. Tractors and fertilizers were made available to the collective farm through the establishment of central tractor stations. By 1938 nearly three-fourths of the land was plowed with tractors and half the harvesting was done by machines. This rationalization of agriculture was facilitated by a movement of the surplus labor from the countryside into factories in the urban areas. The forced draft industrialization of the economy prior to World War II made this possible. The burgeoning peasantry now had available to them, another means of livelihood thus relieving the pressure on agriculture to support a growing population. By 1939 one-third of the Russian people worked in the new industries and other non-agricultural jobs.

The Russian Revolution too had this broader meaning and purpose. The Russian economy in 1917 could no longer support adequately the growing population without further technological development. The struggle over the inadequate surplus produced by an antiquated agriculture became more oppressive to the dominated majority until it exploded in revolution. The communists—Lenin in particular—understood that the answer was industrialization and through their success in this respect established themselves as the new ruling elite in the country.

EUROPEAN REVOLUTIONS

European revolutions generally assumed different characteristics. The technological lead achieved by the Europeans after the middle of the second millennium of the Chirstian era enabled them to increase productivity and relieve the pressures of increasing population in the perennial struggle over the distribution of the wealth. The relief was twofold. First, the Europeans, with the development of the full rigged deep keeled ship and firearms achieved domination of the newly discovered lands and peoples of the western hemisphere and eventually most of Asia giving them not only great scope for plunder but providing their increasing population with new means of livelihood as pirates, slavers, seamen, traders and related commercial callings. Second, and much more important, this burst of technological creativity elevated these countries to a high plateau of productivity based on machinery and chemical energy so that there was more national production for all to share. Agriculture was no longer the only means of livelihood for the vast majority of people.

Industrialization had two basic effects. It elevated increasingly more of the so-called middle class on which democratic politis could be based. greater interest in the conduct of political affairs. There gradually emerged the so-called middle class on which democratic politics could be based. Equally important, it created a new source of wealth and these business and industrial interests clamored for admittance into the ruling class. The result was a realignment of power within the industrializing societies. In most cases it was a reasonably peaceful change. In some cases, as the French Revolution, it was accompanied by violence and bloodshed.

In England, which led the Industrial Revolution, the change was mostly peaceful. The 17th century was a time of great turmoil for the British. The struggle for supremacy between the Monarchy and Parliament raged fiercely with the new commercial interests supporting the Parliamentary forces. But many of the landowners, those who were turning from tillage to pasturage to reap greater profits from the production and processing of wool, turned against the Monarchy. A rebellion erupted in 1642. The commercial and manufacturing interests in the south and east, the new foreign trade sector, were for Parliament. The landed aristocracy, the north peasants, the church, including Catholics, stood behind the King. Throughout this struggle religion—a Catholic restoration—was an important issue. Oliver Cromwell gained leadership of the parliamentary forces which overwhelmed the Royalists in 1648. The Rump Parliament, so-called, from which 140 Royalist members were summarily expelled, voted for the execution of Charles I and he was beheaded on January 30, 1649.

In 1660, after a decade or so of Cromwellian dictatorship, the Monarchy was again restored under Charles II. Charles had no zest for government and gave Parliament little or no trouble. Perhaps the beheading of his father was too grim a reminder so he spent his reign in leisure and pleasure. His son and successor James II, however, proved to be another matter. Unlike his father who, it was said, lived like an atheist and died a Catholic, James was an ardent believer. He set out to restore catholicism in England—even hoped to pursuade the Anglican church to reconciliation with Rome—and in his efforts challenged the supremacy of Parliament. His protestant daughter Mary, now the wife of William III of Orange was his only heir. When the queen bore James a son on June 10, 1688, whom the king planned to bring up as a Catholic to succeed him, the protestants of England offered the throne to William and Mary. William, with the support of Louis XIV of France, sailed for England with an armada of fifty warships, 500 cavalry and 11,000 infantry on October 19, 1688. James capitulated readily and was allowed to escape to France where he lived out the remaining years of his life.

A convention was assembled of lords, bishops and members of Parliament in which William and Mary were offered the crown. The offer was accompanied by a Declaration of Right, later reenacted as the Bill of Rights by Parliament, which explicitly asserted the legislative supremacy of Parliament and excluded Roman Catholics from the throne of England. This has come to be known in English history as the Glorious Revolution.

The Glorious Revolution confirmed the landed aristocracy in power. It was, however, within a democratic framework that not only gave voice to the growing business interests but recognized their importance to the economy of the country. Moreover, many of the landowners were commercial minded. Through enclosures they turned much of the land and commons of the country into pasturage for sheep to profit from the lucrative wool trade of England. The enclosures could have had a damaging effect on the peasants had they not been afforded other enconomic outlets. But England was now becoming a dominant power in the world with colonies and world wide trade. An Englishman could go to America, the West Indies and other colonies; he could find employment with the East India Company in Far East trade or in the emerging metallurgical, textile and other industries in England. Foreign trade needed both a merchant fleet and a navy to protect it. So, Englishmen became seamen. By 1700 less than a third of the population was dependent on agriculture for a livelihood and about half of them owned the land they tilled. The struggle between landlord and peasant that brought on violent revolution elsewhere never developed in England because of the technological creativeness of the English which made national productivity less dependent upon agriculture.

Parliament provided an institution that permitted full scope for Pareto's law. The newly emerging commercial and industrial wealth could rise to power in the House of Commons. The landed aristocracy viewed it with tolerance. This was a time when an Englishman went out poor and came back rich. When he returned he usually bought his way to Parliament. When Clive returned from India, rich at age 35, he bought enough boroughs to control a bloc of votes in the Commons. He had himself elected to Parliament from Shrewsbury. This became common practice with the commercial and industrial *nouveau riche*.

In 1800 the ruling elite consisted of 287 lords (princes, dukes, earls, viscounts and barons), 26 bishops, 540 baronets, 350 knights, 6000 or so squires or gentry and some 20,000 "gentlemen" or "ladies" (people who had unearned incomes). The baronets and knights were entitled to use the prefix "Sir" before their names. This elite comprised less than one per cent of the population of 9 million even if you include members of their families! The aristocracy dominated the government because of its wealth. The 287 peers and lords alone had 29 per cent of the national income according to the census of 1801. Most of their wealth was in land at the time but as industrialization took hold in the 19th century industrialists, colonists, lawyers, journalists, labor leaders, intellectuals and others were admitted to the aristocracy through knighthood or otherwise. Some were even admitted to the peerage. Yes, even intellectuals. The renouned economist John Maynard Keynes was admitted to the House of Lords as Baron Keynes of Tilton. England was a land of free and liberal thought. It was one of the hallmarks of its greatness.

Finally the Glorious Revolution brought forth a free press to crown the democracy of England. There can be no democracy without a free press. Under both the Tudors and Stuarts the English press was controlled though the Licensing Act. William III and his whig supporters let the Act expire in 1694. Thereafter the press has been an important foundation of England's democratic institutions.

In France, on the other hand, the shift of power from a landowning to an industrial elite was more tortuous. At the end of the 18th century France already had a population of some 25 million. All but about 2 million were peasants! A striking contrast with England during the 17th century when the English effected their peaceful revolution.

While feudalism was abolished the peasants suffered considerable oppression from the landowners and ex-feudal lords. There were an estimated 26,000 of these seigneurs, together with the provincial administrators and parish priests, who constituted the agrarian elite in the countryside. Some of the landowners managed and operated their estates, but most lived in the towns or capital and collected rents and feudal dues.

The landowners owned about 55 per cent of the land, which they rented to the peasants for a percentage of the crops or other production. The other 45 per cent of the land owned by the peasants, mostly in uneconomic small holdings, was encumbered with feudal dues. As inflation reduced the value of these dues the seigneurs contrived various ways to increase them or revive other ancient charges. They were collected by merciless professional agents. In addition the government imposed taxes, including the *corvee* which by 1789 was commuted to cash payment. Finally the church collected its tithes and dues. The peasant had to support the state, church and the aristocracy. These rents, dues, taxes and other impositions had become unduly oppressive by 1789.

The French landlord, moreover, differed from his counterpart across the Channel. He was not commercially minded with the exception, perhaps, of the vineyard owners. But wine exports were never as important to the French economy as was the wool trade to England. The landowning interests had no concept of the meaning of industrialization to the future of France.

Two other factors made the situation in France different from England. Industrialization lagged by a century or so. And the French were latecomers on the international scene. Portugal and Spain launched European domination of the world in the 16th century. England entered the scene in the 17th century and eventually came to dominate it in the 18th century. French colonialism did not start in a substantial way until the 19th century. Its early attempts in America and India were frustrated by the English. The French colonial empire, or Greater France, in Africa and Indo-China did not arise until the mid 1800's. The French did not, therefore, have the same economic outlets in foreign trade and industrialization that was available to the English a century earlier. It is estimated that only 75,000 families depended on factory employment in Paris at the time of the Revolution. The pressure for the distribution of the surplus within a predominantly agricultural economy became enormous with the increasing population by the end of the 18th century.

The Revolution was sparked in Paris. The situation in the capital in 1789 was similar to that in Petrograd in 1917. The Bourbon dynasty was decadent. Louis XVI was an ineffectual ruler. The court lived in luxury at Versailles while the factory workers and small tradesmen starved. The situation was aggravated by two bad harvests caused by drought and a violent storm on July 13, 1788 that devastated the crops in the north. Ironically the storm left the vineyards in the south untouched. The grape harvest was the best ever and the price of wine sank to its lowest. Too much cheap wine and too little bread, in the view of one French historian, created a volatile situation in Paris in 1789. It is, perhaps, as good an explanation as any for the madness that followed.

The first thing to note about the French Revolution is that it was without effective leadership. It was certainly without direction and purpose, except, regarding the latter, to destroy the old order. There was no recognition, such as Lenin and Mao had, that France had to industrialize in order to support its burgeoning population. Perhaps, it was too early at this stage of technological development. But then, the English sensed the future even earlier. To destroy an order without replacing it with a new order and purpose had to end in disaster. And so it did.

The leaders of the Revolution were a disparate group. There were aristocrats (Rochefould, Mirabeau, LaFayette, Condorcet et al) and lawyers and advocates in great numbers (Petion de Villenueve, Robespierre, Danton and Vergniaud among others). There were no peasant leaders. Philippe, the Duke of Orleans, made some efforts to win the support of the peasants but it was for ulterior purposes. He had hoped to succeed to the crown after his cousin Louis was deposed. But Philippe too lost his head in the Terror.

The peasants, as they did in Russia in 1917, made their own revolution. As early as April in 1789, after effective rule from Paris ceased, the peasants repudiated payment of feudal dues. Everywhere peasants assembled, exchanged and compared grievances, armed themselves, attacked the estates, destroyed the manorial rolls, burned the homes of the resisters and even murdered some of the seigneurs. In August the nobility announced it would no longer demand the dues, but by then it was a *fait accompli*. Taxes and church tithes, likewise, were repudiated, resisted or compromised. All over France the peasants destroyed the registers, set fire to tax offices and dealt harshly with the tax collectors. The peasants freed themselves from oppression but not poverty. There were too many for the land to support in decent livelihood. The repudiation by the peasants of the landed aristocracy and the church in the countryside in 1789 was the only thing that resembled a genuine revolution. The rest was destruction and terror.

After the sack of the Bastille on July 14, 1789 the revolutionaries in Paris tried to set up a Republic. Constitution succeeded constitution. The various clubs of Paris vied for political control with the Jacobins, headed by Maximilien Robespierre, coming out on top. The Directory—a committee of five—was established in 1795 as the executive of the Republic.

Louis was beheaded on January 21, 1793 by the guillotine, a mechanical head chopper designed by Dr. Guillotin, who miraculously escaped losing his own head on the contraption. Thereafter a period of terror ensued where today's purged was yesterday's purger. Robespierre who headed the committee on public safety during the early days of the Reign of Terror perished by the guillotine himself on July 28, 1794.

Equally devastating was fiscal mismanagement by the Republic. The revolutionaries knew nothing about money management and begot a horrendous inflation. They could not collect taxes so they printed money (assignats, later mandats) by the bushel. Prices soared until a loaf of bread cost 150, a pound of sugar or coffee 1,600 and a pair of shoes 20,000 livres. The rate of exchange against a Louis d'or (a gold coin worth about $25 when based on gold at $35 an ounce) moved from 24 to 70 livres by the time of Robespierre's fall, to 2600 by the end of the Republic in 1799. Inflation brought forth wild speculation and unearned fortunes. A new landowning class arose buying up land of bankrupt peasants. Gold was hoarded by all who could, even the revolutionaries. The assignats became a joke. It was said a "crown is a crown, but assignats are so much toilet paper." The Republic responded with a derogatory campaign against gold referring to it as so much "dung". Little did they understand that throughout history past and present the only defense against money mismanagement is gold.

The Republic was in total disarray and bankruptcy by mid-decade. Organized gangs roamed the countryside robbing travelers and peasants. Chaos prevailed in Paris. Inflation had ruined everyone except the speculators. At this stage the revolutionaries, proclaiming themselves pacifists at the start, turned imperialistic. They decided to transport the Revolution abroad under the banner "Liberty, Equality, Fraternity." For the next two decades the French terrorized Europe with their armies.

Recruitment for the army proved easy and successful. France had an abundance of idle and unemployable manpower. The army provided young Frenchmen with food and adventure. It was, of course, inevitable that the result should be a military dictatorship. And a suitable man rose to the occasion.

Napoleon Bonaparte was an imperator *per se*. Steeped in Roman history his great desire was to emulate the Caesars. He wanted to conquer the world but got unceremoniously stopped by the British in Egypt. Thereafter he reduced his ambitions. He overextended his power in Russia and met disaster. The English, of the now powerful British empire, finally defeated him at Waterloo in 1815.

After Napoleon there was a Bourbon restoration under Louis XVIII and Charles X. They made no concerted attempt to restore the old order. The guillotine was too vivid a memory. The aristocracy could not reverse the peasant revolution of 1789. But the old revolutionaries, Lafayette in particular, kept agitating for a Republic. In 1830 Charles X fled when revolutionary fervor began to build, but the revolutionaries were apprehensive about setting up another Republic. The memory of the terror and assignats was still too strong. They opted for trying out the Orleans branch of the Bourbons and offered the throne to Louis-Phillipe. Louis Phillipe was a liberal and peaceful monarch but he and his supporters refused to establish a constitutional monarchy based on universal sufferage. The secret societies kept up a mounting tide of rebellion leading to the Revolution of 1848 which finally rid France of the Bourbons. The Second Republic elected a Bonaparte, a nephew of Napoleon I, who subverted the revolution and established the Second empire. Two successive plebiscites confirmed him as President for 10 years after which he made his dictatorship hereditary. He silenced Parliament but did grant workers the right to unionize.

Like his uncle, Napoleon III was a war maker. His imperialism led to the Franco-Prussian War of 1871 which collapsed the Second empire. The Revolution of 1871 nearly repeated the excesses of 1793. A commune was set up by the workers but the nascent communists had no well thought out program of socialism. They respected private property. After considerable burning (the Tuileries and Hotel De Ville—and almost the Louvre and Sainte-Chapelle) the revolutionaries settled for a republic. The Third Republic established a Parliamentary system of government that lasted until World War I. The President was a mere figurehead. The President, or Premier, of the Counsel held the real power, but because of a multi-party system the government was mostly one of unstable coalitions.

But France finally had a political system that provided facile admittance to power for the commercial and industrial interests. After Napoleon I France started to industrialize. Factories sprang up powered by steam and, later, electricity. By 1877 there were 30,000 miles of railroad tracks and 128,000 miles of telegraph wires. Steamboats replaced wooden sailing vessels.

Frenchmen made some notable technological contributions. In 1816 Niepce and Daguerre invented the first camera. Henri St. Claire Deville developed a process for producing pure aluminum from aluminum salts in 1845. Serpollet pioneered in the development of the automobile as early as 1887. Clement Ader flew a power driven monoplane fashioned after a bat about 300 yards in 1897. Bleriot flew the channel in a machine heavier than air in 1909. Bleriot's monoplane design became eventually the airplane of the future. Cros invented the phonograph at the same time as Edison.

But France never became the industrial power that England, Germany and America did. Her coal deposits could not match those of England. French technology was never as creative as that of the English and Germans. She had to contend herself with second place. Her peasants were not innovative. They did not use reapers, harvesters and threshing machines until the end of the century. France has always depended more on agriculture than other European countries for her national production. Hence, her different socio-political development.

This lagging and inferior technological development was, perhaps, in large measure the reason for the tortuous transition of power from an agricultural to an industrial elite in France. A conservative and backward looking landed aristocracy together with a late developing and weaker commercial and industrial elite failed to bring about a facile development of a democratic political framework as transpired in England during the 17th century.

After 1848 constitutions were adopted by all the states of Europe. Moreover, a unification of the states of Italy and Germany took place after the Franco-Prussian War of 1871. These constitutions varied but generally provided for universal suffrage and limited greatly the rights of the monarchy. The degree of complete democracy varied. In Germany the monarchy held wide and considerable power until World War I. Most of these changes were peaceful. They all provided in different ways, a political framework that allowed freely for the elevation of the new commerical and industrial elites to power.

Europeans had two advantages that enabled them to change their power structures without the violent revolutions that occurred in Russia and China. European technological ingenuity made their economies more productive and able to sustain population growth. The same technological prowess enabled them to dominate the world. New lands and economic opportunities in the colonies relieved the population pressure on domestic production. European emigrants flowed to the United States, Canada, Australia, South Africa and South America in torrents during the 19th century. Others derived their livelihood from trade in India, China and other Asian and African countries. The new wealth derived from industrialization and colonialism demanded admittance into the ruling class. The old landed aristocracy gave way peacefully. The French Revolution was somewhat unique in this process. It occurred before an industrial elite formed. Its leaders, unlike those in the Russian and Chinese Revolutions, did not understand they had to lead the country toward industrialization. It could, therefore, be only a peasant revolution which came like a flash in 1789. Thereafter, the French Revolution, for which it is notorious in history, was a case of humanity gone berserk. It proves, if anything, the propensity of man to lapse into irrational behavior. Despite the excesses, though, the French Revolution did propagate all over Europe the democratic ideas and ideals that a century or so later prevailed throughout the continent.

REVOLUTION IN INDIA

India won her independence from British rule in 1947. It was a peaceful change. Unlike the revolution in China, freedom from foreign domination was not coupled with a violent revolution against the Indian ruling elite. But like the Communist party in China the new Indian ruling elite also decided that their country must be industrialized in order to step up rapidly national production to alleviate the poverty of the mass of the Indian people. The big difference, however, was that Indians proposed to do so within the democratic framework they inherited from the British. The paramount question in 1947, as it still is a generation later, was whether this was possible under democratic auspices. Japan, an Asian country, had done so but not under a democratic government. The Japanese employed draconian methods not unlike the forced draft industrialization of the communists in Russia and China. India proposed to do so without force and violence.

The peasants in India were as poor as any in the world. Moreover, there were 350 million Indians in 1947. As of 1975 there were 600 million. Three-fourths of the people derive their livelihood from agriculture. Agriculture comprised 4890 crores of a total national income of 9530 crores of rupees (approximately $20 billion) during the fiscal year 1950–51, the beginning of the First Five Year Plan. Population pressure on the distribution of this inadequate national production was acute at the time of independence.

There is no history of large scale peasant revolts in India such as was detailed above in China. There were minor skirmishes against tax collectors, religious inspired fracases between Hindu peasants and Muslim landlords, and vice versa, and the like. It is difficult to understand why this is so when peasant revolts are common in most other societies. That the Indian is as violent a man as any other is evident from the bloodshed over religion the world has witnessed during recent times. There may, however, be other reasons.

The pressure on agriculture was not as great as elsewhere. The warm climate of India reduced the provision for clothing and shelter to a minimum.

Food was the only necessity. Moreover, the climate made double cropping possible. Megasthenes and other Greek ambassadors during ancient times were greatly impressed by this agricultural productivity.

The peasants during Hindu times were mostly free. Land was owned by the king but the peasant enjoyed possession as long as he cultivated it well. There was no system of large estates. There were some large farmsteads cultivated with hired labor and the kings owned large demenses worked by hired hands. The king however, had a right to a share of the produce. The sacred texts prescribed no more than one-sixth. By Mauryan times differentiation was made for good soil and availability of water through irrigation and the *Arthasastra*, a treatise on administration compiled during the reign of the first Chandragupta, prescribes the king's revenue to range from one-fourth to one third depending on the fertility and water resources of the land. Remissions were made for bad harvests. The *Arthasastra* also prescribes eviction of peasants failing to cultivate the land efficiently.

Indian agriculture, however, has always been subject to the vagaries of the monsoon. The monsoon normally has a five year cycle ranging from very poor to good rains and every generation or so there would be two or three bad years in a row. This would produce famines which have recurred in Indian history since time immemorial. But these famines did not beget peasant rebellions as the cultivator realized they were not the fault of the rulers. In fact, the Arthasastra advised the king to store grain for such famines and granaries were maintained for such emergencies by the ancient Hindu rulers.

It would seem also that the caste system contributed in large measure to the peaceful demeanor of the Indian peasant. Caste is a prominant feature of Indian culture. Its origin is somewhat obscure. Doubtless caste originated from social stratification, a sociological phenomenon characteristic of all human societies. In India, though, this social stratification grew more rigid as time went by instead of ameliorating as it did elsewhere. There is evidence that greater mobility among classes existed in India prior to the advent of foreign invasion and rule. The French historian Amaury de Riencourt puts forth an interesting thesis that a retreat into caste by the Indians was a means of defense against the cultural impact of foreign rule which in time ossified Hinduism.

Muslim domination merely hardened the caste system. It was unable to break it down. Muslim converts came mainly from the outcastes. The western impact of democracy and industrialization, however, promises to do so. Caste thrives best in rural India. Urbanization promises to ameliorate caste rigidity and eventually to eliminate it. The building of Jamshedpur, the modern steel city of India, gives a preview of this process. Although it was slow and uncertain in the beginning, differences of caste and creed were overcome as the employees and their families were induced to share common vocational training courses, company eating facilities, recreational outlets and living areas. Similar breakdown of caste is transpiring all over India as factories rise and industrialization progresses.

Religion and philosophy are intimately related to human conduct in India. Every aspect of life is regulated by a code of morality and ethics appropriate to the caste and status of the individual. This is called dharma. Moreover, a person's place or purpose is also fixed and beyond his temporal control. An individual is born into a certain caste because of his behavior in a previous embodiment. His behavior in this life determines his status in the next. Thus a sudra by obeying the moral and ethical code of Hinduism could elevate himself to one of the higher castes. But if he lived an evil life he would suffer further degradation after death through rebirth in the form of some animal life such as a dog or a worm. The process of connection with the past and future is called the transmigration of the soul or the doctrine of rebirth. This religious dogma is without doubt the most ingenious ever invented by the mind of man for maintaining social discipline and order. It has been a chief reason for the great stability of the Indian society.

A peasant so indoctrinated by the ruling elite was given a way to rationalize his miserable plight that held both him and his oppressor blameless. He accepted his dharma and prepared for a better reincarnation after death. This was a far more insidious inculation of Fate in the Indian peasant than that existing in China which the communists found so difficult to overcome. Hindu India, it would appear, did not have the violent conflict over the distribution of wealth that was found elsewhere.

Under Muslim domination, which lasted from 1192 to 1757, divided equally between the Delhi sultanate and the Mughal empire, there is greater evidence of peasant oppression. The sultans increased the revenue up to one half the produce of the land. It was collected from the Hindu chiefs and landlords and Muslim military officers who were given grants of land. In addition, there was the traditional *jizya*, a tax on non-Muslims. Some of the sultans like Ala-ud-din (1290–1321 A. D.) collected the taxes relentlessly. Others like Firoz Shah (1351–1388) were more benevolent. After Timur's devastating raid on Delhi in 1398 the sultanate lapsed into disintegration and most of India broke away from Muslim rule. Sher Shah, the last of the Afghan Lodis, was not only a benevolent sultan but an administrative genius who changed the land revenue to a fixed payment based on actual production over a period of years instead of the old Hindu system of a percentage of the actual produce.

After the Mughals deposed the ineffectual Lodis and Akbar consolidated Mughal rule over Hindusthan his able finance Minister, Raja Toadr Mal refined the new system instituted by Sher Shah. The demand was fixed on the basis of average produce and the ryot, or cultivator, could pay in cash or in kind. The assessment was supported by a cadastral survey and classification of the land according to its use and fertility. Land records were kept for this purpose. No provision for, or practice of, periodic reassessment appears to have been made by the Mughals.

The revenue assessment was made directly with the ryot, and the collection of the revenue was farmed out or assigned for services (mostly military) to a host to tax gatherers, the most notable of whom was the zamindar. He was alloted a definite area of the country from which he was required to return a certain amount of revenue to the emperor, retaining a fractional balance as compensation for his efforts. Where revenue was assigned, the assignee called a jagirdar, was usually required to support a fixed military contingent (reckoned in so many horses) for the emperor from the revenue proceeds but did not have to forward any part thereof to him. Such assignments were revocable at the will of the emperor. While the Mughal empire remained strong, the zamindars were kept under control, but when its power declined, they began to assert proprietory rights in the allotted or assigned area to impose additional burdens on the ryots who cultivated the land. As Mughal power devolved from one weak successor to another the independence of the zamindars grew and flourished, particularly in the areas farthest from Delhi.

This situation obtained when the East India Company came into possession of the Diwani (revenue collection) of Bengal in 1765. For some time, the company muddled along with the system without understanding it, but as more and more friction developed between its collectors and the zamindars the revenue system was placed under elaborate scrutiny by Lord Cornwallis. As already noted this resulted in the Permanent Settlement of 1793, which declared the zamindars to be proprietors of the area from which they collected the tax, subject to an annual revenue payment to the government. The payment was fixed in perpetuity at ten-elevenths of the rent collected from the ryots at the time, with the remainder left to the zamindar as renumeration for his responsibility. The zamindars were, therefore, confirmed in their tenure by the East India Company either because of a misunderstanding of their status or for fiscal expediency. Since the company reserved the right to institute measures for the protection of the ryots, the settlement appeared eminently fair for all concerned at the time it was made.

At first, the stringent distraint regulations caused much hardship to defaulting zamindars and ryots. Many were dispossessed during the generation or so following the permanent settlement, but agricultural production rose during the ensuing period of internal order. The rural population increased and idle lands were brought under cultivation. It was also a period of rising prices. This enabled the zamindars to collect more rent from their lands so that the amount of the revenue under the permanent settlement diminished to a fraction of the rents the zamindar collected from the ryots. The rigidity of the system caused the government to bear the entire burden of monetary inflation.

Outside Bengal, a different system of land revenue was achieved, called the ryotwari settlement, under which the amount of the land revenue was fixed directly with the ryot. In the Punjab and United Provinces the settlements known as the mahal settlements were made with chieftans or groups representing the villages, who in turn allotted the assessment to the cultivators.

The foregoing land revenue systems, continued after independence. The permanent settled zamindari system remained unchanged since 1793, with the result that the government's share of agricultural production kept diminishing until it was in Bengal only about 20 per cent of the rents collected by the zamindars. In the temporary settled ryotwari, mahalwari, and zamindari systems, periodic revisions were made and assessments underlying the settlements gradually changed from a gross produce to a net produce basis. This gave the temporary settlement systems somewhat more flexibility with the result that Madras and Bombay were imposed upon to make up deficits in Bengal. But the revenue system as a whole was characterized by its rigidity being unduly oppressive in times of adversity and unproductive in time of agricultural prosperity.

During foreign rule the taxation of agriculture was a form of tribute and the foreign rulers set out to tax the cultivator to the bearable limit. Fortunately, there was yet no pressure on the land in India during these times as there is now, so that the cultivator could give up his field when the burden became intolerable and seek land in another area where the tax collector was more lenient. This was particularly true under the sultans who at times were unable to control many parts of the country. Under the Mughals there are numerous references to absconding ryots. It was, perhaps, this factor more than any other that made the land revenue system of the Muslims tolerable to the Indian peasant. In fact, it was estimated by Grant during the study preceding the Permanent Settlement of 1793 that only about 20 per cent of the land in Bengal was under cultivation. Competition for cultivators, therefore, tended to temper the rapacity of the tax collectors during Muslim times. Nevertheless, it is estimated that revenue collections were between one-third to one-half of the gross produce of agriculture immediately prior to British rule.

During the past century, particularly the last two decades, the "settlement" feature of the land revenue system operated to change the character of agricultural taxation in India. As population increased, more land was cultivated and agricultural production increased. Under the permanent settlement this increased output could not be taxed. The zamindar's interest became so valuable that it led to the practice of subinfeudation, which resulted in the socially undesirable zamindari system abolished after independence. The several-fold price inflation also benefited the zamindar entirely, at the expense of the state. In the temporarily settled areas, periodic resettlements provided means to the government for overcoming some of the disadvantages of the permanent settlement system, but in view of the long periods of settlement, the state was always at a disadvantage. Most of these resettlements were usually in arrears. They were first postponed because of the war. Moreover, as British rule weakened the British were hesitant to undertake resettlements that would increase the land revenue lest they undermine their waning support in the countryside against independence. Meanwhile, prices increased fourfold and the country undertook a vigorous plan of agricultural development resulting in increasing agricultural production. Whereas revenue policy under Mughal and early British rule aimed at collecting one-third of the gross produce, and at times collected as high as one-half, the inherent rigidity of the settlement system caused the pendulum to swing to the other extreme since that time. During 1950–51, only 51.6 crores were collected in land revenue, representing merely a little over one per cent of the value of the output in the agricultural sector.

After independence the Indian government promptly launched programs of land reform designed to eliminate the proprietary rights of the zamindars, jagirdars and other intermediaries for which they were compensated with long term (up to 40 years) non-negotiable interest bearing bonds. The ryot now holds directly from and pays his rent to the state. Some of the Reform Acts also have provisions enabling the ryot to acquire proprietary rights in the land he cultivates. Additional reforms limiting the land holding to 50–60 acres or so, limitations on rents imposed on tenants and the like were also enacted. The effectiveness of these reforms is often questioned. Since the states are granted power over agriculture by the Indian constitution the land reforms vary from state to state not only in the provisions of the Acts but in the administration of the reforms. In general, though, the intermediaries have been eliminated and the size of landholdings and terms of tenancies have been brought under control.

There are no large landholdings in India. The First Five Year Plan contains an analysis of land ownership. In the fertile and irrigated Doab of the Gangetic plain less than one per cent of the holdings exceed 25 acres. Eighty per cent of the holdings are five acres or less. Fifteen acres or so, however, of this rich alluvium, well watered and susceptible to double cropping, including a cash crop like sugar cane, provides for a very good livelihood. Even in the non-irrigated areas that are completely at the mercy of the unreliable monsoon few of the holdings exceed 100 acres. In Bombay (now Gujerat and Maharasthra states) only 8 per cent of the farms fell in the 25–100 acre category in 1951.

These free peasants of India are very well off. They are now benefiting from the country's industrialization. They are buying tractors, fertilizers and improved seeds. The land revenue is still only about one per cent of output. There is some additional tax burden through indirect taxation such as excise, sales and such like taxes, but these taxes probably add no more than 5 percent to the peasants tax burden. Although the planners in New Delhi keep advocating heavier taxation of agriculture to provide the capital needed for industrialization the Congress party, which has held political power since Independence, refuses to do so. The Congress depends upon the peasant vote to win elections. The state and central ministries are, in effect, the captives of the wealthy or wealthier peasants.

This does not mean there is no revolutionary potential in rural India. There are over 100 million landless laborers in the countryside living on the verge of starvation. They are the first victims of the recurring bad monsoons. Their main source of livelihood is employment by the land owning peasants during harvest time and for other menial work in the villages. When the crops fail there is no employment and no wages with which to buy food, even though there may be no overall shortage of food in the country. Many starve before famine relief reaches them. Starvation is more often a factor of unemployment rather than a shortage of food.

Yet this economically deprived agrarian proletariat does not appear to manifest revolutionary propensities. The ineffectual communists in India have not been able to move them to rebellion. They have not even tried. The only revolt of significance fomented by the communists was in 1946–7 in the Warangel area of Hyderabad. The Razakars led by Kasim Razvi took over about 2000 villages and organized them into soviets. The newly independent government of India fixed upon this rebellion as a reason to depose the Nizam and incorporate this biggest princely state into the union. The Indian army arrested Kasim Razvi and broke up the Razakar organization. This revolt was based upon the wealthier peasants and not the landless laborers. It had mainly religious and regional motivations as the Nizam was a Muslim ruling a predominantly Hindu population.

Since Independence the Indian communists have operated as a political party within the country's parliamentary system. They managed to gain power in states like West Bengal, Kerela and Andhra Pradesh, usually in a coalition government, only for temporary periods. Their base of power is usually the labor unions and the industrial proletariat is still too small to support a revolution through the ballot box or otherwise.

Nothing meaningful could, of course, be accomplished through a redistribution of the small holdings (the average farm in India is 4.7 acres) to the landless laborers. The only solution is rapid industrialization to increase the national production and to permit the unemployed to share in its distribution through more job opportunities. The ruling elite in India recognize this fully but they are faced with two obstacles that may prove insurmountable.

First modern industrialization is capital intensive and provides less employment than (say) around 1900. A modern multi-million dollar steel plant employs only 400. There cannot, therefore, be enough scope for drawing the landless laborers in the countryside into the factories. Yet it has been seen that a peasant or landless laborer from the Punjab countryside, for instance, can be converted into a skillful lathe operator in a piston factory in Patiala very readily. But the jobs are not being created in sufficient numbers.

Second, a vastly increased rate of industrialization is hampered by lack of capital. Industrialization needs two factors of production—advanced technology and capital investment. The modern technology, in the early stages has to come from the technologically advanced countries. Capital investment too can come from abroad but this is expensive and cannot be a long term matter lest the industrializing country lose its economic independence. In the long run most of the capital must be generated at home.

During the second and third Five Year Plans (1956–65) India did a remarkable job of securing and mastering the most advanced technology from America, Europe, Japan and the Soviet bloc. For example, after independence India was importing all its motor vehicles. The government restricted imports in 1953 to those foreign manufacturers who instituted with Indian partners the progressive manufacture of the motor vehicle. In 1967 motor vehicles (cars, jeeps, trucks and buses) were produced in India with 80–90 per cent indigenous content! Similar progress transpired in almost every area of the industrial structure so that by 1970 India was self-sufficient in modern industrial technology. Indian engineers and technicians could design and construct steel plants, refineries, fertilizer factories and other industrial units and supply them, with minor exceptions, with machinery and equipment manufactured domestically. The only technological assistance required was on the frontiers of technology such as petrochemicals, electronics and the like.

Yet by 1970 industrial progress stagnated because of lack of capital. During the period 1956–65 considerable amounts of capital came from abroad not only for industrialization but for general economic development. The western countries and the Soviet bloc offered foreign aid. The World Bank provided loans. Foreign companies entered collaboration agreements for technical assistance and equity participation. India is reluctant however, to take more of this foreign capital as the cost of the loans and foreign investment is about 10 per cent annum and it does not earn enough foreign exchange to service much more of this foreign capital.

At the same time India is not generating enough capital from within, largely, because under its democratic form of government it cannot appropriate an adequate amount of its agricultural output for investment in more rapid industrialization lest the political elite, the Congress party, lose support of the peasants. Russia and China appropriated and continue to appropriate a third or more of their agricultural output for industrialization enabling them to develop more rapidly than India. Japan too took a third or more of the peasants produce for its spectacular industrialization. India cannot hope to match these records with a land tax of one per cent on its agricultural sector!

India's population grows over two per cent per annum. If this continues unabated there will be a billion Indians by the end of the 20th century. It will require greater economic growth than has been achieved the past 25 years to provide jobs for so many people. The pressure on the distribution of an inadequate national product is bound to intensify. Whether this burgeoning rural *cum* increasingly urbanized proletariat might rebel against the prevailing order for a greater share of the national production is impossible to foresee. It would appear, at the moment, that there is no effective leadership for such revolt. It would require extremely astute leadership to break through the caste system and religious indoctrination of the rural proletariat. Urbanization operates to break down these age old barriers so that as the rural unemployed drift into the cities they might, in conjunction with the industrial workers, develop into an angry proletariat susceptable to capable leadership toward a revolution.

It should be noted, in conclusion, that the situation in India is unique. In Europe industrialization produced a middle class that demanded participation in the political life of the country. Parliamentary and other democratic politics followed. In countries outside western Europe, like Russia and China, when the population pressure on the agricultural production resulted in an unfair and oppressive distribution of wealth, a peasant revolt destroyed the old order and the new ruling elite, the communists, launched forced draft industrialization of the country. There was no room or scope in this drastic socio-economic change for democratic institutions. India, on the other hand, inherited a democratic political system with independence from British rule without prior industrialization or a peasant revolt. It had only a tiny middle class on which to base a parliamentary system. Less than four per cent of the Indian population is fluent in English, the official language of parliament and the courts. The world now awaits with interest whether this tiny minority can industrialize the country in order to produce more wealth for its fair and adequate distribution to an exploding population while maintaining a functioning democracy.

POPULATION GROWTH

The problem of a fair and just distribution of wealth within a society remains unsolved. The struggle continues even in the highly industrial societies. Human greed knows no bounds. As the national product increases so do human expectations. The demand escalates from one to two cars per family, then to a car for every child, then two homes, a boat and so on. These demands will soon place an intolerable strain on the world's resources of materials and energy. Unless man bridles his avarice technological innovation and development will not ameliorate the age old struggle over the distribution of wealth but will only serve to intensify it. "For," in the words of Aristotle, "it is more necessary to equalize appetites than property."

But equally troublesome in this respect is the exploding population of the world. Six billion people are expected to reside on earth by 2000 A. D.! It requires little thought to realize what this will do to the perennial struggle over the distribution of wealth at that time. The pressure on land, mineral resources and available energy, even with the rate of accelerating technological development, may well prove intolerable particularly when coupled with the currently rising expectations of individuals for a greater share of the national wealth.

The migration of the exploding population from the countryside into the cities is another matter of grave concern. In 1800 only 25 million people lived in cities. In 1975 the population of just two cities—New York and Tokyo— was 25 million. And by 2000 the population of Tokyo alone is expected to be 25 million. In 1975 over 1.5 billion people lived in cities. This is expected to double by the end of the 20th century. Fifty per cent of the population will be urban; two centuries earlier it was less than ten per cent!

This will present two different problems. In the underindustrialized countries of Asia, Africa and Latin America the major problem is and will continue to be stepping up national production rapidly so that there can be a better share for everybody. In the industrialized countries, which produce adequate wealth to provide a fair share for everyone, the problem will be devising a new system of distribution of wealth for the current job system will prove increasingly obsolete as advancing technology eliminates human labor as a factor of production.

In all countries there will be a constantly increasing urban proletariat. In Asia, Africa and Latin America the rural unemployed will drift into the urban areas where the slow pace of industrialization will not be able to provide jobs for them. The first thing a world traveler observes in these countries is the extensive shantytowns that form large areas of the cities. These squatter residents comprise 30 per cent in Mexico City, 60 per cent in Ankara, Kinhasa and Bogota and as high as 90 per cent in Addis Ababa. In view of the scarcity of industrial jobs these rural migrants crowd into domestic service, street vending and other marginal activities contributing little to the national production. In the industrialized countries rapid technological innovation and development is reducing job opportunities for the burgeoning populations, producing a growing urban proletariat. Unemployment will continue to increase in the youth sector of the population.

IX
Nationalism, Religion and War

Dominant individuals and societies are motivated by more than the appropriation of a greater share of the surplus wealth produced by human technological development. They must also impose their ideologies, religions, socio-economic philosophies, views of life and other beliefs upon their fellow man. Nationalism and religion have consequently been factors of war as important as economics. The two have usually been intertwined with the economic factor so that at times it was not always clear which was the dominant one. Most noteworthy in this respect is the *jehad*, or holy war, of the Arabs when religion and plunder were associated motivations in the building of the Arab empire during the 7th and 8th centuries of the Christian era. The Arab soldier was properly indoctrinated in the justness of Allah, promised prompt ascent into Paradise in case of death in the conflict, and, to enhance the religious aspect of his cause, was awarded a fair share of the plunder. God and gold were the twin factors of the Spanish conquest of Mexico and Peru. Atahuallpa, the Inca, discerned, however, that gold was more important than God to the conquistadors and tried to secure his freedom with an unprecedented tribute of gold and silver.

Most human societies felt they were a superior race of men, had superior gods, superior philosophies and ways of life and that their city, state or nation was foremost in every way. Sometimes the mere existence, let alone challenge, of another peoples different beliefs and ways was an affront to that feeling of superiority and dominance which invited assault and subjection. Nothing infuriated the Muslim conquerors of Hindusthan more than the firm belief of the Hindus in the superiority of their religion, philosophy and way of life. This was often reflected in small and irrelevant ways like the Muslim's fury over the Hindus refusal to use their beautiful slim necked bulbous water container with a goose necked spout for morning ablutions instead of the more prosaic beaker type pitcher preferred by the Hindus.

With the evolution of the concept of the one God came the "chosen people of God" syndrome. The Hebrews, who probably invented the unitary God, appear to be the first afflicted with this complex. The Israelites, however, did not inflict much harm on humanity with it as they were never a powerful nation. The conflict it engendered was largely defensive, as in

Roman times when the Israelites resisted Roman dominance. During the diaspora that followed the Jews endured much suffering and persecution on this account particularly at the hands of the Christians in Europe. Today, again, they are the nexus of strife and violence over the creation of a state of Israel in the Middle East.

The Muslims and Christians, who inherited or developed a similar complex were a different matter. They broadened the original Hebrew concept of the exclusive God by a desire to impose Mohammedanism and Christianity on others and the slaughter and suffering brought upon humanity by this particular vintage of the superiority complex is well nigh incalculable. When Pope Urban II called for the crusade to free the Holy Land from Muslim rule he addressed his fellow Frenchmen as follows: "Oh race of Franks! Race beloved and chosen by God!" This special virus appears to have manifested itself in the Mediterranean civilizations particularly those dominated by the Judeo-Christian-Muslim religions. The Asian civilizations also adopted the unitary God concept in Buddhism but as far as one can discern from history the spread of Buddhism throughout Asia was a peaceful movement.

Wars are made by the ruling elite. But the rulers cannot make war without the support of the vast majority of their subjects. This principle was less true in olden times when wars were on a smaller scale and impinged less upon the common people. And when the common people were unable or unaccustomed to express themselves politically. But Hanibal was severely limited in his invasion force when 10,000 of his subjects refused to accompany him across the Alps. It was even less true when the war was conducted with mercenaries. The principle was, however, always latent. Today, when people are drawn more deeply into the conflict it is an all prevading principle. Presidents Johnson and Nixon failed in Vietnam because they did not have the support of the Americans at home for the war effort. It is safe to assay the matter by stating that the ruling elite in a democracy cannot successfully take their country into war without having 90 per cent or more of the people in support of the venture. There will always be dissenters but if they rise above an insignificant percentage the political leaders will be in trouble. Contrast the success of the Americans in World War II with their failure in Korea and Vietnam. The first had the overwhelming support of the people, the latter, when the people awakened to the full implications of the war, had less than majority support. No leadership can conduct a war successfully under a democratic form of government with only a slim or even substantial majority backing.

War propaganda, therefore, becomes important to the ruling elite. The enemy must be portrayed as evil, anti-Christ, the very devil incarnate. Nationalism, religion, ideology and numerous other kinds of emotional appeals are resorted to to enlist the support of the people for the war. War propaganda is a study by itself, but it is usually based on nationalism, religion or ideology.

NATIONALISM

While religion and nationalism have been frequently intertwined as aggressive motivations nationalism has and continues to exist as a motivating factor itself. The word imperialism is also used to describe nationalistic aggression. This motivation, of course, operates both within civilizations as between civilizations. Nationalism between states of a civilization date back to ancient history. As power centers rose within a civilization this power manifested itself in expansion over other states within the same civilization. Eventually, one state overpowered the rest and unified that civilization into one empire subject to the same religion, ideologies, philosophies, beliefs and way of life. The result was usually a unified and homogenized human culture with its own architecture, art, cuisine and other attributes of national livelihood.

During the period 500–300 B. C. the Indian civilization went through a period of nationalistic wars. During the preceeding millennium the Aryans had consolidated their presence in the subcontinent. The Hindu culture was now fully developed and matured. According to Megasthanes and other Greek travelers the country was enormously properous. The numerous tribes were consolidating into states. By 500 B. C. four strong and warring nations evolved. They were the kingdoms of Kosala, Magadha, Vatsa and Avanti. A century or so later, under prominent rulers like Bimbisara and Ajatasastra, the Magdhan kingdom achieved hegemony over the Gangetic plain. Mahapedma Nanda, who ruled about 350 B. C., was the last important ruler. After his death the Magadhan empire lapsed into chaos in a struggle over succession.

Chandragupta Maurya, the founder of the Mauryan dynasty, overthrew the Nandas and established his rule over the Gangetic area. Alexander's invasion of the Punjab in 326 B. C. undermined the power of the tribes and nations in the Indus valley and when the Greeks withdrew Chandragupta extended his rule into the Punjab, thus unifying into one empire most of the sub-continent.

Chinese history reveals a similar experience. It is called the Period of the Warring States (circa 481–221 B. C.). Toward the end of the Chou period (circa 1028–257 B. C.) the thousand or so feudatories became consolidated in some 14 large and powerful nations. The state of Ch'in (present Shansi and eastern Kansu) eventually subdued the others to establish the first Chinese empire in 221 B. C. Due to centuries of independent development the various states evolved different dialects, philosophies and ways of doing things. The state of Ch'in promptly launched its ways and livelihood upon the conquered peoples. Weights and measures were standardized. The gauge of tracks for wagons was regulated. At this time the roads were constructed with deep cart-tracks embedded naturally in the loess soil of north China and were unusable by wagons of different axle lengths. The philosophy of the legalistic school was imposed on all in place of Confucianism. The Han dynasty (206–220 A. D.) which gained control over the new Chinese empire, however, soon restored Confucianism as state philosophy.

The city states of ancient Greece have a similar history. Athens which defended itself successfully against Dorian conquest began asserting its dominance over the other Greek cities in Attica during the 5th century before Christ. It derived its wealth, for the purpose, from the silver mines of Laurium. After successfully leading the Greek cities to defeat the Persian invasion in 480 B. C. Athens continued its expansionist policy. Thucydides leaves us an interesting account of Athens' policy of domination of the Greek world. As hostilities were underway during the debilitating Peleponnesian war Athens and Sparta were vying for the alliance of the various Greek states. In 416 B. C. the Athenians sent an expedition under Alcibiades to the isle of Melos comprising 30 ships, 1600 heavy infantry, 300 archers together with additional forces of their allies with the objective of winning the Melians over as allies or destroying them for wanting to remain neutral in the war. The assault, according to Thucydides, was preceeded by a conference with the following interesting exchange of views and philosophies:

Athenians.—For ourselves, we shall not trouble you with specious pretences—either of how we have a right to our empire because we overthrew the Mede, or are now attacking you because of wrong that you have done us—and make a long speech which would not be believed and in return we hope that you, instead of thinking to influence us by saying that you did not join the Lacedaemonians, although their colonists, or that you have done us no wrong, will aim at what is feasible, holding in view the real sentiments of us both. Since you know as well as we do that right, as the world goes is only in question between equals in power, while the strong do what they can and the weak suffer what they must. . . . .

Melians.—You may be sure that we are as well aware as you of the difficulty of contending against your power and fortune, unless the terms be equal. But we trust that the gods may grant us fortune as good as yours, since we are just men fighting against unjust, and that what we want in power will be made up by the alliance of the Lacedaemonians, who are bound, if only for very shame, to come to the aid of their kindred. Our confidence, therefore, after all is not so utterly irrational.''

Athenians.—When you speak of the favour of the gods, we may as fairly hope for that as yourselves; neither our pretensions nor our conduct being in any way contrary to what men believe of the gods, or practice among themselves. *Of the gods we believe, and of men we know, that by a necessary law of their nature they rule whereever they can. And it is not as if we were the first to make this law, or to act upon it when made; we found it existing before us, and shall leave it to exist for ever after us; all we do is to make use of it, knowing that you and everybody else, having the same power as we have, would do the same as we do.* Thus, as far as the gods are concerned, we have no fear and no reason to fear that we shall be at a disadvantage. But when we come to your notion about the Lacedamonians, when their own interests or their country's laws are in question, are the worthiest men alive; of their conduct towards others much might be said, but no clearer idea of it could be given than by shortly saying that of all the men we know they are most conspicuous in considering what is agreeable honorable, and what is expedient just. Such a way of thinking does not promise much for the safety which you now unreasonably count upon. (Italics added)

There is much more to this interesting discourse. But in the interest of brevity only the essence is set forth.

Nationalism has been a prominent characteristic of the presently dominant Western civilization. After the fall of Rome Europe was left in political chaos. There were, of course, no people in history afflicted with nationalism more than the Romans. During the period of Roman dominance of the Mediterranean area (circa 200 B. C.—400 A. D.) Rome was the center of the world. All roads led to Rome from the psychological as well as a physical basis. To be a Roman was everything. The Romans flaunted their superiority to the full extent of their economic and military power. The decline of Roman dominance left the people of Europe—barbarians in the eyes of the Romans—in disarray, but over the centuries they were welded into a new civilization under the banner of Christianity.

For a long time the new civilization of Christendom consisted of countless feudatories, cities and princely states with a loose allegiance to the Pope in Rome. Eventually power centers began to form within the new civilization. The first was the Merovingians of France followed by the Carolingians. At the beginning of the 9th century Charlemagne achieved hegemony over western Europe now consisting of France, western Germany, parts of Austria and Italy north of Rome. Pope Leo III dubbed him the Holy Roman Emperor. But it was never a true empire. After Charles's death the "empire" fell apart into its constituent parts—feudal France, German dukedoms, Italian cities, Anglo-Saxon Britain with the Hungarian and Slavic

.states in the East. Spain and Portugal joined the christian brotherhood after the fall of Muslim domination during the 13th century. Thereafter three nations vied for supremacy—Spain, England and France.

Spain was defeated by England in 1588. England thereafter became the mistress of the seas. France was the strongest nation on the continent. The two powers fought for world leadership during the 18th century with France suffering defeat by the English in America and India. In the 19th century the European civilization dominated the world under British hegemony and Pax Brittanica! It was one of the most peaceful and productive centuries known to man.

While British influence was felt all over Europe Great Britain refrained from exerting its political power on the continent. It left the continent to French domination. But as German nationalism arose, after the unification of the German dukedoms during the latter part of the 19th century, and challenged French supremacy on the continent England joined the fraticidal struggle. The result was two debilitating Germanic wars during the first half of the 20th century that rent asunder the fabric of Western civilization.

German nationalism was particularly virulent. *Alleman uber alles.* It was to be Germany over all! Nazi Germany predicated its thrust on racial and national superiority. Millions of Jews were sacrificed on the alter of German racism. Countless others lost their lives during Germany's brief period of domination of Europe.

The two Germanic wars may go down in history as the undoing of Western civilization and its domination of the world. It is already clear that they destroyed the British empire. In 1913 Great Britain was the supreme power. It was often said that the sun never set on the British empire, circling the earth from Canada via Africa, the Mid East and India to Australia. But by mid-century Great Britain had lost its empire and was reduced to a small powerless island. The same fate overtook France. Yet Germany was unable to take over the leading role in Western civilization and world domination. The baton passed instead to the Americans, those energetic and productive descendants of the Europeans, across the Atlantic. How well and how long America will continue the western dominance of the world remains to be seen. Serious challenges are emanating from the East—China and India— once again. And from Russia which is caught between the East and West. In the last part of the 20th century, therefore, humanity is going through a period of realignment of world power and domination and the only thing certain is that those people who prove to be the most technologically innovative and productive will continue to dominate the world.

Nationalism appears to have two phases in its manifestation. There is first the constructive phase during the development of a civilization, when the various nations vie for supremacy, in the welding of the civilization into a dominant empire. At the height of empire the dominant civilization becomes imperialistic and usually commits the mistake of overextension of its power over nations and people outside the civilization. It suffers defeat, thereby weakening itself. More on this historical phenomena later. At this time a destructive nationalism often takes hold resulting in fraticidal wars within the dominant civilization. These nationalistic wars, like the Germanic wars of Western civilization, frequently deliver the coup de grace to the erstwhile dominant civilization.

RELIGION

Nothing, with the exception of wealth perhaps, has motivated man more than his religion. Religion evolved to fill a gap left as man's intellectual growth outpaced his accumulation of knowledge. Three things bothered early man profoundly—the elements, the reproductive process and death.

The flash of lightening followed by a roar of thunder must have terrified early man. Scientific understanding of the phenomena was still thousands of years away, but man desperately needed a rationalization then. So, he ascribed lightening and thunder to a supernatural power. Gods like Zeus, Jupiter, Indra, Thor and others were conjured up and invested with the power of lightening and thunder. A study of the early religion of man shows that almost every elemental force known to and effecting man's life on earth was deified. The sun, moon, earth, light, fire, sea, wind and other universal forces were worshipped. Human arts and emotions were also deified—Aphrodite, the goddess of love and beauty, the Nine Muses, goddesses of poetry and music and others. These early pantheons contained many gods.

The reproduction of life was equally baffling. Early man observed that both plant and animal life renewed itself periodically. After he invented agriculture his food supply depended upon this regeneration of life. The spring sowing and the autumn harvest were two of the most important events of his life. Ascribing fertility and growth to the gods, man propitiated them to the utmost for a good harvest. Bloody sacrifices of animal and human life were often made to the gods. Countless other myths and taboos were observed. Sir James George Fraser details them in his famous *Golden Bough*.

The myth of Demeter and Persephone is appropo. The youthful Persephone, representing fertility, is captured by Pluto, the lord of the dead, and made his wife. Her mother Demeter, Goddess of the grain, vowed she would let nothing grow until her daughter was restored to her. Men ploughed and sowed but nothing grew. The gods became alarmed and Zeus ordered Pluto to restore Persephone to her mother. To assuage Pluto Zeus ordered that Persephone should spend two-thirds of every year with her mother (the growing season) in the upper world and one-third with Pluto (the dormant winter) in the netherworld. This assured the corn and other crops to man over whom the Gods ruled. Fraser details a great number of Gods, myths rituals and practices connected with the fertility of the earth.

Human and animal reproduction also baffled man. He observed that sexual connection between male and female was somehow the cause of the new life but beyond that he did not understand the regenerative process. As elsewhere lack of knowledge and understanding prompted him to deify it. Phallic worship was a prominent feature of early religion. It is still very much so in Hinduism with the worship of the lingam. Fertility goddesses— Isis, Sati and Ishtar, for example, were worshipped. Also fertility gods Osiris, Hapi, Tammuz, Shang Ti and others. In fact the earliest plastic art of man was the fertility goddesses or figures of Cro-Magnon. The Bull and the Ram were objects of worship. The temples of the Neolithic society of Catal Huyuk appear to have been devoted entirely to the Bull of the Auroch, an early ox that inhabited that part of Anatolia during Neolithic time.

The fear of death, however, propelled man to religion more than any other feature of his life. Men simply refused to accept the fact that life was terminal. It doubltess took most of his life on earth to date to realize it. In fact, man is the only form of life that realizes that death is inevitable. For a million or more years man saw his fellow man die by accident or exhaustion in the struggle for survival. It was only recently when technological development produced a surplus of food that man no longer struggled for survival. Somewhere in this evolutionary process it dawned on man that even with abundant food man's life still came to an end. And when he realized this forbidding fact he refused to accept it, conjuring up instead the idea of an afterlife. He realized that the human body could not continue in such afterlife as it putrefied upon death so he came up with the concept of a soul or spirit which left the body to continue the existence after death. The Egyptians who were obsessed with death more than any other civilization developed elaborate mumification techniques in the hope of preserving the human body for its role in the after life.

Most religions, particularly the Judeo-Christian-Muslim theology, do not foresee the departed soul ever returning to earth again. It either goes to Heaven for eternal bliss or to hell for eternal damnation. The Hindus, however, came up with the ingenious idea of the rebirth of the soul in another embodiment here on earth. It should be noted that the Hindu concept of soul or self differs considerably from the Christian. It is more the essence of life in the universe than the personalized spiritual being of the Christians. The new embodiment need not necessarily be human. It could be some form of animal life. Structured into the rebirth is the concept that the new embodiment depends upon the moral and ethical conduct in the previous life. If the conduct was good or exemplary a lowly man, say a sudra, would be reborn a man of higher caste, a vaisya or even a brahman. But if the conduct was bad or evil he would be reborn an insect or dog or some other form of lowly life. There is no heaven in the Christian sense but a Hindu could attain nirvana which is both a state of bliss and freedom from the eternal and tedious process of rebirths. Similarly there is no hell in Hindu theology, the possibility of a lowly rebirth is considered sufficient damnation for an evil life. The doctrine of rebirth has generated a more tolerant and respectful attitude toward non-human life in the Hindu. A Hindu will not crush a worm underfoot, or otherwise snuff out casually another form of life. Some religious sects (the Jains) in India carry this respect for human life to the extent of wearing a gauze over their mouth to avoid swallowing inadvertantly a flying insect.

At the same time Hindu theology is more in harmony with scientific reality than the Judeo apparented religions in recognizing the relationship and sameness of human and animal life. It may even be said that the transmigration of life has a modicum of scientific plausibility if shorn of its animism, for all life on earth emanates out of the dust and clay of the earth and returns again to this dust and clay. It has been written that every atom in one's body once floated in the universe as cosmic dust and gas.

Eventually religion evolved to the universal God—the one God concept. The Pharoh Akhenaton (circa 1375–1358 B. C.) was perhaps the first religious reformer who wished to eliminate the early elaborate pantheons of man in favor of one God. He fixed on the sun as the one God whom he called Aton for the Egyptians to worship. In a way, this was very precocious of Akhenaton as man now knows that the sun is the source of all being on earth. Akhenaton's one God, however, did not survive his death for long and the Egyptians reverted to their many Gods. Similar movements toward a single God were extant in the fertile crescent during the second millennium before Christ. It was the Hebrews, however, who came forth with a viable and durable God that was to effect profoundly the history of man. They called him Yahweh. Eventually the unitary deity of the Judeo-Christian religions came to be referred to simply as God. The Muslims refer to him as Allah which means God in Arabic.

The Judeo apparented religions ascribe to the one God all the powers of the universe. He created the earth and man in six days. Although the Old Testament reckons the time loosely in generations that was not precise enough for the "scientific" minded Christians who fixed the time of creation more precisely as 4,004 B. C. Bishop Ussher was even more definite when in the 17th century he fixed the exact time and date during the year 4004 B. C. as Sunday, October 23 at 9 o'clock in the morning!

The Hindus, it seems, always had a concept of a universal God, certainly a millennium or so before Christ. It was Brahma who encompassed the entire universe and from whom everything emanated. But they also believed in many other Gods who were manifestations of Brahma the universal deity. In fact, the concept of Brahma the universal deity, is far more in keeping with scientific reality than the Judeo religions. It has already been pointed out in Chapter I that Hindu cosmology has a time factor not too different from that now ascribed to the universe by astrophysics.

Buddhism, which issued out of Hinduism, was also predicated on the concept of the one God. Buddhism arose in 6th century B. C. in India during a period of great intellectual ferment. Many philosophical schools flourished, but most prominent were those of Mahavira and Buddha, the founders of Jainism and Buddhism. Both rebelled against pantheistic Hinduism and the materialistic nature of Hindu society.

Gautama Buddha did not think he was founding a new religion. He simply enunciated a philosophy of life predicated on freedom and emancipation from the basic emotions of greed, selfishness, dominance, hate and other biological instincts and motivations of man. He preached that nirvana could be attained only if man followed the Noble Eightfold Path based on good conduct and the attainment of knowledge and observed the cardinal virtues based on non-violence and abstinence. Some of this philosophy is already contained in the Upanishads the latter day religious texts of the Hindus. Buddha's philosophy, along with Christ's teachings, are some of the most enlightened aspects of the religions of man.

Philosophical Buddhism—known as Hinayana or Theravada Buddhism or the lesser vehicle—achieved a firm grip on the Hindu mind for some thousand years (circa 500 B. C.–500 A. D.). It got its greatest boost from Ashoka, one of India's great kings, the last of the Mauryan dynasty (circa 274–236 B. C.). The story is told that Ashoka started his reign in the belligerent ways of his predecessors. During a war of conquest in Kalinga (modern Orissa) he was repelled by the slaughter and suffering he was inflicting on the people. He forthwith terminated the war, renounced violence and adopted Buddhism. Buddhism was made the state religion, the royal hunts were abolished, the slaughter of animals for food was reduced. The practice of vegetarianism among the higher castes in India is thought to have originated during Ashok's rule. Hinayana Buddhism spread to Ceylon, Burma, Siam, Laos and Cambodia. Hinayana Buddhism was more philosophy than religion. It preached salvation through unselfish and non-agressive human conduct and relationship. Buddha is revered more as a teacher than a God. During the latter part of the first millennium of the Christian era a Brahmanic revival took place in India. Buddhism was absorbed into Brahmanism as a sect and Buddha added to the Hindu pantheon as an incarnation of the Hindu God Vishnu. When the Chinese pilgrim Hsuan-tsang visited India seeking Buddhist texts during the reign of Harsha about 600 A. D. he reported that Brahmans were being favored over Buddhist monks at court and elsewhere. The Brahmanic revival apparently was already in full swing.

As Buddhism spread to north Asia it became a religion. It was called Mahayana Buddhism, the greater vehicle. Mahayana Buddhism evolved in north India around the beginning of the Christian era. Taxila with its famous university was one of its centers. At this time there was considerable Greek and Asian influence in this part of India and Buddhism became infected with non-Indian ideas. Buddha became a God with many manifestations. There arose countless disciples (or saints) called Bodhisattvas. The concept of nirvana became more of a paradise hereafter located somewhere in the West. The Chinese in particular liked the Hindu idea of rebirth as they interpreted the doctrine to mean that their role and that of their immediate oppressors would be reversed in the next life. Mahayana Buddhism spread to China, Korea, Japan, Vietnam, Tibet and Mongolia.

The evolution of religion in China took yet another path. Like other peoples the early Chinese had many Gods. During the Shang dynasty (circa 1600–1028 B. C.) there were many nature deities, especially fertility Gods. Shang Ti, the God of Fertility, received the greatest worship. But by the 6th century B. C. the Chinese appear to have lost faith, or interest, in these early deities in favor of worldly philosophies. This was a period of great intellectual activity with many schools of philosophy. Foremost among them was that of Confucius who advocated a way of life based on a rigid social structure and personal authority. The basic social units were the family and the clan under the ruler, the Son of Heaven. Family ancestors were revered. Every man had his prescribed duties and role in life. Second in importance was the philosophy of Lao-Tzu, which attempted to rationalize man's place in the universe. Taoism did not prescribe any rules or duties for men's conduct. It was more mystical. In fact, unlike Confucianism it advocated man's withdrawal from organized society. A Taoist lived a life of quiet seclusion, with a few chosen friends and pursued life of limited achievement. Needless to say Confucianism won out as a state philosophy and persisted until recent times providing a basis of stability for two thousand years in China.

Confucianism and Taoism did not satisfy the common man. He yearned for more emotion and promise in his religion and eagerly embraced Buddhism from India. After the fall of the Han dynasty (206–220 A. D.) when China went through a period of disorganization and foreign invasion from the north Buddhism spread rapidly in China. The Chinese peasant liked the promise of nirvana (more of a heaven under Mahayana Buddhism) and the idea of the rebirth of his oppressors as lowly creatures. It helped to alleviate his oppressed life here on earth. Buddhist monastaries acquired great wealth in land and metals (bronze) and prestige during this time. China sent pilgrims for Buddhist texts and it is through these chronicles of the Chinese pilgrims that much of India's history of this period has been reconstructed for posterity. Thereafter Confucianism, Taoism and Buddhism existed side by side in harmony and great tolerance toward each other. In fact, it was not uncommon for Chinese to espouse all three at the same time, finding nothing incompatible among them in so doing.

It is interesting to note, in this connection, the flush of intellectual vigor that possessed mankind in the 6th and 5th centuries B. C. In China it was the Age of the Sages—Confucius, Lao Tzu among many others. In India an intellectual ferment produced many schools of philosophy, that of Gautama Buddha, Mahavira of the Jains and others. In Persia it was the time of Zoroaster or Zathathrustra. The Israelites produced the Prophets, Jeremiah, Ezekial and the Unknown Prophet who laid the foundation for Judaism and Christianity. And a century or so later there were the Greek philosophers, Socrates, Plato, Aristotle and others. It was as if men, obviously not in communication with each other, were in the advanced civilizations of the world reaching out for a new understanding and rationalization of man's life and place in the universe finding the old religions and philosophies no longer adequate for the purpose. Mankind took a tremendous step forward in its intellectual development at this time. It would be hard to prove from the pages of history that man has advanced much in understanding and wisdom thereafter. He has, however, made great advances in his technological development. In fact, it would be easier to prove that there have been periods of great retrogression in religious and philosophical thought since those creative centuries.

It is now in order, (nay) it is imperative, that man make a similar leap forward in his philosophy so that his remaining life on earth may be conducted on a rational basis. The old religions that served man during a difficult period of inadequate knowledge about the universe, the earth and life within it now appear obsolete and erroneus. In fact, it may even be concluded that the old religions, particularly the Judeo-Christian-Muslim religions are now obstacles to the mind of man in rationalizing his life on earth in the light of the latest knowledge and understanding of the universe and man's role therein.

Religion has performed a two fold role. It tried to explain man's life on earth and the elemental forces of the universe upon which his life depended. This pseudo-knowledge, while it served its purpose at the time, has now been superseded by scientific research and perception. The other function of religion, particularly the most recent ones, has been its moral and ethical code for human relations—the Ten Commandments, the Analects, the Institutes of Manu, the Eightfold Path, the Koranic laws and the like. These moral codes buttressed by sanctions of damnation were extremely instrumental in the maintenance of civilized societies. They assisted in keeping within tolerable limits the biological instincts of dominance, aggression and violence. The old religions, therefore, cannot be dismissed lightly. Civilized societies may be more dependent on them for social order and stability than is realized. Ibn Tufail, the noted Muslim philosopher of 12 century Spain, felt that even if the rulers found religion inadequate and at variance with the truth they must nevertheless propagate it with the unlettered masses as an effective means of maintaining social order and discipline. But religion has also been used by the ruling elite to exploit and oppress the dominated majority.

Philosophy and religion have always been intertwined. The advanced religions are, in large part, philosophies. And many philosophies embrace the supernatural. Some are hard to classify. For instance, is Buddhism a religion or philosophy. Christianity is clearly a religion. Confucianism is a philosophy. The difference really does not matter as both religion and philosophy attempt to rationalize man's life on earth. The defect of religion at this stage of man's cultural evolution is that the pseudo-knowledge upon which it is based is now obstructing man from making the necessary surge towards rationalizing his being for his ultimate salvation.

The most disturbing aspect of religion, however, has been its bigotry. It was, perhaps, not surprising that man's dominance instinct should come into play where his religion was involved. After men conjured up their Gods or God it was only natural to develop the corollary belief that they were the "chosen people of God". Others were goys, infidels, pagans, heathens, unbelievers and the like. They were either excluded, converted by the sword or simply put to the sword. Some of the more pathetic episodes of man are the evocations to their God—many times it is the same God—for victory prior to battle. But as a cynic said "God is always on the side of the big battalions."

Religious wars and religious imperialism constitute a large segment of history. The first clear instance of aggression rationalized by religion is the story contained in the Bible. Moses, Joshua, Saul and David led the Israelites in taking Canaan away from the people settled there for centuries on the justification that it was the Promised Land alloted to them by God. Ever since, though, the justification of aggression in the name of God has been a part of the Judeo apparented religions and nowhere was this more so than in Mohammedanism.

THE HOLY WAR

Mohammedanism, or Islam (true believers), whose followers are called Muslims was founded during the early part of the 7th century A. D. It burst upon the Mid East scene rather suddenly. The Prophet Mohammed Ali lived *circa* 570–632 A. D. He was a caravan merchant who became religiously inspired in middle age, achieved a loyal following and before his death controlled a sizeable area in western Arabia centered around Medina, the Prophet's headquarters and city.

The religion he founded was based solidly on the Judeo theology of the One God who is known as Allah (God in Arabic) to the Muslims. Mohammed embraces the entire geneological descent from Adam and Abraham, recognizes Moses and the other Jewish leaders, embraces Christ and positions himself in this theology as the latest and foremost messenger of the word of God. Neither the Jews or Christians, however, were prepared to accord Mohammed such recognition. Nor were most of his fellow Arabs, for that matter. Thus Mohammed resorted to force to impose his religion upon the unbelievers. In this he was most ruthless. When the Jewish community of Banu-Kuraiza refused to accept Islam he killed all the males, 600 of them, and enslaved the women and children. In this process of religious proselytizing he plundered the wealth of the Jews and rewarded his followers with a fair share. Out of these early incidences during the Prophet's life, of which there were many, the Holy War was born. It was a marriage of religious zeal, which provided the rationalization, and plunder which gratified the greed of the new zealots. It suited the Arab psyche extremely well.

The nomadic Arab was a freedom loving but violent man. He was difficult to lead and organize. At the same time he was poor because he was technologically uncreative. In the words of Ibn Kaldun, the 14th century Muslim socio-historian, sometimes referred to as the father of sociology, "Arabs, are of all peoples, the least versed in the crafts."

Yet within a short span of 100 years the Arabs conquered an area extending from India in the east to Spain in the west including Syria, Persia, and of course, the Arabian peninsula in the middle. Most empire builders depended upon superior technology and wealth for their conquests. But the Arabs had neither. They were, however, able to borrow the advanced technology of the day from their neighbors, hence they possessed the missiles, catapaults, seige machines known to others. At this time mankind was living in a period of technological sterility with little innovation for centuries. Everyone was now familiar with the horsemanship, weaponry and military techniques developed by the Romans, Persians and others a half a millennium earlier. As already postulated when technologies are equivalent other factors make for victory. In this situation it was the new religious zeal of the Arabs.

It should not be lightly overlooked, however, that the Arabs did employ a technique not available to the conquered people. It was the camel domesticated by the Arabs nearly three thousand years earlier. Egypt, Syria and Persia were surrounded by desert from which the Arab attacks were made. When the fighting proved disadvantageous the Arabs simply retreated to the sanctuary of the desert on their camels to renew themselves for another attack. In due time the nomadic Arabs were able to subdue the sedentary civilizations of Egypt, Syria and Persia with this ingenious tactic. It has been said that the Arabs used the desert to conquer the Middle East as the Europeans did the sea centuries later to dominate the world. And most appropriately the camel is often referred to as the ship of the desert.

The Arab conquests were facilitated by another important factor. It was the decadent state of the old civilizations of the Mediterranean area. Europe was in complete disarray after the fall of Rome. Byzantine, the Eastern portion of the Roman empire, was only poorly in control of Egypt and Syria. The Persians were rich and decadent. The nomadic and mobile Arabs greedy for the wealth of these old sedentary societies and energized by the psychology of the Muslim Holy War proved easy victors over them.

The Arabs could not, however, prevail over superior technology, religious fervor to the contrary notwithstanding, which at this time was possessed by the Byzantines. After the capture of Syria the Arabs decided upon an attack on Constantinople. Gibbon reports that the Prophet promised the Arabs who beseiged Constantinople forgiveness of their sins, enormous plunder of the fabulous wealth of the city and succession to the might and mantle of the Caesars. Sea power, however, was necessary for such enterprise and the Arabs were mainly landlubbers. But they acquired seamanship and a navy fast. As soon as Omar's successor Muawiya consolidated Muslim rule at Damascus he set forth to build a navy. The Arab navy enjoyed considerable success in challenging the Byzantine navy along the Egyptian and eastern Mediterranean coast. But when the Arabs launched their attack on Constantinople in 647 A. D., some fifty years after Mohammed's death, they were stopped by a rain of fire from the ramparts. The Byzantines had invented Greek fire, a naptha based concotion, already discussed in Chapter VII, which they catapaulted upon the Arab navy and set it afire. For six years the Arabs repeated the attack only to be repulsed each time by a hail of fire. Thirty thousand Muslims suffered martyrdom in the face of this hell fire, including Ayub, one of the last companions of the Prophet.

The Arabs tried again under Caliph Sulayman in 715–717 A. D. to capture Constantinople and were repulsed as before by Greek fire. A storm finished destruction of the Arab fleet during its retreat. The Arabs left with a healthy respect for the superior technology of the "decadent" Roman empire. Seven centuries were to pass before the Muslims were able to carry out successfully the seige of Constantinople in 1453 A. D. under the aegis of the Turks this time, after the attack by the Fourth Crusade under the Dodge Dandolo had virtually destroyed the Byzantine empire two centuries earlier.

Greek fire prolonged greatly the life of the Byzantine empire. It was kept a secret for some 400 years. The mystique was nurtured among the barbarians and enemies of the empire, according to Gibbon, by a story " . . . that the mystery of the Greek fire had been revealed by an angel to the first and greatest of the Constantines, with a sacred injunction that this gift of Heaven, this peculiar blessing of the Romans, should never be communicated to any foreign nation; that the prince and subject were alike bound to religious silence under the temporal and spiritual penalties of treason and sacrilege; and that the impious attempt would provoke the sudden and supernatural vengeance of the God of the Christians". The God of the Christians prevailed over the God of Islam as usual because the Christians had the superior technology.

The Arabs had no civilization of their own, albeit they had a culture which they retained to date and throughout the centuries of dominance of the Muslim world by others such as the Persians, Turks, and Mongols. To quote

Ibn Kaldun again "Arabs are incapable of founding an empire except on a religious basis." The foundation of the Muslim world was the Persian civilization. "It is strange, yet a fact" writes Ibn Kaldun in his *Prolegomena*, "that the men of learning in Islam whether in the religious or the rational sciences, have been with but a few exceptions, Persians." Omar Khayyam, Al-Ghazali, Ibn Sina (known in Europe as Avicenna), Al Khwarizmi (who transmitted the so-called Arabic numerals and the concept of zero from India to the Muslim world and on to Europe—perhaps the greatest contribution of Islam to the rise of the West) and countless others come to mind.

For a century or two the Arabs ruled the Muslim world as a religio-military caste over the Persian, Syrian, Egyptian, Turkish, Berber and European peoples residing in their empire. A capable and trustworthy resident, called a vizier or wazir, was entrusted with the administration of the country. Most notable, in this respect, was the Persian Yahya Barmakid, the vizier of Harun Al-Rashid, who was one of ablest administrators in history. These viziers became fabulously rich. The Barmakids were reputed to be worth 30,000,000 dinars (about $150 million) at the time of their downfall. The Arabs attended to the military and religious matters. Even the latter was soon handed to devout local Muslims. Due to the intellectual force of the Persians the Muslim world was pretty thoroughly "Persianized" from east to west by the 9th century.

Meanwhile the fierce Arabs were rent by political and religious schisms. Within a generation after Mohammed's death Islam split into two sects, the *Shia* and the *Sunni*. The Prophet provided for no orderly succession to the caliphate. After Mohammed's death Abu Bekr, his able general, was designated *Khalifa* (meaning representative) by the Muslim leaders. Ali, the Prophet's cousin and son-in-law (married to Mohammed's daughter Fatima) felt he was the legitimate successor and withheld his acceptance of Abu Bekr for six months. His uncle Abbas, whose decendants founded the Abbasid caliphate, also disagreed with the selection. Abu Bekr's victories and extension of Islam into Syria subdued the rift temporarily. Upon his death in 632 A. D. he was succeeded by Omar, hence the Omayyad caliphate, who conquered Persia. After Omar's death (assassinated by a Persian slave) in 644 A. D., the Ali rift broke into the open. Ali was at last elevated to the caliphate in 656 A. D. but his glory was short lived when he was assassinated in 661 A. D. His son Hasan succeeded him, but he was deposed by Muawiya, who removed the Muslim capital from Medina to Damascus to resume rule of the Omayyad caliphate. The followers of Ali and Fatima were reduced to a minority but significant faction within the Muslim world. But the Sunni orthodoxy took hold in the heart of Islam, in Syria, Persia, Transoxania and India and became the dominant religious factor in Islam.

In 750 A. D. the caliphate split in two with the Abbasids taking over the heart of the Muslim empire in the Mid East and the ousted Omayyads retaining control in Spain and North Africa west of Egypt. The fabulous

Harun Al-Rashid of Arabian Nights fame, who ruled out of Baghdad from 786–809 A. D. was the most illustrious of the Abbasid caliphate.

Arab dominance of the Muslim world lasted only about two centuries. In 945 A. D. the Persian Buwayhids, from the Caspian highlands, took control in Baghdad. A century or so later the Seljuq Turks burst out of Turkestan across Transoxania into Persia. Many Turks had already insinuated themselves into positions of power when the Arabs used them as mercenaries at court. At first the caliph welcomed the Seljuqs in the hope they would rid him of the Buwayhids, but they soon reduced him to a mere firgurehead. The Seljuqs assumed the title Sultan, meaning master, and organized a Muslim empire from the Punjab in India to Syria in the west where they clashed with the Crusaders over the Holy places of the two religions. The Seljuqs too rested their rule upon the Persian civilization as it was superior to theirs and there ensued a period of great scholarship and learning during their rule.

Two centuries later the Mongols burst upon the Muslim world. Genghis Khan defeated the Shah of Kwarizm in Turkestan in 1220–1. The Mongols had gunpowder, as discussed in Chapter V. In 1256 Hulagu carried the assault into the heart of the Muslim world, sacked and destroyed Baghdad, and established Mongol rule under the Il-Khan dynasty. The Abbasid caliphate came to its end. The Il-Khans ruled from 1256–1337 and built the fabulous capital at Tabriz. European travelers, including Marco Polo, raved about its opulence and beauty.

The Muslim world was now in the hands of the Turks, Tartars and Mongols. The Holy War concept was made to order for these fierce and violent men. Under its aegis they sacked, pillaged and killed from India to Asia Minor and numerous peripheral areas. Timur, the scourge of 14th century central and western Asia was the most famous, or infamous, in this respect. In his autobiography he boasts of killing 100,000 Hindus and idolators during his sack of Delhi in 1398. India had now been under Muslim rule of the Turko-Afghans for nearly two centuries but Timur considered them too tolerant. The Hindus had to be forced to adopt Mohammedanism. But all he did was to leave India rather abruptly with cartloads of spoils in a trail of blood. In 1401 he sacked Baghdad after the Iraqis ousted the men he sent to rule over them. He ordered each of his 20,000 soldiers to bring him a head of a local citizen which he stacked up in hideous pyramids outside the city's gates. Timur's greed and domination knew no bounds. In 1405 he launched an invasion of China with an army of 200,000 but he died at the outset. Without his leadership his army disintegrated.

The last of the Timurid dynasty was Babur who invaded Hindusthan in 1525 A. D. and founded there the Mughal empire. Mughal derives from Mongol as Babur was also a descendant of Genghis Khan on his mother's side. Babur's son Humayan lost the empire for a time to the Afghan Lodis but Humayan's son Akbar, one of India's great kings, regained it and consolidated Mughal rule over India.

Curiously though these fierce and violent men were also scholars. Timur read history, collected art, supported artists, poets and scholars, founded universities and built mosques. Babur was a musician, poet and patron of the arts. He could read Arabic, Persian and Hindi. Both left memoirs or autobiographies. There are some doubts on the authenticity of Timur's. But Babur's is well written, originally in the Turki language later translated into Persian. Babur's memoirs are titillating. He was a bit of a toper albeit that Muslims should abstain from alcohol. In one twenty-four hour period he became inebriated four times! He missed the iced cold drinks he was accustomed to in Kabul and Farghana. There was no ice in India. Not until it was transported there from Boston during British rule.

The Mughals were tepid Muslims, except for Aurangzeb. The great Akbar (1556–1605 A. D.) was a most tolerant Muslim. His queen was a Rajput princess. In the Hall of Worship in his new palace at Fatapur Sikri outside Agra he undertook to find a universal religion that would satisfy all mankind. To the discomfiture of his fellow Muslims he invited Hindu religious leaders, Jain teachers, Parsee priests, Jesuit fathers from Goa and others to discuss religious issues. Needless to say Akbar's noble effort failed. But the religious tolerance of the Mughals enabled Muslim overlord and Hindu subject to live in peace and develop a scintillating civilization in India during the 16th and 17th centuries.

At the western end of the Muslim world in Asia Minor the Ottoman Turks arose from the decadence of the Seljuq dynasty. When the Mongols invaded Persia in the 13th century the Seljuqs fled to Anatolia where they arose again under Ottoman or Osman, from whence the dynasty got the name Ottoman or Osmanli. In 1326 the Ottoman Turks captured Brusa from the Byzantines and made it their capital until they took Constantinople in 1453. In 1402 A. D. the Ottoman, under Bajazet I, suffered a devastating raid by Timur wherein the queen was captured, abused and violated by the Tartars. Thereafter the Ottoman sultans refrained from formal marriage to avoid repetition of such indignity. Recovering from this blow the Ottoman extended their power over Syria, Saudi Arabia, Egypt and North Africa. In 1517 they captured the caliph of Cairo and brought him to Constantinople. Thereafter the caliphate in the Muslim world was identified with the Ottoman sultan.

The most notable Ottoman sultan was Suleiman the Magnificent (1520–1566 A. D.) who terrorized Europe for years. He was defeated at Vienna in 1529. But large areas of southeastern Europe (Greece, Albania, Bulgaria) came under Turkish rule. In the East he extended Ottoman power as far as Baghdad (1543) and Tabriz (1548).

The Ottoman empire persisted until World War I. In part, this durability is ascribed to its unique administrative system. The sultans systematically recruited the most precocious Christian and other boys among their subject people, converted them to Islam and trained them as soldiers/administrators. They were called *yeni cheri* (meaning new soldiers) which has been corrupted into janissaries. The janissaries have sometimes been likened unto Plato's guardians. They did not marry, were completely trained and dedicated to administer the affairs of state and were adequately compensated to avoid corruption. Whether they were incorruptable is doubtful. The system did have another feature for political stability in that it removed from the dominated peoples potential revolutionaries and made them loyal to the Ottoman empire.

There were other notable Muslim regimes. It will suffice here merely to note them; the Mamelukes of Egypt (1340–1517 A. D.), the Safavids of Persia (1502–1576), the Moors of Spain (705–1234 A. D.) and others all of whom subscribed to the idea of the Holy War of Mohammedanism. Under the Safavids the Shi'ites gained ascendency over the Sunnis in Persia. But as European technology gained dominance over the world it blunted the efficacy of the Holy War.

The Muslims did not have a monopoly on the idea. It permeated, as well, the Christian world. For a thousand years Christianity was a peaceful movement proselytizing and converting the Europeans. A militant spirit, however, developed during the 11th century led by the Cluniac monks. They called for church reforms (celibacy, for instance, was instituted for the clergy) and propagated an intense religious feeling among the Christians. Pilgrimages to the Holy Land increased from 16 in the 10th to 117 in the 11th centuries. These pilgrimages began to arm and become increasingly militant. This coincided with the seizure of Jerusalem by the Seljuq Turks. The Christians became incensed that the Holy places should be in the hands of the "barbarous" and "infidel" Turks. Moreover the Turks were threatening the Byzantine empire, a brotherly Christian country. A new spirit of adventure was also emerging among the Europeans. They were anxious for new lands to conquer. All that was needed was the right kind of inspiration and leadership.

That too was forthcoming in a Cluniac reformer Pope Urban II. At the Council of Clermont in 1095 he concluded the session by a call to arms against the infidel Turks. He proclaimed a plenary indulgence—the forgiveness of all sins—to those who would join the Crusade and the promise of heaven if they should die in the capture of the Holy Land. The motivation so provided is hardly comprehensible today. Says Gibbon, "The cold philosophy of modern times is incapable of feeling the impression that was made on a sinful and fanatic world. At the voice of their pastor, the robber, the incendiary, the homicide, arose by the thousands to redeem their souls by repeating on the infidels the same deeds which they had exercised against their Christian brethren."

Pope Urban ordered the clergy to carry out his call for a Crusade throughout Europe. They were assisted by such firebrands as Peter the Hermit and Walter the Penniless who carried the message to the peasantry.

Peter the Hermit was particularly colorful. He rode around barefooted on an ass, garbed in the flowing garments and long beard of the Biblical patriarchs. He had been to Jerusalem and spoke with great conviction and authority. These preachers aroused such enthusiasm among the common people that spontaneous pilgrimages, poorly armed and organized, headed for Constantinople before the Crusade of the knights and nobles could be assembled. They fought with fellow Christians in Hungary and elsewhere enroute mistaking them for infidels. They created civil commotion everywhere which begot retaliation. The Byzantine emperor Alexius was greatly disturbed by these useless "crusaders" although he was anxious for assistance from the Europeans against the Turks. Needless to say most of these purblind enthusiasts did not survive to see the light of day in Asia Minor. As they crossed the Bosphorous they were ambushed by the Turks in the valley of Nice and annihilated by Turkish arrows.

The first Crusade began in 1096. There were 5 independent feudal armies. Godfrey of Boulogne, Raymond of Toulouse and Bohemond of Tarent were among the notable leaders. The various feudal armies were loosely under the command of the papal legate, who was largely ignored. Differences immediately arose between them and with the emperor Alexius. Clashes with the Byzantines ensued. The crusaders besieged and ransacked Byzantine cities enroute to Jerusalem. It was a rag-tag affair. But fortune (or God) was on their side for the Seljuq dynasty was in great disarray at this time. The Assassins murdered Nizam al-Mulk, the capable vizier of Sultan Malik Shah, in 1091. The great Sultan died a year later. A dispute among his four sons over the succession arose. The Turks, therefore, met the crusaders with something less than their customary force. At that, they inflicted gross damage with their mounted archers who could out-maneuver the heavily armored medieval knights of Europe. But in 1099 the Europeans captured Jerusalem, in what is recorded as a most sanguinary affair. Blood flowed in streams as "infidels" were put to the sword. Seventy thousand Muslims, including women and babes in arms, were slaughtered. The Jews were burned in their synagogues.

The crusaders established the Kingdom of Jerusalem. Godfrey of Boulogne became the king. Consummate elation prevailed over the rescue of the Holy places. At the Holy Sepulchre the crusaders sobbed with joy. One crusader even found the holy lance (presumably made of wood) that pierced the side of Christ a thousand years earlier! The crafty Italians (Genoese, Pisans and Venetians), meanwhile, with an eye for profit, staked out the coastal cities of Beirut, Acre, Tyre, Sidon and Jaffa as their exclusive commercial centers. It was their reward for transporting and assisting the crusaders in the capture of Jerusalem.

The Muslim world was now greatly alarmed by the massacre of their coreligionists in Jerusalem. Still badly disorganized they managed to capture Edessa in 1141. A more capable leader, Nur-ud-Din rose among the

Egyptian Muslims. This prompted the Second Crusade which was roundly defeated at Damascus. The crusaders questioned why God allowed his defenders to be so humiliated.

In 1169 a first rate leader named Saladin took power in Egypt. He extended his rule over Syria. He imposed the Sunni orthodoxy on Egypt thus paving the way for collaboration with Baghdad. Fired by indignities heaped upon the Muslims (capture of Saladin's sister, for instance) by Reynald of Chatillon, Saladin called for a *jehad* against the Christians. It was a holy war against a holy war. He captured Jerusalem in 1187. Duke Reynald was put to death when he refused to become a Muslim. King Guy de Lusignan was pardoned and permitted to remain a Christian. The True Cross, allegedly found by the crusaders, was taken to Baghdad as part of the spoils of victory.

This provoked the Third Crusade in 1189–92, the most significant and romantic of the seven or so. The kings of Europe—Frederick Barbarossa of Germany, Richard I of England and Philip Augustus of France—joined this Crusade. Frederick drowned ignominiously in Cilicia and Philip Augustus returned to France ill with fever. Richard remained as sole leader of the Crusade. An indecisive campaign ensued in which Richard and Saladin exchanged battles and courtesies. Saladin ingratiated himself with the Christians. In the end Richard retreated without recapturing Jerusalem promising to return in three years. Saladin graciously agreed to give free access to the Christians to their holy places. A year later he died at age 55. Jerusalem remained in Muslim hands for the next seven centuries!

The remaining Crusades were ineffectual and/or degenerated into outright plunder. The Fourth Crusade (1202–1204) was already discussed in Chapter VII. The Venetians subverted it into an attack on and plunder of Constantinople. The Byzantines empire never recovered from this blow and eventually succumbed to the Ottoman Turks in 1453. These greedy men masquerading in the name of God, in effect, opened the doors of Europe to the hated infidels. The Childrens Crusade of 1212 was most pathetic. Led by a boy named Nicholas of Cologne peasant lads flocked to Genoa and Marseilles to embark for Jerusalem in the hope they could succeed where their fathers had failed. Most ended up on the auction block as slaves. As a Holy War the Crusades, spanning some 200 years, were a failure but they did have other far reaching and more important results already touched on heretofore.

The Crusades did not end the Holy War psychology of the Christians. The Spaniards launched their own crusade during the 11th century against the Moors who conquered and made Spain a Muslim country in 711 A. D. By the middle of the 15th century the Muslims had only Granada, which the Spaniards took from them in 1492, the year Columbus discovered the Americas. The Spanish promptly redirected the Holy War against the heathen of the new world.

God and gold were the motivating forces of the conquests of Mexico and Peru by the Spanish conquistadors. This historical episode has already been detailed in Chapter V, but it is interesting to recall Cortez's position in this respect. In the ordinances Cortez issued to his army he states that the "conversion of the heathen" is the work most acceptable in the eye of the Almighty and that every soldier should regard this as the prime object of the expedition "without which the war would be manifestly unjust, and every acquisition made by it, a robbery." In the retrospect of four centuries of time this sounds both crass and hypocritical. But Cortez truly believed it. So intent was he in converting the Indians that Father Olmedo had to exercise a restraining effect upon him. It reflects instead the devastating effect religious bigotry can have on the activities of man by indoctrinating him with pseudo-knowledge and egocentricism.

Other men in other times seemed less effected by the Holy War idea. Buddhism spread through Asia mostly in peace. And so it would seem to be with the spread of Hinduism to southeast Asia. This thrust occurred during the first millennium after Christ when the Pallavas and Cholas of south India migrated eastward, impelled by trade, and Indianized the people of southeast Asia and the Malaysian archipelago. This included the Indian religions. Angkor Wat in Cambodia and Borobudur in Java are imposing monuments to Buddhism in this area. Though Indian history is sparse there is no reason to believe that this religious conversion was not peaceful.

Thus it would appear that it was primarily the Judeo religions that imbued men with the "chosen people of God" psychosis and the concept of the Holy War that has inflicted such manifold slaughter, torture and misery on mankind. It would seem that it owes its genesis to the idea of the Promised Land found in the Old Testament. It permeated an important theology of man with the conviction that wars of plunder against "unbelievers" were just.

Religious conflict has not vanished from the human scene even though the crass Holy War appears to be ancient history. There are at mid-twentieth century for instance, the religious-based conflicts in Ireland and the Mid East creating great carnage and suffering. Millions were killed in the Hindu-Muslim conflict over the partition of India in 1947. But an equally virulent and similar virus is now affecting mankind in the form of ideological war. Early in the century Lenin enunciated the doctrine of a struggle unto death of capitalism and socialism. This ideological conflict already played a part in the two World Wars. In the first war the British, Americans and others launched an abortive invasion of Russia to prevent the Bolsheviks from imposing communist rule on the country. In the second war anti-communism was a motivating factor in Hitler's imperialism albeit he subsequently and temporarily allied himself with Russia against Great Britain and the West. But the more pure conflicts over the current socio-economic ideological differences occurred after the second war in Greece, Azerbaijan, Korea and Vietnam. The French and American misadventure in Vietnam in the name of anti-communism for some twenty years or so caused far more slaughter and agony than any of the Holy Wars discussed earlier. The use of napalm bomb by the French and Americans on innocent villagers, mostly women and children, has no parallel in history to date in man's inhumanity to man. The only sin of the children of Vietnam was that they were "communists". But the fact was that these innocent victims of American napalm had not the slightest notion of the ideological virus that afflicts mankind today. This twentieth century ideological conflict which has replaced the Holy War of old is only in its infancy. The opposing proponents are armed to the teeth. How much more death, misery and destruction it may impose upon humanity has yet to be recorded.

OVEREXTENSION OF POWER

War has been a way of life of man throughout recorded history whether motivated by plunder, religion, nationalism or simply the desire to dominate. Plunder appears to have receded somewhat since the advent of the Industrial Revolution which gave the nations with the advanced technology the advantage of great capacity for the production of wealth. This gave them the power to dominate others through war and trade. But as population increases, which will beget added demand for available sources of energy and raw materials for maintaining industrial might, conflict and war over these industrial resources will doubtless arise. It would not be consistent with man's past behavior for the mighty to permit the weak to deny these resources to them, albeit that they possess them through geographic happenstance, as long as the dominant nations have the advantage of superior technology.

A further phenomena is worth noting about war. Invariably dominant nations tended to overextend their power only to suffer defeat and (usually) loss of dominant position. In the discussion heretofore it was pointed out from time to time that an aggressor in his reach for empire extended himself too far from home which diminished his power and ended in defeat and retreat. There would appear to be some law of war that a nation's power diminishes proportionately—it may even be exponentially—with distance from home. This was true in ancient times when armies subsisted in large measure off the conquered lands. It is even more true today when armies depend on "life lines" from home. The Americans, for example, had to incur great cost during their two Asian ventures in Korea and Veitnam in supplying roast turkey thousands of miles overseas to their troops for the Holidays in an effort to keep up morale in these unpopular wars. Canned beer and coca cola from home were daily requirements. But even in ancient times when soldiers were content to live off what was available in the conquered lands the pull of home—loved ones, familiar food, well known surroundings—undermined the soldier's moral. The hostility of the people in the foreign lands, furthermore, sapped the morale and the will to fight of the conqueror's armies. Perhaps this was not the case with mercenaries, but here an equally limiting factor arose. Mercenaries had to be paid and the cost of the war increased with the distance away from home.

In Chapter VI we saw that Ramses II was overextended in the Battle of Kadesh (circa 1296 B. C.) when he challenged the Hittites. This served to weaken his power aside from the fact that he undertook the fateful battle with inferior Egyptian technology (a two man chariot against a three man chariot). Ramses defeat ended Egyptian imperialism in the Middle East. The ancient Egyptian civilization declined thereafter and vanished into the dust of history.

The Romans too, a thousand or so years later, were overextended against the Parthians albeit the Parthians possessed superior technology—effective missile warfare. After the initial set backs the Romans were unable to resupply. This was particularly true of Marc Anthony's campaign. After the Parthians destroyed his seige machines the assault on Prasspa was ineffective. Marc Anthony was unable to replace them. He was too far from his base of operation in Palestine. For instance, when the Parthians set fire to his 30 ton battering ram it could not be rebuilt in the hills of Armenia. Marc Anthony vowed to attack again, this time with mounted archers to checkmate the Parthian advantage, but Roman power was unable to extend beyond the Euphrates.

The Persian attempt to subdue the Greeks is, perhaps, one of history's best episodes of the overextension of power. Around 500 B. C. the mighty Persian empire extended from the Hindu Kush to the Hellspont. The Persians decided to extend the empire into Europe. When intimidation failed Darius sent a fleet and 6000 soldiers, who were defeated by the Greeks in the famous battle at Marathon in 490 B. C. A decade later his son Xerxes launched what was the greatest invasion in antiquity. It was perhaps not equalled or exceeded in size until the present century. Herodotus reckons the Persian army numbered 2,641,000 fighting men and again as many engineers, slaves, merchants, suppliers and prostitutes. He adds that when the host stopped to drink the river ran dry. Historians doubt these figures but that it was a mighty host is not denied. The soldiers came from every nationality in western Asia. Even blacks from Ethiopia. The army was supported by a fleet of 1207 ships. At the Hellespont Egyptian and Phoenician engineers built two floating bridges on 674 ships (according to Herodotus) of trireme size heavily anchored and pointed into the fast current. It was the greatest engineering feat of the day. The mighty host took seven days and nights to pass over the bridges into Europe.

The Persian army marched through Thrace, Macedonia and Thessaly into the heart of Greece accompanied by the fleet along the coast. At Thermopylae in southern Thessaly they were detained temporarily by the valiant effort of Leonidas and a small force of Spartans. The other Greeks kept retreating before the Persian force until they were huddled on the island of Salamis off the coast of Attica. The Greek navy, 300 triremes and much smaller than the enemy fleet, retreated into the Bay of Salamis. Here was to be fought one of history's most momentous naval battles.

Themistocles was the genius of the victory. Years earlier he persuaded the Greeks to build a navy. The mines of Laurium, where a particularly rich vein of silver was struck at this time, provided the wealth for the ships. The Greeks were already accomplished sailors from their trade in the Mediterranean area. The Greeks also possessed ships with rams giving them a tehcnological advantage.

In this hour of desperation Themistocles resorted to a clever strategem. He sent a spy into the Persian camp stating that the Greek navy planned to escape from the Bay of Salamis during the night. Xerxes forthwith ordered his fleet into the narrow channel leading into the Bay to trap the Greek navy. This was precisely what Themistocles had intended by his ruse. The Greek sailors operating in difficult but familiar waters were able to outmaneuver the Persian fleet whose sailors speaking diverse tongues became completely disorganized in the narrow channel. The Persian fleet suffered a resounding defeat on September 23, 480 B. C.

Xerxes was now worried that the victorious Greek fleet would cut him off from Asia at the Hellespont. Themistocles proposed to do just that but he could not persuade the cautious Spartans to cooperate. Leaving Mardonius with an army of fifty thousand behind Xerxes proceeded immediately to the Hellspont. The retreat was apparently in some disarray. Herodotus informs us:

> In forty-five days he reached the place of passage, where he arrived with scarce a fraction, so to speak, of his former army. All along their line of march, in every country where they chanced to be, his soldiers seized and devoured whatever corn they could find belonging to the inhabitants; while if no corn was to be found, they gathered the grass that grew in the fields, and stripped the trees, whether cultivated or wild, alike of their bark and of their leaves, and so fed themselves. They left nothing anywhere, so hard were they pressed by hunger. Plague too and dysentery attacked the troops while still upon their march, and greatly thinned their ranks. Many died; others fell sick and were left behind in the different cities that lay upon the route, . . .

When he finally reached the Hellespont the famous bridge was no longer there. A storm and the raging current had destroyed it. He was forced to rely on his decimated navy to ferry him across. Reports Herodotus:

At Abydos the troops halted, and obtaining more abundant provision than they had yet got upon their march, they fed without stint; from which cause, added to the change in their water, great numbers of those who had hitherto escaped perished. The remainder, together with Xerxes himself, came safe to Sardis.

Mardonis and his considerably smaller army of handpicked warriors (Persians, Medes, Sacae, Bactrians and Indians) lived "off the land" in Thessaly during the winter. In spring he invaded Attica again. Pausanias, the Spartan king, led an army of some 30,000 Greeks against him. At Platea in 479 B. C. Pausanias outmaneuvered Mardonius with a solid phalanx attack against the Persian archers and as soon as the Persians flinched their allies deserted them. When Mardonius fell in battle his army fled in retreat. It was saved from utter destruction only by the Persian cavalry (about a thousand horse) covering its rear.

In the second Punic War (218–201 B. C.) Hannibal overextended himself against Rome. His defeat marked the decline and fall of Carthage. After its defeat in the First Punic War (264–241 B. C.) Carthage gave highest priority to the reconquest of Spain. Spain was the prize in the struggle with Rome as it held the gold, silver and other metals that conferred wealth and power. Hamilcar, the father of Hannibal, recaptured Spain in 238 B. C. After his death his son-in-law Hasdrubal succeeded him and ruled Spain. Hasdrubal struck a treaty with Rome whereby the Ebro river in northern Spain was to be the dividing line between the two powers. In 221 B. C. Hasdrubal was assassinated and Hannibal at age 25 went to Spain to take command. It is said that Hamilcar took Hannibal, when a boy of nine, to the altar of Baal-Haman in Carthage and made him swear to revenge his country against Rome. Hannibal never forgot his oath.

When the Romans fomented a *coup d'etat* in Saguntum on the east coast of Spain in 219 B. C. Hannibal put down the revolt summarily. Rome protested. Hannibal replied that Saguntum was a hundred miles south of the Ebro. Rome declared war in 218 B. C. This was the hoped for provocation Hannibal needed to launch an invasion of Italy.

Hannibal crossed the Ebro early in 218 B. C. with 50,000 infantry, 9000 cavalry and 200 elephants. His force consisted mostly of Spaniards and Lybians. Ten thousand of the Spaniards refused to go when they learned Hannibal proposed to cross the Alps. Hannibal had two reasons for choosing this difficult route. First, he could not rely on the Carthiginian navy to protect him in a sea crossing. Also, a sea invasion would have met the Roman army upon landing. Second, he felt he could secure the Gauls living between the Alps and the Poe river, who the Romans had only recently subdued, as allies.

After a summer of harsh marching across the Pyrenees, and battle with the Gauls between the Pyrennees and the Rhone, Hannibal reached the Alps in

early autumn. Where he crossed is not known but it is believed to be either
Little St. Bernards Pass or Genevre Pass. But the pass was already covered
with snow! The descent was worse than the ascent. The roads were buried
by snow or overlain with ice. Men and beasts lost footing and plunged to
their deaths. After 17 days the Alps were crossed but only 26,000 of his army
survived. At this point the venture appeared lost but Hannibal had reckoned
correctly, the Cisalpine Gauls welcomed him and joined him as allies for the
march into Italy.

For the next 17 years Hannibal conducted an inconclusive campaign in
Italy. Whenever he met the Roman army he won, largely, through superb
generalship. The Romans were bewildered and frightened. They changed
dictators often in the hope one would find a way to defeat Hannibal. Quintus
Fabius Maximus, made dictator in 217 B. C., resorted to avoiding battle in
the hope hunger, discord or disease would overtake the invaders. He
became known as Fabius the Delayer. This tactic was again to be used
effectively by Kutuzov against Napoleon as we shall see later. His successor
Caius Terentius Varro, however, chose to fight. He met Hannibal at Cannae
on the Adriatic coast with 80,000 infantry and 6000 cavalry. Hannibal had
19,000 regulars, 16,000 Gauls and 6000 cavalry. He lured Varro into a fight
on a large plain placing the Gauls in the center expecting them to fall back at
the outset. Varro fell for the trap, the Gauls broke and when he charged into
the middle Hannibal closed his flanks around the Roman army. His cavalry
broke through and attacked the legions from the rear. Varro lost 44,000 men,
Hannibal only 6000 two-thirds of them Gauls. The Romans were thoroughly
defeated. The whole nation was in disarray, but resolved not to surrender.

Hannibal next moved his army to Capua. Capua was the center of
pleasure and wickedness in all Italy. After several years of easy living and
dissipation Hannibal's soldiers were no longer the spartans he brought to
Italy. He made one feeble attempt to take Rome but the city's defense was
too strong.

Why Hannibal did not immediately strike at the capital is something of an
enigma. The answer doubtless is that he never felt he had the necessary
power. He had no seige equipment. He received no reinforcements from
either Spain or Carthage. Attrition had reduced his army to less than 20,000
regulars. His Gaulist allies were unreliable.

Meanwhile the Romans, under the redoubtable Scipios, invaded Spain to
keep Hasdrubal, Hannibal's brother, occupied and unable to send reinforcements to Italy. Hasdrubal finally led a small contingent across the Alps in
207 B. C. but was defeated in northern Italy by the Romans. In 205 B. C. the
young Scipio known as Scipio Africanus, who succeeded his brothers slain
in Spain, launched an invasion of Carthage. The Carthaginians appealed to
Hannibal to return to defend his country. He met Scipio at Zama, fifty miles
south of Carthage, in 202 B. C. and, for the first time in his life, was
defeated. Hannibal fought with distinction but his army of mercenaries was

no match for the Roman legions. Scipio, who admired Hannibal tremendously, was generous in victory. His fellow Romans were not so minded and demanded vengeance on Hannibal. The old soldier fled to Syria to the court of Antiochus III. When the Romans defeated Antiochus they again demanded Hannibal's surrender. Hannibal fled to Bithynia. The Romans pursued him. The old general, now 67, took poison in 184 B. C. to avert Roman capture.

There are some instances of overextension by the Chinese in Korea. After the Sui dynasty (589–618 A. D.) took power in China emperor Yang Ti decided to reconquer Koguryo (now parts of Manchuria and north Korea) in his attempt to restore the great empire of the Han. Koguryo was settled by Chinese emigrants and considered a legitimate part of China. Yang Ti needed more land to resettle his soldiers that he wished to demobilize now that he had gained control of China.

The Koreans fought a skillful delaying action drawing the vastly superior Chinese army deep into Koguryo. As Yang Ti marched deeper into the country up to the Yalu river it became more difficult to feed and supply his huge army from the Yellow river basin a thousand miles or so away. A bitter cold and harsh winter set in to aggravate the problem. Yang Ti was forced to retreat without victory.

Yang Ti tried again in 612–13 A. D. and met with even greater disaster for the same reasons. He had overextended his power. When the obdurate emperor planned to try for the third time he precipitated a mutiny and revolt that destroyed the Sui dynasty. It was succeeded by the Tang dynasty.

The Tang emperors were more clever. After defeating the Chinese armies the north Koreans grew haughty and attempted to dominate Silla their small neighbor in south Korea. The king of Silla solicited Tang's help in exchange for suzerainty. Tai Tsung, the Tang emperor, could not refuse Silla's plea for help lest he lose prestige. He sent an army against Koguryo, which employed again the delaying tactic that proved so successful against the Sui emperor. But Tai Tsung was a wiser man and withdrew his army to China before the harsh Korean winter set in.

Koguryo tried once more to subdue Silla in 65 A. D. This time in alliance with Paikche, the third state on the west coast of south Korea. Tai Tsung's son and his remarkable wife the empress Wu conceived an ingenious plan of attack. They launched a sea invasion of Paikche and defeated Koguryo from the rear (a feat General McArthur was to replay 13 centuries later). The Japanese intervened on the side of the north Koreans and were roundly defeated by the Chinese in 663 A. D. The Chinese made Silla the ruler of a unified Korea consisting of the three formerly independent states over which they exercised suzerainty. The Silla period (668–937 A. D.) was a brilliant era in the development of Korea.

The classic example of overextension *cum* defeat was Napoleon's invasion of Russia in 1812. Napoleon's biggest obstacle to world domination was

England. His first attempt to strike down the British empire met defeat in Egypt in 1799. Exactly how Napoleon hoped to wrest or free India from British possession by this ill fated thrust into the Middle East is none too clear. His next thought was to strike overland at India through and with Russia's assistance. But the Russians were allied with the English, Austrians and other French enemies.

Tsar Alexander I sued for peace after Napoleon defeated the Russians at the battle of Friedland on June 14, 1807. The two met on a raft in the Nieman river at Tilsit in Lithuania vowing eternal friendship, and emnity to England. There followed 5 years of uneasy peace. Napoleon thought himself too great to share power in Europe with Alexander. He kept toying with the idea of restoring a Polish state. This alarmed the Russians. The Russians chafed under Napoleon's continental blockade against British goods. It hurt Russia's trade. The Russians avoided it covertly by admitting British goods under the American flag. Napoleon protested. Eventually the Russians ignored the blockade. But when they imposed a duty on French wines Napoleon viewed it as a near declaration of war. Napoleon started withdrawing his troops from Spain and edging them toward Russia. In the spring of 1812 the Grand Army, 600,000 strong, was massed on the Russian border. On June 23, 1812 Napoleon crossed the Nieman river near Kovno and invaded Russia.

It was a great mistake. He had now extended his lines of supply and communications over a thousand miles from Paris. Sir Bernard Pares sums it up concisely:

> Entering a comparatively uncivilized country, Napoleon had to carry the necessities of civilization with him. His mobilization and concentration had been most carefully prepared, but it was impossible for him to invade till the late Russian spring had allowed the growth of the necessary fodder for his innumerable horses. As it was, they began to perish at the most alarming rate from the time when he crossed the frontier. Another thing which he could not carry with him was roads; a series of thunderstorms broke up the superficial tracks at the very outset, and all movements were thereby delayed. The Grand Army included soldiers of many nations; some of them, like the Prussians, most unwilling allies. Discipline began to go to pieces from the start, and large numbers deserted into the nowhere surrounding lines of advance and lived by looting. Napoleon's losses before he reached Vilna were a very large fraction of the whole.

But Napoleon did not intend to occupy Russia. He merely wanted a decisive victory over the Russian army so that Alexander would be a more compliant ally. Moscow, in his view, was to be simply a stopover on his march to India.

The definitive battle eluded him. The Russians kept retreating. They decided finally to make a stand before Moscow at Borodino. A bloody indecisive battle took place on September 7, 1812 but General Kutusov retired beyond Moscow with most of his army intact. Napoleon, entered Moscow, emptied of most of the Russians, without a fight on September 14, 1812. Napoleon called on Alexander to surrender. He got no reply. Kutusov would not give battle. He was prepared to retreat further into the hinterland. As with Fabius the Delayer this strategy proved effective for Kutusov and the Russians. Russia, not the Russian army, swallowed up the invader.

After a month or so Napoleon began to realize the disaster he had begot. The populace was hostile. Moscow was burned down. Snow began to fall. Winter was at hand. On October 19 he ordered a retreat. The Grand Army was in virtual shambles. Many were interested only in their loot. Some even pushed wheelbarrows containing spoils of war as they began the trek back to Paris.

The Russians, army, irregulars and even peasants, harassed the Grand Army all the way out of Russia. It was growing bitter cold and many of the French soldiers had neither overcoats or boots. Many froze to death. Others starved. Marshall Ney and his men crossed the Dnieper crawling on all fours over the ice. Only about 50,000 of the 600,000 that invaded Russia in June came out in November!

The overextension and defeat in Russia doomed Napoleon and his empire. The Allies took Paris on March 13, 1814 and exiled Napoleon to the Isle of Elba. Undaunted, Napoleon returned in 1815, raised an army, but was again and finally defeated by the Allies led by General Wellington at Waterloo on June 18, 1815. This time he was exiled to the island of St. Helena where he died in 1821.

A century or so later Hitler was destined to replay the tragedy. It proves that people either do not read history or learn nothing from it. Hitler's prime enemy too was England, although he was obsessed with communism. Nevertheless, before World War II began on September 1, 1939 he entered into a non-aggression pact with Russia which resulted in the partition of Poland. His rear now secured Hitler launched a spectacular conquest of western Europe climaxed by the surrender of France at Campiegne on June 22, 1940. Russia, meanwhile, joined in the aggrandizement by taking Finland and Rumania. Hitler objected to the latter and pressured Russia to disgorge part of Rumania to Hungary.

Hitler was the master of Europe in 1941. He had no further use for Russia. On June 22, 1941 Germany invaded Russia. The attack was actually a month behind schedule, for on December 18, 1940 Hitler issued an order to his military establishment to prepare for the Russian invasion around mid-May. The unexpected resistance encountered in the conquest of Greece detained him. This was to plague him in September when an early winter occurred in Russia.

Like Napoleon, Hitler too counted on a quick victory. It was predicated on two intelligence miscalculations. First, he underestimated Russia's armed strength. Russia industrialized much more rapidly under the Five Year Plans than was generally realized abroad. The gross output of large scale industry was 12 times greater than at the start of World War I. On the eve of World War II Russia was in a position where she could wage a modern war relying entirely on her own economy. She had developed a heavy industry which could supply its army with up-to-date war machines and ammunition and had organized her agriculture through collective farming and mechanization effectively enough so that it could be depended upon as a source of food supply for the army and the people. This was a sharp contrast with Russia prior to World War I when she was almost completely dependent upon her allies for the means of warfare and her armies frequently found themselves facing the enemy without any ammunition and food. There is some thought that the Russians entered the non-aggression pact with Germany to postpone the inevitable invasion so as to gain time to further their industrial and military strength.

Second, he counted on a fifth column such as had helped him in other countries. It never materialized. As so frequently happens he based his hope on the biased and self serving opinion of Russian emigres who harbored fond hopes the Russian Revolution would be undone.

The Russians again resorted to initial retreat, as they have done many times before, to draw the invader deep into Russian territory. Stalin, who took over the Premiership a few months earlier, ordered a "scorched earth" policy. Nothing of value was to be left behind in the retreat. In a prodigious effort whole factories were disassembled, transported inland and relocated out of reach of the Germans. During 1941, 1,360 large enterprises (mostly war industries) were evacuated to the East. Of these 455 were relocated in the Urals, 210 in western Siberia and 250 in central Asia and Kazakhstan. The Urals and western Siberia were transformed into the most powerful industrial region in Russia during the war. This was, of course, only a fraction of Russian industry. Much was pillaged and destroyed by the Germans.

But Hitler's biggest mistake was overextension into unfamiliar territory. Sir Bernard Pares writes:

> On the other hand, Russia's vast distances are in themselves a great defense. The object of any invader must be to bring the Russian army to a real decision—to encircle it and destroy it. So long as the army is in being and is supplied, Russia is not beaten. It is this that inspired the tactics of Peter the Great against Charles XII and of Kutuzov against Napoleon. But every advance is contested, and in this "back fighting," especially at night, the Russian is a past master. Even the army of 1915, threadbare of all supplies except

the bayonet, was never encircled. This, for the enemy, results in a constant wastage of effective strength. Here the country is almost more important than the army. Napoleon lost more in this way than in any other. Russia, especially in the north and centre, has a greater proportion of marsh than any other country in Europe; in the treeless south, rain churns up the rich black soil into a sea of mud, peculiarly obstructive to mechanized transport; even in the initial stages of the new campaign the early autumn rains brought pitiful complaints from the broadcaster accompanying the German forces. Instead of the metalled roads and built-up areas of France, the invader was surrounded, in the north and centre, by vast and mysterious tracts of no-man's land—forest or marsh or both together—where only the patient Russian peasant could feel at home or find a way. This gave abundant cover for guerrilla warfare all along the German lines of communication, with easy contact, often by parachute, with the Russian rear. Russian agriculture, almost throughout Russian history, had been collective; and now, replacing the antique village communes, which were so effective against Napoleon in day or night warfare at any point on his road, there were the new collective farms, far better organized and led, and with a far closer interest in the soil that they were defending. In the first World War peasant hoarding of food was one of the primary causes of the collapse of the Imperial machine. In the Second it was the Soviet collectivisation of agriculture that maintained the regular distribution of food to both army and people.

Nonetheless Hitler was more successful than Napoleon. He too headed for Moscow—and Leningrad—but was stopped from taking them. The Russian army stiffened its defenses and counterattacked. Winter came early in September. The Germans would have liked to halt for the winter but the Russians would not let them. The army counterattacked. Guerilla units, with women participating, made audacious raids against small units, supply trains and harassed the German soldiers everywhere. The German soldier was inadequately clothed for the severe Russian winter. Many froze to death at their posts.

In June 1942 the tide began to turn. America began to send trucks, jeeps, railway stock, communications equipment and airplanes. Industrial plants and equipment and food were also sent. Eleven billion dollars worth. But most of it arrived in 1943 and 1944. The Red army was now better organized for counterattack. It was well supplied from the new industrial base in and beyond the Urals. England and America were beginning to exert pressure on Germany in the west. The invasions of Sicily and Italy were being planned. Hitler was unable to assign much more of his army to Russia although most of it was already there. Despite this potential help Russia was in 1942 still very much on its own.

The German army was reorganized after the severe winter of 1941–42. Hitler was able to resume the offensive with thousands of tanks and bombers. This time, however, he redirected the attack south to the lower Volga and the Caucasus striking for the oil fields of the Baku area. He was now in desperate need of petroleum products for his war machines.

The Germans got as far as Stalingrad where the Russian Generals Rokossovsky, Vaturin and Yenemenko converged on them and stopped them. Another Russian winter raged and the Germans had to retreat. The attrition of overextension set in with a vengeance. It is estimated that the Germans had by now lost half the forces with which they started the attack. The Germans started their offensive in 1941 with two million men. They were still able to throw a million into the Stalingrad attack. The Russians probably lost 5 million men by now, but their capability for replacement was better as they were at home.

Thereafter, during 1943 and 1944, it was retreat for the Germans all the way. The Russians pursued them *en masse* with well organized and equipped armed units spearheading the counterattacks. Early in 1944 the Germans were ousted from Russian soil. The Germans were thoroughly defeated. Thirteen of Hitler's original 23 armies were annihilated on the eastern front. But the Russian army continued to pursue the retreating Germans across eastern Europe, where they settled some old scores with their ancient Polish and Prussian enemies, into the heart of Germany. In mid-March of 1945 some three million armed Russians stood before the gates of Berlin without a single pocket of German resistance behind them.

The rest is familiar history. The Allies launched invasions in the West. The landing in Italy took place on September 3, 1943. The Normandy invasion was launched on June 6, 1944. After encountering stiff resistance at the Battle of the Bulge during the winter of 1944–45, the Americans and British crossed the Rhine in March 1945 and were before Berlin in April. The German capital was completely surrounded. Hitler stayed with his defenders to the end and committed suicide inside his bunker. On May 2, 1945 the Berlin garrison surrendered.

Hitler's ill-fated invasion of Russia was without doubt the bloodiest war in history. The loss of life is simply staggering. The Russian losses are estimated at 12 to 15 million persons. The Germans lost about 9.5 million people. The American and British losses in the war were small by comparison—948,000 and 574,852 lives, respectively. Only the Taiping Rebellion, which was an internal revolution, comes anywhere near the numbers to match it.

Two decades later we find the Americans, the dominant power on earth at mid-century, repeating the folly of overextension of power with two misadventures in Asia half way around the world from home. The ideological war was now at its height. Under the Truman Doctrine the Americans vowed not to yield a square inch of territory to communism. The Communist Revolution in China found the Americans helpless in the face of it. Demogouges like Senators Joseph McCarthy, Richard Nixon and others started to exploit the communist success in China for their political aggrandizement. Americans fell under a virulent spell of political fear not unlike the Inquisition in medieval Spain. "Communist sympathizers" were figuratively burned at the stake. Americans had to stand up and be counted against communism. A whole generation of Americans was intellectually crippled for any clear objective analysis of the situation in Asia—and elsewhere abroad for that matter. Opportunities for miscalculation and misadventure were soon to arise.

The first came in Korea in 1950. After World War II Korea was partitioned at the 38th parallel with a communist regime under the protection of Russia in the north and a putative democratic government in the south under the tutelage of the United States. Russia opposed a United Nations supervised election to unify Korea. It organized instead a communist state, the Democratic Peoples Republic of Korea in the north and withdrew its occupation. An election was held separately in the south and the Republic of Korea established. The United States left the country in 1948. Border incidents ensued between the two Koreas. On June 25, 1950 North Korea invaded the south.

The Americans sought a U. N. Security Council resolution condemning the invasion and calling for North Korean withdrawal to the 38th parallel. Russia was apparently caught napping by the incident for it had been boycotting the Security Council and was not present to veto the resolution. A second resolution was enacted calling upon the U. N. members to furnish armed forces to repel the North Korean attack. The United States, it turned out, was the only member that provided any substantial and effective armed forces. It became, in the end an American war.

At the outset the Americans thought that U. S. air and naval support to the South Korean army was all that would be necessary. But the South Korean army crumbled like paper maché. After Seoul fell in a few days a U. S. battalion was hastily flown in. On July 8 General Douglas MacArthur was made commanding general of the "United Nations" forces. By the middle of July four American batallions were sent into Korea. But the North Korean advance remained unstopped until the Americans and their ineffectual South Korean clients were huddled in a corner around Pusan. The North Koreans even managed to capture an American General, William F. Dean, in their onslaught.

At this desperate stage General MacArthur resorted to a brilliant maneuver. On September 15, 1950 he undertook an amphibious landing at Inchon with two U. S. divisions and cut off the North Koreans in the rear. He trapped and captured some 100,000 North Koreans below the 38th parallel.

It ended effectively the North Korean invasion. It is interesting to speculate if MacArthur, who was well versed in history, borrowed the idea from the Chinese empress Wu.

Had General MacArthur stopped here and labeled it "mission accomplished" the Korean war would have been a brilliant American adventure. Though a resolution sanctioned military action in the North it was no longer a U. N. matter. What followed was a typical historical overextension of power.

MacArthur was a power unto himself. Even President Truman had no control over him at this stage. Intoxicated with his spectacular success with the Inchon landing he was not satisfied with simply repulsing the North Korean invasion. He forthwith called upon North Korea to surrender unconditionally. It was ignored at first and then rejected on October 10. Meanwhile, the South Korean army, morale temporarily regained, pushed beyond the 38th parallel. American units followed. No resistance was offered by the North Koreans. At the Yalu a South Korean spearhead was summarily annihilated on October 27 by the North Koreans. They did not however follow up on their success. Emboldened by the lack of North Korean counterattacks MacArthur ordered a sweep to the Yalu with 7 full divisions. The offensive was designed to end conclusively the Korean war. It was at this time that General MacArthur made his famous promise to American mothers that they would have their boys home for Christmas.

But when MacArthur reached the Yalu pandemonium broke loose. The Chinese hurled four divisions against him and caught him by surprise. It was an American intelligence failure of the highest magnitude. A bitter North Korean winter had set in to add to the woes of the Americans. Whole divisions were entrapped and had to fight their way out to safety. Many froze to death. An ignominious retreat followed. The Chinese and North Koreans launched a counter offensive which took them below the 38th parallel again by January, 1951. Seoul was once more in North Korean hands. A see-saw war ensued which eventually ended in a truce at the 38th parallel. MacArthur was dismissed from his command in April, 1951 by President Truman.

The American people grew impatient with the inconclusive war. At its height 350,000 American troops were involved. They were supported by a large number of air and naval personnel. Thirty-five thousand deaths and a hundred thousand wounded were already recorded. The war cost the Americans 18 billion dollars and begot a distasteful spate of inflation. The Americans wanted an end to the war. General Eisenhower reaped political profit from this disaffection when he promised during the 1952 Presidential campaign to go to Korea, if elected, to end the war.

The lesson of history, however, remained unlearned. The Americans were to repeat the folly of overextension of power on an even greater scale 15 years later in Vietnam. After the defeat of Japan in 1945 the French returned to Indo-China to reestablish colonial rule. There had already been anti-colonial agitation before the war. An Indo Chinese Communist party, was organized in 1930 by Ho Chi Minh. In 1941 Ho organized a united front of various nationalistic parties known as the Vietminh. It was dominated by the communists. When the Vietminh were frustrated in taking power after the Japanese left they launched a war of independence against the French. The struggle was bitter and protracted. The French retaliated by setting up a rival Vietnam government under Emperor Bao Dai who was more tractable to French interests. The net effect of course, was to convert a colonial war into a civil war.

After 1951 the Americans furnished large amounts of military and economic assistance to the Bao Dai government and the French pursuant to the Truman Doctrine. Jingoists like Vice President Nixon and Admiral Radford agitated within the U. S. government for American armed intervention in Indochina in support of the French to stop communism. But the French effort collapsed after the Vietminh victory at Dien Bien Phu on March 13, 1954. The French people demanded an end to the war. An international conference was convened at Geneva with reluctant United States participation. The Agreements were ingeniously designed for peaceful accomodation of all persons and parties in interest. It was assumed by every one, except the Americans perhaps, that the communists were the dominant power in the country and would take over. Thus, to give ample opportunity and time for those—Vietnamese, French and others—to adapt to the situation by either staying or leaving the country, a two year period was provided during which the Vietminh would administer Vietnam north of the 17th parallel referred to as "the provisional military demarcation line", and the Bao Dai government would administer it in the south. In fact, the Geneva Accords do not even mention the Bao Dai regime simply referring to the French Union reflecting, of course, the subservience of the Bao Dai government to the French. An election was to be held in 1956 to permit the people to choose between Ho Chi Minh and Bao Dai as the head of state. The two temporary administrative zones were not viewed or intended as a partition of the country.

In 1955 Ngo Dinh Deim with the enthusiasm and support of certain Americans like Henry Luce and Cardinal Spellman, both extremely influential men inside the ruling elite in America, ousted Bao Dai and took over the administration in Saigon. The French had by now left the country. The takeover was confirmed by a questionable election in which Diem received 80 per cent of the vote. Most of the non-communist Vietnamese doubtless perferred Diem to Bao Dai. The die was now cast for eventual American involvement in the Vietnamese conflict.

Ngo Dinh Diem repudiated the proposed election of 1956 provided for in the Geneva Accords. He knew, of course, that he would lose to Ho Chi Minh. He gave as his reason that there could be no free election in North

Vietnam. The Americans have been accused of instigating Diem's move, which has not been duly documented, but that they gave Diem their blessing cannot be denied. Aid followed aid and by the end of the decade South Vietnam was a major recipient of military and economic assistance under the foreign aid program. The aid was accompanied by American military and civilian personnel. Russia and China were, of course, providing similar aid to the North. Thousands of Americans were soon involved with both the military operation and the economic development of South Vietnam. Like true bureaucrats since time immemorial they mesmerized themselves on the virtue of their mission. Everything was a glorious success. The truth, in retrospect, was, however, something else.

The Diem regime was corrupt, incompetent and ineffectual. Without its American prop it would have collapsed in a day. After Diem repudiated the 1956 election the communists residing in the south decided he had to be overthrown by force. The National Liberation Front, or Vietcong, was organized for this purpose. At first, the Vietcong were on their own. To be sure, they had the blessing and, perhaps, economic support of North Vietnam but more at this time was not needed. The Vietcong could capitalize on the weakness and unpopularity of the Diem government. Diem's army was totally ineffectual.

By the mid-1960's the situation in Saigon was desperate. The Vietcong held the countryside; the Diem regime was huddled in the big cities. It was a typical peasant revolt as occurred in China a decade or so earlier. Left to its own devices the Diem government would have collapsed.

The Americans were now faced with a horrible dilemma with which its leaders were hopelessly unprepared to cope. The intellectuals were crippled by the virus of McCarthyism so that their contribution was a simple reflex of anti-communism. Many were familiar with history and should have known about the lesson of overextension of power. The contribution of the military establishment to the decision was equally useless. But the military mind has seldom rated over a C minus in the annals of history. There was a notable exception, however, at this juncture. It was General MacArthur, now in his "fading away" years. His advice to President Johnson was "never again involve American fighting men on the continent of Asia", or words to that effect. Unlike most military professionals General MacArthur was a soldier of superior intellect. Although he committed the perennial mistake of overextension he had the greatness of mind to learn from his error. But President Johnson either failed to listen or did not understand. It was perhaps, an act of mercy that General MacArthur did not live (he died in 1964 at age 84) to see his good advice spurned and result in an inglorious defeat of his country in Asia.

Unlike President Kennedy, President Johnson was impressed (nay) overwhelmed by the generals. When they advised him the U. S. military forces could easily defeat the Vietcong he did not question them. Three years later when America was hopelessly bogged down in Vietnam, the aged former Secretary of State Dean Acheson said to President Johnson, "Mr. President you have been led down the garden path by the Generals."

The fateful decision to commit American troops came in February, 1965 after the Vietcong assaulted an American military advisor's barracks in Pleiku. At this time the military instructors had escalated in number to 16,000 or so but as such they did not engage at least formally in combat. After Pleiku, President Johnson gave orders for direct U. S. military action against the "communists". American prestige was on the line. Nothing less than complete defeat of the Vietcong would be acceptable.

The North Vietnamese forthwith committed themselves fully in support of their communist brothers in the south. The number of North Vietnamese soldiers, however, probably never exceeded a hundred and fifty thousand. How much help they rendered before American armed intervention has not yet been reliably established. The Americans promptly labeled the North Vietnamese intervention aggression and tried desperately thereafter to justify their military presence in Vietnam on the grounds of stopping aggression. This position, however, was weak on both fact and international law. The Geneva Accords are clear on the point. No new states were created. There were no North or South Vietnam nations except in the view of the Americans and their South Vietnamese clients. In fact, the population was largely reshuffled and scrambled in Vietnam that a geographic presence was virtually meaningless. Most of the leaders of South Vietnam—President Thieu, Vice President Ky and others—were northerners. Many in the North Vietnam government were from the South. The United States was practically alone in this interpretation and got merely token help from its allies.

The Americans too, like Napoleon, wanted a quick and decisive victory. And like Napoleon they did not want to conquer and occupy any Vietnamese territory. But they got mired down instead in the jungle of Vietnam. For three years they fought a dirty and inconclusive war in which the number of American soldiers and marines reached 405,000. An equivalent number, perhaps, was engaged in providing air and naval support. The bombing of North Vietnam exceeded in magnitude the bombing of Germany in World War II! Hundreds of thousands more Americans manned the long supply lines, the construction of airports, giant naval bases like Cam Ran Bay and the administration of commissaries to provide the luxuries of home to the Americans in Vietnam. Finally, there were the itinerants—officials, congressmen, the media and, not to be overlooked, the entertainers including the ubiquitous Bob Hope. It was a Mighty Host equal to, if not surpassing that of Xerxes invasion of Greece 2500 years earlier.

Frustration propelled the Americans into dastardly acts of inhumanity. Villages were burned with napalm on the justification they harbored "communists". They usually contained mostly old men, women and children. Horrible scenes appeared on American television like the naked 9 year old girl running down a road after a bomb raid on a village. There was the so-called My-lai incident where American soldiers machine-gunned women, children and babies huddled in a ditch trying to escape the war!

The American people were finally shaken out of their torpor. It dawned on them that their leaders had taken the country into a war they did not want or that they could disengage from honorably. The social and political fabric of the country began to rend asunder. President Johnson, Secretary of State Rusk, Secretary of Defense McNamarra, however, kept justifying the war. The Defense Department issued ridiculous and obscene body counts of Vietcong killed, which if tallied would have denuded Vietnam of manpower of fighting age twice over. This false and misleading favorable posture was soon belied by the Tet offensive in February, 1968 whereby the Vietcong, now supported strongly by the North Vietnamese, launched a devastating attack on the cities. The Americans were caught completely by surprise, which demonstrated their utter isolation in the country and their lack of knowledge of the situation in which they were enmeshed. It reflected too that the communists held the countryside with the Americans and their Vietnamese clients huddled in the cities. A perspicacious American said "It seems the only territory we control in Vietnam is the square root on which each GI stands."

The generals, chagrined and humiliated, asked President Johnson to send 200,000 more American soldiers to Vietnam. The president was now confronted with a terrible decision. The American people wanted an end to the war. It was an election year. When it became obvious that Robert Kennedy, who opposed the war, would wrest the nomination from him he renounced reelection for another term and sued for peace. Preparations for a peace conference in Paris were promptly commenced. The bombing was stopped and the withdrawal of American troops planned.

At this point the American people elected Richard Nixon President. He resumed the war (in the delusion *he* could succeed where others failed) and in the process tried to subvert the American constitution. He failed in both respects. To be sure, he could not stop the withdrawal of American troops though he slowed down the process. In the interim he continued a rear guard action in which 20,000 more American boys were killed. He thought that he could bomb the communists into submission. There followed the most intensive bombing in history. Only a very small fraction of it was effective. Most of the bombs fell into the jungle. The bombing begot a horrible headache for Nixon. More bombing resulted in more American pilots shot down and taken prisoners by the north Vietnamese. Their families and friends became alarmed as the imprisonment of the pilots began to mount into years with no end in sight.

Like Napoleon and Hitler before him Nixon struck out for the decisive victory. He invaded Cambodia in May, 1970 with the American troops still in Vietnam. The objective of the Cambodia invasion was to capture the

Vietcong headquarters which Nixon and his generals concluded was "somewhere out there in the jungle" across the Cambodian border. Needless to say they found no communist headquarters. The Cambodia invasion was a failure, but the devastation it precipitated upon the Cambodian people was horrible. Millions of innocent Cambodians lost their lives, property, and means of livelihood because of the American bombing and the communist assault it begot. The end result was a communist takeover.

Nixon's policy was labeled "Vietnamization." It called for building a South Vietnamese army that could, as it was said, "hack it alone". It was nothing new. The French tried it before him. It was the American policy under Diem. Each time it failed but the Nixon Administration thought it knew how to do it better. In 1971 Nixon tested his "Vietnamization" policy by sending the ARVN (army of the Republic of Vietnam or South Vietnam army) into Laos to interdict the famous Ho Chi Minh trail over which supplies flowed from North Vietnam to the Vietcong. It was a disaster. The ARVN was roundly defeated. They fled ignominiously leaving their American tanks and weapons behind for the North Vietnamese.

The 1972 election was now at hand. Nixon was desperate. The troops were withdrawn but the inconclusive bombing continued. The captured pilots increased and remained in Vietnamese prisons. Nixon resorted to diplomacy at this stage. He requested the Russians in 1969 to use their influence with the North Vietnamese. They replied they had no such influence in Hanoi. When requested to stop supplying the Vietnamese communists with arms the Russians said they could not do so while the Americans gave military support to South Vietnam. Now he flew to Peking, with which the United States had no diplomatic relations for two decades because of demogogues like him, McCarthy and others, to seek China's assistance in terminating the war—on American terms of course. He was received warmly and politely told to get out of Asia.

In May, 1972 the communists launched another major attack across the 17th parallel. The ARVN crumbled again. Only the heavy American bombing saved them. Meanwhile the peace negotiations kept dragging on in Paris. In October, 1972, on the eve of the election, Secretary of State Kissinger announced that "peace is at hand." When this turned out not to be so after the election Nixon launched a devastating mining and bombing raid on Haiphong harbor. A peace agreement was finally reached in January, 1973 which confirmed the North Vietnamese and Vietcong in their positions, including most of the south Vietnam countryside. The captured pilots and other POW's were released by the Vietnamese.

The bombing continued. This time to enforce the "peace". Congress finally put an end to the bombing in August 1973. But the war continued by proxy. Large amounts of military and economic assistance poured into South Vietnam. The airfields, bases and other American military facilities were turned over to the ARVN.

At this time the Watergate scandal hit President Nixon. When Impeachment was imminent he resigned on August 7, 1974. A few months later, in April, 1975 the ARVN crumbled under a broad frontal attack on the cities by the Vietcong and North Vietnamese. The collapse was sudden. American officials had to be evacuated by helicopters from a pad atop the American Embassy in Saigon. The defeat of the Americans was now complete and final.

The cost of the war to the Americans was staggering. More than 50,000 GI's were killed; another 400,000 maimed and wounded. Thousands returned as drug addicts. The war cost some 180 billion dollars. The gold drain forced the United States off the gold standard with widespread repercussions on international currency exchanges. It begot a horrendous inflation in the United States. The moral repercussions are immeasurable. American youth has lost faith in its leaders and government. A full assessment of the socio-economic damage inflicted upon the American society remains to be seen and measured.

There was one salutary aspect to the war. For the first time (although the same happened in France) a nation rose against its leaders and declared a war immoral. No such precedent is recorded in other foreign invasions. The people either did not care or did not have the political freedom to express their views. Democracies are more suitable for such expression of opinion. And when the American leaders lost the support of the people their misadventure in Vietnam was doomed to failure.

The Vietnam war was a replay of the Chinese Revolution of 1949. The only difference was the foreign interference by the French and Americans which prolonged the Vietnamese Revolution by 20 years. It was a foreseeable result for anyone with an understanding of Asia. But that was not possible in Washington where the ruling elite was blinded by McCarthyism coupled with an "arrogance of power", to quote Senator Fulbright, an early opponent of the war. The result was a classic overextension of power.

Conquerors and invaders fail to understand that they encounter unknowns when they extend their power far from home. They venture into strange country, encounter unaccustomed weather and, above all, a hostile people. The Russian winter was as effective in defeating Napoleon and Hitler as the Russian army. Hannibal's force was cut in half by the crossing of the Alps. The Americans bogged down in the jungle and heat of Vietnam.

Had the Grand Army been able to meet the Russian army on the plains of Poland Napoleon could have had his quick and decisive victory. If the Americans could have engaged the Vietcong in an open field the encounter would have been decided in their favor in a very short time, for comparatively speaking the Vietcong under such circumstances was a tenth rate power. But when power is overextended into unknown and uncontrollable situations it diminishes greatly.

The invader is a "foreigner". The "fatherland" or "motherland" must be defended against him. It is a powerful factor for human motivation. The invaders are trampling on the peoples food supply. It is that basic. Derogatory epitaphs are hurled at the invader. The Persians were "barbarians" to the Greeks. Napoleon was "anti-Christ" to the Russians. The Americans were "foreign devils" to the Vietnamese. The incredible thing about the Americans was that they did not view themselves as "foreigners" in Vietnam. In fact, they very indignantly considered the North Vietnamese the "foreigners" or "aggressors" in their own country. It betrayed a poor understanding of history.

Guerrilla warfare is as effective against the conqueror as the regular army. The Russian peasants inflicted untold damage on both the Grand Army of Napoleon and the Germans. The guerrilla swims like a fish among the people said Mao Tse-tung. The Vietcong knew every move of the Americans before it was launched but the Americans were always caught by surprise by Vietcong attacks. The invader finds himself at war not only with the army but the entire population and this militates toward a devastating dimunition of his power.

X
Enjoyment of Life—Food and Replication

Man has also found time to enjoy himself—in spite the fact that so much of his energy has been devoted to war and revolution. During the span of recorded history only one year in thirteen has been without war. Donald A. Wells in *The War Myth* writes "From 1496 B. C. to 1861 A. D., a period of 3,357 years there were 227 years of peace and 3,130 years of war."

The impact of this death and misery on individuals has, as usual, been unfairly and unjustly distributed. Some have lived lives completely engulfed by it; others have completely avoided it; but most have been affected. Count Anton Szaray (1740–1809), a general in the Austrian army, fought in 89 battles over a period of 47 years and was seriously wounded in 84 of them! In recent times a whole generation of Vietnamese has lived in war and revolution that spanned a quarter of a century. The Taiping Rebellion decimated and uprooted a generation of Chinese during the 19th century. The schism of Christendom during the forepart of the 17th century, resulting in the so-called Thirty-Years War, embroiled a whole generation of Europeans in death and misery. And so it has been! On the other hand, the Americans have not suffered the agonies of war on their homeland for over a century. Though they have been involved heavily in war abroad most Americans today are incapable of comprehending the horror of war and revolution.

But peace or avoidance of war did not *ipso facto* beget the enjoyment of life. Most of humanity has been and still is gripped by the struggle against hunger, disease and ignorance. Even the fortunate few who have been able to free themselves from the struggle for survival have rarely been able to free themselves of the dominance instinct with its manifestations of greed, selfishness, status seeking and other false values in the perennial struggle over the distribution of wealth. Unsatisfied wants have brought more unhappiness (self inflicted to be sure) than enjoyment to the dominant minority. Few have been able to achieve an enjoyable life in accordance with the principle set forth by Mahatma Gandhi, India's modern saint. Gandhi said that happiness was a formula in which the numerator consisted of a person's "wants" and the denominator the "satisfaction" of those wants. A person could find happiness just as well by reducing (or curbing) the numerator as well as increasing the denominator! Human greed knows no bounds. Those enslaved to it have seldom found life enjoyable. In final analysis, it would be hard to reject on historical evidence Thoreau's famous dictum that "The mass of men lead lives of quiet desperation."

That man strove to and did enjoy life too cannot; however, be gainsaid. History bears this out. The two basics of life—food to provide energy and sexual connection to regenerate man—have been developed into joys of life. The art of cuisine elevated feeding to dining; the art of love changed breeding, the lot of all other animal life, to a highly pleasurable state of human affinity. It lifted mankind, to resort to a pun, out of Nature's rut.

Architecture transported man from the animal lair into a beautiful home appropriately furnished for his comfort. His hairless body he covered with warm and attractive clothing. He has delighted his senses of sight and hearing with painting, sculpture, music and the dance. To titillate his mind man has developed prose, poetry, drama, humor and other forms of literature.

We may now turn to the development of these arts by man which will doubtless prove to be the most enjoyable part of this dissertation.

CUISINE

There are three great and distinctive cuisines. The Chinese, European and Indian. There are others of distinction. Foremost in this respect is Middle East cuisine which would embrace the food of countries ranging from Greece to the Indian subcontinent. Most other national cuisines are either apparented by or related to these great cuisines. Japanese food, for instance, is a variation of the Chinese.

Chinese cuisine is the oldest and, perhaps, the most distinctive in the world. The Chinese were already "dining" when the forefathers of European man, who now dominates the world, were gnawing on joints of meat and drinking their insipid beer from horns or skulls leaving their face and whiskers covered with foam and grease from ear to ear.

The art of Chinese cooking and dining started three thousand years ago. The Imperial court had an official chef as early as 1115 B. C. whose job was not only to supervise the cooking but to advise on the dietary effects of the various foods served. At this time the Chinese were meat eaters including beef and lamb. Whether they also partook of milk products is not clear. The Li-chi, a text written during the Han dynasty (202 B. C.–2 A. D.), sets forth recipes for the Eight Delicacies calling for the use of beef, mutton, and venison among other meats. One of these delicacies was a suckling pig stuffed with dates roasted in a coating of wet clay to seal in the juices. The dried clay was then broken off, the skin removed and mixed with flour into a paste. The piglet was next deep fried to a crisp golden brown with the paste. Then for three days it was placed in aromatically scented steam.

About this time the pressure of population on the food supply dictated a basic change in the evolution of Chinese cuisine. In 400 B. C. the population was already 25 million. Beef, lamb and mutton began to disappear from the diet as the available arable land had to be devoted to cereal production. The cow and water buffalo were kept only as draft animals. Dairy products, if they were ever used, vanished. Curiously though the Hsuing-nu and other nomads from the north who invaded China constantly during this time lived on meat and milk products, but the Chinese never emulated these intermittent foreign rulers.

Around 300 A. D. with the expansion south rice was introduced into Chinese cuisine. Rice originated in Indo-China. Thereafter rice and wheat were the basic cereals of the Chinese diet. Rice became the staple food of the upper classes while wheat was the grain of the poor in north China. Noodles nourished the peasants. Rice was eaten by rich and poor alike in the south. During the Ming dynasty (1369–1644 A. D.) the Chinese developed an ecological balance in the rice fields by raising fish and ducks in the flooded paddies. The fish fertilized the land so that crop after crop could be raised without exhausting the soil. The fish also eliminated the mosquitoes making large areas arable in south China not otherwise habitable because of malaria. Chinese agronomists also developed the quick growing champa rice making possible double cropping.

Tea consumption became widespread during the Tang dynasty (618–906 A. D.) though it was discovered much earlier. Legend has it that tea became known in antiquity when the leaves of the plant dropped into the boiling water of a Chinese sage while partaking his food in the countryside. Tea is taken all day long and on all occasions. There are about 250 varieties. But the quality of the water is considered equally important. Tea drinking developed into a ceremonial art form. The Chinese also drink wines on formal occasions, but these are not like European wines. They are made from cereals, not grapes.

The constant pressure of population forced the Chinese to seek new sources of food. Every variety of sea food was incorporated into their diet. Various and unusual vegetables—lily buds, bamboo shoots, bean sprouts and water chestnuts—were eaten. By 500 A. D. the Chinese had a list of 365 edible vegetables. Pigs and poultry, ducks in particular, became the main meat sources as their keep did not interfere with the arable land. The dog was also a meat mainstay in earlier times. Vegetables not meat, however, came to predominate in Chinese cuisine.

The soybean, rich in protein, substitutes for milk and cheese. Ground and mixed with water it forms a milk like liquid which is made into curds and cheese. The ground soybean is also used for sauce and jams, pastries and condiments. Lastly, it yields an oil that is used in cooking. Chinese cooking does not use animal fat. Peanut oil is most often used.

The Chinese developed from these ingredients over thousands of years a great variety of recipes. There are said to be some 80,000 different dishes. There are 250 ways to cook pork. It was not unusual for a wealthy Chinese to provide 40 or more different dishes for a single feast. There is no main dish in a Chinese dinner. There are many with the diners partaking at random or with the dishes served seriatum to the diners seated at a round table.

A Chinese meal (there is a light breakfast, substantial lunch and a large dinner) is one of contrast and variety—point counterpoint. The notion of the Five Flavors—sweet, sour, salt, hot and bitter has dominated Chinese cooking since ancient times. The idea is to titillate the taste buds with the entire range of flavors during a meal. But the other senses are also delighted with the same idea of contrast and variety. Textures are contrasted and blended—crunchiness against smoothness, crisp water chestnuts in a smooth sauce and so on. Foods are combined to mingle fragrances into wonderful aromas. The eye too is appeased. Vegetables are steamed or lightly cooked to preserve their greenness or other natural color—and, incidentally their vitamins. Rice is cooked to snowy white. Pork and duck are prepared in shades of pink and brown. White and black mushrooms decorate a dish. Even the ear is involved with poetic names for dishes such as jade, ruby and other delightful words. A soup with strips of ham and duck is called "gold and silver broth". Some names for teas are jasmine, cloud mist, water nymph, dragon's beard, silver needle and the like. Chinese cuisine is an aesthetic experience.

Chinese cooking requires complex preparation though the actual cooking time is brief. Much time is spent planning and marketing for the meal. In fact, the market usually determines the nature of the meal as it is built around the best meat and/or vegetables available at the time and place. The cook cuts the food into bite size pieces wherever possible so that the diner may handle the food with chopsticks. Fish is sometimes served whole but so tender the flesh can be picked off the bones with chopsticks. The various foods are then cooked in a wok, a utensil resembling an inverted coolie's hat, with a small amount of water in the narrow round bottom so that most of the food is steamed. The wok was invented out of necessity to maximize heat in fuel short China. The conical shaped vessel is stabilized over the heat in a round collar. It is used for stir frying, deep frying, slow cooking and steaming. By placing the food at different levels and carefully timing the input the whole meal is blended and phased so that everything is ready at the same time with each ingredient retaining its identity. The result is a harmonious blend of flavors, color and aromas unknown in any other cuisine.

Seasonings and condiments are mild and subtle. The basic ingredients are soy sauce, sherry, garlic, ginger root and scallions. Salt, pepper and sugar are used. Chili sauce and tomato paste are recent additions. In Szechwan, which has a hot climate and propinquity with South Asia, hot and peppery spices have been introduced into the cuisine.

Desserts are unknown and sweets are of minor importance. Chinese prefer savories to sweets—dumplings, buns, wontons, egg rolls and such. Fruits and nuts are taken as snacks. Also incorporated in the main dishes. The Chinese have a few sweet dishes for banquets and feasts such as pastries filled with sweet nuts and a rich steamed pudding called Eight Precious rice. Their craving for sweets is mostly satisfied by sweet and sour sauces served with meat and fish. Tea is taken without sugar to avoid any disturbance of the subtle flavors of the many varieties of the beverage.

As in the other great cuisines there are regional variations and differences. Cantonese cooking is, perhaps, the most renowned. Most Chinese restaurants in the West are Cantonese. European trade with China originated through Canton in the 16th and 17th centuries.

Cantonese cooking was always inventive. There were good and abundant food resources in the south. When the Ming dynasty was overthrown in the 17th century many of the ruling elite left Peking for Canton and brought with them chefs and cuisine to enrich the already great Cantonese cooking. As the port of Canton prospered on foriegn trade the wealthy merchants and gentry indulged in good living and dining, which furthered the development of a fine cuisine.

Cantonese cooking emphasizes the enhancement and blending of the natural flavors. Few seasonings are used—soy sauce, ginger root and wine. Quick cooking and stir frying in chicken stock is the technique most often used. Steamed pork and fish, roast pork, fowl and lobster and fried rice are characteristic. Most exotic of the Cantonese cuisine is bird's nest soup and shark's fin soup.

Bird's nest soup is made from the nest of tiny swallows inhabiting the South China Sea. These swallows produce a gelatinous substance to mold their nests which when cooked has a distinctive and pleasing taste. When dried the nests look like finely shredded and glazed coconut, beige in color. The best quality is an unpolluted nest, though used and cleansed nests are also used. Bird's nest soup is considered a mark of the Chinese cuisine for over a thousand years.

North Chinese or Peking cuisine is equally prominent though not as familiar abroad. It was natural for a great cuisine to develop here as it was the seat of the imperial court. Peking cuisine is light and mildly seasoned. Garlic, scallions, leeks and chives are used liberally. Soft fried foods, roasts and wine-cooked meals are common. Peking duck and egg rolls are famous. Due to its proximity to Mongolia and Manchuria lamb and mutton comprise many dishes. These are cooked on the Mongolian Grill, a large open charcoal stove with a fine iron grating on top where the meat is grilled.

Western or Szechwan cuisine is highly spiced—red peppers, chillies, chili and the like—and oleaginous. It has been toned down somewhat by migrants from North China who fled south and west from the invading nomads. Szechwan duck is a variation of Peking duck. Szechwan chicken, on the other hand, is highly spiced.

Central or Honan cuisine is known for its sweet and sour dishes, spiced concoctions and heavy seasoning. East Coast or Fukien cuisine is famous for its sea food and clear soup. Soups predominate at family meals and banquets. Cooking wine is used more often. Fukien is noted for suckling pig. Also its egg rolls.

Along with great cuisine the Chinese developed the art of dining. Meal time is symbolic of the good life. Sharing of food is part of Chinese tradition. Chinese scholars were gourmets and wrote treatises on cuisine. Poets compiled cookbooks. Confucius viewed the enjoyment and sharing of food as a mark of a civilized man contributing to the peace of a society.

The fine arts were employed to make dining more enjoyable. Beautiful and delicate teacups and dishes were developed for the taking of food. Chinese ceramics for dining became renowned and after the 17th century were imported and reproduced in Europe to facilitate the development of European cuisine and dining. The Europeans have always called their cups, plates and other food vessels "china" and "chinoiserie", in recognition of this Chinese contribution to the art of good living.

European cuisine ranks next in importance and emulation. Western dominance of the world brought European restaurants to every metropolis of the world. There are fine French restaurants in Saigon, first rate Italian restaurants in Addis Ababa and English food, certainly not the best of European cooking, penetrated the Indian subcontinent.

European cuisine is the most recent. It dates back, at best, a thousand years. It owes little to its predecessor civilizations. The ancient Greeks were not gastronomes, though at their height Athens boasted a modicum of *haute cuisine*. European cuisine, however, owes much to the Greeks for developing the olive and wine from grapes.

The Romans aspired to be gourmets and ended up mostly as gourmands. But despite this gross manifestation they furthered the cause of good cooking. There is a first-century Roman cookbook written by one Apicus that gives some insight into gourmet cooking of the Romans.

The Romans introduced spices from Asia into their cooking. The old silk road was now in full operation. There was cinnamon and ginger from China. Black pepper and cumin from India. A recipe from the Apicus cookbook calls for the following spices and other ingredients for a sauce for roast meat; pepper, lovage, parsley, celery seed, dill, asfetida root, hazelwort, cyperus, caraway, cumin and ginger.

Two other ingredients, difficult to recreate today, were germaine to Roman cooking. They were liquamen and silphium. Liquamen was a sauce made of heavily salted fish and other seafood gruel which was allowed to ferment for a long time. It was used to season and flavor meats, fish and vegetables. So popular was the concoction that factories arose everywhere to produce it for a broad market. Its closest modern counterpart is probably the fish sauce popular in Indo-China and Thailand called *nouc mam*. It's effect can perhaps be likened unto anchovies in European cooking.

Silphium, a herb from North Africa, was widely, though sparingly used because of the cost. The Persian asafetida was a lesser quality substitute. The resin or juice of silphium was used to flavor condiments and sauces. Its aroma would be considered offensive to most today.

Roman cuisine was broad in scope. Pork and poultry were the dominant meats. Pliny informs us that the pig provided 50 different dishes. Songbirds were highly prized. Seafood, of every kind, milk and cheeses were common. Vegetables of every sort were eaten, cabbages and lettuce, radishes and turnips, squashes and pumpkins, melons and asparagus, lentils and beans. Wines and fruit from all sections of the Mediterranean area. Olives and dates. Even truffles and mushrooms.

The most striking feature of Roman cuisine, doubtless, was the manner of its eating. The satirists Martial, and Macrobius, Juvenal and Pliny the Younger leave us some pretty lurid descriptions.

Dining was concentrated in one huge and elaborate meal late afternoon—the eighth or ninth hour—called the *cena*. The Roman of imperial days rose with the sun, took a drink of water and went about his days work. At noon he partook of a light, usually cold meal, such as bread and cheese. After his afternoon bath he was ready for his big meal.

Typically there would be nine for dinner (the Greeks had five). They reclined on couches, three to a couch, around three sides of a square table (sometimes round) with one side open for serving the food. The tops of the couches were a few inches higher than the table. Each diner had a napkin placed at the head of the couch to protect it from soiling. The diners reclined on one elbow freeing the other hand for eating. Romans ate with their hands. A knife and spoon were the only utensils. The couch of honor was opposite the empty side and the place of honor was the one on the right. The couch to the left took precedence over the one on the right.

A full dress *cena* consisted of at least seven courses—the hors d'ovres, three entrees, two roasts and the dessert or *secunda-mensa*. At huge banquets the courses were multiplied to a score or more. The Romans indulged in bizarre serving of their food. Macrobius describes a cena given by one Tremalchio where, among other excentricities, a large roast wild pig wearing a cap of freedom was brought to the table in a tray. Around it lay suckling pigs made of simel cake with their mouths to the teats of the pig. Two baskets filled with fruit hung from its tusks. This was followed by a boiled calf with a helmet on its head. A servant dressed as Ajax launched a mock attack upon the helpless animal cutting off slices of meat which he passed among the diners with the point of a sword.

The crude manners of the diners were disgusting. A guest thought nothing of overeating, leaving the couch to regurgitate and return to the table to repeat his gluttony. "They vomit to eat, and eat to vomit" wrote Seneca in contempt. Similarly with the wines which were usually taken after the desert. At times the drunken guest would not even leave the couch simply upending the contents of his stomach into a vase brought to him by a servant, and after a small pause resume drinking. The diners would belch with impunity. It seems there was more restraint with respect to the other end of the alimentary canal though it is reported that Claudius seriously considered issuing an edict authorizing such emission of digestive gasses openly and freely. More thoughtful minds, doubtless, prevailed to the contrary.

These gluttonous feasts of the Romans were, perhaps, not the rule. It must be recalled that ancient Rome was a money economy. Men grew rich quicker than they acquired manners. These plutocrats were indulging their egos as much as their desire for good dining. Pliny the Younger describes far more reasonable dinners in which the emphasis was on good food and stimulating conversation. Both Marial and Juvenal describe meals of moderation and delicious cuisine.

When the Romans conquered the Gauls they were appalled by the crude manners and basic food of the Celts. They induced them to drink from a cup instead of Aurock's horns and human skulls. But everyone drank from the same cup. The Romans introduced the spices of Asia—pepper, cumin, ginger—to the Gauls. In exchange they imported from Gaul geese, hams, sausages, cheese and liver pates to enrich the Roman cuisine. Roman cuisine perished with the fall of Rome and Gaul, now emerging as France, reverted to more basic food and eating habits. Even the spices introduced by the Romans became scarce as trade with Asia declined and then virtually vanished after the rise of Islam.

French cuisine, the acme of European cooking, can trace its beginning to Charlemagne (circa 742–814 A. D.). At the end of the Merovingian reign the Franks ate in abundance, mostly meat. Pork and goose, boar and oxen killed in the hunt were cooked on spits. Large fish were grilled. Meat and fish were also boiled together in large cauldrons. The diners sat on straw or hay around low tables set near braziers with the spits and cauldrons from which they helped themselves. In the houses of the rich the food was served more formally on copper dishes with the host carving the meat and serving it to the guests. The Merovingians took pride in their plate and carried it with them from place to place. Barleywater and beer were the common drinks. Wine was drunk only occasionally.

Charlemagne was not exactly a gourmet but he did give the cuisine of the Franks a lift. He promoted the cultivation of fruit and vegetables which were introduced into meals that before were mostly meat. Meat, mostly game as Charlemagne was a great hunter, still predominated. The peacock was the king of the menu. How the peacock got to Europe from Asia at this time is lost in obscurity. It was cleverly cooked so as to retain the beautiful tail feathers to adorn the table. For some 500 years thereafter the peacock was the favorite of medieval cuisine though it reportedly has a tasteless and tough flesh.

The art of dining begins to evolve during Carolingian times. Flowers grace the table. People began to eat with the point of their knives, no longer their hands. They still drank out of the same goblet. "Mulled wine" was taken as an apertif. Charles, however, preferred cider from Normandy. Women were now permitted to join the men at the table. Two meals a day were taken. A light breakfast upon awakening and a big dinner around mid-afternoon.

Further progress was not made until after the Crusades made contact with the people of Asia and learned from them the use of spices, new fruits and vegetables and the refinements of dining. New spices and herbs like cinnamon, ginger, anise, cloves, thyme, rosemary, bay leaves came into widespread use. So did scallions and shallots. Rice and buckwheat were introduced from the East. Peaches, apricots, cherries, dates, lemons and melons were brought back by the Crusaders.

Pepper, which had disappeared with the Romans, was still scarce as it had to come from India. It was not until 1500 or so when pepper was once again more readily available. It is usually referred to in early medieval times as something precious. Law students today, unfamiliar with this history, are always baffled by the examples appearing in old law treatises like Blackstone where real property is transferred for one peppercorn—the peppercorn providing the necessary valuable consideration for the property to constitute a legal and binding contract. In Paris magistrates were bribed with a bag of peppercorns. Pepper is often said to have been an important motivation in the discovery of America when the Europeans sought a water route to India after the Ottoman Turks interrupted the caravans which brought pepper to Europe from India.

The first chef of note in France was Guillaume Tirel Taillevent (circa 1314–1395) who wrote the first French cookbook, the *Viandier*. Note his recipe for cameline sauce—pound ginger, plenty of cinnamon, cloves, cardamon, mace, long pepper if you wish, then squeeze out bread soaked in vinegar and strain all together and salt just right. It speaks for the growing scope of European cuisine after the Crusades. Soups were the favorites of the times. Women favored soup. They felt it kept their chins petit. Chewing meat was thought of as inelegant and deforming to women's jaws. Joan of Arc was reputed to have subsisted on soups—four or five at a meal. It should be noted, however, that the soups of those days were heavier in meat content than those of modern times, more akin to stews.

Catherine de Medici ushered in a great era in French cuisine. She was only 14 when she arrived with a battalion of cooks, ladies in waiting and other escort on October 20, 1553, to marry Henry II. Italy was more advanced in cuisine, particularly in the art of dining, than France at this time. Catherine introduced earthenware from Urbana, glass from Venice, enamelware and silver for the table. Her ladies dressed gayly for dinner. Music accompanied dining.

The fork was still not in use, but was introduced toward the end of the 16th century during the reign of Henry III. Its use was called forth by the ruffs men wore around their necks and wrists. The meat was brought to the mouth by forks to avoid soiling this new fashion in clothes. The knives thereafter became rounded as it was no longer necessary for them to be pointed for picking up meat.

Salad and dessert dishes multiplied. Vegetables were still minimized. Catherine loved artichoke. Asparagus was not yet part of the diet. The emphasis was still on meat. It was the great era of veal, which has thereafter always remained a favorite in Europe. Poultry and fish dishes were popular. The gamey peacock was a thing of the past, replaced by the guinea-hen as the favorite. But desert was king inspired by frangapani which Catherine brought from Italy.

Wine drinking was still a thing of the future. Francois I promulgated an edict in 1536 against drunkeness which provided for cutting off a person's ears after the fourth offense. A person could eat himself sick and a few did, but dared not overindulge on wine.

Dinners revolved about three courses. First course of soups, pates and fricassees; second course of meats and fish and third course of desserts. The dishes in each course could be and were usually many.

Soups were still popular. And what soups. Meals in themselves. Jehan Malvergne, provost of Paris, entertained friends at a dinner on October 30, 1563 where 5 soups were served. The first soup was made of two capons; the second of four partridges; the third of cockscombs and pigeon's kidneys; the fourth of minced capon; and finally, the fifth of partridges and lentils!

Olivier de Serres (1539–1619) broadened French cuisine in scope at this stage by promoting vegetable dishes. He fostered market-gardening to provide fresh vegetables for the table. He was the first to praise the food qualities of the potato introduced into Europe by the Spaniards from America. Serres published two books, at the urging of Henry IV, in 1600 on the art of good living, *Theatre de l'Agriculture* and *Mesnage des Champs*. He discusses cereals, meat, wine and other beverages, fruit and vegetable culture, and sundry advice on homemaking.

French cuisine was now ready for the Age of Louis XIV (1638–1715). The efforts of Olivier de Serres bore fruit. Market gardens and orchards flourished everywhere to increase food supplies. Vineyards produced good wine. It could now be drunk without spicing it. Recipes multiplied where they nearly reached in number and quality, those found today. Roasts and soups were deemphasized in favor in smaller portions of meat accompanied by vegetables and salads. Little suppers for six to eight people became fashionable.

Further innovations were made. Louis loved oysters and, once again, as in Roman times, they became popular. Dom Pierre Perignon (1638–1715) discovered the secret of making champagne. At first no bottles could hold the volatile stuff and it took another fifty years before English glass blowers perfected dark bottles thick and strong enough to contain it for commercial transport. Marie Theresa introduced chocolate as a drink, which had already been popular for years in Spain and Austria. Tea from China came to light. But coffee took the day.

The origin of coffee is somewhat obscure. It was discovered either in Ethiopia or the Saudi Arabian penninsula, as legend has it, when a shepherd boy observed his sheep becoming giddy after eating the berries of a certain tree or bush. How it then found its way into Mid-Eastern cuisine is not clearly known. In the middle of the 14th century it found its way from Aden to Mecca, whence to Constantinople where the first coffee house was established in 1554. From there it wend its way into Europe, first to Italy in 1580, and then as far as England, where the first coffee house appeared in Oxford in 1650.

Coffee was first imported from Yemen, and called Mocha, after its port city. The Dutch transplanted it to their colony in Java. Hence, the name Java for coffee, as European and American markets were supplied from there until coffee growing was spread to Central and South America in the 20th century.

Louis drank it for the first time in 1644. By 1700 cafes sprung up everywhere. The potato got another promotional boost from Antoine-Auguste Parmentier. Potatoes were referred to as "parmentiers". It now took it's place as one of the prime vegetables of French cuisine. Beefsteak and French fried potatoes were destined to become first in the hearts of French gourmets. But in Louis' day the first dish of the table was goose stuffed with various fowl (quail, pheasant, pigeons, woodcock and so on) and aromatic herbs. Many passed up the goose for the forcemeat.

A certain Beauvillier opened the first restaurant in 1782. The word originated earlier with a vendor of soups on the rue de Bailleul, a man named Boulanger, who called his soups "restoratives" (restaurants). It's time had come as there was no place for a visitor or itinerant to eat in Paris. Food preparation had now become specialized. There were not only cooks and bakers (bread was the mainstay of the *hoi polloi*), but confectioners, patissiers and other culinary specialists.

The 19th century, a hundred years of revolution and turmoil that ushered in the industrial era, was not particularly innovative. The Revolution interferred with good eating. Napoleon was no gastrome. A notable advance was the invention of preserving food in sealed containers after subjecting it to heat by Francois Appert in 1795. Appert, however, was deprived of the fruits of his invention when the English substituted the tinned metal can for the glass jar and patented it. Poor Appert received only the title of Benefactor of Humanity from Napoleon together with a purse of 12,000 livres and died in poverty.

Chicken a la Marengo came about accidentally during Napoleon's Italian campaign (June 14, 1800). When the Austrians interdicted the army's canteens the chef substituted olive oil for butter to sauté the chicken and added Maderia and white wine to the sauce. It was an instant success. Unfortunately he died in the fighting that evening. Another great chef who died in the Napoleonic wars was Laguipiere, who General Murat took with him on the Russian campaign. Laguipiere froze to death in Vilna during the ignominious retreat of 1812.

Talleyrand was a great epicure. He supervised his kitchens personally every day. His friend, a lawyer and economist, Anthelme Brillat-Savarin wrote a fine book on gastronomy *La Physiologie du Gout*. In addition to its renown as a treatise on the art of cuisine it is full of philosophical aphorisms. Among others, two comes to the fore—(1) Animals feed; man eats; only a man of wit knows how to dine and (2) By making man eat to live, the Creator invited him to do so with appetite and rewards him with pleasure. Talleyrand sponsored Marc-Antoine Careme who, in addition to being a renowned chef, was the creator of the "center piece" for the dining table. Some of his pieces for state dinners covered several square yards. A boiled red lobster was a favorite prop for his centerpieces.

Louis XVIII (1755–1824) was a distinguished gourmet. He created several renowned dishes of his own—*La Cotelette Louis XVIII* and *L'Ortolan Restauration*. Chateaubriand with bearnaise sauce came into being. It was invented by Montmireil, chef to Monsieur de Chateaubriand.

The Golden Age of French cuisine was, perhaps, reached during the Second empire. Like his predecessor Napoleon III contributed little. But men of letters took a genuine interest. Restaurants flourished. Dumas wrote a cookbook. Flaubert titillated his readers with cuisine in his novels (for instance, the wedding feast in *Madame Bovary*). The short stories of Merimee, *the Souveniers of Maxime* and others abound in descriptions of good food. George Sand's dining room at Nohant was noted for its haute cuisine. Musset, Chopin and other artists dined at Nohant. Rossini married his cook and invented *Tournedos a la Rossini*. He also lost a fortune trying to make macaroni.

How then best to describe and characterize French cuisine as it evolved over the thousand years of history from Charlemagne to the Second empire. From the gourmand meals of numerous roasts and countless soups it evolved into the gourmet meals of five courses or so with wine—always—at every meal.

First the Hors d'oeuvres. These sometimes comprise a meal in themselves. Pate de foi gras is doubtless number one in this respect. Artichoke with hollandaise sauce is another great hor d'oeuvre. Vegetable salads, canapes, fondues, quiche Lorraine, timbales are others. The next course is soup. Onion soup predominates. A tossed lettuce salad with vinagrette sauce (vinegar and oil) follows.

The main course is meat or fish. The latter is sometimes served as an extra course between soup and the meat dish. Beefsteak and French fried potatoes is the favorite dish. Chateaubriand (center cut of the filet) and bearnaise sauce or tornedos (an inch cut of a filet end) are the preferred steaks. Lamb chops also rate high. But these choice meats are expensive as France is not a prime beef raising country. Meat of lesser quality (old cows and hens) is, therefore, the mainstay of French cuisine. It is here where the art of French cuisine reaches its pinnacle. Slow cooking and sauces of meat stock, herbs and wine turn the inferior meats and fish into supereb creations. The wine flavors the recipe as the alcohol evaporates in the heat. Beef bourguinon and coq au vin lead the wide array of such dishes. Cooked in dry red wine (about 3 hours for the beef and 1 hour for the chicken) with onions, garlic, mushrooms, bay leaf, thyme, and other ingredients an aromatic tenderized meat dish with sauce is achieved. These two dishes seem to be better in the home than a restaurant. They improve with time and are better when reheated the next day or so.

Sauces are also prepared separately to accompany or finish meat or fish cooked otherwise. There are two basic sauces, a white sauce called bechamel and a brown sauce of several varieties like bordelaise, perigourdine, madiera and others. Bechamel is made primarily from milk and is used mainly with fish and fowl. The brown sauces are made of meat stock, red or madiera wine, and scallions, shallots, truffles and mushrooms. They are used with red meat and poultry. Sauce bearnaise to accompany chateaubriand is made with white wine, white vinegar, butter, egg yolks, shallots, tarragon and parsley. It is difficult to make as it takes experience to blend the butter with the other ingredients. It is seldom made at home. Lastly there is sauce bigarade for roast duck. The duck juice (fat removed) is mixed with orange juice and orange rinds (or orange marmalade) butter and flour. For a superb bigarade the sauce is flavored with curacaco or grand mariner.

Two other renowned sauces need mention: mayonnaise and hollandaise. The first is made from egg yolks and vegetable oil; the last from butter, egg yolks, milk, lemon juice and arrowroot. They accompany fish, eggs and vegetables in the main. Mayonnaise has achieved a wide variety of uses.

There are countless other variations of these basic sauces. The sauce is the essence of French cuisine. French cooking is characterized by its diversity. It is the sauce that gives the dish its distinctive flavor ranging from the smooth and delicate harmony of butter, cream and eggs to the full-flavored and sturdy mixtures of meat stock, wine and herbs. There is an old saying "La sauce fait passen le poisson"—the sauce is what makes fish palatable. And so it is with inferior cuts of meat. Not only palatable but delicious. French recipes are strict on the removal of fat and oil from the pan before using the meat stock for the sauce. French cuisine is, consequently, not oleaginous in character and quality.

A popular French dish that is not considered part of haute cuisine is cassoulet. It is a meat and bean dish. There are a score or more recipes but three are foremost; the cassoulets of Toulouse, Carcassonne and Castelnaudary. The cassoulet of Castelnaudary is the original recipe—white beans, fresh pork, ham or pork knuckle, some sausage meat and fresh bacon. In Carcassonne they add mutton and sometimes partridge. In Toulouse they add preserved goose or duck. It is the duck or goose that many feel makes a superior cassoulet. Balzac, Flaubert, Dumas and Anatole France have extolled the cassoulet in their novels. Anatole France in *Histoire Comique* sings the praises for one Clemence who "replenishes the pot sometimes with goose, sometimes with pork, sometimes she puts in a sausage or some haricot beans, but it is always the same cassoulet. The basis remains and this ancient and precious substance gives it the savor which one finds in the paintings of the old Venetian masters, in the amber flesh tints of their women. Come, I want you to taste Clemence's cassoulet."

For dessert the French prefer fruit and cheese, though they have created some outstanding desserts. Crepes Suzette for instance. It is a thin omelet, rolled or folded, covered with a sauce of fresh orange juice and orange base liquer. Grand Marnier is best for both crepe and the suzette. It is served hot and flaming with brandy. It is not only ceremonial, and served on special occasions, but subtly tasteful, especially when garnished with whipped cream and shaved chocolate.

The cheeses of France are renowned. Three of the foremost are roquefort, brie and camebert. Roquefort is made of ewes milk and stored in caves where certain organisms invade it to form veins and pockets of blue mold, Today the process is augmented by layering the cheese with molded bread. Brie is also made from the milk of sheep. It is creamy soft with a white or reddish white crust. Both these great cheeses date back far into history. Roquefort may have been discovered in prehistory as early man lived in these caves where the cheese is now made. The famous Lascaux caverns are among these caves where Cro-Magnon left many remarkable paintings. Pliny the Elder writes about a prize cheese from Nimes, a Roman colony in Gaul. While one cannot be sure it is roquefort it probably was as Nimes was situated in the roquefort region. On the other hand it could have been brie as Pliny does not mention blue mold in the cheese. The Romans were fond also of the cheshire and cheddar cheese of their colony in Britain and imported large quantities of it to Rome.

Charlemagne is credited with popularizing both these great cheeses. It is said that on his way back from his battle with the Saracens he stopped at a monastary in Aveyron to rest and refresh his troops. The Bishop served him the blue molded ewes milk cheese. The king began by removing the mold but was told it was the most tasty part. He liked the cheese so much he requested the Bishop to send two cart loads to Aix-la-Chapelle each year for his table. Similarly, on his way back from the conquest of Lombardy he stopped at the monastary of Reuilen-Brie. Here too, the story goes, he was told not to remove the crust, which he and his knights started to do to get at the soft center. The great king was so impressed with this variety of ewes milk cheese that he ordered a shipment of it to his capital twice a year.

Camebert, a later addition, has a similar history. It is mentioned in history as far back as the 12th century. There is a statue to one Mme. Harel, a farmer's wife, in the village of Camebert who is reputed to have perfected the recipe for the cheese. It was popularized when Napoleon was passing through Normandy and was served the soft aromatic camebert. It is said he found it so delectable that he jumped up to kiss the waitress, who served it to him, on the cheek. He had it brought to Paris where it became popular. Unlike the other two camebert is made from whole (the richer the better) cows milk. It is similar to brie. It must be eaten at the peak of ripeness as it is ammonial and distasteful thereafter.

There are many more cheeses in France, but most do not leave their district as they either do not travel well or are produced in limited quantities. They are made of cows, ewes or goats milk. It is an epicurean delight to travel through Ille de France and sample the local cheeses after a good dinner.

Black coffee, in demi-tasse, is taken after dinner, with brandy or liquers. The coffee is strong though not as strong as Italian espresso. The coffee bean is roasted to a dark brown kernel. For breakfast coffee is taken with milk. A french breakfast is light. A brioche or croissant with jam, marmalade or honey. Lunch and dinner, mostly the dinner, comprise the main food intake in France.

There is no meal in France without wine. Wine orchestrates the meal. It enhances the flavor of food. It is not fattening. It is rich in minerals and vitamins. No one drinks the great wines at every meal. Vin ordinaire, or good wines, accompany most meals. French wines are mostly dry—that is, not sweet.

The great wines are the bordeauxs and the burgundies. Both vary with the weather, especially the bordeauxs. There are great vintages, lesser vintages but seldom bad ones. Red wines are always dry; white wines are both dry (chablis) and sweet (sauterne). Rhone wines are also considered good to great, as are the white wines of Alsace. Lastly, but not least, there is champagne, the famous effervescent wine of France.

Contrary to popular opinion the French are not doctrinaire about which wines go with what dishes so long as it is good wine. But generally, white wine (dry) is served with fish and poultry; red wine with meat, poultry and cheese; rosé and champagne with any food. There is nothing wrong with taking a dry white wine with steak if the diner so prefers.

Though French cuisine is foremost there are other great or near great European dishes. Like Chinese and Indian cuisine with its regional variations European cuisine too has its national diversities. While it would be beyond the scope of this dissertation to discuss them in detail it will be in order to mention some of these other national characteristics of European cuisine. The Italians, who led the French in good cooking during the Renaissance, developed marvelous pasta dishes (fettuchini, ravioli, spaghetti), rely more on olive oil for cooking and make greater use of the tomato and pimento in their cuisine. Spanish cuisine too is based on olive oil, greater use of rice and more spices. Paella is one of Spain's great dishes. Italians and Spanish cooking tends to be more oleaginous than other European cuisine. Both countries produce good local wine.

German cooking is stout and hearty. Smoked sausages in great variety, frankfurters, blood and liver sausages (unsmoked), sauerkraut, pickled meats and vegetables and the like. Potatoes in several forms. Sweet and sour dishes permeate German cuisine. Seasoning is light with a bit of garlic, a few herbs and caraway seeds. Czech cooking is similar. The Czechs, in addition, excel in pastries. The famous Czech kolachies filled with cottage cheese and apricot, prune and cherry and other marmalades. Poppy seed filling is also popular. Apricot, plum and cherry trees line the roads and village streets of old Bohemia. No one developed the new fruits brought back by the crusades better than the Czechs. Czech and German beers are the best in the world. For the gourmet interested in the exotic, a meal at the restaurant of the famous Pilsner brewery consisting of sauerkraut with fresh pork, ham and sausage, potato dumplings and a Stepanska (baked omlet) with apricot marmalade for dessert taken with litre size glasses of draft beer from the famous brewery is a truly memorable event.

Hungarian cuisine is characterized by the famous goulashes in sour cream or tomato paste sauces spiced with paprika (sweet red pepper). Chicken paprika is the most famous dish. Equally renowned are desserts like palacsintos (crepes) with different cream and cheese fillings and strudels. Austrian cuisine, however, is most famous for its sweets and cakes. There is apple strudel of world fame. Scores of tortes with nut, poppyseed, apricot and other fillings and various icings. Most renowned is linzer torte (a rich egg and butter dough flavored with raspberry, strawberry or currant jam). Like the Hungarians the Viennese also cook with sour cream and paprika. But their most notable contribution to European cuisine is weiner schnitzel, thin slices of veal dipped in an egg yolk and flour batter and fried in butter.

The place of veal in European cooking requires further comment. Due to lack of grazing areas the Europeans had to kill bull calves. They could not afford to raise them as steers for prime beef as do the Americans, Argentines and others blessed with abundant grazing grounds. Furthermore, the ox, as a draft animal, was superseded by the horse in Europe. Hence, the shortage of prime beef and an abundance of veal in continental Europe. Veal has therefore become a far more important meat in the cuisine of European countries, particularly, the German speaking peoples.

The English speaking people, who were dominant in technological development, have been the last creative in the art of cuisine. Few indeed are the British or American men of letters and the professions who took the time to write a cookbook or treatise on gastronomy. The English have been so preoccupied with their empire that they were mostly indifferent to food. But even so, the English made some notable contributions to European cuisine. The English roast beef dinner is not to be slighted. The Scotch have contributed fish for breakfast. Kippers are the most famous, but poached finnan haddie, well buttered, with scrambled eggs is something to remember. The Americans too have contributed little, albeit they, with the possible exception of Argentina and Paraguay, produce the best beef in the world. The best in American cuisine is the European cooking brought over from the "old country". The Americans have made a notable contribution in the old New England cooking based on rum, molasses and cornmeal. Boston baked beans is the American cassoulet. The Americans have been too preoccupied with technological and industrial development. Like the English they eat to live. The continental Europeans live to eat. Therein lies the explanation.

Indian cuisine is a symphony of spices. It is mostly vegetarian. Vegetables, fruits and dairy products form the basis of the Indian culinary art. The origin of vegetarianism in India is lost in obscurity (as are so many other things). The Vedas reveal that in ancient times the Hindus ate meat freely—goats, sheep, horse, buffalo, ox and barren cows. The milk cow, however, was not eaten and evenutally this proscription was sanctified by religion. In time even barren cows and oxen could not be eaten. It is believed, though, that the reason was economic as in China. As population grew grazing land became scarce. Agriculture needed the bullock and buffalo for power. Moreover, the Hindus, unlike the Chinese, became very fond of dairy products. Keeping the cow for its milk instead of its meat while utilizing the males for agricultural power made the best possible use of the animal.

Buddhism and Jainism dating from the 5th century B. C. were undoubtedly the main progeniters of vegetarianism with their doctrines of non-violence and respect for all life on earth. But the trend must have been gradual as the *Arthasastra*, the treatise on public administration written around 300 B. C., still refers to meat eating as normal and prescribes rules for slaughterhouses and meat inspection. Only later, when Ashoka (circa 277–232 B. C.) converted to Buddhism and accepted its humanitarian principles, did meat eating go out of favor. As Buddhism gripped all of India, particularly the rise of Mahayana Buddhism, vegetarianism became widespread. Fa Hsien, the Chinese pilgrim who came to India seeking Buddhist scriptures in the 5th century after Christ, reported that no respectable person ate meat in India.

Though Indian history (always meagre) does not mention it, it was probably the pressure of population on the available food supply that militated toward vegetarianism as much as Buddhist and Jain doctrine. It is estimated that the population of the Indian sub-continent was in excess of 100 million in the first millennium of the Christian era. It was doubtless therefore, a marriage of convenience between sheer economic necessity and religious doctrine for when Brahmanism supplanted Buddhism as the national religion again toward the end of the first millennium it continued the practice of vegetarianism.

Foreign invasion and rule reversed the trend, in part, during the second millennium. First came the Muslims who were meat eaters. Since the Muslims ate mostly mutton and fowl it was easier for the Hindus to accommodate to the change. Muslims eat beef (not pork) but it was not readily available in the Middle East and India. The British, later, were beefeaters and continued so in India. This the Hindus found difficult to reconcile to and few emulated their new rulers in this respect. Indian Muslims, of course, had no compunction in joining the British in their culinary predilection. But even today the Hindus who eat meat, especially beef, are a very small percentage of the population.

Indians derive their protein mainly from pulses—lentils, peas and beans. The lentils and other pulses are cooked into a thick soup or puree called dhal which accompanies every meal of rich and poor alike. The dhal is variously spiced for diversity and delectability.

Curries are the main feature of Indian cuisine. A curry is simply a highly spiced meat or vetegable dish. It may be dry or with a sauce. Most are stew like dishes. Unlike the European sauces which are thickened with flour, or the Chinese with starch, the curry sauces are thickened, generally, with onions. The onions are finely chopped or minced and fried with ghee or vegetable oil into a puree. This is the essential first step in preparing a curry sauce.

The essence of a curry, of course, is the spices. Contrary to western belief there is no such thing as curry powder. A mixture of spices for a curry dish is called masala. There must be hundreds of masalas in India as, herein, resides the art of Indian cooking. The blending of spices for a particular meat, seafood or vegetable in order to bring forth its natural flavor or temper an overpowering characteristic comprises the culinary art of India.

Indian cooks (mostly men) prefer to blend the individual spices as they prepare the curry, but for convenience some of the most commonly used spices are blended into a masala beforehand (say) a mixture of cinnamon, cloves, cardamom, cumin, nutmeg and mace. It was such a masala that the British brought back to Europe and sold as curry powder. There is nothing wrong with this practice but the spice mixture does deteriorate very fast and loses much of its freshness in a few months. Also, British merchants, for the sake of profit often used inferior ingredients. Curry powder permits no flexibility in the preparation of curry, but then, for the European or American amateur with curries it probably makes little difference.

Curries are said, or believed, to be hot, and some are hot. Most, however, are a subtle blending of spices neither hot or bland. What makes a curry hot is "chili" pepper, or cayenne, in the masala. It can therefore be easily controlled and Indian hosts usually restrict the cayenne in the masala when entertaining foreign guests not accustomed to chili peppers.

Black pepper is indigenous to India and is widely used in masalas. It has been since time immemorial. It is nowhere as hot as chili pepper. Chili peppers, however, originated in Mexico, and did not enter into Indian cooking until after the discovery of America. A "hot" curry is, therefore, a recent development in the culinary art of India.

Indian cuisine utilizes a wide variety of spices. There are a score or more of them. Most of them are grown in India, but the Indians have always been quick to add to their indigenous repertory. Nutmeg, mace and cloves were imported from Java when the south Indians colonized Southeast Asia during the first millennium of the Christian era. Coriander and cumin reached Asia from the eastern Mediterranean during Roman times. Chili pepper and paprika came from Mexico more recently.

The spices are used primarily to provide a wide range of flavors to titilate the palate. But they also possess nutritional and peptic qualities. Chili peppers (cayenne) and pimentoes (all spice) abound in vitamin C. Coriander, cardomom, cinnamon and cloves are antiseptic. The latter two are powerful germicides. This is important in connection with meat preservation in the tropics. Nutmeg and mace mitigate colic. Anise or fennel and cardamom are carminatives. Their seeds are passed around after an Indian dinner to aid digestion. Saffron and tumeric, in addition to flavor, impart color to the curry dishes. Food colorings (tomato red) are also used for eye appeal in Indian cuisine.

Spices are extremely aromatic. The aroma in a kitchen or home where a curry is cooking or has cooked is an experience that can stimulate even the most jaded appetite. The spice section of an old country store still lives in the memory of most Americans.

Mutton and chicken are the meats normally used for curries. Except for Bengal and the Malabar coast seafood is not generally part of Indian cuisine. Vegetable curries are many and varied, but the potato, bringal (egg plant), cauliflower, fresh peas and yams are the popular ones. A notable vegetarian curry is panir matar consisting of Indian milk cheese, cut and fried in quarter inch cubes, and fresh shelled peas with the usual onion and masala (slightly hot) sauce. Khoa matar is similar, but with dried fresh whole milk substituted for the cream cheese.

Spices are used to flavor meats and vegetables without a sauce. Koftas (meat balls) and kabobs mostly made of lamb or mutton, sometimes beef, are very popular with non-vegetarians such as the Muslims. Europeans in India, of course, enjoy this food. Among these grilled dishes is the famous tundoori chicken. Tundoori cooking is a specialty of Indian cuisine found primarily in the north, especially the northwest frontier which is now Pakistan. It is doubtless the result of Muslim (mostly Persian) influence.

The tundoor is an oven built into the ground about four feet deep and two feet in diameter. It has a baked clay semi-spherical top with a twelve inch or so opening. The tundoor is filled half full with charcoal and ignited several hours before cooking. The temperature must be around 1000° F. The chicken (also mutton and large whole fish) is impaled on a stout iron skewer five feet long with a looped end for handling so that when thrust into the charcoal it is suspended a foot or so above the hot coals. In 10–15 minutes it is fully cooked.

Equally important is the marinating and spicing of the meat prior to cooking. The chicken is skinned. Two or three deep cuts, to facilitate the marinating are made across the breasts and thighs. It is then submerged in a marinate sauce of yogurt, lime juice, peppers, tumeric and tomato red for coloring for four to twelve hours before cooking. The result is a tender white meat on the inside with a reddish-brown outside. Fresh lime juice, ghee, ground black cumin seeds and other spices are sprinkled on the grilled chicken.

A semi-leavened bread called nan accompanies the tundoori meat. It is slapped against the inside of the semi-spherical clay top appropriately wetted with warm water to adhere. Just before it is ready to drop off it is removed by the cook fully baked. Hot and pungent pickles or chutneys complete the tundoori meal.

Tundoori recipes vary. Most are secrets passed on from father to son. Some marinate only with lime juice. The spices vary. The foregoing is the recipe and method of preparation used in the renowned Moti Mahal restaurant in Old Delhi. The chef is a Punjabi Sikh, a refugee from Lahore after the partition, who reestablished his restaurant in Delhi in the early 1950's. Another famous tundoori restaurant is Gaylords in New Delhi. Gaylords have opened tundoori restaurants in New York, Chicago and San Francisco.

Indian breads are unique, mostly unleavened or semi-leavened. They are made of wheat. Wheat and rice are the main cereal grains of India in the ratio of approximately one to two, respectively. Wheat is grown in the north; rice in the south and east.

Indian breads are eaten for nourishment and food handling. The Hindus do not use knives and forks; they eat with their right hand. Today, of course, upper class English speaking Indians use cutlery and china for dining. The flat unleavened bread is used as a scoop to transport the curries and other food to the mouth.

The most common is the chapati, a whole wheat pancake type bread much like the Mexican tortilla. A puffed up type called a phulka is eaten by the more affluent. Chapatis are unleavened and baked on a hot griddle without grease. There is also a whole wheat unleavened bread fried in ghee called parautha. A deep fried bread mixed of white and whole wheat flour is called puri. Finally, there are the tundoori breads like nan already discussed. They are semi-leavened and the dough is made with white wheat four, milk and butter and eggs. Rice is extremely popular even in the wheat growing areas of the north. Indian pilaus are famous. Pilaus are spiced and garnished rice dishes. The rice is boiled until half cooked and then steamed until finished. This leaves the kernels plump and free. It is then mixed (or cooked) with vegetables, cheese or meat, spiced with varying masalas and garnished with raisins, nuts and fruit. Matar pilau, a popular dish, is rice, peas and spices garnished with roasted almonds, cardamoms, raisins and other condiments. Pilaus are a Mughal influence. The Mughals were Persophiles bringing with them many Persian recipes. The Persians were very fond of mixing fruit and nuts with their meat and rice dishes. Pilaus, as other dishes deriving from Muslim influence, are most common in the north.

An Indian meal without dairy products is unthinkable. First, dishes are prepared and cooked in ghee. Ghee is clarified butter. When boiled, butter loses moisture and protein residues and keeps without spoiling for months even in the heat of India.

Yogurt is served with rice and curries at every meal. Indians believe that yogurt has antiseptic, carminative and digestive attributes much needed in the hot and moist climate of India. Mention has already been made of Indian dried milk and milk cheese in the preparation of curries.

Desserts too are made mostly from these milk products. Gulab Jaman is one of the outstanding desserts of India. It consists of spherical balls made from a mixture of dried whole milk (khoa) and Indian soft cream cheese (chenna) cooked in an aromatic rose-flavored (gulab) transparent syrup made from granulated sugar. Sugar cane, incidentally, was first grown in India and brought to Europe by the Arabs. These light brown white centered balls submerged in the aromatic transparent syrup are a delight to the eye and taste. Another savory dessert is the Bengali sweet rasgulla. Rasgullas are white, spongy balls an inch or so in diameter made from chenna floating in a transparent syrup flavored with rose and kewra essence. Kewra is a flower from which an aromatic essence is derived. Burfi is a combination of Khoa and sugar, in a 4:1 preparation, in which almonds, pistachios, grated carrots, shredded coconut and other ingredients are incorporated. It is served in flat half inch or so squares covered sometimes with gold or silver foil which, of course, adds eye appeal and bespeaks the affluence of the host.

Indians made a type of ice cream before it was invented in Europe. Kulfi is made of milk, almonds and pistachios frozen in a conical shaped mold 4 to 5 inches in length immersed in a freezing mixture of ice, salt and nitre. Today it is frozen in a refrigerator. Kulfi is served with a corn flour vermicelli called phaluda. There are other ice creams made with milk and eggs and flavored with carmel, bananas, lime and other ingredients. Indian sweets are not all made of milk. There are rice puddings, halvas and other very rich and sweet desserts. Fruits and nuts, too, are plentiful. In this respect nothing supersedes the mangoe. There are said to be a thousand varieties, which must, of course, be taken as hyperbole. Mangoes are in season during the summer and are frequently served as dessert. Mangoes are used liberally to make chutneys and pickles to accompany curries and other foods.

Tea is the most popular beverage in India. It is taken with milk and sugar, hot not cold or iced. Tea is not indigenous; it was brought to India from China by the British in the late 18th century. Coffee is next in popularity; grown and favored in the south. Limeade (called nimbo-pani) is the popular cold drink. Wine and whiskey are British influences; a devout Hindu does not partake of alcohol. But westernized Indians frequently imbibe.

Indian cuisine too has its regional variations. The south is most vegetarian. Its curries are hot and spicy. Fish dominates Bengali cooking. With the further exception of the Malabar coast, fish is not very important in the diet of India. The Bengalis are also famous for their sweets. Indian cuisine in the north and northwest is characterized by grilled and curried meat dishes due, in large measure, to the heavy Muslim influence in this area. In between these major areas are many other local variations. In Kashmir, for instance, the influence of Persian cooking is great and there can be found some extraordinary lamb kabob and curry dishes.

The art of dining did not attain the refinement of that in China and latter day Europe. Due to a predilection for cleanliness the Hindus ate their food off palm leaves and the like and disposed them after each meal. Food was taken with the hands, which had to be thoroughly cleansed before eating. Furthermore, food could be taken and handled only with the right hand. The left hand was used, exclusively again, for eliminatory hygiene and could not touch food lest it pollute it. Muslim influence brought little uplift, but western influence has now brought porcelain and silverware to India for dining. There is, however, a compartmentalized or divided metal dinner dish that is widely used in India suitable for the many and varied foods (served all at once buffet style on a large table).

Middle East cuisine has been effected profoundly by religion. The Muslim proscription against eating pork coupled with the fact that the area is not conducive to beef grazing has narrowly limited meat eating to mutton and fowl. Mutton is, doubtless, one of the fattiest meats. Middle East food, therefore, tends to be oleaginous.

Noteworthy in this respect is the fat-tailed sheep. This particular animal has a tremendous flat tail of almost pure fat, which the Arabs sometimes place on a wheeled trailer while the sheep is still alive to protect it from damage. The tail is roasted with the sheep and served in chunks of rice. Another startling feature of a bedouin feast on a fat-tailed sheep is the offer of the eye of the roasted sheep to the guest of honor. Many a foreign oil executive has quaked at this gesture.

The Persians, from whom the Arabs acquired most everything, introduced fruit and nuts to accompany, perhaps mitigate, the fatty dishes based on mutton. And from ancient time Persians adopted the use of spices and herbs from China and India in their cuisine. This was passed on to the Arabs and other Muslims in the Middle East. The combination of fruit, nuts, sour cream and spices has resulted in some delectable dishes.

The grilling of meat—lamb and chicken—is a highlight of Mid-East cuisine. Everyone likes Shish Kabob. There are many kabobs, including a type made of ground meat. Koftas (meat balls) are also popular. In fact, the famous tundoori cooking of India has Persian antecedents.

But it is the wonderful sweets, made of pistachios, almonds, dates, honey and other ingredients, that are the best part of Middle East cooking. Baclava, made of minced pistachio and almond paste flavored with orange-flower water and sugar in filah (layers of fine pastry), is world renowned. And there is makroud (a date and honey deep fried pastry), sutlage (a milk, sugar, corn flour, orange-flower—water pudding), kishkishat (a cream filled pastry covered with a syrup of sugar and orange-flower-water and chopped walnuts) and others.

The Koran also forbids the use of alcohol. There cannot be European type dining in the Mid-East. Needless to say this proscription is often honored in the breach as it attested by one (and many more) of Omar Kayyam's famous quatrains.

> A book of Versus underneath the
> Bough
> A Jug of Wine, a loaf of bread—
> and though
> Beside me singing in the
> Wilderness—
> Oh, Wilderness were Paradise enow!

THE ART OF LOVE

Nature structured the estrus cycle into life for the perpetuation of the species. One may ponder why this was necessary. The mixing of the genes is the first law of evolution. And as life became more complex, when the mixing of the genes came to be located inside the female body (reasons already discussed) first in the egg of the reptiles, then in the womb of animals, Nature was faced with the problem of achieving the execution of the gene mingling process lest the species fail to propagate. But life is not simply a matter of replication. It is a Parliament of Instincts, to borrow once again Konrad Lorenz's wonderful phrase. These instincts clash and conflict.

Before there can be replication there must be survival. Survival is, there-fore, the first law of life. Life preys upon life for survival. Even cannibalism is barely controlled by Nature's check mechanisms. To be sure, this varies in species. But it is most prevalent among the carnivores. Wolves and tigers have been observed to eat their young and mates. Instead of companionship and trust most animals live in fear of others. A female in nature will repel a mate particularly when borning and rearing the young. In many species sexual union, even with the female in estrus, is something akin to a battle. A female camel will attack the male with her teeth right after copulation. Every studmaster knows he cannot let his stallion approach a mare unsure of being in heat without a solid barrier between them. Zoologists who observed jaguars mating in the jungle found large devastated areas strewn with broken branches and brush where the sexual union occurred. This comes as no surprise to anyone who has witnessed (or been kept awake) by a pair of domesticated cats copulating in his back yard.

Nature found it necessary to compromise these conflicting instincts by placing the female in estrus when she is ovulating and ready to be impregnated with male gametes. All her other instincts are temporarily suspended (very temporarily in some species, to wit, the camel) and she takes on any and every male available to initiate the act of replication.

The males of the specie, who are everready for sexual connection, fight for access to a female in estrus. Here Nature designed the dominance instinct so that the best males of the species are most likely to breed the females. Fights (even unto death in some cases for Nature does not care in this respect) are common and legendary among the males of the specie for dominance in the mating season. The battle for dominance, however, usually ends in defeat not death.

That, oversimplified to be sure, is Nature's way of compromising the two essentials of life—survival and replication. The estrus cycle controls all higher life on earth except, again, that of man. How then did man emancipate himself from the estrus cycle. The answer, of course, is by his cultural evolution. As man lived more and more by the hunt he was forced to mitigate his biological survival instinct that is primarily individualistic and antagonistic towards others of his species. Cooperation and friendliness within the hunting group now became, in fact, more important to his personal survival. And as man moved out of Africa into the temperate zones of Europe and Asia where he was faced with recurring ice ages he was forced to depend, at times, almost exclusively on the hunt. This severe challenge not only generated his great intellectual *cum* technological devel-opment but promoted greater sociability with his fellow man. Moreover, the female became more dependent upon the male for survival as she was gravely handicapped with lesser physical strength and endurance necessary for the hunt (in sub zero weather) and preoccupation with child borning and rearing in the most inhospitable conditions of living on the edge of the glaciers. She could no longer find her own food or contribute to the food supply as a food gatherer as she could in Africa and other milder climates. In these difficult survival circumstances the human males could not afford to fight over possession of the females and the females could not hold themselves aloof sexually from the males. Cooperation and friendliness were now the important imperatives of the day. In this milieu the males had to temper their dominance instinct and the females had to become more cooperative with the males in the matter of perpetuating their kind. A social order began to evolve where all males were given access to the females and the females in turn became available to males at all times, not only when driven to it by Nature. This did not mean the end of the dominance instinct, however, as leadership based on merit was recognized by all the members of the hunting group for their common survival. In the Anglo-Saxon epic *Beowolf*, describing a basic society perhaps not too far afield from the paleolithic hunting group, it is said that a strong chieftan was obeyed by his friends and relatives with gladness as it brought them great joy and prosperity.

In due time men and women began to embrace in sexual union face to face. This must be rated as another milestone in the evolution of man. No other form of life makes such sexual connection as sexual union in nature is essentially an antagonistic act possible only in the truce provided by the estrus cycle. But as man became a social being he converted sexual union into an act of cooperation and friendship. The promotion of its enjoyment became the art of love, which has for better or worse played so important a role in the life and history of man.

One is led to the next question. Why is sexual union an enjoyable act. Is the enjoyment physical or psychological, that is, a product of man's intellectual development. There is no way to know whether sexual union is enjoyable to animals other than man. The very purpose of estrus would appear to refute enjoyment as an incentive to procreation. Moreover, many animal sexual unions are akin to violent conflict. Even the observation of domestic animals breeding gives no clear evidence of enjoyment. The female, at best displays an indifferent or benign attitude; the male a "driven" one. Man has, however, definitely elevated sexual union to an enjoyable experience in life and it can only be ascribed to his greater intellectuality which enabled him to enhance a basic necessity of life with psychic and emotional overtones. In this respect it is like food, where man has elevated a basic necessity into an art form through his cuisine and dining.

It would be wrong to conclude that man has achieved great order and discipline in his sexual behavior. He has, at the same time elevated it to the highest form of art and degraded it into cruelty and ugliness. But then, this is the way of man in all things he touches.

There would appear to have evolved a certain uniformity in sexual discipline, varying in strictness and laxity, among the higher human societies. The nexus of this discipline is pair bonding or marriage. The main objective of marriage is procreation and perpetuation of the specie. Within the marriage sexual freedom is normally complete. In fact, in keeping with male dominance the female is usually without freedom (according to law and mores though not otherwise) to deny sexual congress to the male. The English common law, as well as other legal systems, does not recognize rape in marriage. Modern legislation is starting to make some changes in this harsh rule.

Sexual union prior to marriage is usually forbidden. It is the crime of fornication. Sexual intercourse outside the marriage bond is likewise proscribed. It is the crime of adultery. The latter has always been considered the more heinous of the two.

Civilized societies have varied and vacillitated in the enforcement of the foregoing sexual discipline, most being satisfied with something less than strict compliance, recognizing or indulging the males propensity (some will argue biological instinct) to pursue sexual union with many females. In fact, most societies permit, again with varying laxity, prostitution to satisfy this sexual gregariousness of the male. A double standard has evolved and exists in most societies which permits greater sexual freedom for the male prior to and during marriage than to the female. A female is required or desired to be without any prior sexual experience before marriage. Strictures on the young female for the sake of chastity are imposed in most societies. Yet some of the less developed (in the technological sense) societies, such as the Samoan and others studied by Margret Mead, not only permit but promote sexual freedom of the young prior to marriage. On the other extreme the Puritans of New England fined and punished youth for infraction of the sexual code. Boys were fined and/or forced to marry the girl they seduced. Girls were put into stockades and even branded on the cheek so as to disgrace them publicly temporarily or for life. Adultery has also been dealt with harshly by the different societies. Death to both, more frequently the female, transgressors has been inflicted. Whipping, incarceration and other punishments were inflicted. In New England an adulteress was forced to wear the scarlet letter (a red A) around her neck for public humiliation. In the courtyard of the old castle in Prague stands an iron cage about four feet in diameter and six feet high where Charles IV locked any of his four wives caught in adultery subjecting her to public humiliation. To make her confinement more uncomfortable the floor of the cage is conical making standing on it very difficult.

Marriage has been buttressed by powerful taboos. Foremost is the taboo against incest. It is old and seems to have always existed. There is considerable controversy about its origin and meaning. It was probably established by men for the simple reason of maintaining sexual discipline within the close family or hunting group. Parents, children and siblings could not indulge in sexual relations without undermining any semblance of sexual discipline in the early human societies. To be sure, it is now known that inbreeding has the damaging result of multiplying genes producing human weaknesses, but early man did not possess this scientific knowledge. It works also the other way. In animal husbandry man has resorted to inbreeding to upgrade the productivity of domestic animals. Notable in this respect is the development of the Guernsey and Jersey cows.

A good example in history of the debilitating effects of inbreeding was the strain of hemophelia in the Hanoverian House. It culminated in the birth of a son Alexis to the last Russian Czar Nicholas II and his Hessian wife Alexandra Feodorovna, a granddaughter of Queen Victoria of England. Alexis was a hemophiliac in constant fear of bleeding to death. This situation enabled the clairvoyant and evil monk Rasputin to ingratiate himself with the queen (who had great influence over the Czar) resulting in the misrule that was one of the factors of the Russian Revolution.

On the other hand the Pharoahs of ancient Egypt married their sisters to perpetuate the dynasties. Egyptologists have ascribed the fall of the Pharonic dynasties to these "incestuous" marriages but modern research casts doubt on whether these brother-sister marriages were in fact, sexual unions. There is little or no hard evidence of children by these marriages. In fact, the historical evidence usually is otherwise. The famous queen Hatsepsut (circa 1501–1481 B. C.) was married to her half brother Thutmose II, but Thutmose III, the great empire builder of the 18th dynasty was the son of Thutmose by another wife in the harem. It is now thought probable that these brother-sister marriages were merely for the perpetuation of the royal line as decent was on a matrilineal basis in ancient Egypt.

Related is the taboo against endogamy, that is, marriage within the group, clan or broader social group. The obverse of endogamy is exogamy, that is, the requirement to marry outside the clan, caste or group. The taboo against endogamy was wider than incest as it forbade marriage within the group even though there was no blood relation. This taboo is harder to explain than incest.

An interesting anthropological school of thought postulates that the taboo against endogamy arose out of the taboo against cannibalism. That early man was cannibalistic is clear. Human bones were found, for instance, among animal bones in Choukoutien cave of Peking man. It is unlikely that Peking man buried his dead beneath the ground he inhabited. Moreover, the bones were split so as to get at the marrow. Homo erectus had to eat anything available to survive. Another human, particularly a stranger, was like an animal in this respect. It is not necessary, however, to look for anthropological evidence as there are countless instances of cannibalism in recorded history. The Aztecs sacrificed their war captives to Huitzilopotchli, their war god, and feasted on their bodies. The practice revolted

Cortez and his men. During the famine of eleventh century France men resorted to eating human flesh. If the monk Raul Glaber (circa 985–1046 A. D.) can be believed, he writes that bands of men roamed the countryside attacking wayfarers, mountebanks, strolling minstrels—strangers who would not be missed—killing them and selling their flesh in the nearest market. Little children were similarly abducted and killed for meat. Cannibalism exists even today in some of the vestigial savage societies of Africa and South America. Everyone is familiar with the cartoon of a white missionary sitting in a cauldron of boiling water, topee still on his head, surrounded by savages anxious to feast on him. In order to protect the hunting group against internicine cannibalism the taboo against eating one's kin was instituted. Since food and sex were closely associated and commingled in the mind of early man the taboo against cannibalism brought with it a taboo against endogamy.

Another theory holds that exogamy evolved in order to mitigate conflicts between groups of humans over hunting territories. Intermarriage tended to ameliorate these conflicts through blood ties and friendships. Whatever its origin the taboo against endogamy must have placed a severe restriction on sexual relations. The hunting groups in time confederated into tribes and even bigger social groups but in the beginning when there were only two moieties in a tribe half the persons were ineligible as sexual partners.

In due time this taboo reduced itself to simply a taboo against incest, though the ineligible mates were differently limited in diverse societies. Parents and children, brothers and sisters, uncles and aunts and first cousins are normally excluded mates. The endogamy taboo eventually took on a reverse meaning restricting marriage of persons of one's caste (as in India), race (the Jews), religion (catholics) or other group. Such endogamus groups are usually large so that no undue restriction is imposed upon marriage of its members.

Human marriage has been and is more so today primarily monogamous (pair bonding of male and female). There have been and still are other forms of sexual union—polyandry (one female with several husbands), polygamy (one male with several wives), concubinage (a male and female as the main bond with additional females of lesser status) and group families where the males and females establish one or more sexual liaisons with the group.

Polyandry seems to be an Asian phenomena. Most notable, and frequently studied, in this respect, are the Todas of India. A Toda female is married to a set of brothers. Prior to the birth of the first child one of the brothers is designated the "legal" father (usually the oldest) in the "bow ceremony". Thereafter he is the family head and the property descends through him. The Toda social structure is extremely complex (the buffalo herd has an important place). Too complex to detain us here. Suffice it to say that there are only a few hundred Todas living on some 500 square miles in the Nilgri Hills (a beautiful spot) of Madras. Their quaint marriage custom is, therefore, more a curiosity than a matter of substance. But polyandry has a larger history in India. There is some evidence it was more common in olden times. The great epic Mahabharata, which involves a struggle between two families for the hegemony of North India (circa 1400 B. C.) speaks casually of the marriage of Draupadi to the five Pandava brothers including the hero of the epic Arjuna. Polyandry was also known in Tibet and Mongolia.

Polygamy has been more widespread. The Koran sanctions up to four wives (not enough, of course, for caliphs, sultans, viziers and the like) giving polygamy a religious blessing among the Muslims. The Koran requires, however, that each wife be provided with a separate apartment, or home, which obviously restricts polygamy only to the ruling elite. But the harems of the potentates are legendary. In fact, it was carried to lengths where its *raison d'etre*, if it ever had any outside gratification of the male *macho*, was defeated as a busy monarch could not service several hundred wives for maximum procreation. At the same time the system assured that no other male could impregnate them by castrating the males who guarded and attended the seraglios. Castration did not necessarily assure against sexual connection between the eunuchs and the wives, but this did not apparently matter as greatly.

Polygamy, however, antidates mohammedanism and appears on the pages of history from the very beginning. The *raison d'etre* of polygamy, it would seem, would be a surplus of females in a society. When men began to war over the surplus generated by technological development, following the invention of agriculture, such situations resulted as war killed more males than females. The Middle East has been since the dawn of history such area where nations fought constantly over land, gold, and other riches. Polygamy seems to have thrived best in this region. On the other hand, polygamy has been widely practiced. Hindu kings had plural wives. So did the ancient Egyptians and Greeks. Charlemagne had many wives. Aztecs and Incas, developing independently across the seas, also practiced polygamy among the nobility.

This points up a characteristic feature of polygamy. It was usually the practice or the privilege of the ruling elite. And the reason for it, no doubt, was that it required wealth and leisure to support and maintain many wives. So while the ruling class might have indulged in polygamy the common man was monogomous. This striking characteristic of polygamy leads to the conclusion that it was motivated primarily by the dominance instinct and macho-ism of man and not for maximizing the procreativeness of the society. At the same time polygamy would not be out of line with the laws of evolution as dominant males were intended to propagate their genes with the greatest number of females possible.

A variation of polygamy is concubinage. A concubine cohabits sexually with a man but is not his legal wife for lineal purposes. This was practiced widely throughout Chinese history. The eunuchs, who kept guard over the palace harems consisting of hundreds of wives and concubines, grew into a strong political factor during China's history. Operating through the emperor to whom they had easy access and enlisting the support of favorite females of the harem they were able to challenge the scholars and gentry who comprised the ruling elite. Most notable of these eunuchs was Cheng Ho, already discussed in Chapter V, who built and commanded the famous Chinese navy of the early 15th century during the Ming epoch. How far down the social scale concubinage was practiced is not clear, but again, one can presume that it required some wealth to support additional females. Pearl Buck's *Good Earth* leaves the impression that a peasant who amassed some wealth promptly took on a concubine or two. Today, one hardly need add, the communists have eliminated this practice in China.

Concubinage was not confined to China. It has been practiced widely among mankind. The difference between polygamy and concubinage is merely one of form, not substance. The counterpart of the concubine in the western world is the mistress. Here, however, there is a difference. A mistress is illegal (adultery) while a concubine in most places has been legal.

Communal sexual union too has been practiced but to no great extent. It was usually part of the socialistic communities that sprang up from time to time as solutions of man's innate inability to live in peace and harmony with his fellow humans. While they varied considerably they usually held property in common, lived and raised their children cooperatively and practiced sexual freedom within the group. Notable, in this respect, have been Robert Owen's New Harmony in Indiana (1815–1827), the Onieda Community in New York (1848–1856) and others. Most failed because the participants found they could not get along any better in communal living than in the traditional nuclear family. The most recent example of such communal living is the Kibbutz in modern Israel. It appears to be somewhat more successful than the others. While sexual union is more open and free most sexual cohabitation tends towards pair bonding within the Kibbutz.

The apparent failure of communal sexual cohabitation is a bit surprising. Logic would lead to the prognosis that mankind probably practiced communal sexual relations in the hunting group (and one must constantly remind himself that most of homo erectus and homo sapiens' life during the past million years was so spent). That pair bonding or monogamy evolved out of this cultural development lends force to the conclusion that such one to one sexual union satisfies a felt need of mankind.

Pair bonding, of course, is not uncommon in the animal world. It is not, however, the general practice of primates. It is found, more generally, among carnivores. Birds usually pair bond, but being reptiles they are man's cousin's once removed. When man descended from the trees and left his primate life behind he was forced to emulate the carnivores with whom he now competed for food. This required a home base, a lair or nest like that of the beasts and the birds. A home, it seems, led to the next step, pair bonding and the family as an economic and child bearing and rearing entity. Technological development with its accumulation of wealth fortified and completed the structure. To be sure, man has also practiced polygamy (polyandry can well be ignored) but it is doubtful that it ever effected more than a fractional minority of mankind. It was merely a luxury of the ruling elite. It is doubtful that it ever fulfilled any other need of the human race.

The family that evolved from monogamous marriage, was male dominated. It was patriarchial, patrilocal and patrilineal. Translated it means the family lived in a home owned and dominated by the father and lineal descent and property devolution was from father to son.

How, one may ask, did this come about. The nuclei of the family is the mother and child. Recognition of the fact that the father played some role in the procreation of the child did not come until, perhaps, after the partiarchial family was already established. Early man must have realized that sexual union was a prerequisite for procreation but the science of it was not fully known to man until the 19th century. There is reference in the Bible to male semen as "seed" presumably planted in the womb to beget a child. Even today in the vestigial savage societies sexual union is often viewed as a propitiatory magical act that causes women to conceive but not as an integral part of the procreative process. Malinowski relates that his explanation of the human reproductive process to Trobrianders was met with disbelief. They were convinced that sexual intercourse had nothing to do with the birth of a child. It would seem, therefore, that early human families were necessarily matrilineal as are all primate families today. Only the visible mother-child relation was known to early man.

Matrilineal societies exist even today but only in the retarded sectors of the human race. The Hopi Indians of Arizona, Trobriands of Australia, the Zunis of New Mexico and others trace lineal descent through the mother. The father does not own or dominate the home; he has mere sufference or visitation privileges. But these matrilineal societies are usually avuncular, that is, the mother's brother plays the role of the father and dominates the home of the mother-child family.

There are really no matriarchial, matrilocal and matrilineal families anywhere. The patriarchial family has certainly prevailed in Europe and Asia where human intellectual and technological development reached its zenith. The patriarchial family, doubtless developed when man's survival depended upon the hunt, when man struggled to survive against the onslaught of the glaciers. The woman and child were completely dependent upon the males for food supply. The males took advantage of the situation to gain dominance over the females and as pair bonding evolved the male viewed the mother and child as his property long, perhaps, before he knew that sexual union with the mother begot the child.

When the last glacier, the Wurm, receded about 10,000 years ago making edible vegetation possible women were able to forage once again for their food but by then it was too late to assert their independence from the males. After agriculture was invented (perhaps by the women) the males gained control over the surplus production further augmenting their domination over the females. The patriarchial family has certainly been the main social unit of man since the dawn of history.

The domination of the female by the male in the human community is, without doubt, the most cowardly and dastardly act in the story of man. Man has taken advantage of the woman's weaker strength and incapacity during the gestation, borning and nursing of the child by exploiting her labor and gratifying his lust for power and sex. Yet of the two the male is the least significant in the perpetuation of the human race. Nature could as well have disposed of him once he performed his function of fertilizing the female as it does with the male bee once he fertilizes the queen. Fortunately for the sake of sane humanity there were always men who treated women as equals, helpmeets and companions even in the most vicious and dissolute societies. Will Durant quotes the inscription he found on an ancient Roman tombstone where a Roman pays loving tribute to his wife of forty-one years and vows not to remarry. On the other hand, one must hasten to disabuse any impression that women would be any different in a matriarchial society. Whenever women gained positions of power in the ruling elite of a society they have displayed, at times, violence and viciousness toward others equivalent to man's dismal record in this respect.

History abounds in episodes where women were treated as chattle. Ashurnasirpal III (844–859 B. C.) records that in one foray against his enemies he captured the king's sister, the daughter of the nobles and all the other women—along with 5000 sheep, 2000 cows and 460 horses—for marriage and enslavement. The Rape of the Sabines is notable in history and art. Romulus, it is said, needed wives for his settlers in Rome. He invited the Sabines and other neighboring tribes to Rome for the games. During the races the men were driven off and the women were seized. The Sabine king declared war but Romulus persuaded him to share his kingdom. The two tribes merged. Presumably the women remained the property of the Romans.

It was not unusual in Graeco-Roman times for a woman of rank to be captured by pirates while on a voyage between two Greek isles and sold as a slave to a caravan merchant in the Mid East. While in the hands of the pirates and the caravan merchants she would be violated sexually with impunity. Thereafter fortune would determine her future. If a man of wealth and social standing purchased her she would end up in a comfortable life in a Mid-Eastern harem. On the other hand she might be kicked around ending up as a public prostitute in some Persian city. That she would ever return to her home and family was only remotely possible.

Nowhere have women been more abused by men than in war. The spoils of victory were always gold (and other wealth) and the sexual assault on the women of the vanquished. The psychology of rape in war is complex and deserves greater study but it is clear that more than sexual gratification has always been involved. There was always a large measure of intraspecial dominance connected with rape in war. First, was the dominance of women by men and in a situation where the normal forces of sexual discipline were absent the women of the vanquished became free prey for the victors. But equally important, the violation of the women of the defeated was a manifestation of the superiority of the victors. It differed little from the despoilation of their wealth. After all women were considered chattel.

Lest it be glibly concluded that rape is no longer a factor in modern war the record shows exactly the contrary. To be sure much of modern war is fought remotely and there is little contact with the civilian population. For instance, the trench warfare of the first World War provided little opportunity for rape. So did the naval and aerial bombings of World War II. But where contact with the civilian population occurred rape in modern war was as prevalent as at any other time in history. Mention need only be made of the Rape of Nanking by the Japanese in China in 1937 and the gang rape of Italian and German women by Moroccan soldiers fighting with the Allies, so forcefully dramatized by producer De Sica in the Italian movie *Two Women*. The widespread rape of Russian women by the German army is also well documented. And when the tides of war changed the Russians too committed their share of rape.

Most barbaric, however, have been the rapes of the present decade inflicted on the women of Bangladesh by the Pakistanis in 1971 and on the peasant women of Vietnam by the Americans the past decade. There were some striking similarities in the two situations. Both the Americans and the West Pakistanis were big and brutish men. The "enemy's" women were petite and delicate. The Bengali women are usually very beautiful. The genital disproportion was in itself the cause of much pain and suffering, especially in the case of very young and virginal girls and where gang rapes, of which there were many, were involved.

The record is, as always, very murky. The propensity of the military command to submerge or ignore reports of rape is renowned. It is estimated that upwards to 400,000 women were raped in Bangladesh during the period March, 1971, when the Bengalis revolted against West Pakistan rule, and early December when these domineering rapists succumbed ignominiously to the Indian army in seven days! These towering Pakistanis, who terrorized the little Bengali women (and men) of Bangladesh for nine months turned out to be cowards when confronted with the superior might of the Indian army. This inhumanity of man is characterized by the story of Khadiga, a 13 year old girl abducted by Pakistan soldiers while on her way to school with four other girls. All five were held captive for six months in a military compound in Mohammed'pur where each was regularly violated by two to ten soldiers daily. Other incidents of as many as 80 assaults a night on one girl have been reported. Girls and women from age 8 to 75 were assaulted sexually. Kamala Begum, a wealthy widow who thought she was "too old" to attract attention, was raped in her home one night by three Pakistani soldiers. And so the grisly record continues.

To compound the humiliation of the Bengali women their husbands, fiancees and prospective mates refused to accept them after their violation by the Pakistan soldiers. The Bengalis, like the West Pakistanis, are Muslims who normally adhere to a strict discipline of no pre-or extra marital sexual intercourse by their women. Mujibir Rahman, the leader of the Bengali rebellion and later Prime Minister of Bangladesh, tried valiantly to remove or mitigate this stigma by declaring the rape victims national heroines but the task of reintegrating them into the Bengali society was and still remains staggering. These unfortunate women of Bangladesh have become double victims of man's dominance of women.

Equally barbaric was the rape of Vietnamese women by Americans. Of the more than half a million infantry, supported, perhaps, by another million or two of airforce, naval and base construction personnel only a small fraction (50,000 or so) made personal contact with the "enemy". The great majority "bought" Vietnamese women wholesale in the cities, bases and camps. "Whore houses" in the military establishments were openly tolerated by the American generals. They were called "sin cities", "boom-boom parlors" and the like. The Army's only concern was venereal disease which still managed to get out of hand. No one has yet made an assessment of this "humiliation" to the Vietnamese men of both South and North Vietnam to the ultimate outcome of the war.

And the minority that made contact with the "enemy" population left a record of rape equal to that of any conquering army. Only a few episodes came to light as few soldiers mustered the courage to report on their comrades in arms and the persistance to break through army apathy in the matter. Most feared their comrades would kill them for "squealing" in the next shootout with the Vietcong.

But a court martial of four soldiers for the rape and murder of Phan Thi Mao surfaced when a GI Sven Eriksson, at considerable risk to his life, reported the crime. Phan Thi Mao, a 20 year old peasant girl, was selected for rape by five men on patrol in Vietcong territory. As she was being bound the women of the village pleaded with the GI's. All knew too well her ultimate destiny. As she was being led away her mother, pathetically, ran after them and placed a scarf around Mao's neck. The GI's used it later as a gag over her mouth.

Eriksson would not participate in the rape. He was derided by Sargent Tony Meserve as a queer and chicken. Manual Diaz told the court that he participated only reluctantly as he did not want to be laughed at by the platoon. The soldiers, according to further testimony, practiced unbelievable cruelty on Mao in a sort of competition in brutality. Again, the incident contains more elements of male dominance and macho than any desire for sexual gratification. Ironically Mao's murder was reported as "one VC killed in action" before its true nature came to light! The maximum sentence imposed on the guilty GI's was 8 years imprisonment.

The notorious My Lai incident had its full measure of rape. Much of the massacre was photographed by Seymore Hersh and the military authorities could not ignore it. The rape commenced a month or so prior to the massacre on March 16, 1968. A woman working in the rice field with her baby alongside was gang raped and murdered. During the massacre the GI's singled out a pretty 15 year old girl but when her mother defended her like a tigress a GI shot them both. It seems that the army photographer proved to be an inhibiting or disuading factor. Helicopter gunner Ronald Ridenhour observed a dead woman in the rice field. Flying lower for a better look he reported shockingly "she was spreadeagled, as if on display. She had an 11th Brigade patch between her legs—as if it were some type of display, some badge of honor". Three or so of Charlie Company were formally charged with rape but the charges were quietly dropped.

Three months later another gang rape, involving two officers and several GI's, by the 11th Infantry Brigade occurred at Chu Lai. Two teenage girls, one only 14 years old, suspected of being Vietcong nurses, were according to Captain Goldman's statement to the court "subject to multiple rapes, sodomy and other mistreatments at the hands of various members of the First Platoon of Company B". In the morning the girls were shot to death.

Even more gory stories of rape and murder were told by the Vietnam Veterans Against the War during the protests in the 1970's. The total picture depicted by these conscience stricken soldiers is one of manifold rape and murder of Vietnamese women. The military officers generally condoned or blinked the atrocities merely cautioning the GI's not to do so when photographers were around. A particularly horrible incident was reported by one of these Vietnam veterans. A Vietcong nurse was gang raped and murdered. An automatic grease gun was then inserted into her vagina and her genital tract filled with grease.

Finally, when the Nixon Administration launched the ill-fated invasion of Cambodia using the South Vietnamese army for the groundwork, the ARVN soldiers raped and murdered the Cambodian women with impunity. It must be recalled that the Vietnamese and Cambodians are ancient enemies. Prince Sihanouk singled this out as the most important factor causing the young Cambodians to opt for the Khmer Rouge and deliver Cambodia to communist rule. These subtleties of history somehow always escape the comprehension of the politicans, statesmen and generals who perpetrate ill fated foreign policy and war.

Despite the domination of women by the men in all the technologically advanced societies much of the human race managed to find enjoyment in sexual relations based upon monogamous marriage with its supporting institutions of prostitution, concubinage, mistresses and other escape outlets from the rigidity of monogamy. The story of man is replete with long and happy marriages, tempestous love affairs, affection and altruism in the relations of the sexes. The *Institutes of Manu*, the Hindu code of law and morals, states that there is happiness in a home where the husband is pleased with his wife and the wife is pleased with her husband. The *Kama Sutra*, composed by one Vatsyayana about the third century A. D. (the precise time is unknown), is a manual on the art of love attesting the high priority given sexual relations in the Hindu culture. The idealization of the human figure and sexual embrace, sometimes verging on pornography, in the sculptures adorning the temples at Khajuraho, Bhubanesar, Konarak and elsewhere dating to the ninth to thirteenth centuries A. D. is further evidence of the free and easy attitude toward sexual relations in India. The same can be said of the *Chin p'ing mei*, the Chinese manual of love written in novel form in the sixteenth century. Erotic art and literature of this nature reveals that the attitude and approach to sexual relations in most societies was without guilt or remorse. More on this erotic literature later, however, as there is a glaring exception that should be dealt with first which has poisoned and warped the mind of man on an important phase of life in one of the foremost and greatest civilizations of history.

It was the Christian attitude that sex is evil. Millions of Christians particularly women, were denied sexual enjoyment because of this religious indoctrination. Women were debased and subjected by this belief. Even in the twentieth century millions have not yet emancipated themselves from this guilt complex. Its collateral strictures against contraception and abortion are now complicating unduly mankind's struggle against overpopulation.

The Christian sex ethic is predicated on the premise that sexual relations are evil. Sexual connection is permissable only in marriage sanctioned by the church and allowed only for the purpose of procreation. Any enjoyment, or even the thought of enjoyment, is a sin. It was not the act of procreation that was evil for the clergy needed more "souls" to gratify their dominance instinct, it was the enjoyment of it that was a sin. To be sure, so strict a code was honored only in the breach by many—the irreligious, the tepidly religious, the weak and evil. But the strictures it begot border on the ludicrous.

Everything was directed toward confining sexual relations to procreation and making the sexual act as joyless as possible. Contraception and abortion were forbidden. *Coitus interruptus* was a sin. The *chemise cajoule*, a heavy nightshirt with an appropriate aperture through which sexual connection could be effected, was prescribed for the husband in order to avoid naked contact with his wife. Sexual connection between the spouses was forbidden on Sundays, Wednesdays and Fridays, adding up to nearly half the days of the year! That would probably still give adequate scope for enjoyment with careful planning but to this was added, later, forty days before Easter and Christmas and three days before taking communion. And so on, limiting greatly the time for sexual relations even within marriage. The sexual connection could be made only in the one habitual position. All others, perhaps affording greater pleasure, were sinful. *More Canino* was considered especially abhorrent and called for seven years penance.

How, one is prone to ask, could the church enforce strictures involving intimacy between two human beings. It was done through the device of the confessional. Medievel Christians were so thoroughly indoctrinated that their lives were a constant fear of eternal damnation. Absolution (the forgiveness of sin) followed by communion was the path to salvation. The sacrament could be had only if one confessed his sins in the confession box to a priest. Absolution obtained without full disclosure of sins was not only ineffective but itself a grevious sin. Rather than face such ordeal most Christians, particularly those of stronger will, refrained from violating the prohibitions on sexual relations.

The prohibitions ranged wider than the marriage bed. Sodomy and bestiality were sins. Nuns were said to relieve their sexual frustrations with dogs and other pets; peasants with barnyard animals. Sexual relations with a Jew was considered a form of bestiality. Homosexuality, of course, was forbidden. Even masturbation. Biblical support for this proscription, called onanism, was found in the story of Onan who was put to death for coitus interruptus, described graphically in the Old Testament as "spilling his seed on the ground". This is, however, a misinterpretation of this portion of Genesis because Onan was put to death for violating the old Hebrew law prescribing that a man must provide his deceased brother's wife with child. He practiced *coitus interruptus* with her instead. But this is not the only example where the Christian Church has made a self serving interpretation of the Bible.

It is indeed curious how such an unnatural attitude toward so basic a matter of life came about. It is not easy to trace its genesis. First, it should be recalled that the early Christians were rebelling against and rejecting the life style of the Romans, who had gone to the other extreme with sexual freedom and license. The early Christian tended to be a celibate. Saint Paul's Epistle to the Corinthians (1 Corinth. VII), often misquoted and misinterpreted, may have given early direction to the Christian ethic:

> It is good for a man not to touch a woman. Nevertheless to avoid fornication let every man have his own wife, and let every woman have her own husband. . . . For I would that all men were even as myself . . . But if they cannot contain let them marry; for it is better to marry than to burn . . . If thou marry thou hast not sinned, and if a virgin marry she had not sinned . . .

The early Christian philosophers—Tertullian, Ambrose and Origen, Augustine and Jerome—gradually built upon this rejection of the Roman libertine way of life and eventually but slowly—a thousand years later—embued Christian doctrine with the idea that sex was sinful. Even the theology of original sin was given a sexual connotation. Clement of Alexandria first proposed in the second century that the fall of man was due to Adam's premature sexual union with Eve. This interpretation was revived from time to time. Saint Thomas Aquinas (1226–1274 A. D.) defined original sin as materially "concupisense".

There is an analogy, perhaps, in the Church's proscription against usury. Rome was a moneylending civilization. Exhorbitant interest was the order of the day for Roman businessmen. The Christian edict against usury was, doubtless, a rebellion against this Roman business practice which made debt slaves of so many. It was only under Protestantism, centuries later, that Europe freed itself of the ethic that usury was sinful. A whole theory of the development of capitalism has been built upon this Christian doctrine on interest and profit by sociologists and economists like Max Weber and Richard Tawney.

Great philosophical controversies on the subject raged around 4th century A. D. This was the time it should be recalled of the final breakdown of the family and marriage in the dying days of the Roman empire. Libertinism was rife. The Christians were rejecting the Roman way of life, but had not yet settled on a Christian one. But men of superior intellect began to live chaste lives following the prescription of St. Paul. Onigen went to the extreme of having himself castrated. Monastaries began to spring up for these men of chastity where they could devote their lives to God free of any sexual relations. Similarly, nunneries began to flourish for women.

Jovinian, a monk later defrocked, protested this predilection to chastity and put forth some forceful arguments against it. He argued, first, that God would not have created men with genitals if he had not intended man to use them. Moreover, if everyone practiced chastity it would mean the end of the human race. Certainly God could not have so intended.

Jerome, (circa 340–420), a reconstructed Roman libertine, and Augustine, (circa 354–430), also a former libertine, attacked Jovinian and his followers vigorously. Jerome's *Against Jovianianism* is probably the most renown and ancient treatise on marriage and the family extant wherein the eventual Christian ethic on sexual relations is set forth.

Augustine, too, attacks Jovinianism but reserves his greatest attack on Manicheanism (he directs 14 books against it), a spurious Christian doctrine heavily embued with Hinduism. It was founded by Mani (circa 216–276 A. D.), a Persian from Baghdad, who preached that the way out of the cycle of rebirths (and presumably the attainment of nirvana) was to refrain from procreation. But the Manicheans rejected chastity for the purpose and advocated free indulgence in sexual intercourse with resort to numerous birth control practices including the rhythm method to avoid procreation. According to Augustine, who was a Manichean for 10 years before returning to Christianity, they indulged in sex orgies. It was a philosophy—opposite to the nascent Christian ethic—which professed sexual relations for enjoyment not procreation; hence, it evoked the wrath of the early Christian philosophers.

The doctrine that sex is a sin was not easy to sell to the barbarians of Europe where Christianity took hold and raised a backward sector of humanity to historical greatness. The Celts were free and easy in their sexual relations. The early Christian missionaries emanating from Rome found themselves butting up against a stone wall in trying to impose the newly evolving Christian ethic against sex. Boniface (circa 675–754) complained that the English refused to marry and lived in lechery and adultery after the manner of neighing horses and braying asses. Alcuim (circa 735–804) states that England was submerged in a flood of fornication, adultery and incest. In fact, the early Christian clergy in Europe was sucked into this vortex of free and easy sexual relations. While celibacy of the clergy was an early ideal it was only in the eleventh century that celibacy became mandatory for priests. But eventually, as wind and water wears away the hardest rock, the Christian philosophers and Church fathers succeeded in imposing the "sex is sinful" ethic on the Christians of Europe. Nothing quite like it is found elsewhere in the story of man.

The onus of the proscription fell mostly on the common and upright man and woman. The ruling elite, the Church hierarchy in particular, played fast and loose with the strict ethic. The orgies of the popes and cardinals of Rennaissance Italy are too well known to bear detailing here. The rulers too managed to evade the strictures normally with papal blessing. The story of Henry VIII is well known. Henry had six wives *in sereatim*. He broke with Rome when Pope Clement VII refused to sanction a divorce from Katherine of Aragon, his Portuguese wife. The issue, however, was more political than religious. But Henry's break with Rome gave great impetus to the Reformation.

Eventually the Catholic clergy accepted and adapted to celibacy which gave large support to the Christian ethic on sex. Protestantism adopted the ethic and in many ways furthered its imposition. It did, however, allow its ministers to marry. It was not until the twentieth century that Christians started, at last, to emancipate themselves from the thought that sex was sinful.

How this Christian ethic impacted on the minds of Christians, medieval and modern, or how it affected their enjoyment of sex is most difficult to discern from the pages of history. In the first place most historians omit this aspect of the human story, in part, perhaps because they too are victims of the taboos. But enough has seeped through to indicate the negative psychological impact. There are the stories of the "possessed" nuns which were doubtless manifestations of sexual frustration. The lecherous priests who took advantage of "captive" women in the confessional are legend. But the revelations of modern psychology show that the ethic has produced frigid women and impotent men denied a free and easy enjoyment of sexual relations by a possessed mind. How it affected the peasant and his wife is less clear. Their unlettered minds may have provided a buffer against the psychological impact of the severe ethic. On the other hand history reveals that there were also great love affairs in medieval times in spite of the "sex is evil" teachings of the Church. The romance of Heloise and Abelard comes to mind.

Peter Abelard (circa 1079–1142 A. D.), born in the village of Le Pallete near Nantes, in Brittany, studied philosophy and theology in various monastaries and schools in France with the end in view of entering the clergy. At 35 he had already achieved fame with his lectures at the cathedral school of Notre Dame in Paris. This was the beginnings of the University of Paris. Until now he remained continent albeit he was handsome, charming and witty. He was at this time a canon, not yet a priest, when he was attracted to Heloise the adopted daughter of Fulton, a fellow canon at the cathedral. Heloise, only 16, was not only beautiful but learned having already mastered Latin, and was studying Hebrew, at the convent at Argenteuil. Abelard persuaded Fulton to permit him to live in his house to tutor Heloise. A tempestous love affair ensued and Heloise was soon with child. Abelard wanted to marry Heloise but she refused arguing it would preclude his future in the church (priests were now forbidden to marry) and interfere with his philosophical thought (citing Socrates). Abelard sent Heloise to his sister's home where she bore their son Astrolabe.

To appease the outraged Fulton Abelard married Heloise but agreed the marriage would be kept a secret. This did not satisfy Heloise's family who kept harassing her to make public the marriage in order to restore her good reputation. To avoid such harassment Abelard arranged for Heloise to go to the convent at Argenteuil and take the garb of a nun though not the vows or the veil. This apparently was misinterpreted by her family as a move by Abelard to rid himself of the marriage. One night as Abelard slept they pounced on him and castrated him. Abelard writes in his autobiography, *History of My Calamities,* that his friends avenged him by gouging out the eyes of and castrating two of his assailants. Fulton was dismissed as canon and his property was confiscated by the bishop.

Abelard was overcome with grief and shame. He thought God had punished him for his sins of concupiscence and fornication. He became a Benedictine priest and devoted himself with zeal to the church becoming Abbot of Saint Gildas in Brittany. Heloise too rose in the church and became the prioress of the convent at Argenteuil. When the convent lost its house at Argenteuil Abelard provided Heloise and her nuns with a home at the oratory and buildings of the Paraclete, a retreat he founded near Troyes.

Their love affair, however, was spent. There are some letters (though some doubt their authenticity) wherein Heloise appears to seek a revival of their passion but Abelard responds only in pious ways. The shocking physiological and psychological experience of his emasculation, as revealed in his autobiography, had foreclosed any further thought of passion toward Heloise. A tender friendship continued and when Abelard died in 1142 his body was sent to Paraclete for burial. Heloise survived him by 22 years and was buried beside him in the gardens of the Paraclete. After the oratory was destroyed in the Revolution the bones of Abelard and Heloise were transferred to Pere Lachaise cemetery in Paris where Frenchmen, even today, adorn their tomb with flowers in memory of one of the great love affairs of history.

It was not until the 20th century that the Christians began to free themselves from the "sex is sinful" ethic. Books and journals began to appear on love and marriage. Dr. Van de Velde's *Ideal Marriage*, published in Holland in 1926, was one of the first books to deal with sexual relations on a rational basis. It deals frankly with the physiology and hygiene of sex and details the various modes of sexual union and contraception. In America the early work of Dr. Paul Popenoe on marriage was equally enlightening for the emancipated man and woman. Since then much research and writing has been done on the subject by others (Drs. Kinsey, Masters and Johnson, *et al*) which served to free Christians of the notion that sex is evil. Unfortunately, the field has now been invaded by pornography which only serves to degrade the beauty and nobility of sexual relations of the human race.

Other societies have not passed, it would seem, through a similar syndrome on sexual relations. In the Hindu civilization the male-female relationship was approached with discretion and modesty but without any inhibitions religious or otherwise. In the four stages (ashrams) of life, the second, that of a householder, ranging from the early twenties to fifty or so, a Hindu married and pursued every pleasure of life of which sexual intercourse was foremost. In contrast to the Christian attitude sexual activity was a religious duty. A man was required to have sexual connection with his wife within a period of eight days at the close of every menstration. Sexual relations were viewed since early times as an exalted human relationship for the mutual satisfaction of both parties. A man was adjured to place the satisfaction of his mate above his own. The Hindus believed that a woman could find as much pleasure in the sexual embrace as a man.

This cooperative and mutual approach to the enjoyment of a basic element of life is found in the art and literature of the Hindus. Several texts survive of which the *Kama Sutra*, already mentioned, is the most renowned. It is addressed to the urbane man for India was during the early centuries of the Christian era living in a scintillating period of its long civilization. As one would expect the text goes into great detail on every aspect of the art of love and, in addition, good living. Foreplay is given great emphasis. No less than twelve ways of kissing are detailed. Numerous coital positions are described some of which appear more acrobatic than comfortably effective. Modern medical science and psychiatry have added little to that found in the *Kama Sutra*. Vatsyayana even prescribes clitoral stimulation to the point of orgasm prior to coitus in certain situations thus preceding Shere Hite, who makes a similar recommendation in 1976 with the publication of the *Hite Report*, by two thousand years!

The most striking feature of the Vatsyayana text is the recognition that the sexual satisfaction of a woman is as important as that of a man—without which of course, there can be no art of love. One of the best passages in this respect is found in Chapter VII entitled "The Art of Winning the Confidence of the Wife". When a man marries, writes Vatsysyana, his task "will be to develop in the inexperienced wife a confidence in, and love for, him so that she may derive pleasure from the act of sexual intercourse. For the first three days after the wedding the husband and wife should practice continence . . . For the next seven days they should have ceremonial ablutions, toilet and meals in each other's company, all to the accompaniment of song and music, should visit theatres, etc, etc. Then on the night of the tenth day, the husband should try to be intimate with her in strict privacy by beginning with soft words, so that she may not become nervous or concerned . . . In approaching his wife the husband must not attempt to advance a single step by force. Women, being by nature delicate like flowers, require a tender approach. When they are forcibly approached by men . . . the memory of the violence will often make them unresponsive to sexual intercourse . . . It is recognized that until a husband has been able to gain the confidence of the wife the technique of love-play cannot be applied."

The text continues in considerable detail with the steps involved in a satisfactory foreplay leading up to the consumation of the marraige. Vatsyayana concludes the Chapter as follows:

Why these preliminaries. Why wait and not satisfy one's passion at the first opportunity the husband finds the wife alone? If the man is acting according to the inclinations of his wife and so gains her confidence, she, in return, will place her confidence in him and be the willing slave of his love-desire. If she be always too willing to yield to her master's desire, she will be so passive an agent as to be unresponsive; if she be too unwilling, any attempt at physical intimacy will be a failure. Therefore, a man should see to it that she co-operates in the sexual act of her own free will and with intense pleasure. She should stand neither in awe nor in fear of her husband. The person who knows the pleasant method of attracting a girl's love by gaining her confidence and intimacy and by increasing her own self-esteem at the same time is sure to be very dear to women. On the other hand, the man who neglects a girl because of her shyness is considered by her a fool ignorant of the ways of a maid and as such despised like a brute. The man who, without caring to understand a girl's psychology, attempts to take or takes possession of her body by force, only succeeds in arousing the fear, horror, concern and hatred of the girl. Deprived of the affection and sympathetic understanding she longs for, she becomes obsessed with anxiety which makes her nervous, uneasy, and dejected. She either suddenly becomes a hater of the whole male sex altogether, or, hating her own husband, gives herself to other men as a form of revenge.

To appreciate Vatsyayana's advice fully it should be borne in mind that marriages in India, even now, are arranged by the parents, that the spouses usually do not know each other prior to the wedding and that the bride is often very young. Thus he, in effect, compresses into his "confidence winning" period both the courtship and the honeymoon. But that said, the foregoing advice to the young husband has not been improved upon to date by the best medical and psychiatric wisdom of modern times.

Vatsyayana has been criticised in India and outside for being too clinical and pedantic, but Vatsyayana anticipates his critics in his concluding chapter when he says "there is no reason why a certain procedure or a certain technique must be followed because it has been described in the *shastra* (text) they are to be adapted to fit each individual case or situation." He refutes also that he is writing pornography. "The principles laid down here are intended to ensure social existence in perfect harmony. . . . and not to awaken or foment sexual desire." Many critics are also repelled by his chapters on adultery—how to seduce another man's wife—and on prostitution—advice to the courtesan, concubine and even the lowly whore. But Vatsyayana must be read against the backdrop of his time in history. While historians have not been able to fix the precise time of Vatsyayana's life it is believed he lived and wrote during the golden age of the Imperial Guptas (circa 300–500 A. D.). Golden ages are usually notable for their moral decay. There is no reason to believe it was otherwise in India. Vatsyayana notes that he is writing a comprehensive text on the sexual relations though he may not agree that what is prevalent is right. Quite frequently he deplores the practice as, for instance, the ministration of fellatio by eunuchs in the massage parlors. Throughout Vatsyayana displays open partiality to monogamous love between men and women and deplores the prudery and ignorance that so often prevents it.

Vatsyayana purports to be writing a synthesis citing Charayana, Vabhravya and others as former authorities on the "science of sexual passion." The texts referred to have not survived but the citations serve to inform us that the Hindus have long ago approached sexual relations as a matter of utmost importance in the enjoyment of life.

This attitude is also found in the paintings and sculptures of ancient India. The ideal of feminine beauty is a voluptuous slender waist betwixed full thighs and heavy breasts. The walls and pediments of temples are adorned with these beauties in postures up to sexual embrace. Europeans approaching these figures with a different frame of mind view them as pornography. The Hindu, however, views them as a pleasant fact of life.

Homosexuality is alien to Hindu life. The simitris (lawbooks) condemn it. It is not found in Indian literature. The *Kama Sutra* barely mentions it. Sexual relations have been definitely heterosexual in India. The eunuch too is not common on the Indian scene. The harems were guarded by old men and women. Castration of men and animals, of course, was frowned upon in India in accordance with the Hindu attitude on life.

The Hindus indulged, however, in the unsavory practice of widow burning called *sati*. The word sati, curiously, means "virtuous women" and originated as an act of self-immolation by the wife motivated by intense love of her husband. Moreover, the practice is not endemic to the Indian civilization. The ancient Chinese, the Sumerians and early Indo-Europeans espoused the custom. The aryans, doubtless, brought some version of it to India. The early *smitris* (sacred texts) permit it but do not make it a duty. The earliest memorial to a widow who died by self-immolation is found at Eran in central India dated A. D. 510. But the Greeks who came to India with Alexander in the third century before Christ noted and recorded the practice.

Unfortunately the practice evolved into a mandatory custom because of economy imperatives. Under the Hindu custom a widow could not remarry; hence she became an economic burden on the joint Hindu family. Great pressures were, therefore, exerted on the widow to terminate her existence on the funeral pyre of her husband. Young widows with a zest for life found this unacceptable and there are reports of use of force by the family on such unwilling widow to commit *sati*. Nicoli di Conti, who travelled in south India in the 15th century during the height of the Vijayangar empire states that some 1500 wives and concubines of the kings and nobles were pledged to burn with their husbands.

The British found the practice loathsome and abolished it by law in mid-nineteenth century. The British also enacted the Hindu Widow's Remarriage Act of 1856 permitting the widows to marry again.

Chinese literature too reveals a free and easy approach to sexual relations, to be sure, within a highly structured family system. Multiple wives and concubines provided the escape valve for this rigid family structure. Though sexual behavior has always been a very private matter occasional evidence of it has crept out in literature. The erotic novel *Chin p'ing mai* the adventurous history of Hsi Men and his six wives, written in the 16th century is notable in this respect. Its 1600 pages, among many other things, sets forth the amorous relations of Hsi Men and his numerous wives including details on the technique of foreplay and various coital positions.

Though not written specifically as a handbook on love it serves the same purpose revealing the Chinese attitude toward sexual relations.

The Greeks and Romans also devoted much attention to the art of love. Treatises on sexual relations, coital positions and the achievement of orgasm proliferated during the flowering of the Greek civilization. Many of these we know of only through Athenaeus's *Deipnosophists* (sophisticated manners) a third century B. C. anthology of some hundred or so of these manuals on love. More often than not these treatises advocated the pursuit of love outside the marriage bond as Greek wives were viewed primarily as the bearers and nurses of children. The *hetaera*, was considered the goddess of love as the Greek wife was thought unskilled in the erotic art. But some wives apparently did manage to out-venus Venus.

Most famous of the Greek hetaera was Lais of Cornith. She is reputed to have asked Demosthenes 10,000 drachmas for her favors (he could not afford it), exacted equivalent sums from Aristippus the philosopher at the height of his wealth, but at the same time, conferred them freely on the penniless Diogenes. It appears she was very fond of philosophers. There is a story perhaps apocryphal, that when she disrobed as a model for the sculptor Myron he was so overwhelmed with the beauty of her body that all thoughts of chiseling a replica vanished. He forthwith offered her all his worldly possessions for her love. She refused. Still possessed of an overwhelming desire for her embrace the old sculptor cut his beard, adorned himself with youthful apparel, cosmetics and gold ornaments and called on her once again for her favors. Lais, discerning the attempt at transformation, apparently replied "you are requesting what I refused your father yesterday" or words to that effect. She amassed great wealth, endowed temples and academies and died in proverty. But the Greeks erected a splendid tomb upon her grave the equal to that of any conqueror.

The Romans not only absorbed these Greek manuals but added some of their own. Ovid's *Ans Amotoria* (art of love), composed in 2 B. C. contains three books, two for men, one for women, on the wiles and techniques of sexual relations. It is full of prescriptions on seduction, assignations, adultery and the like. It reaped the wrath of Augustus, who with his wife Julia, were trying to rehabilitate the family system at this time. Ovid tried to retrieve himself by writing *Remedia Amoris* on how one could free himself of sexual passion through hard work, hunting and other ways, but it was too late to restore himself with the emperor. Augustus banished him to Tomi on the Black Sea where he died of loneliness and grief.

The art of love has been practiced within and outside the marriage bond. It may even have reached its greatest height through the courtesan. Mankind, however, has tried with some success to impose sexual discipline through the family system. The family unit is more or less ubiquitous. It has been the basic unit of all human societies. But it has been much more than a system to impose sexual discipline.

Ever since man formed the hunting group and later developed agriculture the family has been the basic soci-economic unit of human civilization. It arose to serve man's two basic needs—food and replication. The first function of the family is to nurture the child. Not only physically but culturally. The accumulated knowledge and wisdom of the society passed from generation to generation primarily through the family. Until quite recently the accumulated technology of man was passed from father to son. The techniques and skills of homemaking passed from mother to daughter. Even the practice of apprenticeship was largely an inter family arrangement. Agricultural technology was transmitted from generation to generation through the family. It is perhaps necessary again to note that agriculture has been the main preoccupation of man for most of recorded history and still is the daily life of most of mankind today. But even in the industrialized societies the acquisition of technological knowledge emanates from the family basis even though the child attends schools and vocational courses outside the home.

It seems only natural, however, that mankind should have also resorted to the family system for the maintenance of sexual discipline. The human specie could have reproduced outside the marriage bond. But it is doubtful whether the accumulated technological and other knowledge of a civilization could have been developed and transmitted to successive generations as effectively without the family system.

As technological development made possible the production of a surplus the family became the repository of the wealth of the society. Property devolved from generation to generation through the family system. The male with his propensity to dominate took control of the property and it usually went from father to son. In most societies women could also inherit and provision was made for the surviving spouse. Moreover, the institution of the dowry was invented to make daughters more attractive for marriage. Prostitution thrived outside the family in virtually every society whereby women, disadvantaged economically in every way in a male dominated economy, were able to trade sexual favors for money or property. Many of the successful courtesans amassed great wealth in practically every society.

The vitality and strength of a society thus became dependent upon the family system. When the family was weakened or undermined by libertinism and divorce the society decayed and vanished into the dust of history. This development infected the Roman civilization as early as the first century before Christ. Efforts to restore the family thereafter, like the Julian laws, proved ineffective. By the 3rd and 4th centuries of the Christian era the Roman family had completely disintegrated and so did Roman civilization. A similar rejection of the family system occurred in 3rd century B. C. Greece. The Greek civilization declined and eventually succumbed to Roman rule.

The Christian church restored the family, in fact, made marriage a sacrament and built upon it the scintillating western civilization. But

Christendom has witnessed several assaults upon the family. It was rejuve-
nated by Luther and the Reformation in the 16th century. Neither the
French or Russian Revolutions, with their attacks on the family, left any
lasting damage. But, it would appear, that 20th century libertinism and the
feminist movements may again have a weakening effect upon the family such
as transpired in the twilight centuries of the Roman empire.

Movements for the emancipation of women are laudible and constructive
up to a point. Women have been wrongfully dominated throughout history.
But woman's liberation to the degree where it shirks her biological responsibility of borning children and cultural responsibility of providing a happy and
enlightening home so that the child can not only effectively carry on, but add
to, the technological prowess of its society during the next generation can
only cause a decline and disintegration of that society. To carry the
argument to its extreme, if women refused to born children the society
would end within a generation. But severe damage to the society can
transpire with lesser neglect or refusal of the women to carry out their
responsibility of perpetuating the specie biologically and culturally. When
the women of Rome became more interested in matters outside the home—
their jobs, professions, theatre, sports and the like—the solid structure of
Roman society from which it was able to master the Mediterranean world
began to crumble.

The waxing and waning of the family system in the Mediterranean and
European societies is well recorded. No such evidence appears in the Asian
civilizations. In fact, the opposite appears to be the case. Both the Chinese
and Indian civilizations were based upon strong family structures. The
Confuscian ethic called for a strong male dominated family as the bedrock of
Chinese society. Concubinage provided an escape valve for such structural
rigidity. The Hindu family, which embraced more than the nuclear father,
mother and children, too, has been the bedrock of the Indian civilization. It
seems, however, that the mother had more power and authority in the Hindu
family than her counterpart in China. Both these Asian civilizations have
survived 5000 years of buffeting, including foreign invasions, and it could be
that their strong family systems were in large measure, responsible for this
remarkable social stability.

XI
Enjoyment of Life—Architecture, Fine Arts and Sports

Shelter and clothing became imperatives of survival when man decided to challenge the glaciers. Early man evolving in Africa required little protection from the weather. It was warm. There was no snow or ice, merely warm rain that was soothing to his sun parched skin. His main concern was the predators. At first he doubtless retreated into the trees, from whence he came, but eventually he built stockades against them.

Life on the tundra was a different matter. During the period of the Wurm glacier (from about 75,000 to 10,000 years ago) the temperature did not go above 50° on a summer day in Europe and Asia. Sub-zero temperatures prevailed during the long winter months. Man found shelter in caves and rock grottos. He protected himself further from the cold by erecting A-frame tents of stout saplings and hides in the caves. A hot fire of thick logs was kept going the year round at the mouth of the cave or rock shelter. The underground retreats also provided a certain amount of geothermal heat to keep early man's habitat warm. Hide tents were erected on the tundra in the warmer months of spring and summer as Neanderthal followed the reindeer, bison and other animals in their grazing grounds.

When the Wurm receded Neanderthal evolving into Cro-Magnon began to live more and more in the hide tents on the open and now warmer plains. Archeological remains at Dolni Vestonice, Czechoslovakia reveal a large hut, with five hearths, about 50 feet long by 20 feet wide dating back some 27,000 years. Four smaller huts surround it. Wooden posts anchored in the ground provided the supports. Cro-Magnon was now building formidable shelters in the open having accumulated the necessary technology and control over fire for the purpose. It would not be unreasonable to presume that not long after Cro-Magnon was building with wood. Magdalenian stone tools were now sharp and strong for hewing rough timber. It was not long thereafter, certainly by Mesolithic time (8500–10,000 years ago) that man invented the polished stone axe.

ARCHITECTURE

The agricultural revolution made architecture possible. Man now had a surplus to invest in things of beauty in addition to matters of survival. And it was perhaps, natural in his stage of cultural evolution at this time that he used his early wealth for religious purposes, including his refusal to accept the fact that life was terminal. Temples and tombs were, therefore, the earliest types of durable architecture. Palaces came next as the ruling elite was able to appropriate more of the wealth for their personal or semi-private use. There were also granaries but they were more functional than beautiful.

Catal Huyuk (circa 7000–5500 B. C.) the remarkable Neolithic city discovered by archeologist James Mellart in Anatolia, possessed grand temples deifying the aurock bull. Two lines of aurock bull horns led up to an alter or pedestal crowned by a sculptured aurock head with embedded horns. Other shrines deified the ram and vulture. Sun dried mud bricks and plaster were now used for the buildings. Accomplished farmers were now migrating across Europe from the Middle East where agriculture was first invented. Not long thereafter prehistoric man covered Europe with giant stone monuments. Some were single upright stones called menhirs (celtic for long stone); some were two or more upright stones capped by a heavy flat stone called dolmens; others took unusual shapes like the six foot diameter chisled stone ring with a 24 inch hole found in Cronwall, England. The menhirs were often set in circles, rectangles, grids or other shapes, doubtless encompassing a burial ground. Most of the megaliths were associated with tombs. Some 50,000 of these monuments have been discovered in western Europe and the British Isles. They date over a 3000 year period from the fifth to the first millenium before Christ.

Most famous of these monuments is Stonehenge on the Salsbury plain of England. It was built over a period of 1200 years starting about 2750 B. C. The main circle of 81 sarsen long stones with lintels was erected around 1800 B. C. The whole structure is oriented to the summer solstice. The rising sun casts its light across the heel stone through the gate to the center of the great circle, where presumably a priest could stand to perform some appropriate ceremony of thanks for the regeneration of life through the seasonal changes dictated by the sun. These astrological orientations caused speculation that Stonehenge was an observatory. But more than likely it had mainly religious motivations involving the heavenly bodies as men's lives were based on the seasons, tides and other meteorological phenomena dependent on the sun and moon. The priests attempted to predict these natural phenomena for their people. In any event the astronomical features of Stonehenge depict a knowledge of the solar system not generally thought to have existed 4000 years ago.

Equally impressive is the architectural and engineering ingenuity displayed by the builders of Stonehenge. The site selected on the Salsbury plain where the summer and winter solstices are at right angles was 20 miles from the nearest source of sarasen (a variety of sandstone) boulders. The boulders were fashioned into huge rectangular megaliths weighing about 50 tons. It is surmised the linear cuts were made by heating the cut line with oil soaked twigs set afire. The hot strip was cooled with cold water causing it to crack. The rectangular stone so hewn was then smoothed with stone mauls.

Next came the formidable task of transporting the 50 ton megalith over 20 hilly miles from Marlbourough down to the site on Salsbury plain. It is believed the stone was lashed to a sledge constructed with stout logs on two runners. The sledge was moved over a series of rollers made from oak tree trunks and pulled and braked by perhaps 100 men over the hills and vales to the site. As the sledge freed a roller behind it was carried forward to repeat its function of rolling the stone across the ground. Millions of yards of fibre rope was used in the operation. The smaller blue stones forming the inner circle weighing about 5 tons supposedly came from western Wales and were most likely transported over water. Additional ingenuity was necessary for loading, and off loading, them on huge rafts.

At the site the 50 ton megaliths had to be levered into holes dug for them in the circle. Even more difficult was elevating the 7 ton lintels atop the 13 foot megaliths. This required a rather sophisticated knowledge of levers, mechanics and other practical physics.

Stonehenge was not alone. Another configuration of menhirs was found in Brittany at Carnac. The grid alignment of the stones indicates they may have been used to study the movement of the moon. Even less is known and understood of the circles and serpentine avenues of megaliths at Avebury to the north of Stonehenge.

Thousands of miles to the east and south the even more prosperous agricultural societies of Egypt and Sumeria were also building tombs and temples. No civilization was more preoccupied with death, and the life after death, than the ancient Egyptians. It was as if life was simply a matter of preparation for an afterlife. The ancient Egyptian would not accept the finality of death. The result was a singularly unique sepulchral architecture that has characterized the old Egyptian civilization ever since.

This funerary architecture took two forms. The pyramids were for kings; the mastabas for lesser members of the ruling elite. Most impressive is the great pyramid built by and for the Pharoah Khufu, sometimes called Cheops, about 2700 B. C. It is at Gizeh near Cairo. From a 755 foot square base it rises to 481 feet at the peak. That would be 48 stories in modern skyscraper terms. Except for two small burial chambers and entrance passages the structure is a solid mass of limestone blocks so neatly hewn and fitted that the space between the joints is less than one fifteenth of an inch. The two and a half ton stones were in step formation to the peak with triangular slabs of polished limestone and granite laid upon the steps to give the pyramid a smooth fine finish. These finishing stones have since been vandalized so that only the stepped limestone structure remains. Two other pyramids, that of Khafra with a 700 foot base and of Menkaura with a 300 foot base, are nearby dating to the third millennium B. C. Associated with the pyramids is the great sphinx, a manifestation of the sun god. It is thought to be contemporaneous in origin.

Herodotus, visiting Egypt in the fifth century B. C., states the pyramid of Cheops took 30 years to build. The stones were hewn east of the Nile, hauled across the river in boats, and drawn up the long causeway to the site. A hundred thousand men worked on the pyramid at all times under an ancient system of corvee. The labor levy was, according to Herodotus, for periods of three months at a time. "One and all" were compelled to labor on the pyramid. Modern research, however, refutes Herodotus. Only about 4000 workers labored on the pyramid at any given time. About 18–20 men were needed to haul a stone up the causeways.

The architecture of the great pyramid is almost perfect. Its sides are laid out so accurately in a square that modern surveying instruments can detect only negligible error. The structure is near perfectly level. The northwest corner is only a half inch lower than the southwest. How did the ancient Egyptians accomplish it 5000 years ago! They apparently dug a trench around the 13 acre site, filled it with water, and used the water surface as the reference point for leveling the stones.

The stones were quarried apparently by cutting a slot with copper chisels and saws into which wooden wedges were driven. The wood was then soaked with water and as it expanded it cracked the rock. The stones were hammered with dolorite tools into rough blocks and hauled to the site where they were finally finished.

The mestabas were more modest structures. Built of brick or stone, all or partly under-ground, or cut into solid rock they were characterized by columned facades at the entrances. Columns were also used in the interior chambers. The column, first founded in old Egypt, was destined to play an important role in the architecture of later Egypt, Persia and the Graeco-Roman civilizations. Temples and palaces became prominent in Egypt during the middle and new empires. Amenhoteph's temple at Luxor, Hatsheput's temple at Dier el Bahri, and Ramses II's temples at Thebes, Karnak and Abu Simbel are some of the most renowned. Several of these were cut out of rock, for instance, Abu Simbel and Deir el Bahri. But in all of them the Egyptian column was a leading feature.

The columns found at Karnak are 70 feet high and 12 feet thick at the base. The flaring bell shaped capitals are 22 feet across. The Egyptian columns, mainly, took two forms. The lotus bud or bell capital and the spreading leaf capital. The columns were many sided (up to 16). A few were fluted. Many were rounded with the hieroglyphic depictions of historical episodes like those at Karnak.

In the fertile crescent the earliest prominent architecture is the ziggurat. None remain as the Sumerians, unlike the Egyptians who built with rock, used clay and sun baked brick. Stone was not as readily available in the Tigris-Euphrates doab. The ziggurat at Ur (circa 2350 B. C.) excavated and reconstructed by Sir Leonard Wooley in 1922–9 is the earliest found to date by archeologists. It is a massive solid structure with ramps to a temple at the top. The idea was to create an elevated place of worship, analogous to a mountain top. The tower of Babylon was 270 feet high. These ziggurats continued to be built up to the rise of the Persian empire. Sargon's great palace was built on a high platform of brick and clay—most likely for defense purposes. A striking feature of the structure was an arched gateway. The Assyrians developed further the arch. Their triple arched palace entrances with huge human headed bulls on either side were monumental predecessors of the Roman triumphal arches centuries later. Their successors the Chaldeans borrowed the arch from the Assyrians for their splendid towers in Babylon. The Persians did not use the arch. It remained for the Romans to resuscitate it centuries later.

The Persians borrowed the column from the Egyptians but they did not improve it much. The tomb of Darius at Naksh-i-Rustam resembles an Egyptian mastaba. The great hall built by Xerxes (circa 485 B. C.) at Persepolis was filled with columns like an Egyptian temple.

It was the Greeks, however, that made a thing of beauty out of the column. First, they placed the columns outside and completely around the building. The inner building was normally very prosaic and functional. Second, they refined their shapes and dimensions for maximum eye appeal to the beholder.

Three styles evolved. All had fluted as well as straight columns. The Doric, being thicker, usually had no base; the slender Ionic had a small base of three or so round moldings. It was their capitals however, by which they were distinguished. The Doric had a simple square; the Ionic a double flaring scroll on the face and back; while the Corinthian had a foliated bell capital.

The Parthenon is Doric. It is perhaps, the most beautiful example of Greek architecture. Built about 450 B. C. on the Acropolis in Athens to replace a temple destroyed by the Persians it delighted and pleased visitors from all over the Mediterranean world for two millennia before it was destroyed in a war between the Venetians and the Turks in 1687. The Turks used it as an ammunition dump during the siege! A Venetian shell hit the ammunition and it exploded! After the Turks were ousted from Athens British archeologists undertook a major study and reconstruction of the Parthenon. Many of the broken pieces, particularly sections of the freize, are now in the British museum.

After the defeat of Xerxes the Greeks were embued with a new spirit and confidence. Pericles decided to rebuild the Acropolis. Architects, sculptures, stonecutters, painters, other artists and thousands of ordinary workers were mobilized for the effort. The rebuilding of the Acropolis was, in a way, an unemployment project. The victorious soldiers of the Persian war needed jobs. And the mines of Laurium were still producing plenty of silver to finance the project.

Phideas was chief architect and sculptor. Callicrates and Ictinus were subordinate architects. The Parthenon had two inner chambers, very plain and unlighted, as they usually were in Greek temples. The main chamber was for the goddess Athena. The word Parthenon means "the virgin's place". The other was a treasury—to store, presumably, the silver from the mines of Laurium. The statue of Athena was 40 feet high, made of wood and covered with ivory and gold. The beauty of the temple, however, resided in the 46 columns (in the proportion of 8 to 17) that surrounded its four sides. Twelve inner columns, six on each side, were placed before the entrances to the chambers.

The greatness of the Parthenon is the attention that was given to detail. The columns were made slightly thicker, called entases, in the middle (only about .07 of a foot) to offset the normal illusion generated by a straight column that its top and bottom are thicker. Both platform and entablature curve slightly upwards—about 4.5 inches—toward the middle for similar reason. And the columns tilt slightly inward to offset the illusion of outward bulge at the top given by a verticle column. All possible optical illusions were thus offset. The 8 by 17 columnade gave a pleasing balance to the rectangular structure. The result was a vision of near perfect form. British architectural historian H. Heathcote Statham concludes "now, here we have something different, in architectural design, from anything hitherto encountered. We are in the presence of an architecture in which details are deliberately shaped and refined, in accordance with an acute intellectual perception to produce their best and most complete effect on the eye; in which detail is an abstract conception of order, form, and proportion; in which both the shaping hand of the artificer and the seeing eye of the spectator are guided by reason and sensibility rather than by mere habit and tradition."

Greek architecture dominated the Graeco-Roman and western civiliza-tions that followed for the next 2500 years. Few public buildings were erected otherwise. There was one major exception, the Gothic, which will be discussed subsequently. The Americans still favored it during the first half of the 20th century when they erected the Lincoln and Jefferson Memorials and the new Supreme Court building. But by the latter half of the century western man no longer favored or could no longer afford the beautiful columns of the Greeks. Modern architecture became prosaic and functional.

The Romans were great builders. They added engineering to architecture. They adopted and developed the arch and the dome. Both Etruscan (round structures) and Greek (columns) were incorporated. The arch was extended beyond the entrance to barrel and cross vaults which formed the basic structure of most buildings. The dome was merely an extension of the arch to a circular base. Columns were used for entrances, porticos, temples and the like. But even where the arch was used the Romans would decorate with columns or half columns between the arches. The coliseum built in 80 A. D. is a good example. While the Romans used all three styles of Greek column they preferred the more ornamental Corinthian which they developed in many floral and leaf motifs. They even combined the Ionic and Corinthian designs into some capitals.

The Pantheon built as a temple by Hadrian in 124 A. D. is a fine example of this mixture of architecture. It has come down in history intact. The building consists of a circular and domed room 142 feet in diameter with a 60 by 110 foot portico upheld by 16 beautiful Corinthian columns with a very delicate leaf design.

Roman architecture, however, was mainly civic. Basilicas for courts and administration like the famous forum. These were large arched buildings with a half circular domed apse at one end. The renowned Roman baths— heavy barrel and cross vault constructions like the baths of Caracalla. Amphitheaters and circuses like the Coliseum.

Great engineering feats like the aqueducts bringing over 200 million gallons of water per day to Rome across miles of countryside and the famous Roman roads made Roman engineers famous. The basic structure of these roads is still followed today. The greatest engineering contribution by the Romans was the discovery of concrete. This enabled them to build cheaply the heavy walls needed to carry the arches and vaults over vast interior spaces. The heavy walls were necessary as reinforced concrete was still 2000 years in the future.

The Romans were never able to build a dome on a square base. The Byzantine Greeks solved the problem by means of pendatives. Pendatives are four arches set in a square on which the dome is set. A pendative base can be fashioned by cutting an orange in half and cutting off four slices to square its diameter. The end of the orange half is then sliced above the four arches. A dome of any fashion can then be erected on the base. The result is a domed square structure. Most famous of this Byzantine architecture is Haghia Sophia (or Saint Sophia) in Constantinople built by Emperor Justinian in 532 A. D. Another is the church of Saint Mark in Venice. Through their trade with the East the Venetians were greatly influenced by Byzantine art. Eastern Christianity became wedded to this architecture and Orthodox Christian churches are still built in this manner today.

Religious architecture in western Christianity, however, took another turn. The early Roman Catholic churches evolved the Romanesque architecture. It starts with the Roman basilica, as this type of building was most adaptable for housing a large congregation. The Roman arch was the basic architecture. The apse was retained and enlarged into the ambulatory where the priests officiated and the choir sang. A transcept was added to make the floor plan in the form of a cross. This established the basic plan of the Christian cathedral. Romanesque was the dominant religious architecture of western Christendom from the 8th to the 11th centuries.

At the beginning of the second millennium of the Christian era a configuration of developments occurred which infused the Europeans with a new spirit. The first millennium Christians firmly believed the year 1000 would be the end of the world and they would face the Last Judgement. This threw a tremendous pallor over the emerging Christian civilization. But the world did not end in A. D. 1000. It took the Europeans a century or so to surmount the shock and to realize that man still had a future on earth. During these same centuries man finally learned how to utilize the full power of the horse through the saddle and stirrup (for military purposes) and the horse collar (for agriculture). Europeans achieved both great agricultural productivity and military prowess. This was particularly true in France and Germany. European man acquired a new sense of power which was destined to build a great civilization. He was ready to reach out to infinity.

He found the Romanesque church too confining and depressing for his new spirit. Unlike the Egyptian, Sumerian and the Greek, the European was a man of the forest. He had bred in him the lofty heights of tall oaks, elms, ash and other trees whose limbs crossed in pointed arches and admitted the sunlight through their leaves to the dweller or sojourner below. He wanted his churches and cathedrals to do the same; to reach out into space to his God. Out of this forest spirit in the 11th century the Gothic cathedral with its stained glass windows was born. Oswald Spengler expresses the gothic spirit dramatically in the following words:—

> The character of the Faustian cathedral is that of the forest. The mighty elevation of the nave above the flanking aisles, in contrast to the flat roof of the basilica; the transformation of the columns, which with base and capital had been set as self-contained individuals in space, into pillars and clustered-pillars that grow up out of the earth and spread on high into an infinite subdivision and interlacing of lines and branches; the giant windows by which the wall is dissolved and the interior filled with mysterious light—these are the architectural actualizing of a world-feeling that had found the first of all its symbols in the high forest of the Northern plains, the deciduous forest with its mysterious tracery, its whispering of ever-mobile foliage over men's heads, its branches straining through the trunks to be free of earth. . . . Cypresses and pines, with their corporeal and Euclidean effect, could never have become symbols of unending space. But the oaks, beeches and lindens with the fitful light-flecks, playing in their shadow-filled volume are felt as bodiless, boundless, spiritual . . . . In the ash, the victory of the

upstriving branches over the unity of the crown seems actually won. Its aspect is of something dissolving, something expanding into space, and it was for this probably that the World-Ash Yggdrasil became a symbol in the Northern mythology. The rustle of the woods, a charm that no classical poet ever felt—for it lies beyond the possibilities of Appollinian Nature-feeling—

No other art of man characterizes a civilization better than its architecture. The purity and perfection of the Greek temple bespeaks the logic and intellect of the ancient Greeks. The functional and hedonistic arenas, circuses, baths, aqueducts and other civic buildings bear the stamp of the plutocratic Roman. The Romanesque too can be said to reflect the doomsday attitude of the first millennium Christian.

The light, lofty, soaring Gothic architecture was achieved by pointed arches resting on tall piers. Naves and transcepts could now be thrust into the sky 150 feet! The walls, no longer required to support the vaults, could be cut freely for windows to admit light. Stained glass became an essential feature of the Gothic cathedral. The piers were supported by buttresses and, as they soared higher, by the graceful flying buttresses. The whole structure was lightweight, well lighted and delicately balanced inside and out. To this eye appeal music was added later in the form of the pipe organ. A Bach or Handel mass performed in this architectural setting is an emotional experience not easy to duplicate elsewhere. It fulfilled in every way the new spirit of second millennium European man. This new spirit and energy was destined to build the most scintillating and highly technological civilization achieved by man to date.

So the cathedrals sprang up all over Europe. Mostly during the 12th and 13th centuries. Some took a hundred years to build. Everyone contributed. Guilds commissioned stained glass windows. Farmers contributed horses for construction and human beings themselves, for penance, perhaps, or out of religious fervor, dragged the stones to the site. Chartres, Bourges, Laon, Amiens, Rheims, Notre Dame de Paris and others in France; Cologne, Ulm, Frankfort, Nuremburg, Frieburg and others in Germany and Salisbury; Durham, Canterbury, Ely, Lincoln and Wells in England are glorious monuments of the new spirit. In America too there are two fine examples, though of a later date. St. Patricks cathedral in New York and the Washington cathedral in the nation's capital.

Gothic was also employed for civic buildings in Europe though most civic structures favored the Graeco-Roman architecture. It was only during the latter part of the 20th century that these two old architectures were foresaken for the new functional structures employing the technologically advanced reinforced concrete, steel, aluminum and other strong and lightweight building materials. This enabled modern man to reach skyward with a hundred floors or more. Some of these modern skyscrapers try to be beautiful but end up being mostly functional.

Muslim architecture is eclectic. It borrowed ideas from the peoples conquered and converted to Islam. The first mosque at Medina was a courtyard roofed with plaster on palm leaves upheld by tree trunks. And this idea of a large enclosed assembly for prayers remained the central idea of the mosque. Arcades carrying a flat roof became the central feature of these early mosques. In the Near East the Byzantine dome was added. The Mosque of Omar in Jerusalem (built in 691 A. D.) is predominately Byzantine. In Spain the mosques were Romanesque. The one at Cordova built in the 8th century is striking with an alternating pattern of black and white stones in its arches. The pointed arch was adopted from Persian architecture and developed to its finest by the Muslims in India. More on it later.

The capture of Constantinople by the Ottoman Turks in 1453 brought further Byzantine influence. Hagia Sophia was made a mosque and used as a model for many beautiful copies, of which the famous Blue Mosque in Istanbul is a fine example.

Islamic architecture did not attain the grandeur and loftiness of (say) the Greek or Gothic. Its purpose was always functional. It was never an edifice to Allah. The Koran forbade such adulation. It was simply a sheltered place, domed or flat roofed, where the devoted could prostrate themselves in prayer bowing their heads in the direction of Mecca. The mosque was consequently always oriented toward Mecca. Its large assembly room was usually marked off in rectangular squares to accommodate the prostrated prayers. The whole atmosphere of the mosque was an earthbound dimly lighted space for the daily prayers of the devoted Muslim.

The one indigenous—and beautiful—addition, the minaret too was functional. It provided an elevated position from where the muezzin could call the faithful to prayers five times a day.

In India a truly indigenous architecture is encountered. Five thousand years ago at Harappa and Mohenjodaro early Indus civilization men already built with fired bricks of standard specifications. Unfortunately only foundations remain so it is not possible to reconstruct the edifices. While no evidence of temples has been found large public buildings such as baths, granaries and administrative quarters have been uncovered. The Harappans did not build with stone. Neither did the Aryans who conquered India around 1500 B. C. Evidence of stone construction is found only during the Buddhist era a millennia or so later. The Aryans apparently built with perishable materials such as wood, of which there was plenty in the forested environment of the Indus-Gangetic plains at the time. Also, as gleaned from the Vedas, the early Aryan was not predisposed to religious edifices. He preferred to worship at an altar and to place his reliquaries on a mound of ground in the open spaces. The carpenter is exalted in the Vedas for erecting the altars on which the Brahman priest performed his sacrifices.

The Buddhists borrowed this custom and from it evolved the stupa. It was simply a hemispheric mound constructed of brick or stone as a shrine to Buddha, or later, a Bodhisattva, often housing a relic at the top. Most famous of those remaining today is the one at Sanchi near Bhopal in Madhya Pradesh believed to have been erected by Asoka in the 3rd century B. C. It was enlarged later by building over the existing stupa to a diameter of 120 feet and a height of 54 feet. An ambulatory (every stupa has one where the devoted circle the dome as part of the act of worship) with railings surrounds the mound 16 feet above the ground. It is reached by a double stairway on the south side. At the top of the dome is a square pedestal supporting a triple umbrella, the insignia of royalty. The stupa is surrounded by a railing of stone with four gateways. These gateways are the architectural highlight of the entire structure. They are some 34 feet high and 20 feet wide with three transverse stone lintels profusely ornamented and decorated with floral and animal (mostly elephant) motifs.

At the same time the Buddhists developed their unique rock architecture. Large caves, man-made, were cut into solid rock for quarters, assemblies and places of worship for Buddhist monastaries. Some were huge galleries 100 × 50 feet with 40 foot ceilings. Pillars, niches and even colonades were constructed inside the cavern. Murals, well preserved to this day, are found on some of the walls.

The most renowned of these rock structures are found at Ajunta and Ellora in western India some 350 miles northwest of Bombay. At Ajunta, in a horseshoe curved rocky cliff overlooking a serene valley, some 28 temples and monastary halls were hewn into the rocky face of the small mountain over the years from about 200 B. C. to 600 A. D. This period spanned the two scintillating Gupta empires which generated the wealth necessary for such architecture. The manual labor required boggles the mind. There is an unfinished cave at Ajunta which, like the unfinished sculptures of Michelangelo in Florence, gives the visitor some comprehension of the man hours needed to carve from solid rock a large space for human use with technology no further advanced than a chisel and hammer! These ancient stoneworkers started at the top, fashioned the ceiling first, and moved downward sculpting the pillars, niches, alters, statues and other features of the temple or monastic buildings as they removed the rock. No scaffolding was necessary for such construction.

Equally noteworthy are the murals found at Ajunta. They are mostly scenes of life at the time from which one may gain a good impression of daily routine in India two thousand years ago. Other scenes depict the life of the Buddha. In one painting a beautiful girl is doing her toilet, including the application of lipstick, in a manner not dissimilar to the fashion of modern times. The remarkable feature of these murals is the preservation of the pigments (red ochre, burnt brick, copper oxide, lamp black and green rock dust) on a plaster made of clay and cow dung mixed with chopped rice husks.

Sixty-five miles away are the Ellora caves and temples. There are 34 in number on a less spectacular site than Ajunta. They date from the 7th century when, for some unknown reason, the Ajunta site was abandoned. While Ajunta was a Buddhist monastary the Ellora site represents Buddhist, Jain and Hindu religious orders. The earliest caves are Buddhist and the latter day are Hindu. This is noteworthy as it reflects the decline of Buddhism and the revival of Brahmanism during the latter half of the first millennium of the Christian era.

Cave 5, probably a classroom for Buddhist monks, is 117 by 56 feet with two dozen pillars. It is the biggest structure at either Ajunta or Ellora. Cave 6, while Buddhist, already contains a statue of Sarasvati, a Hindu goddess of learning. After Cave 12 there are 17 Hindu caves. To the North are 5 Jain caves.

At cave 16 one encounters the most stupendous piece of rock architecture in the world. It is the famous Kailasa temple. It is not any longer a cave, but a free standing temple sculptured out of solid rock. The stone cutters first hewed a rectangular channel 107 feet deep, 276 feet long and 154 feet wide into a hillside of solid rock, leaving a huge stone block in the center from which the temple was carved.

Kailasa temple is dedicated to the god Shiva. It rests on a plinth 25 feet high with elephants, shoulder to shoulder, carved on its sides, leaving the impression the temple is borne on their backs. There is an entrance gateway and a small shrine of Nandi (Shiva's bull) before the steps to the main sanctuary are reached. Around the main shrine are five smaller shrines to Ganesh, the elephant god, Parvati and others. Cornices, pilasters, niches abound everywhere. Above the sanctuary rises a tower in three tiers topped by a cupola to a height of 95 feet. The walls of the rock around the temple contain niches and colonnades for dwelling places for the priests and other temple attendants.

Construction of the temple commenced under the rule of Krishna I, a Rashtrakuta king, in 760 A. D. and took over 100 years to complete. Some writers say it took 250 years. But so it is with Indian history. Needless to say, neither the king or his architect lived to see the completion of their grand design.

There is more of this rock architecture—at Karli, near Bombay, at Elephanta, across the bay from Bombay, in Orissa, on the hills of Udayagii and Khandagari and elsewhere. One may speculate why the Buddhists liked these excavations into rocky hillsides for their monastaries, temples and other religious purposes. Some writers put forth the view that the darkness and mystery of the cave appealed to the mysticism and need for quiet meditation of Indian religionists. But Buddhism was the least mystic of the Indian religions. India is, however, a hot country. Perhaps, the reason is no more profound than that an underground site provided a nice cool place for a Buddhist to meditate. The indestructibility of the caves may have provided further appeal.

At any rate when Brahmanism returned to India the underground architecture gave way to temples in the open of which the Kailasa temple was a precursor. From 900 to 1300 A. D. there was a rash of temple construction all over India of which many examples remain in central, eastern and south India. None are found in north India as the conquering Muslims destroyed them. Nothing infuriated the Muslim conquerors more than the inconvertibility of the Hindu to Islam. Frustrated, he destroyed the Hindu places of worship.

Hindu worship is not congregational. It is a personal intercourse between a man and his god. Hence, the Indian temple is primarily a shrine to a god or gods. In view of the multitudinous Hindu pantheon some Hindu temples are Olympian structures.

A Hindu temple has three or four halls. Most important is the shrine of the idol called vinama. It is topped by a tall tapering tower called a sikhara profusely sculptured with idols, animal and human scenes, and other figures, decorations and scrolls. It is topped with a flat stone disc and a finial. Some temples have an ambulatory around the cella, where the god is enshrined, permitting the worshippers to circumnavigate the idol. In front of the vinama is the mandapa, a small hall for worshippers. It too is topped by a tower of lesser proportion. Next comes the entrance hall, also called the hall of offering, topped by a tower. In between, in some temples, is a dancing hall where the dancing girls of the temple perform for the worshippers. Dancing is a part of Hindu religious ritual. Hindu temples are oriented to the east where the entrance is erected.

Greatly renowned is the Lingaraj temple, dedicated to a lingnam symbol of Siva, at Bhubaneswar in Orissa. It was built between the 10th and 13th centuries. There are four halls—the shrine, assembly hall, the dancing hall and the hall of offerings. The tower is 127 feet high with the figure of a lion crushing an elephant just below the lineal spire. The great beauty of the tower is its incline slightly inwards after it reaches 50 feet in height. The temple stands in a compound 520 by 465 feet.

Bhubaneswar contains many more temples. A similar complex is found at Khajuraho in central India (about 350 miles southeast of New Delhi). Some 85 temples were built between the 9th and 13th centuries. These temples are renowned for their architectural and sculptural excellence. A striking feature of the sculpture is the frank portrayal of love scenes between men and women. Many westerners view it as pornography but to the Hindu it is but the portrayal of an important aspect of life.

The Jains too built grand temples. Jain temples are dedicated to their Tirthankaras (noble souls or saints). They differ little in architecture from Hindu temples. Most famous are those at Mount Abu in western Gujarat.

The temple of Vimala at Mount Abu, dedicated to Adinath, the first Tirthankara, is a structure of white marble 42 feet by 98 feet in a large courtyard with cells for Jain monks. It was built in the 11th century. In the south the Pallava, Chola and Pandya kings erected some of the most beautiful temples in India. The temples at Tanjore, Madura, Srirangam, Conjeevaram and Chidambaram are best known. The distinctive feature of the south Indian temple is the eastern gateway called the Gopuram. The Gopuram is an elaborate ornamented pyramidical structure which usually dominates the entire city. The Gopuram and temples are profusely sculptured, pillared and ornamented.

No palaces or other civic buildings of ancient India survived. They were apparently built of perishable materials. Only the gods appear to have rated stone architecture. But Indian religious architecture radiated far and wide in Asia along with Indian religion. The Buddhist stupa evolved into the beautiful pagodas of southeast Asia. Most striking is the Shwedagon pagoda in Rangoon which enshrines eight hairs of the Buddha! It is a fine example of a Buddhist stupa. The glittering umbrella is overlaid with fresh gold leaf every year by the worshipers. In Java, Borobudur, and in Cambodia, Angkor Wat, are additional monuments to Indian architecture. Both are difficult to classify. Borobudur is Buddhist but highly ornamented like a Hindu temple. It was built about 850 A. D. Angkor Wat, built in the 12th century, is another Buddhist monastary.

Hindu architecture contrasts sharply with Greek and Gothic. It is emotional architecture centering on spiritual and other-worldly values. Logic and purity of form are absent. Diversity, contrast and color appeal to the diffused and spiritual mind of the Hindu. To the logical mind of western man Hindu architecture is often regarded as untidy and disorderly.

The Mughal architecture of India, is, perhaps the most lovely in the country. When the Muslims first came to India in the 13th century they brought with them the Persian dome and pointed arch. No great Muslim architecture prior to Mughal rule, however, is found in India. Pre-Mughal architecture consists mostly of square or hexagon domed tombs of the Afghan-Turko rulers. Forts like Tughluqabad were merely massive fortifications. They were constructed, in the main, of brick and mortar. It was only under the Mughals, starting in the 16th century, that Muslim architecture left its imprint on India. The Mughals built with stone—red sandstone and gleaming white marble. They built palaces, mosques and mausoleums. Architecture in India under the Mughals was no longer confined to religious structures.

The first Mughal building of note is Humayan's Tomb in New Delhi. Next, Akbar (1564–1605 A. D.) built numerous buildings in his capitals at Agra, Delhi, Lahore and Fatehpur Sikri. Fatehpur Sikri was designed and constructed as a new capital some 20 miles north of Agra. Unfortunately, it was soon abandoned due to inadequate water supply. His son, Jehangir (1605–

1627 A. D.) continued the building. But it was Shah Jehan (1627–1658), Jehangir's son, who built some of the most magnificent architectural pieces of the Mughal period. The Red Fort complex, so-called, in New Delhi, where Shah Jehan removed the capital from Agra, and the world famous Taj Mahal in Agra are the best examples.

A Mughal capital or palace is typically surrounded by a high red (perhaps better described as pink) sandstone wall decorated with turrets and cupolas, doubling as lookout towers. Inside the fortress-palace are a mosque, administrative and residential quarters constructed of white marble. The Pearl Mosques, so named because of the white bulbous dome, in the Agra and Delhi forts, are made entirely of white marble. So are the assembly halls and residential quarters in the Red Fort in New Delhi. The Diwan-i-am, or audience hall, with its scalloped pointed archway elicits wonder even today. It bears an inscription "If there be a paradise on earth; this is it, this is it." Here also stood the famous Peacock Throne, a cot (on which the emperor sat cross legged) with four peacocks at each corner constructed of gold and precious gems. It was stolen by Nadir Shah of Persia who made a devastating raid on New Delhi in 1739, when the Mughal empire was in disintegration, and dismantled for its gold and jewels in Iran!

Mughal architecture is a blend of Persian and Indian ideas. The bulbous dome and pointed arch are Persian. But the beautiful scalloping of the arch is said to be Shah Jehan's design. The cupolas and kiosks with their umbrella-type domes are Indian. The lattices or screens carved from marble slabs which decorate many Mughal buildings particularly the Taj Mahal are believed to be Indian. There is controversy about the floral designs of semi-precious gems inlaid in the marble. Some argue it is of Italian origin. Others feel it is Persian. And still others contend it is indigenous. It is well recorded that the Mughals employed architects and artists from Europe, Persia and other parts of the world, hence the marble inlaid work could have been of European origin. It is interesting to note in this connection that if a traveler, after visiting the Taj Mahal, stops to visit the Medici Chapel in Florence, built about the same time, he will find similar marble panels inlaid with semi-precious stones and colored marble in the Italian building!

Space does not permit description of these many beautiful Mughal buildings of 16th and 17th century India. It will suffice to focus on the Taj Mahal. But before so doing brief note must be taken of the Tomb of Itmad-ud-Daulah, the father of Nurmahal, Jehangir's Persian wife, in Agra. It is a small edifice, with four graceful towers at each corner of the rectangular building topped by typically Rajputan round cupolas. A small square second story with a rounded roof is set above the first floor between the towers. The windows are made of marble screens or lattices. Buff colored stone predominates, accentuated with white marble trim. It is without doubt the most delicate and poetic building of the Mughal group in Agra.

It is difficult to describe the Taj Mahal with mere words. To start, it can best be defined as a piece of jewelry 232 feet high! The mausoleum is set on a white marble platform 313 feet square and 22 feet high. At each corner of the platform are tapered minarets 130 feet tall with three evenly spaced galleries topped by a cupola. The mausoleum 120 feet in height is crowned with a bulbous dome 60 feet in diameter and 80 feet high. The entrance has a pointed archway 90 feet in diameter around which verses of the Koran are inscribed with black marble inlaid in white marble. Two stories of arched openings compose the three sided corners. Finally there are two cupolas on the roof besides the dome. Everything needless to add, is constructed in tightly fitted marble blocks.

The inside is white marble inlaid with semi-precious gems—jasper, agate, lapis lazuli, carnelian, bloodstone and others—in various and many floral designs. Muslims, it should be noted, do not depict human or animal life. A single carnation leaf contains 35 different varieties of carnelian. Directly under the dome is the cenataph or tomb surrounded by a marble screen enclosure. The enclosure was originally in gold, but Aurangzeb, Shah Jehan's son, replaced it with marble. Marble screens permeate the building allowing a play of light inside.

The only mar on the beautiful proportions and symmetry is the cenataph of Shah Jehan next to that of Mumtaz Mahal. This was not by design but by dint of history instead. Shah Jehan's grand design included a mausoleum to himself on the other side of the Jumna river in black marble—a counterpart in black to the white mausoleum of his wife. They were to be connected by two bridges across the river, one in white, the other in black marble. In fact, work on the foundation had already started when Shah Jehan fell ill. There was no orderly succession to the Mughal crown, so armed conflict broke out among his four sons. Aurangzeb prevailed, but his father recovered. Aurangzeb would not permit Shah Jehan's recovery to deprive him of his hard won victory so he imprisoned him in the Agra Fort. Aurangzeb provided Shah Jehan with every amenity of life, even a vantage point to view the Taj Mahal, but not his freedom. He cancelled the plans for the black marble mausoleum and entombed Shah Jehan in the Taj Mahal when he died 8 years later. Hence, the unforgivable asymmetry of an otherwise perfect piece of architecture.

The setting of the Taj Mahal is equally impressive. The approach is through a tall main gate of red sandstone inscribed with verses from the Koran. The gate leads to a walled garden with a large rectangular pool containing fountains. The pool is surrounded by dark green cypresses. The visitor first catches the reflection of the dome on the surface of the pool. The two red sandstone mosques flank the mausoleum. The three structures provide a striking view from the other side of the river.

The Taj Mahal presents a visitor with various moods. In the sunlight it gleams and sparkles. At night the white edifice presents a mystical effect.

But it is under a full moon that the Taj exudes its greatest charm. A lavender haze appears to hover over its bulbous dome and spiral minarets. Whether approached by day or night the Taj leaves the impression of floating in the air.

The Taj Mahal is often referred to as a love story. It appears that Shah Jehan was totally captivated by Mumtaz Mahal his second wife of Persian antecedants. She was the niece of the equally famous Nur Mahal his father's Persian wife. No incest, however, was involved as Shah Jehan was the son of Jehangir by a Rajput princess. Her name Mumtaz Mahal, variously translated, means "exalted of the palace", "pearl of the palace" and the like. Surviving paintings show her with black hair, fine features and delicate hands. She had also, apparently a beautiful body as Shah Jehan built a special bath house in his palace in New Delhi containing a large sunken pool-size bath with a marble chair beside it from which he could watch her bathe. She was 21 when they married in 1612 and bore him 14 children. When she died in childbirth in 1630 while Shah Jehan was away engaged in battle it is said he was nearly bereft of his senses. His hair turned white in a few months. He vowed he would build a memorial in her honor second to none.

He marshalled skilled craftsmen and artisans from Europe, Persia, Turkey and elsewhere. Twenty thousand laborers were employed for 17 years in the construction. The white marble had to be transported hundreds of miles from Rajasthan. Huge earth causeways were erected, as in the building of the Pyramids, to elevate the massive blocks of finished marble to their lofty positions.

The Taj Mahal is the gem, the centerpiece, of the many pieces of Mughal architecture that remain to this day in northern India in a triangular area defined by Rajasthan to Kashmir to Bengal. The Mughal court repaired to the Vale of Kashmir 600 miles from Delhi each summer to escape the heat of the Jumna-Ganges doab. They built many lovely buildings, gardens and fountains there, including the renowned Shalimar.

China contains far less durable and substantial architecture than the other civilizations. It was primarily a secular society. Confuscianism hardly inspired an architecture. Buddhist influence on China, of course, was profound and brought with it ideas on architecture and sculpture from India. But these ideas were soon mutated by the overwhelming Chinese culture.

From Chinese historical records—unlike the Indians the Chinese were good record keepers—there is evidence of great cities, palaces and other buildings during the Shang, Choa and Han dynasties. But the buildings have perished as they were built of wood and mud. The most common construction was the "plank building" technique, in which earth was stamped between two boards to form a wall effective against the cold of north China. The common people lived in "burrows and nests", presumably small mud huts or underground dugouts in the fashion of paleolithic man. This enabled them to take advantage of geothermal warmth against the cold. There is

evidence of these dwellings in the ancient Shang capital of Anyang unearthed in 1921.

In the middle of the first millennium of the Christian era Buddhism was
very predominant in China. By the 7th century there were 3716 Buddhist
monasteries in the country. Many were extremely rich, cultivating large
tracts with "temple slaves". They held their wealth in bronze. There was
even a Buddhist "pope" under the emperor. In 845 A. D. there was a
reaction to Buddhism. Emperor Wu Tsung launched a persecution in which
many monks died, their property was confiscated and their monasteries
destroyed. Little or no evidence of this Buddhist architecture survived. The
stone pagoda on Mount Sung in Hanan, erected about 520 A. D., has
distinctive Indian characteristics. It looks like a combination stupa and
shikhara. There is also evidence of rock architecture which the Chinese
pilgrims found in India and central Asia. The Buddhist cave temples and
shrines, some with colossal sculptures of Buddha, at Yun-Shang in Shansi
were constructed during the period 460–535 A. D. There are some 20 large
caves and several smaller ones.

Around 1000 A. D. Chinese architecture submerged the Indian influence
and assumed the characteristic familiar to the world today. It was the
multiroofed wooden pagoda ornamented with tile, ceramic, lacquer and
wood carvings. The beauty and charm resides in the roof or roofs. The idea
of the curved eave is thought to have come from Siam and Indo-China. Tiers
of these delicate roofs identify the Chinese temple. The pagoda in Nanking
had eight roofs which rose 200 feet into the sky. It was destroyed in 1856.
Some pagodas had as many as 12 roofs. But Chinese architecture was more
secular than religious. Palaces and administrative buildings possessed the
same emphasis on the roof. So did the homes of the gentry.

Another Chinese characteristic is the dragon carvings. Marco Polo
describes the dragon pillars in Kublai Khan's palace at Shandu "Round each
pillar a dragon, likewise gilt, entwines its tail, while its head sustains the
projection of the roof, and its talons and claws are extended to the right and
left along the entablature." He also describes the varnished bamboo roof
where split bamboo lengths are laid "concave and convex" to form a rain
proof surface.

Japan adopted this Chinese architecture and raised it to heights of
excellence. The gates and temples at Nikko are a splendor of form and color.
Beautiful pagoda temples and palaces too are found in Kyoto and Nara. Tile,
lacquer and carvings are employed profusely for decoration. But generally
the temples and palaces are not over ornamented.

To complete the survey note should also be taken of the Indian architecture in the Americas. The Mayan pyramids, called teocallis, were steeper
than those found in Egypt, had steps on each of their four sides leading up to
a sanctuary on top where the religious ritual was performed. Best known is
the one at Chichen Itza which rises 75 feet to a massive temple on top.

Earlier Mayan temples were taller. The one at Tikal, Guatemala, rose to 240 feet! These temples were constructed during the period 300 B. C.–900 A. D.

The Aztecs continued the Mayan architecture. They added balconies to display the heads and hearts of their human sacrifices! Bernal Diaz gives us some vivid and lurid descriptions of the great temple in Tenochtitlan where the Aztecs conducted their human sacrifices (including many Spaniards) to their war god Huitzilopochtli.

Temple building was far less emphasized by the Incas, but they have left some imposing urban development for posterity. Macchu Picchu is a city built with stone, atop a saddle lying between two peaks (Macchu and Picchu) about 2000 feet above the Urubamba river as it issues out of the Andes into the Amazon plain. It was a fortified city with a royal palace, temples, sacred plazas, residential compounds and terraces for growing food atop the mountain. One beholds it in wonderment for it defies understanding as to why a city was built on these mountain tops until he learns that the narrow Inca roads (designed only for pack animals and people on foot) ran along the mountain tops unlike those of other civilizations who built their roads in valleys and mountain passes for heavy vehicular traffic.

Further up the Urubamba, twenty-four miles northwest of Cuzco, the Inca capital, is the city of Ollantaytambo. Unlike Macchu Picchu it is built in the valley into the side of a large rock massif. It is an impressive planned city with, surprisingly, terraces cut into the rock mountain for agricultural purposes.

The Incas built with stone (on the coast they used adobe) well fitted so that only a hairline was visible. They possessed only stone tools. They did not know the wheel though they used rollers. Yet they built these remarkable, well planned cities of stones some of which weighed many tons. There is a megalith atop the massif where Ollantaytambo was built, some 100 feet above the valley weighing around 20 tons! How the Inca builders raised it to this height is a source of wonder. Yet one must remind himself that this was only 500 years or so ago when European and Asian men were building Gothic cathedrals and beautiful mausoleums like the Taj Mahal! It is architecture, in final analysis, not greatly advanced over Stonehenge.

DRESS AND ADORNMENT

Clothing became important for survival when man decided to challenge the glacier. In the warm climate of Africa and South Asia, where man first evolved, coverage of the body against the weather was of minor importance and has remained so to date as we shall see later. Why man never developed a fur for protection against the cold is not altogether understood. What is clear is that man evolved in a warm climate and did not need much hair for survival. When he decided to challenge the glaciers he had developed sufficient technology to clothe himself against the cold so that the normal forces of evolution were not called upon for the development of a fur as happened with the bison, mammoth, reindeer, and other animals who lived on the tundra.

How did early man protect his body on the tundra? He borrowed the fur of the animals he killed in the hunt. One of man's earliest tools was the needle. Needles made of bone or ivory were used by Cro-Magnon 50,000 years ago. And it stands to reason that Neanderthal before him fashioned needles out of wood, perhaps, 100,000 years ago. It was only with the invention of the burin that paleolithic man was able to make a needle out of bone or ivory. Flint scrapers to remove the flesh from the hide were used long before erectus decided not to retreat before the glaciers. Vestiges of this way of life still exist today among the Eskimos and Laplanders living in very cold climates.

Agriculture provided a new source of clothing. Man learned how to spin and weave the hair and wool of the goats and sheep he domesticated. Plant fibres such as flax (for linen) and cotton provided further clothing materials. This coincided with the retreat of the Wurm glacier and an increase in temperature of the temperate zones making the new lighter clothing materials adequate to warm the body. Furs were no longer that necessary.

The spindle and the loom were invented to weave the animal and plant fibres into cloth. The earliest evidence of linen cloth has been found in the graves at Badari, Egypt dating back to 3000 B. C. or so. Two scraps of cloth were found in Mohenjodaro, India dating back to the same period.

Sericulture comes later. Fragments of silk cloth have been traced back to the Shang dynasty (circa 1600–1028 B. C.). They reveal a sophisticated weaving technique intimating that weaving was known in China much earlier. Silk was never important to man for protection against the weather. It was a source of enjoyment and distinction for the ruling elites. Its role in history, however, was profound, as already noted from time to time. It prompted the East-West caravans of ancient times and endowed their routes with the pseudonym, the Old Silk Road.

These animals and plant fibres, actually few in number, provided man with his clothing until the 20th century when man invented synthetic fibres from cellulose and petro-chemicals. Rayon, nylon, dacron and others now supply man with much of his apparel. These fibres were not possible of course before the advent of industrialization.

The textile industry, until modern times, was the main manufacturing enterprise of man. China dominated the silk industry and India the cotton industry for millennia. It was only during the reign of Justinian (483–565 A. D.) that the Mediterranean world learned sericulture. Indian muslins dominated the textile world until the 18th century when industrial spinning and weaving superceded the hand loom. Indian prowess was due, in large measure, to the caste system. A boy born into the weaver caste had his role defined for him. His religion told him that through exemplary performance in his role he might elevate himself into a higher, even the Brahman, caste in the rebirth of his soul. He became, therefore, the best weaver in the world. Foreign invaders and traders sought his wares.

It is also noteworthy that the earliest developments of the Industrial Revolution involved the textile industry. The spinning-jenny and the power loom were among the first machines powered by steam. Cheap cotton goods became available for the masses. It spelled the doom of the hand loom industries of India and China. To be sure, the new textile machinery was unable to produce cotton cloth of the fineness and quality of the Indian muslins. This was but an early instance of sacrificing quality for quantity which modern industry begot.

Man did not clothe himself only for protection against the weather. He used clothes, as everything else, for domination. Agriculture provided the ruling elite not only with the wealth they could appropriate for power and dominance but the fibres with which they could distinguish themselves from the dominated majority. Clothes came to be worn for status and authority. The peasants wore rags; the kings and nobles adorned themselves with the finest woolens, linen, cotton and silk. The imperial Inca wore a new suit of clothes each day and passed it down to the lesser nobility for further wear. Eventually, one may presume, it ended up as rags worn by the cultivator. The finest garments produced by the society "clothed" the rulers with power. The dominated majority could only aspire to such raiment but seldom got to wear it.

Bodily adornment has been practiced by men in the tropics too where, obviously, it is unnecessary to dress for warmth. Such adornment often takes the form of painting or otherwise marking the body, plumed and feathered headgear and the like not involving animal or plant fibres. Tortuous acts like elongating the ear lobes, distending the lower lip and inflicting welts on the body have been practiced in Africa and the Amazon basin. Such non-clothing adornment too was calculated to serve the purpose of status and domination.

A new factor in human dress was introduced when technological advance made possible a wider distribution of wealth and the emergence of a middle class. It was fashion in clothes, which dictated a frequent, even annual, change in the mode of dress. The upper and middle class, particularly the women, had to constantly update their wardrobes in order to maintain status and self esteem. Economics played its part as fashion promoted an ever increasing market required for the goods of industrial expansion.

Other factors were involved. Women have always dressed for sexual attraction. It would seem that, in the psychology of sex, a fully or partially clothed woman, or man, is more sexually attractive than one openly naked at all times. Hence, women have always used clothes, subtly revealing or accentuating bosoms, legs, ankles and other appealing features. In fact, it has been argued that men have taken advantage of women in this connection by designing "hobbling" type dress to subject women. The hoop skirt, the bustle and other monstrosities of the 19th century are pointed out as examples. The Muslim chador was obviously designed to keep women subjected. Even the skirt is said to have the purpose of restriction of fast movement.

Modesty about and protection of the procreative and eliminatory parts of the body have been further reasons for clothes. The loin skirt or cloth is not only ubiquitous but was, perhaps, one of man's first items of clothing. When man assumed an upright position his genitals became particularly exposed and vulnerable. He sought ways to protect himself and the loin cloth evolved. The ancient Egyptians are frequently depicted with loin aprons as more clothing was not needed, particularly in the upper Nile. In Europe and Asia more adequate clothing required for warmth also provided for modesty. The Biblical embarrassment over nudity would appear in harmony with the Judeo-Christian position that man was created in the image of God. It became necessary to hide or cloak any reminders of man's animal like functions. Finally, it would be hard to imagine civilized man without clothes. People in the nude would be just another herd of animals.

Man's clothing has, with few exceptions, been of four types, two designed to hang on the shoulders and two to hang from the waist. Trousers and skirts hang from the waist; the shirt (tunic, blouse or chemise) and the coat (mantle, cloak or cape) hang from the shoulders.

In general men have worn trousers and women skirts. Men, doubtless, preferred trousers for the hunt as they permitted greater freedom of movement and provided protection for the legs and genitals. Women preferred the skirt, perhaps because of the comfort and ventilation it afforded the pelvic region. Rock painting in Spain 12,000 years old depict men in trousers and women in skirts! This basic difference in male and female attire has persisted throughout history. No such differentiation, however, is found in garments hanging from the shoulders.

Variations in these four basic garments have, on the other hand, been many. It would be impossible to detail them all. Note will be taken of the more striking. In ancient Egypt men wore short loin skirts and women long narrow sleeveless tunics made of linen. In ancient Greece men and women wore chitons which were long loose fitting gowns hung from the shoulders and girdled at the waist. Men's chitons were usually knee length; women's full skirted with embroidered hems. Flowing clinging gowns of fine silk and cotton, as depicted in marble sculpture, were favored in later centuries. Woolen cloaks and scarves were worn over the shoulders and head in colder weather.

In ancient Rome men and women wore the toga. It was a semi-circular mantle three times the height of the wearer in length. It was draped from the shoulders and worn with great pride as it was forbidden to non Roman citizens.

After the conquest of Greece the women adopted Greek fashions. Due to a colder climate Roman women usually wore several layers of undergarments—a short sleeved tunic next to the body and over it a long robe with shorter sleeves called the stola. A palla or scarf was worn over the shoulders. Roman women became extremely fond of silk and muslin from China and India which drained much gold from Rome and facilitated the bankruptcy of the empire.

Men wore a short sleeved tunic at home. In public they wore a long tunic over which the toga was draped. The Romans used to ridicule the trousers worn by the Gauls in the colder climate of Europe but after the conquest of Europe the Romans began to adapt to trousers particularly in the colonies.

The Europeans favored the trousers. The coat and trouser eventually became the dress of the western man. Women continued the fashion of Greek and Roman women by wearing the gown or dress. But these basic clothes went through some elaborations and even ostentations during medieval times and continued so until the French Revolution. Velvet coats and breaches, long white stockings, ruffed shirts and plumed hats were the fashion of the monarchy and nobles.

The coat and trousers became the badge of the European colonizer around the world. Asian and African men started to emulate the fashion even though it was ill suited for the hot climates of the colonies. To be sure, Europeans also compromised with the weather by wearing the bush shirt and shorts, but the coat and trousers remained the badge of authority. The topee must be noted in this connection. It is a hard lightweight hat or helmet made of paper maché or solapith. It has an inner harness to keep the hat from fitting tightly on the head to permit circulation of air. The topee gave the European the requisite authority, even when worn with the bush shirt and shorts, over the colonials.

Byzantine, Persian and other western Asians wore long sleeved tunics with long cloaks and embroidered breast pieces. The fabrics were usually heavily brocaded, embroidered and embedded with gems, pearls, gold and silver. A short tunic belted at the waist was worn underneath, especially in colder climates. Women wore essentially the same. Common people wore a single tunic girdled at the waist.

Indian clothes differed considerably from that of the Mediterranean area. The men wore the dhoti or longie. The dhoti is essentially a loin cloth. It is usually five yards long and three to four feet wide and made of fine white cotton. One half the length is wrapped around the waist and the other half passed through the legs and tucked into the waist in the back. In some parts, notably Bengal, the dhoti is a yard or so longer so that one end may be flung across the chest and over the shoulder. Mostly, though, the Indian male prefers to be barechested. The longie is an ankle length sarong tucked around the waist and worn in the extreme south, along the Malabar coast. It is also popular in the Indianized parts of southeast Asia like Burma, Siam and Indonesia.

Turbans are also worn by men. They are most popular with the Rajputs and Sikhs. In fact, the Sikh religion prescribes that men refrain from cutting their hair and wear a turban at all times. In the hot climate of India this must surely be considered a form of penance! The Rajputs are also fond of wearing tight ankle length breaches of white linen called Jodhpurs with a form fitting three-fourths length coat. This long coat has now been adopted by the Government of India as official wear. It is sometimes called the Nehru jacket. The Gandhi cap, a political manifestation of the Congress party, is also worth mentioning. It is a plain white cap made of Khaddar (homespun) that can be folded like the army cap of the American soldier. The westernized Indian has adopted the European trousers and jacket of his erstwhile colonial masters but it is ill suited for India, except perhaps, during the pleasant winter months in the north (including New Delhi). During the long hot summer (April–October) Indian officials and businessmen compromise with the weather by wearing only trousers with a bush shirt (straight edged tail worn on the outside of the trousers). No tie. Most of these westernized Indians, however, find refuge from the heat in the far more comfortable dhoti upon their return to their homes from a hot day at the office!

Far more noteworthy, however, is the sari worn by the Indian women. It too is a single piece of cloth six yards or so long and three to four feet wide. The finest are made of muslin, silk and, today, of man-made fibres referred to as art-silk in India. Their most striking feature is the patterns and colors. Most have embroidered or otherwise decorated edges. Many are brocaded and interwoven with gold and silver threads. An Indian lady of the upper classes usually has a fortune invested in her saris. These saris are passed on from mother to daughter for several generations. Fortunately, there is no or little fashion to make them obsolete.

The sari is worn with a choli, a very tight fitting bodice worn without any undergarment. The choli too is made of fine cloth often brocaded and decorated. The sari is tucked and wrapped around the waist with a yard or so left over to fling across the shoulder or head. Such end is usually highly designed and edged with fringe. A half slip is usually worn under the sari. In south India the left over end is pulled through the legs and tucked into the waist in back as is done with a man's dhoti. There is a deviation from the sari in the Punjab where the women, particularly the Sikhs, wear a loose fitting pajama (the word originated here) covered with a long slitted waist to the knees. A colored muslin scarf, an odni, is worn over the head or, more so today, across the shoulders. This mode of dress is due to the Muslim influence in north India. The loose fitting trousers are doubtless of Persian derivation.

Unlike the men an Indian woman is wedded to her sari. Very few forsake them for Western dress. Even when they travel or live abroad they prefer to wear saris. It serves to add an exotic touch to an otherwise drab and colorless gathering.

Indian dress is, perhaps, the most pragmatic of that worn today. Both the dhoti and the sari are adjustable to the variations in obesity of the wearer. Pregnancy does not call for a new wardrobe. This is not true of the choli. A few pounds gain in weight immediately bursts the seams. And saris are immune from the obsolesence of fashion. There have, however, been changes in fashion over the years but ever so slightly. Even today certain saris are avant garde, but it is mostly in the patterns and designs on the cloth. The dhoti and sari have been worn since time immemorial. The only controversy is whether women wore a choli in olden times. Neither history or art give a clear cut answer. Some point to the women of Bali who wear the sari barebreasted as proof that Indian women, particularly in south India, did likewise in ancient times.

The Chinese had to dress more in keeping with the cold climate of China. For everyday wear they have always worn trousers and a short jacket. Royalty and nobility dressed more elaborately. During the Han dynasty (202 B. C.–221 A. D.) both men and women wore the p'ao gown. It had wide sleeves girdled to the waist, and flowed to the floor in voluminous folds. The ruling elite wore the p'ao gown until the Ch'ing dynasty when the Manchus in 1644 introduced the ch'au-fu robe. The man's robe had a pleated skirt, long tight sleeves with horseshoe cuffs and a tight neckband with a detachable wing-tipped collar. The woman's gown was straight with a capelike collar. Everyday wear of the gentry was the chi-fu, a straight robe with long tubular sleeves. A three-quarter length coat was worn over both gowns. A plain long robe, called the ch'ang-fu comprised the informal wear. Chinese women eventually removed the sleeves, shortened it and slit the sides to make the modern Chinese dress. All this elaborate dress, designed for the non laboring gentry, was swept aside by the Chinese communists in favor of the ancient trousers and short jacket. The jacket, or both, are padded with cotton for the cold winters of China.

The Japanese borrowed the Chinese mode of dress. Prior to the eighth century A. D. the Japanese men wore full loose trousers called hakama with a jacket flared over the hips. Women wore a pleated skirt instead of trousers. In the Nara period (710–784 A. D.) the p'ao gown was adopted from China. From the p'ao gown the Japanese developed the kimona for both men and women. The Kimona is a broad sleeved gown that overlaps on the right side and is drawn together by a sash called the obi. The men's obi is usually narrow and plain. The women's wide and decorated. It is often gathered in a large bow in the back. Fashions in fabric, draping and sashing changed and varied. Both men and women have now forsaken the old mode of dress in favor of western suits and dresses in their public life. The old custom of dress is confined to the privacy of the home.

Men and women of all civilizations have employed other adornment of the body. Jewelry from basic metals, for instance, the bronze bracelets of the Unitice culture, to precious gems have been prized everywhere. And in keeping with the dominance instinct the ruling elite, particularly royalty, appropriated for their use, enjoyment *and authority* the most valuable and precious jewelry. In many countries jewelry also serves as a store of wealth. In India, for instance, which has suffered the depredations of foreign invaders for millennia the common people (and wealthy, needless to say) place their savings in gold and silver bracelets, anklets and the like which are worn by the women of the family day and night.

Adornment of the head has also preoccupied men and women. For some reason humans have never been satisfied with their hair or absence of it—in the case of men afflicted with congenital baldness. Ancient Egyptians, both men and women, shaved their heads and wore stylized wigs of human hair. Minoan, Greek and Persian males wore wigs. They were popular in Rome with the women. Faustina, wife of Marcus Aureleus, is reputed to have had two hundred wigs. Roman men, however, did not seem to mind baldness.

Wigs were the fashion in medieval times in Europe. They became a badge of authority with judges and magistrates though it is said the jurists took to them to keep their heads, particularly bald pates, warm in the cold court rooms of the day. But they soon attained the badge of authority of the common law wherever it went even to countries like India where the judicial wig was most uncomfortable in the hot courtrooms of Bombay and Calcutta.

Elaborate coiffures became the fashion of the medieval women. Madame de Pompadour (1721–1764), mistress of Louis XV, popularized the hairdo forever bearing her name whereby a woman's hair was dressed over a pad or artificial frame to raise the tresses high above the forehead. Some of these "pompadours" reached heights of three feet or more just prior to the French Revolution. The women of China and Japan resorted to a similar fashion. These elaborate wigs and hairdos of medieval times were powdered grey, later white, for maximum attractiveness. Women of several civilizations, mostly in the Mediterranean area, dyed their hair. Since, most humans have black or brunette hair the color of distinction to achieve was various shades of blonde or red. Hair has also been curled and decurled to suit changing fashions.

Hats were popular with European men—and women—of 19th century times. Hats displaced wigs with men after the French and American Revolutions. After mid-20th century hats lost their vogue and men, particularly in Europe, began to wear hair pieces to cover their baldness. Hair transplants have now been made possible by medical science.

History also reveals occasional enormities in this connection. Mention has already been made of the elongated ears and distended lower lips of African women. In China for thousands of years women's feet were bound with bandages to achieve petit feet, a badge of distinction and a source of sexual stimulation to men among the gentry. Substantially the same effect could have been achieved, as Lin Yutang sagely observed, with high heeled shoes. Had some genius conceived them he could have spared millions of young Chinese girls much suffering and discomfort over the millennia. The Chinese communists, needless to add, did away with this ancient practice.

Perfumes, ointments and cosmetics were used by the ancient Egyptians, Indians, Romans, Persians, and others. They were used, and still are, mostly to gratify the olfactory sense. And for sexual stimulation. To some extent they were and are used for deodorization of the body. Most civilizations placed high premium on personal hygiene. The elaborate baths of the Romans and the daily bathing of the Hindus are leading examples. European man was a laggard in this respect. He did not begin to bathe regularly until the 20th century!

SCULPTURE

Fine arts date back much further than most people realize. Cro-Magnon left carvings and sculptures in quantity in horn, bone, ivory and stone some of which have been dated back nearly 30,000 years! They fall mainly into three categories—the so-called Venus figures, animal depictions and decorations of batons and tool handles, particularly the spear thrower. The Venus figures, some almost grotesque, portray females with exaggerated pelvic areas and bosoms. They are thought to be fertility symbols. Three score or more have been found scattered throughout Europe and Asia. Quite typical are the Willendorf Venus found in Austria and another, a clay figure, found in Czechoslovakia.

The animal sculptures, on the other hand are much more faithful depictions of life. Unfortunately Cro-Magnon was at times limited by his plastic material, such as a narrow horn or antler, but within these confines his artistry reaches considerable heights of perfection. There is, for example, the leaping horse, 15,000 years old, found at Bruniguel, France carved from a reindeer antler. The front legs had to be folded to the body, the head and neck extended forward and the hind legs thrust back to conform to the narrow antler, but it gives the carving tremendous action and poise for a leap into space. It could be that the prehistoric artist actually observed in a hunt a horse in some such posture leaping across a gorge or chasm. The geometric designs on tool handles and batons too reflect a high degree of sophistication.

Neolithic man continued to sculpt and engrave. His technology had advanced substantially and he was able to polish stone by this time. He worked a wider range of materials including chalk, pumice, alabaster, soft calcite and burnt clay. Fifty or so statuettes have been found at Catal

Huyuk, the Neolithic city in Anatolia representing dieties. Most are mother goddesses with well endowed bodies not too unlike the Cro-Magnon Venuses.

After the dawn of history a leading characterization of civilizations was their sculpture. Much of it has been religious art or otherwise highly stylized. Two have however, attained great realism and emotionalism. The Greek and the Indian.

The Greeks emulated, at first, the Egyptian, Minoan and Mesopotamian sculpture which consisted mainly of stiff frontal and unnatural figures. This early Greek sculpture is often referred to as archaic. But by the middle of the 5th century B. C. the classical sculpture, for which ancient Greece is renowned, reached its full development. The six great masters of Greek classical sculpture were Myron, Phidias, Polyclitus, Praxiteles, Lysippus and Scopos. Phidias was the master sculptor of the Parthenon. Sculpture was always closely associated with architecture in ancient Greece.

Much of Greek classical sculpture lives only by description as the artists worked in wood and bronze, the first perishable and the latter found more useful by succeding generations for armaments and other purposes. Even Phidias' Athena in the Parthenon was made of wood, covered with gold and ivory. Toward the end of the classical period, the fourth century, white marble became the main medium of Greek sculpture. Men were usually nude and muscular, for example, the many famous "Apollos" but the women were draped with flowing chitons and the folds artfully sculpted to reveal the sensous body underneath. The figures were now posed freely and were no longer painted. The artists were able to polish the white marble so it felt and looked like flesh. Venus de Milo, now at the Louvre, is among the best examples. The lovely Nikes, of which the Winged Victory of Sammothrace, also at the Louvre, sculpted around 305 B. C. is a good example, are even better renditions of the flowing chiton draping the female figure.

Equally famous are the bas-reliefs which decorate temple moldings, friezes, metopes and pediment backgrounds. The Elgin marbles, in the British Museum, from the pediment of the Parthenon sculpted by Phidias, are among the best of this sculpture. The riders and horses in the cavalry procession appear so real it is hard to believe that the relief is only about 2 inches thick!

Greek sculpture proliferated after Alexander's conquests during the Hellenistic Period. Most of what has survived was created during these centuries. The work remained of a high quality but the subject matter broadened. Children and old people were portrayed realistically.

The Roman conquest of Greece in 146 B. C. gave Greek sculpture further distribution as the newly wealthy Romans became art collectors. The Romans had a tradition of Etruscan art but it was quickly overcome by the Greek influence. Under Roman dominance Greek sculpture deteriorated in quality if not in quantity. By the time of the empire it had degenerated to portraiture. The musemums of Europe today are overwhelmed with busts of Roman emperors, empresses and other dignitaries.

After the fall of Rome the art of sculpture vanished in the Mediterranean area for centuries. It was slowly revived in the beginning of the second millennium for religious purposes. Both the Romanesque and Gothic figures in and on the churches and cathedrals were highly stylized stiff and unyielding figures. The Virgin Mother was a favorite portrayal. It was only in the Renaissance that the natural expressive spirit of classical Greek sculpture emerged again. Michelangelo (1475–1564) was its chief exponent. His David, Moses and other figures are life itself in marble! Michelangelo far outdid the Greeks in sculpting muscle and anatomy. Donatello, Bernini and even the earlier Nicola and Pisano also sculpted in the Greek tradition. The tradition carried over into the 18th century with such great sculptors as Antonio Canova (1757–1822). His beautiful semi-nude portrayal of Napoleon's sister Pauline Bonaparte Borghese residing in the Borghese Gallery in Rome is in the tradition of the great Praxiteles. Thereafter sculpture in the West degenerated once again into portraiture as best seen by the statues of English dignitaries cluttering up Westminster Abbey.

Indian sculpture originated in the early Indus civilization (3000–1500) B. C.). Several pieces have been unearthed at Harappa and Mohenjodaro. There is a red stone torso of a man, a grey statuette of a dancing girl and the famous bronze dancing girl of Mohenjodaro. All reflect good knowledge of human anatomy by the artist. Many bas-reliefs have also been found (mostly seals) depicting realistically animals and plants.

After the Aryan conquest (1500 B. C. *et seq.*) all evidence of sculpture vanishes for a thousand years or more. It is possible the non-urban Aryans worked in wood which has perished. It was only during the Buddhist period, beginning about the 3rd century B. C. that Indian artists started to work in stone. This early Buddhist sculpture, called the Mathura School was religiously inspired and highly stylized. It usually depicted a seated (sometimes standing) Buddha or Bodhisattva (analogous to a saint) in a serene and meditative mood. To a Buddhist these figures convey much feeling and meaning not readily evident to the uninitiated. These greatly stylized figures symbolize the divine wisdom of Buddha, serenity and peace in a chaotic world.

Far greater realism, however, is found in other figures. The capitals of the Ashoka pillars depict life more freely. Best known of these capitals is the one found at Sarnath with four lions facing outward. It now forms the seal of the government of India. Most noteworthy, however, are the famous yaksis, the voluptuous female figures that graced the stupas and other shrines. Some of the yaksis tend to be over voluptuous but others comprise some of the most sensuous plastic art of man. One of the finest examples is found in the Museum of Fine Arts in Boston. It is a torso of a young female from Sanchi dating back to the first century B. C.

Indian sculpture was influenced by the classical Greek. Alexander the Great came to India in 327 B. C. Thereafter Greek satrapies were set up in the Punjab. But the Mauryans, under Chandragupta I, soon recaptured the area. In the second century B. C. Ashoka converted to Buddhism and it became the dominant religion of India. After the decline of the Mauryan empire an indigenous kingdom of Gandhara arose in the area, which today is West Pakistan and Afghanistan, that lasted from the first century B. C. to the fifth century A. D. Greek influence continued. Trade with the Roman empire also flourished. Under both contacts the Indians were exposed to classical Greek art. Many of Buddhist and civic sculptures in the area at this time bear a strong Greek influence. Some of the Buddha figures are even draped. There are Athena-like female statues—distinguishable from Greek sculpture only by the non-Greek or Roman face. This sculpture has come to be known as Gandharan art.

Gandharan sculpture spread far and wide. It influenced Chinese and other Asian Buddhist art. The Greek influence gradually vanished in India so that by the time of the Brahmanic revival little Greek influence is noted. During the great Hindu temple building era (9th to 13th centuries) sculptures were depicting gods from the Hindu pantheon instead of Buddhas. But the sensuous female figures continued to decorate the temples. A particularly striking statue is one from the Shiva temple at Khajuraho of a beautifully proportioned female nude. She is scantily clad in a jeweled and ribboned girdle and viewed from the back in a quarter turned position of the head and shoulders.

Hindu sculptors focused on the female body. Love-making scenes are common. All the various coital positions described by Vatsyayama are depicted somewhere on Hindu temples. This feature of the Hindu view of life has already been discussed.

Noteworthy too is Indian metal sculpture. Most are miniature figures only inches high, though a few can be measured in feet. They are produced by the *cire perdue*, or lost-wax process. The figure is first sculpted in bees wax. It is then covered with several layers of fine clay mixed with charred rice husks, minced cotton, salt and other ingredients. Holes are left for the wax to flow out and the metal to be introduced. The mold is placed in an oven to melt the wax and bake the mold. The molten metal, which is copper, brass or bronze, is then poured into the cavity left by the melted wax to reproduce exactly the statue carved by the artist in wax.

The dancing girl of Mohenjodaro was produced by the lost wax process. That was 5000 years ago and, perhaps, the first evidence of the process. An even greater lacuna is encountered in metal sculpture. Fine metal sculpture was created during the Gupta period (320–500 A. D.) but only a few survive like the life size Buddha from Bihar, now in the Birmingham Art Gallery. Most of these bronzes were destroyed and purloined by the Muslim invaders purblind on the subject of idolatry and greedy for the metal they contained.

The Indian bronzes that survived are either from the south or Nepal where Muslim dominance failed to extend.

The finest examples belong to the Chola Period (10th–13th centuries) and the most outstanding figure is the dancing Nataraja. It represents the creation and dissolution of the world. Shiva, with his right foot on the demon of ignorance and his left in air, is delicately balanced in a halo of flames. He has four hands. The upper right holds a drum sounding creation and his upper left a ball of fire denoting destruction. His lower right is in the gesture of assurance and the lower left outstretched in a dancing position. These Natarajas range from a few inches to a few feet in diameter.

The Nataraja (meaning the lord of dance) bronzes contain much Hindu religion and philosophy. It strikes one as odd that the same God, Shiva, should represent creation and destruction. But in Hindu thought there is no absolute destruction, merely change. Hence, destruction must precede creation of a new life, a new universe and so on. Thus the Nataraja represents change in life and the universe.

The south Indian bronzes depict the Hindu pantheon. Lakshmi, the goddess of wealth, Parvati, Shiva's wife, and Vishnu, an incarnation of Krishna, are popular figures. A particularly endearing statuette is Lord Krishna as a baby crawling and holding a ball in his right hand.

In Nepal, Tibet, Ceylon, Burma and elsewhere in southeast Asia the Buddhist dieties are encountered. A popular figure is Tara, the virgin goddess of the Buddhist dieties. These Taras abound in Nepal and Tibet some with Aryan and others with Mongolian faces. The Nepali and Tibetan bronzes are often gilded or painted and sometimes studded with jewels. Some are gilded only in front. The gold wash was accomplished by dipping in or painting them with an amalgam of mercury and gold. The majority of them are cast hollow and the inside sealed with prayers, messages and even jewels. The date of production is sometimes found inside.

The Indian bronze art is thought to have reached Nepal during Gupta time. But the major influence was from Bengal during the Pala dynasty (780–892 A. D.). After the devastation wrought by the Muslim invasions in India the development of Nepal bronze sculpture proceeded on its own. It tended to refinement and miniature, causing the Indian art expert, Dr. A. K. Coomaraswamy to conclude that it "suggests the hand of the goldsmith rather than a modeller".

Chinese sculpture was greatly influenced, perhaps inspired, by Indian sculpture under the aegis of Buddhism. As already discussed the Chinese worked with bronze casting as early as the Shang dynasty (circa 1600–1028 B. C.). But these castings were rarely sculpture comprising mainly utilitarian vessels and objects.

Most of the Buddhist bronzes were destroyed in the reaction against Buddhism under Emperor Wu Tsung of the Tang dynasty in 843 A. D. The Buddhist statues in the cave temples at Yunkang and elsewhere are the best repositories of the Chinese Buddhist culture. There is a 45 foot high Buddha in front of cave XX at Yunkang! These sculptures bear the influence of the Gandhara School but later the Indian impact is thought to have come up from southeast Asia, notable Champa (Cambodia). The Buddhas begin to take on a Mongolian face and fat bodies reflecting the Chinese influence. Greater Chinese influence is seen after 1000 A. D. as Buddhism never recovered its former status after Emperor Wu Tsung's persecution. The religion itself became introspective merging with the Taoist philosophy. This became the Chen sect and Zen Buddhism in Japan. The Mother Goddess (of mercy) Kuanyin comes to be venerated and her highly stylized statues became common.

There is also some purely indigenous Chinese sculpture. Most spectacular are the huge figures in stone of animals and men lining the Ceremonial Way, near Peking, the two mile route to the tombs of the Ming emperors. They are not particularly good. Most distinguished are the porcelain figures of the Ming dynasty (1368–1644 A. D.). A fine example is the three color under glaze of Kuanyin in the Musee Guimet in Paris. Miniature figurines in ivory, jade and semi-precious stones were quite common during the Ming and Ch'ing periods. But on the whole sculpture was not the leading art of the Chinese. They excelled instead in porcelain for utilitarian and decorative purposes.

The same Buddhist influence with Chinese mutation carried over to Japan. The Japanese became predisposed toward large statues of the Buddha as seen in the famous Diabutsus. The most notable at Kamakura is 97 feet in circumference and about 50 feet high. It was made of bronze in the year 1252. Equally huge is the Diabutsu in the Todai-ji temple in Nara. The Japanese were also fond of the Chinese Goddess Kuanyin which they called Kwannon.

The Chinese led mankind in the development of ceramics. Perhaps it was a natural corallary to their fine cuisine. Pottery is the earliest and most ubiquitous of the arts of man. He needed a container for his food and drink. A vessel of fired clay was invented in Neolithic times. Pottery finds in Japan date back 10,000 years! The potters wheel was invented in Sumeria at the end of the fourth millennium B. C. Prior thereto the pot was hand-formed, which included the use of a turntable. About 500° F. is required to fire the clay pots but it is believed the Chinese developed kilns for their pottery capable of temperatures of 2000° F or more before recorded history. Next came underglazing whereby the decoration was applied to the clay pot after it was fired. A mixture of minerals such as lead, feldspar, borax and others was overlaid and fired again. When these minerals fused they left a transparent glassy coating over the decoration.

Double firing, however, was not the method used by the ancient Greeks on their historically famous pottery. After the Greek vases were formed on the potter's wheel they were allowed to dry. While semi-dry and plastic the artist applied the decoration. The reddish-orange was achieved by a coating of yellow ochre, the metallic black by iron oxide on the Attic clay. The oxidation, reduction and re-oxidation in the firing fixed the distinctive red-orange and black color glazes on the vases.

Many centuries elapsed, however, before the Chinese invented porcelain. Good stonewares were made from the 4th century of the Christian era. It required firing to 2250° F in order to fuse the China-stone (a feldspar mineral) and fine white clay to a glassy matrix.

Thereafter, the porcelain improved in quality, design and beauty for some thousand years until the creative genius was spent. Despite foreign rule during the Yuan dynasty (Kublai Khan) great advances were made. But new heights were achieved during the Ming dynasty when the famous blue on translucent white porcelain was created. Marvelous porcelain continued to be manufactured during the early part of the Manchu dynasty (1644–1911 A. D.). New colors were added like iron rust, tea dust, famille rose and famille verte (green). Overglaze painting was developed permitting refined decoration. Polychromatic effects were achieved. By the 18th century creativeness ended and only imitation and repetition continued.

Korea and Japan also produced ceramics of high quality. Japan lacked clay and feldspar until deposits of kaolin were discovered on Izumi Yani in the 17th century. Thereafter, the Japanese developed and exported their famous Imari ware decorated in blue, red and gold. The name Imari derives from the port of Imari from where the Japanese porcelain was exported to Europe.

Chinese ceramics radiated around the world. As early as the T'ang dynasty (618–906 A. D.) Chinese pottery was exported to and copied in Persia. A thriving ceramics industry sprung up in Baghdad to supply the Caliph's court. The Muslims added some innovations of their own like the opaque tin glaze to achieve whiteness and new designs and decorations in the glazes. From the Near East porcelain made its way to Europe via the Crusades and Venetian traders. But the greatest impact of Chinese ceramics on Europe came through Portuguese trade with China from the 16th century onwards. Porcelain factories concentrated in Canton for the European trade. The Dutch, French and English joined this trade in the 17th and 18th centuries.

Thereafter ceramics works sprung up in Europe, as at Delft where Dutch potters imitated the blue and white Ming porcelain by covering a soft clay body with tin enamel. True porcelain was not achieved in Europe until the 18th century when Johann Friedrich Bottger at Meissen, near Dresden, discovered the secret of making porcelain. He added a fluxing agent (alabaster and marble) to the infusable Saxony clay to achieve porcelain. He fused them in a kiln heated to 2500° F. He also developed an appropriate glaze for the porcelain. It came to be known as Dresden china.

Though the Meissen factory guarded the secret, as well as the Chinese had for a thousand years, the French at Sevres and the English at Staffordshire achieved the production of porcelain and Europe had a ceramic industry equal to that of China. The English developed the so-called bone porcelain or china. Early in the 19th century Josiah Spode II used up to 40 per cent bone ash in the porcelain mixture. It made a more durable and cheaper porcelain. The name china and chinoiserie has, however, remained in the European vocabulary for porcelain ceramics.

Glassware, on the other hand, was a Mediterranean development. Glass is usually made from sand (silica) mixed with various oxides such as soda, lime, potash or lead and boric oxides. The mix must be heated to temperatures of 2000–3000° F for long periods to attain the desired chemical properties. Glass originated in Egypt as early as 4000 B. C. It was first used for glazing of stone beads and pottery. Then it was molded. Beads were made of pure glass by the Egyptians as early as the 15th century B. C. But it became an art with the invention of glassblowing.

The origin of glassblowing is lost in obscurity. It is believed to have been developed in Sidon, Syria about the First century B. C. It spread westward to Rome and from there into Gaul and Germany. The vessel or object is shaped entirely with the air bubble at the end of the blowpipe (therein resides the art) or blown into a sculptured mold. After the glass cools it is engraved (the Romans used diamond points) or etched with hydrofloric acid for decoration. Colors are also introduced into the glass while it is molten.

After the fall of the Roman empire the art was lost in Europe. It continued, however, in the Mideast under the Muslims from where the Venetians brought it back once again to Italy in the 15th century. Venetian glassmaking was located mainly on the island of Murano. Ground quartz pebbles, for silica, were mixed with burnt seaweed for alkali and lime to produce a fine glass. Syrian glassmakers immigrated to Venice with their skills. The Venetians rediscovered the use of manganese to make greenish glass white. It was called cristallo, after rock crystal. Thereafter, clear glassware has been called crystal. The Murano glassmakers attained artistic heights. They colored the glass and embedded threads of white opaque glass. They engraved and enameled the wares.

From Venice the art spread to France and Germany despite the attempts by the Venetians to keep their techniques secret. Murano artisans, in spite of heavy penalties, emigrated to northern Europe taking their art with them. In the 17th century glassmaking was highly developed in Germany and Bohemia. The English and Irish became superior glassmakers in the 18th century. The English used flint for silica which tended to crack. They introduced lead to counteract it resulting in leaded glass which resembled rock crystal even more than Venetian glass. The Irish produced fine cut leaded glass at Waterford, Cork and Dublin. Excellent engraved glassware is produced today by Orrefors in Sweden and Stuben in America.

PAINTING

No substantial evidence of painting has survived beyond the last half millennium or so. The reason, of course, is that the art involves perishable materials. There are only a few situations where the painting of man has survived in unusual and fortuitous circumstances but these preservations tell a tremendous story. They attest both the old age and ubiquitous nature of the art. That man should have turned to painting for enjoyment is quite natural as no advanced technology is involved. The materials for color (manganese, iron oxide, carbon black and ochre) were all around him. Grinding them into powder and mixing them with water or animal fat was easy. Vegetable fibres and tufts of hair formed rough and ready brushes. Cave sides, mud walls and perhaps, the hide sides of furs formed the first surfaces.

Some 20,000 years ago man was already painting. We know this from the surprisingly striking cave murals found at Lascaux in southern France and Altimira in northern Spain. The founding of Altimira is a story worth noting. Don Marcelino de Sautuola was but dimly aware of the existence of the caves on his summer estate in northern Spain. In 1878 he visited the Paris International Exhibition where he viewed some artifacts of ice-age man found in southern France. Surmising that the caves on his property might also contain such tools and engravings he set out in 1879 to explore them accompanied by his 12 year old daughter Maria. While he explored near the entrance of the cave Maria squeezed through a small four foot tunnel some 85 feet from the entrance to find herself in a cavern the sides of which were covered with many red animals. Maria ran back to her father in excitement. He followed her into the inner chamber stooping through the small entrance. Looking toward the ceiling he beheld some 25 painted bison, two boars and other animals, colored in browns, reds, yellows and black. Some were contorted to conform to the uneven rocky sides. A rounded haunch was painted over a protruding stone with extremely realistic effect.

The academic world greeted the find with skepticism and even accusations of fraud against the Don—a not unusual reaction of the professional to the amateur—but the paintings were eventually authenticated and accepted as the work of Cro-Magnon man. Don Marcelino, after suffering the scorn and insults of the academicians, locked the caves and died in 1888. Twenty years later the caves were reopened. They are now among the most famous of painted caves.

The main cave at Lascaux is equally striking. It was discovered in 1940 by two school boys. The cavern is U-shaped about 330 feet in length. The paintings are more free and varied. Rhinoceros, bulls, bison, horses, deer, antelope, cats and other animals are depicted.

Much speculation has ensued on the meaning of the paintings. A popular theory is that they were created for magical reasons; that Cro-Magnon believed that the depiction of the animals he hunted would promote success in the hunt. Perhaps, Cro-Magnon could also have painted for pure enjoyment. There must have been times during raging snow-storms and spells of sub-zero weather when Cro-Magnon was forced to retreat to the caves. Such forced leisure may have prompted his art. These inner chambers were warm through geothermal heat even though he had to make his fire near the entrance for facile elimination of smoke. The paintings may have been done to beautify these living or gathering quarters. Then too the inner caverns may have been Cro-Magnon's cathedrals where he retreated for religious and spiritual experience. Cro-Magnon artists may have painted the walls and ceilings as Michelangelo did in the Sistine Chapel millennia later.

That the paintings are of animals is not surprising. Cro-Magnon lived by the hunt. Animals were more real to him than to modern man. He lived in awe and need of them. Some of the depictions are far more real than found in modern paintings. The crouching bison in Altimira is a good example. The bison was king of the animal world and the Cro-Magnon artists gave it a regal powerful look.

The ancient Egyptians were prolific painters. Their funerary architecture served to preserve many original specimens in the tomb paintings. The three ducks from the wall of a tomb at Medun (circa 2613–2494 B. C.) in the Cairo museum are extremely vivid and realistic. Paintings of humans, on the other hand, are very stylistic. Painted reliefs are as common as flat wall paintings. In fact, the Egyptians painted everything—wooden coffins, statues of wood and stone, beaten gold reliefs, even their heiroglyphics. Everything, of course, was religiously oriented and associated with the afterlife.

Six main colors were used of finely ground or powdered minerals—red (iron oxide or red ochre), yellow, (orpiment or yellow ochre), blue (azurite or blue frit), green (malachite), blacks (carbon black) and white (gypsum or whiting). The minerals were mixed with water, sometime, including gum. The paint was applied to the dry wall, usually over a thin wash of plaster. The paintings were not frescoes. The artist used a stumpy brush of grass or palm fibres.

Greek painting is known to posterity mostly through ancient literature. Most were done on wooden panels, walls or other nondurable materials that have perished. Masters like Kimon (6th century), Mikon and others (5th century), Appolodous (end 5th century) and Zeuxis, Aristides (4th century) have been applauded by Greek writers. Great painting was achieved during Alexander the Great's time. Apeles considered the most famous Greek painter worked at this time. And there were others. None of their work survived.

We do, fortunately, have some knowledge of Greek painting from vase decoration. Since the vase decoration used primarily red and black colors the pigment virtuosity of ancient Greek painting is only poorly represented on the pottery. But the themes, styles and life scenes give an idea of ancient Greek painting.

The eruption of Mount Vesuvius in A. D. 79 fortunately preserved more specimens of Roman painting. Excavations in the buried Roman cities of Pompeii and Herculaneum unearthed a wide range of styles of Roman painting around the fall of the republic and the rise of the empire. Virtually nothing survived prior to the first century B. C. Some of the walls of the buried villas were painted to imitate marble slabs. Most important, however, are the perspective wall paintings of landscapes and architectural scenes. Others are walls with a number of decorative scenes placed within architectural framework. The paintings bear Greek influence and were done mainly by Greek artists. A noteworthy example is the encaustic wall painting found in the house of Lucretius Fronto at Pompeii. Encaustic painting mixes pigments in molten beeswax and resin.

The styles found in the Companian towns buried by the eruption of Vesuvius persisted thereafter in the surviving walls in Rome and Ostia. The paintings of the early Christians found in the catacombs of Rome, however, depart from the classical and tend to be more impressionistic, spiritual and symbolic.

During the Dark Ages painting, as did other art, vanished in Europe. Since 330 A. D. Graeco-Roman art migrated east to Constantinople where it came under heavy western Asian influence and became Byzantine art. The new synthesis developed under the aegis of Christianity. It was largely religious art.

The great Byzantine art was mosaic. The Byzantine church, in contrast to the reach into space of the Gothic cathedral, was an artificial heavenly dome of sparkling glass and gold mosaics. Painted walls and panels, however, were foresaken. Mosaics, murals and paintings evolved a distinct religious art where Christ, the apostles and saints acquired a semi-oriental character that has persisted in western Christian religious art to this date. Every catholic parish church in Europe and the Americas (and also in Asia) bears the style of Byzantine art even in the twentieth century. The halo around the head of the religious figures is Byzantine.

Byzantine art radiated north into Russia and west into Europe. Ravenna, Italy was an early Byzantine art center but by the 6th century it was lost to the "barbarians" and Byzantine art returned to Europe in a substantial way only with the rise of Venice to power in the 11th century. Saint Marks, begun in 1042, is pure Byzantine art.

The early western Christians rejected all Graeco-Roman art as idolatry. This was part of the general rejection of the Roman way of life already discussed. But the passage of time, as it always does, assuaged this temper and by Carolingian time the nascent European civilization was again becoming interested in the arts. Charlemagne turned to Greek artists, as there were few if any native artists, who naturally brought with them Byzantine art.

The church, leaving behind its early gloom at last, began seeking decoration for its monastaries and places of worship. Moreover, the Christians now wished to depict Christ, the apostles and saints and above all, the Virgin Mary. For this they borrowed from Byzantine art which had already done so centuries earlier. Gold and gem studded vestments and mitres of priests and acolytes, the chalice and other artifacts for the celebration of the Mass bore and still bear the stamp of Byzantine art. Even the Byzantine triptique became popular in Europe during this time. Byzantine artists, or Venetians trained in Byzantine art, were found in all the cities and monastaries of Europe in the early centuries of the present millennium.

A new civilization, however, was aborning in Europe which was destined to develop its own art. The first creation was Gothic architecture. Next came European painting. The Italians led the way. Stylism gave way to realism. Early Italian painters like Giotto (circa 1276–1337) started Byzantine and ended Italian. There ensued a creative period concentrated in Florence and Venice during the 15th and 16th centuries which brought forth such renowned painters as Filippo Brunelleschi, Andrea Mantegna, Michelangelo, Leonardo da Vinci, Bottecelli, Veronese, Tintoretti, Raphael and others. The Italian genius was perspective. Their technique was the use of oil paint. Byzantine mosaics and paintings were flat in keeping with their objective of depicting religious and other figures. Scene and background were irrelevant. People in their natural settings, however, was the objective of the Italian painters. The great architect and sculptor Filippo Brunelleschi is regarded as the inventor of the one-point perspective. Also the diminishing size of objects as they recede from the eye of the viewer. This together with other techniques such as a window with a distant landscape developed into a system of perspective that has been until the advent of modern art, the foundation of the greatness of European painting.

In the 17th century, often referred to as the golden age of European painting, perspective and oil painting spread to every land. In Flanders there had already been a concurrent development. The Van Eyck brothers (circa 1317–1450), generally regarded as the founders of the Flemish school, probably developed oil as a medium before the Italians but there is no positive verification of the fact. Their most famous work is the Ghent Altar piece for the Cathedral of St. Baron in Ghent. It is a three tier polyptych of 20 panels some 17 by 18 feet in size depicting the prophets, patriarchs, apostles, saints and other religious figures against a panoramic background. It was completed in 1432 after eight years of work. Most of the Van Eyck and other Flemish paintings were religious. But like the Italian paintings they were realistic and with scenic backgrounds. By the 17th century the Flemish and the Italian schools blended together into a European art form.

In the 17th century Europe was bursting with energy. New sources of power were harnessed with the water-wheel and windmill. The full-rigged ship was developed for mastery of the seas. Cortez would never have subdued the Aztecs without his brigantines. And no one captured this new found energy of a burgeoning civilization better on canvas than Peter Paul Rubens (1577–1640).

The Rape of the Daughters of Leucippus (Munich Museum), the Rape of the Sabine Women (London National Gallery), the Outbreak of War (Pitti Gallery), the Anger of Neptune (Fogg Museum), Cavalry (Brussels Museum), Henry IV at the Battle of Ivry (Uffizi), the Raising of the Cross (Antwerp Cathedral) and countless more studding the museums of Europe and America reflect enormous bursts of energy. Many involve the horse which European man had developed into a most effective source of energy with the stirrup and horsecollar by this time. Even his more peaceful scenes are peopled with robust men and voluptuous women exuding procreative energy for the perpetuation of the new civilization.

The new spirit of the 17th century European painting referred to as Baroque art (an unfortunate term) dominated all of Europe. In Italy it was the work of Caravaggio, Carracci, Bernini (including sculpture, for example, his Ecstasy of Saint Theresa) and Tiepolo. France produced Nicolas Pousin, Claude Lorraine and others. In addition to Rubens, Flanders produced Van dyck; Holland had Rembrandt, Frans Hals and Jan Vermeer. Spain luxuriating in the wealth from Potosi, too had its great moment in painting with Zuban, Valasquez, and Murillo.

Spain also had El Greco. The Greek. But his paintings do not reflect the new spirit of Europe. In fact Domenikos Theotokopoulos, his real name, was merely in Europe but not ''of Europe''. His background was Byzantine. He was born in Crete then a Venetian colony, and trained in the Cretan school of icon painting. He next went to Venice and studied under Titian. Finding Italy unreceptive he went to Spain when he was already 40. In Spain too he received a mixed reception.

His paintings were different. They had a macabre quality. His figures were elongated and emaciated. His perspective was distorted. His colors were unusual and today considered striking. Icy blues and greens (View of Toledo), livid pinks, purples and pale yellows. Many compositions were dark and sombre like the Burial of Count Orgaz in the Church of St. Thomas in Toledo, probably his greatest work. His subjects were largely religious. The paintings reflect emotionalism and mysticism.

France and England failed to produce any really great artists during the golden age. When Henry IV wanted to produce the Medici cycle he employed Rubens, a foreign painter. Sir Joshua Reynolds, William Hogarth and Thomas Gainsborough came to the fore only in the 18th century when the genius of great European painting was spent. Their painting was mainly portraiture.

The 19th and 20th centuries brought a reaction against the realism of the great masters. The impressionists dominated European painting by the end of the 19th century. Instead of delineating clearly and realistically a scene or subject the artist by a play on color and light let the viewer develop the scene in his mind from these impressions. The impressionists developed a particular technique of short rapid brush strokes, each daub effecting a separate impression of light and color. Outdoor scenes were the best subjects and the impressionists most frequently painted outdoors instead of in studios.

The word impressionist derives from Claude Monet's "Impression; Sunrise" painted in 1872. Needless to say, the impressionists were received with hostility and derision by the art critics of the day, but eventually became the dominant school. Most famous are Renoir, Monet, Manet, Degas, Cezanne, Pissarro and others in France, where this art form originated, Turner in England and Van Gogh in Holland.

The 20th century brought cubism. Founded by Cezanne and furthered by Picasso of Spain it dominated painting the first half of the century. Cubism departs further from realism. Its distorted geometric depiction is designed to induce a subjective impression or reaction in the viewer. By mid-century even further departure from realism evolved in surrealism and other abstract art. Salvador Dali of Spain, with his limpid watches, is the leading surrealist.

Painting, after music, is the leading art form of Western civilization. Sculpture was always secondary. Good art reflects the temper of its age. Western painting too appears to do so. In its infancy it reflected the Christian foundation of the new civilization. The realistic, robust and energetic painting of mid-millennium exuded the vitality of the blooming culture leading up to the Industrial Revolution. The last two centuries reveal maturity, uncertainty and, perhaps, disintegration of the West.

The earliest evidence of painting in India is found in the Ajanta caves. Sanskirt literature, however, reveals that the rulers in Vedic times maintained art galleries (chitra shalas). None of these pre-Buddhist paintings have survived.

In the famous play Shankuntala by the Sanskrit playwright Kalidasa (circa 5th century A. D.), which Goethe admired greatly, there is a passage about a painting of the beautiful Shakuntala which portrays her as a flower in an idyllic background. A bee hovers around her lips to signify that Shakuntala is like a flower to the bee. The setting of the story is in earlier Brahmanic times.

The paintings in the Ajunta caves reflect a highly developed and sophisticated art. They were painted from the first to the eighth centuries A.D. They are not true frescoes, though often so referred to, but painted on a plaster over the cave wall an inch or so thick of clay and cowdung mixed with chopped rice husks and animal hair. The plaster was covered with a thin layer of gypsum or lime on which the painting was done. It was first outlined in cinnabar red (mercuric sulfide) before the final colors were added. The paintings have a reddish-brown hue that matches the body color of the Indians.

The subjects of the murals are both religious and secular. Many are scenes from the Jatakas (legendary accounts of the Buddha's life) like the one in cave 1 (6th–7th century) portraying the prince among a bevy of beautiful maidens at the royal court announcing his decision to renounce the throne. These early Indian artists achieved a good degree of perspective as seen in the mural in cave XVII (5th century) depicting the prince and his consort sitting on a four poster bed.

The murals at Ajanta represent a fruition of painting tradition that developed (perhaps) over a millenium in ancient India. A sophisticated art form was in existence as seen from such texts as the *Kama Sutra* and others which set forth the rules of painting covering both technique and substance. The canons prescribed among other things, a realistic depiction of natural objects and the infusion of grace, action and feeling into the composition. These texts emphasize the relationship between the arts of painting and the dance. One notes, in this respect, the dance like gestures of the hands and bodies in many of the Ajanta paintings.

The genius of Ajanta appears to have spent itself by the end of the millennium. Architecture and sculpture dominated the arts thereafter until the 13th century when the Muslim invasions set in. The next era in Indian painting arose in the middle of the present millennium. It is the miniature paintings of the Mughal period.

There is evidence of miniature paintings on palm leaves in Gujarat and Bengal as early as the 11th century. They were done for religious purposes, the first by the Jains and those in Bengal by the Buddhists. As paper became more easily available the technique was adopted for secular enjoyment in western India particularly in Rajasthan. It was Akbar, the great Mughal emperor, who popularized miniature painting. As will be recalled it was Akbar's policy to fraternize with the martial Rajputs. In the process he became fond of their painting and established at his court in Fatepur Sikri a school for painting where he awarded periodic prizes for the best miniatures. This stimulated interest in the art all over India and the 16 and 17th centuries garnered a harvest of miniature paintings that now reside in the museums and collections of the world.

These miniature paintings are seldom larger than 8″ × 10″, the size of a piece of typing paper. The miniatures are usually unsigned and the artist remains anonymous. They are frequently profusely colored and detailed. The multicolored Indian garments are a prominent feature of the picture. The themes are most often based on Hindu religious or epic lore, particularly those of the later period. An especially charming one is *Radha's Complaint*, painted in 1775, in which Lord Krishna is playing his flute surrounded by seven beautiful and admiring maids while Radha sits disconsolately to the side conversing with a female friend. Krishna's body, as always, is painted blue. The background is a lovely hilly scene on the banks of the river Jumna. The picture has fine perspective. It is now part of the N. C. Mehta collection in Ahmedabad. Mr. Mehta is one of the foremost authorities on the Indian miniature paintings.

The early Mughals fostered the art, but when Aurangzeb, the purist ascended to the throne in 1658 A. D. he forbad the paintings at court in accordance with the Muslim proscription against representing human and animal life! The artists, who were mostly Hindus, retreated to Rajasthan and Kashmir where the art flourished until the early 19th century. Many different schools arose such as the Mewar, Malwa, Bikaner and others named after the particular area of which the Kangra school in Kashmir is the most renowned. *Radha's Complaint* was a product of the Kangra school.

A word is, perhaps, in order at this point on Muslim painting. The Arabs had no art, but they were always prone to adopt the art and technology of the conquered people. They emulated the arts of the Byzantine and Persian peoples with one overriding modification that there be no representation of human and animal life. That reduced mosaic, painting and other arts to decorative dimensions. But as Mohammedanism extended its hold on non-Arabic peoples with indigenous cultures the proscription against representational painting got compromised.

The Persians and Turkish people produced great miniature paintings during the Timurid (1335–1486 A. D.) and Safavid (1486–1736 A. D.) periods. The schools of Herat and Shiraz produced many miniatures now in the museums of Europe. In fact, there was even a school of Kabul which produced a handsome miniature of Babur the Great in 1505, now in the British Museum, in the Timurid style. When the Mughals came to India they were therefore, familiar with the art of miniature painting and promoted a happy marriage between the Persian and Rajasthan techniques.

Chinese painting is unique and truly indigenous. It is basically monochromatic, with minimum emphasis on color. Oil painting is unknown. The one or single point perspective is not a feature of Chinese painting. Instead, Chinese artists used the "shifting perspective" or the many points of view in their landscape paintings. They "walk you through" the picture as it is sometimes said. This technique may have been inspired by the practice of painting on a scroll. A viewer can unroll the scroll and observe the landscape from scene to scene. In fact, Chinese artists prided themselves on how many li of landscape they could compress into their scrolls. To be sure, these scrolls are now hung fully unrolled in museums. But the artist did not intend the viewer to see it all at once. Michael Sullivan in his *Short Story of Chinese Art* enlightens us on this point as follows:

> In the passage I have quoted above, Shen Kua explains, the attitude behind what we might call the 'shifting perspective' of Chinese painting, which invites us to explore nature, to wander

through the mountains and valleys, discovering fresh beauty at every step. We cannot take in so great a panorama at a glance; indeed, the artist intends that we should not. We would need perhaps days or weeks to walk the length of the stretch of countryside he presents in his scroll; but by revealing it to us little by little as we proceed, he combines the element of time with that of space, in a four-dimensional synthesis such as western art has never achieved. The nearest parallel is to be found not in European art, but in music, in which the theme unfolds and develops in time. As we unroll as much of the great panorama as we can comfortably pass from right hand to left (never opening it out fully as is often done in museums), we find ourselves drawn unwittingly into the scene spread out before us. The artist invites us to follow him down the winding paths, to wait at the river-bank for the ferry boat, to walk through the village—disappearing from view for a few moments, perhaps, as we pass behind a hill—to re-emerge and find ourselves standing on the bridge gazing at a waterfall; and then perhaps to saunter up to the valley to where the monastery roof can just be seen above the tree-tops, there to rest, fan ourselves after our exertions, and drink a bowl of tea with the monks.

The earliest evidence of Chinese monochromatic painting goes back to the Period of the Warring States (481 B. C.–256 B. C.). It was found in the Changsha graves and done by a painter in the ancient feudal state of Ch'u. Sketched on silk with deft stokes it depicts a full dressed women with a pheonix and dragon. It already possesses the brush technique and other qualities of the classical paintings a millennium or more later. The impact of Buddhism on Chinese art during the first millennium of the Christian era, unlike that on sculpture, does not appear to have effected painting profoundly. Painting has always been a more important art than sculpture in China. In the cave murals that survived there is evidence of Indian and western Asian influence, particularly in the subject matter. Scenes from the Jatakas and paintings of the Boddhisattvas proliferated. Most have not survived. After the decline of Buddhism Chinese painting became thoroughly indigenous and bloomed during T'ang (619–906 A. D.) and Sung (960–1279 A. D.) times. Favorite subjects were landscapes, with a large mountain or massif, and delicate renditions of birds and flowers. Paintings of bamboo were highly regarded. In fact, philosophically regarded, because of the strength and resilience of the bamboo. The bamboo has had a more profound impact on Chinese life and thought than is generally understood abroad. We saw in Chapter IV how it impacted on Chinese naval technology. The same effect is now noted in Chinese painting.

A school of painting was established at court by Emperor Hui Tsung, who was himself a painter, in 1104 A. D. Hui-Tsung and his artists were

particularly fond of painting flowers. Kuo Hsi (circa 1020–1090), a great
mountain landscape painter. Ching Hao (circa 900–960) and others were the
masters of the northern Sung period. Li Tang (circa 150–1130) and Ma Yuan
(circa 1190–1224) were the prominent painters of the southern Sung period
when, perhaps Chinese landscape painting reached its apogee. The aim of
the 13th century painters was to "express 10,000 li (about 3500 miles) of
space on one foot of silk." River landscapes were favored. They painted on
hand scrolls of paper, using ink and ink tones to build up lyrical and plaintive
scenes. The idea was to stir emotion and feeling in the heart of the viewer.

Unfortunately most of these paintings have perished. And those that
survived have been hard to attribute to any particular artist. In large part,
this is due to the principle (one of six principles of painting enunciated by
Hsieh Ho an art critic of the 6th century) which instructs painters to copy the
paintings of old and reputable masters so as to acquire the feeling and
emotion of executing the painting. This practice, obviously, proliferated the
reproductions of great paintings until the original was lost in their midst.

During the succeeding centuries Chinese painting did not deviate or
change appreciably from the classical period. Artists during the Yuan
dynasty, most of them in exile from Mongol rule, continued the style of the
southern Sung school. The plum blossom and the bamboo were favorite
subjects. Bamboo painting served to assert a feeling of independence of
foreign rule. The most famous artist of the early Ming period that followed
was Wang Fu (1362–1416 A. D.) who favored bamboo and landscape
subjects. Later two schools flourished. The Che school and the Wu school,
the latter in the tradition of the southern Sung. The Four Wangs, successors
of the Wu school, predominated during the early years of the Manchu or
Ch'ing dynasty (1644–1912). Greater individualism and experimentation
developed at this time. More color was used with the ink lines and strokes.
These individual artists according to Michael Sullivan "made the first
century of the Ch'ing dynasty one of the most creative periods in the history
of Chinese painting." Thereafter, a steady decline in creativity gripped
Chinese painting. Court painters became insignificant figures. Whether
classical painting will revive under the communists or some new style evolve
remains to be seen.

Japanese painting followed the Chinese tradition. Little secular painting is
known before the present millennium. Buddhist influence was substantial
prior thereto. Some wall paintings dating back to the 8th century survive at
Nara. Scroll paintings became popular during the 11th and 12th centuries.
These scrolls unfolded from left to right to present a continuous story or
landscape. This tradition continued until the Momoyama period (1573–1705)
A. D.) when folding screen painting became the dominant art. Two six-fold
screens, some 30 feet long usually contained a single composition or
landscape. Japanese artists employed more color than their Chinese counterparts. After contact with Europeans during the 16th century greater

perspective was introduced into the paintings. Full color woodblock printing, up to 10 colors, was developed after 1700. This made possible
production of beautiful prints for the newly rising merchant class of Edo. It
was, perhaps, the first venture into popular art by a civilization.

Calligraphy, the art of beautiful writing, was closely associated with and
greatly influenced Chinese painting. In fact, the Chinese regarded calligraphy as a greater art than painting. Affection for the written word is the result,
in large measure, from the complex written language which has developed to
more than 10,000 basic characters. It originated with simple pictograms (say)
of the moon or sun. Pictograms were combined for ideograms. Finally to the
ideographic or radical element was added a phonetic element for pronuncia-
tion. This wide range of expression provided a broad scope for the art of
calligraphy.

A person's personality and character became associated with his writing.
"Not only is a man's writing a clue to his temperment" writes Michael
Sullivan, "his moral worth and his learning, but the uniquely ideographic
nature of the Chinese script has charged each individual character with a
depth of content and association the full extent of which even the most
scholarly can scarcely fathom."

Writing became an art during the 3rd century B. C. when the brush was
introduced making possible beautiful strokes for forming the ideograms. The
clerical and draft scripts were developed at about the same time. The latter
was designed for rapid informal writing but soon developed into the art we
know today.

The Chinese grew fond of introducing calligraphy on to their paintings
consisting of a narrative or poem associated with the subject. It was a
natural coalition and became more prolific during the Yuan, Ming and
Ch'ing periods.

The Chinese draft script was adopted by the Japanese into a syllabic
alphabet called the *hiragama*. Calligraphy is also highly esteemed in Japan.

The Muslims too have held a high regard for calligraphy. The flowing
Arabic script lent itself readily to beautiful writing. The oldest was called
kufic after the city of Kufa in Iraq. It was a vertical script. A more rounded
and flowing script called *naksi* was introduced around 1000 A. D. In the 16th
century a more slanted script was adopted which was the *nastalig* and has
been the dominant Islamic script ever since.

Calligraphy received greater emphasis in the Muslim world as orthodox
Muslims were forbidden representative art. Calligraphy, however, can be
very decorative as observed on the Taj Mahal where fifteen chapters of the
Koran in Arabic script are inlaid with black marble in the white marble of the
archways of the mausoleum.

Egyptian hieroglyphics too were calligraphy. The ancient Egyptians took
great pride in the beauty of their writing and used it widely for decoration of
temples and monuments. Hieroglyphics (so named by the Greeks, meaning

"sacred writings") are a combination of ideograms and phonograms. Lacking vowels, however, the ancient Egyptians never developed an alphabet. Combining ideo and phonograms made possible the formation of words. There was no spacing or punctuation to break the flow of words. They could be written horizontally or vertically. Despite this lack of facility hieroglyphics served as a written language for some three millennia (3100 B. C. to 394 A. D.). About 700 B. C. a popular form of hieroglyphic writing, the *demotic*, evolved for secular purposes. A simplified hieroglyphic called *hieratic* continued to be used by the priests.

Color was used in the ideograms creating some vivid cartouches (cluster of ideograms denoting a royal name) and papyruses. Base reliefs of hieroglyphics (some in gold) are beautiful art.

For millennia men of the Mediterranean area puzzled over the hieroglyphics until French troops found the Rosetta Stone while digging trenches in Egypt during Napoleon's ill fated invasion in 1799. It contained a memorial to Ptolemy V in 196 B. C. in three languages—hieroglyphics, demotic and Greek. Twenty-three years later the French linguist Fancois Champollion was able to unlock the meaning of the hieroglyphics from their Greek and demotic counterparts. It served to unfold much Egyptian history contained in the hieroglyphics in graves, on monuments and temples.

The Byzantine civilization developed mosaic into a representational art. The mosaic technique—the creation of a pattern or picture by embedding small colored objects called tesserae into a flat matrix—dates back to the 3rd millennium B. C. Pebbles, stone, marble, shells, glass, baked clay and even gems have been used. But until the Byzantines made pictures with mosaic the technique was used mostly for decoration. Mosaic floors and pavements were common in Roman times. Pictures in mosiac, however, did start in Roman times as early as the 3rd century B. C. but they were not common.

It was, therefore, natural for the Byzantines—this was, after all, the eastern Roman empire—to turn to mosaics when they wished to depict the Christian god and saints in pictures for the devout to worship. The western Christians adopted the form for their holy pictures, but as the new European civilization assumed a vitality of its own it converted the technique into stained glass. Stained glass was almost a necessary feature of the Gothic cathedral, whose pointed arches reached out into space, for the admission of light into God's new house of worship.

Stained glass is a European art. It is found almost nowhere else. It comprises mosaics of colored translucent glass held together by strips of lead to form decorative or pictorial windows. The glass was colored while molten by the addition of metallic oxides. Cobalt oxide, for instance, creates a blue color. The colors were limited—blue, red, purple, green and yellow. The colored glass was then cut into shapes to fit the window design. A grozing iron was used before 1500—after that a diamond-cutter—to cut the pieces. Details like facial expressions, hair and beards, garment folds and other features were effected with grisaille, a mixture of powdered glass, a metallic oxide and gum which was traced and baked on the colored glass in a kiln. After the glass was cut and grisaille applied to the appropriate pieces the segments were assembled between strips of lead soldered together. A strip of lead was placed around the entire design and inserted into a window frame for installation into the masonry wall.

Stained glass flourished between the 9th and 15th centuries, mainly as a religious art. It is found mostly in the cathedrals of Europe. The 13th century was its high point. The Gothic cathedrals of Chartres, Bourges and Rouen in France, Cologne and Ulm in Germany and Canterbury in England contain some of the best known stained glass windows. The cathedrals in Assisi, Florence, Arezzo and Milan in Italy too have some fine windows. But without doubt the greatest experience in the art of stained glass can be found in Saint Chapelle, completed in 1248 A. D., in Paris. Whole walls glow with stained glass creating a paradise of visual delight.

After 1500 the painting of glass windows evolved as an economy measure and the art of stained glass declined. It was revived on a modest scale during the 19th and 20th centuries. A good example of modern stained glass can be found in the Hienz cathedral in Pittsburgh, Pennsylvania done primarily in blue hues. The design is decorative not pictorial.

The Europeans also elevated tapestry to a high art. The technique, however, dates back to antiquity. Almost as soon as man learned to weave cloth he introduced designs into the warp and weft. The design is made with the weft, which is normally done only in the area the color is wanted. Tapestry woven designs in linen have been found in Egypt dating back to the Eighteenth dynasty (1567–1320 B. C.) in the tombs of Tutankhamen and Amenhotep II. The Coptic Christians depicted scenes in linen during the 3rd to 7th centuries A. D. The Muslims continued the art in the Middle East. Chinese tapestry dates back to the T'ang period (618–906 A. D.). But it was during the 14th and 15th centuries that tapestry was brought to Europe. The somewhat amateurish Bayeau Tapestry commemorating the Norman invasion of England, already mentioned, dates back to the 11th century, but the art reached its height around the 17th century.

The finest work was done in France and Belgium. Most renowned was the Gobelin factory in France. In consequence, tapestries are sometimes called Gobelins. Religious, mythical, pastoral and other scenes were represented. The *Unicorn in Captivity* in the Metropolitan Museum in New York done in the 15th century is noteworthy. A profusion of flowers and plants is woven into a dark blue (warp) background with a white unicorn resting in captivity inside a fenced enclosure. Great perspective was effected so that some tapestries are like the best paintings. The *Adoration of the Magi* a 16th century tapestry is a good example of the finest perspective, lighting and colors.

Color durability gave the early weavers difficulty due to lack of nonfading dyes. They had to content themselves with 15-20 colors. By the 16th century Flemish weavers were using over 100 colors. The Gobelin factory used about 150 colors by the end of the 17th century. In the next century the number was widened to 500 and weavers could emulate the color virtuosity of the greatest paintings. The quality of the wool also improved commensurately.

After the 18th century the art declined. A modest revival has developed in recent times. Tapestry was highly favored by the ruling elite in medieval Europe to cover the cold stone and masonry walls of castles, manor houses and other buildings. Its portability and durability added to its value for this purpose.

Floor coverings—rugs and carpets—have also been used for decorative purposes. This is a Persian art. The Turkish people took up the art subsequently and excelled in it. They carried it with them to China and India. There are, consequently two major types—Persian and Turkish carpets.

The technique involves the tying or knotting of a short length of yarn around two adjacent warps of a woven fabric. The knots are alternated with two or more wefts. As each row of knotted yarn is completed across the width of the loom it is pressed down against the previous row so that the yarn sets perpendicular to the fabric base. The knotted yarn is then trimmed to the desired pile. The knots range from 300 to 2,400 per square inch in good carpets, but the quality of the carpet does not depend upon the intensity of knots alone. The colors, design and other artistry are important. The Ardebil Carpet, made in Persia in 1539, now in the Victoria and Albert Museum in London, considered one of the world's greatest carpets, has only 325 knots per square inch.

The origin of the carpet is lost in obscurity. It seems clear though that the art originated with the nomadic horsemen and shepherds of the Caucasian and northern Persian steppes. The Scythians used carpets (mostly heavy woven fabric) instead of saddles in riding horses long before the Christian era. The Hermitage in Leningrad has a fragment of a pile carpet dating back to 3 A. D. found in the frozen subsoil of a nomad chieftan's grave in Mongolia. It is thought that the idea for a tufted carpet may have been inspired by a sheepskin rug used by the nomads for floor coverings and other purposes. But the verifiable facts about carpet making do not date much farther back than the 15th century. Prior to 1500 knowledge of carpets depends upon literature.

There is, for instance, the fabled story of the Spring Carpet made for the palace at Ctesiphon during the reign of Khosru I (531–579 A.D.). It was allegedly about 84 square feet (an 8' × 10' rug) made of silk and laden with jewels. Its main feature was the garden scene it depicted with pathways, streams, flowers and birds. When the Arabs captured Ctesiphon in 635

A. D. the famous carpet was cut up and divided as booty among the soldiers in keeping with the doctrine of the holy war.

The Persians were fond of depicting garden and other outdoor scenes. The Muslims, of course, ended this practice and the carpets that have survived consist mostly of geometric designs. The design would often emanate symetrically from a medallion in the center or a series of smaller medallions spaced over the surface of the carpet. During the Safavid period (1486–1736 A. D.) when some of the greatest Persian carpets were made, the central medallion design predominated. Floral decoration was tolerated as in the renowned Ardebil Carpet made in 1539 for the mosque at Ardebil in Persia. It has a medallion design (a large gold medallion on an indigo field) from which radiate profuse vine and floral patterns. Made of wool knotted on silk it is a huge carpet some 35 × 18 feet. There were actually two carpets, badly damaged, from which the surviving carpet was reconstructed.

A noteworthy feature added to the art by the Muslims was the prayer rug. A devout Muslim prostrates himself in prayer, where ever he is, in the direction of Mecca five times a day. Hence, the practice arose of carrying a small prayer rug to place on the ground or floor for the purpose. The rug is usually 5 by 7 feet designed like a prayer niche in the mosque. It has a decorated upper side which is laid toward Mecca on which the prayer bows his head. The lower side has only a border. The prayer rug is easily rolled up and carried about at all times by the devout Muslim.

After the Ottoman Turks captured Tabriz, a Persian rug-making center, they adopted and continued the art. Most of the rugs known in Europe during the 16th and 17th centuries were Turkish. As demand for the rugs grew in Europe the Turks began to depart from the traditional Persian designs to cater to the tastes of the European market. Floral designs became more common. Eventually Europeans began to make their own carpets in the old (albeit) corrupted Persian patterns.

Turks carried the art into China. The Chinese, even though Mohammedans, quickly departed from the non-representation of life idea and introduced dragons, horses, flowers (lotus and peonies) into the designs. Colors were also varied, with preference for yellow backgrounds and wide use of blue and white. The Mughals brought the art to India. There had been no indigenous carpet making before as the hot climate was not conducive to the art.

MUSIC

Music is the art Western civilization bestowed on mankind. The Europeans perfected notation and polyphonic music during the three centuries of the 17th to 19th of the Christian era. Neither was invented but both were highly developed by them.

Music is obviously a much older art but its history can only be dimly perceived. Since every human being is biologically equipped for the production of sound it may be unhesitatingly concluded that man learned to make pleasant sounds by humming, whistling, yodeling and singing almost as soon as he learned to talk. But the ephemeral nature of the art—it is created out of thin air and after a moment of enjoyment vanishes—made any preservation of it impossible until notation which did not develop in any substantial way until the present millennium. Some fragmentary notation has survived from Greek times but it tells us very little of Greek music.

Musicologists must therefore resort to secondary sources. The earliest evidence is the depiction on the wall of a cave in Trois Freres, dated 40,000 years ago, of a shaman masked as a deer pursuing several reindeer while playing a musical bow, such as is still used in parts of Africa today. Music was apparently thought to have magical qualities that could promote success in the hunt. That music was closely associated with magic and religion by early and even ancient man seems clear. There is a painted wooden stela dating back to the 10th century B. C., now in the Louvre, showing an Egyptian musician with a harp propitiating the birdheaded God Ra-Han-akhte. There is even a score dating back as recently as 1641 A. D. for music to cure a tarantula bite!

Egyptian representative art indicates the fondness for music by the ancient Egyptians. There is adequate evidence of the instruments employed. They were mostly strings and flutes, from which it can be deduced the music was soft, and perhaps, shrill.

The Greeks brought philosophy and mathematics to music. In fact, it is to the Greeks that modern man owes the derivation of the word music. It was called *mousike*, the art of the Muse. Principles of musical rhythm were developed by the philosophers. Pythagorus was foremost among them. Plato stated that education in music was the mark of a refined man. Although the Greeks developed a notation based on their alphabet virtually none has survived and the few that have are of questionable authenticity. In part, this may be due to a gulf that existed between the philosophical and ordinary approach to music. The professional performer on the *aoulas* (a double piped instrument) was not educated or articulate in music. He performed and transmitted it orally.

The Romans carried on this oral tradition and developed much secular music for their entertainment and enjoyment. Music was heard in the theatre, circus and at military and ceremonial functions. Bronze wind instruments were used for battle signals and general fanfare. They borrowed the *cithara* (a string instrument) and the *aoulas* from the Greeks. Drums, cimbals, tambourines, bells and other percussion instruments were borrowed from Africa and the Near East. They even developed a hydraulic organ. Here too, despite Roman familiarity with Greek notation, no written evidence of Roman music has survived. Like the Greek, the sound of Roman music too remains an enigma.

The early Christians rejected Roman music, particularly instrumental music, as it was associated with the licentiousness and immorality of a way of life they repudiated. The early church fathers, in particular converted Romans like Tertullian (circa 150–230 A. D.), urged Christians to shun music. He writes: "Musical concerts with viol and lute belong to Apollo, the the Muses, to Minerva and Mercury, who invented them; ye who are Christians, hate and abhor these things . . . " Augustine, however, a century or so later takes a more conciliatory attitude viewing with favor the singing and playing of the Psalms of David in the church.

Meanwhile the eastern church in Constantinople was developing independently and unbothered by the virulence of anti-Romanism. It soon developed a liturgy of psalms and hymns with strong Greek and oriental overtones. Jewish psalmody, only natural, was influential. The western church too developed a similar liturgy though, perhaps, more cautiously. It is known as plain chant or plain song. It doubtless too bore a foreign flavor. Oriental influence on Rome in the days of empire was substantial.

In the 6th century Pope Pelagus II sent Gregory to Constantinople as the papal legate where he became familiar with the liturgy of the eastern church. Upon his return Gregory became pope and was instrumental in the reorganization of the liturgy of the church of Rome. It came to be known as the Gregorian Chant and formed the foundation of Christian music until the end of the first millennium.

Byzantine influence on Christian church music during the first millennium is more difficult to demonstrate than the Byzantine impact on European painting. There is, however, some clear evidence of it. The prominent use of the chant *Kyrie Eleison* (Lord have mercy) is Greek and Byzantine influence. It survived until the present time even when the Roman church adopted a Latin liturgy in the 3rd century. Alleluia, Amen and Sanctus, too, derive from the East.

But be that as it may, the West was ready for its own music at the start of the second millennium. Europeans built a new House of God in the Gothic cathedral. Its pointed arches reached into space. Stained glass windows brought in the sun and the sky. A more spatial music than the monotonous Gregorian chant was required. European genius came to the fore with polyphonic music. In the words of Oswald Spengler, "The Cathedral *is* music."

Polyphony is two or more melodies sounded harmoniously at the same time. Other civilizations and even primitive peoples employed polyphony, but none based their musical system on it. Greater intensity and resonance could be achieved by superimposing melodies upon each other. The transition from monophony to polyphony evolved almost naturally by layering one or more melodies upon the Gregorian chant for the sonority befitting the Gothic cathedral.

Vocal polyphony developed in Europe during the 10th and 12th centuries. The earliest form was called organum. It was merely diaphonic with a superimposition of the same melody upon a Gregorian chant at a different pitch. Many voiced music, true polyphony, was perfected later in the 12th century in the School of Notre Dame. Leonin and Perotin were the prominent composers of the new music. Both were organists. Organ music was included in their compositions.

Instrumental music was first rejected by the church when it was in the grip of intense anti-Romanism. It flourished outside the church and was roundly condemned by the early Christians as sinful. But it persisted. By the 12th century the troubadors in France were entertaining the nobility, (in fact, many were *of* the nobility). Most famous in this respect was Richard the Lion-Hearted. At first with monophonic, but by the 13th century with polyphonic songs. Many of these French songs, monophonic and polyphonic, called *chansons* survive and can be heard on modern recordings. Instrumental dance music also grew in popularity.

The troubadors may also be responsible for the concept of romantic love in Western civilization. They would address their *chansons* to a particular lady whom they would extol and idolize. Much of it was platonic. Doubtless the good feeling and emotion so generated evolved frequently into greater intimacy. The troubadors managed thereby to elevate the status of the Christian woman above the sinful status attributed to her by the early church fathers.

The next few centuries witnessed the growth of secular and instrumental music and a departure in church music from the Gregorian chant. Conductus replaced organum in the 13th century. It was newly composed, not tied to the Gregorian chant. Next came the motet which dominated from the 13th to the 15th centuries. The motet broadened the polyphonic scope. Counterpoint was emphasized. By the 14th century there were many different schools—the Italian, Franco-Flemish and the English. New masses were composed.

Secular music became popular with the newly emerging mercantile class. Advancing technology in woodworking, machine tools, metallurgy made new instruments possible. Keyboard instruments were perfected. Wind instruments were refined. Viols were broadened in scope.

Notation developed *pari passu*. Medieval notation consisted of *neumes* written above the text of the Gregorian chant to indicate the rise and fall of the melody. In the 11th century the monk Guido d'Arezzo devised the four line notation with clefs on the lines to indicate pitch. This precocious monk is thought also to have developed solmization—relating the notes of the melody to the pitches of specific syllables of the tune. This made it possible for a vocalist or instrumentalist to sing or play the melody without previously having heard it. This technique is still in use today. Thus, at first, only pitches were noted. In the middle ages rhythm and tempo were added. Secondary features like dynamics, agogics, instrumentation and other refinements followed. The invention of printing about 1500 gave notation great scope.

The development of Western music now took on a scholarly character. More so than even by the Greeks, science and mathematics were applied. Music is sound; and sound is energy. European man was reaching out for new sources of energy at this time. Perhaps it was natural that he should do so for enjoyment as well as power. In any case, it was music, the art of energy, that was destined to become Western man's greatest contribution to the enjoyment of life.

Notation made possible the composer. No longer was it necessary for the creator and performer of the music to be one, as we shall see, in the case of Indian music. Swiss musicologist Romain Goldron writes:

> At all events, music, which had up to now been transmitted orally and remained more or less homophonic, was to take on a visual form, which would render it objective—the score; and the demands of accuracy would become more and more exacting. Other voices came to join the main melody in obedience to certain laws. The simultaneous sound that resulted from polyphony fostered in musicians a completely new idea, that of *harmony*, which in turn generated its own grammer and syntax. The role of the performer, which till now had been paramount, would be diminished for the benefit of the composer, whose importance and whose demands increased more and more as it became possible to write down everything.

Walter Woira, professor of musicology at the University of Keil sums up as follows:

> Western culture produced the completely notated musical work of art and created a formal theory of composition. Before that, music, like the dance, had existed primarily as improvisation along certain guidelines. Now, however, it acquired a mode of existence like works of literature and for the theater. That the composer little by little came to prescribe all the elements of music means also that these became constituent parts of composition.

By 1600, after centuries of slow maturation, notation, polyphony and the additional and refined instruments were ready for the full flowering of the new music of the European civilization. The creative genius was to be the province of the composers. Subsequent history, therefore, revolves around these composers. Within four centuries this creative genius was spent and the future of Western music in the 20th century is an unknown matter.

Johann Sebastian Bach is the first composer of renown during the period. In fact, until quite recently the history of Western music was thought to have started with Bach. But now it is realized that there were many centuries of development before Bach's music could appear on the scene in full bloom. An equally famous contemporary was George Fredrich Handel. Both were Germans but Handel made his fame in England. Bach did so at the court of Prince Leopold of Anhalt where he composed the famous Brandenburg concertos in 1721. Polyphonic music had now graduated to the more complex fugue in which a number of short themes are introduced and reintroduced in contrapuntal manner. Bach drew heavily on Vivaldi, Torelli and Corelli, the three eminent composers of the late 17th century.

The Italians were also foremost in the development of opera. Vocal music was brought out of the church for secular enjoyment. It was far more adaptable for entertainment as it could be incorporated into drama for the theatre. Composed first for private entertainment (for salons, weddings and the like) it was soon graduated to public amusement. The first public opera house was opened in Venice in 1627. By 1800 Italian opera was highly developed and spread to every capital in Europe. Indigenous variations developed, particularly in Germany. The virtuoso singer was the central factor of Italian opera. Some were women. A unique development was the *castrato*, the castrated male singer, who could give the normally female voices of soprano and contralto, greater volume and range. Young boys with good voices were also castrated to preserve their adolescent tones for the choir. These *castrati* were a familiar feature of the cathedral choirs of Europe.

A counterpart of the opera was the oratorio. It was a musical rendition of a biblical or other religious story. It was usually in the nature of a narrative. Handel was famous for his oratorios like the *Messiah, Judas Maccabeus* and others.

The period 1600–1700 A. D. is referred to by musicologists as the Baroque, that unfortunate term once again. This is followed by the Romantic Era which lasts until the late 19th century. The early part of the Romantic is sometimes called the Classical Period. Three names predominate during this time; Hayden, Mozart and Beethoven. They were the giants of Western music.

Hayden was born in 1732, Beethoven died in 1827. Mozart lived, all to briefly, in between. It was a century of creative genius in Western music. There was good music before and after but none reached the heights of Hayden's string quartets, Mozart's operas and Beethoven's symphonies. Beethoven's nine symphonies, many string quartets and numerous piano concertos are generally regarded as the greatest music ever composed. Hayden was the most productive—a hundred and more symphonies, 83 string quartets, many piano concertos, sonatas and other works. Mozart produced over 400 pieces during his short span of life (1756–1791). He started composing, however, while still a child. His finest work was, probably, *the Magic Flute*, his last opera. Beethoven was not so prolific, but then he composed while deaf most of his life!

Polyphonic music was now highly developed in harmony and counterpoint. Instrumental music was dominant. The best music was now in the concert hall, no longer in the cathedral. The sonata-form dominated composition in which the melody or theme was introduced, developed and repeated in, normally, four movements; the first, fast, the second, slow, the third, minuet or scherzo (dance music), and the fourth, fast. The sonata structure was employed in most of the compositions—string quartets, concertos and symphonies. The development of the theme and its repetition provided variety and unity.

The music was intended to evoke emotion and images. Compositions were given names. Beethoven's 6th symphony is called *Pastoral*. The first movement invokes bucolic impressions; the second, scenes by a brook, the third, merrymaking and dancing in a village, the fourth, a violent thunderstorm and the fifth, the calm and serenity after the storm. The images evoked are of course, subjective, but it is not difficult to conjure up a scene in the fourth movement of a sudden summer thunderstorm with people scurring for cover and flashes of lightening around the vanes of the village windmill, the highest point in the countryside. Then, in the fifth movement, the passing of the dark clouds and rain, the sunlight glistening on the wet grass and trees, a rainbow, perhaps, calm and serenity, once again, restored. The music of the fifth movement is the loveliest and most peaceful melody found in any composition. And so it is with others. In Beethoven's *Eroica*, the 3rd symphony, one can visualize Napoleon marching the Grand Army of the Republic across Europe under the banner Liberte! Egalite! Fraternite!

The high point was, perhaps, the so-called chamber music. It was ensemble music for small groups of instruments. The string quartet was the most popular. Great clarity is possible since only one instrument of a kind is used. It comes close to absolute music. All three of the great masters composed it; Beethoven's string quartets are thought by many to be his best work. Oswald Spengler considered chamber music the high point of the development of Western music. He concludes:

> *Here, in chamber-music, Western art as a whole reaches its highest point.* Here our prime symbol of endless space is expressed as completely as the Spearman of Polycletus expresses that of intense bodiliness. When one of those ineffably yearning violin-melodies wanders through the spaces expanded around it by the orchestration of Tartini or Nardini, Hayden, Mozart or Beethoven, we know ourselves in the presence of an art beside which that of the Acropolis is alone worthy to be set. (sic)

To Spengler, and many would agree, the development of Western music after Beethoven declined.

The great technological development of this period was the piano. The harpsicord lacked range and was, therefore, monotonous. The piano by using hammers to strike the strings with different intensities broadened the range of sound between loud and soft. It was first invented in Italy in the late 17th century but was not fully developed until the late 18th century in Vienna and London. The English version was heavier permitting great tension on the strings. Beethoven preferred it. It was only natural that the English should make this breakthrough as they led the world in metallurgical technology at this time. By 1860 the tension on the cast iron frame of a concert grand was 16 tons. The tension has been doubled in modern times.

Henceforth, the piano became the king of the solo instruments. But, if that is true, the violin still remained the queen. Entire compositions were devoted to it. Beethoven composed an enormous number of piano sonatas. His *Emperor* concerto is probably his most famous. It has tried the genius— and the fingers—of countless virtuosi since it was first performed at Leipzig on November 28, 1811. It was composed while Napoleon captured and occupied Vienna, where Beethoven lived, and incorporates the sounds and temper of the time. There followed a great number of piano composers and/or virtuosi. Franz Schubert (1797–1828), Robert Schuman (1810–1856), Frederich Chopin (1810–1849), Franz Liszt (1811–1886) Johannes Brahms (1833–1892) and Peter Tchaikovsky (1840–1893). Chopin and Liszt were eminent performers. In this connection mention must be made of Nicolo Paganini (1782–1840) who was the composer-performer on the violin of comparable genius.

The nineteenth century also produced great masters of the opera. The Italians, as before, led the way with Gioacchino Rossini (1797–1868), Gaetano Donizetti (1797–1848), Vincenzo Bellini (1801–1835) and the incomparable Guiseppe Verdi (1813–1901). *La Traviata, Aida, Riggoletto*, to name a few of Verdi's fine operas. France, brought forth, Georges Bizet (1838–1871) Charles Gounod (1818–1893), Jules Massenet (1842–1912) and others.

But it was Germany that gave music the great Richard Wagner (1813–1883). Many consider Wagner the foremost composer of all time. Needless to say Wagner evoked controversy over his music. He joined symphony to opera, with a chromatic harmony that gave his operas a distinct and original sound. *Tristan and Isolde*, composed in 1859, is, perhaps his most renowned work. Wagner wrote both the libretto and the music!

Wagner was fond of literature. In particular the epic poems of the German race. He was often accused of being a racist. His most monumental work, his *magnum opus*, is the series of the four operas of the *Ring of the Nibelung*, based upon the religious and epic lore of the Germans. It was completed in 1876 after twenty years of work interrupted by his scandalous and profligate personal life and other works. The entire Ring cycle was premiered in the Bayreuth theatre, erected as a shrine to Wagner, in August 1876 with royalty (Ludwig of Bavaria) and countless music colleagues

(Liszt, Tchaikovsky, Saint-Saens and others) in attendance. It was the supreme triumph of Wagner's life. He was now accepted in the world of music and art and had become, finally in the twilight of his life, a wealthy man free of the debts that plagued him throughout most of his earlier years.

The late 19th century also witnessed the spread of music among the Slavs of eastern Europe. Chopin was of Polish descent on his maternal side. After Peter and Catherine oriented Russia toward Western Europe there emerged several major composers—Peter Ilich Tchaikovsky (1840–1893), Nicolai Rimsky Korsakov (1844–1908), Modest Mussorsky (1839–1881), Alexander Borodin (1833–1887) and others. Tchaikovsky became a great composer of music for the ballet, to wit, *Swan Lake, Sleeping Beauty, Eugene Oneigin* and others. Equally noteworthy is the work of the Czech master Antonin Dworak (1841–1904).

In the 20th century Western music found itself at a crossroads. By 1850 the art was fully developed. Instrumental music was now predominant. The instruments have changed little during the past century. The symphony orchestra is composed today substantially the same as it was in 1850. A rebellion, against this tradition, however, set in toward the end of the 19th century. Dissonance, rather than harmonious melody, became *avant garde*. Weird noises were coaxed out of traditional instruments and new sound makers (cow bells, gongs and the like) were introduced. It was frankly referred to as "barbaric style". Bela Bartok (1881–1945), with considerable insouciance, called one such composition *Allegro Barbaro*. Prokofiev's *Scythian Suite*, composed in 1914, and Stravinsky's *Le Sacre du Printemps*, composed in 1913, are further examples of dissonance and exotic sounds.

A major innovation was the twelve-tone technique, or dodecaphonic music, pioneered by Austrian born Arnold Schoenberg (1874–1951). It consists of arranging the twelve tones in an octave with each tone given equal importance instead of having one tone predominate. Whether it has any future still remains to be seen.

Twentieth century technological advance has had two significant impacts on music. The first is the recording of music on plastic discs or tapes. The phonograph, or gramophone, was invented contemporaneously by Alexander Graham Bell in America and Charles Cros in France in 1877. Since then the simple mechanism has evolved into stereophonic, and even quadraphonic, recording. Recording of music dating back 500 years—thanks to notation—was made possible. Good music could now be enjoyed in the home of every cultured person.

Electronic music—produced or modified by electronic means—is the latest technological innovation. Instruments like guitars are amplified. Entire performances are modified with the microphone. Whole compositions can be performed electronically from the score without human performance. Electronic production and modification has virtually no limits on the range of sound possible.

Whether it is good music is questionable. Undisciplined sound is not music. There is a fine line which when crossed makes the production of sound simply noise. In the words of musicologist Wiora:

> Music is the play of tones, that is, of fixed, clearly defined quantities. Other sounds, like glissandos, cries, noises, may occur as inserts; if they are numerous the result is partly musical; if they predominate, it is no longer music in the proper sense of the word.

Art normally reflects the temper of the age. Dissonant music may be reflecting the breakdown of cohesion, discipline and harmony of Western society. Perhaps it is merely echoing the noises begot by industrialization—the ten ton truck roaring on the superhighway, the screeching jet taking off at the airport and the like.

Indian music is a half turn away from Western music. It has no notation and no polyphony. Nonetheless it is great music with a long tradition.

The central feature of Indian music is the raga, which may best be defined as a tune pattern or framework to which the performer must conform. But within that framework he is free to create and improvise. The performer is both composer and musician. Each performance, even by the same musician, is different within the confines of a particular raga. Since there is no notation each composition vanishes into air once it is performed except insofar as it may be orally remembered and reproduced or near reproduced once again. Today, however, it can be recorded.

Such tradition obviously makes it difficult to reconstruct a history of the music. Fortunately, there is some literature from which a dim picture can be perceived. The Vedas, the ancient religious texts, intimate that the Brahman priests sang liturgical hymns which were perhaps like the medieval plainsong or Gregorian chant. In the 2nd century before the Christian era the sage Bharata wrote a treatise on drama, dancing and music called the *Natyasastra* which sets forth a system of music differing little from the present classical tradition. It is, therefore, concluded by musicologists that the ragas we know today in India were the same or similar to those performed two thousand years ago. How Indian music evolved from the Brahmanic chant to the raga will probably be lost forever in obscurity.

The traditional instrument is the vina, a seven stringed instrument with two gourd resonators, ten or twelve inches from each end. It is played with a plectrum. The vina is about three and a half feet overall with a finger board twenty-one and three-fourths inches long. Two of the wires are steel the other five brass. The sitar is similar, favored in the north, with six strings and only one pear shaped or round resonator at one end. To some extent this reflects the two schools of music. The Karnatic system, the most traditional, prevails in the south and relies mostly on the vina; the northern or Hindusthani system, influenced by the Muslims, uses the sitar. In the performance the difference within the two schools is not very significant.

The vina or sitar is accompanied by the tambura, a four or five stringed instrument, which is played in a continuous drone as a backdrop for the main instrument. Far more important, however, is the tabla, a pair of drums which give great dimension to the raga. The right hand one is tuned to the tonic or dominant and the left is the bass. A paste of flour and water is usually applied to the drumhead and allowed to dry before the performance, after which it is removed, to achieve greater resonance. Indian drums have a distinct ping that is not found in Western drums. A great musician and his tabla player achieve a rapport that is near mystical. The tabla player will with his drums playfully coax, challenge, but never interfere with, the sitar player to bring out his best performance. And when the result is creative genius it is not uncommon to see tears of joy flowing from the admiring eyes of the tabla player. Sounds of approval and praise are also ejaculated by him.

The ragas are primarily heptatonic. Five or six tones or notes, are used in lesser or subsidiary ragas. A raga must use at least five notes. The seven notes are elaborated with half and quarter tones.

There are countless ragas. Since the Natyasastra (which enumerates over thirty ragas) six have been considered basic. They are classified for time of day and various emotions. There is a raga for the morning, evening and late evening and a raga associated with spring, the rainy season, love, peace and colors and so on. Ragas are considered masculine. There are female counterparts called Raginis. Also sons called Putras. It is a prodigious task, indeed, to commit all these forms to memory. The great poet-musicologist of the 13th–14th century Amir Khusrau said "It is an art so refined, so complex, so subtle, that after twenty years of study I only began to understand its beauty."

The raga has a fixed structure. It begins slowly, with the Alap, to invoke the raga form and to familiarize the audience and accompanists with the tones to be used. Next the rhythm scheme is introduced in the Jor. This is followed by a fast movement in the selected rhythm. At this point the tempo slows and the drums join for the first time. This part is known as the Gat. The tempo changes from slow to medium to fast and ends with a crescendo, very fast, known as the Jhala. The drums beat out the rhythm pattern, called Talas, and maintain the time-cycle of the Gat.

A raga performance is intended for a small audience. It is something like the chamber music of the West. A great performance will evoke a sympathetic response from the audience in the form of elicitations of joy and approval, but never handclapping which would be discordant. An accomplished musician can make the sitar cry, moan and emote like a human being. The rapport between sitar player and his drummer has already been noted. The raga performance is a truly memorable emotional relationship between performer and auditor.

In addition to the classical ragas there is music for the dance, drama, temple and other purposes. The orchestra for these performances consists of

drums (always), strings, flutes and other wind instruments. The orchestra
has not attained the heights found elsewhere as the great musicians of India
opt for the classical ragas. Vocal music too has not attained pre-eminence.
The voice is treated as an instrument and tends to be throaty and nasal
instead of natural.

Western music has grown in favor in modern times especially by the
English speaking and educated Indians. In fact, Indians can now boast of a
great conductor of Western music in Zuban Mehta, a Parsee from Bombay.
Cinema music also bears a strong Western influence.

Near East (Muslim) music is similar to Indian music. The maqam is like
the raga providing a pattern or form for the composer-musician. The Arabs
were already familiar with such music before Mohammed from their
intercourse with Syria and Persia. Mohammed frowned on secular music
and prescribed that good Muslims would indulge only in the religious hymns
and other mosque music like the muezzin's chant but in due time secular
music regained popularity. As already noted the Arabs borrowed heavily
from the cultures of the people they conquered in the Near East and Persia.
Harun-al-Rashid was very fond of music and his renowned court at Baghdad
was filled with musicians and dancing girls. Strings and lutes were the
favorite instruments of the Arabs. A distinct type of Muslim music evolved
in southern Spain known as Andelusian. It reflects Gypsy and European
influence. The guitar is a prominent instrument in Andelusian music.

China has a long tradition in music. It is rooted in the sounds of nature;
metal, stone, silk, bamboo, calabash, terra cotta, skin and wood. Bells were
made from bronze, sixteen stones comprised the instrument Pien-ch'ing for
a full range of tones, silk was used in string instruments, bamboo for pipes
and flutes, calabash for a mouth organ, terra cotta for an ocarina, skin and
wood for drums. There are some 130 different instruments. Legend has it
that Emperor Hoang-ti around 300 B. C. or so sent his Master of Music
throughout his empire to seek out good music. In a secluded valley he found
some fine bamboo trees from which he cut stems to reproduce the twelve
notes of the scale. He returned with the full scale on which Chinese music
thereafter was based. Bamboo again! The role of bamboo in Chinese culture
has already been noted.

Chinese notation consists of ideograms for the tones of the scale. There is
no time marking. Hence, much of the music must be learned and transmitted
orally. The music is mostly monophonic. It is sometimes played with
rhythmic backgrounds and secondary melodies.

Chinese opera originated during the T'ang period (618–906 A. D.). It has
flourished ever since. Its greatest period was during the Ming epoch (1368–
1664). Male singers customarily assume female roles as men and women are
not permitted to appear on stage together. There are also all women casts,
with women taking male roles. The singing is highly stylized.

Japan has a similar tradition. Until the 12th century Buddhist music was predominant. After 1200 A. D. narration set to flute music and the No drama with the stereotype singing and music developed. A form of chamber music emerged around 1500 A. D. with a 13 string zither and a 3 string lute. A flute was added for ensemble music. Singing often accompanied the instrumental music. The kabuki and bunraku (puppet) theatre music was a later development. Japanese instruments and singing are combined with an orchestral effect for the narrative and dancing.

The gamelan orchestra of Indonesia provides a rather unique kind of music. The orchestra consists of a wide variety of exotic instruments mostly metallophones, xylophones and drums. The melody instruments are the suling, a flute usually with six holes, the rebab, a heart shaped bowed lute with two strings and the saran, a metallophone of six to nine iron slabs placed across a wooden trough. Bamboo slabs are sometimes used instead. A metallophone of ten to fourteen small bronze gongs resting on a mesh of strings with earthenwear resonance pots below is used as a paraphrasing instrument. The gender, consisting of thin metal strings placed above a bamboo resonator tube is also used. A xylophone of wooden slabs and large gongs is used to ornament and punctuate the melody. Finally, there are drums to indicate and maintain the tempo.

Two tonal systems predominate. The slendro, named after the Indian kings of the Sailendro dynasty (circa 8th to 10th centuries), referred to as the masculine or "severe" system, is extremely complex in the tones. The pelong, the female or "friendly" system, is based on the seven tone system. Both vary considerably from Western or other Asian music. The leading orchestras of Java are equipped with two sets of instruments for each of the systems. Gamelan music is, indeed, unique among the tonal systems of the world. The melody has a rolling exhuberant effect with ornamentation and punctuation from the various exotic instruments developed by the Javanese.

The music of Bali is more refined and gentle. Drums and gongs are deemphasized. Vocal music is favored. The Indian influence is more pronounced. The Balinese are very fond of music. Every village maintains its own gamelan orchestra. Claude Debussy was impressed by the gemelan orchestra from Bali he heard in 1889 at the Exposition Universalle in Paris and incorporated some of the tones in his compositions.

DANCE

Dance and music are intimately associated. Graceful and even rhythmic movements can be executed without music but they are not a dance. They are calisthenics. Rhythmic bodily movements come innately to man as he is part of the rhythm of the universe. Day and night, the seasons, sexual cycles, locomotion and the life processes all obey regular and rhythmic patterns. Associating bodily movement with the rhythm of sound, therefore, comes naturally to mankind. Hence, the dance. An old persian proverb says "He who danceth not knoweth not the ways of life." To which Confucius adds "A nation's character is typified by its dances".

Dancing is, perhaps, the oldest enjoyment of man. All peoples have had their folk dances for joyous occasions—harvests, weddings, holidays and so forth. After a bountiful harvest was stored away safely for the impending winter man would dance spontaneously out of joy and satisfaction. As technology advanced making possible a more affluent middle class ballroom dancing evolved for the joy and relaxation of a more complex industrial society.

But dancing was also associated with magic, religion and war. In some instances it was indulged for emotional intoxication. A notable example was the whirling dervishes, a Sufi sect of Islam, who spun to the music of the flute out of religious fervor until completely entranced. The eminent Muslim philosopher El Ghazzali was a member of this sect.

Unlike some of the arts such as sculpture and painting enjoyed mainly by the ruling elite, dancing and music have been enjoyed generally by all of mankind. But dancing too has been elevated to a classical art. As it would be beyond the scope of this dissertation to discuss the many folk and national dances of mankind emphasis will be focused on the two most classical of the dances evolved by man, the Ballet of the West and the Bharatanatayam of the Hindus.

Early Christianity frowned on dancing during its flush of anti-Romanism. Unlike music the church never incorporated dancing into its religious ritual. Dancing therefore, flourished only among the peasants. In medieval times the increasingly affluent courts of the nobility sought new forms of entertainment and enjoyment. Sedate and elegant dances were held. Books were written on the art of court dancing. Narratives or dramas were performed into which dancing was introduced. They came to be called court or banquet ballets and thrived first in Italy during the Rennaissance. The first choreographer of note was Bergonzio de Botto whose banquet ballet composed in 1489 created a stir at the time. Spanish courts had a similar but lesser development. Many of the folk dances of the time were incorporated into these early ballets.

Catherine di Medici (1519–1589) brought the ballet to France where it was developed into the art we know today. She brought with her an Italian dancing master Balthasar de Beauvoyeulx (French adoptation of his Italian name) who staged two court ballets that have been noted in history. The first in 1573, *Le Ballet des Polonaise*, to commemorate the election of Catherine's son Henry as King of Poland. An orchestra of "30 viols" glorified Henry and Catherine. In 1581 he staged his famous *Ballet Comique de la Reine* to celebrate the marriage of Margaret of Lorraine to the Duke of Joyeuse. It was a lavish production watched by some ten thousand guests. It lasted from 10 p. m. to 3 a .m .!

Until now the dancing was done by members of the nobility. Louis XIV loved to dance. His favorite role was that of the sun in *Le Ballet de la Nuit*. But in 1661, when he was too fat and old to dance, Louis established the Academie Royale de Danse with thirteen dancing masters. It was intended for the nobility but in due time became a school for professionals. The first professionals were males. Female roles, subordinate at this time, were danced by ladies of the court. Gradually female professionals came to the fore. Most famous was Marie Comargo (1710–1770). Almost equally famous was her rival Marie Salle. Comargo developed leaping steps and to enable her skill designed a shortened skirt. Marie Salle danced in a sheer muslin dress that revealed the graceful movements of her body. She captivated the English with her performance of *Pygmalion* in London in 1734. Little did they know they were the forerunners of the ballerina that was to dominate the ballet in the succeeding centuries. The 19th century witnessed the rise to primacy of the prima ballerina. Marie Taglioni was first renowned. She elevated the ballerina to her toes to give the illusion of floating in air. A hard blunt toe on the slipper, still used today, was designed and perfected for dancing on the pointes. The tutu, a wide gauze skirt was developed next to afford freedom of movement for the legs. At first, in keeping with Victorian modesty, the tutu was ankle length, later it was elevated to the knees as portrayed by Dega's paintings. Eventually it became a short frilly skirt around the hips known to ballet goers today. The tutu now adds to the spatial and elevated performances of the ballerina.

Marie Taglioni was the daughter of an Italian dancing master at the Paris Opera who vowed to make her a supreme ballerina. She exercised and practiced leaps, arm and body movements for six hours a day which, incidentally, has been the regime ever since for aspiring ballerinas. At 20 she had acquired great elevation and feathery landing, a light and floating grace that caused the critics to call her dancing angelic. Her performance of *La Sylphide* at the Paris Opera on March 12, 1832 became a milestone in ballet history. It was the beginning of the Romantic period. Other famous ballerinas of the day were the Austrian Fanny Elssler, the blonde Italian Carlotta Grissi of *Giselle* fame and the Danish dancers Lucille Grahn and Adeline Genee.

In 1760 Jean-Georges Noverre (1727–1810) published his *Letters on Dancing and Ballet*, generally regarded as the beginning of classical ballet. It was an attempt to formalize ballet steps and movements. The basic principles of ballet technique were set forth. The five positions of the feet and the eight body movements like the soubresauts, pirouettes, entrechats, fouettes and the arabesques. Stretching and bending exercises for suppleness of the arms and legs were prescribed. All this was based upon scientific study of the human body for possibilities of elevation, gliding and gyration. These basic principles have been retained ever since. Noverre's pupil Jean

Dauberial (1742–1806) and his pupil Salvatore Vigano (1767–1821) followed these principles in their ballet creations.

The choreographer was now born. No longer was it left to the dancer to create and improvise. Every step and movement was prescribed. The dancer's virtuosity consisted of the perfect execution of the classical movements and the application of drama and emotion to them. In fact, the *raison d'etre* of classical ballet was to routinize the dance movements so that the dancer could concentrate on the technique, emotion and drama of the ballet.

The ballet was on the wane in western Europe by the second half of the 19th century. But it was to find a new home in Russia. There was classical ballet in Russia, however, before the French choreographers began to arrive. First came Jules Perrot in 1848, then Saint-Leon in 1859 and finally the great Marius Petipa (1822–1920) in 1862. Petipa's influence was monumental. He teamed up with the eminent Russian composer Tchaikovsky to produce *The Sleeping Beauty* (1890) and *Swan Lake* (1893) two of the finest ballets ever created. Lev Ivanov his pupil did the choreography for Acts II and IV of the latter. In 1885 a succession of Italian dancers and choreographers visited St. Peterburg and succeeded in adding more emotion and fire to the Russian ballet. At the turn of the century the Imperial Ballet in St. Petersburg was the foremost dance company of the day.

In the 20th century two Russians extended and popularized the classical ballet on a world wide basis. The first was the great impresario Serge Daighilev; the other, Anna Pavlova, the supreme ballerina of the day, if not, of all time.

Born in 1872, the son of an officer in the imperial guard, Daighilev, bounced around the world of the arts during his early years in St. Petersburg. He was more interested in painting and music but knew all the artists of the Imperial Ballet. In 1908 he took Russian opera to Paris and followed the next year with Russian ballet including dancers Anna Pavlova, Tamara Karsavina and the legendary Vaslav Nijinsky along with the striking choreography of Mikhail Fokine. It was an overwhelming success. For the next twenty years, until his death in 1929, Daighilev took his company far and wide across Europe and North and South America. London took the Daighilev Ballet to its heart. John Maynard Keynes, the 20th century's leading economist married one of the Diaghilev ballerinas in 1925, the blond and beautiful Lydia Lopokova who remained his faithful and loving wife for life. International economists and financiers recall touchingly the story of how she nursed him tenderly at the time of his unfortunate heart attack at Bretton Woods during the negotiations in 1944 for the establishment of the World Bank and International Monetary Fund. Tamara Karsavina married British diplomat H. J. Bruce and remained in London helping with the birth of the English ballet.

The twenty years, 1909–1929, are referred to as the Daighilev era in the annals of ballet. Until then ballet was dominated from the narrow perspective of the choreographer. Daighilev added dimension by emphasizing as well the costumes, settings, staging, the theme and the music. The art of lighting was his particular contribution. During his twenty years he introduced to the Western world several great choreographers—Fokine, Massine and Balanchine and numerous dancers—Nijinsky, Pavlova, Karsavina, Danilova, Markova, Dolin, Lifar and other luminaries. The Diaghilev era is frequently divided into three periods. The Fokine period from 1909–1914; the Nijinsky—Massine period 1914–1922; and the last from 1922–1929, which was in effect a period of exile as Russia was now a closed society after the 1917 revolution.

Pavlova was something unto herself. She left the Diaghilev Ballet after a few performances in 1910 to tour abroad on her own. She bought a house in London, the famous Ivy House, where she lived until her death in 1931. Her solo performances took her all over the world, including North and South America, Australia and the Far East. Some questioned her taste in choreography, music and costume but none her dancing. *The Dying Swan* was her most famous performance. As ballet historian Ferdinando Reyna says "Anna Pavlova was winged grace itself." She inspired a whole generation of young girls from Lima to Sidney. How much of the revival of classical ballet after World War II is owed to Anna Pavlova cannot be measured.

While the Russians were promoting classical ballet around the world the forepart of this century there was a revolution against it spearheaded by the American dancer Isodore Duncan (1878–1927). Eschewing the hard toed slipper and tutu she danced in her bare feet. In similar manner she rejected the classical positions and movements in "an effort to express my being". Her movements consisted of running, skipping, leaping with flowing arms. A similar expressionist movement transpired in Germany. Another American dancer Martha Graham (born 1893) introduced primitive dance rhythms from Africa and the Caribbean into modern dance. Such rebellion against the classical form also transpired, as we saw earlier, in painting and music but in the dance it has been overshadowed by the Russian ballet earlier in the century and by the revival of the classical ballet after World War II.

The communist revolution might have snuffed out the classical ballet in Russia. But it did not. After the revolution the Imperial Ballet was in disarray. Many (about 40 per cent) of the choreographers and dancers reestablished themselves abroad but those that chose to stay in Russia gradually restored the art. And the new Soviet government gave it encouragement and support. Greatest credit must be given Agrippana Vaganova who trained the ballerinas Semyonova, Ulanova and Dudinskaya, that resuscitated Russian ballet, and published a book entitled *Fundamentals of the Classic Ballet* which became the basis of the Soviet ballet. In fact, it has been translated into many languages and is widely used outside Russia.

Vaganova's male counterpart was Asaf Messener who taught most of Russia's great dancers of today. Imaginative choreographers came to the fore. Fedor Lopochov, Lydia's brother was one; Leonid Lavrosky another. The latter's *Romeo and Juliet* to Prokofiev's music was one of Ulanova's triumphs in 1940. By mid century Russia again had two of the foremost ballet companies in the world, the Kirov and the Bolshoi, which have delighted audiences all over the world during the past two decades or so.

Equally accomplished companies emerged in Europe and America. Most famous, perhaps, was the Saddler's Wells Ballet, now the Royal Ballet of London. It produced the scintillating ballerina Margot Fonteyn who may go down in the annals of ballet as the Pavlova of her generation. The Royal Danish Ballet of Copenhagen, the Stuttgart Ballet of Germany and the Ballet of the Twentieth Century of Brussels are other renowned companies. In America the American Ballet Theatre and New York City Ballet have achieved great excellence. Some of these companies especially the American are affected by modern dance whereas the Russian and English companies remain primarily classical.

The Bharatanatayam, the classical dance of India, is more than two thousand years old. It originated as religious ritual performed in the temple by beautiful girls called devadasi. When the sage Bharata compiled his treatise on drama and dance, the *Natyasastra* (circa 200 B. C.–200 A. D.) the dance was already highly formed. The name Bharatanatyam derives therefrom.

After a time the devadasi sank to low repute. The ruling elite, the rajas and landlords, perverted them into prostitution. Orthodox Brahman priests conducted a campaign to purge them from the temple. The classical dance, however, survived in the homes and courts of the wealthy Hindus. In the late 19th and 20th centuries the Bharatanatayam has been restored to its former pristine status.

Gestures and facial expressions are as important as rhythm in the Indian dance. Most beautiful are the movements of the hands called mudra. There are over a hundred primary poses of the arms and legs known as haranas. Some 32 angharas which are combinations of haranas. Mastering them requires years of training.

The gestures are designed for communication with the audience. The Bharatanatayam is obviously meant for the cultured. The untutored can enjoy the graceful and elegant movements, but are unable to derive the meaning of the dance.

The Bharatanatayam is danced almost exclusively by women. Indian gurus (instructors) are very particular about the girls they accept as pupils. In the words of the late A. K. Coomaraswamy, India's leading art critic, "The danseuse (Nartaki) should be very lovely, young, with full round breasts, self confident, charming, agreeable, quite at home on the stage, expert in gesture, with wide open eyes, able to follow song and instruments and rhythm, adorned with costly jewels, with a charming face, neither very stout nor very thin, nor very tall nor very short''.

The dance costume is equally beautiful. The dancer wears a tight fitting silk choli and a brightly colored and embroidered sari draped tightly around her hips. It is heavily pleated in front to permit freedom of the legs. The pleated skirt opens like a fan when the dancer parts her knees. Her long hair is braided in back and decked with jasmine and marigolds. Diamonds are set in her pierced nostrils and rings, gold bands and bracelets ornament her fingers and wrists. A bracelet of tiny silver bells encircles her ankles. Her eyes are accentuated with make-up (khol), a round red mark is painted between her brows and her palms and soles are dyed rose pink. As she dances her sari ripples and her flower bedecked braid swings to the rhythm of her movements. It is the essence of graceful femininity.

The dance lasts about two hours and is normally divided into six parts. In the ala rippu (prologue) the dancer walks gracefully upon the stage, bows to her guru and the audience with folded hands and strikes the formal pose. The music begins. She goes through three interpretive and pure dances. Next is an interlude of padams. Padams are songs in sanskrit or a south Indian language sung by a member of the orchestra. The dancer dramatizes the chants with facial and other expressions. Her art is suggesting all possible interpretations of the song. The final part is the tillana. It is a fast and vigorous dance consisting of parabolas, spirals, circles with the torso contrasted with angular and arched movements of the limbs. The dancer engages in leaps and jumps. The tillana ends with three clangs of the cymbals and joyful shouts of the singers while the dancer concludes with a series of jumps thumping her feet to tinkle the bells on her ankles.

The Bharatanatayam has a masculine counterpart called Kathakali. It is a dance-drama executed in pantomime. The actor wears a heavy hard paste makeup (grotesque to the untutored) that takes hours to prepare, appropriate to the character part (usually scenes from the Mahabharata or Ramayana) he will portray. The actor does not speak. The drama is communicated through the idiom of mime using facial and dance movements. A Kathakali actor has a glossary of 500 or more gestures. It is an extremely vigorous dance, done mostly by men. In many ways it is similar to Chinese opera or the No and Kabuki theatre of Japan.

Prior to the Muslim invasions Bharatanatayam was performed all over India. Kathakali, however, developed later during the 17th century in Kerala, South India. After Muslim rule was imposed in the north during the 13th century the classical dance retreated to the south which until today has been its sanctuary. The best gurus, schools and dancers came from the south. But under the Indianized Mughals a new dance form developed called the Kathak. The Kathak is a blend of Persian and Indian influence as is the case of other Mughal art. It is primarily footwork to complex rhythm patterns. There is no rigid technique as in the Bharatnatayam. The dancer doubles and quadruples the rhythm with mathematical precision. She whirls and spins. It is a vigorous dance done by both men and women.

A fourth dance, the Manipuri, is usually considered classical in India though it is more in nature of a folk dance. It developed in the isolated valley of Assam where the people are extremely fond of dancing. Both men and women dance it. It was unknown outside Manipur until Rabindranath Tagore brought it to his school at Santiniketan and introduced it to the rest of India.

The dancer wears a loose fitting colorful blouse and stiff, full skirt with round mirror pieces embroidered into it. Her hair is rolled up in a crown with chains of white blossoms. Sandalwood paste dots her forehead and luminous mica powder is applied to her face. The dance is slow with swaying and gliding movements. It is graceful and feminine.

A concluding word on ballroom dancing. As the Industrial Revolution brought forth an affluent middle class the folk dance was brought up, or in another view, the court dance was brought down into the public ballroom. The court dances—pavan, gavotte and minuet—were ballroom dances in a sense but enjoyed only by the ruling elite. Ballroom dancing is enjoyed by the new middle class of an industrial society.

The waltz is, perhaps, the first ballroom dance designed for a couple rather than a group. It evolved in Austria and Bavaria around the turn of the nineteenth century. The word "waltz" means "to roll" or "to turn". Johann Strauss and his son gave the waltz a great boost when they adapted it for their light concert compositions, with the younger Strauss' incomparable *Beautiful Blue Danube* and *Tales from the Vienna Woods*. By mid century the waltz was the popular dance of Europe.

Next in popularity was the polka which originated in Bohemia around 1830. In contrast to the gliding rhythm of the waltz the polka has a strong downbeat and jump step. From Bohemia it quickly spread throughout Europe. Smetana introduced it into his concert compositions.

Both the waltz and the polka were extended with emigration to the United States. A slower version called the Boston or hesitation waltz was developed during World War I. About the same time the Americans evolved the foxtrot a moderate dance tempo consisting of an alternating one and two step rhythm which has ever since become the most popular dance step of the Western and westernized world.

During the interwar period several Latin dances spread to and became popular in America and Europe. The tango originated in Argentina and gained prominence in Europe. Not so in America where two others grew in favor instead. The rumba from Cuba and the samba from Brazil, both with strong African overtones. The samba with a strong double or single (called marcha) downbeat is the easiest of the two. The rumba because of a sophisticated shifting of bodily weight from hip to hip is a more complex dance to learn. Once the shifting of weight is mastered the step is a simple one-two-three pause rhythm. Both are heady intoxicating dance rhythms.

The latest dance creation by the joy loving Cubans is the cha-cha-cha. It originated in the 1950's and was brought back to America and Europe by the tourists. It is a more difficult dance consisting of two slow and three fast beats or steps.

There are some other ballroom dances which may merely be mentioned as they have not attained the sustained popularity of the above. The jitterbug originating in America, the calypso and reggae in Jamaica, the merengue in Haiti and Dominican Republic, the conga, from Cuba again, and the mambo. In the 1960's there was a degeneration in the dance, in America in particular, with the introduction of vulgar bodily movements and gestures. Most have been passing fads.

Western domination spread ballroom dancing to virtually every country of the world. Indian ladies in saris, Vietnamese girls in ao-dais, Chinese women in slit skirts could or can be seen doing the fox trot and rumba in the hotel dining rooms of New Delhi, Saigon and Shanghai or Honkong during the present century. Curiously, though, ballroom dancing has suffered a partial eclipse in America during the 1960's and 1970's. There is some indication that ballroom dancing is reviving again.

LITERATURE AND DRAMA

When man began to write, (nay) even before, he composed prose and poetry for the preservation of his accumulating knowledge and amusement. The invention of writing, one of man's greatest achievements, is thought to have occurred late in the 4th millennium B. C. in ancient Sumeria. The earliest poem known today is the *Epic of Gilgamesh* which has come down in history in 12 clay tablets composed by Babylonian scribes in Sumerian cuneiform about 2000 B. C. They were found in the library of the Assyrian king Ashurbanipal (circa 669–626 B. C.) at Nineveh.

Gilgamesh is depicted as a demi-god. Like most epic heroes he is all powerful and sexually irresistible. He is "fearsome like a wild ox" and seduces "the maid", "the warrior's daughter" and "the noble's spouse". He becomes a threat to both men and the gods. The Sumerian mother-goddess Aruru, therefore, creates a powerful brute Enhidu, who consorts with animals, to overcome Gilgamesh. They become friends, however, and travel together in pursuit of knowledge and immortality. The latter proves a hopeless quest. The theme of immortality is critical also in another Sumerian epic of Inanna, the goddess of love and fertility, who the Babylonians called Ishtar. Noteworthy also is the kinship of man and animals, the sameness of life on earth, which was later rejected by Judeo-Christian theology.

The eleventh tablet contains the legend of the Flood in substantially the same form it is later incorporated in the Bible; the story of Noah and the

Ark. The legend of the great deluge is found elsewhere in the myths and legends of the Near East that it has caused speculation about its veracity. A possible explanation is the glacial cycle. Large areas of the Persian Gulf were dry land at the height of the Wurm glacier. When the Wurm began to recede around 8000 B. C. these areas were again submerged in the sea. It is altogether possible that due to some geological or meteorological factor the rising sea broke through the entrance into the Persian gulf in a flood tide causing a sudden deluge of these littoral lands sometime during the 5th or 4th millennium before Christ. Lacking scientific knowledge and explanation of the phenomena prehistoric man sought explanation in the supernatural.

This was, it should be noted, the site of one of man's earliest civilizations. The Israelites too originated in Ur at the head of the Persian gulf. There is a growing belief based upon increasing scientific knowledge that the Arabian penninsula adjoining the gulf was a verdant land (say) around 5000 B. C. and not the desert it is today.

Early literature with the exception, perhaps, of the Chinese, was of the religious type or epic form. Most notable is the Bible. It is not possible to authenticate the authorship or time recordation of the Old Testament. It was compiled over centuries. Genesis was probably written around 1000 B. C. although it records events that transpired a millennium or so earlier such as Abraham's departure from Ur for Canaan. It is thought the entire text of the Old Testament was completed during the 5th century B. C. The New Testament on the life and teachings of Christ was compiled during the first century of the Christian era. The Old Testament was written in Hebrew; the New originally in Greek and later in Latin for the Roman Catholic church. The Koran too rests on the Old Testament adding onto it or merging it with the life and teachings of Mohammed. It was compiled early in the 7th century A. D. in Arabic. It is considered untranslatable by the orthodox Arab Muslim though it was rewritten in the languages of the conquered peoples. Every Muslim learns to read from the Koran and it remains thereafter the greatest literature of his life.

The Old Testament is the most interesting. It is more than religion. It is history, philosophy, folklore and practical wisdom. To be sure, it is heavily biased, but when the bias is taken in stride it is some of the most fascinating literature composed by man.

Egyptian literature too was heavily religious. It did not, however, produce any epics. But the ancient Egyptians wrote some of the earliest secular prose and poetry. *The Protests of the Eloquent Peasant*, written about 2000 B. C. is the story of a cultivator who was bilked or robbed by an official so he pleads his case in nine appeals to the Pharoah's chief steward and wins the restoration of his property. It reflects a striking bit of social justice not generally thought to exist at that time.

The *Story of Sinhue*, written a few centuries later during the Middle Kingdom, is a story of an Egyptian who fled to Syria, after implication in an assassination of the Pharoah, where he prospered greatly but always longed for Egypt. Like all Egyptians at this time he regarded Egypt as the only place for worthwhile living. Finally in his old age, he is permitted to return by the new Pharoah. He contemplates the return to his homeland and the bliss of an Egyptian burial with great joy. A touching passage is the relief he feels when he discards his heavy Syrian clothes for the cool Egyptian linen.

The New Kingdom (1567–1085 B. C.) produced some charming love poetry. Akhenaton's *Hymn to Aton* equals some to the best poetry of man. Prose also reached great heights, particularly the so-called wisdom literature—words of advice by wise old men to the young. Many of these passages found their way into the Old Testament.

The Greeks, along with the Indians, were the great epic compilers of mankind. Every literate person of the Mediterranean area thereafter became familiar with the *Iliad* and the *Odyssey*. These two epics have had a profound influence on the art and literature of the Western world.

They were composed by the blind bard Homer during the 8th century B. C. The two poems embrace the religion, myths and legends of the Mycenaean age. And they do more. Homer's characters from the lowliest swineherd to nobles like Achilles and Odysseus portray the everday life of the ancient Greeks.

The Iliad is the story of the abduction of a queen, Helen, the wife of Menalaus, by Paris, the prince of the Trojans. The Greeks assault Troy and recapture Helen. But it takes ten years! The Greeks win with the famous ruse of a gift of a wooden horse containing Greek soldiers to get inside the city walls that they were unable to scale for a decade. After Helen is recaptured everyone starts for home. But Odyssues, who devised the strategy of the wooden horse, got lost in the Mediterranean for ten years before he returned to his faithful wife Penelope. Penelope's resistance of numerous suitors, more interested in Odyssues's property, is a portrayal by Homer of the ideal Greek wife. The voyage is filled with mythology—the Lotus Eaters, Cyclops, Circe, Scylla and Charbydis—that has ever since permeated Western literature and art.

For centuries the Iliad was considered mythology until the amateur German archeologist Heinrich Schliemann discovered in 1870 the site of ancient Troy in Asia Minor near the entrance to the Hellspont. Since then the renowned walls of the Iliad have been uncovered. No one doubts any longer that the famous siege took place. Historians fix the date of the battle around 1200 B. C. But whether the attack was motivated by the abduction of Helen or some more prosaic reason such as the Trojans interferring with the passage of Greek ships through the Hellespont for much needed wheat from the Black Sea area is an open question. But for the sake of literature it is best to let the romantic motive prevail.

The Romans borrowed the Greek epics for their early literature. The Odyssey was translated into Latin in 275 B. C. by one Andonicus, a Greek slave, who was a teacher in the Roman household of Livius Saltinor. Two centuries or so later Vergil (70–19 B. C.) composed the *Aeneid* which is largely an adaptation of the Iliad and the Odyssey for an epic on the foundation of Rome. The hero Anneas wonders through the Mediterranean on his return from Troy, including a trip to the netherworld, ending up with a conquest of Italy.

There followed a golden age in Latin literature with the poetry of Horace and Ovid, the History of Rome by Livy and others. During the days of the empire Roman literature produced Seneca and Pliny, the historian Tacitus, the biographer Plutarch and, last but not least, the satirists Juvenal and Martial. Concurrently some Christian writers came to the fore, notably, Tertullian of Carthage (circa 160–230 A. D.), Ambrose, bishop of Milan, Jerome and the great Augustine (345–430 A. D.). Augustine's *City of God* is one of the finest pieces of Christian literature.

During the twilight of the Republic and the early empire literature for public consumption and amusement developed. Books proliferated throughout the empire and were simultaneously published in Rome, Athens, Lyons and Alexandria. They sold for as little as five sesterces (75 cents); a fine edition of Martial's epigrams sold for about five denarii (3 dollars). The *nouveau riche* bought books as status symbols but never read them. Sulla decried the practice. A traveler seldom failed to leave on a journey without a book or two to amuse him enroute. Roman books were not the bound copies we know today. They were scrolls or rolls (volumen) kept in a round wooden box called a capsa. The books were hand copied as the technology of printing was not yet developed at this time.

Such a market begot a degeneration in literature. Everyone from a fool to a philosopher wrote poetry bemoaned Horace. Politicians and generals wrote their memoirs for profit. Writers resorted to obscenity and pornography to lure readers. Catullus (circa 84–54 B. C.) is particularly notable in this respect. While he published some tender and beautiful poetry he was merciless toward those he disliked, writing obscenely about their homosexuality, lack of hygenic manners and the like. Will Durant writes "Catullus vascillates easily between love and offal, kisses and fundaments". Such writing came to be known as street corner urology. Martial was also guilty of similar obscenity. Both defended their writing by saying they were forced to compile such dirt in order to hold their audience.

After the fall of Rome Western literature sank to a low point. The Greek heritage was lost or shunned. The Arab philosophers, notably Ibn Rushid, or Averroes, of Spain (1126–1198) translated Greek works which filtered into Europe. A reawakening to Greek literature and art took hold in Italy during the Rennaissance (14th–16th centuries) from where it spread to the rest of Europe. The Greek heritage, once again, flowed in the veins of Western literature.

Three influences now coalesced to provide the foundation of the literature of the evolving European civilization. The Graeco-Roman heritage, the Judeo-Christian biblical tradition and the epic lore of the Germanic tribes. The epic poem appears to be an Indo-European propensity. The same, as we shall see, was also true of the Indians.

Beowulf was first reduced to writing in old English, it is thought, in the 8th century by an English monk. That it was orally transmitted for centuries before seems clear. Beowulf was the prince of a royal house of the Geatas who lived in Sweden. He frees his uncle Hrothgar, the king of Denmark, of the troll Grendel that haunted the palace and ate a few members of the court during each nightly visitation. This entails a battle beneath the sea. In the end Beowulf dies defending Geatland against a dragon.

Another Germanic epic *Tristan and Isolde* was reduced to writing only in the 12th century. *Chanson de Roland*, in old French, was written in the 8th century. There are many others—the *Cid*, in old Spanish, the Icelandic *Elder Edda*, the *Nibelungenlied* in middle high German and the Arthurian legends of old England. The *Chanson de Roland* is genuine history though overlaid with myth. It is the story of the repulse of the Muslim invaders in the Pyrennes by Charlemagne's army, of which Roland was the foremost knight. All of these epic poems are a mix of history, mythology and even religion. There was most likely a Beowulf but not a Grendel. After the archeological proof of the story of the Iliad modern man no longer views these ancient epics as pure fiction and mythology.

Europeans continued to write epic, or neo-epic poetry. there is Dante's *Divine Comedy* and Petrarch's *Africa* in the 14th, Spencer's *Faerie Queen* in the 16th, Milton's *Paradise Lost* and Bunyan's *Pilgrim's Progress* in the 17th centuries.

Thereafter Western literature became realistic, though fictional, with the birth of the European novel. Cervante's *Don Quixote*, published in 1605–15, is usually considered the first true novel. Voltaire, Rousseau, Balzac, Flaubert, Zola, Hugo, France, Provost, Malroux in France; Defoe, Fielding, Scott, Dickens, Thackery, Emily Bronte, Trollope, Hardy in England; Geothe, Schiller, Mann in Germany; Pushkin, Gogol, Tolstoy, Dostoevsky in Russia; Cooper, Hawthorne, Melville, Mark Twain, James in America. This formidable list still omits many worthy of mention, particularly some in the 20th century who have still to meet the test of time.

Great history was also written. The first historians were the Greeks. Herodotus, the father of history, covered the Persian war period. Much of his writing was considered, until recently, myth or fiction but modern archeology has now verified most of the doubted portions. Thucydides covered the Peloponnesian war. The Romans, however, were second rate historians. Tacitus was, perhaps, the ablest; Plutarch's *Lives* also contain good history. Mention is in order here of Flavius Josepheus who wrote about the first century of the Christian era, particularly the history of the Jewish race. It was the Europeans, however, who made history great literature. Moreover, they evolved a philosophy of history. Edward Gibbon's *Decline and Fall of the Roman Empire* (1776–1794) was the first monumental interpretation of Roman history. This was followed by another outstanding *History of Rome* by Theodor Mommsen in 1854–55. In addition to first rate history both are written in language and grammer that has since vanished from the pen of Western man. In the 20th century historians became occupied with the meaning of history. Oswald Spengler's *Decline of the West* (1923) and Arnold Toynbee's *Study of History* (1933–1955) are the foremost works in this respect. Man had now evolved intellectually to the point where he looked analytically at his past for a key to his future.

The mass market for literature returned again in the 20th century and with it the degeneration of prose. In order to capture a market for their novels authors felt they had to introduce sex and violence and obscenity into their composition. Rhetoric descended to the vernacular. America became the mecca for this kind of literature. Whether it will survive the test of time or perish like its Roman counterpart two thousand years ago is for the future to judge.

The Indians created two great epics, the *Mahabharata* and the *Ramayana*, which have had profound impact on the cultural life in India and throughout Southeast Asia. The earliest Hindu literature, however, is the sacred Vedas, religious lore, composed about 1400 B. C. or earlier. There are four Vedas consisting of hymns and prayers, chants, sacrifice formulae and the private or personal aspects of religion. Later the *Brahmanas* were added as guides for the priests for the sacrificial performance. The *Upanishads*, compiled about 800–500 B. C., reflect the development of rational thought in India and form the basis of Indian philosophy. In general they proclaim salvation through knowledge and understanding. There is profound speculation on the origin of the universe, the beginning of life and the interrelation of all things. Asceticism and disdain for material goods are advocated. Non-violence and abstinence are virtues in the Upanishads.

There is also a body of secondary sacred literature known as *smritis*, "that which is remembered". The Vedas, Brahmanas and Upanishads are known as *srutis*, "that which is heard". The smritis and srutis are the revealed wisdom of the Hindus, where the two conflict the srutis prevail. The smritis are supposed to convey the teachings of the Vedas to the common people. They consist, in the main, of the two epics, the Puranas, the Sastras, Vedangas and Dharmas. The Dharma sastras regulate the political, religious and social life of the Hindus. There are 22 smritis on the law codes starting with the Institutes of Manu. Another, the Nataya sastra, the formal book on drama and dance has already been noted. The two great epics are the most renowned of the smritis.

The *Mahabharata* is the longest epic poem in the world's literature containing over 90,000 stanzas. It was allegedly composed by the sage

Vyasa in sanskrit around 500 B. C. In the main it depicts a battle that raged for 18 days between two Aryan clans the Kurus and the Pandus for control of the capital city of the Ganges-Jumna doab called Indraprastha, the site of modern New Delhi. The hero of the epic is Arjuna, who along with his four brothers, led the Pandus to victory. The five brothers were married to one woman, the Princess Draupadi, which poses something of an anomaly in the poem as the Hindu ruling elite was generally polygamous. The *Bhagavad Gita*, called the Lords Message, is an ethical passage of 700 verses in the *Mahabharata*. It is highly revered by the Indians. It is an important feature of Indian religion and philosophy.

The *Ramayana*, more popular, is less phisophical. It is attributed to the sage Valmiki and composed in sanskrit a century or so before the Christian era. It depicts a later episode in Indian history connected with the expansion of the Aryans into south India. The *Ramayana* involves the abduction of a queen, Sita the wife of Ram, by Ravanna the king of Lanka (Ceylon). The epic consists in the main of the campaign by Ram with his trusted friend Laxsman to rescue Sita. Hanuman, the monkey god, leads a contingent of primates to assist in the assault. Its simple philosophical theme represents the victory of the forces of good over the forces of evil.

The *Ramayana* is very popular with the Indians. Their two chief holidays commemorate it. Dussehra, which occurs in October, hails the victory of Ram over the king of Lanka. Divali, occurring three weeks later, known as the festival of lights, celebrates the homecoming of Ram with Sita.

These two epics have been adopted by the peoples of Southeast Asia. They were brought to this area during the period of trade and colonization in the first millennium of the Christian era by the Pallavas and Cholas of south India. There is a quarter mile long mural in the palace in Bangkok depicting scenes from the *Ramayana*. The Wyang puppet dance in Java also depicts the Indian epic.

The novel has not been part of Indian literature until modern times when the European novel was emulated. Drama, however, is another matter as we will presently see.

Chinese literature is secular. There are no great epics such as those discussed above. The Confucian classics consist of five texts—Book of Changes, Book of History, Book of Songs, Book of Ritual and the Spring and Autumn Annals. They were supposedly edited by Confucius in the 6th century B. C. There have been several commentaries on the classics. An early one by Cheng Hsuan (127–200 A. D.), a later one by Chu Hsi (1130–1200 A. D.).

Chu Hsi develops the Great Learning and the Doctrine of the Mean from the Book of Ritual. These two commentaries together with the Analects of Confucius and the Book of Mencius comprise the Four Books of Chinese learning.

The Chinese cherish poetry. The earliest is found in the Book of Songs. During the Tang Period (619–906) two types of composition were followed, the old style of 8 lines and the new style of 4 lines. Poetry was associated with painting and calligraphy. There is usually a verse on a painted scroll.

The Chinese developed good prose. They were always fond of narrative, particularly, during the T'ang period. Hsuan Tsang wrote vividly of his pilgrimage to India (629–645 A. D.) in *Hsi Yu Chi* which has ever since been a reliable source book on Indian history. Indian fables brought by Buddhism formed the basis for some narrative. Novels appeared around the 16th century. The *Chin P'ing Mei* (Metal Vase Plum-Blossom) already referred to, is a story about Hsi Men and his six wives, a wealthy and polygamous merchant. The *Hung Lou Meng* (Drum of the Red Chamber) written around 1770 is generally regarded as the greatest Chinese novel. It was written by Ts'ao Hsueh-chin. It is about his family, engaged in the manufacture of textiles for three generations, ending in ruin.

The Chinese were keenly mindful of their history since early times. The Book of History covers the time from the third millennium to the sixth century B. C. The *Shi Chi* by Ssu-ma Ch'ien (145–86 B. C.) also covers early history. It established also the form for historical writing which is largely a compilation of original source material—annals of the emperors, monograms on canals, rivers and other state projects, biographies of leaders and the like. It is, consequently, genuine and objective history. The *Tzu Chih T'ung Chien* by Ssu-ma Kuang (1019–1086 A. D) covers the period 400 B. C. to 960 A. D.

The 20th century witnessed a rebellion against the classics. From 1917–1927 there was a spate of translations of Western literature. The Chinese communists returned again to indigenous sources with much revolutionary overtone.

The Japanese emulated Chinese literature and gave it an indigenous flavor. Poetry acquired a lyrical quality. They outdid the Chinese with the novel. An early masterpiece was the *Tale of Genji* written by a court lady, Murasaki Shikibu, around 1000 A. D. The story is about a prince of heroic proportions and keen sensibilities, a lover of nature, beauty and women. It is rich in psychological nuance. It is the worlds first true novel.

The tradition continued thereafter. Buddhist influence was felt during the medieval period (1200–1600 A. D.). Popular fiction evolved, with the invention of printing, during the Tokugawa period (1603–1867). A quantum of vulgarity crept into the literature of this period. Realistic novels set in the shops, streets and pleasure houses proliferated. A Western influence is noted during the Meiji period (1868–1912).

Drama provided an even greater source of enjoyment. It was able to reach many people beyond the literate through the theatre. In fact, the word theatre derives from the Greek word *theatron* which means "a place for seeing''. Some drama as shall be seen, is pantomine and meant purely for seeing. But the great drama of man is designed for both seeing and hearing.

Drama and theatre had their maximum development in the West beginning with the ancient Greeks. The ancient Egyptians indulged in ceremonial plays that did not attain the stature of dramas. The Greeks developed two types of drama, tragedy and comedy. Each is thought to have had a different genesis. The Doric Greeks first developed the choral song and dance into a literary performance. In the 6th Century Thespis of Icaria (hence the word thespian for actor) designated a member of the chorus to step forward to impersonate some character and engage in a dialogue with the chorus. From this small beginning grew the Greek tragedy. In due time the actors donned masks and costumes depicting the characters portrayed. The chorus from whence the actor emanated remained a central feature of the Greek drama. Greek tragedy included poetic dialogue, music of the flute or lyre and dancing by the chorus with gestures. It reached its maximum development in Athens at the Great Dionysia during the 5th century B. C. with the plays of Aeschylus, Sophocoles and Euripides. Their dramas are great literature.

Comedy is thought to have evolved out of nonchoral farce performed particularly by the Dionysiac worshippers during their revelries in which they sang, danced, joked and lampooned bystanders. Gradually these farces burgeoned into plays with repeated performances. The chorus was borrowed from the tragedy and the full fledged comedy began to vie with the tragedy at the Great Dionysia in the dramatic competitions. The most notable composer of old comedy was Arsitophanes. A new comedy evolved in the 4th century which de-emphasized the chorus and the actors dressed in ordinary clothing though still masked. Menander was the leading composer of the new comedy.

The Greek theatre was an open air structure normally built into a hillside. The stage was circular with tiers of seats for the audience wrapped around it in a semi-circle. In back of the stage was a building called a shene (whence the word scene) containing entrances to the stage and dressing rooms for the actors. Its roof was used as an elevated stage when required. Machines were used to transport the actors from the lower to the higher stage and for the descent of dieties unto the stage. Elaborate costumes and masks were worn by the actors. Mary Renault made a comprehensive study of the Greek theatre and drama which is vividly described in her *Mask of Apollo*, published in 1966.

The Romans took over the Greek tradition, particularly the new comedy. Terence (195–165 B. C.) imitating Menander, was the leading Roman playwright. Plautus (254–65 A. D.) wrote tragedies. The Romans changed the structure of the theatre. They reduced the stage to a semi-circle, since the chorus had now become obsolete in the new comedy. The stage was placed against the back wall of a rectangular building set on flat ground. The seats were arranged in a horseshoe pattern. There was no roof.

The literary quality of the performance was far below Greek standards. It was more in the nature of a farce and burlesque which soon gave way to vulgar and spectacular gladitorial shows and other performances. The theatres grew bigger and bigger until they became the famous amphitheatres that dotted the empire. Such elaborate performances as mock sea battles in flooded arenas were performed in these Roman theatres. It was pure entertainment with little or no literary content.

After the fall of Rome drama vanished in Europe for a thousand years. In the second millennium the church began to stage plays in the nave at Christmas and Easter time of the nativity and the crucifixion adding a few lines of discourse, in Latin, to the regular chants. These performances became so popular that the church saw fit to restrict and ban them. They were then performed outside the church, and known as mystery cycles, on scaffolds in open space surrounded with wooden seats arranged in a straight line as in the nave or in a semi-circle.

During the 15th century the Rennaissance opened up access to the plays of Terrence, Seneca and others which were translated into Italian and other European languages. A treatise in Latin by the renowned Roman engineer Vitruvius on the construction of the Greek and Roman theatre was also found.

In the 16th century troupes of professional actors ranged over Europe to perform for anyone or anywhere they could find employment. Such itinerant actors are portrayed in Shakespeare's *Hamlet*. They varied greatly in the quality of performance.

While the theatre began to revive in Italy, Spain and France, it found its most enthusiastic acceptance and greatest development in England. The Elizabethian Theatre was an open air building in circular or octagonal shape. There were three galleries of seats with a roof over the top tier. A large square stage jutted into the open space inside the galleries with two pillars on it supporting a roof. The stage had a balcony in the rear and a small dormer-like structure on top from where a trumpeter sounded a call for the start of the performance. Most famous of these Elizabethian theatres was the Globe in London.

The dominant figure of Western drama is William Shakespeare (1564–1616). Starting as an actor he suddenly erupted as a playwright in 1592 with his *Henry VI*. During the next two decades or so he produced 37 plays and 154 sonnets. His plays ranged across the entire spectrum of drama—comedies, tragedies, tragi-comedies and histories. His history is so accurate that doubts arose later that a man of allegedly narrow education should be so learned and gave rise to the so-called Baconian theory—that the eminent scholar Francis Bacon wrote the plays under Shakespeare's name. There were other like claims. None has sustained the burden of proof.

Shakespeare drew heavily on prior literature. Plutarch's *Lives* are the source for his illustrious plays on Greek and Roman history. *Romeo and*

Juliet is based on Brooke's narrative poem of that title published in 1562. His knowledge of English history was befitting an educated Englishman. Many an Englishman learned his history from Shakespeare. Marlborough stated frankly that all the history he knew was so derived.

Shakespeare was great because of the human wisdom incorporated into his drama. He plies no particular philosophy, but merely accepts life as it is with its comedy and tragedy. He believed man should live his brief existence on earth to the full extent of his powers and accept the end calmly, life being terminal. In *King Lear* Edgar consoles his maliciously blinded father, the Duke of Glouster, with the following words:

> . . . Men must endure
> Their going hence, even as their coming hither.
> Ripeness is all . . .

When Shakespeare has Richard III exclaim in the heat of battle "a horse! a horse! my kingdom for a horse!" he was expounding a bit of profound wisdom for at that time of man's technological development the horse was the greatest source of energy at his command. A man without a horse, particularly in battle, was a man bereft of power. Such penetrating perception of human affairs is the essence of Shakespeare's drama. It is, perhaps, for this reason that Shakespeare (along with Confucius) is the most quoted author of the world.

The drama, the theatre, continued as a chief source of enjoyment in the West to the present time. The theatre was roofed, the protruding stage retracted and seats for the audience placed in the orchestra. The modern theatre, in fact, is primarily orchestra with one or more galleries or balconies in the rear.

Each generation had its leading playwrights but none surpassed Shakespeare in stature. Mention should have been made earlier of Christopher Marlowe, a fine dramatist whose misfortune was to be a contemporary of Shakespeare. His *Tamurlaine the Great* (1588) is equal to that of a Shakespeare play. Succeeding generations produced such outstanding playwrights as John Dryden (1631–1700), Oscar Wilde (1856–1900) and George Bernard Shaw (1856–197). The French came to drama only in the early 19th century with such dramatists as Alexander Dumas (1802–1870), Victor Hugo (1802–1885), Alfred Musset (1810–1857) and others. The Russians too, emulating the French, became playwrights. Most notable is Anton Chekhov (1860–1904) with such outstanding plays as *The Cherry Orchard* (1904) and *The Three Sisters* (1901). Pushkin and Tolstoy also wrote plays. The Norwegian dramatist Henrik Ibsen during the 19th century and the American playwrights Eugene O'Neill and Tennessee Williams during the 20th century also produced great plays. In the 19th century drama was composed in prose instead of poetry.

In the 20th century drama was profoundly effected by technological innovation. It could now be recorded by motion picture cameras and sound reproduction equipment. The cinema, movie or film, as it came to be referred to, could now be replayed for audiences far and wide. By mid century it could be transmitted electronically by television. As was to be expected such broadening to a mass audience had the result of degrading the literary quality of the drama. Pornography obscenity and vulgarity, let alone sheer inaninity, crept into the performance despite censorship to control it. But the cultured minority could still find drama of the highest literary quality even in this milieu. Notable were the two series *Upstairs Downstairs* and *the Pallisars*, the latter based on the novels of Anthony Trollope, that appeared on the British and American screen in the 1970's.

India's drama and theatre date back as far as that of the Greeks. The basic source is the *Natyasastra* by Bharata composed·between 200 B. C.–200 A. D. which restates the legend that Brahma created the drama based on the four elements of speech, song, mime and sentiment in response to the god Indra's suplication that some form of diversion "which must be visible as well as audible" be provided for the common people. The *Natyasastra* collected and formalized the various traditions in drama, mime and dance that had developed in ancient India and it has been the bible of dramaturgy in India ever since.

Much of Indian drama is based upon the two great epics. But there is also a body of secular drama. The golden period of sanskrit drama was the first millennium of the Christian era. The most notable play was *Shakuntala* by the famous poet and dramatist Kalidasa (circa 375–445 A. D.). It made a large literary impact in Europe when it was translated in 1789 by Sir William Jones. Geothe was profoundly impressed by the play and modeled the prologue of his *Faustus* after its counterpart in Shakuntala.

The story of Shakuntala is a love affair between a king and a commoner (actually of royal and celestial heritage), too complex to detail here, permeated with profound misunderstanding and sorrow. But like all sanskrit plays, it ends in reconciliation and happiness. It evokes great emotional and sympathetic reaction from the audience and has been played in India for over a thousand years.

The Little Clay Cart, composed by King Shudraha (circa 400 A. D.?) is a popular and famous comedy. Love, intrigue, court rivalry and jealousy and disreputable scenes of life are found in the play. The play is renowned for its strong characterization. The main plot is a love affair between a courtsean and a Brahman already wed to another. This poses a double barrier—caste and marriage. After a series of intrigues, a miscarried murder of the heroine and the like, the king frees the courtsean of her lowly profession enabling her to live a respectable life and marry her lover. The *Little Clay Cart* has been performed and acclaimed abroad in Paris, Oslo, Moscow and New York.

The title derived, incidentally, from a toy clay cart of the Brahman's son which he disliked so the courtsean replaces it with one of gold.

Six principal dramatists stand out in sanskrit drama. In addition to the former there were two additional kings, Harsha (circa 606–647) and Visakhadatta and Bhasa and Bhavabhuti. Bhasa came to light only in 1910 through the consumate effort of T. Ganapati Shastri of south India. Thirteen of his plays have been restored. There is some belief he may have written the *Little Clay Cart* as King Shudraha is a bit elusive in the history of India. King Harsha, however, is real and was a great monarch in his time.

There is much more theatre in India than the literary. Kathakali, the pantomimic drama-dance, has already been discussed. Puppet theatre too has been popular throughout the ages. And there is a wide variety, by regions, of folk theatre.

The famous Wyang puppet theatre of Java owes its genesis to Indian cultural impact in Southeast Asia. The plays usually depict scenes from the *Ramayana*. Puppet plays have been popular world-wide since ancient times. The Egyptians of antiquity, the Romans and more recently the Japanese and Europeans (particularly the Italians) found puppet entertainment enjoyable. The Punch and Judy shows in England are well known.

Chinese drama has not reached the literary peaks of the Greek, English or Sanskrit plays. It is more in the nature of entertainment. It is highly formalized. The scenes are largely unemotional, the staging implied (mounting an imaginary horse) and the music thin, sounding often shrill and clangy to one accustomed to Western music. The costumes are elaborate and colorful for maximum eye appeal. There is no Chinese Aeschylus, Shakespeare or Kalidasa.

Japanese theatre is similar. The oldest and most formal is the No play, the classical lyric drama of Japan. It is the end product of a number of dance dramas of Buddhist and Chinese derivation (the Gigaku and Bugaku of the 6th to 9th centuries) which was perfected in the 14th century. It may even owe its origins to the Kathakali dance drama of India.

It consists of lyrical declamation, mime and dance, a drama language of its own which even few Japanese fully understand. The actors are formally costumed with faces masked or pasted. There is a chorus which chants a description of the action.

The No plays are short one act dramas depicting scenes in the past about gods, emperors, warriors and persons of high rank. They were obviously intended as entertainment for the ruling elite. Several of these plays follow one another during the program.

In fact, the No was forbidden by law as entertainment for the common people. There followed in consequence a rather bizarre development during the 16th century that led to the rise of the renowned Kabuki theatre of Japan. In 1586 a dancing girl named O-Kuni performed a semi-religious erotic drama-dance in the middle of a dry river bed (to evade the police it is said) in the city of Kyoto. It captivated an audience and she expanded it into the beginnings of a theatre for the common man as well as the nobility. After her death (in 1610?), however, her Kabuki degenerated into the Pleasure Women's Kabuki which became a vehicle for prostitution. The nobility, in particular, sought assignations with female dancers after the performances. This disturbed the Tokugawas and the Shogun, fearing that it might undermine the morality and order of the society, banned the Pleasure Women's Kabuki. But the common man yearned for the dramatic aspect of the Kabuki and it revived toward the end of the 17th century with male actors performing female roles. Men's Kabuki grew quickly into a major art form. It eventually became the dominant classical drama of the country with the No plays receding into obscurity. The Kabuki, however, borrowed heavily from the No.

The Kabuki too is based on a combination of chant, mime and dance. The elaborate costumes continue. Paste replaces masks on the face. The acting is less formal. There is more stage property. Instead of an imaginary horse, as in Chinese opera, there is an extremely realistic velvet horse animated by two actors. Some Kabuki actors spend a life time perfecting their perform-ance as the fore or aft part of the horse. In the end though the Kabuki performance is still highly formalized and ritualized and only those familiar with the form can truly enjoy it. A striking feature of the Kabuki theatre is the hanamichi, a passageway through the audience to the stage for proces-sionals, dances and elaborate exits by leading actors. It creates more intimacy with the audience. A revolving stage was another innovation.

The plays range from tragedy to farce. Tragedies often end in death unlike sanskrit plays. Courtseans too were favorite characters. The greatest Kabuki playwright was Chikamatsu (1660–1724). He is sometimes referred to as the "Shakespeare of Japan". Dramatists do not generally regard the Kabuki plays as having the literary quality of Greek, English or Sanskrit drama. It is perhaps presumptious on the part of Western oriented man to be over critical on Chinese and Japanese drama, for having different cultural roots, he is doubtless unable to truly appreciate it. The Kabuki can bring a Japanese audience to tears and peels of laughter and that is what drama is all about.

The Japanese also developed a unique puppet or doll theatre called Bunraku. Puppets were introduced from abroad in the 9th century largely for the amusement of children but in the 16th century the puppet shows rose to the height of dramatic shows. The technology of constructing and manipulat-ing the puppets was brought to a high level of artistry. The puppets or dolls are about one-third the size of an adult. The tongue, eyes and brows are moveable affording virtuosity for facial expression. The hands and feet also move. Even the belly swells on some of the dolls. Three men operate a doll—one for the head and right hand, another for the left hand and the third for the feet. The dolls are made up and costumed in the classical drama style.

In fact the puppet theatre always provided keen competition for the Kabuki and influenced it often to emulate its performance.

In modern times Asian drama has adopted the cinema or movies of the West. India, in fact, produces more film footage than America. The films are very popular in the villages. Great movies have been produced by both the Indians and Japanese which have won acclaim abroad and prizes at international film festivals. The outstanding Indian producer is Satijay Ray. His *Pather Panshali* has won universal recognition. The Japanese film *Roshomon* is another great movie produced in Asia.

Drama and literature bring up the matter of humor. What is it that makes people laugh. Man is the only form of life with the capacity to laugh. Laughter denotes enjoyment. But there is a vicious side to laughter. Laughter at the misfortune or discomfiture of others is cruel. It derives from the dominance instinct of man as such laughter gives the laugher a sense of superiority. Thomas Hobbes (1588–1679) ascribed laughter to this cause. "And it is incident most to them, that are conscious of the fewest abilities in themselves who are forced to keep themselves in their own favor by observing the imperfections of other men" writes Hobbes in his *Leviathan*. A truly self confident person does not laugh at the misfortune of others. It is mainly those with inferiority feelings who derive temporary flights of glory from another's discomfiture. But of those there are many in the human race. Drunkards, hen-pecked husbands, cuckolds and the like have always been the universal object of laughter in dramas. Closely related is the laughter at the pomposity and pretensions of the ruling elite. This too is found in drama. While cruelty is also involved in this case it is generally felt that the humorous situation is the creation of the discomfited and not caused by misfortune or fortuity.

But most humor is harmless to others. The incongrous situation or utterance evokes much laughter. A good example is the pronouncement by the bishop in Shaw's play *Getting Married* that he "cannot as a British bishop, speak disrespectfully of polygamy". The incongruity resides in the fact that the British empire contained many polygamous colonials so that to criticize polygamy would be inconsistant with British imperialism. This line is, perhaps, not so humorous to an American.

The witty or satirical aspersions cast at human institutions, conformities and follies are, perhaps, some of the best humor. Martial's famous dictum that "she who marries so often does not marry at all", with its obvious implication, is a good example of satire.

People and nations have always laughed at themselves. It affords relief from the pressure of social discipline. This is usually reflected in their literature, most notably in their magazines. The English have their *Punch*, the Indians *Shankar's weekly*, the Russians *Krakodil*, the Americans the *New Yorker* and so on.

SPORTS AND AMUSEMENTS

The foregoing discussion deals with the enjoyment of life mostly by the ruling elite. The vast majority of mankind eats to live but does not dine, knows little of the art of love, does not possess the literary capacity to enjoy the fine arts. What then has been its sources of enjoyment.

Allusion has already been made that some of the fine arts have their pedestrian counterparts. Folk music, folk dance and folk drama provide a great source of enjoyment for the hoi polloi, the proletariat or other designations for the dominated majority. In fact, the higher forms of music, dance and drama emanated from their "folk" counterparts. In this area the differences in enjoyment are merely one of degree with the ruling elite enjoying the higher forms and the dominated majority the lower forms of the art. Also it should be pointed out there has always been considerable crossing of the line whereby a lowly commoner finds enjoyment of great music, for instance, and a person of rank seeks his amusement in sports and burlesque. The propensity of the nouveau riche is noteworthy in this respect. In their eagerness for acceptance by the ruling class the newly rich will purchase boxes at the opera and season tickets to the symphony which they do not enjoy because of inadequate knowledge of the art.

Sports, spectaculars and other amusements have provided the most enjoyment for the dominated majority. The ruling elite not only tolerated it but usually promoted such amusement in the interest of social peace and stability. The legend of the Hindus is appropo in this circumstance. It is said that when India passed from the golden age to the silver age, that is, more general prosperity, the people began to grow restless—greed, envy, desire and anger filled their hearts—and the gods became disturbed about the situation. The god Indra implored Brahma for some form of amusement to mollify the people. "We want a form of diversion which must be audible as well as visible. Since the four Vedas are forbidden to the lower caste, be so kind as to create another Veda which will be shared by all the people." Brahma whereupon created the arts of song, mime and dance for the amusement of the lower castes.

While the legend may be apocryphal it contains great historical prescience. Most notable, of course, is the Roman experience with its "bread and circuses" to prevent the unemployed proletariat of Rome from rebellion. Fronto (2nd century A. D.) writes about Trajan "his wisdom never failed to pay attention to the stars of the theatre, the circus, or the arena, for he well knew that the excellence of a government is shown no less in its care for the amusements of the people than in serious matters, and that although the distribution of corn and money may satisfy the individual, spectacles are necessary for the contentment of the masses."

The Roman experience was not planned by the ruling elite; it evolved from simple beginnings, mostly connected with religion or religious festivals. The

Saturnalia was the most famous with its varied entertainment, including the liberties permitted to slaves and the plebs. Horse racing formed, perhaps the most popular sport at these festivals. Beginning as early as 221 B. C. the Circus Flaminius (later Maximus) was inaugurated in the narrow level valley between the Palatine and the Aventine. Two posts were erected at each end around which the chariots turned. The race was normally seven laps (about 5 miles). The spectators simply swarmed over the banks to watch the races.

The circus grew over the centuries. First wooden, then tufa stone and later marble seats were erected on the banks. The upper tiers always remained in wood. A sand track was installed. There were stables for the horses. In Caesar's time, the Circus could accommodate 150,000 spectators. In the latter days of the empire about 250,000 seats—some estimates are as high as 385,000—were available. Replicas of the Circus Maximus were everywhere; two more in Rome, three in the suburbs and one in every large city of the empire.

Competition and gambling were part of the spectacle. Four factions or colors (the red, blue, white and green) eventually formed which provided the horses and the charioteers. These were corporate organizations of the rich for profit. The owners and the public placed heavy bets on the race.

The charioteers were heroes and compensated accordingly. They were most often of lowly birth and estate, mainly emancipated slaves. But once they achieved fame and riches they navigated in the upper eschelons of Roman society. The successful ones were referred to as *miliarii*, not because they were millionaires but because they won the prize at least a thousand times. Pompeius Musclosus won 3,559 times, Scorpus 2,048 and Pontius Epaphroditus 1,467. Diocles won 1,462 times out of 4,257 races and retired at an early age in 150 A. D. with a fortune of 35 million sesterces (about $5 million). Once famous and rich they were idolized, their names passed from lip to lip, their portraits everywhere, women, many of high station, offered themselves freely. When a charioteer died he was accorded an elaborate funeral, with ovations befitting an emperor, particularly if he died in the race.

The charioteer's life was not without danger. The trick of the race was to round the post with minimum time and travel. This often resulted in collisions in which both men and horses were killed or maimed. Some of these collisions resulted in monumental tragedies. Fuscus was killed at 24 after 57 victories, Crescens at 22 and Aurelius Mollicius at 20. All were already millionaires even at this early age. This gore together with the gambling provided the magnetic pull of the Circus on the populace of Rome.

Next to the races the theatre and the amphitheatre provided the Romans with amusement. The literary theatre, as already noted, found no home in Rome. Song and mime were preferred, and spectacles, for which the theatre graduated to the amphitheatre of the empire where the Romans lust for blood and violence was sated.

The Roman opera was reduced in time to the popular singer and mime. He continued to be called an actor. The entire song drama centered upon him. He alone characterized the action whether singing, miming or dancing. These actors, like the charioteers, gained fame and riches. Pylades was famous, or infamous, during the reign of Augustus. Riots occurred under Tiberius between followers of rival actors. Nero banished them but was forced to recall them by popular demand. They grew fabulously rich and moved in the highest social circles even though usually of inferior antecedants. Women proffered themselves willingly. Even the Empress Domitia became involved with the actor Paris.

The quality of the performance degenerated. The singing was delegated to a choir so that the actor could concentrate on mime and dance. Some of the pantomimes became virtuosos in expressing without words a full range of emotions and actions with their face, hands and bodies. But the mimes soon concentrated on erotica. The actors performed suggestive sexual movements with their pelvises. It threw women into orgastic ecstacies. Juvenal writes contemptuously "Tuccia cannot contain herself; your Apullian maiden heaves a sudden and longing cry of ecstacy as though she were in a man's arms; the rustic Thymele is all attention, she learns her lesson."

The amphitheatre satisfied the Roman thirst for violence. While there was a wide assortment of bloody conflicts the central feature of the amphitheatre was the gladiators. The gladiatorial dual had its humble beginnings in the religious human sacrifice of antiquity called the *munus*. It was of Etruscan origin and performed primarily at the funerals of great men. The first one noted was at the funeral of Brutus Pera in 264 B. C. In 216 B. C. 22 gladiatorial combats were performed at the funeral of Marcus Lepidus. Thereafter the contests spread and gladiatorial shows were resorted to even by politicians for votes during the last days of the Republic. It was private parties and public festivals which provided the chief outlet for the gladiators after the first century B. C. Eventually they grew into the colossal spectacles in the amphitheatres involving a thousand gladiators or so.

The gladiators were slaves, war captives or condemned criminals. Occasionally some freeman (a rogue of a good family) opted for the arena. The Emperor Commodus while young participated freely not only as a gladiator but in the animal contests. As slaves became more expensive during the days of the empire the gladiators were mostly condemmed criminals. Only disobedient and incorrigible slaves were sacrificed. Crimes for which offenders were condemned to the arena were limited to murder, robbery, arson, mutiny and sacrilege. Christians and other dissidents were, unfortunately lumped into the category. Training for the arena was conducted in special schools called *ludus gladiatorius* owned by the lanistas and operated for profit. These schools were conducted scientifically so as to provide the proper diet, exercise, rest and other amenities to make a good fighting man. Even women were provided for sexual satisfaction. In fact, the life was so good that many a gladiator who earned his emancipation returned for another term. Most, however, hated and rebelled against the enslavement.

The combats were normally in pairs, but there was also a group contest where the winners fought each other until one survived. In a group combat of 100 gladiators the survivor had to kill 7 opponents! Augustus is said to have given such mass battles during his reign involving 10,000 gladiators. The emperor had to be present and attentive as part of the ritual. Caesar was criticized for reading state papers during a gladiatorial show. A defeated gladiator would beg the emperor for mercy. In response to the wishes of the crowd the emperor would spare his life with a thumb up gesture or condemn him to death with a thumb down signal. If the vanquished fought valiantly his life was usually spared—but only to fight again another day.

The gladiators were classified by their arms. The *retiari* fought with a net and trident; the *secutores* fought with shield and sword; the *dimachae* with a short sword in each hand and the *laqueatores* who were slingshooters. At first blush this strikes one as mismatches, but the advantages and disadvantages of the various weapons afforded equality in the duels.

If a gladiator was fortunate or clever enough to survive his prescribed term—two or three years—in the arena he was emancipated. During his fighting days he could win lucrative prizes and amass riches. But only a few reached this happy end.

Equally spectacular was the animal slaughter in the arena. Terrible spectacles were staged. Bear against buffalo, buffalo against rhinoceros, rhinoceros against elephant unto death! Criminals were condemned to fight ferocious beasts like lions, tigers, panthers. The story of Androcles and the lion is appropo. Androcles, a runaway slave, was condemned to fight a lion in the arena. It so happened that Androcles had removed a thorn from the paw of the lion in an earlier encounter in Africa. The lion remembered and refused to hurt Androcles. Androcles was pardoned and made his living thereafter exhibiting his friendly lion in taverns. Freemen would also daringly attack the beasts, assuring beforehand that the advantage was with them. Commodus deported himself accordingly. At one time from the safety of his box in the Colosseum he shot 100 tigers with 100 arrows to display his prowess in archery. Another time he arranged for a panther to pounce upon a condemned criminal shooting the panther with an arrow before he landed. Five thousand animals were killed in one day when Titus inaugurated the Colosseum in 80 A. D.! There *venationes*, as they were called, had one beneficial attribute, at least, in that they rid the empire of a lot of ferocious beasts.

The gladiatorial contests were first held in the circuses and theatres. The first amphitheatre in Rome was built in 29 B. C. It was destroyed by fire in 64 A. D. A new durable stone structure was erected in 80 A. D., which came later to be known as the Colosseum where most of the great spectacles were held. Its ruins still remain in Rome today from which tourists can derive some conception of its splendor in its day. Replicas of the Colosseum soon dotted the empire during its golden age.

The Romans defended the killing on the grounds it merely executed criminals and provided a deterrent to crime. Even Juvenal is found nowhere to criticize it. The capacity of man for rationalizing the action he desires is, of course, the great escape valve of life. Cicero and Seneca deplored the slaughter.

No civilization exceeded or equalled the Romans, with the possible exception of the Americans, in providing entertainment for its people. Christianity terminated the gladiatorial combats. Byzantine continued the chariot races but not the gladiators. In fact, the chariot races in the Hippodrome in Constantinople were the highlight of Byzantine life for nearly a thousand years. Acrobats, animal processions and the like also performed in the Hippodrome. In the West the Europeans entertained themselves more modestly with church processions, public parades, traveling minstrels and acrobats and jousting knights at the tournaments. The nobility engaged in hunting. Falconry, borrowed from Islam, became extremely popular. Ladies of high rank were particularly enthusiastic about the birds. But mass entertainment did not return again until the 19th and 20th centuries with the ballgames. More on this later.

The Indians too had a taste for violence in their mass amusements. Animal fights were extremely popular. Cocks (in particular a fierce little Indian quail), rams, bulls, buffaloes and elephants were pitted against each other. Elephant fights were favorites of the Mughals. There is some evidence of gladiatorial duels. Boxing and wrestling before public audiences were favored by the masses. Archery was preferred by the soldiers. Chariot racing (including a special breed of trotting oxen which could run as fast as horses) is also mentioned in the literature. Polo was introduced and became popular during Mughal times.

Bull fights were held in the south. The men entered the arena unarmed and tried to subdue the animal by superior wit and strategem, much like the American rodeo or the ancient Cretan's acrobatic bullfight. Apparently, the men were gored frequently rendering it a violent spectacle. None of this entertainment assumed the proportions of the huge spectacles of the Roman circuses. There are no archeological remains of amphitheatres in India.

The Chinese appear to have been largely disinterested in sports. A popular source of entertainment throughout the ages for the Chinese people was the acrobats and tumblers who toured the countryside playing to paying audiences.

The twentieth century saw the biggest proliferation in mass entertainment known to man to date. It was due, in part, to the technological development that made it possible to bring sports, singing and acting to every neighborhood theatre and living room. But, in large measure, it was the perennial motivation to satisfy the people in their craving for entertainment that spurred the development. Much of it, as in Roman times, was based on sex and violence from which the people derived vicarious satisfaction. Whether the orgastic reaction was induced by an Elvis Presley before a microphone in America or Pylades on the Roman stage the social psychology involved remains the same.

The mass entertainment explosion was led by the Americans. Europeans followed in the wake. Western civilization had now reached its peak bringing great prosperity to its nations. It could afford to allocate a large proportion of its wealth for the amusement of.its people. Moreover, it was a source of immense profit for the ruling elite.

It is often difficult, even for an American, to realize how recent has been this development. It was only in the second quarter of the century that the explosion was initiated with the development of sound recording and motion pictures. Radio, and the invention of television in the third quarter, completed the electronic development for the mass entertainment revolution.

Ball games now dominate sports. Horse racing still persists. Boxing and wrestling may be said to be vestigial remains of the gladiatorial fights. But it is the ball game that provides the basis for the modern spectacular.

Ball games of diverse sorts date back to antiquity. The ancient Egyptians engaged in a bat-and-ball game that originated in a religious fertility rite as early as 2000 B. C. Later, villages formed teams and competed widely with each other under priestly supervision. Polo was highly developed by the Persians by 230 A. D. It is believed to have originated with the nomadic horsemen of the steppes. From Persia it found its way to India and China around 600 A. D. and eventually to England and the United States. The Mayas and Aztecs played a game which called for throwing a ball through a ring on a wall.

The ball game began to evolve in Europe, mostly in England, about 1600 A. D. Cricket and baseball derived from stool-ball (first mentioned in 1330) where a ball was thrown at an upturned milking stool, called a cricket, and the batter, with his hand or stick tried to hit it away before it landed on the stool. Later a second stool was used as a marker for the batter to run to after the hit. It was played in America as early as 1621 and still called stoolball. In the 18th century after additional markers were added to run to or around it was called baseball in both England and America. The English, however, preferred the single-base cricket while the Americans favored the multi-base ball.

The development of the game in America is lost in obscurity. But by 1850 it assumed professional status and organization and by the turn of the century it was the "great American pastime". Two leagues evolved with the seasons (April through September) winners playing each other for the "world" championship in early October called the World Series. The game struggled along, always in financial difficulties, until after World War I when it achieved wide popular support in the prosperity of the 1920's. Great stars rose like the famous Babe Ruth, the home-run-king, who was paid in 1930 the then princely sum of $80,000 per year.

The American people at mid-century gave their biggest attention, however, to football. It was more violent and provided greater excitement. Football had a different genesis. It originated in the colleges and universities and they are still used as the training schools for the highly professionalized game today.

Football originated in England around 1600 or even earlier as a kicking game in the villages during religious festivals like Shrove Tuesday. The ball was usually an inflated bladder of a pig and has been called a pigskin ever since even though the balls are made now of cowhide. It was a free-for-all with adversaries being kicked as often as the ball. Due to its roughness it was banned from time to time and played mostly by the lower classes.

In the 19th century it was taken up at schools like Eton, Harrow and Rugby purely as an intramural sport. The rules varied but the ball could not be carried or passed. In 1823 William Webb Ellis at Rugby, out of desperation in a dull game, caught the ball and ran with it for the first touchdown. The game of rugby was born but the English preferred the pure kicking game which developed into modern soccer. Soccer is played wherever the British left their imprint from Jamaica to India and most everywhere else in the world.

The Americans, however, built upon rugby. The first game played between Rutgers and Princeton at New Brunswick on November 6, 1869 was more in the nature of soccer. Rutgers won 6–4 under its own rules. A week later at Princeton playing under its own rules won 8–0. This sort of chaos prevailed among the colleges in the East vacillating between the soccer and rubgy type of football until 1882 when Walter Camp of Yale, considered the father of American football, attempted to create some order and discipline in the game. He introduced the scrimmage rule that required a team to yield the ball to the other side if it failed to advance it five yards in three tries or downs. In 1906 the forward pass was introduced and the Americans now had a special football of their own.

The game remained mostly in the schools until the 1920's when the college stars became interested in continuing to play the game for pay after graduation. The pay was little in those days but in the Depression of the 1930's it provided temporary employment. Red Grange, the great half-back from the University of Illinois, gave professional football a big boost when he joined the Chicago Bears in 1926. Thirty-six thousand fans watched him play with the Bears against the Cardinals. The National Football League formed in 1921 (with a franchise fee of only $100) was dominated by the Green Bay Packers, Chicago Bears and the New York Giants during the

Roaring Twenties and the Depression years. In those days the big event was the Bear-Packer game.

The Green Bay Packers were the phenomena of the early days of professional football. The name derives from the Acme Packing Company which was granted a franchise in 1921 and where Curly Lambeau, the first coach, and several of the first players were employed. Lambeau, a Notre Dame graduate took the Packers to national championship three times during the early Depression years. The Packers won the National League championship again in 1936, 1939, 1944, 1961, 1962, 1965, 1966 and 1967. They won the first two superbowl games—1967 and 1968.

Green Bay was a small city of 40,000 during these early days of professional football when teams in the big cities kept going bankrupt. The Chicago Bears and the New York Giants were the only others that managed to survive the Depression. The citizens of this northern Wisconsin city supported the Packers with a dedication and enthusiasm found on few college campuses. When the Packers encountered financial difficulties a voluntary levy was undertaken by the fans to defray the deficit. Attendance at the games was always up to capacity. Farm boys would save their nickels and dimes for a fifty cent seat behind the goal posts during the Great Depression.

After World War II professional football became a spectacular. Big money came to dominate the game. The pressure for training the players on the colleges grew acute. Scholarship money flowed freely for the purpose. Scholastic requirements were lowered to accommodate boys with athletic prowess but deficiency in scholastic ability. Some educators complained that colleges were being transformed into *ludus gladiatoriums*. Negroes with their superior athletic skill entered the ranks in disproportionate numbers. By 1975 over half the players were black whereas negroes comprised but ten per cent of the population. The road to fame and riches for the socially disadvantaged black boy was the ballgame as it was the circus and the arena for his Roman counterpart two millennia ago.

In the 1960's the American League was formed and the winners of each League met in the superbowl for the "world" championship. Handsome purses were awarded to the winners. The season was stretched from July to early January when the superbowl game was held. Some coaches and players were now paid a quarter of a million dollars or more each season! Stadiums, modeled after the Roman amphitheatres, were constructed by every city for the games. Some could accommodate over 100,000 fans.

But it was television that elevated the football game (and other ballgames to a lesser extent) to the greatest spectacle of all time. In fact, the television camera was able to give the viewer a better sight on the plays, particularly after the "instant replay" technique was evolved, than he could have in the stadium even with a seat on the fifty yard line. The TV viewer, however, was not able to participate in the emotional chemistry of the crowd which had always afforded a peculiar intoxication for arena and stadium spectators. Television enlarged the stadium so that as many as 50 million Americans could watch the superbowl! The circus was now brought into every living room in America.

Football and baseball are only two of the many games offered to the Americans for entertainment. Basketball, hockey, tennis, golf, bowling and others have their devoted fans. The English and others are devotees of cricket and soccer. The latter, in particular, has swept the world and, except in America, is the dominant sport of the Western and westernized countries. In Rio de Janerio a hundred thousand wildly cheering Brazilians pack the Estadio Maracana each week for the soccer game.

Next in importance as mass entertainment in modern times was the motion picture. In historical prespective they too are a recent phenomena. Experiments with moving pictures, however, date back to the 19th century in both Europe and America. Thomas Edison perfected his Kinetoscope in 1894, which was essentially a peep-show with fifty seconds or so of continuous film. In 1896 he developed a machine to project the film on a screen. It was inaugurated at Koster & Bial's Music Hall in New York. A similar cinematographe was unveiled in Paris a year earlier.

In 1906 the Edison company produced the first film with a sequential story—*The Great Train Robbery*. Edwin S. Porter was the technical genius of the production. For two decades the film industry now centered in Hollywood struggled with and improved the technique. Since there was yet no sound these early motion pictures were essentially pantomime. And the greatest pantomime of the era was Charlie Chaplin. In 1926 Hollywood produced its first spectacular—*Ben Hur*. It was, in part, a spectacular on the spectaculars of another age.

In 1927 Hollywood brought out its first sound "talkie", *The Jazz Singer*, starring Al Jolson. The technology was now completed. It was the culmination of the genius of Thomas Edison as it welded together his phonograph and his kinetoscope. Despite the Depression, Americans received the "talking picture" with great enthusiasm. Attendance at the movie theatres rose to 100 million per week! In fact, the movies diverted the attention of idled Americans from their pressing economic problems. In the 1930's a ticket to a double feature lasting up to four hours cost only twenty-five cents!

Hollywood became magic land for American youth. There were no social barriers to stardom which brought instant fame and fortune. Like their Roman counterparts the Hollywood stars were immediately accepted in high social circles irrespective of humble antecedants. For every success there were thousands of failures. The moral, psychological and even physical damage inflicted upon the American society by this craze has still to be measured. For example, millions of young girls who were induced to smoke cigarettes out of emulation of the stars during the 1930's are now dying of lung cancer!

The most famous movie produced by Hollywood prior to World War II was, doubtless, *Gone with the Wind*, an epic about the American Civil War. It starred Clark Gable, the leading male actor of the time and Vivian Leigh, a British actress. Other great actors and actresses were Rudolph Valentino, Greta Garbo, John Gilbert, Helen Hayes, the Barrymores to mention only a few. This was Hollywood's golden era for after war it was overtaken by television.

Television appeared as a vehicle for mass entertainment in 1948. But its technological development spanned many years. The discovery of the element selenium in 1817 by Jons Berzelius of Sweden—and the subsequent discovery by Louis May of England in 1873—that it was a superior conductor of electricity when exposed to light laid the foundation for television. In 1878 Sir William Crookes invented the cathode ray tube. Paul Nykow of Germany put together a mechanism for a rudimentary electronic transmission of a picture in 1884. In 1907 Russian and British inventors using photoelectric cells in the camera and cathode rays to reconstitute the picture in the receiving set advanced the technology further. By 1920 John Baird, a Scot, and Charles F. Jenkins of the USA started to market the first television sets. At this stage the big American companies became interested—Westinghouse, General Electric, RCA and AT&T—and jointly undertook its perfection. The foremost scientist in this effort was Dr. Vladimir Zworykin, a Russian immigrant, who worked first for Westinghouse and later for RCA. Two independent inventors Philo T. Farnsworth and Allen B. Dumont also received patents on television technology. Experiments on color television started in 1940. In 1948 the Columbia Broadcasting System (CBS) and, a year later, the National Broadcasting Company (NBC) succeeded. NBC was awarded the patent since its system could transmit to both color and black and white receivers.

A nationwide broadcasting system, too complex to detail here, evolved rapidly. In 1950 there were 104 television stations and 10 million sets. In 1960 there were 50 million sets. By 1975, 70 million, a TV set in virtually every living room in America.

In the beginning TV shows were live performances, but soon they were filmed beforehand and run—and rerun—on the screen. The center of production shifted from New York to Hollywood once again as motion picture production did during World War I. Television now dominated mass entertainment.

Television entertainment covers a wide spectrum—drama, musicals, comedies, panel discussions, documentaries, news, childrens shows and sports. There is something for everyone. As already mentioned, some first rate drama is offered on the TV screen. The documentaries are extremely educational. But since it is designed for mass entertainment most of the shows are puerile and inane. Many of the shows contain violence—police and criminal stories, underworld struggles, war and the like. There would appear to be something in the psychological makeup of man that causes him to be fascinated with violence. The violence that fascinates and amuses the Americans is not the sanguinary kind of the Roman spectacles. This may, however, be due only to technological development that permits TV violence to be simulated. It is an open question whether there is any difference in the social and psychological impact on the viewer of the two different types of shows.

Television has been duly circumspect to date on violations of the moral code. Not so, the motion pictures or magazines. European produced films have gone so far as to screen the performance of the sexual act for public viewing. American magazines thrive on nude photographs. None of this is unknown elsewhere in human affairs. The Indian love scenes on their temples have been noted. The ancient Greeks idealized the nude in sculpture. But no other society has resorted to such depiction for mass entertainment.

Finally note should be taken of the popular or "pop" singer because of his Roman counterparts. He too has been able to captivate women through the sexually suggestive timber of his voice or bodily movements. Elvis Presley (1935-1977) was the American phenomena in this respect. He had a following of millions of American "Tuccias". Frank Sinatra, another example, was an earlier version of the same phenomena. Both became millionaires like their distant cousin Pylades of ancient Rome.

Private games too have fascinated man as pastimes throughout the ages. They are countless so only two can be discussed here—chess and cards. The ancient Egyptians enjoyed many games like *Tau*, the game of robbers, which the Romans took over and called *Ludus Latruneulorum*. Draught boards or chessboards were used. There was a game of bowl. And others. But the most renowned and widespread game throughout history has been chess.

Chess originated in India. It was called *Chaturanga* in sanskrit. The Indians appear to have been addicted to gambling. Before chess they gambled with dice. The *Mahabharata* begins as a tale of woe. Yudishthira gambles away his kingdom, his four brothers and their common wife Draupadi with dice. When they are restored to him he loses them once again at chess. Thereafter the five brothers with Draupadi are banished to the forest. This story in the Mahabharata attests to the antiquity of chess in India. There is some question when these references to chess found their way into the epic poem. Some scholars believe the purana discussing chess was written much later than the first compilations of the poem, perhaps, as late as the 10th century A. D. Though the date of origin may be uncertain the origin of chess in India is not.

Chaturanga was from the beginning a game of war. A maharaja and his contingent—counselor, chariots, horses, elephants, and soldiers—goes into battle with another raja and his contingent on a board (battlefield) of 64 squares. In the *Mahabharata* there is a long passage in which the sage Vyasa instructs Yudhishthira how to play the game.

From India the game radiated throughout the world. In the 6th century A. D. it was played in Persia. Legend has it that an ambassador to the court of Chosroes I (531–579 A. D.) brought it as a gift from the Indian people. The Persians added greatly to its development into the present game. After the conquest of Persia by the Arabs (circa 650 A. D.) the Muslims disseminated chess throughout the Mediterranean area. From Spain it began to filter into Europe at the start of the second millennium of the Christian era. The Crusades gave its growing popularity in Europe an extra boost. At each step westward the game was mutated but it remained essentially the same. The Europeans changed the emphasis from battle to courtly behavior. The raja became the king, the war counselor the queen, the horses knights, the chariots (or ship) the rooks, the elephant the bishop (a strange transformation) and the soldiers, pawns. Early sanskrit literature intimates that the number of moves was determined by a throw of the dice. This feature apparently disappeared even before the game emigrated from India.

A similar dissemination to the East occurred. There is some claim the Chinese originated chess as far back as 1000 B. C., but the latest view is that it was a different game. The first genuine evidence of chess in China is dated about the sixth or seventh century which would coincide with the Buddhist influence from India. From China it moved to Korea and Japan undergoing a more profound change than occurred in its transit west. *Shagi*, as chess is called in Japan, diverges considerably from its Chinese apparentation. A southeast radiation through Burma, Siam, the Malaysian penninsula to Borneo and Java took place simultaneously. It is thought that chess reached Russia originally through central Asia and not from Europe though the game played in Russia today is of European heritage.

It would seem appropo that the Hindus should originate chess. They are the original mathematicians. It is, therefore, appropriate to conclude with a legend that prevails in India with respect to chess. The king was so delighted with the game that he turned to the sage who invented it and said that he would grant his uppermost wish. The sage asked that the king reward him with an amount of rice equal to the sum starting with two grains doubled on each of the 64 squares of the chess board. The king agreed readily to what, at first blush, appeared like a modest request but when the amount was calculated it was so much rice that it would have rendered the kingdom bankrupt!

The origin of playing cards is more obscure. It would appear they originated in China. There is a reference in a 17th century Chinese dictionary that the game was invented as a pastime for the emperor's concubines. The Crusaders brought cards back to Europe from the Near East where the Muslim world was familiar with them. Gypsies also introduced them into

Europe from the East and used them for fortune telling. Playing cards did not come into widespread use until the invention of printing in the 15th century as they were difficult to manufacture earlier.

The forms of playing cards has remained substantially unchanged since the 16th century. The royal motif of the English court, the black and red colors, the four suits (already in China) designated spades, clubs, hearts and diamonds. Their designations are allegedly of French origin representing the four estates—nobility (sword or spade), clergy (heart), bourgoise (diamond) and the peasants (club). In the 19th century the double ended card was devised for easier handling. After the French Revolution an attempt was made without success to change the royal motif. Attempts to introduce four colors and a fifth suit also met with failure.

Two score or more games have been played with cards from the simple solitaire to the sophisticated bridge. Bridge derived from whist. It was introduced at the Portland Club in London by Lord Brougham in 1894. Contract bridge had its antecedents in France. Harold S. Vanderbilt grew fond of it at the Traveler's Club in Paris. He and his friends developed a set of rules in 1925 which were published by the Knickerbocker Whist Club in New York. The game was an instant success, particularly in America. Bridge clubs blossomed like flowers in the 1930's. A noted player Eli Culbertson published a book on the game. Annual tournaments between American and European teams were held.

On the darker side the Americans also developed poker. Playing cards always lent themselves to gambling. Games similar to poker were played for stakes in Italy, France and England as far back as the 15th century. Such early gambling was not extensive.

Poker started in New Orleans early in the 19th century where it was brought from France by the French settlers. It was called *pocker*, "to bluff". It was carried north on the Mississippi steamboats. Pioneers carried it west. By the end of the century it was the leading gambling game in America.

XII
Rise and Fall of Societies
Mediterranean Civilizations

Societies rise and fall. That appears to be a prime lesson of history. No nation has been able to defy this inexorable destiny. And there is no reason to believe that any people will do so in the future.

There is no regularity to this decree of history. Neither is there a prescribed pattern or formula for the rise and fall. Spengler tried to trace a thousand year cycle but he was only slightly successful. Toynbee thought, or hoped, that Christendom could avoid such demise by evolving a universal state for the whole world with a return to Christianity as a universal religion. In the end he appears to have lost faith in this hope.

It is largely a matter of fortuity. A sector of humanity suddenly becomes inspired and energetic, developes or acquires the advanced technology for command of greater energy, produces or otherwise acquires the wealth to manifest that energy to dominate others and to enjoy a good livelihood and after a period of time (sometimes centuries) loses its energy and lapses into obscurity. When it loses its power it usually succumbs to the rule of a more energetic society or, if spared that fate, simply lapses into stagnation from whence, phoenix-like it sometimes regenerates itself to regain its long lost power and supremacy. The latter, as shall be seen, transpired in the oldest known civilizations of ancient Egypt and India. In this kaleidoscopic rise and fall from power there appears to be an overriding factor. The dominant societies to date, with only a few exceptions, have been the Indo-European and Mongolian peoples. Why this has been so is not readily apparent. It may be however, that this sector of humanity met the challenge of the glaciers and in the process developed a greater capacity and facility for technological innovation and development.

The first human societies developed independently and remotely of each other. Man's technological development did not provide him with the facile communication and transportation facilities he enjoys today until recent times. These early civilizations did not know or were only vaguely aware that other like societies existed. The Europeans and the American Indian societies were not aware of each others being until the 16th century. The

Sumerians and the Harappans may have known each other vaguely. Neither knew of the Chinese. But today the entire human race is welded together by modern communications. Yet, there is no universal brotherhood. But it is clear that history is no longer regional, though one cannot be sure what that portends.

These early regional civilizations had one thing in common. They emerged in the fertile river valleys within the same latitude range of the world. This is not difficult to understand. Man's first technological leap toward civilization was the invention of agriculture around 8000 B. C. The well watered and fertile alluvium of the great river valleys was the natural site for the new technology. But agriculture was not founded in the river valleys. It was developed instead in the foothills of the Zagros and Taurus mountains, a hilly range above the Fertile Crescent, starting in western Iran and northeast Iraq running through southern Turkey, down the Mediterranean coast to the Jordan valley. It is here where the wild wheat and barley grew that became man's first foodgrains. This was also the habitat of the wild sheep and goats, man's earliest domesticated animals.

These first farming communities were small and remained so, perhaps, for millennia. Archeologists are only now beginning to reconstruct their dimensions. Jarmo in northeast Iraq, dating back to 6700 B. C. consisted of about 25 houses or families. Beidha in the Jordan valley, dating back to 7000 B. C. was of similar size. They were villages, at best, but even so there is evidence at Beidha that social stratification had already set in. Bigger houses for the rich were found among the ordinary houses. The struggle over the surplus doubtless started almost from the beginning of agriculture. As these first farming villages exhausted the soil around them they were forced to seek other land. Beidha was abandoned in 6500 B. C. These first farmers soon realized that the most productive areas were the rich bottom lands of the river valleys. And where there was no dependable rainfall which they enjoyed in the foothills they learned how to control the water of the rivers to irrigate the rich alluvium. The two most scintillating civilizations of antiquity, the Sumerian and Egyptian, were founded upon irrigation.

An early site was the Konya plain of Anatolia where the first city now known to us as Catal Huyuk has been found dating back to circa 6000 B. C. Since wild wheat and barley are not indigenous to this area agriculture must have been brought to the plain from the other side of the Taurus range.

British archeologist James Mellart discovered Catal Huyuk in 1961. After three seasons of digging he was able to identify twelve different cities that existed during an eight hundred year period between circa 6500–5700 B. C. About 5600 B. C. the site was abandoned for a new site across the river. His work was not completed due to an altercation with the Turkish government, too complex to detail here, known as the Dorak Affair. So, the full story of this first Neolithic city still remains to be completed.

What Mellart did find, however, is truly remarkable. Nearly 9000 years ago there existed on the Konya plain a complex society sustained by a highly developed agriculture. At its height the population was about 6000. The buildings were made of sun dried rectangular brick of standard specification on a timber framework. The roof was constructed of thick mud plaster on bundles of reeds supported by stout beams. Entry into the houses was through the roof, presumably for security purposes, with appropriate ladders. The smoke from the hearth and oven escaped through the same hole. Raised platforms for sleeping were arranged along the walls. There were bins for the storage of food. The buildings adjoined each other, with courtyards and storerooms, for additional protection. The size of the houses ranged from 11.25 to 48 square meters.

Catal Huyuk teemed with shrines and sanctuaries. Forty of the 139 living quarters excavated were devoted to religion. Murals with a full range of pigments decorated the walls. Plaster reliefs of goddesses and animals were everywhere. The head of the Aurock bull predominates. The goddesses are normally buxom female figures, doubtless fertility symbols. One figure is of a goddess supported by two leopards giving birth to a child.

Burial was beneath the platforms of the houses. The bodies apparently were first stripped of flesh by vultures on special exposed platforms before the skeleton was interred beneath the dwellings. Gifts of jewelry, figurines, statuettes, pottery and even tools were buried with the skeleton.

The economy of Catal Huyuk was diversified. Some fourteen grains and plants were cultivated. Wheat, barley and peas were the main grains. Almond, acorn, pistachio, apple, juniper and hackleberry were important food sources. Sheep, goats and pigs were bred for meat and milk. It is not clear if the cow was domesticated. The wild Aurock was hunted and worshipped but probably not yet part of the barnyard. Deer, fox, wolf, leopard and gazelle were hunted. The hunt was still very much a factor in the livelihood of the people.

Full time pursuit of the arts and crafts is very much in evidence. Stone was ground, polished and perforated into axes, saddle querns, mortars and pestles, bowls, cosmetic palettes, beads and rings for jewelry. Wood was worked for bowls, vessels, dishes, storage boxes and buildings. Pottery, however, was not highly developed. The potters wheel was not known. Copper and lead were smelted as early as 6400 B. C.

Mats and baskets were woven. Also carpets were found on many floors. Wool and mohair were used for cloth. The cloth was dyed. Animal furs and skins were made into garmets, belts and other items. Whether tanning was practiced is not clear, but the acorn was well known and used.

Mellart believes that Catal Huyuk was a great trading center. Its obsidian mirrors, jewelry, razors and knives have been found as far away as Jericho and Beidha. So also its greenstone axes and other tools. Among the skeletal remains unearthed to date were a mix of races pointing to the conclusion that foreigners (presumably traders) lived at Catal.

The wide scope of the arts and crafts known to the people of Catal Huyuk nearly equals that found in later civilizations. But they had not yet developed a script, music or kept records, hence they probably cannot qualify as a civilization.

Another noteworthy Neolithic city is Jericho situated in a desert 1000 feet below sea level between the Sea of Galilee and the Dead Sea. Its value as a site is due to an artesian spring, part of the underground flow of the Jordan river, which gushes forth a thousand gallons of water per minute. It was settled and fought over even before the invention of agriculture. It is not clear when it became an agricultural community. It may have preceded Catal Huyuk. There is some dubious evidence that irrigation was practiced about 7000 B. C. At any rate, it was a highly developed city during the 6th millennia B. C. with buildings made of brick and mortar. The floors were plastered. The houses were rectangular. No shrines or temples have been found. Pottery was not made. But Jericho had walls. Many of them even as late as biblical times as every Christian knows. The first one was built about 8000 B. C. It was over 6 feet thick and over 12 feet high. New walls, even double walls, were built over old ones destroyed by earthquakes and erosion. Erecting these walls called for concerted community action from which it is presumed that a complex urban organization existed. The walls were obviously needed to protect ownership of this valuable oasis in an otherwise forbidding desert. Jericho is thought to have flourished substantially off its trade in salt from the Dead Sea. Obsidian and greenstone found in the Jericho remains date back to 6000–7000 B. C. No evidence of the salt the people of Catal Huyuk received in exchange, of course, can be expected to be found among its ruins. Jericho too had no script.

The story of man moved next into the fertile river valleys. The earliest and most renowned sites required irrigation for which more complex social organization was necessary. Greater surpluses were produced in these fertile lands enabling man to develop further his arts and crafts. Foremost, among them, was the invention of writing. A script made possible recorded history and it has, therefore, become a watershed in human cultural evolution. Civilization is generally regarded as beginning when man learned to write. This assumption may well be challenged but it is perhaps as good a place as any to date the beginning of the civilization of man.

There have been essentially three fountainheads of civilization. The most turbulent and creative in the Mediterranean area and the other two in India and China. Most others have been affiliated to or apparented by these three. There is a fourth, the Indian societies of the Americans, the Mayas, Aztecs and Incas. It has been annihilated by the Europeans, but its contribution to the civilization of man has been negligible. Technologically the American Indians contributed little or nothing. Culturally not much more. Their major contribution was certain food and other agricultural products—corn, potato, tomato, peppers and tobacco—perhaps more properly attributable to geography.

As shall be seen the vicissitudes within these three areas varied considerably. The Mediterranean area, which encompasses the Near East (including Persia), North Africa and Europe, is the most diverse and yet contains a cultural homogeniety with roots in Sumerian and Egyptian history. The succeeding dominant peoples or nations founded their societies on the technology, arts and way of life of the past mutating them, to be sure, as the centuries passed. The Christians and Muslims who have dominated the area during the past two thousand years consider the Old Testament as their religious origin. Much of the religious lore in the Old Testament is of Sumerian origin and much of the wisdom was borrowed from the Egyptians. Both have built upon the Greek culture that preceded them. And the Greeks borrowed heavily from ancient Egypt.

The heart of the civilizations of the Mediterranean area, the Fertile Crescent, was geographically vulnerable to invasion from the north by the Indo-Europeans and from the Arabian penninsula by the Semites. Dominance of this first and oldest area of civilization has been a struggle between these two races. The Indo-Europeans (Hurrians, Hittites, Persians, Greeks, Romans, Celts, Germans, Slavs and others) dominated the area most of the time due largely to their superior technology and wealth. The Semitic peoples (Amorites, Assyrians, Hebrews, Phoenicians, Arabs and others) wrested dominance from the Indo-Europeans intermittently when motivated, in most instances, by religious fervor and organization. They were not creative technologically with the possible exception of the Phoenicians, and had, therefore, to borrow the superior technology and plunder the wealth of others for the power needed for dominance. Their dominance was usually short lived by historical standards.

SUMERIANS

The Tigris-Euphrates doab cradled the first civilization of man. Its script dates back to 3600 B. C. To this marshy site, which is called the Plain of Shinar in the Bible, the people from the Zagros foothills and possibly the Jordan valley brought their wheat and barley, their sheep, goats and cows to found an extremely prosperous agricultural economy. They had to drain the marshes and dam the river flow to irrigate the fertile alluvium between the two rivers as the doab does not receive sufficient rain fall (less than seven inches annually) to ripen a crop of wheat and barley. Five thousand years ago (today the delta extends another 130 miles into the Persian gulf) the doab comprised an area approximately 170 by 40 miles, about the size of the state of New Jersey. Yet at its height the doab and its environments supported a population of, perhaps, a million.

The racial origin of the Sumerians is obscure. They were not Semites as they spoke a non-Semitic tongue. In fact, there are Mongolian overtones in their language. They most likely emanated from the north. They were probably the same or akin people to those who inhabited Catal Huyuk as they shared several features in common. They brought with them the cow, which they revered like the latter day Hindus, that was domesticated in Anatolia around 6500 B. C. They also buried their ancestors below the floor of their homes. Whether they first exposed the corpse to vultures for removal of the flesh is unclear. Such exposure of the corpse, it should be noted, was also the practice of the ancient Persians.

The doab was not settled suddenly. Groups of people in search of fertile land doubtless drifted into the area over many millennia. The Ubaidians settled in what became Sumerian Eridu as early as 5300 B. C. Farmers from the foothills, doubtless, staked out fertile oases in the area between the two rivers long before the Sumerians organized their irrigation system. The Sumerians came after these early settlers had already occupied these independent farming villages between the rivers. The Sumerians may have come from Elam (later Susa) in the Zagros foothills of western Persia. Evidence of an advanced culture dating to 4500 B. C. has been found there. Moreover, these people may have come originally from Central Asia as their culture resembles another unearthed at Anau in southern Turkestan dating back at least to 5000 B. C. They may have been an advance contingent of the Indo-Europeans who emanated in later centuries from the Caucasian-Aral sea area. There is growing evidence that this area and not Mesopotamia (which incidentally means doab—land between two rivers) may be the cradle of civilization. Unfortunately the first Indo-Europeans did not develop a script so they necessarily belong to pre-history. More and more though it is becoming clear that this central Asian area produced a highly developed agriculture and evolved an advanced technology before that known to us from Mesopotamia after the dawn of history. It is therefore open to speculation that the Sumerians were precursors of the Indo-Europeans who gained control of the Tigris-Euphrates doab because they brought with them an already superior technology. A Sumerian legend, which cannot be ignored, holds that they came by sea through the Persian gulf and up the two rivers to conquer the doab. This would not necessarily be at variance with their issuance from Central Asia as they may have launched an invasion from southern Iran by boat. "And it came to pass" states the Bible, "as they journeyed from the *East,* that they found a plain in the land of Shinar; and they dwelt there." Since the Semites did not issue out of Persia this bit of biblical lore must refer to the Sumerians. If such presumption is correct it too supports the theory set forth above. But, be that as it may, the origin of the Sumerians as of this time necessarily remains open to speculation.

By 2800 B. C. when their queen city Uruk (biblical Erech) boasted a population of 50,000, ancient Sumeria had developed a technology and culture to which not much was added for several millennia. They invented the wheel. Hitched the ox to the plow and the ass to the wagon. They developed metallurgy—copper, lead, tin and bronze. But not iron. Pottery (including the potters wheel), weaving of baskets and cloth (wool and linen), lapidary, gold and silver smithing were known to them. But their greatest achievement was a complex irrigation system with well defined property and water rights.

It is thought that this complex economic organization begot writing. Records of production and revenues, property and water rights had to be kept. Commerce and trade in the cities called for written contracts. In fact, most of the oldest tablets are concerned with economic matters. The writing was with a stylus, or reed tip, on a soft clay tablet which was sun dried and sometimes baked. This left a durable record enabling archeologists to reconstruct Sumerian history more fully and readily. The Sumerian script, called *cuneiform* (meaning "wedge" in Latin), consists of some 600 signs for ideograms and phonograms. The unraveling of the Sumerian script and language was the feat of British historian Henry C. Rawlinson, who in 1835 risked his life to read the inscription to Darius on a sheer stone cliff 300 feet above the ground at Behistun in western Persia where the accolade is written in cuneiform and old Persian. In due time the new art of writing was employed to record history (the geneology of kings, for instance), write literature and promulgate laws. A library of neatly stacked tablets was uncovered at Tello dated to 2700 B. C. The Epic of Gilgamesh was written on tablets about the same time. A Sumerian king named Ur-Nammu promulgated a code of law circa 2100 B. C., several centuries before the famous code of Hammurabi.

The great prosperity of Sumeria already produced a complex social structure. At the top were the kings, priests, and the large landowners. Next came the farmers or free landowners. As time passed these diminished while the large landowners grew in number and holdings. At the lowest level were the slaves and propertyless unskilled workers who did the menial jobs like water carriers. As the cities grew a class of craftsmen and artisans developed. Finally there were the scribes, a class of learned professionals, who were employed by the ruling class to keep the law and records. The scribes were an intellectual elite who had to study hard (for there were some 2200 ideo and phonograms to memorize) but enjoyed a life of secure and prosperous employment. They can be likened unto the lawyers, accountants and other professionals in modern society.

An arithmetic was invented for all this record keeping. It was based on the number 60 which is divisible by more numbers than any other. Some of its derivations—the foot, 60 minutes, 60 degrees—are still used today. Money was not yet known. Transactions were in kind. But the Sumerians already employed the concept of interest with rates recorded as high as 15–33 per cent. Though inflation is generally associated with the mismanagement of money, these high interest rates still unassociated with money must bespeak some kind of economic misery not yet apparent from the Sumerian record.

The bountiful surplus begot war and plunder of each others wealth. The doab was not a single political unity during Sumerian times. It was subdivided into many farming areas each with its central city from where the ruling class administered the complex irrigation and landholding system and gradually developed an urban life of arts and crafts. Preeminent among these city-states were Ur, Uruk, Eridu, Nippur, Umma, Kish, Adab and Lagash. Abraham was born in Ur. Lagash subdued Ur and so on. War enhanced the power of the kings, at the expense of the priests, and created more slaves, who in turn displaced the free farmers as tillers of the soil for the landlords. It's an old story that keeps repeating itself throughout ancient history.

The wealth of Sumeria fostered architecture and fine arts. Unfortunately little of it survived as the Sumerians were forced to build in sun-dried, and later fired, brick for lack of stone in the doab and its immediate vicinity. Stone was almost precious as it had to be transported from the mountains at great cost. But through literature and archeology it is known that the Sumerians built grand temples with lofty towers for a shrine or alter at the top to their gods. The foundation of the Ziggurat of Ur, built in 2100 B. C. of fired brick, still stands from which artists' reconstructions have been made. It is an imposing monument. These Ziggurats found their way into the Bible with the story of the Tower of Babel. There is more history in this bit of biblical lore than meets the eye. Scintillating civilizations since time immemorial have always attracted foreigners because of better employment and trade opportunities. The ancient Greeks called them *metics*. They were "in" but not "of" the society. They spoke a foreign tongue until, and even later when, they mastered the language of the city. It was doubtless this situation on which the story of Babel (historical Babylon) was predicated.

The Sumerian prosperity was soon coveted by its neighbors. Semitic migration into the doab had been going on for centuries. To the northwest about 200 miles of the Sumerian cities the Akkadians were growing in power. In the 26th century B. C. they produced a great king, Sargon I, who conquered all of Sumeria. Sargon was a bastard, the son of a temple prostitute. A legend, Mosaic-like, grew up about his origin, probably true, in which his mother seals him in a basket-boat with pitch and places him in the river. He is discovered by a palace workman and taken into the royal household where he is raised as a cup bearer to the king. He grows in favor and power and, in the end, usurps the throne. No sooner did he become king of Akkad when he launched an invasion of Sumeria and conquered all the cities to the mouth of the two rivers. From this Akkadian-Sumerian empire he conquered far and wide, to the West up to the Mediterranean coast, northwest to the foothills of the Taurus range and east to Elam. The recently discovered ruins of the ancient Semitic city of Elba (near Aleppo) reveals it was conquered by Sargon. Elba had by then been under Sumerian influence for centuries adopting cuneiform for its script. His grandson Naram-Sin extended the conquests to the upper Tigris. But after a century or so the line of Sargon disintegrated and the Sumerian cities, once again, resuscitated under the leadership of the city of Ur, enjoyed a century of peace and prosperity.

It was now Sumer and Akkad, a nation of Sumerians and Semites. The Akkadians had no script and they too adopted cuneiform for their language. Akkadian, is thus, the first written semitic language. In fact the Akkadians had little civilization of their own and adopted the culture of the conquered Sumerians.

Two new invaders of the doab now emerge into history. The Elamites, non Semites from the East and the Amorites, Semites from the northwest. For two centuries these two war like peoples fought over the domination of Sumeria. At this time the great king of Babylon Hammurabi (circa 1945–1905 B. C. per Breasted) ousted the Elamites and the doab became Babylonia. The doab was destined to be fought over by the Semites and the Indo-Europeans for a millennium and more, until the rise of Persia in the 6th century B. C. The Sumerians disappeared from history.

EGYPTIANS

The Egyptian civilization was unique due to its singular geography, geology and meteorology. It sat astride the Nile alluvium for some 750 miles with its triangular delta on the Mediterranean comprising in all a territory no bigger than the states of Connecticut and Massachusetts. The tributaries of the Nile originated some 4000 miles away in the watersheds of Ethiopia and Uganda at Lake Victoria so that the fertile soil and rainfall of half a continent was brought down annually in perpetuity for good agriculture in this small part of the earth. This narrow strip of fertile land, moreover, was flanked on each side by miles of life defeating desert protecting the newly developing society from unwanted intrusion. Furthermore, the river flowed north and the wind blew south providing cheap water transportation to knit the economy together. The Egyptians were indeed a twice blessed people and they rose to the occasion by building one of mankind's earliest and most scintillating civilizations.

Wild wheat and barley are not indigenous to the area. Hence, it is presumed that agriculture was transmitted to the Nile valley from the Near East. But the distance from the Jordan valley to the Nile delta is short albeit the passage was across forbidding and swampy terrain. Even this may have been conducive to agriculture as the Neolithic settlers, perhaps, migrants from the Near East found landed oases in the semi-flooded delta with good soil for their wheat and barley seed. From these oases agriculture spread up the Nile along the alluvial strip which measures anywhere from one to fifteen miles wide for hundreds of miles. The delta is about 150 miles wide. That agriculture was transmitted to Egypt soon after its founding in the foothills of Western Asia is evidenced by an exhumed body of a man 6000 years old at a neolithic site near Badari between Cairo and Karnak with undigested barley in his stomach.

The racial origin of the ancient Egyptians is not clear, except that they were white. There is evidence of paleolithic cultures but hunting and food gathering could not have been bountiful in the mostly desert areas of northeast Africa. More than likely the Nile valley was settled during Neolithic times by people of the Near East who brought agriculture to the area. These migrants were very likely a mixture of Indo-Europeans or their predecessors and the Semites.

As was the case elsewhere these first neolithic farming communities were doubtless scattered throughout the delta and up the Nile, perhaps, to the first cataract (where the Aswan dam is now built) a stretch of 750 miles. Eventually these two areas were to become contending political divisions called Lower and Upper Egypt dividing at Memphis, near modern Cairo. This unique geography promoted strong provincial polities that were called nomes. Politico-economic organization became necessary as unified control of the waters of the Nile was essential to ancient Egypt's agriculture. In the delta surface drainage and irrigation was used, but agriculture along the banks of the Nile above the delta required lifting of the river water from lower to higher channels by as many as three or more successive lifts until the level of the fertile strip was reached. The invention used was called a *shadduf* consisting of a fulcrumed lever with a leather bucket at one end counterbalanced at the other end with a lump of sun dried clay. These lifts were kept going day and night during the growing season and required the mobilization of much manpower.

The villages and cities with their sun baked brick houses, temples and tombs of stone and other buildings were sited on the desert immediately above the fertile strip where the dry desert sand preserved most of the enduring ones for posterity. It is in these artifacts with their hieroglyphics that the history of ancient Egypt is found as it had no Herodotus to relate its story. Due largely to the ancient Egyptian's obsession with life after death the tombs, in particular, have proved an archeologist's dream from which the story of this old civilization has been vividly reconstructed.

About 5000 B. C. a strong chieftain united the nomes in the delta into a kingdom of Lower Egypt and another did the same above the delta into a kingdom of Upper Egypt. The former conquered the latter to form the first union sometime during the latter centuries of the fourth millennium. Its capital was established at Heliopolis, below modern Cairo, and named after the sun. Great advances were made in agriculture during this time. The strange Egyptian hoe (a curved wooden stick with a straight wooden handle loosely attached but with a reed rope affixed a foot or so from the juncture to provide rigidity for the stroke into the soil) was modified by extending the handle and hitching it to a pair of oxen with a yoke across their foreheads beneath the horns. A handle, later a double one, was affixed to the juncture to guide the curved point through the soil. Adding animal power increased greatly agricultural production. This antiquated plow is still used by the fellaheen today 6000 years after its invention! This bespeaks not the backwardness of today's fellaheen but the technological perspicacity of the ancient Egyptians for the use of a moldboard plow in the Nile valley, so essential to European and American agriculture, would result in the loss of precious moisture. Vast areas were brought under cultivation through better organized irrigation. Complete understanding of the characteristics of the Nile, its flow and ebb, the inundation and drainage of the delta, its droughts and floods, was mastered. The geometry of land survey, which had to be replotted after each inundation, was perfected. Their mathematics, however, did not go much beyond simple arithmetic. A calendar of seasons— inundation, cultivation, harvest and drought—each lasting three months, was developed. A calendar of 365 days was used. But the greatest achievement was the invention of writing. It originated with record keeping for a highly organized agriculture. Unlike the Sumerian cuneiform the Egyptian script was mostly pictorial. Concurrently they invented paper and ink. The paper was made of the papyrus reed (hence the word paper) that grew abundantly in the delta. After peeling the rind the papyrus stem was sliced into strips. These strips were laid side by side on a flat stone with another layer placed crosswise on top. A cloth was laid over the double layer of strips and beaten with a wooden mallet until the reed strips fused into a sheet which was dried and polished into a fine piece of paper. The sheets were pasted together into long scrolls. Ink was made from soot (pure carbon) mixed with water thickened with vegetable gum. A pointed reed was used as a pen. This development of writing which followed on the heels of its earlier invention in Sumeria was likewise the flowering of the Egyptian civilization.

The first union fell apart after a few centuries of glory for reasons not yet clear from the record and the next lasting union was achieved by the semi-legendary king from Upper Egypt known as Menes about 3100 B. C. A new capital was established at Memphis in the apex of the delta. He founded the first of 30 dynasties that span Egyptian history from 3100 to 341 B. C. The Egyptians now mastered metallurgy which augmented their already productive agriculture and facilitated their foreign trade. They mined and smelted the rich malachite ore in the Timna valley of the Negev desert and developed in the Sinai the greatest copper and bronze industry of antiquity as already described in Chapter IV.

About 2700 B. C. at the beginning of the Third dynasty Egypt entered a golden age known as the Old Kingdom that lasted through the Sixth dynasty for some 500 years. The Egyptians had now mastered construction and sculpture in hard stone. The great pyramids at Gizeh for the Pharaohs

Khufu, Khafre and Menkaure (or Cheops, Chephren and Mycerenus as Herodotus rechristened them) and the Sphinx belong to this period. They are among the most notable accomplishments of man even today. A labor levy, like a corvee, was imposed upon the peasants and artisans during the periods of the drought and inundation when the fields required no attention. The monument builders were well fed for their labor by the Pharaohs, including plenty of garlic and onions relished by the ancient Egyptians. It was a happy and prosperous time in Egypt.

It led, however, to a socially disturbing maldistribution of wealth. Monument building proved costly. At the same time an avaricious and parasitic priestly bureaucracy established itself which appropriated to itself a disproportionate share of the wealth. Despite the fact that the Pharaoh was considered a god and the religious head, the priests insinuated themselves into a dominant role within the ruling elite. Economic hardship and disorder ensued. The irrigation system broke down. Rebellion seethed in the land of the Nile. It reached its climax under Pepi II, who ruled for 90 years, the last Pharaoh of the Sixth dynasty. The governors of the nomes took power and Egypt disintegrated into many principalities which quarreled and fought one another.

Social stratification in the Old Kingdom was rigid and hierarchical. At the top was the Pharaoh who was king and god. Beneath him was a civil and priestly bureaucracy consisting of priests, nobles, administrators and scribes. The scribes were the professionals of the social order. The dominated majority comprised the peasants, artisans and unskilled laborers. Finally, there were the slaves who were not significant under the Old Kingdom as the Egyptians were not a warring people at this time. Notably too, there was not yet a military establishment.

Had Egypt not been surrounded by desert at the time of its politico-economic disintegration (circa 2200–2000 B. C.) it would doubtless have succumbed to foreign domination and its history might have been different. But after two centuries of disarray it was once again reunited by powerful Pharaohs emanating from Thebes of the Twelfth dynasty (circa 1991–1796 B. C.). This period is often referred to as the Middle Kingdom. The irrigation system was restored, copper mining in the Sinai highly developed and political dominion was extended to the third cataract. The gold mines of Nubia (Sudan) were exploited to augment the wealth of the nation. The god Amon was brought to the fore to break the Re priesthood of the Old Kingdom. Egypt was again restored to greatness.

But it did not last long. In the 18th century, during the Thirteenth dynasty (circa 1786–1633 B. C.), the country lapsed once again into disorder. Civil war between Lower and Upper Egypt erupted. A Theban regime established itself in an area stretching some 125 miles below the first cataract. Nubia broke away from Egyptian rule. And this time a foreign invader with superior technology took over Lower Egypt. It was the Hyksos from western Asia, thought to be Indo-Europeans, who came with horse and chariot, powerful bows and arrows made of wood and horn, scimitars, daggers and body armor. The Egyptians had no armor and fought with rudimentary weapons. They ruled for two centuries during the Fourteenth-Seventeenth dynasties (circa 1786–1567 B. C.). Hyksos domination did not extend much beyond the delta, never as far as Thebes.

It was during the Hyksos period that the Israelites migrated into the delta. Every Jew, Christian and Muslim is familiar with the story of Joseph in the Old Testament and the Koran. He was sold into slavery by his brothers and taken to Egypt. Joseph was a precocious lad who ingratiated himself with the Hyksos king and became his chief administrator. This would not likely have happened had there been an Egyptian on the throne. From this high position and authority he brought his people into Egypt and settled them in the delta. This too would not have been possible under an Egyptian Pharaoh as the Egyptians forbade immigration except in bondage into the delta. And as soon as the Hyksos were ousted the Israelites were enslaved to work as brickmakers and construction labor.

The Egyptians, after a time, mastered the horse and chariot for military purposes, copied the new weapons, ousted the Hyksos and launched an age of imperialism that spanned the Eighteenth-Twentieth dynasties (circa 1567–1085 B. C.). It was another scintillating period. Plunder added wealth to its prosperous agricultural productivity. The treasury at Thebes bulged with gold and silver. Great monuments were built into and from hard rock, this time far up the first cataract at Karnak, Luxor, and Abu Simbel. Thutmose I extended the empire to the fourth cataract and into Palestine and Syria up to the Euphrates where he was stopped by the Mitannis. A professional army now arose for the first time to defend the empire. Egypt was master of the Mediterranean world.

Thutmose was succeeded by his daughter Hatshepsut who married her brother Thutmose II and ruled in his stead. When he died leaving an infant son Thutmose III by a wife in the harem Hatshepsut ruled in his name as regent. But for all practical purposes she was the Pharaoh. She assumed masculine manners, had statues of her sculptured wearing the royal beard and deemphasizing her femininity. A great temple-sepulchre was built into solid rock for her at the Valley of the Kings. She also completed the great temple at Karnak in Thebes. Empire building was suspended for two decades. Hatshepsut concentrated on internal development and foreign trade. Peace and prosperity were the order of the day. She had an eminent vizier, a certain Senmut, as her helpmeet in her good governance. Senmut, however, fell from favor and power when Hatshepsut discovered he had surreptitiously arrogated for himself space in the royal tomb.

After twenty years Thutmose III marshalled the necessary backing among the nobility to regain his throne. Like his great grandfather he too was an outstanding monarch. He promptly resumed foreign conquest but as in the case of the first Thutmose, he too was stopped by the Mitannis when he tried to extend the empire beyond the Euphrates. This proved to be the limit beyond which Egyptian power could not be expanded. The empire now found its scope which reached from Syria to the Sudan. The Egyptians, however, did not rule directly, except in Nubia, choosing instead to dominate the areas through local rulers. This indirect rule was augmented by taking sons or brothers of these local rulers to Egypt as hostages where they were thoroughly Egyptianized and returned home warmly disposed toward Egypt.

Thutmose III organized the empire so well that it endured a century of neglect by his successors. Most notable was his grandson Amenhoteph IV who initiated a revolutionary religious reform, in large part, to free the country of a parasitic priesthood that had once again regained dominance. In part he also wished to replace the multitudinous pantheon with a single deity. He conjured up a sun god called Aton as a single universal god, the source of all life on earth. He changed his name to Akhenaton, or Ikhnaton, meaning servant of Aton. The capital was moved from Thebes to Akhetaton (Horizon of Aton) where Tell el Amarna stands today. The noble effort failed for the people were too addicted to their old and comfortable gods. The dispossessed priesthood doubtless conducted an effective propaganda campaign against Akhenaton. Akhenaton used the military bureaucracy to oust the priests, but his reform was doomed when the army joined the civilians and priests against his new god. Hereafter, the three branches of the bureaucracy became extremely powerful and succeeding Pharaohs had to be duly deferential.

Akhenaton's successor Tutankaton, his son in law, died as a youth but only after he capitulated to the priests for the restoration of the god Amon. His name was forthwith changed to Tutankhamen. His claim to fame resides in his magnificent tomb, which somehow escaped the tomb robbers, that gave mankind millennia later when it was uncovered in 1922 A. D. an idea of the wealth and magnificence of imperial Egypt. It would be remiss to pass on without mentioning Akhenaton's beautiful Queen Nefertiti. Assuming the bust of her that has been passed on to posterity is a faithful reproduction, Nefertiti (the beautiful one is come) was a woman of incomparable pulchritude that evolution has not improved upon to date. Atop a long aristocratic neck the bust portrays a face with delicately balanced features and serene eyes. Akhenaton's premature attempt to create a unitary deity for man may have failed but he succeeded as a husband and making happy a most beautiful woman. And that is no mean accomplishment.

Imperialism was resumed by the Pharaohs of the Nineteenth and Twentieth dynasties eleven of which bore the renowned name Ramses. The empire was neglected by the last kings of the Eighteenth dynasty. It was in a state of virtual disintegration. This is revealed clearly in the so-called Amara Letters, a collection of 300 clay tablets in cuneiform part of the royal records of Akhenaton's reign wherein the princes of Western Asia beg and implore the Pharaoh for military assistance against invaders from the Arabian desert and to quell revolts. No help was forthcoming. Meanwhile a powerful Hittite imperialism was thrusting into Syria and Palestine. Ramses II, who reigned for 67 glorious years, set forth to reestablish the empire. But before he launched his campaign he sent an expedition to Nubia to mine the gold he needed to finance his expedition. In 1296 B. C. Ramses set forth to fight the Hittites and suffered a severe defeat at Kadesh on the Orontes river in northern Lebanon. The Battle of Kadesh, detailed in Chapter VI, is one of history's notable events. It was the turning point in Egyptian imperialism. After it Egypt went into irrevocable decline and disintegration albeit its greatness persisted for several centuries.

Many factors contributed to Egypt's decline and fall. Not the least significant was the loss of technological prowess. Technological development had now reached the iron age and Egypt possessed neither the iron ore or the technical skill to produce it. The Phoenicians and Greeks in addition were developing better ships—sail and triremes—for control of the Mediterranean. Nothing dramatizes this disadvantage more than the letter sent by the Pharaoh to the Hittite king virtually begging for some iron which the Hittite king refuses! It is important, however, to bear in mind historical perspective in this connection. While the Hittites smelted iron it probably did not contribute much to their power. Their technological superiority rested on the horse and chariot. Iron was too expensive and scarce to be a factor in war at this time. That came later during the last millennium before Christ when Egypt suffered foreign invasion after invasion by peoples from the north armed with iron swords. Egypt which had dominated the Mediterranean area with the bronze dagger was now destined to be forever dominated by others with an iron sword.

But equally important was a gross maldistribution of wealth to non-producers in the swollen bureaucratic society of imperial Egypt. There were now three parasitic bureaucracies—the priests, the army and the administrators, mainly a large host of tax collectors. Everything was taxed to support the bureaucrats. The taxes were collected in kind. Money was not yet invented. This required an ever expanding revenue administration. The priests who had overburdened the Egyptians before were, once again, the masters of the Pharaohs. They appropriated to themselves a lions share of the wealth. The high priest of Amon is estimated to have owned as high as 30 per cent of the arable land of Egypt! The military establishment too, to whom the Pharaoh became more and more beholden during the imperial age, was unduly compensated for its "defense" of the country. Until the advent of imperialism the army depended largely on a citizens levy, in times of need, at no cost to the people. Now it was a professional bureaucracy that wielded much power and consumed much wealth. This pressure of consumption by a growing legion of non-producers would doubtless have resulted in great inflation had ancient Egypt been a moneyed economy. Instead wages were paid in kind—bread, beer, beans, meat, onions and other consumables. In 1170 B. C. there was a hunger strike when the government fell behind two months payment in the rations. People resorted to robbing graves, work stoppages and other drastic action. Productivity declined. Hard times ensued.

But Egypt remained attractive to foreign invaders because of its great agriculture. First came the Libyans from the West. Next the forerunners of the Greeks—the Mycenaeans and the Dorians—that the Egyptians called the "sea people" as they came across the Mediterranean. The Egyptians were able to repulse them, at first, and won a notable sea battle at the mouth of the Nile in 1190 B. C. The Nubians pushed in from the south and controlled part of Upper Egypt for 70 years. The Assyrians moved in for a short while. In 525 the Persians overran Egypt and dominated it for two centuries. Alexander wrested Egypt from the Persians in 332 B. C. and established Greek rule and influence under the Ptolemies. Egyptians were treated as second class citizens by the Greeks. The 30th dynasty came to an end.

Alexandria became a center of learning for the entire Mediterranean world. Euclid wrote his *Elements* and Eratosthenes calculated the circumference of the earth there. Rome took over from the Ptolemies (in one of the great romantic dramas of history involving Cleopatra, Caesar and Marc Anthony) in 48 B. C. and Augustus incorporated it into the Roman Empire in 31 B. C. The Arabs wrested it from the Byzantines in 639 A. D. and converted it into the Muslim country it is today. Egypt was for a thousand or so years the pawn of the struggle between the Indo-Europeans and Semites which broiled in the Mediterranean area during the millennium before Christ. So, through the past three millennia Egypt's role in history has been as the granary of the successive dominant peoples of the Mediterranean area. Even this has now come to pass as Egypt is today a deficit grain producing country dependent on imports of wheat. The ancient Egyptians have long ago been submerged in these successive inundations of foreign invasions. They are known to us only through their tombs and monuments.

As a postscript on the ancient Egyptians it can be concluded that they were indeed a great people. Their social structure was strong. Stable families, hard working peasants and clever artisans. Yet this rigid structure provided for opportunities for social mobility. There are instances on record of men of humble birth rising into the ruling elite. In the Old Kingdom a man named Uni rose from a worker in the royal warehouse to governor of Upper Egypt. Later the army provided another facile avenue for entrance into the ruling class. Amenhotep, the son of Hapu, rose from a scribe in the army to vizier under Amenhotep III. And so on. Their undue preoccupation with the afterlife, however, sapped much energy and wealth that could, during their decline, have been better put to use in the defense of the country. All peoples at this time refused to accept life as terminal but the ancient Egyptians outdid all others in this respect. If the ancient Egyptians can be faulted it would be for their egotism. Few other peoples have so overworked the pronoun "I". A good example, detailed earlier, is the account of the "glorious" victory of Ramses II at Kadesh. Their decline and fall from power must have been an extremely humiliating experience. What they could not understand, of course, was that their days of glory belonged to a stage of technological development when agriculture and copper metallurgy, in which they excelled, were foremost. When other peoples mastered the horse (which they adopted but were never familiar with) the trireme and the smelting of iron they were destined to be dominated by them.

THE INDO-EUROPEANS

Beginning around the middle of the second millennium B. C. wave after wave of peoples from the north—the Caucasus, Black sea and Europe—started pouring into Western Asia where they fought the Semites from the Arabian peninsula for domination of the Mediterranean world. A millennium or so later the Indo-Europeans were masters of the area and the Semites, until the rise of the Arabs another millennium later, remained a subject people. The Indo-Europeans owed their success, in large measure, to the energy of the horse and the smelting of iron which gave a new cutting edge to their weapons and agricultural implements. These two technological innovations together with vastly improved vessels for navigation lifted mankind to a higher level of economic and military development after remaining on a plateau for some two thousand years following the development of agriculture and its related techniques of irrigation, draught animals and the like under the Sumerians and Egyptians.

Such a churning of peoples tended to blur the racial lines. In fact, the racial identity of some of the people is not clear. There is doubt, for instance, about the Phoenicians who are generally regarded as Semites by historians. That a people spoke a semitic tongue is not necessarily a reliable indication that they were Semites. The semitic language was very attractive and many non-Semites adopted it in preference to their own. Moreover the Semites invented the alphabet which made their language very convenient for trade. Aramaic became the *lingua franca* of the caravans around 1000 B. C. The Philistines, an Indo-European people, used a semitic language. The accepted practice in war in those centuries was to kill or enslave the men of the vanquished and to add the women to the harems of the victors. It would be naive to think that this did not commingle the genes of future generations. The degree of racial purity thus depended upon geography. In the north and south the lines tended to be more pure. In the middle—the Fertile Crescent—where the two races clashed the commingling of genes was most prevalent. The prominent nose of some Hebrews is generally thought to be of Anatolian genetic origin. The Assyrians, for example, are considered to have been an Indo-European-Semitic mixture.

Hammurabi, sixth in line of the Amorite kings that imposed their hegemony over Akkad-Sumeria during the fore part of the second millennium before Christ, ushered in a scintillating though short lived age. Historians are unable to agree on the precise time of Hammurabi's rule. Breasted fixes it *circa* 1945–1905 B. C; Durant *circa* 2123–2081 B. C.; Toynbee *circa* 1792–1750 B. C. The latter is probably nearer the mark. The *circas* tend to be somewhat elusive as scholars reach back into history. The Babylon (there were others) of Hammurabi found its way into history as a fabled and romantic place. It was an obscure city to the north of the main Sumerian cities where the two rivers almost meet when Hammurabi decided to make it the capital. Hammurabi was a great administrator who attended to every detail, including the spring sheep-shearing, repair of the canals and the like menial enterprises. Substantial prosperity revived under such order and discipline. Thousands of letters wherein Hammurabi directs his governors have survived giving a detailed picture of his rule. Trade and commerce flourished on top of a reorganized agriculture to bring vast wealth to Babylonia.

Unlike the Akkadians the Amorites established their own god Marduk as head of the pantheon. The Sumerian goddess Innini was renamed Ishtar to become the Babylonian goddess of love and fertility. The people, however, continued to worship the old Sumerian gods. Great temples were built on the ziggurat models with high towers and arched doorways. The temple of Babel mentioned in the Bible probably refers to Hammurabi's temple in the capital.

The Amorite society was built upon the Akkad-Sumerian. Little or nothing was added technologically. Most noteworthy is the Code of Hammurabi, a 3600 line compilation of man's earliest laws and rules. It codifies, in the main, the old Sumerian laws for which there was a centuries old precedent in the Code of Ur-Engur. It contains largely, a retributive criminology—an eye for an eye, a tooth for a tooth—which at times resulted in great injustice. For instance, if an architect built a house which fell and killed the son of the owner the architect's son was put to death!

Hammurabi's Babylon hardly survived his death. The Indo-Europeans descended upon it with the horse and chariot and dominated it for the next six centuries. The Kassites came from the East. The Hittites from Anatolia made a devastating raid and plundered Babylon around 1600 B. C. but they did not stay to rule. That was left to the Kassites who dominated Babylon until the Assyrians rose to power early in the last millennium before Christ.

Between the Kassites and the Hittites, in upper Mesopotamia, were the Hurrians. Their domain was called the Kingdom of Mitanni. For centuries they maintained suzerainty over the Assyrians. These lords of Mitanni bore Indian names and worshipped some of the same gods as the Hindus. They presumably derived from the eastern sector of the Indo-Europeans that moved into Persia and India around 1500 B. C. The history of these Indo-Europeans is still poorly understood. In fact, until quite recently the Hittites were thought to be a figment of biblical imagination. There was "Ephron the Hittite" who sold Abraham a cave to bury his wife. Also Uriah the Hittite whose beautiful wife Bathsheba David coveted and other references. Some of these biblical references were, of course, to the remnants of the Hittites scattered around the Near East after their empire was destroyed by another wave of Indo-Europeans around 1200 B. C. Purblind Egyptologists tended to ignore and even dismiss as erroneous the respectful references to the Hittites on Egyptian monuments and in their other documents. No one was quite sure what to make of the "Hittites" with pointed shoes curved backward toward the shins like the Jaipur slippers still found and worn in India to this day.

But the Hittites finally broke through the light of history in 1830 when French archeologist Charles Felix-Marie Texier discovered the ruins of their capital Hattusa in the Anatolian plain. Diligent activity ensued thereafter by European archeologists but the full story was not revealed until the Hittite script was unlocked. In the ruins many cuneiform tablets were found but a new hieroglyphic script predominated. The breakthrough came in 1915 when a Czech scholar Bedrich Hrozny surmised it was an Indo-European and not a Semitic tongue. Philologists were baffled for some time by its format until it dawned on them that the lines read alternatively from right to left and left to right unlike other scripts that are written in one or the other pattern! After Hrozny's discovery it took still another generation or so before scholars were able to interpret the Hittite script facilely. The complete history of the Hittite civilization still contains many gaps that scholars hope to fill one day with additional archeological finds. For example, no account by the Hittites of the Battle of Kadesh has yet been uncovered! History has only the biased Egyptian account.

The origin and the disappearance of the Hittites are an obscure part of their history. It is believed that they migrated to Anatolia from Europe above the Black Sea. In Anatolia they must have found a highly developed civilization, as can be surmised from the ruins of Catal Huyuk, which they conquered. The earliest reference to the Hittites around 1900 B. C. is found on tablets discovered at the Assyrian trading post at Kanesh in the Taurus mountains.

By the 17th century B. C. the Hittites had mastered chariot warfare. In addition they fought in bronze armor with bronze daggers, bronze tipped arrows, spears and lances. Their bows were made of wood, horn and sinew. They were highly skilled metallurgists, including the smelting of iron. But when and to what extent iron was used for weapons is not clear.

It is not certain whether the Hittites brought the horse and chariot with them from Europe or adopted it from the Hurrians. The latter is most likely the case and there is a treatise on horse breeding, feeding and training written by a Hurrian dated around 1350 B. C. which was found among the Hittite ruins that would tend to support this view. But whether they developed or adopted it they soon had a light weight chariot mounted on a single axel and spoked wheels made of wood and rimmed with metal. The cab was made of wood covered with leather.

About 1680 B. C. Labarna I undertook the founding of the Hittite nation by conquering some of the neighboring cities. Labarna II continued the conquests, established the capital of the new kingdom at Hattusa and changed his name to Hattusili ("man of Hattusa"). His grandson Mursilis I defeated the Amorites destroying Babylon around 1600 B. C. thereby gaining control of the Euphrates trade routes. After Mursilis' death the Hurrians attacked and occupied much of southern Anatolia. Around 1500 B. C. Telipinu consolidated Hittite rule around central Anatolia and brought to an end a period sometimes referred to as the Old Kingdom.

There followed a century or more of disarray and decline in Hittite prowess. The powerful kingdom of Mitanni kept the Hittites in check. The Egyptians too advanced into Syria under Thutmose I, conquered Aleppo and made the Hittites pay tribute. There were power struggles internally over succession to the crown. In 1386 B. C. Suppiluliuma ascended to the throne and resumed Hittite empire building. First he rebuilt the defences of Hattusa, reorganized the army and subjected the rebellious peoples of Anatolia. In 1374 B. C. he made his first foray against the Hurrians and was defeated. But he profited from the set back by gaining knowledge of the terrain in the upper Euphrates area and taking full measure of Hurrian defenses. In 1366 he captured the kingdom of Mitanni. In the same year he marched into Syria and captured Kadesh. In 1353 B. C. he rounded out the empire to the East by capturing the important city of Carchemish located at a crucial juncture on the Euphrates trade route. At the beginning of the 12th century (1300 B. C.) the Hittite empire extended from the Aegean sea in the west to the Tigris river in the east and the Orontes to the south a territory about the size of France and Italy. Suppiluliuma was succeeded by his son Mursili II in 1347 B. C.

A curious episode transpired while Suppiluliuma was besieging Carchemish. A messenger handed him a letter from the widow of Tutankhamen who died without a heir. She requested marriage to one of Suppiluliuma's sons who would become the Pharoah of Egypt and, hopefully, produce by her a son for the continuance of the 18th dynasty. Suppiluliuma's suspicion and procrastination (several exchanges of letters over a year) proved fatal for when he finally sent his son to Egypt an Egyptian priest had seized both the widowed queen and the throne. The Hittite prince was forthwith put to death by the usurper. The confrontation between the two empires, which might have been averted by the marriage, was now ordained and it came in 1296 B. C. in the Battle of Kadesh already discussed earlier.

After the battle a century of peace ensued between the two ancient powers. In 1284 a non-aggression treaty, inscribed on silver tablets, was signed. Ramses II married a Hittite princess and made her a chief wife. The Egyptian-Hittite alliance was remarkable, not only in its duration, but its friendship. When the Hittites suffered a drought the Pharoah sent them grain relief.

But Hittite peace did not endure. By 1200 B. C. the Hittite empire vanished, somewhat mysteriously, and the "land of Hatti" was settled thereafter by the Phrygians. The Phrygians, a lesser people, do not appear to have done in the Hittites. Theories abound from internal revolt (which may have weakened but not destroyed the society) to different foreign assaults. The most plausible is that the Hittites were annihilated by the so-called "sea peoples", on which more later, who are known for such devastating raids. At any rate, the Hittites dispersed throughout the Near East and continued as little principalities, to which many of the Biblical references apply, bearing at times a not too faithful continuance of the Hittite culture. These Neo-Hittites, as they are called, even forsook the Hittite tongue for various Semitic languages extant in the area. The Phrygians who took over the Anatolian plain were an undistinguished people. They live in history mainly through King Midas, of the legendary golden touch, and King Gordius, of the Gordian Knot. Finally even the Neo-Hittites disappear around 700 B. C. with the rise of the Assyrian empire.

Hittite arts were not particularly distinguished. They built and sculptured in stone but roughly. The palace at Hattusa was more of a fortress than a piece of architecture built in and on top of a stone promontory overlooking the Anatolian plain. Immediately beneath the palace was an immense temple built of stone, the foundation still remaining.

Hittite wealth derived from agriculture, which was about the same as practiced in neolothic Catal Huyuk, and a vigorous production and trade in metals. Copper and bronze comprised the main production. Iron smelting was a Hittite monopoly. Silver was produced in abundance and, cast in bars or rings, used as a medium of exchange. The foundation of the economy was the independent farmer and metalsmith.

Hittite law was highly developed. It was more humane than the Code of Hammurabi. An arsonist, for instance, was not put to death but required to rebuild the house he burned. The people were expected to honor their obligations and obey the laws.

Unlike the other bygone people that leavened the civilization of the Mediterranean area it is hard to find any lasting effects of the Hittites. Their greatest contribution was the promotion of iron technology. Their religion, language and arts made no enduring impact.

Around 1200 B. C. another wave of Indo-Europeans inundated the eastern Mediterranean area. The Egyptians called them the "sea peoples" as they burst open the Nile delta from across the Mediterranean. Their history is still only vaguely understood. But the accumulating archeological evidence indicates they were mostly proto-Greeks from southeastern Europe. The Mycenaeans are thought to have migrated into the Greek penninsula with the first wave of Indo-Europeans the early part of the second millennium before Christ and developed a flourishing civilization during the period 1600–1200 B. C. Around 1400 they conquered the Minoans of Crete. They were a warring people, with chariots and bronze weaponry, who indulged in plunder and piracy in the Aegean sea area. The siege and sack of Troy, the story of the great epic *The Iliad,* was one such marauding expedition. Ugarit the proto-Phoenician city was similarly sacked and destroyed by the "sea peoples" around 1234 B. C.

The best record of their marauding raids is left us by Egyptian chroniclers. About 1220 B. C. the Pharoah Menneptah defeated an invasion of the delta by a joint enterprise of Lybians and five "sea peoples". Actually, it was more of a migration as these "sea peoples" had their families and possessions with them bent on settlement in the fertile Nile valley. Among them were the Achaeans and the Tyrsenoi (Etruscans). The inscription mentions that the "sea peoples" also raided the east coast of the Mediterranean (to wit, Ugarit), that Canaan had been sacked and Israel ravaged. Curiously, there is no mention of such raid in the Bible. This same inscription contained the notation that "Hatti is at peace" intimating that at this time the "sea peoples" had not penetrated into central Anatolia.

Early in the 11th century during the reign of Ramses III (circa 1198–1161 B. C.) the "sea peoples" made two more raids, actually migration attempts, into the delta by sea and inland down the Mediterranean coast. It was during these raids that the "sea peoples" are thought to have destroyed the Hittite empire. While they did not penetrate the delta they settled in various places in Palestine and Syria. The most notable of these settlers were the Philistines who situated in the rich coastal area (roughly) from modern Tel Aviv to Gaza. The rise of the Phoenician cities—Tyre, Sidon, Berytus and others—in the coastal area above the Philistines at about the same time has led to a view that this too many have been part of the migration of the "sea peoples" to western Asia. Ugarit, which was an old Semitic city on the coast was utterly destroyed by the first wave of the "sea peoples". The logic of history would support the thought that the Phoenicians too were of these same "sea peoples" who took over this coastal strip, subjected the Semites living there and exercised thereafter domination over the area. Their maritime prowess, their political organization of city-states and, most convincing, their rise to dominance at the time of turmoil created by the raids and migrations of the "sea peoples" lends weight to the theory that they were of Greek antecedents. That they spoke a semitic tongue does not necessarily prove they were of semitic origin. The Philistines too adopted a semitic language when they settled in Canaan.

The Mycenaean cities on the mainland also were devastated and destroyed around 1200 B. C. Many of the Mycenaean kings that mustered before Troy in the Iliad found their palaces sacked and burned upon their return. These raids were made by another proto-Greek people, the Dorians, who migrated into the Greek penninsula from the Danubian area of Europe. This area, at Hallstatt, was one of the earliest iron making regions of antiquity and the Dorians probably came with iron swords. By 1050 iron was common in the Aegean. The Mycenaeans fled before the Dorians seeking new places to settle. Being a warring people they launched raiding *cum* migrating ventures in (mostly) the eastern Mediterranean area. In these ventures the Dorians may have joined them for they too were on the move for new places to settle.

After the destruction of the Mycenaean civilization the Aegean world sank into a 450 year Dark Age out of which the brilliant Greek civilization eventually rose about 750 B. C. The so-called "sea peoples" destroyed the Hittite empire and contributed to the decline of the Egyptian, leaving a vaccuum in the Near East. Palestine and Syria were now open to migration and settlement by smaller nations until the rise of Assyrian power around the ninth century B. C. The most renowned confrontation of this period, already detailed heretofore, was that between the Philistines and the Israelites for the control of Palestine.

THE SEMITES

Semitic tribes were moving into Palestine and Syria during, and even before, this time. In addition to the Israelites there were the Maobites, Amorites, Edomites, Amonites and Aramaeans. Outside the domestication of the camel the Semites brought no new technology to the area. But they made two notable contributions to man's cultural evolution. The first and most important was the invention of the alphabet. The second, more controversial but of profound impact on the civilization of the Mediterranean region, was monotheism.

The evolution of the alphabet is lost in obscurity. All that is certain is that it occurred among the Semites living in Canaan sometime in the last centuries of the second millennium. The Egyptians came close to an alphabet and there is some thinking that the Semites took off from this point as some of the earliest evidence of a rudimentary alphabet has been found in the copper mining areas of the Sinai that were for centuries under Egyptian domination. Around 1000 B. C. or so the Phoenicians carried the alphabet westward into the Mediterranean region and the Aramaeans eastward by way of the caravans. Aramaic was the *lingua franca* of the inland trade. The Semitic alphabet, however, was incomplete as it contained no vowels. It was left to the Greeks to finish the alphabet around 800 B. C. to form the basis of writing thereafter for the Graeco-Roman and Western civilizations.

The development of monotheism followed a more tortuous path with credit for the religious innovation due mainly to the Israelites (also known as Hebrews or Jews). The history of the ancient Israelites is also notable for their fast rise and fall. They became a nation under David and after a brilliant half century or so under Solomon fell into disunion, disintegration and foreign domination lasting only a century or two as an independent integrated society. More is known about the Israelites than the other Semites—the Edomites, Moabites, Amonites and others—because of the Bible. The others have no written history and we know of them only indirectly. It should be noted that there is almost no corroboration of the biblical story elsewhere in history. Egyptian records leave no specific mention of the Israelites residing in Egypt. There is no other record of the three kings, Saul, David and Solomon. But for the Bible no one would know they existed.

This begs the question—how reliable is the Bible as history. Archeologists are becoming increasingly convinced that there is more history in the Bible than was at first thought. To be sure, the Bible cannot be read literally, but only substantively, as history. That is true, of course, of all epic lore. The story of the Bible was written down only after the 9th century B. C. Theretofore it was conveyed as folklore for centuries and as such suffered the attrition of time and memory. For instance the Age of Patriarchs supposedly covers 400 years or so yet the Bible asserts there were only three generations—Abraham, Isaac and Jacob (also known as Israel)—quite obviously that flies in the face of reality. Doubtless the generations passed as elsewhere among humanity but these men were the outstanding members that folklore retained in memory. Then to reconcile the discrepancy they were endowed with unnatural longevity. Abraham, it is said in Genesis, lived to age 175. Noah, it is said lived 900 years! But such discrepancies need not obviate the history residing in the folklore. Also, there have been misunderstandings due to the inadequate translation. For example, the King James version of the Bible has the crossing into Sinai in *Exodus* at the "Red Sea" when a later more accurate translation places it at the "Sea of Reeds", that is, the swampy area in the delta of the Nile. The Sea of Reeds was doubtless navigable by foot but not by the Pharoahs' chariots.

What is the roughly hewn history of the Israelites from the Bible. They first migrated into the doab from Arabia somewhere before the turn of the second millennium before Christ. Abraham departs from Ur in Sumeria for Canaan, the "land of milk and honey", shortly thereafter, the early part of the millennium, where he lives with his family among the Canaanites. It would appear that many Hittites lived in Canaan at this time as several of his progeny took Hittite wives. They were, however, reluctant to do so and Isaac sends Jacob to Haran in upper Mesopotamia 350 miles away to seek a wife among his distant relatives. Jacob returns, after a considerable sojourn, with two wives, the daughters of Laban, and two concubines. From them he fathers twelve sons, who later beget the twelve tribes of Israel. Apparently Canaan was never the land of milk and honey of their dreams for the

Israelites were frequently starving because of drought, locusts and other adversities. They migrated to Egypt in order to survive as related in the Story of Joseph detailed earlier. Jacob and his sons came peacefully and by invitation from the Hyksos Pharoah, under whom Joseph had attained the high post of vizier. But the Hyksos were ousted by the Egyptians and "there arose up a new king over Egypt which knew not Joseph." The new Pharoah placed the Israelites in bondage where they remained until Moses led them out of Egypt around 1225 B. C. The Israelites had lived in Egypt for 430 years according to the Bible.

When they arrived in Canaan they found the Promised Land occupied and settled by others—a mixture of Semites, Hittites, Philistines, Phoenicians, and others. Moses had a near revolt on his hands as many of the Israelites wanted to return to Egypt where, at least, they had enough to eat. But after sojourning on the outskirts of the Promised Land they began infiltrating peacefully and by force wherever they could the hills and valleys of Jordan. They possesed very backward technology, whereas the Canaanites had horses and chariots, iron and bronze weapons. Archeologists have found evidence that where the Israelites managed to gain control technology retrogressed, for instance, the replacement of metal sickes with stone ones. But by luck (attributed to their god) or clever stratagem they managed some notable victories. Joshua crumbled the walls of Jericho with a trumpet blast—doubtless a timely earthquake intervened—and captured this important Canaanite city. The Song of Deborah gives us an account of the capture of the city of Hazar. The Canaanites attacked the Israelites, who were virtually without weapons, with 900 chariots. A torrential rain storm mired the chariots in mud and the Israelites, taking advantage of the disarray of the Canaanites, defeated them in hand to hand combat. When the Midianites launched a raid on an Israel settlement west of the Jordan with weapons no better than those of the Israelites but with a camel corps Gideon stampeded the camels at midnight with trumpet blasts and fire torches throwing the entire Midianite army into disorder and defeat.

During these early centuries the Israelites remained a loose federation of twelve tribes led by Judges—wise men or counselors, sometimes priests, who were consulted in times of crisis. Samuel is the most renowned of these Judges. Whether these twelve tribes were geneologically pure is doubtful. They lived in Egypt for generations while the Egyptians dominated Palestine and Syria from where they brought Semitic slaves who were likely commingled with the Israelites in Egypt. Also the Israelites while infiltrating and capturing the Semites, and non-Semites for that matter in Canaan, doubtless intermarried with them. But despite these possibilities they apparently managed to maintain their socio-political organization on the basis of the twelve tribes.

By the middle of the tenth century the twelve tribes gained control of most of the hilly terrain west of the Jordan but could never muster the power to take the rich coastal areas held by the Philistines and Phoenicians. These battles are detailed in Chapter VI. Moreover this was the century of maximum Philistine power which not only kept the Israelites out of the coastal area of the Promised Land but subjected many of the Israelites settlements in the Canaan hills from whom they exacted tribute. The Philistines refused to divulge their iron technology to the Israelites—they even required them to have their agricultural implements sharpened by Philistine smiths.

In order to throw off the Philistine yoke the Israelites decided to submit to a king and upon Samuel's recommendation selected Saul as their first ruler. But Saul suffered defeat after defeat by the superior Philistine armies and finally lost his life as well as his three sons in the devastating battle on the Plain of Jezreel. He was succeeded by David around 1000 B. C. under whose rule Israel became a nation. David repulsed the Philistines who retreated to their coastal cities where they remained a small independent nation until subjected by the Assyrians. The Bible contains no account of great victories over the Philistines which could mean that their power waned as much through some internal disintegration as the growth of Israel might. It is not clear whether the Israelites mastered the horse and chariot by Davids' time. There is a reference that Absalom, David's rebellious son, mustered horses and chariots and yet in his moment of defeat and death he is riding a mule. At any rate, David turned his attention inland and brought the Moabites, Edomites and Ammonites under Israel rule. At his death Israel stretched from the Euphrates to the Sinai penninsula. He established the capital at Jerusalem where he brought the Ark of the Covenant. Finally he forged an alliance with Hiram, the king of Tyre, for use of his port for access to the Mediterranean. He left this empire to Solomon, his son by Bathsheba, upon his death circa 971 B. C.

Solomon was certainly one of the great kings of history. He ruled gloriously for 40 years (circa 972–932 B. C.). In Solomon's time the Israelites knew the horse and chariot. In fact, Solomon built a lucrative trade in this respect. In his infinite wisdom he realized that the best horses were reared in the pasturelands of Anatolia and the best chariots were manufactured in Egypt. He put the two together and sold the war machines throughout Western Asia at great profit. Solomon thus became the first armaments merchant in history unsurpassed, perhaps, until modern times by the Americans.

He exploited the copper mines of the Sinai. Also fabled gold and diamond mines, whose location has not yet been established. Through the ports of Tyre and Aquaba in the Sinai he conducted a prosperous international trade including luxury items like ivory, apes and peacocks. Wealth poured into Israel. And Solomon lived accordingly. His stable of horses was famed. Also his harem of 700 wives and 300 concubines (doubtless exaggerated). He used marriage to forge alliances. A daughter of the Pharoah became his wife—

there were other intermarriages with royal houses. Also a romantic liaison with the queen of Sheba, the issue of which formed the geneological lineage of the Ethiopian kings down to Haile Selassie of modern times.

When Solomon decided to upgrade Jerusalem commensurate with its new wealth he found the Israelites did not possess the architectural and building skills to erect a temple and palace. He was forced to seek technical assistance from the Phoenicians. He levied a corvee of 150,000 men. Construction continued for 20 years. Heavy taxes were imposed on citizens and subject peoples alike to finance the building.

The Israelite kings were vicious, selfish and avaricious men in tune with the temper of the times. Saul tried to kill David when he became a popular hero. David found sanctuary with the Philistines. David took Bathsheba into his harem and sent her husband and his friend Uriah deliberately into battle to get him killed. Solomon assassinated all possible pretenders and obstacles to the throne. All of this was apparently condoned by Yahweh, the god of the Israelis, for Yahweh was still a war god.

Solomon's rule begot a gross maldistribution of wealth. After the construction boom subsided the laborers, who were drawn off the land into the cities, were unemployed and they formed an angry proletariat. Economic hardship and social disorder prevailed. To add to Israel's woe Sheshonk, the Libiyn Pharoah of Egypt, made a devastating raid on Jerusalem (circa 926 B. C.) and made off with all the gold stored by Solomon in the Temple.

This brought forth a succession of religious social reformers known as the Prophets who transformed Yahweh from a god or war to a god of compassion and love. There was Amos, Hosea, Isaiah, Jeremiah, Ezekial, the Unknown Prophet and others who left their imprint on the Bible. They railed against the ruling elite, pilloried them for their selfishness and greed while the majority of people lived in hunger and misery. They predicted disaster and punishment for the people of Israel for their sins. And it came.

After Solomon's death the Israelites split into two kingdoms, the kingdom of Israel (or Ephraim) in the north with Samaria as its capital and the kingdom of Judah in the south with its capital at Jerusalem. For two centuries they existed side by side as unhappy and unprosperous states. The Assyrians conquered Israel circa 721 B. C. and deported 200,000 into slavery. Judah suffered similar fate circa 597 B. C., at the hands of the Chaldeans who removed most of its population into captivity to Babylon. The kingdom of the Israelites was deflowered. All that remained were the peasants on the land who were made to pay tribute to the Assyrians and Chaldeans. When they were finally freed from captivity by Cyrus, the Persian, in 538 B. C., the Israelites filtered back to Jerusalem—many chose not to return—and under Persian rule restored the Temple and resuscitated a Jewish state that was only a modest replica of its former self. As before the Israelites found themselves unwelcome for other Semites had settled in

Canaan and without Persian help might not have reestablished themselves in the Promised Land.

In all this suffering and adversity Judaism became a monotheistic religion. Its evolution is difficult to trace for the Semites were generally politheistic. The first idea of a unitary, exclusive and universal God was the Pharoah Akhenaton's Aton, which was the Sun. In many ways one cannot be but impressed with Akhenaton's idea, for the sun is the genesis—origin and continuance—of all life on earth. There is a theory that Akhenaton's religious ideas influenced Moses. At any rate, until the advent of Moses the god of the Patriarchs was a personal god and they worshipped in addition other gods. There is the incident related in the Bible when Rachel makes off surreptitiously with Laban's idols and Laban accuses Jacob of stealing "his gods". Also the Golden Calf incident in Exodus, which was doubtless an Egyptian carryover for while in Egypt the Israelites emulated the worship of parts of the Egyptian pantheon particularly the Bull. In fact, the Israelite god did not even have a name, until Moses asked him what name he is to give the Israelites. God replied to Moses, tell them "I am," which then became Yahweh. Some historians however, think Yahweh was an adaptation of Yahu a god worshipped by other Semites in Canaan.

At any rate, Yahweh was not an exclusive or universal god at first. Even the First Commandment only proscribes that "You shall have no other god *before* me." Other gods and idols continued to be worshipped. Micah, the wealthy Israelite of the tribe of Ephraim had two idols made of silver and a shrine for them with a priest to officiate. Solomon allowed his foreign wives to worship their gods and even constructed shrines for them in Jerusalem, without a twinge of conscience, as a small price to pay for their love. Yahweh was, however, the main god but, at this time, an exclusively tribal and national god of the Israelites preoccupied mainly with their aggressive efforts to capture the Promised Land. He castigates them constantly for their sins. He was unforgiving at this time. Yet he tolerated the grossest injustice. He blinked David's possession of Bathsheba through seduction and murder (violation of two commandments) though Nathan, the priest, was displeased initially. He rewarded Solomon, who murdered his way to the throne, with infinite wisdom.

The Prophets, however, remade Yahweh during the Israelite's centuries of adversities. Yahweh became a god of the dispossessed and the humble, full of compassion and love. The Prophets railed against the greed of the rich, their violence and licientiousness, the worship of Baal and other gods by the people. During the reign of king Josiah, Jeremiah's exhortations inspired him to undertake a religious reform to propitiate Yahweh and invoke his protection against the Assyrians. The Bible was revised and updated. In timely fashion the priest Hilkiah discovered some documents purporting to be the "Book of the Covenant" written by Moses. In fact, the

Israelites appear to have forgotten about Moses by this time—Amos and Isaiah never mention him—and the Ten Commandments.

Isaiah promised the Israelites a redeemer, a messiah, who would restore them to unity, prosperity and peace. Centuries later Jesus Christ, following in the footsteps of the Prophets, spoke of Yahweh as a compassionate and peaceful god for all mankind who would redeem the dispossessed. Christ was accepted, not by the Israelites, but by the Indo-Europeans who built a new civilization upon Christ's teachings. Another Semitic tribe, issuing once again out of Arabia, the Arabs took the god of the Israelites and remade him into a god of their own.

There is great poignancy in this bit of history. The Israelites started no different from other peoples of the time. They were cruel, greedy and immune to human suffering motivated only by the dominance instinct. But due to centuries of suffering and humiliation they evolved a religio-philosophy that favored the deprived. Christ preached that the meek would inherit the world. The meek will probably never inherit the world but at least they now had a philosophy that recognized their existence. Western liberalism has been predicated upon this religious philosophy. And the liberalism of Western civilization that speaks for the dominated majority has been a shining light in the history of man.

Meanwhile two other powers developed at the other end of the Fertile Crescent, the Assyrians who were a racial mix, and the Chaldeans who were Semites. The Assyrians date back to the beginning of the third millennium B. C. but they remained an obscure kingdom dominated by others until the early part of the first millennium. Situated on the tributaries of the Tigris river in the foothills of the Zagros mountains they flourished on the fringes of the Sumerian and Babylonian civilizations with their capital at Ashur.

In the second millennium something not yet fully understood happened in the lower doab that made it less attractive to immigrants. The Semites of Arabia began moving into the western end of the Fertile Crescent, which was now the "land of milk and honey." And the Sumerians and Akkadians moved northward into the upper part of Mesopotamia where Ashur was located. A possible explanation is that centuries of river irrigation in the lower doab without proper drainage caused the soil to become salty and infertile. This phenomena is well known to modern agriculturalists and river irrigation projects today are structured to avoid salinity of the irrigated area. The less productive soils of upper Mesopotamia and the Jordan valley dependent on rainfall not irrigation would have escaped similar ruination. Egypt, too, avoided salinity as the Nile valley was inundated annually with fresh water to wash away the salt deposits.

The Assyrians, however, remained hemmed in by the visissitudes of history. During the second millennium Western Asia was the imperialistic playground of the Egyptians and the Hittites blocking the Assyrians from access to the Mediterranean. Two Indo-European peoples, the Hurrians and the Kassites kept the Assyrians under domination in Mesopotamia until about 1000 B. C. with their superior technology. As Egyptian and Hittite power receded the Philistines, Phoenicians, Israelites and Arabians established themselves in Palestine and Syria and posed a formidable obstruction against the Assyrians to keep them from breaking through to the Mediterranean. But the Assyrians grew in power. They adopted the horse and chariot from their Hurrian overlords. When the Hittite monopoly on iron was broken the Assyrians took readily to the new technology. Their armies were soon equipped abundantly with iron weapons. Later they used cavalry, a technique they borrowed from the Medes on the other side of the Zagros range. To the horse and chariot and iron weapons they added very effective siege machinery to forge the greatest and fiercest army of antiquity. They first had to secure their rear. During the reigns of Ashurnasirpal II, Shalmaneser II and Adadninari III (circa 885–783 B. C.) they conquered the Kassites in Babylon, pushed the Urartus (proto-Armenians) north and conducted a punitive expedition against Elam in the east. In 732 B. C. Tiglath-Pileser III captured Damascus and broke up the coalition in the coastal area. Thereafter for a century or so the Assyrian armies terrorized Western Asia under the dynasty of Sargon II (722–626 B. C.) which included his equally famous successors Sennacherib, Esarhaddon and Ashurbanipal. A decade after Ashurbanipal's death the empire was in decay and disintegration.

Toward the end of the 7th century the Assyrians swept through Palestine to the borders of Egypt subjecting the Philistines and the Israelites. Samaria fell in 721 B. C. Israel was reinvaded by Sennacherib in 701 B. C. Two hundred thousand Israelites were taken into captivity and dispersed throughout the Assyrian empire as slaves. Ten of the twelve tribes simply disappeared. Judah was spared at this time as the Assyrian army was overtaken with a plague in the Nile delta and was forced to retreat. Sennacherib had also to look to his rear. Babylon was annihilated (once again) for its rebellion. It was left to his son Esarhaddon to capture the Nile delta in 671 B. C. The Assyrians also brought most of Anatolia under its control. In 700 B. C. Sennecherib defeated the Greeks in Cilicia. This area was the source of most of the metals needed for its army. In the 7th century B. C. the Assyrian empire comprised most of Western Asia.

The Assyrians were a vicious and insensitive people. At the height of their power a common scene in Western Asia was long lines of captives with the men in the van, the heads of their kings and princes hanging from their necks as gruesome pendants, followed by the women and children and the animals and booty in the rear. It was part of the policy to remove the ruling elite of a subject peoples, disperse them throughout Western Asia so they could not regroup, and rule the peasants through their own administrators for the tribute they could exact. In fact, Sargon II boasted that, in so doing, he left a better Samaria in being.

Their power was based on plunder and the iron technology of their erstwhile rulers the Hurrians and Hittites. This ill gotten wealth begot a splendid empire. Sennacherib built the famed city of Nineveh as a new capital east of the Tigris (across from modern Mosul). He built, perhaps, the first elevated acqueduct of stone masonry a thousand feet long as part of a thirty mile irrigation system conveying water from the mountains to the Nineveh plain. Illustrious palaces and temples were constructed of stone, an art acquried from the Hittites, in which the arch was predominant. The Assyrians were good sculptors and are now renowned for their bas-reliefs. The Assyrians gods were an odd mixture. Ashur headed the pantheon. Their leading goddess Ishtar was borrowed from Babylon.

The Assyrians added little to the civilization of the Mediterranean area. Their technology was borrowed; their wealth mostly plundered. There were some redeeming features. They introduced cotton from India to Western Asia. Ashurbanipal built a magnificent library of 22,000 tablets at Nineveh, including the *Epic of Gilgamesh*, which has survived for 2500 years (now in the British Museum). Their great impact, however, was the field of political organization of a far flung empire upon which later empires like the Persian and Roman were modeled.

The deadweight of their military establishment was their undoing. To maintain the empire required manpower and wealth. Domestic productivity declined as peasants were recruited for the army. Rebellion of subject people not only required more soldiers but diminished the tribute flowing into Nineveh. Foreign mercenaries were hired eroding the wealth of the nation and the loyalty of the army. The cities were filled with aliens brought there as captives and attracted otherwise who owed no loyalty to the nation. foreign pressures increased.

The end came fast. The Chaldeans captured Babylon in 616 B. C. The Medes from the east took Ashur in 614 B. C. The two joined forces to attack Nineveh. It fell in 612 B. C.! The Assyrian army, however, escaped. The Israelite Prophet Nahum exclaimed with jubliation "Nineveh is laid waste." His rejoicing was premature.

The Chaldeans now assumed dominance of the Fertile Crescent. Nebuchadnezzer, their great emperor, defeated the Assyrian army supported (strangely) by the Egyptians in its hour of doom with finality at Carchimesh in 605 B. C. In 586 B. C. Nebuchadnezzer destroyed Jerusalem and deported the last two tribes of Israel (Judah and Benjamin) into captivity to Babylon. Some 50,000 Israelites were deported.

The Chaldeans had been migrating into the doab from Arabia for centuries. The decline of Assyria provided the opportunity to take over the area. Nebuchadnezzer rebuilt Babylon again into a fabulous city with its famous Hanging Gardens (roof gardens) which the Greeks considered one of the Seven Wonders of the world. He enlarged its environs by building a bridge, perhaps the first of its size, across the Euphrates. This was the Babylon of the Bible.

The development of astronomy was the greatest contribution of the Chaldeans to civilization. Astronomical records had been kept over the centuries in Akkad-Sumeria. From these records the Chaldean astronomers Nabu-rimanni and Kidinnu complied the movements of the moon, earth, planets and sun which were only a second or two off from those prevailing today. The Greeks based their astronomy on these calculations. In most other respects the Chaldeans were uncreative and after Nebuchadnezzer's long reign of 40 years in 538 B. C. succumbed to the domination of the Persians.

THE PERSIANS

A new factor had now entered into the equation of nations that favored the Indo-Europeans. It was the mounted warrior. As already detailed in Chapter IV the peoples of the pasturelands of the north—the Scythians, Sarmatians and others—mastered the art of mounting the horse during the fore part of the first millennium before the Christian era. After a thousand years or more of domestication they had bred and reared a larger animal capable of carrying a man on its back. Riding the horse increased the warriors mobility and efficiency, though not power which had to await the invention of the stirrup a thousand years later. The awesome military prowess of the Assyrians was still based on the horse and chariot for its shock force though they began to rely on cavalry toward the end of their regime. but the Assyrians lacked the big horse of the north which they had to acquire through trade or force from the Medes, for whom, unlike the peoples of the west, they always held the highest respect. Assyrian records refer to them as the "mighty Medes of the East."

The Medes, as well as the Persians, were part of the eastern sector of the Indo-European family. They began filtering from the Caspian-Aral seas area into the Zagros mountains and the adjoining Iranian plateau, perhaps, as early as 2000 B. C. Here like their brethern, the Hurrians, Urartus, Cimmerians and others they found good pastures, including alfalfa, for their horses. They were a rough people, with no script and a nomadic way of life. By Assyrian times they were quite powerful and, as we saw, defeated the Assyrians at Ashur and Nineveh during the latter part of the 7th century. The Medes made their capital at Ecbatana on the Hamadan plain to the east of the Zagros range.

After the demise of Assyria the Medes and Chaldeans formed a loose alliance with Nebuchadnezzer inheriting the southern portion of the Assyrian empire and the Medes the upper portion. The Chaldeans were in constant fear of the more powerful Medes. They cemented the friendship with the marriage of an Median princess by Nebuchadnezzer for whom he built the famous Hanging Gardens in Babylon to assuage her pining for her verdant homeland in the hills. The Median king Cyaxares promptly marched into Anatolia to claim his domain where he encountered the indomitable Lydians (also mounted) who defeated him six times in his efforts to reach the Mediterranean. An uneasy truce was struck with the Halys river as the demarcation line.

To the south of the Medes were the Persians, who settled on the less desirable land of the erstwhile Elamites that were destroyed about 640 B. C. by Ashurnasirpal. They were, at first, subjects of the Medes. In 559 B. C. Cyrus II who's heritage is subject to much romantic speculation but need not detain us here, ascended the Persian throne. Cyrus is another outstanding king in history. The Medes had now, after several decades of peace, prospered greatly and quickly assumed a life of ease. Their king Astyages made himself unapproachable and unliked, so when he marshaled his army against this upstart (allegedly his grandson) to the south, the army mutinied and defected to Cyrus. The tables were turned. Cyrus now ruled the Median-Persian empire, adding to his army the capable Median soldiers. The Medes and Persians melded into one people and to the outside world nothing had really changed except the ruler. Cyrus immediately clashed with Lydia ruled at this time by the legendary Croesus. As will be recalled Croesus, who dominated the Greeks of Ionia, consulted the oracle at Delphi before launching his attack on the Persians. The oracle replied that if he crossed the Halys "He will destroy a great empire." Failing to note the double meaning of the oracle he attacked the Persians with purblind confidence in 547 B. C. and lost his crown.

Both sides had cavalry so, with technology equated, superior generalship came to the fore. Cyrus knew horses instinctively feared camels so he placed his camel corps, with which his horses had grown familiar, in the van. The Lydian horses reared out of control when they caught the odor of the camels giving the Persian army the necessary advantage for victory. Cyrus proposed to burn Croesus on a pyre. According to Herodotus, Croesus, in his predicament, began mumbling about the futility of life recalling a philosophical discussion he had years earlier with Solon, the Greek lawgiver, to that effect. Cyrus was impressed by these philosophical moanings reflecting that the same fate could befall him someday. Croesus then called out to Apollo to save him from his plight, whereupon a sudden rain storm developed and quenched the fire. Cyrus, with respect increasing, freed Croesus and made him a trusted counselor. Anatolia was now subjected.

Cyrus next turned his attention to Mesopotamia which was to be the bread basket of his empire. He defeated the Chaldean army in 538 B. C. and entered Babylon as a welcomed conqueror. Navonidus, the Chaldean ruler, had lost the loyalty of his people, largely, through his religious deviations detracting from the worship of Marduk. Cyrus wisely, restored Marduk and even claimed the Babylonian god selected him to be their king. Cyrus disturbed nothing, forbade any looting by his troops but installed his own administration.

The Jews welcomed him as their savior—as the Unknown Prophet had predicted. Cyrus not only gave them freedom to return to Palestine but also financial assistance to rebuild Jerusalem and their temple. Without Persian help the small minority would have been unable to reclaim their former land, as it was now settled by other hostile Semites.

During captivity in Babylon the remnant of the Israelites developed the worship of a single universal god—a compassionate god of the dispossessed—which was thereafter known as Judaism. Their new state was called the Kingdom of Judea. Cyrus had by his policy of religious tolerance effected significantly the future of history in the Mediterranean world. Judaism not only survived but apparented Chrisitanity and Mohammedanism two powerful religious forces that effected the Mediterranean civilization down to modern times.

Persian religious thought too had a profound impact upon the Judeo religions. The concepts of good versus evil, the final judgement with its reward or punishment in heaven, purgatory and hell and the invention of the Devil all derive from Zoroasterism. Sometime in the 6th century B. C. there was born among the Medes a prophet of monumental dimensions. He was Zarathustra, whom the Greeks rechristened Zoroaster. Zarathustra preached an almost pure monotheism, the worship of a supreme being called Ahura-Mazda who created the universe and everything in it. He was opposed by Ahriman (the devil) who ruled the netherworld. Mazda created the forces of good and evil—the truth and the lie—and everyone was given the free will to choose between them. Every person faced a final judgement by Mazda as to whether he lived a life of good or evil. If the former his eternal life would be blissful; if the latter torment and damnation; if somewhere in between he was required to serve 12,000 years in purgatory before being admitted to heaven.

Like most prophets Zarathustra was rejected by his own people, the Medes, but was accepted by the Persians. The Persians corrupted his teachings substantially to accomodate traditional beliefs but the fundamental principles of Zarathustra survived and Zoroasterism became the religion of Persia for a thousand years. It was eclipsed for a time by the Greeks. The Muslim conquest of Persia in the 8th century A. D. virtually extinguished it. It survives today only among a small group of Iranians in southwest Iran and with the Parsees of Bombay, a contingent of Persians who emigrated to India to avoid focible conversion to Mohammedanism during the 8th century A. D. They comprise today only about 100,000 of the vast population of India albeit that their prominance on the Indian scene far exceeds their number.

Persian religious tolerance generated a relatively happy empire. The Phoenicians and Arameans were delighted with the trade and commercial prosperity that ensued under Persian peace. Since the Persians had no script of their own they continued the use of Aramaic for business purposes. In due time they borrowed the alphabet to develop a script for the Persian language. Commerce and business were largely in the hands of the Semites, including the Jews. The Persians chose the role of warriors and administrators.

The Persians were masters of organization. Cambyses II succeeded Cyrus and extended the empire into Egypt in 525 B. C. But he was unpopular and survived only eight years. He was succeeded by Darius, a distant cousin, after some still unclear court intrigue involving the murder of Cambyses's brother Smerdis and the ousting, by Darius, of a Magi priest who usurped the throne while Cambyses was in Egypt. Darius, while justifying his legitimacy, extended the empire from Egypt and Anatolia in the west to the Indus river in India. It was the biggest empire known to man at this time.

The ruling elite consisted of the Seven Families which derived from the men who murdered the usurper and assisted Darius to the throne. From their ranks were drawn not only the satraps who governed the provinces, but the administrative and military officials of the central government. There may have been a hundred satrapies (the Book of Esther states there were 127) although only 20 major ones are generally enumerated. The empire was governed by strict laws and regulations, the "Laws of the Medes and the Persians" referred to in the Bible. Complete and accurate fiscal records were kept of the revenues and tribute collected and expended. This fostered a large bureaucracy of judges and scribes. The scribes had to be erudite in four languages—Persian, Aramaic, Babylonian and Elamite. A very effective communications system was established to knit this vast empire together by a system of roads and couriers riding horses in relays—a sort of pony express—to speed messages between the capital and provinces. It took only 7 days to send an order from Susa to Sardis (in Anatolia) a span of 1600 miles. Caravans took 90 days to cover the same distance. Light signals blinked in a visual code from hilltop fire towers supplemented the courier system to cope with emergencies such as local uprisings.

Though an inland empire, Darius was mindful of the need for sea power and for water transportation. For this he employed the willing Phoenicians and even the reluctant Greeks who were the foremost seafarers of the day. He constructed a canal to connect the Red Sea with the Mediterranean through the Nile delta. One Scylax undertook a voyage, under Darius's sponsorship, down the Indus river across the Indian Ocean and Red Sea to Suez to chart a water connection with India. Persian army engineers were masters at the art of crossing rivers on pontoon bridges constructed on boats tied side to side.

Beneath the ruling elite were the cultivators, artisans, smiths and others who produced the wealth of the empire. Commerce and finance was the preserve of the Semites centered in Babylon. Some of them like Egibi and

Sons, a Babylon banking family, grew extremely wealthy managing large estates, operating slave farms and other enterprises.

Much of the wealth appropriated by the rulers was spent on magnificent palaces and royal buildings. Babylon, which was the financial and commercial capital, was rebuilt by Cyrus. His son Cambyses used it as his political capital. Darius however, settled on four capitals in Iran. Ecbatana was continued as a summer capital. The old Persian capital at Pasagadae was retained as the coronation city. Darius established his administrative capital at Susa, the capital of the Elamites. But the temperature reached 130° in summer so he built a new capital in the mountains at Parsa (called Persepolis by the Greeks). Its ruins attest to its grandeur and splendor. The court moved in great caravans between these capitals in accordance with the seasons.

The Persian army was the strength and undoing of the empire. Every Mede and Persian male had to be prepared to serve between the age of 15 and 50 years. The Persian cavalry was the heart of the army. But as the empire grew each subject nation was required to furnish a levy. The soldiers and their equipment consequently varied widely. It became difficult to maintain an effective command. Moreover, the Persian soldier required the utmost comfort during the campaigns so that a fantastic retinue of camp followers—heralds, scribes, eunuchs, concubines and prostitutes—encumbered the army. This cumbersome army proved a failure in Xerxes' invasion of Greece in 480 B. C.

The Persians, outside the mounted warrior, added little to arts and crafts. They did excel in architecture as is seen from their ruins, but no new forms were evolved. Agriculture and industry were left to the subject peoples. The Persians did not interfere as long as the revenues and tribute were forthcoming. This left the peasant and artisan at the mercy of the landlord, banker and tradesmen. Large Babylonian banking firms like Murashu Bank, Egibi and Sons and others became economic empires owning and managing large tracts of land in the doab.

The result was a gross maldistribution of wealth. The Persians exacted heavy tribute and taxes and lived in utmost luxury. In fact, they were unable to spend their revenues and hoarded the balances in their treasuries at Persepolis, Susa and elsewhere. When Alexander sacked Persepolis he found three billion dollars of gold and silver in the treasury. The bankers extended credit to the agriculturists and industrialists to defray their taxes and in the process acquired more of their property. Prices of food and essentials kept rising constantly. An insidious inflation pervaded the economy.

THE GREEKS

Meanwhile another power center was developing across the Bosphorous in the eastern Mediterranean. It was the Greek civilization. The Greeks were part of the western branch of the Indo-Europeans, who emigrated initially into Europe during the first migratory wave the early part of the second millennium B. C. They are known as Mycenaeans (Acheans in the Iliad). Prior thereto the Peloponnesus was occupied by peoples of unknown origin referred to as the early Helladic culture.

For a long time the Acheans were considered legendary figures but the indomitable Heinrich Schliemann, the verifier of the Trojan War, refused to accept the conclusion and in 1876 found the ruins of Mycenae, the kingdom of Agamemnon who led the attack on Troy. The reality of the Mycenaean civilization began to emerge.

The *Iliad* was now taken as serious history. Like the Bible it too has to be interpreted substantively not literally, for by the time Homer reduced it to literature the story had been passed down orally for 500 years!

Earlier a scintillating civilization developed on Crete and in the Cyclades. Its origin is even more obscure and believed to have started as far back as the 5th millennium B. C. The people probably emanated from Anatolia and may have been of the same stock as those inhabiting Catal Huyuk. Their agriculture and crafts were highly developed. Commerce with the Egyptian civilization is evident. This Minoan civilization was extremely attractive to the Mycenaeans and they came to dominate it around the middle of the 2nd millennium. Noteworthy in this connection is the Island of Thera in the Cyclades which was destroyed by a tremendous earthquake and tidal wave somewhere about 1500 B. C. that submerged most of the island and gave rise to the legend of the lost Atlantis. Archeological discoveries relate its culture to that of the Minoan civilization.

The Mycenaean civilization is difficult to fathom. There is evidence of considerable wealth, but whether it was produced, pillaged or wrested by trade is unclear. The Mycenaean tombs yielded much gold and valuable artifacts. The records (in the so-called Linear B script scholars have only recently deciphered) bespeak a complex society of peasants and artisans ruled by kings and nobles scattered among the vales between the mountains and hills, mostly in the Peloponnesus. Foremost among them was Mycenae commanding the rich Argive plain. Minoan *cum* Egyptian influence is evident. In the 14th century B. C. the Mycenaneans extended their domination over Crete and, it would appear, a Mycenaean civilization now dominated the Aegean sea including the coast of Anatolia. There are respectful references to the "King of Ahhiyawa" in Hittite records. Ahhiyawa is being interpreted as colonies or outposts of the Acheans in Anatolia (perhaps Rhodes). The Mycenaeans, like their Indo-European cousins, the Hittites, too were masters of the horse and chariot (they even shipped them to Troy for the attack as related in the Iliad) but it is not clear whether they knew iron technology for, at this time, the Hittites exercised a monopoly over the production of iron.

As already mentioned, by the end of the 12th century the Mycenaean civilization vanished. Scholars contend over the causes and there is some indication of both internal decay and disarray and external invasion. It was probably a combination of the two. The Iliad alludes to the rivalries of the Achean kings. Upon their return from Troy some of the kings found their castles destroyed or usurpers on the throne. The epic *Seven against Thebes* attests to internecine warfare. The classical Greeks held the belief, as expounded by Thucydides, that a new wave of "backward Greeks", the Dorians, overwhelmed the Mycenaeans and took over the western portion of the peninsula. Presumably the Dorians came down the valley east of the Pindus range and crossed the Corinthian Isthmus into the Peloponnesus. This would accord with the Doric-Ionic cleavage of ancient Greece. But whether the Dorians overwhelmed the Mycenaeans or simply filled a vacuum left by the decay of the Mycenaean civilization will probably never be clearly known. Also these invasions or incursions may have lasted decades if not centuries.

The Dorians were, doubtless, culturally backward but they may have possessed technological superiority for there is evidence they knew iron technology. They may have already pounced upon the Mycenaeans with the shorter striking iron sword that was to become during the next thousand years or more the major weapon of the Graeco-Roman civilization. This would be in accord with the history of iron technology. As will be recalled iron smelting was developed in northeast Anatolia by the Chalybes and guarded as a monopoly by the Hittites until their destruction around 1200 B. C. Thereafter it spread rapidly around the Near East. The Phoenicians and Philistines had the technology in the 11th century, the Assyrians shortly thereafter. It must also have spread into Europe. Hallstatt (Austria) became a famous iron making center early in the first millennium. Just how soon the technology reached the Danubian area is not known but it could have been as early as the 11th century. A puzzle of archeology is that there is little or no physical evidence of iron smelting anywhere, including Anatolia, prior to 1000 B. C.

At any rate, the Greeks now entered upon a Dark Age that lasted 450 years. Life was primarily agricultural. But the Greek terrain, unlike the Nile valley and Mesopotamia, was poor farming land. Hesiod in his *Works and Days* leaves an account of the harsh life of the Greek farmer around 700 B. C. The numerous plains and vales nestled among the mountains of the rugged peninsula developed their own capitals where the landed aristocracy resided. They became the well known city-states of ancient Greece. Athens, which managed to escape the Dorian holocaust with its stronghold on the Acropolis including an enclosed water well, preserved most of the Mycenaean culture and became the leader of the Ionian east. Sparta, with its strong Dorian influence superimposed upon the Mycenaean, became the leader of the Doric west.

Around 750 B. C. the Greeks emerged from their agricultural shell and launched a vigorous colonization effort around the Mediterranean. The primary motivation was population pressure on the limited arable land. Greek colonies were established in southern Italy, Sicily, southern Gaul, eastern Iberia, Cyrenaica (Lybia), Ionia (Anatolian coast) and the Black Sea. The western colonies were predominantly Doric while those in the east Ionic. Sea-faring revived and Greek trade began to prosper. The Greek colonies produced many raw materials (for instance tin for bronze) and, most important, grain which they were eager to trade for the wares of the motherland. Greece possessed another advantage. Though its land was limited for foodgrains its hillsides were good places to grow the olive and the grape. Olive oil and wine became two of its earliest major exports. Gradually trade led to manufacture of pottery, metal and other artifacts in demand around the Mediterranean. The beautiful vessels in which the wine and olive oil were shipped became more desirable than their contents by the colonials. Artisans, smiths and other craftsmen soon began to populate the cities.

The greatest boost, perhaps, to its wealth was the discovery of a lode of silver at Laurium in Attica about mid-millennium. A rich vein was struck in 483 B. C. Athens was the primary beneficiary. It catapulted Athens to the fore among the Greek cities. Themistocles wisely used the silver to build a formidable navy that was to win the war against the Persians.

Silver facilitated trade which begot additional wealth for the Greeks. Money, which has and still creates so much grief for mankind, was by this time well developed. Though invented by the Lydians, it was the Greeks, who realized its potential. The Persians seemed not to understand money as they hoarded most of their precious metals and much of their trade continued on the barter basis. The Athenian *owl* which they kept faithfully pure for years, became the leading foreign exchange of Mediterranean trade.

Adoption and adaptation of the Phoenician alphabet around 800 B. C. greatly facilitated trade. It was far more facile for the Greek language than the Linear B script of the Mycenaeans. Shortly after its adoption from the Phoenicians for commercial purposes it became the vehicle for Greek thought, poetry and prose that has distinguished the Greek civilization in history. The great epics the *Iliad* and the *Odyssey* were reduced to writing by Homer around 800 B. C.

The landed aristocracy that dominated the Dark Age was now at bay. Population pressure on limited land and the growth of a merchant *cum* artisan class in the cities created socio-economic disarray. The old kings and oligarchies were challenged. Tyrants (a term that has since become odious) led rebellions of the dispossessed against the ruling elite. The insidious effect of money aggravated the situation. The landowners lent money at high interest rates to the peasants with land as security which they acquired when the debt became unrepayable. Despite the colonies that the aristrocracy thought would provide an alternative for the dispossessed (and it certainly did) the struggle over the distribution of wealth became acute.

The most renowned tyrant (perhaps he should not be so labeled) during the period of revolution (circa 660–500 B. C.) was Solon of Athens. His rise to power in 594 B. C. was peaceful as the aristocracy acquiesced in his absolute power with the end in view that his reforms would avoid violence. Solon cancelled all debts, proscribed enslavement for non-payment, forbade the export of wheat (Athens could no longer afford to do so with its burgeoning population) and stimulated instead the cultivation of the olive and the grape for the export of oil and wine. In addition he introduced a limited democracy with his reform of the constitution. All free men were admitted to the assembly though the Archons (elected officials) had still to belong to the equestrian (propertied) class. Civil strife, however, continued and in 546 B. C. another tyrant, Pisistratus, assumed power. He ruled within the Solon constitution through manipulation of the elections. Pisistratus improved the lot of the peasant by state loans on easy terms and secured a reliable source of grain from the Pontus (Black Sea area). Cleisthenes (an aristocrat turned merchant) assumed power in 510 B. C. and broadened the electorate permitting more of the liberal elements of the population to participate in the elections.

Similar trends toward democracy, particularly in the east, were transpiring in many other cities. In Sparta, however, the trend was toward a hardening of the monarchy. This was due, in large part, to its peculiar system of land tenure. When the Dorians superimposed themselves upon the indigenous population in large parts of the Peloponnesus they reduced them to serfs—called helots. These formerly free peasants obviously chafed under such tenure. It required repressive rule from the top. Sparta became an autocratic closed society eschewing outside influence, particularly the democratic ideas of the East. For instance the Spartans even refused to adopt silver coinage continuing to use, instead, the old iron spits as a medium of exchange. Young boys were removed from their families and trained for war and administration. Sparta had the only professional army among the Greeks which was to serve them well against the Persians. Luxurious living was shunned for the "spartan" life of austerity and discipline.

These two ways of life were hostile to each other. Sparta even tried without success to subject Athens in 506 B. C. The only thing that held the two types of Greeks together was a common enemy. And the common enemy was the Persians.

The two Mediterranean powers, like the Egyptians and Hittites years earlier, were now on a collision course. The Greeks of Ionia chafed under Persian rule and were in a constant state of insubordination. In 499 B. C. the Greeks in Ionia and Cyprus rebelled against their Persian satraps. Athens sent help but Sparta refused. The Athenians penetrated inland and raided

Sardis. This provoked Darius to send a punitive expedition across the Aegean of 600 ships and 20,000 men. The Athenians under the capable leadership of Miltiades defeated the Persians at Marathon in 490 B. C.

A decade of respite was granted the Greeks. Egypt rebelled which preoccupied the Persians. Darius died in 486 B. C. This deterred Darius's successor Xerxes for a time, but he never forgot the Persian grievance against the Athenians. Themistocles, who was involved in the battle of Marathon achieved leadership in Athens and put the interval to good advantage by broadening the democracy and, more to the point, building a great navy. In 480 B. C. Xerxes marched across the Hellspont against the Greeks. His defeat has already been detailed in Chapter IX.

Ancient Greece was now at the height of its power. But peace merely permitted the Greeks to indulge in their internecine rivalries. Sparta achieved heroic status with its defeat of Mardonius and the Ten Thousand, the Persian army left behind by Xerxes to resume the attack in 479 B. C., but was unable to take advantage of its supremacy because of unrest in the Peloponnesus. Athens waltzed into the breach by organizing the Delian League (478–477 B. C.) an alliance of the Greek cities (some 250 of them) against the Persians which it gradually subverted into an Athenian empire in the eastern Mediterranean. Its rule became arrogant and ruthless until it suffered a disastrous defeat when it overextended its power in Egypt in support of a rebellion against the Persians. Boeotia broke away. After a decade of aggression Athens settled down to mind its domestic affairs.

There followed a generation of sparkling development in the arts, architecture, philosophy, history, medicine, science and other intellectual accomplishment that has forever stamped upon history the glory of classical Greece. It was the golden age, the age of Pericles, who assumed leadership of Athens by 443 B. C. the Parthenon was begun in 447 B. C. and completed in 432 B. C. Ictinus, Callicrates and Phidias were the architects and sculptors of the great monument. Aeschylus, Euripides and Sophocles composed illustrious plays. Socrates and Plato philosophized. Herodotus and Thucydides wrote history. Hippocrates of Cos practiced advanced medicine. Leucippus and Domocritus postulated the atomic theory of matter. Many more men of learning and wisdom too numerous to detail came to Athens at this time for it had become the intellectual center of the Greek world.

Democracy was fully established in Athens. The Assembly was supreme. Every man, except slaves and metics (aliens) could vote, be heard and accept office. But all offices were short termed, except the generals who could be reelected annually. Pericles was a general. Flushed with success the Athenian became prideful and insufferable to other Greeks. The autocratic ruled cities like Sparta resented the insouciant liberalism of the Athenian.

In 431 B. C. war broke out between the Spartans and Athenians and their respective allies. It was a stupid war fought over petty and irrelevant issues as is usually the case in fratricidal warfare. Great destruction was inflicted upon the economy. The Spartans cut down all the olive trees in Attica while the Athenians were beseiged within their city walls. It takes an olive tree 30 years to reach full productivity! The war spread to Sicily involving the respective colonies of the two factions. It lasted 27 years with one year of peace or truce. Thucydides, who participated in and observed the struggle, leaves us a good account in *The Peloponnesian War*. In the end Athens was humiliated in defeat. Pride preceded the fall—in accordance with the ancient wisdom of the Greeks!

Sparta proved an inept master of the Greek world. Its autocratic rule was obnoxious to the Greek cities in the east. Around 370 B. C. Athens was able to restore much of its democracy and some of its former intellectual brilliance with Aristotle, Aristophanes and others. The tyrant Dionysius of Syracuse, the victor in the Sicilian phase of the Peloponnesian War, was able to exert great power and influence on mainland Greece during this time. The Greeks were unable, however, to restore their eminence of the 4th century B. C.

Athens and other Greek cities reached that state of socio-economic decadence that bedevils most societies prior to their decline and fall. There was gross maldistribution of wealth. Land became concentrated in large estates worked inefficiently by slaves, accumulated in wars, who dispossessed the free peasant. In the cities too, slave labor predominated. The free Greek could find no employment. A census taken by Demetrius about 310 B. C. sets forth the population of Athens as comprising 400,000 slaves, 10,000 metics and 21,000 citizens. There is doubt whether the slave population could have been that high but that it was high is not in doubt.

Inflation seized the economy. This is always the case when a society tries to consume more than it produces. There was a 400% rise in prices between 480–330 B. C. Interest rates rose commensurately. Mortgage loans called for 16–18% interest. Commercial loans 18%.

Banking and speculation were rife. The two marched hand in hand. The manipulation of money was largely in the hands of the metics. Pasion and Phormio, former slaves from the East, became fabulously rich as Athenian bankers (the Rothschilds of the Greek world).

Class struggle was everywhere. Sporadic revolutions erupted. The common man felt no loyalty to his society. Nor quite obviously did the slave. The metics were there merely to make money. Rich men provided entertainment through games and even fed the proletariat in the hope of restricting their hatred and violence.

The rich veins of silver at Larium were depleted. The gold mines of Thrace were in Macedonian hands. Athens no longer could afford to maintain a navy to protect her merchantmen. Piracy was again rampant in the Mediterranean. Profits from trade diminished. Athens no longer had the loyalty of the people to field an army as it did at Marathon two centuries earlier.

Meanwhile a new power was aborning in Macedonia, the hinterland of the Greek world. Philip II, of Greek descent and considerable intellect and great capacity for leadership, ascended the throne. His vision was broad with the end in view of uniting the warring Greek cities into an empire. He developed his famous phalanx—a massed formation of infantry 16 ranks deep with 14 foot spears—to move like a juggernaut against and through the enemy ranks. Equally important was his cavalry, which derived from the propinquity of the Macedonians to the mounted nomads of the steppes of southeastern Europe. He financed his military ventures by exploiting the gold mines of Thrace that yielded him some $8 million annually. Through aggression and diplomacy, including marriage alliances, Philip united most of the cities in the north. By 352 B. C. he reached Thermopylae and prepared to march on Delphi. Athens remained undecided to take the field against him. Isocrates felt Persia was still the main threat and favored a common course with Philip for an offensive in Asia. But he was thwarted by the fiery oratory of Demosthenes who prevailed on Athens to join Thebes to resist Philip. Philip defeated them in 338 B. C. in Boeotia. While he punished Thebes severely he refrained from sacking Athens whose intellectual brilliance he greatly admired. Moreover Athens was now isolated and harmless to his purpose.

Philip had grander visions in mind. It was the conquest of Persia whose wealth would enable him to build the greatest empire in the Mediterranean area. Unfortunately he was murdered (by Olympias his queen, it was rumored though not proven, out of jealousy over a younger wife Philip had taken) in 336 B. C. He was succeeded by his 20 year old son Alexander, tutored by Aristotle since he was six, who was to realize his father's dream.

Taking a year or two to consolidate his rule over the Greeks, which included the sacking of the city of Thebes for its rebellion and an unusual meeting with the blond Celts across the Danube, Alexander crossed into Asia in 334 B. C. He had in reality an extremely small army of 35,000 men for so ambitious a venture consisting of a very effective cavalry of 5000 horse and the famous Macedonian phalanx. Alexander knew he had to have heavy cavalry to equate the Persian horsemen.

He quickly liberated his fellow Greeks in Ionia, defeated Darius III at Issus in Syria in 333 B. C. and then besieged the Phoenician city of Tyre for a year concluding rightfully that it was necessary to destroy the Phoenician fleet to protect his rear in the Aegean. Alexander had no navy, a serious weakness in his assault. He refrained from making a levy for ships on the maritime cities like Athens and Corinth. Why he did so is not clear. Perhaps he felt he could subdue the Phoenicians, who furnished and manned the navy for the Persians, by land. The Phoenicians, however, defended themselves stubbornly on their stoutly walled island a thousand yards or so off the mainland. By building a causeway and eventually securing ships from the Ionian Greeks Alexander captured Tyre in August 332 B. C.

The way was now clear to Egypt. The Philistines offered resistance at Gaza and were destroyed mercilessly by Alexander. Jerusalem surrendered without a fight. So did the Egyptians who crowned him Pharoah after Alexander duly related himself to their god Amon. This set the foundation for the Ptolemic dynasty. He immediately conceived plans for the city of Alexandria at the mouth of the Nile, which was for centuries thereafter to be the center of learning in the Mediterranean area.

From Egypt Alexander swept back into western Asia through Syria to find and destroy the Persian army. They met at Gaugamela, east of the Tigris, in 331 B. C. where Darius had regrouped his polyglot army 600,000 strong, consisting only in small part of Persians and Medes. Nonetheless Alexander quaked before the mighty hosts of Darius and had to be fortified in his resolve by his courageous fellow Macedonians. But by adroit use of his phalanxes and cavalry playing the two together like a fine instrument, he soon put the Persian army to rout. Darius was something of a coward and when he fled in mid-battle his Persian horsemen followed suit. The foreign levies, of course, were glad for the opportunity to give up the fight.

The Persia of Darius III was not the Persia of Darius I two hundred years earlier. The empire was in a high state of socio-economic disintegration. The productivity of the people was drained off by high taxes and tribute. Inflation gripped the economy. Financial hardship was widespread. The loyalties of the subject people was frayed. The royal house, due to no law or tradition of orderly succession, was beset by regicide. After Xerxes' rebuff in his attempt to extend the Persian empire into Europe there was a succession of Artaxerxeses and Dariuses, usually through murder at the top which had to include children who might later challenge the succession, until the crown devolved on Darius III. He was an ineffectual monarch. Twice he deserted his army before Alexander. A Persian noble Bessus assassinated him in 330 B. C. at Hecatompylos after the second retreat from Gaugamela.

The four capitals were forthwith open to Alexander and he sacked their treasuries seriatim. Billions of dollars worth of gold and silver, exacted over the centuries by the Persians from the subject peoples, were purloined by the Macedonians. Alexander rewarded and spent lavishly. In fact, he found it difficult to mobilize the large ass and camel train required to carry off the treasure. Alexander burned Persepolis, but why he did so is not clear. He was incensed against the Persians by the sight of many fellow Greeks he encountered en route to the capital who were deliberately maimed and crippled by them earlier. It is also said he did it at the instigation of a courtesan at the court in a fit of drunken orgy. He may also have intended to do so as a symbolic act of the ultimate triumph of the Greeks over their centuries old enemy.

Alexander was possessed by an uneven and erratic personality. He was capable of the highest compassion and the utmost cruelty. When Darius abandoned his family in his cowardly retreat from Issus Alexander extended them kindness and protection. At Gaza, where the Philistines blocked his passage to Egypt, he let his men murder and rape the populace into extinction. Twice, in Egypt and in Persia, he had himself deified contrary to Greek tradition. He tried to meld the Greeks and Persians into one brotherhood (not knowing, doubtless, that they were distant cousins) by ordering his men to take Persian wives. He married, first, the Bactrian princess Roxanne and then two ladies of the royal line. He murdered any Greek, even old friends, suspected of disloyalty and grieved almost pathologically over the death of Hephaestion, his best friend and comrade in arms. He had his body cremated on a pyre 200 feet high at the most extravagant funeral ever celebrated. He indulged in unbelievable drunken orgies (six quarts of wine in one night). His feats in battle bordered on the foolhardy.

After capturing the Persian capitals he marched into eastern Persia to subject the Provinces. There he lifted his sights on India, where he almost met disaster. He crossed the Indus. Near Vitasa (modern Jehlum) in the Karri plain stood the mighty army of the Indian king Paurava or Porus as the Greeks called him. Porus deployed his elephant corps of 200 beasts in front of his infantry of 30,000 foot. At the wings he had chariots and 4000 cavalry. The elephants panicked the Macedonian cavalry but the Greeks ultimately regained control of their steeds and, in turn, stampeded the elephants with their repeated charges and belly thrusts. Alexander was taxed to the utmost but his heavy cavalry won the day. Noteworthy in this connection was the effectiveness of a contingent of Scythian mounted archers who stunned the Indian cavalry with their deadly missiles. He magnanimously spared the life of Porus and restored him to his throne. Alexander's beloved horse Bucephalus, who was his better half in battle for nearly two decades, died in this encounter. Alexander named a city he founded in India Bucephala in honor and memory of his precious steed. After defeating Porus Alexander wanted to invade the Gangetic plain but his men refused to follow him. He marched down the Indus to the sea instead. At Multan he was severly wounded leading a scaling of the walls only to find himself alone amongst the enemy when the ladder broke. He was almost killed before his followers could get over the wall to join him. He recovered though greviously wounded.

Alexander returned to Susa in 325 B. C., after nearly succumbing to the heat in the Baluchistan desert, where he seemed at a loss as to what to do with his newly won and immense empire. He harbored dreams of invading the Arabian penninsula and the western Mediterranean. But his time was spent regaling himself as an oriental monarch and in countless drunken orgies. His men grumbled about his Persianization and some began to doubt his sanity. Many yearned for their homeland. In June of 323 B. C. when the heat in Babylon was insufferable, Alexander contracted a fever and died at the early age of 33. What more he might have accomplished had he lived another 25 years, as should have been his due, has been the subject of much speculation ever since. Many feel he would have conquered the western Mediterranean and much of India. It would have been an empire such as was not to be known to history until the rise of the British empire fifteen hundred years later.

Alexander's impact was far broader than his military conquests. He Hellenized the Mediterranean world. The Greek culture was added to the old Sumerian and Egyptian as the foundation of the presently dominant Western civilization. The original classical Greek art and literary forms were variously altered to suit a broader area and alien people but they remained essentially the same throughout for two millennia.

Alexander died intestate. In the scramble for succession Saleucus won Western Asia; Ptolemy seized Egypt and Antigonus gained control over the Greek mainland. The Celts, of which we shall soon learn more, were already pressing hard on the Greeks from their homeland above the Danube. The house of Antigonus held power in Greece until the Roman conquest in 168 B. C.

The Seleucids were unable to hold Western Asia together for long. India broke away under Chandragupta who formed the first Indian empire by 300 B. C. The Parthians resuscitated the Persian empire around 250 B. C. The Greeks in Anatolia broke away early in the 3rd century. The Seleucids, however, retained control over Syria until the rise of Rome.

The Ptolemies ruled the longest. At first they made Egypt prosperous by reorganizing agriculture in the fertile Nile valley. Alexandria became not only a great intellectual center but a commercial capital. The Ptolemies invited the Jews to settle in the new city and as much as one-fifth of the population was Jewish. The Greeks ruled as foreigners over the Egyptians but as their power waned they became Egyptianized. Cleopatra was more Egyptian than Greek. When Caesar came to Egypt in 48 B. C. the Ptolemies were in a high state of decadence. They offered no resistance.

Judea, unfortunately, got caught in the struggle between the Ptolemies and Seleucids for control of Palestine. Under the Ptolemies the Jews were given their freedom but had to pay a heavy tribute. When the Seleucids gained control over Judea in 198 B. C. they set out to Hellenize the Jews. Judea was ruled by a High Priest and an Assembly of Elders. It was a strictly religious society. Intermarriage with non-Jews was forbidden unlike their Israelite predecessors. The people were mostly farmers. They possessed little or no arts. Enjoyment of life was eschewed. The Seleucids decided to introduce Greek arts and ways of living but the orthodox Jews refused to cooperate. Many of the youth, however, were won over to the Greek way of life as it offered more pleasure.

In 167 B. C. Antiochus sacked Jerusalem, slaughtered thousands of its inhabitants, looted the temple and dedicated it to Zeus, made circumcision a crime, ordered the Jews to eat pork and sold most of the population into slavery. Many Jews fled into the hills including the family of the Maccabees. Judas Macabee led a guerrilla war against the Greeks defeating the Seleucid army in 166 B. C. In 164 B. C. he recaptured Jerusalem and rededicated the temple to Yahweh. The rededication (Hanukkah) has become a holiday for orthodox Jews ever since. Antiochus was planning another attack on Jerusalem when he died in 163 B. C., but his successors continued the aggression. When Simon Maccabee won the support of Rome in 142 B. C. the Seleucids reluctantly recognized the independence of Judea. Simon became High Priest and founded the Hasmonean dynasty.

THE ROMANS

The struggle for domination of the Mediterranean world shifted after Alexander to the West, which had for centuries been the frontier of the ancient civilizations. The Greeks established colonies there for their excess populations during the 8th century. But even earlier the area was a refuge for the displaced. During the great migrations around 1200–1000 B. C. some of the so-called sea peoples that threatened Egypt and the eastern Mediterranean eventually settled in the West—The Sicels in Sicily, the Shardana in Sardinia and the Tyrsenians (Etruscans) in Etruria.

The origin of the Etruscans in one of history's enigmas. Their script remains unlocked. But archeologically Anatolian antecedants predominate. Herodotus states they were emigrants from Lydia. Vergil's Aeneid traces their origin to a contingent of defeated Trojans who migrated west under their leader Aeneas after the Trojan war. Whether they were Indo-Europeans is unclear. Their language apparently is not, yet their script flows back and forth occasionally in the manner of the Hittites. The most plausible deduction is, at this time, that they were part of the great migration initiated by the Indo-Europeans though they may have been other people from Anatolia dispossessed by these marauders.

At any rate they brought to Italy a highly developed technology and culture, including the horse and chariot and metallurgy. The area where they settled between the rivers Tiber and Arno abounded in metal ores. Furthermore, the island of Elba, only six miles offshore, was rich with high grade iron ore. By 600 B. C. at Fufluna, the Etruscans had an iron works of a magnitude unknown in the ancient world with the exception, perhaps, of Hallstatt in the Danube area. Their trade in metals around the Mediterranean brought them great wealth. They lived luxuriously. Women enjoyed wide freedom. But they were unable to organize into a nation preferring the city states of the Greek world.

When the Etruscans came to Italy they found an indigenous people with a lower level of technology and culture. It is known as the Villanova culture. Indo-Europeans via Europe had already migrated into the penninsula, perhaps as early or shortly after the first migration, certainly by the time of the later migration around 1000 B. C. that brought the Dorians into Greece. Among these Indo-European peoples were the Latins who settled south of the Tiber. In the 6th century B. C. they came under Etruscan domination when Lucius Tarquinius established himself as the king of Rome.

Tarquinius Superbus (the Proud), the last of the Etruscan kings, was ousted in a rebellion in 509 B. C., precipitated by the Rape of Lucretia, a lady of high rank, by Sextus Tarquin the king's son. Lucretia, a woman of exemplary virtue, forthwith stabbed herself to death. The citizens of Rome, now a mix of Latins and Etruscans, seized upon this *cause celebre* and decided to terminate the monarchy and establish a Republic.

The Republic was an aristocracy *cum* democracy with a complex system of checks and balances. There were two Consuls, the Senate and two Assemblies. The plebian, the common man, had a vote only in the Assemblies but the voting was heavily weighted against him on the basis of property. The wealthy—the landed aristocracy (the patricians) and the rich businessmen (the equities) dominated the Assemblies, which elected the Consuls. The patricians—old families like the Julii, Claudii, Fabii and others—dominated the Senate. The Senate became supreme—it had executive, legislative and judicial powers. Fearing dictatorship the Consuls were not only granted veto power over each other's acts but could serve only one year in a decade. It was recognized, however, that in times of emergencies and crisis absolute power had to be reposed in a good leader. The constitution therefore, allowed for the election or appointment by the Senate of a dictator for a short period. A dictator was also expected to relinquish the power before the expiration of the appointment if the emergency passed. Cincinnnatus is always held up as an example of a good dictator. He was granted dictatorial powers for six months to repel an invasion of the Aegui in 458 B. C. Legend has it that Cincinnatus dropped his plow, repelled the invasion in 16 days, promptly relinquished the dictatorship and returned to his furrow. It is a sad commentary that in the end this (probably) necessary feature of the constitution proved the undoing of the Republic.

Theoretically a plebe was to be one of the Consuls but both were usually patricians or equities as the office provided no salary and required some education. The political arena was a constant struggle between the wealthy and aristocratic, the patrician, and the common man, the plebian. In the 5th century the plebians won a great victory by the creation of the Tribunate of the plebes. The Tribunes, elected by an assembly of all the plebes had the power to veto (I forbid) any act of the Senate and Assembly. This political balance between the ruling elite and the dominated majority affording a certain degree of mobility worked rather well for five centuries until the Republic fell with the rise of Caesarism in the First century B. C.

The government was administered in accordance with law—the Twelve Tables of the Decemvirs. Prior to their promulgation about 450 B. C. Roman law was a mixture of customs, royal decrees and priestly interpretations. The Twelve Tables were a severe code resting upon the old paternalism of an agrarian military society. Plebians were forbidden to marry patricians until 287 B. C. Enslavement was the penalty for theft, debt default and other breaches of social discipline. Death was inflicted for serious crime.

Every citizen was liable for military service from age 16 to 60. The Roman farmer-soldiers were ready to exert their power and influence against their neighbors by the 4th century B. C. In 390 B. C., however, they suffered a humiliating defeat at the hands of the Cisalpine Gauls who exacted a ransom of 1000 pounds of gold. It took fifty years to recover from this setback. But shortly thereafter the Romans rapidly subdued not only the Cisalpine Gauls but other tribes—Sabines, Samnites, Umbrians and others—of the penninsula. The Greeks on the foot of Italy and in Sicily were another matter. They could seek aid from their motherlands in Greece. Pyrrhus of Epirus invaded Italy pursuant to such request and defeated the Romans near Heraclea in 280 B. C. He lost 4000 men and allegedly remarked "another such victory and I am lost!" Costly triumphs have ever since been called "pyrrhic victories". Rome eventually defeated Pyrrhus and dominated the entire penninsula.

They had next to confront the Carthagenians who were masters of the western Mediterranean. There ensued three Punic wars during the period 264–146 B. C. in which Carthage was erased from history. Rome had no sea power in the beginning while Carthage was the master of the western sea. But with the help of Greek architects the Romans constructed a fleet of 100 quinqueremes in sixty days modeled after a Carthagenian ship washed ashore in Italy. They added something, however, that made the difference for victory. It was a gang-way with an iron spike on the end, called a *corvus*, which was dropped on the deck of the Carthagenian ship so that Roman peasant soldiers could board the enemy vessel and engage its crew in hand to hand combat. The Carthagenian mercenaries were no match for the Roman warriors. Much of the struggle was over Spain for its strategic gold, silver, copper and other metal ores. The second war involved Hannibal's daring invasion of Italy across the Alps, detailed in Chapter IX, that almost succeeded.

Carthage was founded by the Phoenicians about the 8th century B. C. In due time these emigrants from Tyre wrested large areas of fertile land from the Lybians for a prosperous agriculture. They grew wealthy, however, after they conquered Spain and exploited vigorously its rich gold, silver and copper deposits. Carthage was ruled by an oligarchy of rich merchants and landlords. It was a money economy. Everything was bought including its soldiers and sailors.

They built a great navy and for centuries before the rise of Rome fought the Greeks on Sardinia and Sicily for domination of the western Mediterranean. Most renowned of their rulers were the Barcids of which Hamilcar and his son Hannibal are best known. They dreamed of empire but unfortunately encountered the rise of Roman power enroute.

After Carthage the Romans turned their attention to Greece and the eastern Mediterranean. Philip V of Macedonia provoked the Romans by supporting the Carthagenians which ended in the Macedonian's defeat in 167 B. C. and the domination of Greece by Rome. Antiochus III of Syria intervened against the Romans during the Greek campaigns and was roundly defeated at Magnesia in 190 B. C. Antiochus escaped to Syria but thereafter the Seleucids remained under Roman control.

Rome continued its aggression during the First century before Christ. In western Asia the Romans subdued Anatolia and the Near East, but when Crassus tried to cross the Euphrates and march on to India, in the footsteps of the much admired Alexander, he suffered a devastating defeat by the Parthians at Carrhae in 53 B. C. The historic Battle of Carrhae has been detailed in Chapter VI. Mark Anthony tried again in 33 B. C. and was similarly rebuffed. The Euphrates became the easternmost extent of Roman power.

The Roman encounter with the Jews turned out to be a major milestone in the history of the Mediterranean civilizations. In 63 B. C. Rome asserted its rule over Judea. The Jews resented their new masters and seethed with rebellion. Crassus incensed them further by raiding their temple for gold on his way to conquer Persia. Two important events transpired in Judea during Roman rule. A Jewish prophet Jesus Christ (circa 0–33 A. D.) arose and a new religion Christianity evolved out of his teachings. It became a foundation stone for the European civilization that 15 centuries or so thereafter was to dominate the world. The Jews continued their rebellion and were cruelly decimated once again as a nation. A protracted revolution erupted in 66 A. D. According to Josephus more than a million Jews were killed. Their temple was burned in 70 A. D. Countless others were sold into slavery. The Jews were now dispersed throughout the empire where many had already settled earlier. Abroad they were treated tolerantly by the Romans. Synagogues were permitted. Augustus even excused them from civil duties on their sabbath. In 132 A. D. the Jews made a futile attempt under Simeon Bar Cocheba to recover Jerusalem. It outraged the Emperor Hadrian who forbade Jews to enter the city except on one day a year fixed by the Romans so they could come and weep at the ruined walls of their bygone Temple. For two millennia Judea was to be inhabited by others, while the Jews lived in small communities scattered around the Mediterranean but held together as a nation, though without a country, by their religious faith.

The Romans thrust their power into Europe where they encountered the Celts. The Celts too were Indo-Europeans who migrated into central and western Europe, and eventually the British Isles, from 2000 B. C. onwards. They brought the horse and chariot and metallurgy with them. Around 1500 B. C. they developed a leading bronze center at Unitice in Bohemia where tin and copper ore was abundant. Later at Hallstatt (near Salsburg) beginning around 1000 B. C. they founded a very successful iron works. The Celts were using iron agricultural implements much earlier than most people. Caesar was impressed with their iron technology such as iron rims sweated on their chariot and wagon wheels.

Unfortunately the Celts are known mostly through archeology as, like other Indo-European peoples, they did not know writing. That they were otherwise highly civilized is now generally agreed. The Greeks and Romans warped their history out of perspective by calling them by the odious term "barbarians". They were, however, a rough and ready people always warring with one another. In fact, it was out of this tribal rivalry that Caesar intervened and conquered Gaul.

The Celts pushed into the Po valley around 400 B. C. where they encountered the Etruscans who proved no match for their martial spirit and vigor. In 390 B. C. these Cisalpine Gauls made a devastating raid on Rome. The Romans eventually (150 years later) subdued them but they were always rebellious. In 217 B. C. the Cisalpine Gauls defected to Hannibal when he invaded Italy through the Alps. The Celts also invaded Greece but were defeated at Pergamum in 230 B. C.

The Romans controlled the Celts between the Pyrenees and the Alps and in southern France when Julius Caesar was sent to Provincia in 58 B. C. as governor. Caesar was vying with Pompey and Crassus for supremacy at this time and had his sights set on conquest. He defeated first the Helvetti, then the Belgae and by 57 B. C. conquered all of Gaul. The Celts rallied under an able warrior Vercingetorix in 52 B. C. It taxed Caesar's ingenuity to the utmost. In 45 B. C. Caesar's able generalship prevailed. He captured Vercengetorix and paraded him as a trophy of victory in Rome before executing him. Gaul was subdued.

Augustus tried to extend the empire beyond the Rhine but was repulsed by the Germans. The Romans settled for the Rhine and the Danube as the frontier of their empire in Europe. Claudius rounded out the empire in Europe by conquering Britian in 43 A. D.

The empire surrounded the Mediterranean completely. It did not thrust as deeply into Persia as the Romans would have liked. But all the peoples who had been developing the civilization of the Mediterranean area since the beginning of recorded history were now under a single rule. The Roman empire was destined to endure for five centuries during which time a Graeco-Roman stamp was irrevocably placed upon this sector of humanity.

Rome owed its military prowess mainly to three factors. The brave and loyal citizen-soldier, a well disciplined army and, above all, to Roman engineering. The chief weapon of Mediterranean warfare at this time was the iron sword. He who could wield it best won the day. But every offense begets its defense. And the best defense against the enemy with the sword was a stout wall. Roman engineers demolished and surmounted these walls with their technological ingenuity enabling the superb Roman soldier with the sword to dispose of the inhabitants. Mention has already been made twice of the corvus, the ingenious gangplank for boarding an enemy ship reducing naval warfare to a duel of swords. This was not exactly original with the Romans for the Egyptians employed grappling hooks to board enemy vessels, but the Roman corvus was a more efficient mechanism for the purpose. Even more ingenious machines were developed by Roman engineers for scaling or battering enemy walls. Assault towers, ramps, battering rams, catapults, ballista capable of hurling 100 pound stones, onagers, crossbows, flame-throwers and the like found no enemy rampart unassailable. Moreover Roman organizational ability could always mobilize the timber, stones and other materials as well as the food and other necessities of life for its soldiers from the countryside of the enemy. The seige of Avaricum in Gaul was maintained by Caesar for 27 days.

Cavalry, curiously, was not a central feature of Roman warfare. It proved crucial against both the Germans and the Parthians. Twice the Parthians, who were otherwise disorganized and undisciplined, decimated the Roman legions with superb horsemanship and missile warfare. The unconquerable Roman soldier with his sword was completely ineffectual against a deadly arrow delivered from 500 paces. The Germans too relied on cavalry to defeat the Roman legions venturing beyond the Rhine. Alexander knew he had to checkmate the Persian cavalry to march beyond the Euphrates. The Romans never understood this fact and failed to extend their power to India.

During the days of the empire, when the citizen-soldier was a feature of the past, Roman engineering remained as good as ever. The walls, strongholds, and barracks on the limes were sturdy and comfortable for the men guarding the frontiers. The soldiers were mercenaries and mostly foreigners drawn from the provinces. Not only was this costly but the loyalty of these mercenaries was unreliable. As Rome progressed toward bankruptcy the troops were paid in grain, from Egypt, and even allocated land near the strongholds to support themselves. At this stage discipline degenerated and they were little more than a weak militia against the Germans. Even more insidious was their interference in the selection of a new emperor. By giving support to a particular candidate they, in effect, held the ultimate power. In the 4th century a Roman emperor ruled by German sufferance. In 392 A. D., after recovering Gaul for Rome, the Frankish general Arbogast arranged for the murder of Valentinian and had his puppet Eugenius made emperor. Arbogast conferred the title Augustus on his son Arcadius and groomed him for emperor. Theodosius, the eastern emperor, however, thwarted Arbogast's design to usurp the Caesarship.

Rome grew wealthy on plunder and tribute. But as this enormous wealth poured into Rome it soon begot socio economic disorder. Gross maldistribution of wealth ensued. The rich grew richer. They bought up the land and worked it with slaves who were a glut on the market, selling for a dollar a head during the last days of the Republic. The latifundias dispossessed the sturdy peasant farmers of old who crowded into Rome as an unemployed and angry proletariat. Most were citizen soldiers who found themselves in Rome, after helping to conquer the Mediterranean world, without a place and purpose in their own society. Many of the slaves seethed with rebellion. Slave revolts, mostly futile in the face of Roman power, erupted during the last two centuries before Christ. Most famous was that of Spartacus in 73 B. C. The rich Roman lived in fear of the slaves and the proletariat.

Politics became polarized in the last days of the Republic between the conservative and rich, the optimates, and the liberal and dispossessed, the populares. Rome was still governed by the rich. But reformers sprang up, some from the aristocracy. Most notable were the Gracchii brothers (163–121 B. C) who advocated land reform for the unemployed. Both were cleverly eliminated by premature death through the machinations of the landed aristocracy. At the same time Roman politics veered strongly toward authoritarianism. Around the turn of the last century before Chirst Rome witnessed a duel between two would be dictators Giaus Marius, leader of the populares and Lucius Cornelius Sulla, an optimate. For three decades (107–79 B. C.) these men had themselves repeatedly elected to the consulship so that their rule was near absolute. The old rule that a consul could hold office only one year in ten was now honored mostly in its breach.

Marius professionalized the army and this reform, more than anything else, brought about the demise of the Republic. Roman soldiers no longer had to be men of property. They were paid instead by the state or by rich generals. The legions grew to be more loyal to their generals than to Rome, particularly the Republic. by 70 B. C. a struggle for power arose between three generals of aristocratic heritage, Gnaeus Pompey, Julius Caesar and Marcus Licinius Crassus that led to the downfall of the Republic and the rise of Caesarism. Pompey, a lieutenant of Sulla, distinguished himself militarily in Spain, Anatolia and by the elimination of the pirates in the Mediterranean in 67 B. C. Caesar conquered Gaul in 58–50 B. C. Crassus lost his head (literally) trying to conquer Persia in 54 B. C. leaving the field to Pompey and Caesar. A general was not permitted to take his troops into Rome without the approval of the Senate. Occasionally the Senate would vote a "triumph" to honor a great victory allowing the victorious general to march into Rome with his legions.

Pompey's army was therefore camped outside Rome. He had, however, the support of the Senate. Caesar was ordered by the Senate to disband his army. But he marched his legions across the river Rubicon, the southern boundary of Cisalpine Gaul, for Rome where he bivouacked them outside the city limits. Pompey promptly withdrew his army into Greece. A civil war raged. The two armies finally joined in battle at Pharsalus in Thessaly in 48 B. C. Caesar's legions won decisively. Pompey fled to Egypt where the youthful Ptolemy's vizier had him assassinated. When Caesar arrived in Alexandria he learned he was the master of Rome. In Egypt he rather foolishly succumbed to the charms and wiles of Cleopatra. It took nine months for him to recover his senses and return to Rome where he had himself proclaimed dictator for life by a cowed and humbled Senate.

Caesar ruled with compassion and wisdom. He tried valiantly to arrest Rome's decadence. He slowed for awhile the creeping welfarism gripping Rome by reducing the welfare rolls from 320,000 to 150,000. Rome had a population of about a million. The free entertainment provided the slaves and proletariat at great expense to the state was restrained. The administrative system was reformed to cope with the rule of a great empire. He gave the Graeco-Roman world and ultimately the world the Julian calendar based on the Egyptian almanac. But on March 15, 44 B. C. he was stabbed to death in the Senate by his enemies, who resented his destruction of the Republic.

After Caesar's assassination the civil war erupted again. An uneasy truce ensued with Octavian, Caesar's legal heir, taking command in the West, Marc Anthony, ruling the East and Lepidus, Caesar's lieutenant, assuming control in Africa. The three shared rule in Italy. Octavian first ousted Lepidus and then defeated Marc Anthony and Cleopatra at Actium in 31 B. C. He now possessed complete control and rule of the empire. Octavian was given the title Augustus (august) by the Senate and ruled with absolute power for 40 years. He and his successors were also called Princeps (the first) and Imperator from which the word emperor derives.

Thereafter emperor followed emperor either by designation or usurpation, confirmed meaninglessly by the Senate, for more than four centuries. Assassination ended the term of many an emperor. Some were men of considerable ability, even philosophers, others were idiots and a few madmen, but mostly their rule was capable and the Caesars gave the Mediterranean world peace for nearly half a millennium.

Augustus was a competent ruler. He too tried to stem the tide of decadence which had by his time permeated the body social. The strong family structure that underpinned Roman society was in disintegration, especially among the wealthy ruling elite. Divorce was rampant. Women were more interested in their careers, professions and activities outside the home. They eschewed or neglected their role as mothers of the future generation. Young men avoided marriage and family responsibilities in the sexual freedom of the times.

Augustus worried about the dilution of the Roman stock. Rome was now the leading metropolis of the Mediterranean world. It was a magnet for metics. Slaves, freedmen and other aliens from the conquered nations poured into the capital. They bred without restraint while the purebred

Romans shunned parentage through avoidance of marriage, abortion and contraception. Marriage between Romans and metics was on the rise. At this rate, Augustus reasoned, the metics would soon dominate Rome with their numbers. The defense of the empire was at stake as the old dedicated and loyal peasant-soldier was disappearing. The metics were in Rome only for money and economic betterment. They had little or no loyalty to Rome.

Augustus promulgated the Julian Law designed to restore the old family, arrest the dilution of Roman blood and promote the propagation of loyal citizens of Roman heritage. Among other measures he imposed a tax on bachelors and denied them inheritances unless they married within a hundred days. Spinsters too were taxed and could not inherit after age fifty. Members of the Senatorial class could not marry metics, actors or actresses or courtesans. Fathers of many children were favored for government appointments. These restrictions proved unpopular. Needless to say they did not arrest the social decay.

Augustus also tried to stem the growth of welfarism. The rolls had again, after Caesar's restriction, grown to 300,000. Abuse and corruption crept into the system. Old slaves, for instance, were freed and placed on welfare, as freedmen qualified, to avoid the obligation of supporting a spent worker. Augustus reduced the rolls to 200,000. But the growth of welfarism continued.

Rome could not afford the cost of its welfare system. Nor the cost of its military establishment. Nor its luxurious living. It was never a productive society. In days of old it had a fairly bountiful agriculture, which nurtured, in addition, good and loyal soldiers at little or no cost to the state. But agricultural productivity was ruined by land concentration and inefficient cultivation with slaves. The peasant farm vanished. Wheat and other food stuffs were imported mainly from Sicily, North Africa, Gaul and Egypt. Manufacturing, however, was never highly developed by the Romans. They profited by commerce and trade but not to the extent of the Greeks and Phoenicians.

The wealth of Rome came mainly from plunder and tribute. The former enabled Rome to build the empire; the latter to sustain it. But as consumption (luxuries, defense, welfare, entertainment) outpaced the production and acquisition of wealth, the empire succumbed to a debilitating inflation.

The Romans tried to solve the crisis by the manipulation of money. The Romans became the first notable and notorious mismanagers of money in history. This politico-economic malady has plagued the human race ever since. In its pristine stage Rome had only the copper *as* for money. After it made contact with the Greeks it issued a silver coin called *denarius*. Later it issued a gold *aureus*. But the denarius was always its main coin. The denarius was kept pure until about 100 A. D. Gold and silver circulated in a ratio of 1:12, fluctuating a point or two therefrom, depending upon the current supply of the precious metals. The gold and silver was first looted from the temples and treasuries of the subdued people and later augmented from the mines of Spain, Thrace, Nubia and elsewhere that fell under Roman control.

The Romans resorted to both devaluation and debasement to inflate their currency. The ultimate technique was plated coins, a wash of silver over a baser metal usually copper. The Roman did not invent plating as the Athenians used it albeit temporarily during the Peloponnesian war. On the whole the Greeks refrained from manipulating their money as did the Persians. Rome resorted to currency manipulation already under the Republic in times of dire emergencies like the invasion by Hannibal, the Servile wars and the Civil wars but not in any substantial way. Money management was the perogative of the Assembly and, during the last century, of the Senate. Generals were usually authorized to mint money in the Provinces. The Caesars took the matter in hand after the fall of the Republic and inflation became rampant during the days of the empire. Augustus refrained from any money profligacy but with and after Nero all restraints were dropped. In the 3rd century Roman money collapsed.

Nero reduced the silver content of the denarius to 90 per cent, Trajan to 85, Commodus to 70 and Severus to 50. The aureus, originally one fortieth of a pound of gold, was reduced by Nero to one forty-fifth, Caracalla to one fiftieth, Diocletion to one sixtieth and Constantine to one seventy-second.

Interest rates rose to 12 per cent from the 4 per cent prevailing during the time of Augustus when money was relatively stable. In fact, they would have soared higher had it not been illegal to charge more than 12 per cent.

Hard facts on prices are not available, particularly for Italy proper. But the inflation was empire wide. In Palestine prices advanced a thousand per cent between the first and third centuries. The price of wheat in Egypt rose 15,000 per cent over the same period! Egyptian bankers refused to take Roman coins.

Diocletian (284–305 A. D.) repudiated the denarius. This was tantamount to a declaration of bankruptcy of the empire. His attempt at monetary reform failed. In 301 A. D. he issued his famous Edict fixing prices of some 800 items of goods and services. Death was the penalty for violations of the Edict. The bureaucracy burgeoned to administer the price controls adding to an already costly administration Rome could not afford. Taxes rose to support the parasitic bureaucracy. Business men caught between rising costs and fixed prices were ruined adding to the unemployed proletariat in the cities. The Edict boomeranged. Goods disappeared from the market and black market prices prevailed for the dwindling supplies. A peck of wheat fixed at 100 denarii rose to 10,000 denarii in a few decades! Gold and silver were hoarded; only the debased coins circulated. The final blow was an order that the debased coins had to be accepted at face value as legal tender but that taxes had to be paid in gold and silver! In the 4th century the Roman empire in the west was in utter and irrevocable economic ruin.

Diocletian, a remarkable man, was forced to take further drastic economic measures when his monetary reform and price controls failed. First, he started to collect taxes in kind—in commodities—wherever it was feasible. Soldiers and administrators in turn were paid in grain and other goods. More insidious, however, he undertook a comprehensive census in which every citizen's economic situation was determined and fixed for life. Sons were obliged to carry on their fathers calling. This rigid socio-economic structure was formalized by Constantine. The once free Roman citizen became an economic serf. It was the only way that productivity could be maintained to support the mammoth administrative and military bureaucracy of the decaying Roman state. The seeds of European feudalism can be founded in these edicts of the dying Roman empire.

Bullion had been flowing to the East for some time. The luxuries the Romans craved, but could not afford, were manufactured in Asia. Diocletion followed this wealth by moving his capital to Nicodemia, across the Bosphorus, and appointing a co-ruler in the West. This eventually split the Roman empire in two. Constantine moved the eastern capital to Byzantium in 324 A. D. which was renamed Constantinople. Rome, no longer able to afford a defense against the Germanic tribes, succumbed to barbarian domination. The eastern sector of the Graeco-Roman civilization continued, dominated by the Greeks, as Byzantine until 1400 A. D.

As Rome decayed it lost the affection and loyalty of its people. Few could remain unalienated in a society that brought them economic ruination and offered them only hoplessness. Indignity was heaped upon despair by the luxurious and licientious living of the dwindling ruling class. Roman religion had become religiosity. It offered little or no solace to the masses. The disaffected began to turn to the religions of the East for sanity and comfort. And they embraced with their hearts the teachings of the Hebrew prophet Jesus Christ. Hardly a Roman, not stationed in Judea, was aware of the crucifixion of Christ on Golgotha outside Jerusalem in 33 A. D. Yet three centuries later the religion founded upon his teachings was to dominate the dying Roman empire. Christ taught man to avoid and reject the things of the world (that is, the decadent Roman civilization) for the Kingdom of Heaven. Though the new faith offered little on earth it promised much in Heaven hereafter. Such a philosophy found receptive ears and minds. Things Roman became sinful. Usury and profit. Sex. The Arts. An anti-Romanism developed and gripped Christendom for centuries. It still effects the mind of Western man today, as in the matter of sexual relations, already discussed in Chapter X.

The early Christians were persecuted intermittently. Many died in the arena. But Christianity spread steadily so that by the end of the third century the Roman government realized the futility of continued oppression. In 311 A. D. the Caesar Galerius gave it legal sanction. Constantine continued the policy and when he himself became a convert in 337 A. D. Christianity was destined to become the dominant religion of both the eastern and western sectors of the empire. A schism eventually developed between the Eastern (Greek) and Western (Latin) Church though both rested on the teachings of Christ.

The West was taken over by the Germanic tribes—the Goths, Franks, Bergundians, Alemmani, Lombards and others. The Huns from central Asia were pressing them from the rear. Attila penetrated as far west as Italy in 453 A. D. before the Hunnish threat expired. Africa was dominated by the Berbers. The one remaining civilizing institution was the Christian Church which was now firmly established in Rome. These so-called barbarians accepted and adopted Christianity as their religion and, thus, placed themselves under the spiritual and even temporal authority of the Bishop (later Pope) of Rome. When these barbarians repeatedly sacked Rome during the 4th and 5th centuries they refrained from destroying it out of awe and deference to the fact that it was the seat of their spiritual leader.

As for the rest of the Western empire there remained little else but the land—it was otherwise in economic ruins. The livelihood of the people depended solely on agriculture. The Germanic chieftans and nobles carved out areas of control in which the cultivator was bonded to the land in perpetual serfdom. The manorial system became the economic order of the day. This economic imperative gradually evolved into the feudal system from which issued the European civilization that was to dominate the world in the 19th century.

Economic ruination also spawned the monastery system of Christendom. The church began acquiring tracts of land and attracted men of superior intellect and ability to manage them. There were now few other economic opportunities in the bankrupt empire for men of competence and integrity. Romans, revolted by their degenerate society, converted to Christianity. One such patrician named Benedict, after years of penitential living, founded the Benedictine Order in 529 A. D. on the heights of Monte Cassino which, more or less, established the structure of the life and organization of the European monasteries. The monasteries provided not only economic security but an intellectual haven. The learning of the Graeco-Roman empire was preserved and carried on in these tranquil and secure retreats. The monasteries even undertook such matters as agricultural research to improve the productivity of the land. They provided another essential feature for a healthy and developing society as the clerical route was about the only path available for a poor but congenitally gifted boy to rise into the ruling elite in the feudal society.

The eastern sector, on the other hand, made a far better economic recovery and adjustment. First, it became the repository of more of the bullion of the dying empire. Constantine reformed the currency based upon the gold *bezant* containing one-sixth of an ounce of gold. The bezant enabled Constantinople to become the trade center of the Mediterranean. The eastern sector possessed more industry allowing it to avert reversion to a primarily agricultural state. And when, under Justinian, the Byzantines acquired silk technology they were able to build a prosperous textile industry based upon sericulture in the Peloponnesus and dying, spinning and weaving in Syria. The clandestine acquisition of this technology by two Nestorian monks has already been detailed. Finally, the invention of Greek Fire, also discussed earlier, provided the Byzantines with a defensive (and offensive) military technology that enabled them to fend off invaders for centuries assuring their endurance as a dominant power in the eastern Mediterranean longer than may have been the case otherwise.

The eastern sector had, however, a formidable challenger for control of Western Asia in a renacent Persian empire under the Sassanids, who overthrew the Parthians in 226 A. D. and took over rule in Ctesiphon. Meanwhile, a revolt occurred in Syria by a Roman governor who ruled the eastern provinces from Palmyra. He was succeeded by his wife, the fabled and beautiful Zenobia, who was defeated by the Roman legions and brought to Rome in a resplendent triumph in 275 A. D. The unrest continued until Diocletion finally put it to rest in 284 A. D. In fact, this defection of the eastern provinces prompted Diocletion to establish his rule at Nicodemia. Zenobia's provincial empire had the effect of keeping the Persians behind the Euphrates. Persians, however, sat astride the Old Silk Road and controlled the supply of silk and other luxuries from Asia flowing to Constantinople until the Byzantines were able to build an indigenous silk industry. The Byzantines also avoided the Persians by circumnavigating them by sea to India and China.

People in both sectors of the dying empire considered themselves Romans. Byzantine was a name unknown to them and given the eastern sector by historians. Many of the Roman elite emigrated to Constantinople after the economic ruination of the western sector and brought with them the Roman way of life. Constantinople was built as a replica of Rome. Chariot races and games were continued though not the bloody gladiatorial spectacles. A huge circus called the Hippodrome was constructed. Luxury living continued, though not the drunken sexual orgies. Christianity had a civilizing influence in this respect. But the essential beast in man was not purged. Decapitation was a normal mode of transfer of power to the Byzantine crown. The manifestation of luxury was primarily in dress and adornment. Thus, the importance of silk.

This early Roman elite rested upon a mass of Greeks, who no longer spoke classical Greek but a vernacular more akin to its modern counterpart. Latin was the official language until the 7th century. Latin continued as the language in the West (it was the language of the church until the 20th century) and spawned a whole family of Romance languages—Italian, Spanish, French and Romanian.

Perhaps, the greatest continuum was the codification of Rome law by Justinian known as the *Corpus Juris Civilis*. In 528 A. D. the emperor appointed a commission of 10 jurists to codify and reform the law of Rome that had evolved as a jumble of ordinances, edicts and decisions handed down by various authorities. Nothing, except perhaps Byzantine Art, had a greater effect upon the succeeding European civilization.

Justinian was an outstanding emperor (483–565 A. D.). His uncle Justin I rose to the throne through the army. He was a Bulgarian peasant. As aide to his uncle Justinian was well schooled for rule. He married the remarkable Theodora, a prominent actress and courtesan, whose father had a bear act in the Hippodrome. Justinian had to change the law forbidding a man of Senatorial rank from marrying an actress. Theodora proved to be a worthy empress.

Justinian had visions of resuscitating the Roman empire. He conquered Italy and established a capital at Ravenna. This had a profound Byzantine impact on the art and religious pomp of the infant European civilization. Justinian's dream failed and his modest conquests in the West soon terminated.

By the 7th century the Roman civilization was submerged in an alien sea. Roman blood, as Augustus rightfully feared, was a mere trickle in the veins of the people who now possessed the territory of the Caesars. In the east the Roman empire got a new lease on life thereby extending its power for several centuries. It evolved, however, into a hybrid civilization more and more Greek and Asian as time passed. By 1000 A. D. there were hardly any traces of it's Roman apparentation. In the West too the Roman heritage was absorbed and submerged as it civilized the Germanic tribes who now possessed the land. It was the Europeans however, who were destined to evolve a new civilization in the Mediterranean area with a burst of energy and technological innovation that would dominate the world. By 1000 A. D. this movement was well underway. But before its fruition there was to be one more, perhaps the last, Semitic challenge to the Indo-Europeans for domination of the Mediterranean area.

THE ARABS

The history of Islam has already been detailed in Chapter IX. Fired by religious zeal under the prophet Mohammed in the 7th century, who purported to be the latest and truest voice of the Universal God that was evolved in Western Asia under Judeo-Christian theology, the Arabs conquered the Mediterranean world from Persia to Spain in the course of a century! The Arabs possessed no superior technology nor great wealth for such a formidable accomplishment. But they had the great fortune to launch their conquests at a time when the civilizations in the area were suffering decadence, exhaustion, or overextension. The Sassanids of Persia after four centuries of rule were in a state of degeneration similar to their forefathers at the time of Alexander's invasion. The Byzantines were greatly overextended in their rule over Egypt, Palestine and Syria. Their power rested on their navy and Greek fire, both ineffective in these locations. Moreover, the Byzantines and Persians had exhausted themselves warring each other during the period 572–628 A. D. Arab cavalry, supported by camel corps, was sufficient to conquer the Persian and Greek lands in Western Asia. North Africa and Spain were equally defenseless as the western sector of the dying Roman empire was in even greater decay. At the turn of the 8th century the Islamic empire stretched from Sind in India to the Pyrenees in Europe. Most significantly the Arab domination of the Mediterranean had effectively isolated Europe from Asia for several centuries.

The Arabs, nonetheless, made a considerable contribution to the advance of civilization in the Mediterranean area. They were a catalyst between the cultures of the East and West. They transmitted the higher mathematics of India to Europe without which the Industrial Revolution would not have been possible. They preserved much of the Greek learning. It eventually filtered into Europe via Islamic Spain. Persian scientific knowledge too was transmitted to Europe. But the Arabs were not a creative people. The Arab philosopher Ibn Kaldun summed it up well when he said the Arabs possessed no crafts and that their civilization rested mainly on a Persian foundation.

THE EUROPEANS

In the 5th century the Huns exploded out of Asia to terrorize the civilized world from China to India to Europe. The Germanic tribes, whom the Romans kept at bay behind the Rhine for centuries, sought refuge in Gaul, fleeing in terror from the Huns. They came with or without Roman permission, as the empire in the West was no longer in a position to deny them ingress. The Huns vanished almost as swiftly as they came, but not before their leader Attila stood before Rome in 453 A. D. He was dissuaded by Pope Leo I from sacking the city. Actually Attila was overextended and when disease permeated his army he was forced to retreat. He died in Hungary. The Hun army disintegrated leaving Europe for good. Some Huns remained to become the Hungarians. But the Huns left the Germanic tribes in possession of most of western Europe.

Like the Celts the Germanic tribes too were Indo-Europeans who had been in Europe by this time for a thousand years or more. They had gradually become Romanized and Christianized during the last days of the empire. Many entered the Roman army as mercenaries. But they were still a rough people when Europe sank into a Dark Age in the middle of the first millennium after Christ.

The most precocious among them were the Franks, who occupied the northwest of Gaul between the Somme and the Loire. They chose as their leader a chieftan called Clovis whose grandfather Merovee fought with the Romans against the Huns. The Merovingians were the first French dynasty. Clovis cleverly sided with the Pope in the Arian heresy (that Jesus Christ, the Son, was not the equal of God, the Father) and won the support of Rome against the Visgoths and the Burgundians who he defeated in 507 A. D. to gain control over the whole of France. Paris became the capital of the new nation. It was an amalgamation of the Franks and the earlier inhabitants, the Gallo-Romans. The Merovingians ruled loosely and uncertainly over this realm with the Goths and Burgundians in constant rebellion. Administration was vested in Mayors who managed the realm as well as the feudal estates.

A new menace across the Pyrenees arose early in the 8th century. The Arabs conquered North Africa, Sicily, Southern Italy and Spain by 711 A. D. and threatened to move into France. The Merovingians designated one of their Mayors Charles Martel (the hammer) to repel the Arabs. He defeated the Muslim army at Poiters in 732 A. D. in what is regarded as a historic battle. The Arabs had cavalry but Charles Martel's infantry withstood the charge. The Muslim army retreated never again to re-enter western Europe. It is puzzling why the Arabs retreated in view of their military superiority. They were obviously overextended once they crossed the Pyrenees. The cold weather (it was autumn) could not have been pleasant for these desert bedouins. At any rate, they settled for the more hospitable climate of Spain.

Two important consequences ensued. Charles was so impressed with the Arab cavalry that he decided to base the French army on the mounted warrior. In order to finance the more expensive cavalry he confiscated land from the church (which had during the disintegration of the Roman empire acquired vast tracts in Gaul) to distribute to his vassals who were required, in exchange, to maintain a fixed number of warriors for the French army. This furthered and matured feudalism for which the foundation already existed as the peasants were tied to the land since the days of Diocletian. The medieval knight became the foremost military factor of the emerging European civilization.

The restriction on the extension of Muslim power into Europe to Spain, Sicily and southern Italy, which were subject to Arab domination for some four centuries, divided Europeans into two distinct types, the north European of Indo-European blood and the southern European of mixed Semitic and Indo-European heritage. It was the former who was destined to dominate Western civilization through superior technological development.

Charles Martel did not claim the throne but his son Pepin III did, had the Pope bless the takeover, founding thus the famous Carolingian line of French kings. Most renowned was Charlemagne, his son, who ruled from 768–814 A. D. Pepin and Charles extended French rule over all of western

Europe except England, Scandinavia, Spain and southern Italy. Charles was crowned Emperor by the Pope on Christmas day in 800 A. D. in Saint Peters Cathedral in Rome. It was the beginning of the Holy Roman Empire which Voltaire (later) said was "Neither holy or Roman". Charlemagne moved the capital from Paris to Aachen for a more central location in the enlarged realm that included most of Germany. In fact Charlemagne too was of German stock.

Charlemagne was more than a conqueror. Though unlettered himself he took keen interest in learning and the arts. Byzantine influence flowed into France from Ravenna and Constantinople. Good living and gentle manners began to evolve. A Carolingian renaissance set in. Charles fancied himself as the emperor of the West on equal terms with the Byzantine emperor.

But western Europe was hit by another scourge in the 9th century. It was the marauding Vikings from Scandanavia. The Vikings too were of Germanic origin. They owed their prowess to their seafaring. Their craft, which looked like oversized rowboats, could navigate the seas as well as the rivers enabling them to attack deep inland. The Swedes penetrated into Russia. The Danes conquered England. Most significant to the future development of Europe, perhaps, was the conquest and settlement of Normandy by the Norsemen. The rise of the Normans and their acquisition of England was the beginning of the might of the north Europeans and their subsequent domination of the world. The story of William the Conqueror, the Battle of Hastings in 1066, has already been detailed in Chapter VI.

Charlemagne's weak successors were unable to keep his fragile "empire" together. It was eventually divided into three parts among his grandsons—France, Germany and a buffer state in between containing Lorraine that was to remain thereafter an area of contention between the two peoples. France was united by the Capetian line of kings for some four centuries, but Germany remained disunited except for occasional strong monarchs. Such a great German king was Otto I (912–973 A. D.) who became the Holy Roman Emperor over Europe minus France. This second Holy Roman Empire endured somewhat loosely until the 13th century. Across the channel a strong England arose after the Norman conquest in 1066 A. D. These peoples or nations were to become the leading states of the budding Western Civilization vying with one another for supremacy.

The Roman Catholic church was throughout a strong and unifying institution in Europe. It had a superb hierarchial organization seeping down from the Pope through archibishops, bishops and priests to the people. The church had conquered Gaul long before the Germans. Land and other wealth was accumulated over the centuries through gifts and legacies from the devout in the hope of attaining the Kingdom of Heaven. At one time the church owned one-third of the land in France! The monastery of Saint Martin of Tours had twenty-thousand serfs. The monasteries were also industrial centers with many crafts—weavers, shoemakers, metal smiths

528 MAN IN UNIVERSE

and the like. Most important they were centers of art and learning, reproducing manuscripts, harboring artists and conducting schools.

By the end of the first millennium churchmen had become venal and immoral. Church offices were bought and sold. It was called simony after the magician Simon Magus who allegedly offered to buy from Saint Peter the power to confer the Holy Spirit. Priests and prelates were allowed to marry and many carried their sexual activities to the verge of licentiousness. The papacy itself sank into similar degradation.

The church was rescued in the eleventh century by the new monastic order at Cluny founded in south-central France in 910 A. D. The Cluniacs purged the church from the parish to the papacy. Simony was abolished, celibacy was imposed upon the clerics and the efforts of the clergy were redirected mainly to religion. By the eleventh century the monks of Cluny assumed most of the high positions in the church. Gregory VII, a Cluniac monk, became the Pope in 1073 A. D.

Gregory the Great reasserted the authority of the church. Popes were henceforth elected by the college of cardinals and not designated by the Emperor. He was followed by another Cluniac Pope Urban II, who promoted the Crusades, one of the strangest phenomenas in history, when he called for arms at the Council of Claremont in 1095 A. D., against the infidel Turks, to recapture the Holy Land. It seemed that the Europeans were ready for the venture. All that was needed was the inspiration. For two centuries Europeans had been making pilgrimages to the Holy Land some of which had already assumed martial proportions. The Normans had taken southern Italy and Sicily from the "infidels". The Spaniards were beginning to push the Muslims back to the Iberian penninsula. The Crusades continued for two hundred years. The First Crusade succeeded gloriously with the capture of Jerusalem in 1099 A. D. and the establishment of European outposts in Lebanon. But the Holy Land was soon lost to the Muslims. The Crusades are discussed in detail in Chapter IX.

The Crusades were a failure. Moreover, they weakened Byzantium and it succumbed to Muslim rule a century or so later. But they served to energize the budding European civilization. New industries (silk and glass), new foods (apricot, plum, rice, sugar cane) and spices (cinnamon, cloves, nutmeg) were brought back from the Near East. A taste for luxurious living (steam and warm water baths, silks and brocades) arose. This coincided with the Indo-European proclivity for technological innovation which was once again astir.

The full power of the horse was extracted for more productive agriculture through the invention of the horse collar with appropriate harness and the horse-shoe. The moldboard plow was perfected for the moist sod soils of Europe. The wind and water were harnessed for industrial power through greatly improved water wheels and windmills. But most important of all, the deep hulled full rigged ship was built to dominate the seas. The technological development that was to enable the European to rule the world was carried out mainly by the north Europeans. There was, however, one exception. The Portuguese and Spaniards were the first to build ocean going ships. The French, Dutch and English soon reduced their technological lead but not before Spain and Portugal conquered large parts of the new and old worlds. After the Industrial Revolution in the North these two European nations sank into insignificance.

Like their Roman predecessors the Europeans now wanted the luxury goods produced in Asia. But they had little or nothing to trade in exchange. They had no bullion though a money economy was slowly reviving. The Venetians and other Italians slowly restored the Mediterranean trade through Constantinople and other eastern ports. One item that traded well was woolen goods. The wool was produced in England and manufactured into garments in Flanders. The capture of Constantinople, the channel for Asian goods to Europe, by the Ottoman Turks in 1453 A. D. restricted further the access to the luxuries from Asia. The Europeans sought desperately for a new route to India to circumvent the Muslim stranglehold on the eastern Mediterranean.

A historic phenomena now transpired that was destined to propel the Europeans to world domination. It was the discovery of the Americas. Seeking a sea route to India by sailing west Christopher Columbus in 1492 stumbled upon the heretofore unknown western hemisphere. Riding the northeast trade winds his voyage took him to the Caribbean where the first conquests were made. The daring and romantic story of the conquistadors has already been told in Chapter VI. In less than a century the Spaniards and Portuguese conquered most of Central and South America and established sea routes to India and China. Colonization of the new lands followed with the south Europeans taking Central and South America and north Europeans taking North America. This relieved the population pressure in Europe as it did in Greece two thousand years earlier when the Greeks colonized the western Mediterranean.

Fabulous wealth poured into Europe from plunder, silver mines like Potosi and foodstuffs from the newly established plantations. Gold and silver were in plentiful supply. Most of the bullion came through Spain but much of it flowed into northern Europe through piracy. Europe was, once again a money economy. It could now buy freely the luxuries it wanted from Asia. The bullion from the Americas simply flowed through Europe to India, China and other parts of Asia. But the Europeans lived better and many extravagantly. This increased money supply also begot a horrendous inflation in Europe during the 16th and 17th centuries.

The goods from Asia were augmented by new foods from the western hemisphere—the tomato, red peppers, the potato and others. Chocolate became a popular drink during the 16th and 17th centuries. Even tobacco, that was to plague Western civilization with drug addiction thereafter, found its way to Europe. But it was sugar that was to play the important role in European colonization of the new lands.

The Crusades familiarized Europeans with sugar cane but the climate and soil of Europe was not suitable for its cultivation. Central America was just right for the crop. It lacked labor, however, so the Europeans brought African slaves to the islands to work the plantations. Slavery had been receding in Europe but a substantial slave trade existed in Africa to supply the slave markets of the Muslim world. The Europeans tapped this labor source, stimulating the African slave trade in the process, to man the sugar and other plantations of the Americas. The Portuguese were first in the African slave trade but it was soon dominated by the English. Millions of negroes were shipped to the Americas during the 17th to 19th centuries where their descendants as freedmen form substantial minorities in North and South America and majorities in most Caribbean islands.

The initial plunder was followed by colonization broadening considerably the ambit of the burgeoning European civilization in a manner similar to the extension of the Greek civilization into the western Mediterranean two thousand years earlier. There was, however, a very significant difference in the extension of the European civilization into the Americas. The south Europeans less technologically minded and competent, extended their dominance over South and Central America along the already decadent feudal lines of medieval Europe, that is, they organized agricultural and other production on the basis of slavery and serfdom. They subjected the American Indians and imported African slaves for the purpose. The north Europeans, always more technologically minded and already in the uptake of the Industrial Revolution colonized North America along technological lines. They elected not to enslave the Indian but to eliminate him instead in the process of wresting from him the land they coveted in what is one of history's prime examples of genocide. There are no definite figures on the population of North America at the beginning of the 17th century but estimates range as high as nine million. To be sure, the Spaniards too killed millions of Indians but they did not eliminate them as Indian blood today flows freely in the populations of Mexico, Peru and other South American countries. This policy catapulted the North Americans to the highest technological development known to man within two centuries whereas South and Central America remained underindustrialized.

In Europe dramatic politico-socio-economic changes were transpiring during this time. Agricultural prosperity fostered better living and population growth. The introduction of the superior manufactures and appetizing foods and spices from Asia, first by the Venetian merchants, and then by the Crusades promoted commerce and trade providing non-agricultural economic opportunities for the emerging Europeans. At first this budding trade was conducted at fairs under the auspices of the manor lords. Foreign money (florins, bezants, dinars) was the medium of exchange as the European nations were only beginning to coin money and were plagued with lack of bullion. Italian bankers, as moneychangers, accompanied the itinerant merchants. A mercantile law arose to protect merchants and buyers.

These fairs graduated to towns—Oxford, Cambridge, Bruges, Ghent, Innsbruck, Frankfurt, Hamburg and others—to serve as permanent "fairs". They were still small ranging from 2,500 to 20,000 population. The old cities—Paris, London, Florence, Milan—took on commercial attributes. These cities too were small—only 100,000 people lived in Paris in the 15th century. The towns prospered and attracted dissatisfied and precocious lads from the manors. An alternative to agriculture was now present. Moreover, the merchant and the artisan were free of the manorial obligations. Feudalism started to decline.

This new economic class—the bourgeoisie, the third estate, the middle class—was free. Local self government prevailed in the towns. Economic life was organized into merchants and artisan guilds which were self governing but monopolistic. They fixed prices, standards and membership in the crafts. There was great economic prosperity and a *nouveaux rich* of bankers, merchants and industrialists emerged. The church, compromising with economic imperatives, eased its preoccupation against usury and profit. The Christian aversion to usury gave the Jews an advantage in moneylending and they became the first bankers of Europe.

This new constituency strengthened the monarchies, as kings no longer were completely dependent (even captives) on the lords of the manors. Strong monarchies resulted in stable nations and Europe began to take shape as a civilization of nation states that it is today. The 16th and 17th centuries, were times of great monarchs. The most renowned, perhaps, was Louis XIV, who ruled France gloriously for 72 years (1643-1715 A. D.). In England Elizabeth I (1558-1603 A. D.) and Henry VIII (1504-1547 A. D.) were powerful monarchs. The Hapsburgs ruled in Germany and Bohemia. Gustavius Adolphus (1611-1632 A. D.) ruled in Sweden.

The powerful monarchies clashed with the Papacy. The Protestant Revolution created a schism in Christendom in which England, Scandinavia, the Netherlands, and most of Switzerland and Germany refused to recognize the Papal *curia*. The Protestants predicated their religious doctrine upon the Bible instead of Papal doctrine. The Bible, thus, became more important to the Protestant than to the Roman Catholic. The most prominent leaders of the Reformation, as the schism is also called, were John Hus of Bohemia (1369-1415 A. D.), the earliest Protestant leader, and Martin Luther of Germany (1483-1546 A. D.). The schism resulted in internecine war and great loss of life. The Thirty Years War (1618-1648 A. D.) decimated and depopulated Germany, dissolved the Holy Roman Empire and set back the evolution of political unity and freedom of the German people for centuries. Henry VIII removed England from Papal suzerainty when the Pope refused to dissolve his marriage to Katherine of Aragon so that he could marry Anne

Boleyn, but it took another century before England was irrevocably Protestant. The shedding of blood in England, however, was minimal.

Protestanism freed the North Europeans of several debilitating economic restraints imposed by the church. The Bible did not proscribe interest and profit. The proscription was part of the anti-Romanism of the early church fathers. Moreover Protestantism, that is Calvinism, made the accumulation of wealth (not consumption of it) a proof of eternal salvation. This new attitude toward profit and wealth is considered by many such as the German sociologist Max Weber and English economist Richard Tawney as an important factor in the industrialization of the North European countries.

In the 17th centuries the absolute monarchies began to give way to democracy and parliamentary government. England was foremost in the development of constitutional government. As early as 1215 the feudal barons exacted the Magna Carta from King John at a meadow on the banks of the Thames called Runnymede. It merely assured the feudal lords their rights against the king. It gave the common people nothing. But it was a small step toward democracy. John's son Henry summoned the knights and burgesses in 1268 to ask their advise on and permission to raise taxes. This was the beginning of Parliament. From its power over the purse it broadened its authority to matters of national policy. For several centuries thereafter there was a struggle between the monarchy and Parliament for supremacy with the latter going into eclipse under powerful kings like the Tudors. But the Parliament took on additional powers judicial and legislative including the unique right of impeachment of the king's officials. The Protestant revolution became a part of the struggle. Parliament marshalled its forces from time to time to prevent a Catholic restoration by Catholic kings. Finally in 1668, in the so-called Glorious Revolution, Parliamentary supremacy over the Crown was established. In its slow evolution the English Parliament became bicameral with the Commons eventually (Reform Bill of 1832, *et seq*) elected by the people. The rise of Parliamentary governments on the continent of Europe was more slow and tortuous as already discussed in Chapter VIII.

The common law developed concurrently. It was indigenous to England as the legal systems on the continent were based on the civil law system predicated upon Roman law as preserved in the Justinian Code. The common law, it may be said, started from scratch and is the basis of the legal systems of the English speaking peoples. It was based on judicial decisions in the Kings *curia* and other courts. At first it involved primarily land tenures as the economy was almost wholly agricultural. Mercantile law evolved only in the 18th century. The common law was not legislated, with some exceptions like the Statute of Wills and the Statute of Uses. It was, in the main, compiled by eminent jurists like Sir Edward Coke (1552–1634 A. D.) in his *Reports and Institutes* and Sir William Blackstone in his

Commentaries. Blackstone's *Commentaries* had a profound effect on the legal systems of the colonies, particularly America.

These two pillars of democracy, the Parliamentary political system and the common law, were a major contribution of the Europeans, the English in particular, to the advancement of civilization in the world. They have conferred freedom and personal security on more people in the world today than have been enjoyed by earlier people. India, for example, is governed by Parliamentary government under a legal system based upon the finest traditions of British justice. So are many countries of Africa and elsewhere which were part of the British empire.

The most far reaching contribution of the European civilization to the advancement of mankind was the Industrial Revolution of the 18th century. Again England was foremost in this respect. The Germans, renowned for their technological competence were unfortunately floundering in political disunity and instability at this time defaulting possible leadership in this connection to the English. The year 1750 is generally regarded as the beginning of industrialization. It was, of course, not that abrupt or definite. European man had been moving toward this goal for centuries by maximizing the power of the horse, wind and water with improved technology. The Dutch and East Anglia windmills were extremely complex mechanisms by the 18th century. It was easy for these millrights to transfer their mechanical genius to the steam engine when it emerged on the technological scene. The major achievement of the Industrial Revolution was not the improved machine but the harnessing of a new source of energy for the machine. Man brought under his control for the first time the chemical energy contained in matter. Throughout his evolution up to this time man was able to control only the biologic energy of life (of himself and animals like the ox and horse) and the elemental energy of the earth like the wind and the flowing water. Now he was able to harness mechanically the chemical energy residing in matter like wood and coal. This constituted another major technological breakthrough like the invention of agriculture eight millennia or so earlier. Within another two centuries western man went even further to tap the nuclear energy in matter to bring within control external energy beyond the wildest imagination of earlier man. That is why technological development must be considered the greatest accomplishment of European civilization. The detailed history of the Industrial Revolution is set forth in Chapter V.

This technological breakthrough enabled European man to eventually dominate the entire world. European colonialism began, of course, much earlier. The Spanish and Portuguese conquests of the New World started in the 16th century. In this part of the world the pre-industrial technology (firearms and the mounted warrior) was adequate to overwhelm the technologically backward American Indian civilizations. Asia was another matter. There the technological gap in the 16th century was not as great. The

European approach, therefore, had to be by trade with the sea as a retreat and sanctuary whenever hostile reception was encountered. Gradually the European traders were able to establish coastal trading centers called "factories" by the English. But any domination of the Asians had still to await two centuries or so.

The Portuguese came first. When Pope Alexander VI issued his famous Papal Bull (1494) dividing the world for exploration, conquest and trade between Spain and Portugal the New World, with the exception of Brazil, fell to Spain. Portugal got Africa and Asia. Thus Portugal was destined to develop a trading empire (including the African slave trade; hence the word negro, meaning black in Portuguese, for the African slaves) whereas Spain brought forth the first European colonial empire. Portugal dominated the Asian trade during the 16th century. Alburquerque conquered Goa in 1510 which developed into a military and commercial center from where Portuguese naval power dominated the west coast of India. Fortified trading factories were established in Malacca in 1511, Yokahama in 1548, Macao in 1557 and other ports in the 16th century.

The North Europeans—English, Dutch and French—refused to be bound by the Papal Bull and started to make inroads into the Asian trade during the 17th century. In 1600 Queen Elizabeth chartered the East India Company which founded its first Indian trading factory at Surat (near Bombay) in 1613. Madras was founded in 1639; Calcutta in 1698. The Dutch founded factories in Gujarat, Bihar, Bengal and Orissa the early part of the 17th century. And France, coming last, founded entrepots at Surat in 1660, Pondicherry in 1673 and Chandernagore in 1690.

At the same time the English tried desperately to find a northwest (also northeast) passage to Asia. This effort by Forbisher (1576), Davis (1586) and Hudson (1610) acquainted the English, Dutch and French with the North American continent. Colonization ensued shortly thereafter. The Virginia colony was established in 1608. The Pilgrims landed in Massachusetts in 1620. The Dutch founded New Amsterdam (New York) in 1624. The French initiated their colonization in Quebec (1608) and later founded New Orleans in 1718. In the 18th century colonization by the north Europeans was in full progress.

Bitter rivalry for colonial domination of North America and commercial supremacy in India developed in the 18th century. The Dutch retired from the fray and concentrated their efforts in Indonesia. The Portuguese, declining in power, sank into a secondary position in Asia. In America the English gained domination after a series of armed conflicts ending in the Treaty of Paris in 1763 which eliminated French power in the New World. In India too three Carnatic wars during the period 1740–1765 resulted in English supremacy over the French in the subcontinent. These colonial wars were merely an extension of the fratricidal wars that raged in Europe for dominance during the 18th century.

At the start of the 19th century Great Britain ruled an empire on which "the sun never set". To be sure, the English lost political control of most of North America but the Americans continued to be closely tied to England through trade and cultural affinity, analogous, again, to the relationship that existed between ancient Greece and the Greek colonies in the western Mediterranean. Even the Monroe Doctrine of 1823, whereby the United States warned all foreign powers to desist from colonial activities in the western hemisphere did not interfere with this affinity of the two English speaking peoples as British interests in America were primarily trade and commerce, for instance, cotton for the mills of Lancashire.

By the end of the century Great Britain had dominions, colonies and spheres of influence in every part of the world—Canada, West Indies, Africa, Egypt, Near East, India, Malaya and China. China was never a colony but after its defeat by England in the Opium Wars of 1842 and 1858 resulting in the unequal treaties China came within the British sphere of influence. It should be noted that the English were far more interested in trade, adequate supplies of raw materials for its industries, food for its burgeoning population and markets for its manufactured goods. Free trade and freedom of the seas were the twin British policies to sustain this economic imperialism. For this purpose England maintained the most formidable navy in history, at first powered by sail, then by steam. France too built an empire, second to Great Britain, in North Africa and Indo-China.

The 19th century was one of the glorious centuries of man. Industrialization bloomed producing more material wealth for more people than ever before. Distribution of the increased wealth was broader creating a growing middle class demanding participation in the political life of its country. Democratic governments based on universal suffrage evolved. The idea of democracy was not new as it existed throughout history but never before was the franchise so broad. Poverty was still the lot of most. To a large extent poverty is relative (in America less than $6500 income is considered poverty but that is 30 times the per family income of India) but there was less of it in Europe and America than elsewhere because of the blessings of industrialization. Industrialization was to bring forth its deleterious effects of chemical and noise pollution, mechanization and depersonalization of work and the like but these enormities were not yet fully realized and appreciated until the 20th century.

British supremacy was soon challenged. First by a renascent France under Napoleon at the beginning of the century. Napoleon was unable to marshall the force to bridge the English channel, the formidable natural water moat that protected England throughout history. His attempt to cripple England economically with the continental blockade against her goods also failed as the desire in Europe for the superior goods of English industry and trade was too overwhelming. He tried also to hit the British at their colonial jugular by breaking through to India in the Middle East but was defeated by the British in Egypt in 1799. When Lord Nelson destroyed the French fleet at Trafalgar in 1805 Napoleon knew he could not challenge the British empire at sea. This was England's second victory for mastery of the seas, the first was the defeat of the Spanish Armada in 1588. Napoleon next tried to reach India by land via Russia. This was his undoing. Napoleon's ill-fated invasion of Russia has already been detailed in Chapter IX. The British supremacy remained unchallenged for the remainder of the century.

In the middle of the 19th century a new power center arose in Europe. It was Germany. The Germans disunited for two centuries were finally brought together as a nation under the hegemony of Prussia. But by now the other European nations had parceled out the world in their colonial and trade expansion. In its thrust for dominance Germany had first to deal with France, which it defeated in the Franco-Prussian war of 1871. It regained the largely German populated areas of Alsace-Lorraine and received an indemnity of five billion francs which proved useful in its industrialization. The Germans lagged in industry despite their technological ingenuity because of the political instability that beset their land. They now had to catch up with Britain, France and the United States.

Around the turn of the century the Germans began to dream of world empire. They managed to gain colonial footholds in Africa and Asia where they clashed with the old colonial powers. A struggle over Morocco with France in 1905 was resolved amicably. But the supreme colonial power was Great Britain. Germany realized it could not challenge the English at sea. Like Napoleon it too deduced that the heart of the British empire was India. From her central position in Europe Germany thought it might be possible to reach India by land. European technology had now developed the steam locomotive and the railroad which made this possible. The Germans conceived the Bagdad railway project which would pass through the Balkans and Turkey. They sought the cooperation of other European nations for both the capital cost and diplomatic support. Great Britain, naturally, was wary of the project as the railway would provide a facile invasion road to India. The British sought control over its easternmost nexus as the price of cooperation. The English and French protested to Turkey about the project but the construction, plagued by shortages of capital and engineering difficulties, proceeded slowly and by 1914 only a few stretches in Turkey and Iraq remained to be completed.

Europe was in a state of nervous agitation over German imperialism at this time. Only an incident was needed to spark a fratricidal war. It came with the assassination of Archduke Francis Ferdinand, the successor to the Austrian crown, in Sarajevo, Bosnia by a Serbian on June 28, 1914. The five powers tried to settle the conflict between Austria and Serbia, but through various alliances soon found themselves drawn into war. Turkey joined the central powers—Germany and Austria—which opened the road to India for a German thrust. The British tried unsuccessfully to block any such purpose by capturing the Dardanelles, the ill fated Gallopoli campaign, in 1915. This proved unnecessary as Germany was already overtaxed fighting a war on two fronts—Russia in the east, Great Britain and France in the west—for any march on India. When America joined the allies in 1917 Germany was overpowered and defeated. The war precipitated the Russian Revolution in 1917 that was to have so profound an effect on Europe.

America now rose to power. After gaining independence from Great Britain in 1776 the Americans launched a vigorous development of their vast and resource rich land. Through purchase (Louisiana) and conquest (from Mexico) the Americans possessed the entire continent between Canada and Mexico. A devastating civil war was fought in 1860–64, ostensibly over slavery but actually to determine whether the new industrial interests of the north would predominate over the agricultural interests of the south. In the Industrial Revolution of the time the result was predestined. After the war America undertook a spectacular industrial development that fifty years later, by the time of World War I, made it one of the highly industrialized nations of the world. During the forepart of the 20th century this pace continued and by mid century America was the foremost industrial power in the world. It industrialized (mechanical power and chemical fertilizer) its agriculture for the production of food and fibre never before known to man.

After the war a powerful communist state began to evolve in Russia. Europe (and the world) was to divide over economic philosophy as to whether the factors of production (land, mines and industries) should be owned by the state or private individuals and corporations. In 1848 Karl Marx and Fredrich Engels published the Communist Manifesto in which they exhorted the workers to unite and wrest ownership of industry from its private owners. In Marx's view such socialistic ownership could come only after industrialization. But as it came to pass the first nation won over to the new economic philosophy was Russia, a preindustrial agricultural economy. Lenin revised communist doctrine to strike at European colonialism which appealed to the Asians and played a vital role in depriving the European nations of their colonies after World War II.

The Slavs were also part of the Indo-European migrations during the second millennium before Christ. They settled in northeastern Europe behind the Germans. In the 5th century A. D. they too were pushed westward by the Huns and some, the Czechs and Poles, settled as far as the Elbe on lands vacated by the Germans. The Slavs also pushed southward to the doorsteps of Byzantium. Half of Europe became Slavonic.

In the 9th century the Vikings invaded down the Baltic waterways. Rurik, the Viking, became the first Prince of the Russians in 862 A. D. with a captial at first at Novgorod, and later moved to Kiev. His heirs ruled Russia for the next seven hundred years. The Russians came under two major influences. The cultural impact of Byzantium and the devastating Mongol and Tartar invasions from Asia. Vladimir (980–1015), adopted Byzantine Christianity because of its appealing pomp and ritual after due consideration of the various faiths (he rejected Mohammedanism, it is said, because it was quite impossible to be happy in Russia without a strong drink). The Poles and Czechs, however, opted for Roman Catholicism.

In the 13th century the Tartars under Batu, a descendant of Genghis Khan, devastated Russia and exacted huge tribute. All Europe trembled before this new scourge from Asia, but the Russians took the brunt of the attack. It set back Russian national development for centuries. Kiev gave way to Moscow, more centrally located with respect to Russia's waterways, as the center of power. East of the Volga the Tartar's held sway and Muscovite Russia paid tribute to the Tartar Khans. But as the Tartars declined Muscovite Russia grew in power. At this stage Russia was half European and half Asian. As Sir Bernard Pares so aptly puts it "Russia is at the back end of Europe, the least European part of Europe."

By the time of Ivan the Terrible (1533–1584) Muscovite Russia was expanding in all directions. More and more of the Tartar areas were conquered. Kazan was taken in 1552, Astrakhan in 1556, Siberia conquered in 1583 and the Pacific reached in 1556. In the 17th century the Romanov dynasty came to power and the eminent Tsar Peter the Great (1689–1725) continued the Europeanization. Russia expanded westward into Europe and acquired part of Poland in 1772 in a treaty of partition with Prussia and Austria. Two successive partitions gave Russia even more of Poland. The Russians became Francophiles with the court and gentry copying and imitating everything French. It is interesting to note that there are more of Gaugin's canvases at the Hermitage than any place else as Russian merchants, prior to the Revolution, bought them before Gaugin achieved his fame just because they were French.

At the end of the 19th century the Russian empire stretched from Vladivostock in the east to Warsaw in the west—an unprecedented land mass under one rule. The Russians constructed the Trans-Siberian railway to knit this vast empire together. But by the turn of the century Russia was seething with rebellion. Population pressure on the limited wealth of a predominantly agricultural society was growing intolerable. To be sure the serfs were emancipated by Alexander's reform of 1861. The land, however, remained concentrated in the gentry, mostly parasitic and absentee, living in luxury in St. Petersburg and Moscow. Industrialization was slow and inadequate to provide a livelihood for the excess population on the land. This gross maldistribution of wealth ultimately exploded in the Revolution of 1917, detailed in Chapter VIII.

Two decades after World War I—the war that was to end all war—a second Germanic war gripped Western civilization. This war comprised even greater madness than the first. Moreover, it involved Asia where

Japan, a new power, tried to build an empire in the Pacific. It was truly a World War.

German frustration over its defeat in the first war begot a virulent nationalism under a paranoid dictator Adolph Hitler. In this madness the Nazis massacred six million Jews, doubtless the worst holocaust of the many this hapless people have suffered over the millennia. Hitler was equally paranoid about communism. When he took on both Russia and England, to whose aid America rallied, it was his undoing. Germany did not possess the wealth, that is, the industrial productivity, for such a two front war. It was defeated in 1945 and partitioned with its eastern sector falling into the communist bloc.

The Japanese miscalculated. They possessed neither the technology nor the industrial capacity to take on the most highly industrialized country in the world. They suffered, consequently, a decisive defeat in 1945, already discussed in Chapter VI.

The defeat of Germany and Japan, however, was not the most important consequence of the war. The British empire crumbled. The two Germanic wars debilitated the European nations and leadership of the Western civilization passed to the United States. After the war America became the most powerful nation in the world. It is interesting to note that the power center of the civilizations of the Mediterranean area has been moving west for three millennia. The power center started in the Fertile Crescent, moved west to Greece and Rome, then to western Europe and across the Atlantic to America.

Russia emerged from the war as a world power, despite the devastation to its economy and people (some ten million lives lost). More significant, perhaps, Russia was able to bring the entire Slavonic world under its hegemony within the communist bloc. Europe was now divided along ideological lines. Part of the German nation was in the communist orbit. Strong communist parties in Italy and France were maneuvering for control in western Europe.

The ideological conflict became world wide. Technological advances in communications and transportation welded humanity into one community for the first time, by mid 20th century. America assumed the political and economic (the Marshall Plan) leadership of the non-communist part of the European civilization. As European colonialism ended after the war the former colonies got caught up in the ideological conflict. China was won over by the communists in 1948. India opted for a Parliamentary government when it gained independence from Great Britain in 1947. Indo-China, that hapless country, went through twenty-five years of war before the communists gained control in 1975.

America made two, mostly unsuccessful efforts (in Korea and Indo-China) to arrest the takeover of Asia by the communists. Russia too tried to extend its power into western Asia (Azerbaijain) without success. By the last quarter of the 20th century the lines were pretty well fixed between the two powers. At this time there is peace between them as neither has the superiority in technology or industrial capacity to dominate the other.

XIII
Rise and Fall of Societies— Asian Civilizations

INDIAN CIVILIZATION

Earth's tallest mountains, the Himalayas, provide a watershed in the Indian subcontinent second to none in the world. Two river systems, the Indus (from whence derives the name India) and the Ganges create an alluvial plain (as thick as 2000 feet in places) stretching in a crescent for some 2000 miles from the Arabian Sea up the Indus river into the Punjab and over to the Junma-Ganges doab to the Bay of Bengal. The Gangetic plain is fed furthermore by the watershed of the Vindhya mountains in central India augmenting an already abundant flow of water from the Himalayas.

The Himalayan range not only nurtured this area with fertile alluvium and abundant water but provided a formidable barrier against intrusion from without unlike the defenseless Euphrates-Tigris doab. Though, as we shall see, India was always attractive to foreign invaders it enjoyed, particularly in its earlier days, greater freedom to develop a truly indigenous civilization unlike the turbulent Mediterranean area just discussed.

It is not surprising, therefore, that one of the first and foremost civilizations sprung up in this region of the world. It was in the Indus basin that man first developed in the subcontinent an agricultural society similar to that in Mesopotamia and the Nile valley. The development of the Gangetic plain came later.

HARAPPA

The early Indian society is often referred to as the Harappa civilization after the name of one of its two great cities. Harappa was situated on the left bank of the Ravi River, one of the five (there may have been six at this time) tributaries of the Indus system; Mohenjodaro, the other city, was some four hundred miles southwest on the banks of the Indus in Sind. Around this axis covering an area of about one thousand miles in length and five hundred miles in breadth flourished a well-developed, highly urbanized civilization during the period 2500–1500 B. C. Recent excavations reveal that the Harappans extended their domination as far south as Gugarat and east into the Jumna-Ganges doab, making it the largest empire of its time.

Each metropolis, (around 50,000 population) had well appointed buildings, streets, drains and other public facilities constructed of burnt brick of standard specification. The houses had tiled bathrooms connected with municipal sewers directed to soak pits outside the city. Rubbish shoots leading to bins on the street, where presumably it was collected and disposed of by the municipality, were built into the homes. Such refinement in sanitation is unknown in history elsewhere, with few exceptions, until modern times.

Cotton textiles were made. Cotton cloth is India's gift to civilization. Bronze and other metals were worked. There is no evidence of iron as iron technology was still unknown to man.

A citadel was located strategically in each city. There were large public baths. Central granaries have also been found which would indicate some type of agricultural planning and perhaps taxation in kind. The main foodgrains were wheat, barley, peas and sesame. Animals of all types including the cow, goat and fowl, but apparently not the horse, were domesticated. The chicken was still another contribution of mankind by the Indus civilization.

There is a Harappa script yet undeciphered. Unfortunately, there is no rosetta stone nor is there likely to be to unlock its secrets. The script is unique and bears no resemblance to the Sumerian. Plastic art was well developed as portrayed by the famous bronze dancing girl of Mohenjodaro.

The genesis of this earliest Indian civilization is somewhat obscure. Though there is evidence of amalgamation of racial stocks from western and central Asia, the indigenous strain was presumably Dravidian. The Dravidians were dark-skinned, broad nosed, thick lipped, round-headed men of Austroloid origin who apparently peopled the entire sub-continent at this time.

There is archeological evidence of trade with Mesopotamia. Harappan seals have been found in considerable numbers in the Euphrates-Tigris doab. But this is not difficult to comprehend as there was (and still is) a facile waterway from the Persian Gulf to the mouth of the Indus without losing the sight of land. If the Sumerian myth that they came into the Euphrates-Tigris doab by sea from Iran proves to be true history it is just as likely that a contingent of these early migrants may have sailed eastward and up the Indus river to settle in this equally hospitable land for man's new agricultural technology. Sir Mortimer Wheeler feels that there was more affinity between the Sumerian and Harappan civilizations than archeological remains reveal. He postulates not only a common racial genesis, presumably by land from Central Asia, but more trade and commerce both overland and by sea than is presently known. But he concludes that due to geographic remoteness and absence of facile communications at the time the two contemporary cultures developed independently and differently.

In the 17th century B. C. the Harappan civilization lapsed into decay. Urban life seems to have deteriorated. The artifacts became of lesser quality. This is known as the Jhuhar and Jhanagar cultures. The reason for the decline is not clear. There may have been a climatic catastrophy such as an earthquake or flood which destroyed the agricultural organization that sustained the vigorous Harappan civilization. At Mohenjodaro some 30 skeletons have been found in situations where death was caused by some sudden calamity. The decline may have been caused by simple socio-economic disintegration that, as we have seen, caused other societies to fall. And the Indo-Europeans who were migrating from the Caspian-Aral seas area into Europe and Western Asia invaded the Indus valley during this time.

Much archeological work remains to be done on the early Indus civilization before the whole story is known. The discovery has been made only in recent times since the first world war, but considerable knowledge has been gained through efforts of such archeologists as Sir John Marshall and Sir Mortimer Wheeler.

THE ARYANS

The Indo-Europeans that came to India around 1500 B. C. belonged to the eastern branch of the family and are called Aryans. The Persians and the Mitannis belonged to this same branch. The Aryans who came to India were part of the mass migration of an energetic race bursting forth on to the sedentary civilizations of western and southern Asia, which they reinvigorated with new blood, and into Europe where they founded civilizations of their own. The Indo-European a tall, fair-skinned, thin-lipped, sharp-nosed, long-headed man was destined to ultimately dominate the Indian civilization as, we saw earlier, he did the Persian, Graeco-Roman and European societies.

To what the Aryan owed his energy is unclear. His domestication of the horse was however, his main source of power. He may also have known the use of iron. The horse gave him superior mobility and military technique. Astride or more commonly behind his horse in a two-wheeled chariot he possessed a sense of power and a zest for life no longer existing in the old civilizations of the time. It was, therefore, relatively easy for the Indo-European to overwhelm and dominate his neighbors to the south.

It should not be thought that the Harappans succumbed in one fell swoop. The Aryan incursions into the Indus Valley were many and frequent, probably disorganized, lasting perhaps over several centuries. Thereafter the history of India for some twenty-five hundred years, at least until the period of foreign domination, was the interaction, amalgamation and synthesis of Aryan and Dravidian stocks into a single culturally integrated Indian Society. The fusion is, however, by no means complete either physically or sociologically. As anyone familiar with India today notes—the Aryan racial type predominates in north India while Dravidian characteristics are most common in south India. North Indian languages are Sanskrit based whereas south Indian languages are of Dravidian origin.

After the Aryan invasions the Indian civilization reverted to a non-urban agricultural state. This was frequently the case elsewhere in history, to wit, Europe in the middle ages, after barbarian invasions. The Indus area was heavily forested at this time in contrast to its treeless arid condition today. Other areas of India were sheer jungle. In this semi-primeval atmosphere a new robust culture began to flourish in the dying embers of the Harappa civilization.

The early Aryan period was an heroic age during which the numerous tribes settled in that part of India known today as the Punjab and vied with one another for supremacy. Unfortunately the early Aryan was uninterested in recording history and it can be pieced together only from vague references in his sacred works called the vedas and epics. And these too were unrecorded for several centuries but kept alive from generation to generation by the prodigious memory of the priests, the Brahmans. As yet no archeological evidence has been unearthed but this is unlikely to happen as the Aryan was slow in reconstructing an urban civilization.

The Aryans lived in wood and bamboo houses of which no trace remains. They worshipped outdoors with their priests officiating before wooden altars on mounds of ground. Unlike the Harappans they did not build with brick. They had no art, at least no evidence of it remains. There is thus no archeological evidence of the early Aryan period. And, more important, they had no script. It is the absence of the written word that makes it so frustrating, almost impossible, to reconstruct the history of the Indo-Europeans that were destined to dominate the civilizations of man during the succeeding millennia. In fact we know them mainly through myths, epics and religious lore which had necessarily to be carried by memory until it could be reduced to writing centuries later. And so it is with the aryanization of India for which history has only the religious and epic lore of the Aryans to interpret India's history before 500 B. C.

The original religious Hindu text is the *Rig Veda* (book of knowledge) consisting of 1028 hymns composed, it is believed, during the period 1500–1000 B. C. It is the oldest religious text in the world. This is followed by the Brahmanas, which are commentaries on the Vedas and guides for the performance of the sacrificial rites. The Vedas portray a life of conquest of the dark-skinned people (dasas, which came to mean "slave") by the "wheat colored" Aryans. The Aryans had horses and chariots, bows and arrows and bronze weapons. They were beefeaters, heavy drinkers of alcoholic beverages and great gamblers with dice. There were many tribes one of which, perhaps the leading one, was known as Bharata (a word often used for India). They divided into three classes. The king (raja) and his warriors were the Kshatryas, the priests were the Brahmans and the common people—the agriculturalists and tradesmen—the Vaishayas. A fourth class, the Sudras, who did the menial work, were the enslaved Dravidians referred to as dasas (dark skinned). This social stratification developed into the caste system that has distinguished and still characterizes the Indian civilization. The sanskrit word for the caste system is *varna* which derives from color of the skin. A sharp color consciousness developed during the early Aryan period when the small minority of Indo-Europeans with superior technology conquered a large indigenous population of dark skinned Dravidians. It was a means of keeping the purity of the Aryan blood that Augustus would have envied. Each varna, or caste, was thenceforth associated with the color of its skin—white for the Brahman, red for the Kshatrya, brown for the Vaishya and black for the Sudra. This distinction makes sense except for the Kshatrya unless the color red was meant to refer to the sanguinary duties of the warriors. The Brahmans who did not work in the fields obviously had the lightest skins; the Vaishya peasants, tradesmen and artisans were browned from the sun and the Dravidians, the Sudras, were genetically black.

In practice the caste system was as not rigid as it was portrayed in the religious texts or even as it came to be during the period of foreign invasions. The French historian Amaury de Riencourt sets forth an interesting thesis in his *Soul of India* that a retreat into caste by the Hindus was a means of defense against the religious cultural impact of Muslim rule that in time ossified Hinduism. During Vedic and Buddhist times caste lines became blurred, the Kshatryas almost vanished, the Vaishyas forsook agriculture for trade and the Sudras became the agriculturists and artisans. When a Sudra gained political power a Kshatrya lineage was conjured up for him. In fact, the main Kshatrya class today, the Rajputs, are descendants of the Scythians (sakas) and Huns (huras) who invaded India during the period 300 B. C.–500 A. D. and were assimilated into the Hindu society. Nonetheless the caste system provided a stable social structure that many feel contributed greatly to the political stability and durability of the Indian civilization.

Political organization centered on the tribe headed by a king called raja who was responsible to a council, the sabba. In some instances there were only tribal councils. These early Aryan republics were, therefore, not absolute monarchies. There was a large measure of democracy in the early Aryan governments. Their political organization was, perhaps, similar to that in the Greek cities.

The Aryans pushed out of the Punjab into the Gangetic plain eastward to the Bay of Bengal and south to the Vindhya Mountains of central India in a fashion, possibly, reminiscent of the settlement of the frontiers in America and Siberia of recent times. The tribal republics were consolidated into nations and eventually empires. When the Greeks under Alexander made contact with India in the third century B. C. they found a highly urbanized civilization stretching across the Indus and Gangetic plains with its capital in the east at Patiliputra, the site of modern Patna, in Bihar state.

In the interim—that is 1500–300 B. C.—the Aryanized culture bloomed into the Indian civilization known to us today. How much is of purely Aryan origin remains still to be unraveled by archeologists and historians. The relation may be similar to that of the Graeco-Roman and European civilizations where, to use Toynbee's term, the former apparented the latter. In this process of cultural growth Indian thought and wisdom developed. The numerous Vedas, Puranas and Brahmanas were succeeded by the Upanishads which embody the philosophy and ethics of the Indian civilization. The great epics, the *Mahabharata* and *Ramayana,* containing both historical and philosophical insights, were composed during the latter part of this period. It can therefore be said that by the middle of the first millennium before Christ the Indian civilization had developed and matured.

The epic *Mahabharata* (meaning greater Bharata or India) depicts a struggle that transpired sometime during the last centuries of the second millennium B. C. for dominance of the capital city of Indraprasthra (site of modern New Delhi) between two Aryan clans, the Kurus and the Pandus. The center of power had by now shifted from the Indus basin to the Gangetic plain. The doab (between the Ganges and Jumna rivers) is described in the epic as heavily forested. The *Mahabharata* was written around 500 B. C., supposedly by the sage Vyasa and, is a further source of Indian morals and ethics. The *Bhagavad Gita,* sometimes called the Lords Prayer, is an ethical passage in the *Mahabharata* of 700 verses and highly revered by the Indians.

The Uphanishads composed about 800 B. C. reflect the development of rational thought in India. The Uphanishads were, in large part, a revolt also against the ritual and religiosity of Brahmanism. In general they proclaim salvation through knowledge and understanding. There is profound speculation on the origin of the universe and the beginning of life. The interrelation of all things gave rise to monism in Indian thought. Asceticism and disdain of material things were highly valued. Non-violence and abstinence were other virtues of the Uphanishads. Buddhist ethics and morality stem from the Uphanishads. The noble eightfold path for the attainment of Nirvana is based on non-violence and abstinence.

BUDDHIST ERA

No sooner had the Indian civilization matured when it was beset by troubles. The Hindu society had become oppressive and self indulgent. The people began to resent Brahmanic dominance. Religion had degenerated into religiosity. Greed and licentiousness were rampant as the story of the Buddha informs us. There was great intellectual ferment in sixth century

B. C. India. Many philosophical schools flourished, but most prominent were those of Mahavira and Buddha, the founders of Jainism and Buddhism.

Siddhartha Gautama, the Buddha (enlightened one), was a Kshatrya whose royal family ruled the small state of Sakya (lower Nepal today) in the foothills of the Himalayas which fell within the suzerainty of the powerful state of Kosala in the Gangetic plain. He was born in 573 B. C. and as a young prince lived a life of privilege and luxury. At 30 he questioned his pointless life of wealth and ease and, in the spirit of the Uphanishads, sought to discover the meaning of man. He wandered through the woods for six years and traveled through the kingdom of Magadha, the most powerful state at the time. After wide observation and meditation he concluded that man's selfishness and aggression were the main cause of the suffering and unhappiness of mankind. Abstinence and non-violence, he concluded, were the means of eliminating human strife and misery; the pursuit of knowledge and understanding the way to happiness. Siddhartha lived and taught accordingly thereafter and soon amassed a large following. It was not intended to be a new religion—more of a philosophy of life—but it became the foundation of one of the world's great religions.

The story of Vardhamana Mahavira is similar. He too was born a Kshatrya (*circa* 540 B. C.) who rejected the Brahmanic religiosity. Mahavira was the son of the chief of the Jnatrika tribe in the eastern Gangetic plain who forsook, like prince Siddhartha, a life of ease and luxury to become an ascetic. He established a new sect. The Jains were named after Jina (conqueror) the title bestowed upon Mahavira by his disciples. The Jains carried the principle of self denial to an extreme. Salvation was death through starvation. It took Mahavira thirteen years to starve himself to death. The Jains believe that everything on earth—rocks, worms, and humans—were all imbued with varying degrees of life. Non-violence in every respect became an essential rule of life. In fact, some Jains wear a gauze over their mouth to avoid swallowing an insect accidentally. The Jains even went to the extreme of forsaking agriculture because cultivation of the soil involved the killing of life. The Jains today are mostly business men and bankers and concentrated in western India in the state of Gujarat. Due probably to its extremism Jainism never achieved the widespread acceptance of Buddhism. But both profoundly affected Hinduism with their tenents of non-violence and abstension.

An observation here is in order. Few peoples of the human family have pondered as deeply as the Indians on the meaning of man's existence. The Upanishads, Buddhism, Jainism and other religio-philosophies have sought the causes of the misery and strife. In general the great Indian thinkers concluded that the chief causes of this misery and strife were egoity and violence. They are of course the twin manifestations of man's biologic instinct of dominance. Rejection of hostility toward others together with self denial and asceticism were prescribed as the ideal for man. Though they may have gone too far, perhaps, with respect to abstinence (certainly not regarding non-violence) such a way of life could serve as the salvation of man. Unfortunately these great philosophies were and are given mostly lip service inside and outside India. It appears that man then and even now, has not yet evolved culturally sufficiently to submerge his biologic instinct of dominance to live a non-violent and selfless life envisioned by the eminent Indian thinkers.

Political strife was likewise the order of the day. By 500 B. C. the tribes had been consolidated into four strong and warring nations. They were the kingdoms of Kosala, Magadha, Vatsa and Avanti. Pre-eminent among them was the kingdom of Magadha which at this time had prominent rulers like Bimbisara and Ajatasatra who pursued expansionist policies against their weaker neighbors. By 400 B. C. a Magadhan empire with its capital at Patilputra (modern Patna) gained hegemony over the Gangetic plain. The last important Magadhan king was Mahapedma Nanda who ruled about 350 B. C. After his death there was a struggle over succession to the crown which left the empire in chaos.

At this time the Aryans had brought the fertile Gangetic plain under cultivation with irrigation. Great prosperity prevailed. There was much wealth for which to contend both within and between the warring states. It is believed that the reason Magdha prevailed was due to the rich iron ore within its state. Even today the iron ore in Bihar assays 60 per cent! It is not known whether the Indians developed iron technology by themselves or whether it was transmitted to India from western Asia. Later migrants from Persia may have brought the technology to India. Recent archeological finds date iron artifacts in India to the forepart of the last millennium before Christ. In any event, the Magdhans were best situated to utilize the new technology and it doubtless enabled them to dominate their neighbors.

Meanwhile Alexander the Great intervened in Indian history with his invasion of the Punjab in 326 B. C. Even earlier, under Darius, the Persians exercised domination over parts of the Indus area for a time during the 5th century. Alexander's invasion undermined the power of the tribes and nations in the northwest creating a political vacuum in the Indus valley. These conditions were propitious for the emergence of India's first emperor Chandragupta Maurya the founder of the Mauryan dynasty which was destined to unify the whole of India. Chandragupta defeated the Nandas to gain control of the Magadhan crown and then conquered the northwest driving out the Greek satraps. By 300 B. C. Chandragupta ruled over the first Indian empire. Friendly diplomatic relations, however, were maintained with the Seleucid empire in Persia.

Chandragupta had an able and ruthless Brahman advisor known as Kautilya, or Canayka, who composed a machiavellian treatise on politics called the *Arthasastra*. If formed the basis of a Mauryan administration extremely totalitarian though apparently just according to Megasthenes the Greek ambassador to Chandragupta's court in Patiliputra.

Legend has it that Chandragupta adopted Jainism and fasted to death in the fashion of Jain saints after a reign of twenty-four years. He was succeeded by his son Bindusara who maintained the empire for his son Asoka the most renowned ruler of India and one of the world's greatest kings.

Asoka ruled from 269–232 B. C. during which time he transformed Indian society internally and projected her culture externally. He started out in the aggressive vein of his forefathers by conquering Kalinga on the east coast. The horror of war shocked him into rejecting force and aggression for spiritual conquest. He adopted Buddhism and propagated its humanitarian ethics both inside and outside India.

Within India justice was tempered with humanity. All form of life was respected. Slaughter of animals for food was dissuaded. Hunting expeditions were discouraged. The consumption of meat at the palace was reduced to negligible proportions. Vegetarianism, the origin of which is lost in obscurity, probably owes its genesis in India, in large measure, to Asoka's view of life.

During Asoka's reign Buddhism went abroad and became a world religion. The Buddhist monk Mahendra, thought by some to have been Asoka's son, converted Ceylon to Buddhism. Other monks spread their religion to Burma, Siam and Central Asia from whence it spread to China.

Asoka is famous for his moral and ethical edicts, issued for the guidance of the people, which were inscribed on rocks and tall rock pillars capped by the famous Asoka capitols. The so-called Arabic numerals are found on some of the pillars. One found at Sarnath consisting of four lions facing outward now forms the seal of the Government of India. These edicts preserved in stone are the oldest Indian historical documents and attest to the wisdom of ancient India.

Asoka's successors were lesser men and soon after his death the Mauryan empire was in disintegration. Provincial governors asserted their independence and numerous quasi-feudal kingdoms emerged. Moreover a period of foreign invasion from the west ensued.

FOREIGN INVASIONS

After the fall of the Mauryan empire that extended over the whole of the sub-continent with the exception of the extreme south there ensued a period of political disintegration of a half a millennium or so (200 B. C.–300 A. D.) with repeated invasions into the Punjab from central Asia and Persia. First came the Greeks from Bactria who had broken away from Seleucid rule about 250 B. C. The Bactrian Greeks conquered the Punjab early in the second century and established their rule at Sagla (modern Sailikot). Their king Menander (Indianized to Melinda) converted to Buddhism. Another succeeding line of Bactrian kings ruled from Taxila until 50 B. C. Two notable developments transpired during Graeco-Bactrian rule in the Punjab. There was a fusion of Greek and Indian art, primarily in sculpture, known as Gandhara art, that was to have a profound impact on Buddhist art in central Asia, China and Japan. Gandhara was at that time the name of this region. The familiar seated meditating Bodhisattva (a saint) emanated from Gandhara art. The other was the birth of Mahayana Buddhism that found its way across central Asia to China and Japan. Taxila was a leading center of learning in the Buddhist world at this time.

The Bactrian Greeks were disseized by the Scythians and Parthians, known as Sakas and Pahlavas in India. As noted before the Parthians (of Scythian ancestry or affinity) had taken over Persia around 200 B. C. and in 54 B. C. won a historic victory over the Romans at Carrhae. They were now in an expansive mood. The Scythians, on the other hand, were hard pressed by the Yueh-chih an Indo-European speaking peoples in central Asia who, in turn, were fleeing the Hsiung-nu or Huns from Mongolia. The Sakas ruled the Punjab from about 50 B. C. to 50 A. D.

Next came the Yueh-chih who wrested the Punjab from the Pahlavas and Sakas, driving them into western India where they prospered, thoroughly Indianized, until the rise of the imperial Guptas in the 4th century A. D. Greatest of these Kushan kings was Kanisha who extended his rule into the Gangetic plain as far as Benares. He established his capital at Purushpura (modern Peshawar) near the Khyber pass. His empire included Bactria and Kashmir. Kanisha ruled around 100 A. D. The Kushan dynasty lasted until about 250 A. D. when it was overthrown by a resurgent Persia under the Sassanids.

A vigorous East-West trade flourished at this time around the Old Silk road. Northwest India (the Khyber pass) was the outlet of trade from India where it joined the main route between the eastern Mediterranean and China. Muslin, silk, ivory, jewels, pepper and spices flowed to the Mediterranean area in exchange, mainly, for gold. The gold drain to India (and China), as already mentioned, was decried by Pliny, the Caesars and other Romans. In India the merchants grew fabulously rich on this trade. They endowed temples (particularly the Jains) and other works of art. The Kushans too grew wealthy from the trade although much of the goods emanated from central and south India.

The rest of India continued under indigenous rule though politically fragmented. The powerful Andhra dynasty ruled the Deccan (central plateau of the subcontinent) for some four centuries or so after 230 B. C. In 27 B. C. the Andhras captured Magadha which had been ruled by the Shungas after the demise of the Mauryans. The Kalinga kingdom revived in the east (around Orissa). In the far south three Tamil kingdoms vied for supremacy in Tamiland, the Cheras in the west, the Cholas in the east and the Pandyas in the center. In 325 A. D. a new dynasty, the Pallavas conquered Tamiland and dominated the area for some five centuries. The origin of the Pallavas is obscure. Their name would imply Pahlava descent though other evidence points to local antecedants. The Cholas were great sea-farers and carried on extensive trade with Southeast Asia where they founded colonies in Siam, Cambodia, Java, Bali and elsewhere in the area.

This intermediary period of foreign intrusion and absence of political unity was, nonetheless, a time of further development and maturation of the Hindu civilization. South India became thoroughly Aryanized. This is portrayed by the epic *Ramayana*, composed about 200–100 B. C. The Hindu way of life embraced the entire subcontinent, including the assimilated foreigners.

The Indian way of life was based on *dharma* (law, status, duty, responsibility) and *ashrama* (stages of life). Every aspect of life was regulated by a code of morality and ethics appropriate to the caste and status of the individual. Moreover, a person's place or purpose was also fixed and beyond his temporal control. An individual was born into a certain caste because of the behavior of his soul in a previous embodiment. His behavior in his present life determined his status in the next. Thus a Vaishya by obeying the moral code of Hinduism could elevate himself to a Brahman in his next life. But if he lived an evil life he would suffer further degradation after death through rebirth in the form of some animal life such as a dog or a worm.

The process of connection with the past and future is called the transmigration of the soul. This religious doctrine is without a doubt the most ingeniour ever invented by the mind of man for maintaining social discipline and order. It has been a chief reason for the great stability of the Indian society. Such religious dogma, however, did not induce fatalism among Indians. It provided a rationalization for man's estate in life whether high or low which left him with no sense of guilt as does the Christian doctrine of original sin and afforded him another opportunity to improve his status in the process of the passage of his soul into successive rebirths. He could thus enjoy life providing he did so within the strictures of Hindu morals and ethics.

Life was divided into four stages or ashrams. The first was that of a student generally from the ages 6–12 (after his investiture with the sacred thread) to 20 or so, when the boy lived with his Guru (teacher). He was required to concentrate on studies and remain celibate during this stage, which proved at times trying when the Guru's wife, generally much younger than the Guru, was attractive and seductive. After studying the Vedas, phonetics, grammer, etymology and astronomy the boy returned home, married the girl selected by his parents and entered the second stage of life as a family man. During this period he begot children, acquired wealth and generally enjoyed life. The pleasures of love (kama) including sexual enjoyment (rati) were given high priority. It was his responsibility to keep his wife happy, raise his children, amass riches and support the Brahmans. When his first grandson was born (around age 40 to 50), thus having assured the continuity of his line, he retired to the forest (today forests are scarce in India) for a life of meditation without further responsibilities to family and society. His wife might accompany him. The fourth ashram was a final life of ascetism where the Hindu rejected all worldly goods and responsibilities and begged for food. Presumably his wife had predeceased him by this time. These last two stages of ascetism and semi-ascetism remained more of an ideal as few high caste wealthy Hindus would dispossess themselves of all their worldly goods for the life of a hermit, with the exception of the medicants and monks. But such was and still is the ideal. Actually it does not differ greatly from the life of the well born in other human societies.

The ashrams applied to the life of the Hindu male. The women's role was that of a wife and mother. As a young girl she was instructed and trained by her mother in womanly and household arts and generally in music, dancing and the fine arts. Though the Hindu way of life was male dominated the women of India were usually more secure and assertive than elsewhere.

Buddhism dominated this period. Jainism also flourished. But Brahmanism remained alive. There was no serious strife among them. The stupas and cave temples (Ajanta, Ellora and others) date originally to 200 B. C. The Institutes of Manu, the earliest legal code of the Hindus, was compiled around 200 B. C.

There was considerable exchange of ideas with the Mediterranean world and China which accepted Buddhism at this time. Astronomy from Mesopotamia was transmitted to India under Bactrian rule. But in two areas the Indians were most creative. The first was mathematics. The details are set forth in Chapter V. Algebra, trigonometry, spherical geometry, calculus and other higher mathematics were known to ancient Indian mathematicians. Sanskrit was well developed in its grammer. So highly developed that it became difficult to cope with by the common man and more popular languages, called prakrits, evolved from which most of the present day north Indian languages derive. Sanskrit became a dead language.

THE GUPTA ERA

In 320 A. D. a second Chandragupta (unrelated to the first) arose to found the Gupta dynasty that was to unify northern India into a splendid empire again for two centuries or so. Like the Mauryas, the Guptas too made their capital at Patilputra and based their power on the rich iron ore deposits of Bihar. The famous iron pillar, now at Kutab Minar in New Delhi, erected around 400 A. D. on a hill in Ambala (in the Punjab) as a memorial to Chandragupta II attests to India's highly developed iron technology at this time. This extraordinary pillar is nearly 24 feet high and weighs approximately 6 tons. It is constructed of welded discs of wrought iron. Its method of production has been called a mystery greater than the building of the pyramids. Most remarkable is that after 1500 years it shows no sign of rusting, a proof of the purity of the iron unmatched until the present time.

The Guptas first secured their power in the eastern Gangetic plain, then thrust it northwest into the Punjab and Kashmir and east into Bengal. In 388 A. D. Chandragupta II defeated the Sakas by capturing Ujjian their magnificent capital in western India. The Guptas never ruled directly in the Deccan but they exercised dominance and exacted tribute over its northern areas. In the latter part of the 5th century the Huns invaded the Punjab. (This was the century of the Huns. Atilla stood before Rome in 453 A. D. The Huns captured Persia in 484 A. D.). Skandagupta exhausted the treasury and the dynasty fighting them. Early in the 6th century the Huns ruled the Punjab and large parts of the Gangetic plain.

The Gupta era (circa 320–525 A. D.) is probably the golden age of India. Fa-hsien, the Chinese pilgrim who came to India around 400 A. D. and spent six years in the country collecting Buddhist scriptures left to history a diary on his visit. He notes the absence of crime, the consideration of the people for each other and the gentle administration of the country. Vegetarianism was now widespread among the higher castes. Patiliputra was a beautiful city of palaces, temples and hospitals free of charge to the poor. Buddhism still predominated though, Fa-hsien notes disconcertingly, Brahmanism was enjoying a revival, particularly at court. In fact, Samudragupta is reported to have celebrated the ancient Brahmanic "horse sacrifice" to commemorate his successful empire building.

Vatsayama's *Kamasutra* dates back to this era, as further evidence of a prosperous and refined existence. The mural in the Ajunta cave depicting a sensously attired maiden doing her toilet, including lipstick, is further testimony to sophisticated living at this time. The renowned playright Kalidasa belongs to this period. His plays, particularly Shakuntala, reveal sensitiveness to beauty, cultured dialogue and other attributes of an advanced civilization. Architecture and the fine arts reached a high point at Ajunta, Ellora and elsewhere. The form of the Hindu temple was already emerging with the revival of Brahmanism but its glory was still several centuries in the future.

Economic prosperity prevailed. Agriculture was based on the peasant villages with a share of the production taken in revenue for the royal treasury. Rice, wheat, sugar cane, fruits of wide varieties (including mango), spices and the cherished dairy products were produced abundantly. Foreign trade flourished oriented, perhaps, more in the direction of China now due to Buddhist affinity. Bullion continued to flow to India as the merchants preferred gold and horses from the West in exchange for their muslins, ivory, jewels, spices and other wares. Silk, tung oil, musk and amber were imported from China. The wealthy Vaishya merchants contributed lavishly to the support of the Buddhist and Jain monks and artisans who built and maintained splendid temples. Ajunta and Ellora alone bespeak a tremendously wealthy society during the early centuries of the Christian era when many of them were constructed.

The Huns did not last long. Their great king Mihirakula was forced to retreat to Kashmir by 530 A. D. The Huns soon lost their identity and were absorbed into the Hindu society integrating into the Rajput clans, a hearty warrior class that defended India against the Muslims during the ensuing centuries. Northern India lapsed again into disintegration but it was reunited for a time under a remarkable monarch named Harsha Vardhana (a descendant of the Gupta line) around 600 A. D. Harsha ruled for 41 years from a new capital at Kanauj near modern Lucknow. Two sources of information are available on Harsha's rule. There is a biography of Harsha written by a Brahman courtier named Bana, which tends to over-glorify the energetic monarch. Another Chinese pilgrim Hsuan-tsang sojourned in India from 630–644 A. D. He describes much disorder including two robberies committed against him. Harsha was forced to move around the provinces ceaselessly to maintain law and order. The Brahmanic revival was apparently well advanced during Hsuan-tsang's visit. Hinduism grew in popularity with worshippers offering flowers, fruits, sweets and other delicacies to the gods. The Hindu temple developed accordingly for such "diety" worship. Tantric rites (including secret and orgiastic rituals) associated with female manifestation evolved at this time. Even Buddhism accommodated femininity by introducing female divinities known as taras.

After the death of Harsha northern India lapsed once again, into fragmentation and internecine warfare. The Palas of Bengal gained dominance in the eastern Gengetic region under powerful monarchs like Dharmapala (circa 770–810) and Devapala (circa 810–850). The Palas were patrons of Buddhism and introduced it into Tibet. After the Palas the Gujara-Pratiharas (Rajputs), who emanated from western India dominated the Gangetic plain to the borders of Bengal. Their most powerful kings were Mihira Bhoja (circa 840–885) and Mahendrapala (circa 885–910). They defended India against the invasion of the Arabs who occupied Sind in 712 A. D. During their two centuries of rule they suffered repeated invasions by the Deccan Rastrakutas who captured their capital at Kanyakubja (near Lucknow).

Around 1000 A. D. the Turkish rulers of Ghazni (Afghanistan) started conducting raids into the Punjab carrying back slaves and booty. But instead of uniting against the Muslims the north Indians continued their internecine strife. Three new kingdoms succeeded the Pratiharas, the Cahamanas (Rajputs) in western India, the Gahadavalas in the east with the Candellas in between. And there were lesser dynasties. North India was hopelessly divided on the eve of the Muslim invasions. The three most powerful kingdoms were involved in a triangular war at the end of the 12th century. Most renowned of the Indian kings at this time was Prithviraj Cahamana.

The 10th–13 centuries, as already discussed in Chapter XI, witnessed a period of Hindu temple building analagous to the Gothic cathedral activity at about the same time in Europe. The Hindu galaxy of gods and religious worship had by now fully evolved and the temple was the focus of it all. Bubaneswar in Orissa, Khajuraho in central India and the Jain temples at Mount Abu in Gujarat all date to this period. There were, perhaps, similar temples in north India which were destroyed by the intolerant Muslim conquerors.

Political division also prevailed in the Deccan and Tamiland during the first millennium of the Christian era. Unlike the Mauryas the Guptas never achieved dominance of any duration south of the Vindhya mountains. The Vakatakas dominated the western Deccan at the time of the Gupta empire losing out to the Chalukyas soon thereafter. The Chalukyas ruled from Badami in Hyderabad, which Hsuan-tsang visited, a prosperous city of temples, palaces and forts five miles in circumference. The Chinese pilgrim found the people hard working, peaceful and obedient to their king. Greatest of their kings was Pulakeshin II (circa 609–642) who defeated Harsha's army when he tried to invade the Deccan. The Rastrakutas succeeded the Chalukyas in 757 A. D. and established their capital at Ellora (near modern Aurangabad) ruling for two centuries. They are renowned for their invasions into the Gangetic plain, as noted earlier, and the commissioning of the famous rock temple Kailasanatha, discussed in Chapter XI, by their king Krishna I. The Chalukyas regained control of the Deccan in 973 A. D. and ruled until 1189 A. D.

In Tamiland the Cholas gained control over the Pallavas in the 9th century and dominated the extreme south, including Ceylon, until 1267 A. D. The Cholas colonized in Southeast Asia. Most notable was the naval expedition to Indonesia by the Chola king Rajendra (1014–1042). A brisk trade via sea between South India and China flourished at this time. The Cholas were succeeded by the Pandyas in the 13th century as the dominant power in the southeast.

MUSLIM INDIA

The Muslim conquest of Hindustan occurred in 1192 A. D. when Mohammed of Ghur defeated Prithviraj, the last of the great Hindu kings of medieval India. But the Muslim impact was felt earlier. During the heroic age of Islam the Arabs extended their power into Baluchistan and Sind in 712 A. D. As already discussed the Arab phase of Islam lasted about two centuries and the borders of India was the extent of their power eastward. Moreover, the Arabs quickly realized they had encountered a superior civilization and chose to live in peace (with the imposition of the jizya, the special tax on unbelievers, instead of the sword) and learn the mathematics (which they called hindsat, the Indian art), astronomy and philosophy from the Hindus. The Hindus, in their customary fashion, largely ignored these early Muslim intruders.

A lesser but nonetheless significant result of the rise of Islam was the Parsee community in western India that has and continues to play an important role in the country. Refusing conversion from Zoroastrianism to Mohammedanism "by the sword" many Persians emigrated to India in the 8th and 9th centuries A. D. where they were free to continue their religion and way of life by the tolerant Hindus. To be sure, their way of life was not too different as they were Aryan cousins and in due time the Parsees melded easily into the Indian scene. These precocious foreigners, never exceeding 100,000 in number and concentrated mainly in the Bombay area, have always loomed bigger in the country and have contributed immeasurably to the professional and entreprenural life of India.

The real Muslim impact, however, came from Central Asia centuries later after the Arabs converted the Turks to Islam. The jihad (holy war) philosophy of Islam suited the temperment of these fierce warriors of the Asian steppes. Their first kingdom was founded at Ghazni (Afghanistan) in 962 A. D. which lasted until about 1170 A. D. Mahmud of Ghazni made some 17 raids into the Punjab each winter around 1000 A. D. to steal gold, jewels and women carrying them back to Ghazni through the Khyber pass. In these raids he penetrated as far as Kanauj (Lucknow) in the Gangetic plain and the Kathiawar peninsula where he sacked the fabulous city of Somnath and denuded its many temples of their riches. At the time of Mahamud's death in 1030 A. D. the Ghaznivads exercised defacto rule over much of the Punjab. About 1170 A. D. another tribe, the Ghurids, took over Afghanistan and in 1175 A. D. under Sultan Muhammad began their raids into India. The Turks owed their prowess to superb horsemanship (they had the stirrup) and the facility to use the bow and arrow at full gallop. In 1192 A. D. Muhammad of Ghur captured Delhi leaving his army commander Qutb-ud-din Ayak in charge of the newly conquered empire. This was the onset of the Delhi Sultanate that was to rule over northern India for three centuries. The sagacious Qutb-ud-din gradually gained independence for his regime from Ghazni to launch the first of five successive Turko-Afghan dynasties that ruled the Indus-Gangetic plain until the advent of the Mughals in the 16th century. His dynasty, the first, is known as the slave dynasty since Qutb-ud-din, and his original associates, came to India as slaves (mamelukes) of Muhammad of Ghur.

The Rajputs (Chalukyas, Chauhans, Paramaras and Pratiharas) resisted the Turko-Afghans for years but the Muslims found little difficulty extending their rule into Bengal. In fact, the Muslim rulers of India had greater difficulty preventing the Mongols under Genghis Khan and his successors from invading Hindustan.

The slave kings were succeeded by the Kaljis in 1290 A. D. The Kaljis too were Turks who came to India via Afghanistan. Most notable of this line was

Ala-ud-din (1296–1316 A. D.) who succeeded in extending the Sultanate deep into the south. Under Ala-ud-din the Sultanate reached its peak of glory and power. Land revenue of fifty per cent of the crop was exacted from the Hindu farmers, but prices of food and cloth were kept low so that the people were generally well off. The Khalji philosophy was to keep the Hindus poor so that they would be more submissive. The Muslims were a military caste atop the Hindu society and Muslim nobles were granted large estates called jagirs, from which they were expected to maintain an appropriate contingent of cavalry for the Sultan.

The Muslims tried to convert the Indians but it was too large a task. Buddhism was pretty well destroyed, including the sacking of the University of Nalanda at Benares, the Buddhist center. Temples and sculpture were destroyed so that today the Indus-Gangetic plain is devoid of Hindu-Buddhist cultural remains. This can only be found in the Deccan and Tamiland in the south where the Muslim writ ran weak and Nepal which remained untouched by them. This first Muslim period left nothing notable behind in architecture and the arts, except the pedestrian square and hexagonal cenotaphs that dot the Delhi-Lucknow area and massive forts such as Tughluqabad a few miles outside New Delhi.

Hinduism retreated inwardly and, in many ways, became fossilized in order to survive the Muslim impact. In the process Brahmanism absorbed Buddhism. The Buddha became an incarnation of Vishnu. It was thereafter practiced as a separate religion only outside India.

The Khaljis were succeeded by the Tughluqs in the 14th century. Ghiyas-ud-din Tughluq, the founder of this dynasty, was the son of a Turkish slave at court and a hindu mother. He distinguished himself as a soldier in the northwest fending off the Mongol invasions of Hindusthan. Most famous or infamous of this line was Muhammad-bin-Tughluq (1325–51 A. D.). He was cultured and vicious at the same time, a characteristic not unusual of his race. The Moorish traveler Ibn-Batuta, who was in India at this time, describes numerous acts of inhumanity by the Sultan, such as the execution of his enemies by elephants with iron blades affixed to their tusks. He was prone to impetuous ill-considered acts. In 1327 he ordered the people of Delhi *en masse* to move to Daulatabad 700 miles to the south. Many died on the way. Those who survived were most unhappy in the new environment. It had no assured water supply. Realizing his folly he ordered the people back to Delhi. Few survived the two journeys. The once beautiful capital of Delhi was in ruins after this misadventure and took years to recover. Stanley Lane-Poole calls it "a monument of misdirected energy." The scheme however, was not entirely without merit. Tughluq wished to have his capital further away from the Mongol threat. Also, a capital in the Deccan would afford better control over the wealthy provinces in the south. But he failed to understand the human element involved in so drastic a change.

Still another misadventure was marching an army into the Himalyas in 1337–38 to subdue some rebellious tribes where all but a few perished in the inhospitable geography and climate. His experiment with fiat money proved equally disastrous. Impressed by the printing of paper money by Kublai Khan in China he decided to issue copper coins of monetary value exceeding the worth of the metal. He failed, however, to protect his copper coins against counterfeits. Any smith and artisan was able to strike similar coins. The result was ruinous inflation and a bankrupt royal treasury.

The Sultanate was by now in a high state of disintegration. In addition to the human calamaties inflicted on the people the country was hit by a severe seven year (1335–1342) failure of the Monsoon such as has plagued the subcontinent at least once a century. A terrible famine ensued. The furthermost provinces began to secede from the Sultanate. Bengal declared its independence in 1338. In the south a new kingdom of Vijayanagar was established by the Rajput warriors of western India fleeing Muslim rule. It maintained dominance over the south until 1565 A. D. It was a power when the Europeans made their early contacts and many accounts of its splendor and affluence have been left by these early western adventurers.

Muhammad's cousin Firoz succeeded him in 1351 and tried to restore the Sultanate to its former glory. He was an able man and succeeded, in part, though he was unable to recover the lost provinces. He had the good fortune of normal monsoons so that a modicum of prosperity returned. He rebuilt the capital which he renamed Firozabad, consisting of mosques, colleges and beautiful gardens, the ruins of which can still be viewed in New Delhi today. Within a decade after his death Timur of Samarkand, the scourge of Central Asia during the 14th century, broke through the Khyber pass into the Punjab in 1398 A. D. and at Delhi butchered in cold blood 100,000 of its inhabitants. Heads and mutilated bodies of Hindus (infidels) were stacked high in gruesome towers. For fifteen days the population was pillaged and raped. Delhi was completely ruined. Timur's raid was followed by a famine. Timur left India in a trail of blood with ladened booty wagons and enchained slaves in the tens of thousands.

The Delhi Sultanate lapsed into decay in the 15th century. Two dynasties officiated during its demise. First the Sayyids of Turkish antecedants who were succeeded by the ineffectual Lodis of Afghan descent. Most of the Sultans of western India broke away from Delhi rule. Bengal remained independent. The Lodis retained control only over a small area in the Gangetic doab and the Punjab until deposed by the Mughals.

THE MUGHAL EMPIRE

The founder of the Mughal empire in India was Babur, a descendant of Timur on his father's side and Genghis Khan on his mother's side. After Babur gained control of Kabul he started to design the invasion of Hindustan. At first he was invited to India to take sides in a fight between two Lodi factions, but he quickly pitted himself against them for control of Delhi. He defeated Ibrahim Lodi on the historic battlefield of Panipat in 1526. A year later he met and defeated the Rajputs in the battle of Khauna.

Babur died four years later in 1530 in Agra. He was succeeded by his son, Humayan, who proved incapable of consolidating the empire. The Rajputs remained unsubdued and the Muslim nobles revolted under the leadership of Sher Shah who was able to effect an Afghan revival. He ruled for five years. During this time he devised a brilliant administration including a land revenue assessment which was to form the basis of subsequent land revenue systems.

The Afghan revival did not survive Sher Shah's death. There ensued a struggle for succession which continued until 1555 when Humayan, with Persian help, recaptured Delhi and Agra. He died in an accidental fall (when under the spell of opium it is said) from the staircase of his library at Delhi in 1556 and was succeeded by his thirteen year old son, Akbar.

Akbar was another great king of India. He defeated the Afghans who rose against him again after Humayan's death. For the next forty years, Akbar conquered and annexed until the whole of north and central India was under Mughal rule. Most difficult to subdue were the Rajputs. This Akbar wisely facilitated through intermarriage and appointments at court. But the Rajputs of Mewar were never completely dominated.

Akbar was a tolerant and open-minded sovereign. He refused to treat Muslim and Hindu differently. He married a Rajput princess and appointed Rajput generals of his army. Another Rajput, Raja Todar Mal, who served under Sher Shah, became Akbar's chief finance minister and introduced the famous land revenue system of the Mughals.

The land revenue was fixed at one-third of the average produce of the land. The cultivator could pay in cash or in kind. A cadastral survey was made classifying the land according to its use and fertility and determining its average production. The assessment was made directly with the cultivator (ryot) and the collection of the revenue was farmed out or assigned for services (mostly military) to a host of tax gatherers. The most notable of whom was the zamindar. He was alloted a definite area of the country from which he was required to return a certain revenue to the emperor, retaining a fractional balance as compensation for his efforts. When revenue was assigned, the assignee (called a jagirdar) was usually required to support a fixed military contingent (reckoned in so many horses) for the emperor, but did not have to forward any of the revenue to him. The appointments were revocable at the will of the emperor. While the Mughal empire remained strong, the zamindars and jagirdars were kept under control, but when its power declined they began to assert proprietory rights in the alloted or assigned areas and to impose additional burdens on the cultivators.

The Mughal administrative system was equally effective. The officials were called mansabdars. Since they too served at the will of the emperor they were diligent and productive. There were twelve provincial governments each ruled by a subadar. Some of the subadars maintained courts almost as splendid as that of the great Mughal.

Broad prosperity prevailed in India under the efficient administration and reasonable taxation of the Mughals. The population of India during Mughal times was already a hundred million. Indian agriculture, susceptible to double cropping, can be very productive during periods of peace and political stability. The water table in the Indus-Gangetic plain is only about ten feet below ground so that supplemental irrigation is easily available with wells dug only twenty feet below the surface. Persian wheels (water buckets fixed to a chain belt turned by a bullock or camel moving in a circle around the well head to lift the water from the shallow well) dotted the country side. Equally productive were the smiths, artisans and weavers. India produced the finest cottons, woolens and silks in the world. Foreign trade with Asia and Europe flourished in these manufactures during the Mughal period.

Akbar was a builder. He built the Red Fort of Agra where the court resided. But his most famous construction was Fatehpur Sikri, his new palace outside Agra, where he spent the happiest days of his life. It was there in the Hall of Worship where Akbar undertook to find the universal religion which would suit all mankind. He invited, to the discomfiture of his fellow Muslims, Hindu religious leaders, Jain teachers, Parsee priests and Jesuit fathers from Goa to debate religious issues. The discussions had two effects. First, Akbar asserted the supremacy of the temporal over the religious power of Muslim India. Second, he evolved his new religion of catholic comprehension to unify the faith of mankind. But this noble experiment was destined to fail. Akbar was accused of foresaking Islam which appears to be untrue. He was, however, a most tolerant Muslim.

Akbar died in 1605 after a reign of fifty years. He was succeeded by Jehangir, his son by a Rajput princess. Jehangir and Shahjahan, his son (whose mother was also a Rajput) ruled from 1605–1666. Both were lesser men but they held the empire together and even expanded it until it covered all of India except the extreme south.

Prominent during Jehangir's reign was his Persian queen Nurmahal (light of the palace), also known as Nurjahan. She was beautiful, brilliant and ambitious. Her father emigrated to India during Akbar's rule and rose to high position at court. He came to be known as Itmud-ud-Daulah for whom Nurmahal had a tomb built in Agra of lacey white and buff marble that is one of the finest pieces of Mughal architecture. Nurmahal was extremely powerful at Jehangir's court and virtually ruled the empire during his failing years. Among other things she arranged the marriage of her niece Mumtaz Mahal (pearl of the palace) to Shahjahan but later opposed him as successor to the throne. Persian influence at the Mughal court was great. Persian was the language of the court. Persian ways and manners were emulated. Mughal architecture was a blend of Persian and Rajput forms. Miniature painting, popular in Persia, received enthusiastic patronage in the Mughal court.

Their reigns, particularly that of Shahjahan, are distinguished by their architectural achievements and their active and considerable foreign trade with the countries of Asia and Europe. This was a period of European advent into India by way of trade. It was considered to be the golden period of Mughal rule in India. Shahjahan built the famous Taj Mahal at Agra, a mausoleum intended as a memorial to his beloved queen, Mumtaz Mahal. He moved the capital to Delhi where he erected a magnificent palace complex known as the Red Fort. It contained the famous Peacock throne.

The chief weakness of the Mughal empire was the absence of an established succession to the crown. Consequently a struggle for succession usually ensued. A fierce war broke out for succession to Shahjahan even before he died when he became seriously ill (of strangury from excesses in his harem) in 1657. Aurangzeb eventually won. Aurangzeb (a son of Mumtaz) was a Mughal differently constituted. He was an intolerant Muslim. The defaced sculpture and architecture of Delhi and Agra created by his predecessors is a lasting monument to his zealous sunni orthodoxy. Among other things he also reinstated the jizya—a special tax on unbelievers. His religious fanaticism (he spent more time at prayer than in his harem) sincere as it may have been, undid the harmony between Muslim and Hindu which his predecessors assiduously cultivated. Aurangzeb's long reign of fifty years was consequently marked by strife and rebellion.

A devastating inflation overtook the economy. Aurangzeb taxed severely. The zamindars and jagidars (who found it difficult to maintain their cavalry in the inflation) exacted more from the cultivators, who fled the land in the face of intolerable taxation decreasing productivity. Zamindars chose to rebel rather than starve. The Jats and Sikhs in the Punjab, who supported Aurangzeb's brother in the war of succession, remained in a state of revolt.

The rise of the Marathas in western India was, perhaps, the most important historical phenomena of this period. Much credit goes to their brilliant leader, Shivaji. He was a daring soldier, a successful military conqueror and a great administrator. He blunted the Mughal power in India and extended Maratha rule across central India. The Marathas became the dominant power in India during the eighteenth century while the Mughal empire sank into disintegration and dissolution.

After the death of Aurangzeb the Marathas continued to erode the Mughal empire. Meanwhile the weakness of the Mughals tempted Nadir Shah of Persia to launch a devastating raid on Delhi in 1739. Among other things, Nadir Shah stole the famous Peacock Throne and dismantled it for its precious jewels. Ahmad Shah of Afghanistan followed suit. In 1751 the Marathas formed an alliance with the Mughals to repulse Ahmad Shah for which they received territory in the Punjab. In 1761 the Marathas suffered a humiliating defeat by Ahmad Shah at Panipat from which it took decades to recover. But for this disaster the Marathas may have achieved hegemony over India and British domination may never have arisen. So once again, as on many occasions before dating back to the Mahabharata, Indian history was decided on the plains of Panipat.

ADVENT OF THE EUROPEANS

In the beginning the Europeans came to India as the Turko-Mongols before them, with a militant religion, seeking the superior manufactures of the country. Unlike all previous invaders they came by sea. This gave them an advantage of being able to retreat at will without suffering annihilation at the hands of a more powerful adversary on land. Moreover, it afforded them a less obtrusive contact with the Indian people.

The Portuguese, not the Spaniards, were the first Europeans to come to India. When Pope Alexander VI divided the world between the two Christian powers for exploration and conquest, India fell to them. Alfonso de Albuquerque established Portuguese power in India with his capture of Goa in 1510 which he developed into a military and commercial center from whence Portuguese naval power dominated the west coast of India. Other coastal settlements at Diu, Daman, Salsette, Bassein, Charil and Bombay on the west coast, and San Thome on the east coast, were established. Attempts at colonization failed because of persecution by the Deccan Muslims and the greater attraction of Brazil for the Portuguese.

A century later the Protestant nations of Europe, who came primarily for trade, displaced the Portuguese. The Dutch established factories in Gujarat, Bengal, Bihar and Orissa, moving deeply inland into the Ganges valley, the early part of the Seventeenth century.

In 1600, Queen Elizabeth chartered the East India Company which founded its first Indian factory at Surat (near Bombay) in 1613. Sir Thomas Roe was sent to the Mughal Court at Agra as Ambassador for the East India company. Madras was established in 1639. Calcutta was founded later in 1698. The center of English activities on the west coast, meanwhile, was shifted from Surat to Bombay, which Charles II acquired in 1668 as part of the dowry of Catherin of Braganza, his Portuguese queen. He transferred it to the East India Company for an annual rent of £10. These three ports became from then on, the centers of English power under the East India Company and came to be called the Presidencies of Bombay, Madras and Calcutta.

The French came last when, at the instance of Colbert, the Compagnie des Indes Orientales was formed in 1664. The first French factory was established at Surat in 1668. Pondicherry was founded in 1673 and Chandernagore in 1690. Bitter rivalry ensued thereafter between the Europeans for commercial supremacy in India. The Portuguese and Dutch were the first to retire from the fray and the field was left to the English and the French.

The English and the French fought for supremacy in the Carnatic, the area along the east coast of India, between Madras and Calcutta, where their respective trade centers were Madras and Pondicherry. The fighting was precipitated by the outbreak of war between England and France in Europe over the Austrian succession in 1740–45. At first the two mercantile companies attempted to remain neutral. But three successive Carnatic wars ensued during the period 1740–1765 in which fortune favored one side and then the other. The French governor of Pondicherry, Joseph Francis Dupleix, deported himself brilliantly and might have built a French empire in India had he obtained better support and understanding from Paris. In the end, the English gained supremacy over the French. In the struggle both sides became heavily involved in local politics which eventually developed into British political domination over India.

BRITISH INDIA (1757–1947 A. D.)

The Battle of Plassey in 1757 is generally regarded as the beginning of British domination of India. But by that time the East India Company had been trading in India for 150 years. In the beginning the East India Company operated as a peaceful trading body. But toward the end of the 17th century, India was in political ferment. The Marathas raided Surat in 1664 and 1670. Mughal rule over Bengal was weakening. The company decided, therefore, to establish fortified settlements. A few abortive attempts were made to wrest Indian territories at Hugli and Belsore, but soon it was thought wiser to come to terms with the Mughal emperor in Delhi. In spite of its disintegration, the Mughal empire under Aurangzeb was still too formidable to be challenged by a few adventurers. In 1698 the company was granted the zamindari of three Bengal villages, one of which was Kalekata, where Calcutta was later established. In addition the Mughal emperor ordered the Nawab of Bengal to issue a firman commuting the company's custom duties to an annual payment of Rs. 3000.

But difficulties with the Nawab of Bengal, one Siraj-ud-Daulah, continued. Although the war with the French was mainly in the south the English thought it necessary to fortify Calcutta against the French attack from the sea. The Nawab misinterpreted this as a military move against him and he attacked them at Calcutta in 1765. The assault resulted in the notorious Black Hole of Calcutta, wherein 146 English prisoners were confined in a room 10 × 15 feet in 100° temperature for a night and all but 23 perished (a recent study puts these figures at 64 and 21 respectively). Robert Clive was sent from Madras to retrieve the English cause. Clive recovered Calcutta in January 1757 and decided to depose the Nawab who had, in addition, incurred the emnity of the Hindus and Mir Jaffar, an important Muslim officer of the Court. In alliance with these dissident Indian elements, Clive marched against the Nawab and defeated him at Plassey on June 23, 1757. Indian treachery and Clive's able generalship were important factors in the Nawab's defeat. Mir Jaffar was installed in his place. Siraj-ud-Daulah's body was seen floating down the Hugli river a few days later. Thereafter, the Nawab of Bengal was in effect an English puppet. When Mir Jaffar refused to take orders from the English, he was replaced by Mir Kassim who became equally intractable.

As their power grew, the English interpreted the exemption from custom duties to include also domestic trade thereby obtaining a great competitive advantage within the country. Mir Kassim decided to remove this advantage over Indian traders by abolishing the duties on internal trade. Enraged the English marched against the Nawab defeating him at Buxar on October 22, 1764. Mir Jaffar was again reinstated as Nawab of Bengal.

Although the English now possessed complete control over the Nawab they decided, out of customary fondness for due process of law, to legalize it. Clive requested and obtained from the Mughal emperor in Delhi in 1765 the appointment of the East India Company as the Diwan of Bengal, Bihar and Orissa. Under the Mughal administration, revenue and finance were separated from general administration. The Diwan collected the revenues and, after making provision for provincial administration, remitted the remainder to Delhi. The Subadar (a nawab if Muslim and raja if Hindu) was responsible for law and order in the area. The Company was henceforth entitled to collect revenues from Bengal, Bihar and Orissa, allot a fixed amount to the Nawab for administration and remit a fixed amount to the Emperor in Delhi. Control over Bengal was now complete and legitimate.

After Plassey and Buxar a period of extension of the power of the Company over the rest of India ensued. The Mughal empire continued to disintegrate. Ahmad Shah, the Afghan, made no attempt to establish his rule in Delhi after defeating the Marathas and Mughal forces at Panipat in 1761. North India lapsed into disorder. Bengal was now under English rule. Oudh (Uttar Predesh today) was semi-independent of Delhi. The Sikhs, under their powerful leader Ranjit Singh, gained control over the Punjab.

In central and south India the Marathas had regained a large measure of their former power. The Nizam of Hyderabad made himself independent of Delhi. Further south Mysore was growing in power under Hardar Ali and Tipu Sultan. This resulted in a three-cornered struggle for supremacy in central India in which the winner had every intention of ousting the English from India. The English, harassed by French interference, defeated or compromised all three.

The Company evolved a flexible policy of annexation and alliances with Indian rulers under which the latter recognized the Company as the paramount power in India, but remained as ruler within his respective territory. All external affairs were handled by the Company. This came to be called the doctrine of paramountcy which enabled the British to rule India with the minimum of force and administration. By the end of the Eighteenth century, Mysore, Oudh and Hyderabad were brought under British rule or dominance. The four great Maratha states—Gwalior, Indore, Baroda and Nagpur—were brought into the system during the first two decades of the Nineteenth century.

All that remained of importance was the Sikhs in the Punjab. Two Sikh wars were fought in 1846 and 1849 after which the Punjab was annexed. The Sikhs, known by their beards and long hair underneath colorful turbans, originated in the Sixteenth century as a dissident sect of Hinduism. Their founder Guru Nanak spread the doctrine among the Jats of the Punjab. The Sikhs became militant when persecuted by the Mughals and gained dominance over the Punjab under their great leader, Ranjit Singh, after the disintegration of the Mughal empire. It was only after his death in 1839 that the English decided to bring the Sikhs under British rule. Though numbering only about 6 million today their importance on the Indian scene now and under British rule looms much greater.

As British rule thrust into the northwest the British had to deal with the Afghans. This resulted in two Afghan wars and the annexation of Sind in 1843. In the east two Burmese wars resulted in the annexation of lower Burma in 1852. This gave the British complete control of the Bay of Bengal and an eastern buffer for Calcutta. The British empire in India was now fulfilled. On the eve of the Mutiny of 1857–58, the Company exercised direct rule over two-thirds of India, while the other one-third was composed of about 600 princely states over which the Company asserted paramountcy.

In this process of empire building, two governor-generals were prominent. They were Wellesley (1798–1805) and Dalhousie (1848–1856). Wellesley added more territory to English rule than any other governor-general. Dalhousie developed the doctrine of lapse under which the Company would annex a princely state where the ruler died without an heir. He refused to recognize an adopted heir as was the custom of the Hindus. A dispute arose over the small state of Jhansi in central India where the Raja died without a direct heir but had, according to Hindu law, an adopted son to succeed him. Dalhousie refused to recognize the adopted son as successor and annexed Jhansi in 1854. This made an undying enemy of the young Rani, the ruler's widow, who subsequently became the heroine of the mutiny. Dalhousie also incurred the emnity of the pretending Peshwa of the Marathas, Nana Sahib, by terminating the pension which the Company had been paying his father. The grounds were that he, too, was an adopted son and not entitled to succeed to the throne of the erstwhile Maratha confederacy. Finally, the Company decided to depose the Mughal emperor as he had long ago ceased to wield any effective power in India. This disturbed the Muslims who were already unhappy about the deposition of the Nawab of Oudh.

At this time, too, many Indians, Hindu and Muslim, were growing alarmed about the strong western influence entering the country which was changing their age-old customs. There was the introduction of the railway and telegraph, the advent of western education, the abolition of sati (widow burning) and infanticide, the Hindu Widows Remarriage Act of 1856 and other changes. But political and social discontent would have been submerged if the sepoy army had remained loyal. Here too, certain ill-advised steps were taken. Recruitment had shifted from Bengal to the higher caste Hindus and Muslims of Oudh and Punjab who were less subject to discipline. Caste difficulties arose when it became necessary to send Indian troops over-seas. High caste Indians are not permitted to leave India. Dalhousie's order in 1856 that all recruits must be prepared for overseas duties disturbed the Indian army. Moreover, the Indian soldier became somewhat disenchanted with the British officers because of their poor performance against the Afghans. But the supreme folly was the introduction of the Enfield rifle with cartridges greased with animal fat. This offended both the Hindus who thought it was cow fat and the Muslims who thought it was pig fat. It was the spark that kindled the fires of rebellion.

The mutiny was short-lived. It's back was broken in six months and it was completely over in a year. It did not affect the whole of the country and remained confined to central India in a triangular area defined by Delhi-Gwalior-Lucknow. Calcutta, Bombay and Madras knew of it only by hearsay. The Sikhs remained loyal, the Ranas of Nepal remained aloof and the Afghans did not see fit to profit from the discomfiture of the British. The rebellion failed primarily because its objective was to restore something that was historically dead. Its purpose was the restoration of the Mughal empire and the Maratha nation. How this political incompatibility was to be resolved had the rebellion succeeded is not clear.

The mutiny shook the British to the core. Until this time Britain ruled India not directly but through the agency of the East India Company. Many Englishmen were uncomfortable with this unusual set-up. There was doubtless much misgivings about exercising political rule over an overseas empire through a private corporation whose charter was designed for carrying on trade and commerce. After the acquisition of the Diwani of Bengal greater government control was asserted over the Company. North's Regulating Act of 1773 introduced parliamentary control. Pitt's India Act of 1784 established the Board of Control consisting of a Secretary of State, the Chancellor of the Exchequer and four privy councilors appointed by the king to supervise the Court of Directors of the Company. It became thereafter a purely administrative agency of the crown. Thus prior to the mutiny there had been a gradual transfer of power from the Company to the crown. The Company had become something of a fiction and its abolition was precipitated by the mutiny. Thereafter, Great Britain took on direct rule in India.

The Government of India Act of 1859 terminated the dual authority exercised by the Board of Control and the Court of Directors of the East India Company and vested it in the Secretary of State for India with rank of Parliamentary minister. A Council of India was set up to advise the Secretary of State. The Council soon lapsed into a consultative body with little control over the Secretary of State. The Secretary of State like other ministers, was responsible to the British Parliament but few members of Parliament possessed sufficient knowledge of India to effectively question his decisions. In practice, therefore, the Secretary possessed unlimited authority over the Government of India.

The Indian Council's Act of 1861 increased the power of the Viceroy, as the Governor General was now called, and made him more independent of the Legislative Council by adding "not less than six no more than twelve" additional members of which not less than half were to be non-official. But it restricted its legislative functions. Prior sanction of the Viceroy was needed for introducing any legislation concerning the public debt, public revenue, Indian religious rights, military discipline and policy toward Indian states. No law could be enacted at variance with acts of Parliament. The Viceroy could veto any law passed by the Council. Moreover, he was empowered to issue his own ordinances which had the force of law. Finally, the British Government could annul any law enacted by the Legislative Council. The Act also restored legislative functions to the provincial councils. Such legislative councils were established in Bengal in 1862, North-Western Province (Uttar Pradesh today) in 1886 and the Punjab in 1898.

The policy towards the princely states also changed after the mutiny. In a proclamation of 1858 the British Government renounced any further annexations and honored the treaties made with the Company. Their relationship to the British Government was further facilitated by the Act of 1878 which proclaimed Queen Victoria Empress of India. This established the sovereignty of the crown over the Indian states as the paramount power in India. To assure perpetuity of rule in the Indian states where no natural heir survived, the Hindu rulers were permitted to adopt sons and Muslim rulers to arrange for such succession as sanctioned by Muslim law. The British, however, reserved the right to depose a ruler guilty of misgovernment which was exercised on several occasions. A separate political department was established for relations with the Indian states under which a resident agent was assigned to each state or group of smaller states to "advise" the ruler.

The primary political problem of the first half century after the mutiny was the northwest frontier. The objective was to check Russian imperialism in central Asia. This involved flirtations and wars with Afghanistan and control of the fierce Pathans of northwest Punjab. On the whole, the British were reasonably successful in this purpose. A similar objective was pursued on the northeast frontier. In this case it was out of fear of French imperialism in southeast Asia. It resulted in the annexation of upper Burma in 1885 whereby the whole of Burma was brought under British rule.

The Indian army was reorganized during this period. Up to the mutiny each Presidency maintained its own army under separate commanders. In 1863 all military units were placed under a single commander-in-chief and divided into four territorial units—Bengal, Madras, Bombay and Punjab— each under a Lieutenant General. The Indian army was reorganized again in 1904 by Lord Kitchener into three army commands and nine divisions. The composition of the army also changed. After the mutiny the ratio of European to Indian recruits was raised. In 1863 there were 65 thousand European to 140 thousand Indian troops. This ratio was maintained until World War I. The artillery, however, was manned exclusively by British soldiers. The recruitment of Indian troops was from all castes and creeds instead of the higher castes as before the mutiny. Greater recruitment from the martial races—the Sikhs, Pathans and Gurkhas—was also undertaken after the mutiny.

INDEPENDENCE MOVEMENT

There was, naturally, a reaction to the impact of the West. First, several movements towards a Hindu reform and revival took form. The earliest, the Brahma Samaj, was an attempt by Raja Ram Mohan Roy to adapt Hinduism to the new western ideas. His successor, Keshab Chandra Sen tried to achieve a synthesis with Christianity. Worship of one God and social reforms such as abolition of infant marriages, remarriage of widows, intercaste marriages and the like were its objectives. On the other hand, the Arya Samaj led by Swami Dayananda with its slogan "Back to the Vedas" was a reactionary movement.

Most important of these movements was the Ramakrishna Mission founded by Swami Vivekananda, a disciple of Ramakrishna. The objective of this movement was a synthesis of western ideas and Hinduism. Vivekananda carried the mission abroad and made a great impression in America. There was also the Theosophical Society, founded in the United States. Annie Besant, an English woman, represented the Society in India. It allied itself with the Hindu revival movement. Mrs. Besant, however, started calling for the independence of India. As Jawaharlal Nehru says "Annie Besant was a powerful influence in adding to the confidence of the Hindu middle classes in their spiritual and national heritage."

These Hindu reform and revival movements generated the beginning of new national consciousness. They did not, however, take on the proportions of political agitation though they perhaps laid the foundation for the independence movement. In the end any nationalistic movement that had a chance of success had to be based upon the new ideas of the West. Such a movement had its start in the organization of the Indian National Congress in 1885.

The Congress was an organization of the English educated Indian middle class. It is interesting to note that the Congress was organized however, by a retired English civil servant, Allan Octavian Hume. The Congress was scrupulously non-militant in the beginning. It always professed loyalty to Great Britain. It concerned itself chiefly with criticism of the government and demands for social reform. Attention was constantly called to the abject poverty of India. Various revenue measures, more precisely the salt tax and the Arms Act, limiting the possession of weapons by Indians, were severely criticised. But it was the agitation for allowing more Indians into the Indian Civil Service which proved the greatest cementing force of the early Congress movement. The ICS examinations were conducted only in England which placed the young Indian at a disadvantage. English educated Indians, therefore, clamored for simultaneous examinations in India in order to remove this handicap.

At the start the Government was sympathetic to the movement, but as the Congress became more critical the friendly attitude changed. Two charges, particularly rankled the British. The first, that Indians were the victims of the colonial system. It was alleged "that the interests of India had been sacrificed to those of Lancaster." The second, that the Indian Army was used to further British imperialism in Asia with the Indians paying the cost. The official British attitude, in return, was that the British educated Indians, as an infinitesimal minority, had no right or claim to represent the views of India.

Though the end in view of the Congress movement was an independent India, based on western institutions and ideas, it was only natural that such modern institutions would have to be built upon the Indian civilization of the past. Unfortunately, around the turn of the century, this was perhaps carried too far—to the point of reactionary Hinduism. The dominance of the Congress during this time by the extreme right wing is associated with Bal Gangadhar Tilak, a man of great erudition, ability and dynamism. Tilak was a Maratha, a Chitpavan Brahman of the caste of the Peshwas, with a passion for regenerating the past glory of the frustrated Maratha nation. He carried his rightist nationalism to such extremes as opposing the Age of Consent Bill which forbade consummation of child marriages until the bride was twelve years old. He organized an anti-cow-killing society. Tilak's lead was taken up by the Bengalis in 1905. "Arya for the Aryans" became the Bengali slogan. This reactionary direction of the Congress gave rise to militancy and terrorism. Some British officers were murdered. An economic boycott called the Swadeshi, or Buy-India movement, was launched. And in 1906 the Congress made the first official demand for Swarej or self-government.

In 1907–8 the moderates regained the upper hand after the Morley-Minto constitutional reforms of 1908 granted greater Indian participation in the government. Some of the militancy receded. Moreover, Lord Curzon was replaced by the sympathetic Lord Hardinge as Viceroy in 1910. In 1911 the King and Queen of England made a good-will visit to India which was made the occasion for the announcement of the change of the capital from Calcutta to Delhi and the undoing of the partition of Bengal. But this was offset by the passage of the Press Act in 1910 making inflammatory writing a criminal offense. At any rate, when war broke out in 1914, the Indian scene was relatively peaceful again.

Meanwhile, the Muslims were experiencing a tardy nationalistic resurgence. The Muslims resisted western education and acceptance of western ideas much too long. The Muslims were the ruling class the British displaced. Consequently, the Hindus grasped the opportunity under British rule to gain ascendance over their former rulers. Moreover, the Muslims had no cultural roots in India and had to look outside India to the Middle East for their cultural genesis. Hence, unlike the Hindus, they could not fall back upon Indian civilization for national regeneration.

There was also no Muslim middle class to lead a national movement. Most of the Muslim elite were feudal in outlook and status. The Muslims were in India as rulers and took little interest in trades and professions. The one exception, the Muslim jurists who expounded the Koranic law, were rendered largely obsolete by the introduction of the English law under British rule.

In 1875 Syed Ahmed Khan, alarmed by this loss of advantage, started a movement to promote English education among the Muslims. He founded the Anglo-Oriental College of Aligarh, which did much to foster higher education and modern culture among the Muslims. Syed Ahmed Khan, however, advised Muslims to refrain from joining the Congress. At first Muslims joined the Congress readily and by 1890 comprised 22 per cent of the delegates. But the militant Hinduism that ensued disaffected many Muslims. Moreover, constitutional reforms were heading for a free electorate in India which raised fears on their part of being a perpetual minority in a free and democratic India. It was, therefore, felt that Muslims needed their own political organization which resulted in the founding of the Muslim League in 1906. Agitation for separate electorates became, thereafter, the cornerstone of the Muslim League policy. The British tended to aid and abet this rift between the Muslim and Hindu communities as a factor for perpetuating British rule. The war, however, strained the British-Muslim affinity due to the British attack on the Ottoman Empire. This promoted a rapprochement between Congress and the Muslim League. The result was the Lucknow Pact of 1916 wherein the Muslim League endorsed the demand for independence and the Congress accepted the principle of separate electorates.

The Congress supported the British and the allied cause enthusiastically during the war and Indian troops rendered valuable service to the Empire.

For this the Indians expected to be rewarded with constitutional reforms granting a large measure of self-government. England also felt honor-bound to recompence such loyalty with political reforms. The result was the Montagu-Chelmsford Report which, however, proved unsatisfactory and disappointing to the Indians. Even more disturbing was the passage of the Rowlatt Acts in 1919 authorizing detention without trial for political agitation.

But a new factor had now entered the freedom movement. It was Mahatma Gandhi who took the issue of independence to the Indian villages. Until now the Congress support did not extend much beyond the English educated Indians who constituted, at best, three per cent of the Indian people. This led many British to the conclusion that the freedom movement could be held at bay so long as the district officer kept the villagers content and submissive to British rule. Gandhi recognized quickly that it was here where the British were vulnerable. Moreover, he was a clever politician. He gave support, for example, to the Khilafat Movement so important to the Indian Muslims. Upon termination of the war, the Muslims feared the Allies would destroy the Khilafat embodied in the office of the Turkish Sultan and the Muslim world would lose its spiritual head. Gandhi espoused the cause of preserving the Turkish Khilafat and won in return the cooperation for the time being, of the Muslim League.

After the disappointing constitutional reforms of 1919 and the enactment of the Rowlatt Acts, Congress realized independence would come only after a struggle. Many Englishmen, though not all, espoused the objective of Indian independence. But it was to be in the indefinite future. Gradualness loomed differently to those on opposite sides of the issue. Gandhi realized that "gradualness" could be accelerated if the Indian people could be induced to make British rule difficult. For this he devised his noncooperation and civil disobedience movement. Gandhi's disobedience movement was adopted as a policy by Congress in 1920 and it became thereafter the strategy for independence.

The movement evoked a hearty response throughout the country. Gandhi sent Congressmen into the villages to stimulate the demands for independence. Many got acquainted with village India for the first time in their lives which served them in good stead after independence. Civil disobedience flared all over India. The jails were soon overflowing with political prisoners. Imprisonment for civil disobedience became a badge of honor for the Congressmen.

The postwar cooperation between Congress and the Muslim League was short lived. The Khilafat movement petered out when Kemal Ataturk, not the British, destroyed the Turkish Sultanate. A series of communal riots broke out in 1923 and the Congress and the Muslim League were again at odds in the freedom movement. Muhammad Ali Jinnah was favorably disposed until Gandhi came to dominate the Congress. A personality clash caused him to leave the Congress in 1930 and in 1934 he became the resolute leader of the Muslim League. The Muslim-Hindu split resulted in a bitter three-cornered struggle with the British by the 1930's. On January 1, 1930, Jawaharlal Nehru, the Congress President hoisted the national flag of India and Independence Day was celebrated on January 26, 1930. Thereafter, on this day, the ceremony was repeated annually and it has become a cornerstone in the history of India's struggle for independence.

Several attempts were made to find a constitutional formula satisfactory to everyone. In 1927 a commission under Sir John Simon undertook the task. Before the Simon Committee reported the Viceroy, Lord Irwin, announced the goal of dominion status for India. Meanwhile Congress set up a committee under Motilal Nehru which made a constructive report in 1928 on the constitutional issue. It accepted the goal of dominion status "without restricting the liberty of action of those political parties whose goal is complete independence." It visualized a federated union. It recommended direct election by adult sufferage. It failed, however to deal with the question of minorities and rejected the principle of separate electorates.

In 1929 the Muslim League set forth its demands. They called for a federal constitution with complete autonomy and all residuary powers vested in the provincial assemblies. Separate communal electorates were urged. Moreover, Muslims must have weightage, or disproportionate voting rights, where they were in a minority. Finally, Muslims must have a statutory share in the central and provincial cabinets.

The Simon Report recommended a federal union which would include the Indian states as well as the provinces of British India. But the central government was to come into being only after a "healthy development" of self-government in the provinces to which full political responsibility was to be granted immediately. Meanwhile, the central government was to remain in British hands. Needless to say, these recommendations received little support from the Indians.

There followed three roundtable conferences in which the British received varying degrees of cooperation and non-cooperation from the Indians. The conferences nevertheless provided material for the Joint Committee of both Houses of Parliament whose proposals formed the basis of the Government of India Act of 1935.

The Act of 1919 (which went into effect in 1921) introduced the principle of division of powers between the central and provincial governments which was to become the foundation of subsequent and the present constitutions of India. Equally important, it was the beginning of a federated government. The central government was assigned defense, external affairs, railways, post and telegraph, currency and coinage and other national concerns. The provincial governments were assigned internal law and order, administration of justice and jails, irrigation, famine relief, land revenue administration and similar local matters.

In the provincial governments the powers were further divided into reserved and transferred subjects. The former included police, justice and prisons, irrigation, forests, famine relief, land revenue administration and inspection of factories. The latter consisted of local self-government, education, public health, sanitation and medical administration, public works, agriculture, excise, cooperative societies and development of industries.

The provincial governments were reconstructed for this purpose. A dual government was established known as dyarchy. The Governor with his executive council was granted control over the reserved subjects for the administration of which he was responsible to the Viceroy not the provincial legislature. The transferred subjects were placed in charge of the Governor acting with his ministers who were appointed by the elected members of the provincial councils. The Indian ministers, however, served at the pleasure of the Governor. Moreover, they were required to retain the confidence of the legislature. Furthermore, the governor's powers of interference with respect to transferred subjects were extensive.

The central legislature also underwent changes by the 1919 Act. A bicameral body was constituted consisting of a Council of State and the Assembly. The central legislature was empowered to act on all subjects but prior consent of the Governor-General was necessary for the introduction of bills in certain fields—measures affecting the public debt or public revenues, foreign relations, defense and others. Moreover, the Governor-General had the right to have a bill passed if he certified it as essential for the safety and tranquility of India. He could also promulgate emergency ordinances. In money matters the powers of the legislature were very limited. Hence the Viceroy still remained dominant in central legislation.

The Viceroy's executive council was again enlarged and opened up for Indian membership. Though the Act did not so prescribe it became practice to admit three Indian members. Lord Sinha was succeeded by Sir Ali Aman as law member. Thereafter some eminent Indian lawyer was invariably the law member. The education portfolio was headed by an Indian.

The 1935 Act embodied two main objectives, (1) provincial autonomy with a government responsible to an elected legislature, and (2) a federated central government consisting of the provinces and the Indian states. All powers were to be divided between the center and the provinces. Dyarchy was to be instituted at the center with certain powers such as foreign affairs, defense, and the like reserved to the Viceroy. There was a complete transfer of power at the provincial level and a partial transfer at the center. Dyarchy was abolished in the so-called Governor's provinces, numbering eleven now, namely Madras, Bombay, Bengal, United Provinces, Northwest Frontier Province, Bihar, Assam, the Punjab, Central Provinces, Orissa and Sind. In these provinces the Act vested the authority of the province with the Governor, himself, as the representative of the crown. He was provided with a council of ministers to aid and advise him in the discharge of the entire sphere of provincial government except in certain matters like law and order, for which he had special responsibilities and which were in his sole discretion. The ministers were to be appointed by the Governor from amongst the members of the local legislature and were to be responsible to it.

The Act of 1935 was another substantial step toward independence. The Congress, however, criticized it severely. They disliked the idea of the Indian princes nominating representatives to the Indian Parliament. They were apprehensive about the reserved powers, particularly excluding Indian parliamentary control over defense and external affairs. Finally, they were not prepared to accept the retention of the functions and powers of paramountcy over the Indian states by the British. They were also irritated by the provision in the act declaring *ultra vires* any legislation which would discriminate against British commercial interests. The Muslim League was equally critical of the new constitution and it looked again as if the two communities were about to enter a period of amity in the independence movement.

The Congress, nevertheless, decided to cooperate at this time and contest the elections. It was eminently successful. The Congress candidates ran on a platform of social and economic reforms. Congress ministries were formed in eight of the eleven provinces. Muslim League ministries were formed in Bengal, Punjab and Assam. The Congress administrations were highly successful in working the reforms. In the words of Sir Percival Griffiths in his *British Impact on India* "They maintained law and order well; they conformed to the normal principles of government finance; they learned how to utilize the knowledge and industry of the civil services; they went ahead with their plans for reform. As was to be expected they legislated too much and too hastily but they were not revolutionary and they desired stability as earnestly as their official predecessors." Congress popularity consequently increased among the people. Party membership rose from one-half to five million during the next three years. But a schism developed between the followers of Gandhi and Subhas Chandra Bose who eventually split off to form a new party, the Forward Block. On the whole, however, the period of 1936–39 was a peaceful one on the road to independence.

Then came the outbreak of World War II. Indians were disturbed that India should be dragged into the war without their consent. Congress issued a strong declaration refusing cooperation in the war effort and asked the British Government to state whether its war aims included the treatment of India as a free nation. When no satisfactory reply was made the Congress ministries resigned in autumn of 1939. Congress kept demanding a provisional national government at the center which the Viceroy refused to concede but offered instead on August 9, 1940 to set up a constituent assembly to adopt a new constitution, nominate additional Indians to the Viceroy's executive council and appoint a war advisory council consisting of representatives of British India and the Indian states.

The offer was regarded as unsatisfactory by the Congress. Gandhi inaugurated an individual civil disobedience campaign. The deadlock continued until May 8, 1942 when, while things were going badly for the British in the war in the Pacific, Sir Stafford Cripps was sent to India to conciliate the dispute. He promised dominion status and a constituent assembly to adopt a new constitution after the war was over but no immediate change in the government toward greater independence. Two conditions were attached, however, that any province not satisfied with the new constitution could secede and the rights of minorities would be guaranteed by treaty with Great Britain.

Both Congress and the Muslim League rejected the offer. Mr. Jinnah now started demanding a separate nation for the Muslims. He feared a democratic India, even with separate electorates, in which the Muslims would be a minority. He revived the idea of Pakistan as a sovereign state and it was formally endorsed by the Muslim League in 1940. Many Indian Muslims did not share this view point. Most notable among them was Maulana Abdul Kalan Azad, one of the greatest of Indian Muslims, who was Congress President for a number of terms.

After failure of the Cripps mission, Congress adopted a resolution on August 9, 1942 in favor of launching a large scale mass struggle for independence. The government retaliated immediately on August 9, 1942 by arresting the Congress leaders and declaring the Congress illegal. Riots and disorders broke out in the form of train derailments, cutting of telegraph and telephone lines and the like. More than 60,000 Indians were arrested, 18,000 detained without trial, 940 killed and 1,630 injured by the police during the last five months of 1942. To compound matters Subhas Chandra Bose, with Japanese assistance, inaugurated the Government of Free India at Singapore and advanced with an army via Burma, now in Japanese hands, to the frontier of India.

On May 6, 1944, Gandhi was released from jail on grounds of health. Meanwhile, Lord Wavell became Viceroy and came forth with a plan approved in London to appoint all members of the executive council, with the exception of the Viceroy and the Commander-in-Chief, from India on the basis of parity between the Muslims and Hindus. He called a conference in Simla to select personnel but the Congress and League could not come to an agreement.

The struggle for independence had now reached an ominous stage. The outcome could have been bloody. But events outside India were destined to determine the peaceful turn it took. It was at this point the English people decided to change their government from the Troy to the Labor Party. The Indians were all too familiar with Winston Churchill's statement "I have not become the King's first minister in order to preside over the liquidation of the British Empire." They were also familiar with his earlier statement "England, apart from her empire in India, ceases forever to exist as a great power." "The only realities" responded Jawaharlal Nehru, writing in prison "were Britain's determination to hold on to India at all costs and India's determination to break this hold." To be sure, all Englishmen did not feel about India as did Churchill but he and his party were in political control at this crucial period.

Moreover, when the war ended, Great Britain was prostrate. She no longer possessed the resources to maintain an empire, particularly one seething with rebellion. The Labor Party, therefore, decided to come to terms with the situation in India. The Labor government announced that fresh elections were to be held, the Viceroy's council was to be reconstructed with Indian membership as proposed by Lord Wavell and a constituent assembly convened as soon as possible. The mutiny of the Indian Navy on February 18, 1946 added further to this determination. The elections were held in early 1946 and resulted in a sweeping victory for the Congress generally and for the Muslim League with respect to Muslim seats.

Two major problems confronted the constitution makers as independence loomed. The Muslim-Hindu rivalry and the integration of the Indian states. The former was hardening not ameliorating. Partition, however, was not taken seriously as a solution. Jawaharlal Nehru could not believe the demand was genuine as "Those who today demand separation would be the greatest sufferers from it," for "if the division is made so as to separate the predominantly Hindu and Muslim areas, the former will comprise far the greater part of the mineral resources and industrial areas. The Hindu areas will not be so hard hit from this point of view. The Muslim areas, on the other hand, will be economically backward, and often deficit areas which cannot exist without a great deal of outside assistance." Partition also was rejected by the second Cripps mission in 1946 as impractical. There is reason to believe that even Jinnah himself did not really want it but put the demand forth to increase his bargaining position for constitutional provisions favoring Muslims. The problem, unfortunately, was emotional, not intellectual, and partition proved the ultimate solution.

The miracle of Indian independence was the facile way the Indian states were integrated into the Indian Union. Failure in this respect would have been far more serious for the future of India than the separation of the Muslim areas. For this India today owes a large measure of gratitude to Sardar Vallabhbhai Patel whose political skill prior to and immediately after India's independence brought the Indian states into the union.

The princes had a privileged and comfortable position under British paramountcy. They disliked the Congress and feared for their privileges in an independent and democratic India. Many British, particularly those serving in the political department of the Viceroy's government which maintained relations with the rulers, sympathized with them. Moreover,

Great Britain was grateful for the loyalty, a self-serving one to be sure, of the princes. Both Congress and the Muslim League were disturbed by the provision in the Act of 1935 which retained paramountcy for the crown. The Cripps mission of 1946 equivocated on the issue in its report by stating "It is quite clear that with the attainment of Independence by British India whether inside or outside the Commonwealth the relationship which has hitherto existed between the rulers of the states and the British Crown will no longer be possible. Paramountcy can neither be retained by the British Crown nor transferred to the new government. At the same time the states are ready and willing to cooperate in the new development of India. The precise form which their cooperation will take must be a matter of negotiations during the building up of the new constitutional structure and it by no means follows that it will be identical for all the states." In the end the Indian Independence Act of 1947 left the Indian states completely independent and free to join either India, Pakistan or neither. Fortunately, the princes had no place to turn once the protection of British paramountcy was gone except to one of the unions.

The Government of India even prior to independence created an Indian States Department on July 5, 1947 and placed Sardar Patel in charge. Patel, with Lord Mountbatten's influential backing, negotiated instruments of accession which provided that, pending promulgation of a constitution by the constituent assembly in which the states would be adequately represented, the Indian Parliament would legislate for the acceding states relating to defense, external affairs, communications and the like. Most of the states agreed to accession. The small ones were integrated into the existing provinces or amalgamated into new states which were subsequently called part B states under the new constitution.

Two states, however, proved difficult. Hyderabad in central India was predominantly Hindu but ruled by a Muslim, the Nizam. Negotiations proved abortive. But a putative communist rebellion and disorder broke out inside Hyderabad which spilled over into India. This provided an occasion to send Indian troops into Hyderabad causing the Nizam to accept the inevitable accession to India.

Kashmir was different. It was situated between India and Pakistan and bordered foreign countries. Moreover, a Hindu prince ruled over a predominantly Muslim population. The Maharaja would probably have opted to remain independent but when Pakistan marched troops into his land he quickly acceded to India and asked the Indian army to repel the invaders.

At the end of the war when the Labor Party decided to grant India independence events moved fast, perhaps too fast. A cabinet mission under Sir Stafford Cripps was sent to India in March, 1946. No agreement was reached but the mission recommended, among other things, a three-tiered federation which satisfied no one. A constituent assembly of 296 members elected on a communal basis by the provincial legislatures was to be formed.

Furthermore, an interim national government comprising the Viceroy's executive council chosen from the leaders of the different parties was to be constituted immediately.

The interim executive council under the leadership of Jawaharlal Nehru was sworn in on September 2, 1946. But the Muslim League refused to participate in the constituent assembly. The constituent assembly was, nevertheless, formed and met on December 9, 1946 selecting Rajendra Prasad as President. Various committees were formed to draft different parts of the constitution.

Meanwhile, the Muslim League started protesting these developments. This precipitated bloody communal riots in Bengal during August 1946. The atmosphere continued to be tense and unsatisfactory until February 20, 1947 when the British Government announced it intended to "quit India" by June 1948 and sent Lord Mountbatten to replace Lord Wavell as Viceroy to implement the new policy decision. Lord Wavell was adament against partition but Lord Mountbatten decided the "quit India" resolution could not be accomplished in a year without it. Partition became possible when Congress agreed to it. Thereafter events moved swiftly. A boundary commission under Sir Cyril Radcliffe was set up to partition the Punjab and Bengal. The India Independence Act was passed by the British Parliament on July 1, 1947 setting August 15, 1947 as the date for transfer of power to the new dominions of India and Pakistan. At midnight August 14 a special session of the constituent assembly was held in Delhi. It declared the independence of India as a part of the British Commonwealth and designated Lord Mountbatten the first Governor-General of the new Indian dominion.

INDEPENDENT INDIA

After independence (following six and a half centuries of foreign rule) India and Pakistan faced the monumental problem of industrializing their antiquated agricultural economies for the economic betterment of their burgeoning populations. Both wished to do so within a democratic political framework. Pakistan failed (as Jawaharlal Nehru forsaw) for it was from the start a misbegotten political entity. The Punjabi and Bengali Muslim had nothing in common except the thin thread of religion that proved insufficient to hold the two regions together. In the civil war of 1971 the Bengali sector split away into the independent state of Bangladesh. Both truncated Pakistan and Bangladesh are presently struggling along in dire economic straits under military dictatorships.

India, on the other hand, has maintained its Parliamentary form of government. Jawaharlal Nehru was Prime Minister for the first 17 years of its independence. He guided India successfully both in its external affairs and in its economic development. After his death in May 1964 the country lapsed into political disarray and economic stagnation. How much of the loss of economic momentum the past decade or so is attributable to political instability and how much is due to fundamental problems of economic development remains unclear at this time.

In June 1975 Prime Minister Indira Gandhi, Jawaharlal Nehru's daughter, promulgated an Emergency Order that begot a massive constitutional crisis. It was designed primarily to cope with the growing economic problems but unfortunately resulted in repressive measures against her political opponents. Many within and outside India thought the country had succumbed to political dictatorship. Mrs. Gandhi's father too was often accused of political dictatorship as he ruled strongly but by dint of forceful personality rather than dictatorial propensity. His daughter unfortunately lacked such tact and sterling qualities. But like her father she too was dedicated to democratic principles and permitted free elections to prevail. She lost the Parliamentary election of March 1977 to an opposition coalition led by the Janata party a political grouping of former Congress party members. India today is still reaching for the political stability she enjoyed during its first 17 years under Jawaharlal Nehru, who will doubtless go down in history as one of the great statesmen of the 20th century.

The mere survival of democratic institutions, however, cannot solve India's basic problem of inadequate productivity. In fact, many feel that there cannot be maximum economic development within a democratic framework. In 1950 India's population was 360 million; in 1975 it was 600 million! Peace, better food production and public health measures increased population rapidly making economic betterment more difficult. Stabilizing population growth should be the highest priority but in this respect India has had only a modicum of success. The sociological and political factors involved pose near insurmountable problems.

India has had both success and disappointment in economic development. The First Five Year Plan (1951–55) merely restored and consolidated production after years of social strife and upheaval caused by the partition. But the Second and Third Five Year Plans (1955–65) were very successful. Through collaboration agreements with Western and Soviet bloc corporations and governments, supplemented by foreign loans and aid, the Indians acquired most of the modern technology for industrialization of the economy. In that short span of time, for instance, the Indians, starting from scratch, produced indigenously most of a motor vehicle. Steel production was increased from one to nine million tons. But more important Indians achieved the technological competence to design, engineer, construct and supply most of the machinery for future steel plants, refineries, fertilizer factories and other industries on their own! But there has been unsatisfactory progress during the decade of the 1970's. It was projected earlier that by 1975 India would have an economy based upon 15 million tons of steel production but steel production was not even up to the 9 million ton capacity established in the 1960's.

The political and economic future of India, at this time, is open to speculation. That it is the dominant power in South Asia is without doubt. India has achieved nuclear power capacity. The country is self-sufficient in armaments—jet aircraft, tanks, vehicles and small arms. It possesses the most advanced industrial technology, except in some areas on the frontiers of modern industry. Agriculture too has been upgraded with additional irrigation, chemical fertilizers, mechanization and improved agronomy. Food production has more than doubled since independence. But the population has also nearly doubled. Thus the per capita income has increased only modestly from Rs. 284 ($60) in 1950 to Rs. 670 ($80) in 1977.

CHINESE CIVILIZATION

Geology and geography conspired to create a singular culture on the far eastern end of the Eurasian continent. The tectonic plate on which rides the Indian subcontinent was thrust underneath the Eurasian land mass forming the Himalayas, the highest peaks on earth, and behind them the 12,000 foot high Tibetan plateau of broad dimensions some 500,000 miles square. The southwest Monsoon drops immeasurable quantities of water on this elevated area from whence it flows south to form and nurture the vast India-Gangetic plain and eastward similarly in the Yellow-Yangtze river basins. The Brahmaputra that flows into the bay of Bengal, the Irrawaddy that waters Burma and the Mekong that nourishes Cambodia and South Vietnam too originate in the vast Tibetan watershed. To the northeast of the Tibetan plateau are immense deserts, the Ordos and Gobi, from whence the northwest winds deposited over the eons tons of fine silt with and upon the alluvium of the Yellow river forming the characteristic loess soil of North China. Here too in the eastern watershed of the great Tibetan plateau (the roof of the world) was formed another river valley where man founded one of his foremost civilizations.

This unique geography had yet another result. It made the migration of paleolithic and nelolithic man to and from the region difficult, almost impossible, so that a distinct race of man, known as Mongoloid, developed in this genetic isolation. The Mongoloid differs considerably from his Indo-European counterpart to the west on the other side of the formidable mountain-desert barrier. He is generally shorter, with yellow pigmented skin, hairless body, brown eyes and straight black hair. While the Chinese are predominantly Mongoloid other racial strains have been absorbed during the course of history and prehistory. Professor Eberhard in his *History of China* describes eight prehistoric cultures that melded into the formation of the Chinese people some of which were not Mongoloid. The people of the Liad culture, for instance, were Austroasiatics. A significant Turkish strain came later from the west resulting in a taller and heavier built Chinese in the northwest. Thai, Chuang and Chingchai elements entered from the south where a lighter petite people evolved.

It appears though that Mongoloid man was as competent in technological innovation and development as his Indo-European counterpart. Chinese technology prior to the Industrial Revolution was as highly developed (and developed independently) as that in the Mediterranean area. In fact, in some ways, navigation and gun-powder, for instance, it was more advanced. This is now convincingly confirmed by the prodigious research done by Joseph Needham and his staff (mostly Chinese) at Cambridge University and set forth in a 7 volume (two still unpublished) work entitled *Science and Civilization in China*. Mongoloid man too met the challenge of life on the bitter cold and forbidding tundra during the ice age.

The invention of agriculture, it would appear, came several millennia later than it did in western Asia. Too little is still known about the Neolithic age in prehistoric China. But the earliest evidence of agriculture to date is at a site called Pan-p'o in Shensi where cultivated millet stores dating back to 4000 B. C. were found. Millet is indigenous to China and grows well in the loess soil of the horseshoe bend of the Yellow river. Evidence of wheat, which is not native to the area, date back only to about 2500 B. C. in the northwest where it must have been brought from the west. Rice did not appear until the Yangtze basin was developed as its cultivation was unsuitable to the soils and climate of North China. Even wheat had to await the cultivation of the Yellow river alluvium in the east as it does not grow readily in the heavy loess soils of Shensi and other western provinces. The cultivation of the soybean around 1500 B. C., however, formed the mainstay of Chinese agriculture for it provided the much needed protein for human energy. It seems, however, to have displaced the cow as milk products have never been a staple in the Chinese diet. But pig breeding was already part of the northeast culture (in Hopei province) around 2500 B. C.

THE SHANG DYNASTY (CIRCA 1600–1027 B. C.)

Chinese history is dated generally from 1600 B. C. with the founding of the Shang dynasty in the Yellow river basin. But there is an even earlier obscure Hsia dynasty whose existence is mostly legendary. The Chinese were mankind's earliest historians but scholars remained skeptical on the accounts of the Shang kings until archeologists unearthed the Shang city of Anyang in Honan province in 1927. Anyang was founded by the Shang king Phan Keng about 1300 B. C. Anyang confirmed the ancient texts and provided considerably more knowledge on the Chinese people at this early date.

For decades prior to 1927 the farmers of Hopei and Honan were ploughing up inscribed animal bones, which scholars concluded contained an early verion of the Chinese script already known from inscriptions on the Shang bronzes. These so-called "oracle bones" derived from a practice of divination during and preceding Shang times whereby tortoise shells and the blade bones of animals were heated and the resultant cracks interpreted by Shang oracles to foretell future events. These interpretations were inscribed on the cracked bones in the form of questions and answers. For example the query raised could be "is it time to plant" and the answer might be yes or no. These questions and answers (not always recorded as the cracks supposedly provided the answer) afford much information on the life of the early Shang. Though not clear it is believed that the Chinese script originated with these oracle bones.

But by the Shang period the Chinese civilization had already taken on peculiar characteristics of its own, refuting any notion that it was an import from the west. There is, for example, the unique pottery called a *li* consisting of a cooking vessel with three hollow legs to straddle the fire permitting a different liquid to be boiled in each of the legs. A second pot with a perforated bottom to set atop the *li* was also in use for steaming the food. Chinese cuisine was already refined at this early date. The semilunar knife (made of stone at first) and the composite (sinew backed) bow are other neolithic Chinese inventions not known elsewhere. The latter may have been brought to North America across the Bering Straits by the Amerindians. The famous Shang bronzes too reflect a technique different from bronze casting in western Asia.

The Shang ruler exercised a loose suzerainty over some thirty or so dependencies in an area probably no more than 200 by 200 miles square centered around Honan province. It was not yet the China of todays dimensions. It was also not the feudalism that prevailed during the succeeding Chou period. The societies were hierarchical with great appropriation of wealth by the ruling class as evidenced by the burial sites of the Shang rulers. Servants, horses, chariots, and various artifacts were entombed with the kings and nobles. Slaves through conquest in war constituted a large segment (about 25 per cent) of the population estimated by Professor Eberhard at about 4–5 million in the Tenth century B. C.

A script of some 3000 characters was in use. Writing, the hallmark of civilization, appeared in Sumeria two thousand years earlier pointing up again the later development of the Chinese civilization. The principle of the Chinese script differs from that of other peoples. The ideographs or characters are not phonetic. C. P. Fitzgerald, the English authority on China, likens them unto our numerals (say) the number 5 which is sounded as *five, fünf* or *cinq* in different European languages. This has enabled Chinese of different dialects to understand each other in writing though not in speech. This scriptal universality has played a significant role in uniting the Chinese people.

Religion during the Shang period consisted primarily of nature dieties. The supreme god was Shang Ti, the god of vegetation. The earth was a mother goddess who bore the plants and animals fathered by Shang Ti. To promote fertility great sacrifices, including humans, were made to these gods.

Agriculture was the mainstay of the Shang economy. Drainage and irrigation were practiced. Cultivation was still by hand. Animal plowing was not yet in use. Millet, wheat and soybean were the staple crops. The dog, pig and fowl were the main animals. The meat of cows and sheep was also eaten but there is no evidence of the use of milk or milk products. The horse (always expensive in China) was still owned only by the nobility. Sericulture was already practiced. Linen was also grown for fibre. Woolen clothes were not yet in use.

Technologically the Chinese were quite advanced in Shang times, more so than the people of the Mediterranean area in some respects. They fired their kilns up to 3000°. Instead of casting bronze artifacts by the lost wax technique they soldered bronze molds (cast in clay forms) with imperceptible seams. It is believed that the bronze technology came from the south. The recent find in northern Thailand of Bronze technology dating back to 3600 B. C. lends support to this view. Bronze (dating back to 2500 B. C.) has always played a significant role in China where metals were scarce. It was too dear to be used widely for implements and weapons. Bronze was used as money. Its use served as an economic barometer for during periods of deflation bronze implements and artifacts were turned into coins and the reverse during periods of inflation. This scarcity of metals is believed to have been an important factor that propelled the Chinese into the development of porcelain for vessels and fine implements for daily use.

The Chinese had the horse and chariot in Shang times. But it is thought to have come from the west with the explosion of the Indo-Europeans into Asia during the second millennium B. C. The horse was always an expensive source of energy for the Chinese as they had inadequate pasturelands for rearing the animal. But it played a vital role in Chinese history in the struggle with the Hsiung-nu and Mongols from the steppes of Mongolia and Siberia.

CHOU DYNASTY (CIRCA 1027–257 B. C.)

The Shang were overpowered by the Chou, a vassal state to the west in the Wei valley (Shensi province) in 1027 B. C. Who the Chou were is not clear. That they were thoroughly sinified, even intermarrying with the Shang, is known. But they distinguished themselves from the people of the North China plain by referring to them derogatorily as "black haired people" implying an ethnic differentiation. Professor Eberhard sets forth the thesis that they were originally Turks and Tibetans who settled first in Kansu and western Shansi and eventually in eastern Shensi because of barbarian pressure (the same that brought them to China earlier) from the west. In eastern Shensi they fell under the spell and hegemony of the Shang and became Chinese. Yet their dominance of the emerging Chinese civilization infused it with new blood and ideas. It appears also that they possessed overwhelming technology not so much in kind as in quantity for they seemed amply equipped with the horse and chariot. Situated in the northwest they had better access to the horses reared on the steppes of Siberia and their proximity to the Shang gave them easy access to the metal and wood technology of the Chinese for the production of chariots. It should be noted that the Chinese chariot was a heavier wooden wheeled vehicle and not the light weight finely spoked carriage of western Asia.

The Chou introduced two salient features into the Chinese culture. They possessed a strong patriarchal family tradition that subsequently became the foundation of Confucianism. In the beginning they were also very clannish referring to themselves as "the hundred families". They introduced the "son of heaven" concept into China's religion (if it can be so called) whereby the Chinese ruler exercised his authority under the mandate of heaven. He was never deified or ruled by divine right as in the Mediterranean area. Both these concepts contributed substantially to the great stability of the Chinese society.

In order to rule the Chinese people the Chou instituted a feudal state. The "hundred families" were distributed over the country in garrisons and fiefdoms ruling over the Shang population of the area. The Chou ruler (the first was named Wu-Wang) ruled directly only over the original Chou state in the Wei valley with its capital near modern Sian. The rest of the country was ruled by the feudal lords (who created sub-fiefs and lesser nobility within their fiefdoms) of the Chou clan and such other former Shang vassals incorporated into the new feudal system.

The Chou dominated the new feudatories. Many brought with them their slaves and serfs to cultivate the land disseizing thereby the Shang peasantry. The dispossessed Shang turned to trade so that the word Shang came to mean "merchant". The Shang priesthood too was rendered obsolete with the introduction of the Chou "religion". The ex-priests found a new outlet though, by becoming scholars, scribes and advisors to the Chou on Chinese ways and proprieties. China thus became the first and only civilization with no priests. It was thereafter a predominantly secular society. Otherwise the Chou simply built upon the culture of the Shang developing it further into the future Chinese civilization.

The Chou "family" ties gradually weakened with the passage of time and memory and the feudal states began asserting their independence of the emperor. Nonetheless, there could be only one "son of heaven" so the Chou ruler, called Wang, maintained his suzerainty over the feudal lords. But in 771 B. C. the Chou emperor Yu was killed in an attack on his capital by an alliance of barbarians and feudal lords from the north. The capital was forthwith moved to Loyang in the North China plain where Chou emperors ruled without a territory but further away from the barbarian northwest. This devastating blow weakened the Chou suzerainty and China lapsed eventually into internecine warfare known as the Period of the Warring or Contending States (481–256 B. C.) that Toynbee, in his characteristic wont, renamed the "time of troubles."

There were at first, perhaps, two-three hundred states (Eberhard says a thousand) but the strong swallowed the weak over the centuries so that by 500 B. C. or so there were some 14 contenders for supremacy. The two strongest were Ch'in which now occupied the former territory of Chou in the Wei valley to the west, and Ch'u in the south, astride the newly developing Yangtze river valley area.

In the 5th century B. C. the internecine warfare grew more deadly. Iron technology made it possible to arm large peasant armies. The mounted warrior now entered the fray. Prior to this time the wars between the states were conducted chivalrously reminiscent of warfare in 16th–17th century Europe. It was forbidden for instance to slay a noble who lost his chariot. The battle was temporarily suspended until he found another one. Territories could only be raided not occupied. There occurred probably countless gracious capitulations such as that portrayed by Valazquez in *The Surrender of Breda* in 1625 A. D.

Mounted horsemanship emerged in western Asia, as discussed in the previous chapter, the forepart of the millennium and found its way east via the nomads of the steppes of central Asia and Mongolia. The first state to adopt cavalry from the nomads (called the Hsiung-nu) was the northern state of Chao, which put its army on horseback around 500 B. C. This also ushered in a profound social change in China as it introduced the trouser to replace the cloak for men's dress. It was derisively referred to as "barbarian" dress, but riding horseback made it necessary.

It was the Ch'in, however, who were destined to utilize the new technology for victory. They had the best access to horses, being situated in the northwest. There were already at this time notable horsedealers who bought horses in Mongolia and sold them to the Chinese armies. Moreover, being barbarians once removed themselves, they took more facilely to the new technique. The Ch'in also had easy access to the rich iron ore deposits of north Shansi, particularly after they defeated the Chao in 259 B. C.

The Ch'in were more ruthless and lived by an authoritarian code. They relied heavily on Chinese advisors from the east and the school of philosophy they espoused was that of the Legalists. The Ch'in ruler boasted of massacring 400,000 men in his defeat of the Chao! The figure is doubtless greatly exaggerated but it bespeaks a high order of ruthlessness.

In 223 B. C. Ch'in defeated its great rival Ch'u and in 221 B. C. the Ch'in ruler Huang Ti proclaimed himself the Emperor of China (the name deriving from Ch'in) having now subdued all the other states. Huang-Ti was a ruler of considerable stature and dimension. He ascended the Ch'in throne at 13 and promptly began work (near Sian) on his tomb of monumental proportions. He had his artisans produce a life size replica of his elite corps 6000 strong in terra cotta, including their horses, chariots and weapons and placed in battle formation underground to guard his sarcophagus. The flat roofed subterranean area covered three acres. Some 700,000 forced laborers worked 36 years on the project. The Communist government of China initiated an archeological program to exhume the terra cotta figures many of which are still intact after 2200 years despite the cave in of the subterranean tomb.

But this was only one of his accomplishments. The Ch'in were great builders of hydraulic works. Huang Ti continued the irrigation works and canal construction of his predecessors. He integrated and completed the Great Wall of some 1500 miles by 207 B. C. Parts of the Wall had been built as early as 300 B. C. by various northern states (Yen, Chao, Ch'in and others) to keep the Hsiung-nu from raiding their territories. Owen Lattemore asserts, interestingly, that the purpose of the Wall was mainly to keep the peasants from migrating (presumably to settle on free land) outside their states. In any event, the Wall never really kept the Huns and Mongols from invading China.

Huang Ti also built a magnificent new capital at Hsien-yang (near Sian) to which he removed the rulers and nobles of the states he subdued in order to reduce the risk of rebellion. They lived in splendid buildings (replicas usually their former palaces) but virtual prisoners of the emperor. Huang Ti decreed he was to be designated the "first emperor" and his successors numbered sequentially for the next "ten thousand years." It was a grand vision. Unfortunately his dynasty lasted only 14 years. In 207 B. C. it was succeeded by the Han dynasty which survived for four centuries.

In his rule as emperor, Huang Ti accomplished much to consolidate and unify China. He standardized coinage, weights and measures and the gauges of chariot and wagon wheels to fit into the deeply rutted roads in the loess soils. Administration was centralized with the country divided into provinces (and provinces divided into prefectures) with officials and military commanders responsible to the emperor. Above all he standardized the script, though most of his kin could not read, for it was necessary for a unified administration of the country. The Chinese script has remained so since.

There had been much economic progress and social change during the Period of the Contending States despite the warfare and bloodshed. Much additional land was brought under cultivation, especially in the west and the south. The plow and iron implements were used widely. Manuring (including human excrement) and fallowing were highly developed. Rice became a leading cereal with the development of the Yangtze valley. Beef and lamb virtually disappeared from the diet as population pressure on the land increased. Professor Eberhard estimates the population in 400 B. C. was already 25 million. At that time the territory of the Chou states was only about one-fourth of China today. Land became alienable as the feudal lords were ousted during the warfare. New land brought under cultivation avoided the old feudal tenures. Primogeniture gradually gave way to equal inheritance by all sons automatically breaking up the large holdings. Merchants grew in numbers and wealth (to wit, the horse traders already mentioned) with the new iron and horse technology. In the unsettled times they placed their wealth in land, perhaps, the only safe and secure investment of the day.

There was much intellectual ferment in those troubled times. The great thinkers pondered the meaning of the strife and misery that had gripped their civilization. There were a "hundred schools" of philosophy (secular not religious) that arose during the period 500–250 B. C. The three most prominent and/or enduring were those of Confucius, Lao Tzu and the Legalists.

Confucius (circa 551–479 B. C.) traced his antecedents to the Shang. He was reared in the state of Lu in the Shantung peninsula where the Chou feudal order remained intact longer than in the west. Like other scholars of his time he was an itinerant advisor to the nobility serving for a time as head advisor to the ruler of Lu. He achieved a following but attained little stature and recognition during his life.

Confucius espoused a philosophy of life based on social order and discipline. It was predicated on a strong patriarchal family structure and a ruling elite of the gentry. To be a gentleman was everything. Loyalty and responsibility to one's family, the ruler (the son of heaven) and reverence for one's ancestors was the ethical way of life.

Lao Tzu the founder of Taoism (the way) is a more elusive figure. His antecedents are unknown. Even his time of life is uncertain being placed anywhere from the 6th to 4th centuries. There is some belief that he may even have visited India. At any rate, Taoism is very much like Buddhism. Lao Tzu too taught rejection of the wicked world. A life of seclusion away from the cities in harmony with nature was "the way" of the good life. Like the Buddha, Lao Tzu too wanted to rid mankind of gross desires, envy and evil.

The two philosophies were not exactly incompatible. A Chinese could espouse both particularly for different stages of life. Confucianism as a youth and father; Taoism in old age especially if he acquired the wealth to live comfortably in the country. This is not too different from the ideal Hindu way of life. And when Buddhism came from India centuries later a Chinese was not greatly disturbed about incorporating its basic tenets in his panoramic outlook on life. Taoism could not, however, compete with Confucianism as a philosophy of state, with its anarchy and detachment.

Confucianism did not become the philosophy of state, however, until under the Han dynasty. The philosophy of the Legalists had more appeal for the more barbarian Ch'in. Most famous of this school was Shang Yang who died in 338 B. C. His followers pretty thoroughly infiltrated the Ch'in court. Their tenets called for a strong central government with strict laws and policies enforced on the people. Warriors and peasants were given highest priority in the state, the first, to enforce the law the latter to grow food for the enforcers. Scholars, merchants and others were considered useless. It was a political philosophy similar to the *Arthasastra* by which the Mauryas ruled the first empire in India. Both philosophies were machiavellian in their approach to empire and the Ch'in viewed everything right and fair in their subjection of the other states of China. The Legalists, of course, dominated the administration of the first emperor Huang Ti. Scholars, particularly the Confucianists, were disdained and persecuted and executed. Huang Ti is reputed to have buried countless scholars up to their necks and then lopped their heads off at ground level. Books were burned. A reign of intellectual terror prevailed such as has been repeated from time to time in all human societies.

HAN DYNASTY (206 B. C.–220 A. D.)

After Huang Ti's death in 209 B. C. there ensued a period of assassination of heirs and other pretenders to the throne. In fact maneuvering for power broke out promptly after his death delaying internment in the magnificent tomb he built until his body started to putrify. His executors found it necessary to place a cartload of decaying fish in the funeral cortege to camouflage the putrescense. In 206 B. C. Liu Chi, or Liu Pang, assumed the title of emperor and founded the Han dynasty that was destined to rule for four centuries. Liu Pang was born a peasant, then became a local official, and turned to banditry in the political upheaval of the time. Gradually he built an army, subdued the other bandits and renascent feudal lords and assumed rule over the empire founded by Huang Ti. There was, at first, some reversion to feudal rule and political disarray but the empire founded by Huang Ti and restored by Liu Chi proved strong enough to withstand dissolution. For the next two thousand years there would be periods of division and reunification but China would remain whole.

A new class of landed gentry arose under the Han dynasty to replace the old feudal order. It was based on a strong patriarchal family. The gentry adopted Confucianism (it completely displaced the Legalists around 100 B. C. who disappeared thereafter from the China scene) as their philosophy, for it better suited their way of life and thought. From this gentry class were drawn the officials who dominated the administration of the country. Unless the emperor was a strong personality he was completely dominated by the gentry *cum* official class. The renowned Mandrin (the name given a Chinese official by the Portuguese) examination system arose under the Han and became thereafter the route for upward mobility in the Chinese society. The gentry-official class remained the ruling elite in China for the next two thousand years.

This social structure had several strange effects not present in other societies. Merchants and artisans were relegated to the lowest scale of the social order. Scholars were highly regarded as erudition became the avocation of the leisured gentry. There was naturally great intrigue at court by the gentry, first, through the placement of family members in high official positions and secondly, by relating to the emperor and/or his heirs through marriage. A family whose daughter was able to become an empress, or better yet a regent to an infant heir, wielded great power. Chinese history is replete with such intrigue, involving naturally a good deal of homicide. The prominent role of eunuchs in the Chinese courts was another phenomena of the system. Chinese emperors wishing to free themselves of the domineering gentry placed eunuchs (usually of lowly origin) in important and confidential positions as they could not become heads of powerful gentry families. But the eunuchs proved corruptible, gained power through their access to the emperor's harem and generally added to the intrigue at court. The gentry-official, or Mandrin system as the Europeans called it, had a notable feature that facilitated the stability of the Chinese society. The examinations for office were open to everybody though the overwhelming majority of the positions were secured by the sons of the gentry as they had the leisure and wealth to acquire the classical education on which the examinations were based. Nonetheless a gifted and ambitious son of a peasant could participate and achieve high office. Once the office was achieved it was easy to acquire land and become part of the gentry. This not only reinvigorated the ruling elite with new blood but compromised many potential revolutionaries.

China was very prosperous under the Han dynasty. Peace and stability unknown in the country for centuries, brought forth great agricultural productivity. New areas to the south and southwest were colonized and brought under cultivation. This expansion was largely peaceful as the tribal people in these areas were easily overcome and sinified.

The trouble for the Han was in the north. The Hsuing-nu possessed a tremendous technological advantage in the mounted warrior. For some two centuries or so the Chinese tried to keep this formidable enemy at bay with the Great Wall. A wall thirty feet high could not be crossed by horses. But it was costly to garrison the 1500 mile fortress. The great Han emperor Wu (140–86 B. C.), the sixth ruler of the dynasty, decided to meet the challenge by invading Mongolia to destroy the Hsuing-nu. China was now wealthy enough to afford the venture and it had perfected a new weapon, the crossbow, to stop the mounted Hsuing-nu. The new weapon could easily fell a horse. But there was one disadvantage for it took time to draw and cock the cross-bow with a winding mechanism. The Han armies would therefore form a square with the cross-bowmen in the center and as the Hsuing-nu charged the infantry would open ranks to permit the bowmen to release the highly energized arrows against the charging enemy warriors. After the salvo the infantry would again close ranks to permit the cross-bowmen to recock their bows. This cumbersome procedure, though it failed at times, proved quite successful against the nomad warriors. Final victory, albeit temporary, was won over the Hsuing-nu in 51 B. C.

The struggle with the Hsuing-nu brought China even more directly in contact with the West. The emperor Wu sought an ally in the rear of the enemy. He had heard about the Yueh Chi and the fine horses they raised. China needed a new source of supply since the horse trade with the Hsuing-nu had been interrupted by the hostilities. Wu sent Chang Ch'ien to find the Yueh Chi, who had been forced further west by the Hsuing-nu (in fact, we encountered them earlier in India at this time). Chang Ch'ien had difficulties finding them (he was captured enroute for a time by the Hsuing-nu). But when he found them he learned of a new world besides China. Chang Ch'ien visited India, grew familiar with the Hellenized societies of western Asia and found a world filled with fine horses.

The king of this central Asian country that Chang Ch'ien called Ta Yuan (modern Bokharo) refused to sell the Chinese horses so emperor Wu sent an expedition in 104 B. C. which, after considerable hardship and reversal, made Ta Yuan a tributary. A good supply of horses was thus assured. Also greater security was created for the caravans from the west.

Wu's imperialism created internal socio-economic disorder. The military ventures were expensive (especially the high cost of imported horses) requiring additional taxation of the peasants. Moreover, the peasants were forced to raise horses reducing further the food production of the country. Meanwhile the gentry families were conspiring and vying for power. When the weak Emperor Wu died in 32 B. C. and left an eighteen year old son Ch'eng Ti (32–7 B. C.) the Empress Dowager ruled in his name. She placed members of her family in positions of power, including her nephew Wang Mang, who insinuated himself into supreme authority at court. When Ch'eng Ti died without issue Wang Mang placed a number of successive minors (including a year old baby) on the throne and in 8 A. D. usurped the throne himself.

Wang Mang's usurpation, as it is known, split the Han dynasty into two periods. The first phase of the dynasty was, after two centuries, bankrupt in more ways than one. Land concentration reached inequitable dimensions. Taxes and rents improverished the peasants. The people seethed with rebellion. Wang Mang effected several reforms in the attempt to alleviate the matter. He confiscated some of the estates (mostly of his enemies) and redistributed the land. He instituted the "even granary" program, that was to recur from time to time thereafter in China, by buying up grain (and other essentials) in times of plenty and selling them in times of shortages to keep prices stable. He created many state monopolies (wine, iron, salt and others). Wang Mang freed the slaves. He is often called "the first socialist" in China, but most of his measures merely enriched the royal treasury.

Joseph Needham credits Wang Mang with the advancement of science and technology in China. In 4 A. D. he convened the first assembly of scientific experts to discuss, among other subjects, mathematics, music, botany and the calendar. The invention of the compass is thought to have originated during his reign.

Wang Mang, however, miscalculated greviously when he planned another war with the Hsuing-nu. In part, he thought the war would divert attention from the economic troubles at home. But mainly he hoped to destroy the Hsuing-nu so that the cost of the military establishment in Turkestan (maintained, among other reasons to protect the caravans) could be eliminated.

The campaign was aborted by a peasant rebellion in 18 A. D. led by the secret society called the Red Eyebrows. This was the first peasant revolution that was to recur again and again in China for the next two thousand years until it culminated in the Communist Revolution of 1948. This dialectic of chinese history has been discussed in detail in Chapter VIII. It has been a struggle over the agricultural surplus. The gentry and the court would appropriate as much of the surplus as possible in rent and taxes and when the situation became intolerable for the peasants there would be a bloody revolution ending the existing dynasty. An adventurer, frequently a peasant, would eventually gain power and establish a new dynasty. But the gentry, as a class, would survive albeit many of the old former families would lose both life and land. The new emperor could not rule China without the gentry. In part, this was due to the complicated Chinese script in which the revenue, irrigation, land and other records were maintained. Only the scholars could manage the difficult writing and the gentry had a monopoly of scholars. Land would be distributed to the peasants quelling thereby, their rebellion. The surviving gentry, licking its wounds, regained official positions under the new dynasty and thereby gradually reacquired the land. The cycle would repeat itself.

These peasant rebellions were usually fomented and led (misled might be a better word) by the secret societies with intriguing names—Red Eyebrows, Yellow Turbans, White Lotus and the like. They were never able to overthrow the gentry until the Communists gave the peasants the necessary leadership in the 20th century. Foreign invasions too, unlike the story in the Mediterranean area, did not eliminate the gentry though the Mongols eclipsed them for a considerable time. No other ruling elite, with the exception of the Brahmans in India, has been able to perpetuate itself so persuasively for so long.

Millions of Chinese lost their lives in the Red Eyebrows peasant revolt. Wang Mang's soldiers defected to the Red Eyebrows. The Han princes took advantage of the situation by organizing the gentry in Honan under the leadership of prince Lui Hsui to stop the revolt. Lui took power in 25 A. D. and restored the Han dynasty. Wang Mang's head was lopped off by a soldier in 22 A. D. and the skull was kept in the treasury for two centuries!

The massacre reduced the population and made land available to the surviving peasants. Money lenders too were killed relieving the peasants of their debts. A fresh start was made toward prosperity and well being of the peasants. The capital was moved to Loyang in Honan, a rich agricultural area, where the gentry was able to regroup quickly to oppress the peasants once again. In 180 A. D. another massive revolt led by the Yellow Turban society erupted that contributed in large measure to the end of the Han dynasty in 220 A. D.

The later Han period was less distinguished than the earlier. A destructive intrigue developed at court. The eunuchs became extremely powerful. A vicious conflict developed between the scholars and the eunuchs. Cliques evolved among the gentry leading eventually to a division of China into warring states. A manifestation of the eunuch-gentry struggle was that the power of the eunuchs was confined to the central government. In the provinces the gentry *cum* officials were in full control. But the provincial powers-to-be could not aspire to the establishment of a new dynasty without securing the Imperial Seal. This often resulted in the abduction of the emperor and retaining him as a captive in the hope of obtaining the seal for legitimate succession.

The second Han period is notable for its contact with the Mediterranean area. During the period 73–102 A. D. the famous general and Viceroy Pan Chao extended Chinese suzerainty to the Caspian. His envoy Kan Ying visited Persia and, it is believed, made contact with some of Rome's eastern provinces around the Black Sea. In 166 A. D. Marcus Aurelius Antonius (referred to as Antun in Chinese records) allegedly sent a Roman envoy to China. It is, of course, known from Roman history that silk and other Chinese products reached Rome regularly via the caravans at this time.

The Han period is renowned for its literature and scholarship. The gentry possessed the necessary leisure for the scholarship. Encyclopedias (Shan Hai Ching), histories (the famous Shih Chi) and philosophical treatises (Lun Heng) were compiled. Poetry flourished. Painting was done on silk. Buddhism brought with it Gandhara art from India and Central Asia.

Science was not greatly favored by the gentry as their economic interests were tied to agriculture. Nonetheless, there were great innovations in technology during the Han period. Notable advances were made in porcelain manufacture. Tiles and decorated bricks were produced. Paper was invented. From its contact with the West the Chinese imported such new plants as alfalfa (for horses), grapes and peaches. Oranges, lemons and lichis were brought from the south.

DIVISION, INVASION AND BUDDHISM (220–580 A. D.)

In the early centuries of the Christian era China entered a turbulent period of internal division, foreign invasion and rule by the Huns (Hsuing-nu),

Turks, Mongols and Tunguses from the north and the impact of Buddhism from India. In many ways it is astounding that the Chinese could withstand all three and come out whole.

In 140 A. D., the last census under the Han, the population was approximately 50 million. Moreover the Chinese had extended their rule into Szechwan, up to the Tibetan massif, and south of the Yangtze valley to the China seas. The empire proved unmanageable by the Han bureaucracy contributing in large measure to its division into three areas where the defecting generals established new dynasties. The division followed natural and geographic lines. The oldest and most populated Yellow river basin became the kingdom of Wei which had gained control of the Imperial Seal. The westernmost (modern Szechwan) and smallest, the kingdom of Shu in the well irrigated lands of the Ch'entu plain. The Shu dynasty claimed relation to the Han and therefore, greatest legitimacy. The lower Yangtze river valley area and parts to the south became the kingdom of Wu.

Wei was the most important for several reasons. It contained the great majority of the people (29 million to 12 million in Wu and 7.5 million in Shu). It was the area of the old cultures of the Shang and Chou. It had to face the Hsuing-nu and other invaders from the north. Finally it absorbed the major impact of Buddhism in China.

The conflict with the nomads of Mongolia is one of the central features of Chinese history. In these particular centuries the "Huns were on the move". We encountered them in India under the fierce king Mihirakula. Atilla stood before Rome in 453 A. D.! Though the Hsuing-nu are thought to be the same as these Huns by most historians that is not entirely clear. Too little is yet known about the nomads of the steppes who mastered the horse and terrorized the sedentary civilizations of the Mediterranean area, the Indian subcontinent and China for a millennium and a half. The western nomads (Scythians and Sarmations) were clearly Indo-European; the eastern ones (Tunguses and Mongols) were Mongoloid; but those between (Turks, Yueh Chi, Hsuing-nu) appear to have been a mixture of the two. The foremost scholar on the Huns, Otto J. Maenchen-Helfen, concludes the Hsuing-nu were a Europoid-Mongolian racial mixture. Some Turks spoke a Sanskrit language. Mostly the nomads had no script of their own which makes it so difficult to reconstruct their history. Generally they engrafted themselves on the sedentary civilizations in the river valleys of the earth that they raided and/or conquered and by whom they were absorbed. In time they disappeared into these superior cultures. No where was this more true than in China.

Buddhism entered China from Central Asia (to a lesser extent from Burma and Siam in the south) during the 1st century B. C. with the caravans from India. Indian merchants leaving home for several years a journey brought along Buddhist monks to minister to their religious needs. For several centuries the Buddhist clergy was foreign, mostly Indian, and confined to the commercial centers. But in the depressed times of the later Han period the deprived of China began to find solace in the foreign religion. We saw this same social phenomena in decadent Rome. It appears to be a leading indicator of a civilization in extremity. Secular Confucianism may have satisfied the gentry but it provided little or no enduring satisfaction for the peasants. Taoism was too ethereal. Mahayana Buddhism with its promise of a better and enjoyable afterlife provided the emotional content lacking in the secular philosophies. The lowly found comfort in the Indian doctrine of transmigration of the soul for it not only gave them hope of redemption but perverse delight in the thought that their oppressors would be reborn lowly creatures in the next life.

Buddhism brought with it the monastery system providing yet another haven of security for the dispossessed. A new entity had now emerged on the China scene that permitted ownership of large estates in perpetuity to which ordinary people, not members of the gentry families, could attach themselves for a good and secure life. It is doubtful that the gentry would have permitted the growth of the monasteries had they not found themselves insecure and at bay during these politically disturbed centuries. By the 7th century there were 3716 Buddhist monasteries in the country. They cultivated large tracts with "temple slaves". They worked industries and kept shops. Much wealth held in bronze was accumulated by the monasteries. Architecture and sculpture took on an Indian character. The Buddhist cave temples at Yun-Shang in Shensi, constructed during the period 460–535 A. D., resemble those at Ajunta and Ellora in India.

The spread of Buddhism was aided and abetted by the foreign rulers. The Indian and Central Asian monks were more acceptable to the Mongol, Turk and Hun chieftans. Moreover, they needed them as advisors at court for much of the Chinese gentry fled the northern areas for the south. Gradually the lowly Chinese became Buddhist monks and, in a way, the Buddhist monasteries filled the role played by the gentry in the foreign dominated areas of the north. Buddhist scriptures were laboriously translated into Chinese. This was, in fact, a prodigious undertaking for not only was there a fundamental difference in the script but also in the thought processes of the Indians and the Chinese. Earlier in the discourse on Indian history we encountered the Chinese pilgrims in India, Fa-hsien from 399–414 A. D., and Hsuan-tsang from 630–644 A. D., seeking Buddhist scriptures. These Chinese monks, furthermore, brought back new ideas on mathematics, science and technology (for example, the stirrup) from India that the foreign rulers found interesting and useful.

In 265 A. D. the Wei kingdom was taken over by Wu Ti (265–289 A. D.) who reconquered the kingdoms of Shu and Wu to reunify China until 317 A. D. In an attempt to restore agricultural productivity Wu Ti decreed a demobilization in 280 A. D. so that the soldiers could resume life as cultivators. This merely favored the nomads—the Huns, Tibetans, Toba

(Turks) and the Hsien-pi (Mongols)—who now poured into North China and dominated it for nearly three centuries. Some 16 dynasties, of which five were Huns, three Tibetan, three Turkic and five Mongol ruled the whole or part of the Yellow river basin. Most prominent were the Toba, who ruled North China from 385–550 A. D.

The Toba were primarily Turkic people, with an admixture of Mongol. In due time they subdued the Huns, Mongols and Tibetans to rule the entire Yellow river basin from Tibet to Korea. It was during Toba rule that Buddhism made its greatest impact on China. In fact historians often allege that the Toba used the Buddhist monks deliberately in their fight to diminish the power of the gentry. The Buddhist cleverly incorporated Turkish (and Chinese) myths and beliefs into their religion. The emperor was designated an incarnation of Buddha. This fitted nicely with the "son of heaven" concept of the Chinese emperor. The Toba emperor, in turn, made Buddhism the state religion with the chief monk as its head. He was like a Pope of China. War captives and criminals were turned over to the monasteries to work their land as "temple slaves". The Chinese people in the north were now thoroughly Buddhist.

The Toba instituted a profound land reform in 485 A. D. as further curb on the power of the gentry. Everyone had a right to a limited amount of land for life, but could not pass it on to heirs. Land was thus redistributed each generation. The purpose of the "land equalization system" was to prevent the growth of large estates. Land planted in mulberries for silk production was excepted. The land redistribution law remained in effect until 750 A. D.

But the Toba emperors strove, above everything else for Chinese legitimacy. They purported to be a continuation of the Wei dynasty. They married Chinese princesses. The administration was relegated to Chinese. The Toba ruled as a military caste, with a foreign religion, over this Chinese substructure. Like the emperors the Toba nobles too intermarried with the Chinese gentry and regarded themselves as Chinese. By 500 A. D. the Toba were absorbed and integrated into the Chinese society. The Chinese gentry again had regained much of its former power. The Toba emperor Wen Ti (471–499) regarded himself as Chinese. He made Chinese the official language. Chinese clothing and manners were reestablished. The capital was moved from northern Shansi to Loyang in 493 A. D. Confucianism was reestablished as the official religion at the court.

In 550 A. D. the Toba, now thoroughly sinified, split into the Northern Chou (in the west) and Northern Chi (in the east) and in 580 A. D. the Sui dynasty reimposed Chinese rule. Moreover, the Sui reunited once again the whole of China into one empire. The south remained free of foreign rule during these centuries. There was a wholesale emigration of the gentry to the south which was something of a frontier or colonial area, where they carved out great estates. The eastern Chin exercised a loose rule over the south from 317 to 419 A. D., followed by the Lui-Suing (420–478), Southern Ch'i

(478–501), Liang (502–556) and Ch'en (557–558) until the area was reconquered by the Sui in 580 A. D.

THE TANG DYNASTY (618–905 A. D.)

The Sui dynasty was short lived, less than four decades, but it accomplished much. There is an analogy to the Ch'in dynasty that lasted only 14 years but in that short period unified China into a great empire. Its founder Yang Chien (who ruled as emperor Wen Ti) thoroughly sinified but of barbarian lineage, was an energetic man. Reorganizing the empire after three and a half centuries of division was no easy task especially in view of the vast cultural differences that developed. The north and south no longer spoke the same language (though they used the same script) and there were many dialects. Population shifts had taken place to the northeast and south leaving the northwest thinly peopled. Yang Ti, his son, an equally energetic ruler, moved the capital to Loyang and undertook construction of the Grand Canal that interconnected the Yangtze and Yellow river systems into one comprehensive internal waterway. Some five million forced laborers under a police guard of 50,000 were employed (dragooned) for the canal works. About two million men were said to have lost their lives on the project. Quite obviously such cruelty and privation did not make the Sui popular.

Furthermore, the continuing war with the Turks and Koreans was costly requiring greater taxation of the gentry. Yang Ti was also a spendthrift. Wen Ti had already alienated the ruling elite by favoring Buddhists at court (he himself was a devoted Buddhist). Internal disorder erupted again in 615 A. D., when the Sui suffered a defeat by the Turks, and it was only after eight years of fighting that the empire was restored under a unified rule by the Tang. Li Shih-min, the real founder of the new dynasty, was a mixture of Chinese (related to the Sui) and Turk. He built an empire with its capital at Cheng-an again that lasted three centuries.

Chinese historians (and some Western historians too) regard the Tang period as the golden age of China. China remained thereafter, even under further foreign rule, a unified state. Li Shih-min, who ruled as emperor T'ai Tsung, reformed the Confucian examination system already revived under the Sui, making it free to everyone particularly the learned gentry. The original system started under the Han had lapsed into disarray with administrative appointments made by recommendation, mostly by the generals. This placed the emperors at the mercy of the military. The new administrators holding office by virtue of free and open examination tended to be more loyal to the court. This reform, perhaps T'ai Tsung's greatest change, separated thereafter the civil and military administration of the country with the former generally the ascendant. T'ai Tsung also updated the Toba land reform law for greater distribution of the land to the peasants but it served merely to slow not stop the accumulation of the land by the gentry and the monasteries.

T'ai Tsung kept the Turks at bay, in part due to dissension within their own ranks and in part due to the Arab invasions of Central Asia during the 7th century that witnessed the meteoric rise of Islam. His son Kao Tsung (650–683 A. D.) finally conquered Korea in 661 A. D.

China was at this time the center of attraction in the world. Foreigners flocked to it, establishing trading colonies not only in the capital (at Chang-an again) but at every trade center along the caravan route. Sea routes to South China also flourished at this time. The foreigners brought with them their religions—Zoroasterism, Nestorian Christianity and Manichaeism—which began to attract the attention of the Chinese. Jews and Arabs began to make their appearance. The foreigners bought mainly silk but also everything else (especially ceramics) that caught their interest.

The Chinese were fond of and excelled in astronomy. The big dipper was identified as early as Shang times. Later the celestial phenomena known as a supernova was identified. There is the record (the earliest known) of the Crab Nebula that exploded in 1054 A. D. The Tang erected imperial observatories at Chang-an which, curiously though, were manned largely by Indians. Most notable was Gautama Siddarta whose name appears on an astrological almanac published in 729 A. D. that embodies, for the first time in China, the concept of zero. A Buddhist monk I-hsing invented the first clock—a great astronomical water-powered mechanism employing an escapement—constructed at the palace in Chang'an in 721 A. D. Eclipses were forecast with accuracy (they were portentous events to the Chinese) with the amillary sphere (a nest of rings dividing the sky in imaginary circles) invented as early as the Han period.

Buddhism was in its glory during the Tang period. Even the gentry espoused it along with Confucianism. The gentry cleverly turned the doctrine of transmigration in their favor by interpreting it to mean a man had to serve the government and the gentry well to attain a better rebirth. It gained a following at court. The Turks and other nomads were Buddhists. It was during Tang times that Buddhism made its greatest thrust into Korea and Japan. The Japanese were sinified in every way during the Tang period. Trade flourished between the two countries. Buddhism also took on an introspective aspect at this time, known in China as Ch'an and in Japan as Zen, that was tantamount to a return to the original meditative philosophy of Buddha.

Buddhism, at its height, was destined for a shock from which it would never recover as the leading religion of China. The Tang empire lapsed into decline and disintegration during the latter part of the 8th century. Land concentrations in the hands of the gentry and the monasteries had increased. Moreover, the latter were exempt from taxation. But the need for revenues was mounting. First, there was the tribute that had to be paid to the Uighers, who helped save the dynasty from the Tibetans. Second, the cost of the central administration was increasing enormously with more officials, who had arranged attractive pensions for their old age (fifty percent of their salaries at retirement). The cost of the military establishment was gargantuan. Luxurious and profligate living (eunuchs and concubines everywhere) at court was expensive. Tax revenues were insufficient to meet all these requirements.

In desperation the Tang emperor Wu Tsung decided to confiscate the wealth of the monasteries. The Edict of 843 A. D. prohibited all alien religions. The monks were ordered to dress like Chinese and become Chinese citizens (defrocked as Toynbee puts it). The monasteries were secularized and their movable wealth, mostly in bronze statues, confiscated. Professor Eberhard asserts the Edict was not motivated by religious persecution but by the government's need of the wealth held by the religious orders. Yet Taoist monasteries were exempt. But they did not pose the same economic problem. Buddhism survived as a religion. It was too well entrenched with the Chinese people. But the affluent powerful Buddhist monastic order came to an end. The world of art unfortunately, lost most of the Chinese Buddhist sculpture of this period. There was, however, a resurgence of the Buddhist order during the ensuing decades followed by a great persecution in 955 A. D. (the gentry had by now become powerful again) whereby the building of temples, the administration of monks and other activities of the Buddhists was placed under state regulation. There was no recovery from this persecution.

The draconian confiscation of wealth failed to save the Tang dynasty. A century or more of undue consumption of agricultural surpluses by the court, the officials, the pensioners and the military establishment impoverished the people beyond endurance. A peasant revolt erupted in 860 A. D. It was led by Wang Hsien-chih, a peasant who failed the examinations (apparently the system failed to compromise all potential revolutionaries). He was assisted by a pauperized salt merchant Huang Ch'ao. The merchants, considered lowly, suffered undue taxation and confiscation of their worldly possessions.

The uprising erupted in the south (present Hopei) and swept north, captured the whole of eastern China, and moved toward the capital. The military governors were unable to stop the sweep toward the capital as their troops, underpaid and equally deprived, defected to the peasant army. The government belatedly offered Wang high office but he declined it. The Tang turned to the Turks for assistance, defeated Wang and beheaded him in 878 A. D. Huang Ch'ao redirected the peasant army to the southwest where he plundered Canton (Arab sources allege some 120,000 foreign merchants were killed). Huang, with ample funds now, moved north again and captured the capital and made himself emperor of his own shortlived Ch'i dynasty. The Tang, again with the assistance of the Turks defeated Huang in 883

A. D. Huang was killed in 884 A. D. The Tang, however, paid a high price for the suppression of the rebellion with foreign aid. The Turkish commander Li K'o-yung murdered the last Tang emperor and took over rule from him in 907 A. D.

It is a noteworthy observation on the turmoil the Chinese people experienced during most of the first millennium of the Christian era that the population at the end of the Tang period was still about 50 million, the same as in the last Han census of 140 A. D.! Foreign invasions, rebellions, poverty imposed upon the peasants through malappropriation of the national production by the ruling elite and other maladies kept the population down. But despite it all great advances were made in the arts and technology.

THE SUNG DYNASTY (960–1279 A. D.)

Fifty years of division, including foreign rule, followed the fall of the Tang dynasty in 907 A. D. It is referred to as the period of the Five Dynasties. But this is misleading as it ignores the more than five dynasties in the south. In 960 A. D. the Sung reunited China again for another scintillating period of three hundred years. The center of gravity, however, moved to the south as the Sung were never able to oust the Khitans (called Kitai by Europeans from whence derives the name Cathay) who had established themselves in the northeast. The Khitans (a mixture of Mongol and Turk) called themselves the Liao dynasty and exacted heavy tribute from the Sung. By the early 12th century they ruled most of North China above the Yellow river with their capital at Peking. The Sung empire was based on the Yangtze valley and the south with its capital at Khaifeng. In the northwest the Western Hsai, a Turko-Tibetan people, held sway to whom the Sung also paid tribute. The Khitan were great horsebreeders. They had a herd of some 10 million horses, which they traded with the Sung for the manufactured products (silk, porcelian, lacquers and the like) of China. The Khitan became quite wealthy from this trade plus the tribute. This gave rise to the fabulous lore about Cathay in the West as they, not the Sung, were the "Chinese" the Europeans and West Asians made contact with via the caravans. The real culture bearers though were the Sung whose empire was to the south.

A reason the Sung were unable to oust the Khitan from the Yellow river basin was their non-military attitude. Upon establishment of the Sung empire its founder Chao K'uang-yin called together his army commanders to dismantle the old system of military governors in the provinces. He awarded the generals high official positions and estates instead. The country was placed on a civil administrative basis. This he did in order to avert a future military takeover of the empire by a strong provincial military general, a practice that prevailed in China since the fall of the Han dynasty. Unfortunately it weakened China against the warring nomads. But the Khitan too lost their militancy in light of their affluence from trade and tribute with the Sung. This *modus vivendi* brought peace to China for some two centuries enabling the Sung to develop further the great civilization of China.

In science and technology, as Joseph Needham puts it, the Sung placed into practice what the scientists and technicians of the Tang period conceived. Hydraulic engineering (lock gates, new surveying instruments) and bridge building (transverse shear-wall and caissons) was advanced. The Chinese junk with its balanced sternpost rudder, water tight compartments, self flooding and bailing fore and aft sections and battened sails rigged on multiple masts staggered thwartwise (to maximize wind power) was perfected. Marco Polo marveled at these vessels. Some had as many as 50 to 60 private cabins for merchants and officials and crews of 200 to 300 seamen. These ships were equipped with magnetic compasses and other celestial navigation instruments. Gunpowder was put to use as grenades, flame throwers and bombs (fired by catapaults) for both land and naval warfare.

The Sung period is known for a green porcelain called "celadon". It was fine stoneware with an etched design under a green feldspar glaze. Temmako, characterized by a rich, dark brown golden streaked glaze, was also highly prized. Near the end of the period the blue and white porcelain that became famous later during Ming times made its appearance.

The characteristic landscape painting of the Chinese reached its apogee during Sung times. The multichromatic murals of the Buddhist painters were now superceded by the monochromatic fine line (closely related to calligraphy) drawings of the landscapes. Flowers and bamboo were favorite subjects. A school of painting was founded by the Emperor Hui Tsung in 1104 A. D. Hui Tsung was himself a renowned artist fond of painting flowers. It is said that the aim of the Sung period artist was "to express 10,000 li (about 3500 miles) of space in one foot of silk".

Literature flourished with the development of block printing. A new body of Neo-Confucian philosophy evolved that united Buddhism and Confucianism. This incorporation of Buddhist metaphysics by Confucianism eclipsed Buddhism in China. Encyclopedias, histories and scientific works abounded. An Imperial Medical Encyclopedia was published in 1111 A. D. Pharmacy and acupuncture were codified. Shen Kua, chancellor of Han-Lin Academy compiled his *Meng Chhi Pi Than* about 1086 A. D., a masterpiece on the scientific knowledge of the time. Covered are such subjects as astronomy, geology (including fossils) meteorology, physics, chemistry, engineering, agriculture, biology and other scientific and technological matters. It contains the first description of the magnetic compass. This magnificent treatise unfortunately has not been translated into any Western language. The Sung period also produced some of the greatest mathematicians, for instance, Chhin Chiu-Shao and Li Yeh. Algebra, derived from India, was brought to its highest development. There was an unfortunate decline in the status of women. Foot binding started during the Sung period to achieve petite feet. Millions of Chinese girls could have been spared this atrocity had some Sung technician invented the high heeled shoe instead that accomplishes virtually the same effect.

The Sung period was beset with grave socio-economic problems. Land concentration proceeded apace. Much of the land was tax free or the gentry otherwise avoided taxation. Government expenditures (military outlays for an ineffectual army, the civil administration and the court) increased by leaps and bounds—seven-fold between 1000–1021 A. D.! To cover the deficit the government issued deposit certificates and paper money for the first time. The printing of paper money was soon out of control. Speculation, particularly in grain, followed. The gentry and merchants grew rich in this situation. Inflation ensued.

To avert revolution, reform and welfare schemes were initiated. The architect of these reforms was Wang An-shih (1021–1086). His aim was better control of agricultural productivity by the government for a more equitable distribution of the surplus. He reinvigorated the "normal granery" idea to stabilize prices of food. Welfare programs such as medical care, food and better housing for the old and destitute were instituted. Public baths and even geisha houses to entertain soldiers away from home were erected. Low interest loans were made available to peasants. And so forth.

Most important, he proposed reform of the examination system—based on the classics—to make it more practical. Official salaries were increased so that gifted lads from poor families could enter the administration. Military expenditures were reduced. Wang had the support of the Emperor Shen Tsung, but his reform measures were rescinded after Shan Tsung's death in 1085. The reforms hurt the gentry and they proved too powerful a lobby.

But an even greater calamity awaited the Sung dynasty from outside. A new enemy rose behind the Khitan, the Ju-chen (a Tungusic tribe) who first conquered the Khitan empire (Peking fell in 1125) and then marched against the Sung capturing Khaifeng in 1126 A. D. Hui Tsung's son, the emperor at the time, and his artist father were taken prisoners ending the reign of the Northern Sung. Another son of Hui Tsung escaped, however, and pro-claimed himself emperor in Hangchou where the southern Sung dynasty persisted until 1279 A. D. This represented less of a change than appears at first blush for the Sung dynasty was based in the south. It did frustrate a Ju-chen (who called themselves Chin) takeover. The Ju-chen too settled for tribute that the southern gentry willingly paid for peace. Professor Eberhard observes, interestingly, that the two peoples referred to themselves filially but the Mongols and Tunguses were the father-in-law, whereas centuries earlier it was the Chinese who were the elder and the Hsuing-nu the younger brother. The changed attitude bespeaks the overwhelming impact of the Mongols and other northern tribes at this time. But in spite of the professions of brotherhood the Sungs soon conspired with the Mongols against the Ju-chen and that proved their undoing. The Mongols defeated the

Ju-chen in 1233 A. D. but continued their conquests against the Sung. In 1276 the Mongols captured Nanking. The emperor fled to Macao where he died in 1279.

MONGOL PERIOD (1280–1368 A. D.)

Until now foreign invasion and rule came mainly from the northwest by the Hsuing-nu and the Turks who ruled only the northern parts of China and were soon sinified. The Mongols and Tunguses in the northeast were extremely backward and barbarian during these centuries. In the 12th century the Mongols became energized and under a great leader Genghis Khan built an empire that stretched from the Pacific to Hungary in Europe. They conquered Central Asia, Persia and northern China after defeating the Ju-chen, and Western Asia in 1234 A. D. Genghis and his sons lost temporary interest in the rest of China for exploits in the west. Agriculture baffled the Mongols. Genghis would have liked to turn northern China into a pastureland for his horses, but was persuaded otherwise by his able Chinese (actually a Khitan) advisor and chronicler Yeh-lu Ch'u-ts'ai. It was only some fifty years later that his grandson Kublai Khan saw the potential of empire in the rest of China and the Mongols conquered the whole of the country in 1276 A. D.

Not only did the whole of China come under alien rule for the first time but the foreign rulers refused to be sinified. The Mongols ruled as a military caste over the Chinese society. They christened their rule the Yuan dynasty. Furthermore, unlike earlier alien rulers they refused to rule through Chinese officials. Instead they employed a host of foreigners—Turks, Uighurs, Muslims and even Europeans. Most renowned of them (to Europeans) was Marco Polo who served Kublai Khan from 1275–1292 including a term as provincial governor in Hangchou. He was intensely impressed by the old Sung capital as there was nothing comparable in Europe or the Near East at the time.

The Mongols tried desperately to keep the Chinese subdued. Mongolian was made the official language. The Chinese were forbidden to learn and use it. Hence, the foreign officials had to be bilingual. The clever Uighurs managed to cope with it to their great advantage. Marco Polo never learned Chinese though he spoke Mongolian. The so-called "nationality legislation" relegated the Chinese to the lowest strata of the social structure. They were forbidden to intermarry with the Mongols, bear arms and other civil rights. It afforded a perfect situation for the foreign official and merchant to exploit the Chinese people.

The Chinese peasant grew desperately poor under Mongol rule. His situation was already intolerable under the Sung—and he was ready for revolution for years—but now he was made to bear further taxation and deprivation. The foreign court lived lavishly. The Mongol garrisons in the provinces had to be supported. The Mongols espoused Buddhism (particularly Tibetan Lamaism) which encouraged a restoration of many monasteries removing more land from taxation. Finally the Chinese gentry, denied offices, became more rapacious. The peasant was dragooned into forced labor to repair the dykes (the Yellow river burst its banks in 1351), extend the canal system to Peking and other work projects of the Mongols. The Mongols took readily to the nefarious Sung tactic of printing paper money to finance the revenue shortfalls which begot further disastrous inflation. The peasant suffered the brunt of it. One sixth of the population (7,600,000 out of a population of 45,000,000 according to Professor Eberhard) was starving. But even this figure based on a 1329 census is probably conservative.

The peasants were ready to revolt under such maldistribution of wealth. The sporadic uprisings were first directed against the gentry. In 1353 a capable peasant leader Chu Yuan-chang arose to unite the uprisings into a national revolt. Chu was supported strongly by a branch of the White Lotus society known as the Red Turbans. The Chinese gentry persuaded Chu to redirect the rebellion against Mongol rule. The Mongols were in a state of disintegration by this time. Their garrisons had become ineffectual after decades of easy living and offered little resistance to the uprisings. Kublai Khan's seven successors (he died in 1294) were lesser men and usually inept. Before the revolution reached Peking they fled to the sanctuary of Mongolia. Chu Yuan-chang assumed rule in Peking in 1368 A. D. with gentry support and founded the Ming dynasty.

The Mongols made little cultural impact on China in their century or so of dominance. They did make notable changes. In wresting Yunan from Burma and Thailand they used Muslim administrators from central Asia who implanted Islam in that province of China. It has persisted to this date. Their near conquest of Indonesia opened up the archipelago for Chinese trade and influence. The establishment of the capital in Peking and with a construction there of a beautiful city made Peking the future capital of China, albeit that the Ming removed the capital to Nanking in the beginning of their rule.

Chinese art and technology was advanced despite the autocratic foreign rule. Shipbuilding and navigation (both inland and sea going) progressed under Mongol exploitation. Kublai Khan built fine fleets. Two invasions were launched against Japan, probably to stop Japanese piracy, both of which ended in disaster. An invasion of Java was undertaken in 1292. The use of gunpowder for warfare was developed further, particularly the metal-barreled cannon. The cannon was used in large numbers by Chu Yuan-chang and his revolutionary army in the capture of Peking.

The Mongols were fond of opera. Their patronage gave the development of Chinese theatre a great boost. Many famous dramas (the Story of the Lute, the Romance of the Western Chamber and others) were written under Mongol rule. Knotted carpets were developed—a technique learned from the Persians. In architecture ideas were taken from the Tibetans and

Indians. Peking still contains some of these Tibetan type multistoried pagodas. Painting continued in the new Chinese style developed under the Sung. Most of the Sung artists retreated into the countryside away from the Mongol centers where they maintained their painting and calligraphy. The bamboo was a favorite subject. Most famous of these painters was Chao Meng-fu (1254–1322) a descendent of the Sungs.

MING DYNASTY (1368–1644 A. D.)

The Ming period is doubtless one of the most illustrious in Chinese history. It is certainly the best known to Europeans as the two cultures, the newly emerging and the old, made close and frequent contact. The much advanced porcelain technology of the Chinese was introduced to Europe and thereafter to this day eating dishes are known as "china" or "chinoserie". It is sometimes said the Ming added little that was new. But they certainly advanced it. As C. P. Fitzgerald puts it "Chinese civilization had been cast in a pattern by the Tang which the Sung developed and the Ming restored." And augmented he could have added.

Chu Yuan-chang ruled thirty years from Nanking during which time he drove the Mongols from China, suppressed to some extent the Japanese pirates and consolidated his rule from the Great Wall to the China sea. Mongol estates (once used as pastureland) were redistributed and brought under cultivation. Soldiers were resettled as cultivators. Irrigation works were restored. The Grand Canal system was overhauled. Highways, bridges, city walls, temples, shrines were repaired and reconstructed. Chu's son Yung Lo, equally capable, ruled until 1425. During this span of 67 years Ming rule was firm and impressive.

Yung Lo removed the capital to Peking and renewed the city. The present palace and many other buildings still remain. A million men were employed. It is said Yung Lo gave them ten years to complete the job but they did it in five! It was a magnificent court. Nanking, however, remained the cultural center of the country.

Yung Lo built a great fleet. He placed it under the command of the eunuch Admiral Cheng Ho. In 1405 A. D. Cheng Ho left with 63 large junks for an expedition into the Indian Ocean. It is still not clear for what purpose this costly and grand effort was made. No colonies or territories were claimed, though obeisance was extracted. The kings of Ceylon and Sumatra were brought back to do homage in Peking. No raids were made, though much tribute (exacted voluntarily out of awe or under duress) was collected. Part of the fleet were the so-called treasure ships. Vast geographic, oceanographic, biologic and other information was collected. Ostriches, zebras, giraffes and other exotic animals were brought back to Peking for the first time. The giraffe baffled the Chinese the most. When a courtier tried to flatter the emperor that it was a mythical animal that appeared only when the country was ruled by a Sage Yung Lo dismissed the statement as nonsense. He concluded the giraffe was real.

After seven major expeditions that covered the entire Malaysian coast of Africa to Madagascar during the period 1405–35 the Fleet was abandoned. It was too large to station in the Yangtze estuary where it would interfere with more essential internal traffic. And, it may be supposed, proved just too costly to maintain. Then too, Yung Lo's successors may not have had the same love for the sea.

Why was it done. There may have been some thought in the beginning to circumvent the caravan trade that was dominated by the Turks under Timur. And it did certainly open up trade. After Timur's death in 1406 the caravans were free of interference. The Fleet was not really used against the Japanese pirates though it might have terrorized them. In the end the Fleet probably served no other purpose than to show the flag and assert the greatness of China. That, it doubtless did, for China was recognized as the foremost power of Asia (to the Chinese, of course, the world) at this time.

The Chinese became extremely nationalistic during Ming times. First, there was the recoil from Mongol barbarianism. This distrust of foreigners was, however, extended to the Muslims and Europeans as well who were pressing at the ports and gates for admittance. No longer were the free and open "foreign" enclaves of merchants, missionaries and the like of earlier centuries welcome. The Roman catholic missionaries could make no advances at all. Matteo Ricci, the Italian Jesuit father, was permitted to take up residence in Peking but largely because the Chinese found him a learned mathematician, astronomer and technologist (astronomical and military equipment). In general, though, the Chinese had only contempt for the Portuguese and when they suddenly became aware of their superior firearms in 1519 they resorted to a subterfuge to steal the advanced technology. The Portuguese were lodged at a hostel in Nanking and invited frequently to the palace for entertainment. While away Chinese technicians stole into their rooms and copied the trigger mechanism (they already had gunpowder which the Europeans got from them) for the production of a rifle by the Chinese.

Agricultural productivity reached new heights under the Ming. Since the land area could no longer be expanded intensive farming, for which the Chinese are renowned, was developed. Improved seeds (champa rice) were borrowed and developed. Fish and ducks were grown in the flooded rice fields. This had a two fold result. It produced more protein food in the same area and the fish and ducks fertilized the fields so that fallowing could be foresaken. Semi-annual cropping was undertaken. Fish also eliminated malaria by eating the mosquitoes making many areas cultivable that were not so before. The multiplier effect of these changes vastly increased the production of food. It had a profound impact on the development of Chinese cuisine already discussed in Chapter X.

Cotton was brought under widespread cultivation. The plant came from India much earlier but it did not thrive well in the northwest. Fukein and Kwang-tung in the south now became the main areas of cultivation. The technique of fluffing the fibre with the vibrating string of a bow enabled the use of cotton for the quilts and padded garments needed in the north. Block printing of cotton (and silk) added to the growth of a vast textile industry. Factories with many looms employing large numbers of people sprung up everywhere in the Yangtze area. Shanghai emerged as the center of the textile industry. It consisted of a network of businessmen who brokered cotton and silk and distributed the finished cloth.

It was indeed a period of great prosperity. The two major economic regions, the Yellow river and Yangtze basins were now equal in productivity and were connected by the Grand Canal system. The procelain industry too grew in the light of its export demand. New techniques, more in the coloring, were developed. But it was the well known blue and white that found its way around the world. The greatest collection, perhaps, is now at the museum in Istanbul as the Ottoman Turks were leading admirers of the Ming porcelains. Even as far away as America—as seen in the museum at Mount Vernon, George Washington's estate—Ming porcelains found their way.

Cities grew with the new industries, but the intensive agriculture could support the urban areas easily. A problem was germinating, however, that was to play such an important part in the history of China during the next three centuries and culminate in the Communist Revolution of 1948. It was the explosive population growth of the 18th to 20th centuries. At the end of the Ming period the population was still not vastly greater than in the last Han census of 114 A. D.—perhaps around 100 million or so. Under Manchu rule the population was destined to increase five-fold which the intensive agriculture, with its satellite textile and other light industries, developed during the Ming times was incapable of supporting.

Progress and change continued in the arts. Storytelling, borrowed from the Indians, became popular. The Chinese novel developed during Ming times. The *Tale of the Three Kingdoms* romanticizing the struggle of the gentry after the fall of the Han in the 3rd century became the classic. The rise of the erotic novel dates back to the Ming. *The Chen-p'ing-mei*, already discussed, was probably written the end of the 16th century. The philosophical giant of the age was Wang Yang-ming. The Chinese opera was further developed. A well tempered "scale" of music was evolved. Chinese painters continued in the Sung style still residing mostly in the south. Wood block printing made available prints of the masters to a wider public.

"An enormous amount of scholarly work was done" during Ming times states Joseph Needham. Comprehensive encyclopedias were compiled of existing knowledge. The *Ta Tien* composed in 1403 under Yung-lo comprised 11,095 chapters. Two thousand scholars worked on it for four years! It grew so large it was never reprinted for distribution. The last copy perished in the Boxer Rebellion of 1901. Lesser scientific treatises were compiled. One series describes exhaustively about 1000 plants and 1000 animals. Similar treatises on medicine, chemistry and technology were published. But it was no longer creative technology. Nothing points this up better than the incident related earlier on how the Chinese purloined the rifle mechanism from the Portuguese. The technological lead was now shifting to Europe. About this time Galileo had invented the telescope (1609), Harvey published his treatise on the circulation of the blood (1628), Newton worked out his calculus (1687) and the Portuguese were already sailing superior ocean going vessels. It was the beginning of Europe's great technological leap that would in a few centuries give the Europeans domination of the world including China.

After the exemplary rule of the first two Ming emperors court politics became a cesspool of iniquity. It was due largely to the old eunuch system. The Ming restored the examination system but it still required considerable wealth for a young man to afford to take them. It usually required many months residence in the capital or provincial center. The new gentry was, however, not as powerful as the old for land was growing scarce as population increased. Thus the gentry officials were losing out again to the eunuchs at court. In fact, it became the practice of the time for a son of the gentry to have himself castrated after passing the examinations (eunuchs were not allowed to take the examinations) as a means to greater power. As a learned eunuch, of course, he had a great advantage. Some of the Eunuchs indulged in unbelievable graft and corruption. One such eunuch, Liu Chin, in 1510 amassed a fortune of 250 million ounces of silver (worth several billion dollars today) together with huge quantities of gold, precious jewels and magnificent real estate. He was finally arrested and his loot confiscated by the emperor.

The eunuchs went further. They manipulated Ming political rule, making virtual puppets of weak emperors and intriguing to place others on the throne. The last effective Ming emperor was Wan-li who ruled from 1572 to 1620 A. D.

The country was now in a state of rebellion. Li Tzu-ch'eng, a bandit, conquered the province of Shensi and proclaimed himself king of his dynasty, the Shun. He captured Peking in 1644 and the last Ming emperor killed himself. Li proved incapable of consolidating his rule. Meanwhile the Manchus had freed themselves of Ming rule, conquered Korea and Manchuria. The Ming general, Wu San Kui, who commanded the Chinese army on the Manchu border invited the Manchus into China to oust Li in the fond hope he could become emperor. But they took over rule in Peking and Wu became their general. Some Ming factions fled south. The southern gentry refused to acknowledge the Manchus. But after a few decades, in 1682 A. D., the Manchus had firm control of China.

MANCHU DYNASTY (1644–1911 A. D.)

Foreign rule was imposed upon the Chinese once again. The south Chinese never reconciled to it. The Manchus in turn were sinified though they of course came under the influence of the north Chinese and spoke the dialect of the north which came to be called mandarin.

The Manchus placed the gentry in power through the old examination system. But with each Chinese official served a Manchu (who did not have to take the exams). In addition the whole country was garrisoned with Manchu troops organized into the Eight Banners. They were stationed in fortified cantonments in Peking and the provincial capitals. The Banners had to be supported by the provinces and came to be resented by the Chinese. After a period of peace the Banners, unused to war, grew effete and useless. But the gentry confirmed in their traditional power by the Manchus kept peace in the countryside. The Manchus finally rid China of the pernicious eunuch system. They doubtless felt their system of Manchus monitoring the gentry officials would keep the latter in check. But as the Manchus became sinified the gentry grew so powerful that the Manchus became totally dependent upon them.

The system worked well under great emperors and the dynasty was fortunate to have three such in K'ang-hsi, Yung-cheng and Ch'ien-lung whose long rules spanned the latter half of the 17th and the 18th centuries. These first Manchu emperors conducted an aggressive foreign policy. The whole of Mongolia and Sinkiang were brought under Chinese rule. Suzerainty was acquired over Tibet. Korea, Vietnam, Siam and Burma were made tributaries. Even Nepal was invaded and conquered. The Chinese empire never controlled more territory. An important consequence was the final termination of the nomadic threat from the north. The Manchu extension into Mongolia coincided with the Russian expansion into Siberia. Russia was the dominant power in Central Asia. The Nomads were now squeezed between two great powers. Even more important, though, was the fact that the horse, on which the nomad power was based, had become obsolete technology. Firearms, steam and metallurgy were the new sources of power and in this respect the nomads of the steppes were sorely deficient.

A cultural renaissance set in with the reinstatement of the gentry. New encyclopedias were compiled. But it was little more than the restatement of old knowledge. The Chinese genius for technological innovation was spent. In fact, the 19th century witnessed a great deal of translation of European works on science and technology, where the center of technological innovation had now shifted. In the arts too, there was much activity. Some of the most famous literary works belong to the early Manchu period. The finest novel, thought so by many, in Chinese literature—*The Dream of the Red Chamber*—was written by Ts'ao Hsueh-ch'in in the mid-18th century. It is a story of a son of impoverished gentry parentage who falls in love with a girl from a highly placed family. New dramas proliferated. One such drama consisted of 240 acts and took two years to perform! Western literature too was translated into Chinese.

The most significant development of the Manchu period, perhaps, was the population explosion after 1750 A. D. In two centuries the population rose from less than 200 million to over 600 million! The intensive agriculture developed during Ming times vastly increased the production of food. Manchu peace and internal order added the other ingredient for greatly increased population growth. By the 19th century the population pressure on the land was intolerable. The ruling elite was unwilling or incapable of any solution of the socio-economic problems that the population explosion begot.

Industrialization would have been the solution. The Europeans were already on this road to greater economic productivity. The gentry, who were now firmly in power, were always opposed to non-agricultural development. Agriculture was their preserve and they were able to fortify themselves against the population pressure on the land through increased rents and other perquisites. The Manchu dynasty that should and could have given China the leadership in this direction had by the 19th century become the captive of the gentry. Moreover, the Manchus had become paranoid about foreign ideas fearing that such foreign influence might beget a rebellion against their rule. The situation could thus get only worse and it did.

European colonialism also aggravated the socio-economic situation within China. When Pope Alexander VI divided the world between Spain and Portugal in 1494, China fell to Portugal. But China proved even less receptive than India and instead of a foothold Portugal could secure only a toehold at Macao for trade with the Chinese. Portuguese missionaries too were not given freedom to proselytize. In the 19th century Protestant missionaries gained entrance and thought they were making progress. The Communist Revolution of 1948 destroyed that delusion.

The Manchus restricted foreign trade to the port of Canton. The Europeans wanted tea and porcelain from China at this time for which the Chinese demanded specie, but these were the centuries of Potosi and the Europeans had plenty of silver in their pockets. By the 19th century that was no longer the case—the mines of Potosi and Mexico had been drained of their rich silver veins. But the Europeans found something else to trade. It was opium to which many Chinese were addicted and to which millions more would soon be with the influx of the drug from Mexico and India where it was grown for the China trade. When the Manchus tried to stop the trade the so-called Opium Wars of 1840–42 and 1858–60 broke out in which the decadent Manchus were defeated and humiliated. England was mainly involved. The English were extremely frustrated by the Chinese. Here they were masters of India, in fact masters of most of the world, and they could get no cooperation from the Manchus. The English (and their colonials in America,

India and West Indies and elsewhere) had become a nation of tea drinkers so the demand for tea and the tea cups for drinking it provided a profitable market. But the stubborn Chinese wanted only silver and opium in exchange and scoffed at English textiles and other manufactures. No one, it seems, European (including the American) or Chinese gave any consideration to the moral implications of the opium trade. Even the Manchus when they tried to stop it did so primarily because they feared it was making the Chinese merchants of Canton too rich (enabling them to revolt against them) and not that millions of Chinese were becoming drug addicts.

The Opium Wars gave the Europeans *carte blanche* in China. Many new ports were opened for trade. Foreign embassies were established. Shanghai became the main entrepot for European trade. The Yangtze was opened for European ships making possible the so-called gun-boat diplomacy of the Western powers in China.

This opening up of China to Western trade had a devastating effect upon the already volatile socio-economic situation in the countryside. English and American manufactures poured into the Chinese markets destroying the handicraft industries that often provided the margin against starvation for the Chinese peasant. Steam navigation and rail transport introduced by the Europeans deprived the Chinese boatsman on the rivers and canals of much gainful employment. The import of cheap rice from Siam, Java, Cambodia and elsewhere kept grain prices low so that the landlords were forced to increase rents impoverishing both the landlord and peasant causing the struggle over the diminishing surplus in the countryside to become more acute. The flow of silver reversed as the European demand for tea and porcelain decreased and eventually dried up. The English began to grow tea in India and Ceylon. Porcelain technology was reinvented or discovered by the Europeans in Germany and England during 18th–19th centuries. There was now little the Europeans needed or wanted from China so the Chinese had to pay with silver. The price of silver rose against copper which further worsened the situation of the peasant as he was forced to pay his taxes in silver and could sell his product only for copper.

Peasant revolts erupted all over China during the 19th century. The Red Turban in Canton in 1854. The Red Band in Szechuan in 1860. The Nien Fei in Honan and Anhwei in 1855. In the northwest Muslim rebellions transpired between 1853–73. Most notable was the Taiping Rebellion that trembled the Yangtze basin resulting in the capture of Nanking in 1853. Thirty million Chinese are thought to have lost their lives in these uprisings.

The Taiping Rebellion was led by a frustrated student, a peasant's son, who failed in the examinations. His name was Hung Hsiu-ch'uan. Hung started his movement in Kwangsi and his army grew by the thousands as he moved eastward. He formed his own dynasty. He called it *Tai-ping Tien-kuo*, which means the celestial kingdom of great peace. As the Taiping army moved through the Yangtze valley unpopular landlords and revenue collectors were executed, land registers and loan accounts were burned and land was redistributed on a communal basis to the peasants.

While Hung ruled in Nanking for eleven years he never succeeded in capturing Peking. The gentry rallied to rescue the Manchu dynasty for they realized their estates were at stake. Tseng Kuo-fan, a powerful landlord, assembled a peasant army for the gentry and defeated the Taiping army in 1864. The Europeans gave him some timely aid such as transporting Tseng's troops in their steamships and even a unit of foreign and Chinese troops under the command of C. G. Gordon.

The Chinese people were now keenly aware of the debilitating impact of Western domination upon their lives. Europeans and Americans were derogatorily referred to as "foreign devils". Equally reviled were the Chinese who cooperated with the "foreign devils" as agents, brokers or managers waxing rich thereby. They were called "running dogs". The Manchus too were blamed for permitting the Europeans and Americans to impose their greed for quick profit upon the Chinese people. In 1900 these pent up hates and grievances erupted into the Boxer Rebellion. The name Boxer given the rebellion derived from the fact that the revolutionaries engaged in boxing matches for sport. The rebellion was initially aimed at the Manchus and gentry, but the Manchus and landlords cleverly redirected it against the "foreign devils" resulting in the sacking of the foreign legations in Peking and other European-American establishments. An international force of Americans and Europeans was organized to quell the rebellion. The Western powers blamed the Manchus and exacted heavy indemnities for their losses of life and property. This constituted a further indignity and humiliation for the Chinese people.

THE REPUBLIC AND REVOLUTION OF 1948

The Manchu dynasty was thoroughly decadent and incompetent as the world entered the 20th century. Many Chinese were now keenly aware of the technological backwardness of China. In 1895 Japan defeated China in Korea largely because it had modern armaments. But enlightened Chinese could not prevail upon the Dowager Empress to initiate the industrialization of the economy as Japan was doing. Japan had now joined the Western powers in the exploitation of China.

Western educated Chinese felt strongly that the Manchus had to be replaced by a republic as a first step toward the economic reforms necessary to alleviate the country's socio-economic problems. They rallied around Sun Yat-sen, a peasant's son, educated in English schools in Hongkong, who spent many years in America. His compatriots were mostly Western educated sons of the gentry. They had peasant support though this was not a traditional peasant revolt. The revolt succeeded easily, but more by default than by assault, and a Republic was established in 1912. After the Dowager

Empress died in 1908 she was succeeded by a two year old heir Pu Ti. The regent foolhardily dismissed Yuan Shih-k'ai the only competent general in the Manchu army. Yuan Shih-k'ai joined the revolt ending the Manchu dynasty. Yuan Shih-k'ai was elected President of the new Republic.

The Republic was incapable of ruling. It was an edifice without a foundation. The gentry did not support it. The peasants were unaware of it. Yuan tried to subvert it by setting up a dynasty but he died before he could effect his purpose. The country lapsed into political disarray and a long period of warlordism gripped the countryside. Sun Yat-sen disassociated himself from the Peking government and established another Republic in Canton under his Presidency.

Sun Yat-sen decided to march on Peking in 1924. The Koumintang (the name of his revolutionary party) now possessed a formidable army, organized and trained by Russian advisors, under the leadership of Chiang Kai-shek. Sun died, unfortunately, in 1925 and leadership devolved on Chiang Kai-shek. The Koumintang had two factions, the communists on the extreme left and a right wing consisting of the western educated and enriched Chinese of Shanghai and other port cities. Both Sun and Chiang married into one of these *nouveau riche* families, the Soongs, a leading banking group in Shanghai.

The march north was eminently successful. Even peasants joined the movement as the communists promised them land. Shanghai fell to Chaing without a struggle in 1927 and he established a new republic known as the Nationalist government with its capital at Nanking.

A split developed thereafter between the communists and the right wing, when Chiang ignored Sun Yat-sen's promise of land reform in order to win the support of the gentry. The communists, at first, made a futile attempt to wrest power through an uprising of the factory workers in Shanghai in 1927. Chiang had no difficulty quelling the revolt. Mao Tse-tung, who believed the revolution had to be predicated on the peasants, gained control of the Communist party after the Shanghai fiasco. He removed his forces into the south and eventually, after the famous Long March, into the more secure northwest where the Communists continued to build their army and peasant soviets in the areas they brought under their rule. Chinese students flocked to Yennan in great numbers as they grew disaffected with the Nationalist government. A civil war ensued as Chiang continued to harass the Communists who he now feared with near passion.

At this point Japanese imperialism intervened in Chinese affairs. Earlier Japan had wrested Manchuria from China. In 1937 it invaded China. In anticipation of the Japanese invasion a truce had been negotiated in the civil war and the formation of a United Front in 1936 to meet more effectively the Japanese thrust. The Communist army was designated the Eight Route Army in the United Front. As Chiang Kai-shek retreated before the Japanese army with his ineffective army deep into the interior to Chungking the Eight Route Army offered the only resistance to the Japanese in the North China Plain from its base at Yennan in the northwest. It liberated large areas not only from Japanese control but from the gentry most of whom had fled with Chiang to Chungking. They instigated land reform and redistribution of the land ingratiating themselves with the 100 million peasants living on the great plain.

When the war ended the Communists held the countryside and could have taken over the cities when the Japanese left, but Chiang with American help, struck an agreement with the Japanese General Nakamura not to relinquish the cities until Chiang could transport his army (with American aid) from Chungking to take them over.

The Nationalists had the cities, the Communists controlled the country-side. The civil war was resumed, but the outcome was inevitable. The Communists had the real power base—the peasants. Chiang Kai-shek had the support of the gentry and the westernized business interests. Moreover he was cursed (though he thought he was blessed) with American support, that supplied him with the best equipped army that had ever appeared on the continent of Asia. Nationalism was an important factor in the communist appeal to the Chinese intellectuals and peasants. To the great surprise of many (especially the Americans) this great military force was easily defeated by the Eight Route Army. The answer was in the contrasting morale and purpose of the opposing armies. This pattern was destined to be repeated again and again so tragically in Korea and Vietnam and would become the stamp of the basic revolution that would shape the future of Asian countries in the 20th century. The anatomy of the Communist Revolution of 1948 in China has been discussed in great detail in Chapter VIII.

The Communists imposed firm rule over China. The gentry, the ruling elite for over two thousand years, was completely eliminated. Agriculture was reorganized into communes in which the peasant received a larger distribution of the surplus. Only about thirty per cent was taken in revenues. There was no rent as the landlord was abolished. But more important, the Communists launched a vigorous program of industrialization to increase the productivity of the economy. Thus building upon the age old technological competence of the Chinese people together with their capacity for hard work and frugal living Communist China has already become a power factor in the present world and is probably destined for great power status in the not too distant future.

OTHER ASIAN SOCIETIES

The other Asian societies were apparented either by the Chinese or Indian civilizations. Korea, Japan, North Vietnam and Taiwan derived their technological and cultural development mainly from China. Burma, Thai-land, Cambodia, South Vietnam, Malaya, Sumatra, Java and Bali developed

614 MAN IN UNIVERSE

under Indian (Hindu and Buddhist) influence. The Philippines and Celebes, due to their later appearance on the historical scene, developed under Christian and Muslim dominance. Islam made an impact in several areas but it never displaced the underlying Indian cultural foundation.

Among them Japan attained greatest importance. Its prehistory is murky. The islands were apparently settled by immigrants from the mainland, the southern ones from the Chinese mainland and Korea and the northern islands by the "hairy" Ainu, presumably from Siberia. There is some record of the "King of the Wa" presenting himself at the Han court which, in Chinese eyes, made Japan a vassal state. Chinese impact followed thereafter in several waves over the succeeding centuries. Around 300 A. D. or so a unified kingdom was established in the Yamato area. The east and north was under Ainu control. The first wave of Chinese influence came around 400 A. D. The Japanese had no script. Chinese books were brought to Yamato by the Koreans from which they adopted the Chinese system of ideographs to the Japanese language. It never really fit. Eventually they modified it to convey the Japanese language. For many years Chinese was the language of scholarship.

A second wave of Chinese influence came in the 6th century with the introduction of Buddhism. Again it came via Korea. Prince Shotoku of the Soga clan, the Regent in the Imperial House, gave Buddhism its greatest boost with the Japanese. He founded the famous Buddhist monastery at Nara early in the 7th century.

During the Tang period (618–905 A. D.) cultural ties and trade increased. The Japanese sought to introduce the Chinese system of government with a strong emperor served by a gentry-official class. It failed to take root, largely, due to the strong clan system whereby powerful families ruled absolutely over their large landed estates. A new capital was built at Nara, modeled after Ch'angan. Eighty years later the capital was moved to Kyoto, to avoid the strong Buddhist influence of Nara, where it remained until 1869.

The emperor reigned but seldom ruled. Power was usually in the hands of a powerful family (normally related to or apparented by the Imperial line) the leading member of which acted as Regent (later called Shogun) to the emperor. These Regents or Shoguns were, in effect dynasties holding power for centuries. The Fujiwara (645–1100 A. D.), Kamakura (1185–1333 A. D.) Ashikaga (1336–1568 A. D.) and the Tokugawa (1603–1868 A. D.). The Shoguns ruled from their own capitals in Kamakura and Yedo to the east of Kyoto. There were occasional restorations of Imperial power but in general Japan was ruled by the Shoguns. It should not be thought that the Imperial House was without influence. The emperor was viewed as the symbol of unity and continuity. The Imperial family possessed vast wealth which gaven them power. Finally, the great clans or families that ruled were related to and intermarried with the Imperial line. But it was the leading families that comprised the ruling elite and made Japan a feudal society. Loyalties flowed to the families, not the emperor. A feature of the system was the Samurai, a military elite corps that was attached to the clans not the emperor. A struggle eventuated between the Samurai and the nobility for control of the manors.

Japan remained, with a notable exception, free of foreign invasion. The Chinese did not deem it fit to develop a navy for imperialistic purposes. Moreover, they found Korea the outermost limit of their power. But the Mongols under Kublai Khan made two attempts to invade Japan both with disastrous results. When Japan refused to recognize Mongol suzerainty Kublai Khan had a fleet built in Korea and embarked with 15,000 Mongol troops and 8000 Koreans in 1274 for the island of Kyushu. The invaders met strong resistance. When stormy weather threatened the Korean sea captains advised withdrawal lest the vessels be destroyed on the rocky coast. Kublai was no seafarer and remained undaunted by the portent of the failure of his first attempt. He tried again in 1281 with a larger fleet and invasion force. Unfortunately the Mongols scheduled the landing in June too close to the typhoon season of August. The Japanese meanwhile were better prepared and after seven weeks of fighting remained unsubdued. On August 15–16th a violent typhoon hit Japan destroying the Mongol fleet. The Japanese annihilated the remainder of the Mongol and Chinese armies left ashore. The Japanese named the timely typhoon "kamakaze" (the divine wind) and credited the Goddess Ise with their deliverance from the Mongol threat. Needless to say that terminated any further dreams of Mongol maritime imperialism.

The Japanese were generally unfriendly to foreigners. The Portuguese gained admittance early in the 16th century when the country was disunited during the last years of the weak Ashikaga shogunate. Some of the western feudal lords (daimyos) admitted them in their areas. Firearms, which interested the Japanese, were introduced by the Portuguese. In 1549 Francis Xavier landed in Japan and began a vigorous proselityzing program. There were some 150,000 Catholic converts by 1580. But the conversions were short lived. Japan was in political disarray at this time. The demise of the Ashikaga shogunate was followed by a war lord period. Most notable of these leaders was Toyatomi Hideyoshi who rose to power in 1587. Hideyoshi is noteworthy for his abortive invasion of Korea (he failed to understand the need of naval support for his army) and the banning of Christianity. When Tokugawa Ieyasu took power after Hideyoshi's death and established the strong Tokugawa shogunate with its new capital at Yedo (Tokyo) the Tokugawas shut Japan off to foreigners with the Exclusion Orders of 1637–38. Japanese were forbidden to go abroad under penalty of death. Only a few Dutch traders were allowed occasional entry. The Japanese were unaware that the Industrial Revolution was transpiring in Europe at this time.

Japan could not retain its isolation. The Western powers would not permit it in their dominance of the world during the 19th century. In 1853 the

American Commodore Matthew Perry forced Japan to open its ports to the Western powers similar to the concessions wrested from China a few years earlier. Internally it had a shattering effect on the already decadent Tokugawa shogunate. Feudalism had become obsolete. The result was the Meiji Restoration of 1868. The ruling elite now comprised the former nobles, particularly of the western Choshu and Satsuma clans together with some influential samurai. Power was exercised in the name of the emperor. In the breakdown of feudalism the redeployment of some 400,000 samurai posed the greatest problem. Eventually they were employed in government and the newly developing industries. The Japanese finally decided to industrialize their agricultural economy and sent their youth to America and Europe to train as scientists, engineers and economists. While abroad they embibed the democratic ideas of the West and began agitating for a parliamentary government. It resulted in the Meiji Constitution of 1881 giving the Japanese a legislative government based on the German model. The ruling elite was growing militaristic, with the Chushu and Satsuma maintaining a hold, respectively, on the war and navy ministries that dominated the cabinet. Militarism gave industrial development a great boost. The Japanese invaded the mainland in 1895, gained the cession of Formosa, ousted the Chinese from Korea (which they took over in 1910) and challenged Russia. In 1905 the Japanese administered a stunning defeat to the Russian fleet that lifted the spirits of all other Asians chafing under colonial rule. They were careful, however, not to aggravate the Western powers in China. After World War I they felt this was no longer necessary and the Japanese launched on their Asian Co-Prosperity Sphere, the building of an empire in the Pacific that would provide access to essential industrial raw materials unavailable in the islands. In 1931 they took Manchuria and in 1937 invaded China. Then they overreached and attacked the United States which ended their quest for empire. This disaster has been discussed in detail in Chapter VI. But after the humiliation and shock of the defeat Japan achieved spectacular industrialization during the post war period attaining near great power in the world.

None of the nations of Southeast Asia ever attained power status nor are they likely to. Most of them are too small. For centuries they have been under European colonialism. And others like the Vietnamese were under Chinese suzerainty for centuries before that. They have, however, developed some interesting variations on the Hindu and Buddhist cultures. There are for example, the imposing Buddhist temples at Angkor Wat in Cambodia and Borobudur in Java. The Wyang puppet dance of Java depicting the Hindu epic of the *Ramayana* is another interesting cultural refinement. Bali remains to this day an almost pure Hindu society.

XIV
THE CROSS OF MAN

Man finds himself crucified upon a cross the upright member of which represents his rationality and the limb his genetical instincts and motivations for survival and replication. The foregoing review and analysis of history can leave no doubt that man has not yet gained control over the basic instincts programmed in his genes by evolution during his reptilian and mammalian past. Rational men do not make war, murder and rape others, enslave and deprive them of their liberty, humiliate and strip them of their dignity. Moreover, man has perverted these genetical instincts and carried them to extremes, by virtue of his technological development, not intended by nature.

These irrational motivations can best be summed up as the instinct to dominate programmed by evolution in all forms of life. The first law of life is survival. It is either prevail or perish. But dominance is also programmed intra-specie so that the genes most advantageous for the survival of the species would be reproduced in succeeding generations. Nature intended that the dominant males mate with the most and dominant females of the specie. This intra-specie dominance became the foundation of the heirarchial societies of man, the primates and other mammals. It is this intra-specie dominance that now threatens man's existence.

Nature's design worked well until man upset it. To be sure many forms of life expired because they failed to adapt to the changing environment on earth, but they always gave way to a more complex organism better able to cope with new situations. Greater cellular complexity required more highly developed nervous and sensory systems culminating in the development of the brain. The brain emerged with the fish. The reptiles still had only a tiny brain. It developed fast with the mammals when they took over from the reptiles. But it was man in whom the brain reached its highest degree of development during the past million years or so.

Man's superior brain became the means of his domination of the earth. But it could now become the source of his demise. Man's intellect enabled him to use energy outside himself through technology. All other forms of life can exercise only the energy with which they are endowed biologically. Through his technology man has built civilizations that gave him material abundance and greater enjoyment of life. At the same time, though, man's technological advancement has created unbelievable misery and unhappiness for the human race. And the reason is that man has not been able to free himself of the instinct to dominate.

Man is a "tyrant" laments Russian philosopher Nicolas Berdeyav (1874–1948). He is a tyrant, says Berdeyav, on a great scale (war, political rule, bureaucratic establishment) and on a small scale (employer, head of family and in his friendships). "There exists an age long tendency to despotism, a thirst for power and mastership. The primary evil is the power of man over man, the lowering of the dignity of man, violence and domination" he writes in his *Slavery and Freedom*. Psychological violence, he adds, has now been added to physical aggression by man's intellectuality as the ultimate tyranny.

It appears, however, that man's tyranny is a perversion of the dominance instinct. Nature structured it as a survival feature in the evolution of life. The dominance of superior individuals was calculated to perpetuate the genes most advantageous for the survival of the species. Nature did not design this instinct for intra-specie killing, rape, mayhem and other physical injury. Reindeer bucks engaged in combat over a doe in estrus will lock horns fiercely, but never thrust them into their opponent's soft underbelly, until the weaker retires in defeat. It was such defeat nature had in mind not murder. A similar check mechanism is either weakly structured in the genes of man or does not exist. The reason may be that primates do not possess lethal appendages so nature did not consider it urgent to structure a strong check mechanism on their dominance instinct. But here too man has upset nature's scheme by acquiring lethal powers through his technological innovation and development. Man is now loose on earth with tremendous power to kill his fellow man and a weak or no genetical check on his dominance instinct.

Man's greed is still another enormity of the dominance instinct. It seems that mankind has contended over the distribution of wealth as soon as its technological development produced a surplus of food and other goods beyond its daily need. This is a central feature of history. Dominant individuals and societies would appropriate inordinate amounts of wealth with total disregard and indifference to the suffering it caused the dispossessed. No other form of life carries this feature of the dominance instinct to such extreme. The leading baboon or macaque will appropriate the first and best orange or banana but he does not hoard them to the exclusion of his fellow monkeys in the group.

Man has made some effort to ameliorate his dominance instinct. During his long life as a hunter he saw fit to cooperate with his fellow humans for their common survival. He developed the family and home based upon pair bonding of male and female and protection of the offspring of the union. He organized the hunting group under the leadership of the most precocious male. This required considerable compromise of the dominance instinct. It was at best a limited compromise though as the family, clan, tribe and later nations and civilizations were built on the heirarchial basis. Nonetheless this cooperative and social aspect of the story of man gives hope for the future.

It demonstrates that man can through his rationality control his dominance instinct if convinced it is for his well being. Unfortunately as man's survival against the dangers of his environment was assured through his technological progress the need for cooperation diminished. But he now had to fear his fellow man so a certain compulsion (law and order) was introduced into human relations to avoid internecine mayhem and provide security for the appropriation of wealth by the dominant individuals. It has at best been a truce of necessity rather than spontaneous cooperation and affinity among men.

This conflict in motivation is now the source of man's dilemma. His powerful intellect tells him he can no longer indulge in aggression and malappropriation of wealth against his fellow man. But his genetic programming propels him toward the manifestation of his instinct to dominate in his human relations particularly in the distribution of wealth produced by his technology. These two motivations clash and in the end the irrational instinct to dominate usually prevails.

Man's efforts to rationalize his plight seems to indicate he is subconsciously uncomfortable about it. It is said that kings rule by divine right or the mandate of heaven. Priests are ordained by God. There are "chosen people of God" which gives them the right to kill or enslave unbelievers, infidels, goys and other foreigners. Colonialism (which usually included racism) was laudingly referred to as the "white man's burden". Today one may kill "communists" or "capitalists", without guilt, depending on which side of the ideological struggle he finds himself. Men may dominate women because they are the weaker sex, the distaff side or similar psychological balm. The propensity to rationalize the dominance of other humans is virtually without limit. Yet it only masks the real reason which is that man is programmed genetically by nature to dominate. As the Athenians said to the Melians "Men . . . by a necessary law of nature rule wherever they can. And it is not as if we were the first to make this law, or act upon it when made; we found it existing before us, and shall leave it to exist for ever after us . . . ".

As man's technological innovation and development progresses this dilemma reaches crisis proportions. The spectre of a man made nuclear holocaust now hovers over mankind. A certain balance of terror at the moment keeps the holocaust in abeyance. But it is only a matter of time, as history presages, that one of the two antagonists will decline in technological innovation and industrial productivity from forces operating within giving the other the opportunity to dominate the world with its superior nuclear power. Perhaps, both may decline in favor of a third power that will achieve the technological superiority to dominate the world. There is even a lesser possibility that the ever developing technology of man may destroy the conditions favorable to the continuance of life on earth by such debilitations as the destruction of the vital ozone layer in the upper atmosphere or chemical pollution of the potable water. But this, at least, should be avoidable by the rational behavior of man.

A nuclear war would not necessarily eliminate man or destroy life on earth. It would, however, maim the human race or certain sectors of it. It could destroy the industrial centers of the earth and, perhaps, set back technological progress by centuries. The average American, European or Russian is little aware of the delicate interdependence of a highly industrialized society. Only a fraction of the population—scientists and engineers—is capable of structuring and maintaining it. The 1977 New York City blackout because of some technological deficiency (or incompetence) was a grim reminder of the dimensions for even greater disastrous breakdowns. In an all out nuclear war between America and Russia the generation of electricity upon which almost everything else depends would be the first casualty of the holocaust. The water and sewage systems would be next. The intricate food distribution system would come to a halt. Far more people would starve to death than would fall in the explosion of the nuclear war heads. Most Americans, for example, have not the slightest idea where their food comes from (outside the supermarket) and would be totally incapable of producing it themselves. The engineers and technicians who survived would probably be incapable or would have no incentive (after all they were never rewarded one tenth the amount paid a crooner or TV anchorman) to start the complex industrial plant operating again. There is every prospect that the highly industrial societies of America, Europe and Russia would become irreparably paralyzed leaving those who managed to survive the initial holocaust and fallout to starve to death.

But there would be other areas of the world that might escape the conflagration wholly or sufficiently to continue a highly technological existence. China would be badly hurt but not devastated by the nuclear fallout. At least, its industrial plant should not be destroyed. Farther to the south countries of Latin America, Africa and India might escape a crippling fallout. India, Brazil and South Africa, for instance, are highly industrialized—India even possesses nuclear capability—and could carry on a highly technological existence. In such eventuality, the power centers of the world would shift from America, Europe and Russia to South America, South Africa, India and China. There is no reason why these sectors of mankind could not continue technological innovation and development until they too—not having learned from history as has been the case of mankind to date—engage each other in nuclear war. The old centers of civilization would probably remain uninhabitable for years. The surviving scientists, engineers and other technicians would doubtless emigrate to these new centers of civilization. In due time (could be decades even centuries) the radioactivity should dissipate in the Northern areas and agriculture could resume. But lacking industrial resources and capital investment they would probably be the backward areas of a technological society centered elsewhere.

It is hazardous to contemplate the future course of history. A nuclear holocaust is certainly possible but the outcome of two powers competing for dominance has usually been resolved otherwise than by mutual confrontation and annihilation. America might decline in power because of overconsumption of its wealth. Russia could succumb to revolt against its autocratic rule. Athens can be cited as precedent for the former; Sparta for the latter. But the threat of nuclear destruction of a large sector of mankind will now continue to hover over man.

Is there no solution for man? It can come only through rational behavior in human relations. The genetical instinct of dominance with all the subsidiary enormities engrafted upon it by man's technological prowess such as war, homicide, greed, envy, status, egotism and the like must be purged from human relationship. This ideal is much easier to postulate than to inculcate. Moreover, it is not a new idea or thought. Gautama Buddha enunciated such a philosophy 2500 years ago! He concluded that the misery and unhappiness of mankind was due to the aggressiveness and greed of man. He preached non-violence and abstension. In essence his philosophy was based upon man's emancipation from the manifestations of the dominance instinct. Jesus Christ too, two millennia ago, preached similarly. He advocated human relations based upon brotherly love (love thy neighbor) and more egalitarian sharing of worldly goods, for "it is easier for a camel to go through the eye of a needle, than for a rich man to enter the Kingdom of God." But despite these enlightened precepts it does not appear that man has moved any nearer to his emancipation from violence and greed than he has since the dawn of history.

It is often felt or said that man is progressing toward rational human relationship. Modern man expresses horror when he reads on the pages of history that Byzantine emperors had their eyes gouged out and their heads lopped off in the struggle for imperial power, that Christians were forced to fight wild animals in the Roman arenas, that Scipio Africanus killed 50,000 Carthaginians when he destroyed Carthage, that Timur slaughtered 100,000 Hindus in his sack of Delhi and so on. But do these acts of violence differ from Hitler's slaughtering of millions of Jews in gas chambers and incinerators or the French and Americans burning to death countless women and children in Vietnamese villages with napalm bombs on the dubious provocation that they were "communists". Nothing seems to have changed. Only the technology for slaughter has advanced. It is somewhat encouraging that there was a public outcry in both France and America against these inhumanities, but the average citizen in both countries harbors nary a twinge of conscience about these atrocities perpetuated by his fellow-nationals or the national policy of his country that sanctioned them. And the so-called "good-Germans" of World War II blinked the abominable cruelty against the Jews and today the horrible incident is dim in memory.

There are individuals, and have been throughout recorded history, who can be said to be truly civilized, who have and are capable of submerging and controlling the instinct to dominate but they comprise only a fraction of the human race. The vast majority of men still give full vent to the dominance instinct. Moreover, since these individuals usually take the initiative (by the very nature of the dominance instinct) they dictate national policy and individual actions. The American philosopher John Dewey (1859–1952) summed it up best when he wrote "While saints are engaged in introspection burly sinners run the world."

Emancipation from the dominance instinct cannot await the slow pace of biologic evolution. Whereas biologic evolution did not produce technological development (control of energy outside the specie) it cannot likewise be expected to produce the check mechanism on man's dominance instinct to prevent him from resorting to his technology to dominate others. Man's rationality has been in the making for millions of years and has not yet gained complete ascendency over his basic genetical programming. In due time (reckoned in thousands, perhaps, millions of years) biologic evolution might develop a cerebral cortex powerful enough to overcome the genetical programming still present in man from his earlier evolution through the reptilian and mammilian ages. Anthropologists seem to feel that there has been no appreciable growth in man's intellectual capacity the past 100,000 years or so. A hundred thousand years, however, may be too short a period to permit a measurable biologic change in so complex an organism as man. Then too, the intelligence of individuals varies greatly. Modern man's brain ranges in size from 1100 to 2200 cubic centimeters. The average size is about 1375 cubic centimeters. A bigger brain normally (but not always) confers greater intelligence so that the evolution of bigger brains in humans should increase the rational behavior of mankind. Man himself may, however, have thwarted his own biologic evolution by interfering with the law of survival of the fittest. No longer do the weak—the ones with the lower intelligence—perish. Instead they are enabled to survive and reproduce in the secure socio-economic milieu resulting from man's technological development. If mankind practiced eugenics in its replication, as man has done so successfully in his animal husbandry, its cerebral capacity could easily be elevated to an average brain of 2000 cubic centimeters. Increasing man's intellectual capacity greatly would, however, pose another biological problem. The head of the new born child would have to increase to accommodate the larger brain and that would make human birth, already difficult for women, even more painful. All this makes for interesting speculation but it is unlikely mankind will practice eugenics in the perpetuation of the specie or that normal biologic evolution, assuming man has not arrested its operation, will increase man's cerebral capacity greatly and quickly over its present level.

Man may, however, improve the effectiveness of his brain through his technology. Computers have now been developed that can perform mathematical computations and process information billions of times faster than the human brain. This vastly increases the effectiveness of man's intellectual capability. It is sometimes said (and feared) that computers will be built that would out think man and come to dominate him. But the computer can only do the things that it is programmed to do albeit it can do those things faster than the human brain. At the moment there is little prospect that computers can be made to think like man. The chief reason is that the human brain (nature's computer) is ten thousand times more densely packed with information than a computer. The human brain contains about ten billion bits (binary digits) per cubic centimeter to a million per cubic centimeters of a computer. Moreover, the sensory faculties of man (nature's programmer) have an enormous capacity for feeding the brain with new information. For instance, as the human eye scans the horizon it sends about 5000 bits of information per second to the brain. The Viking cameras could transmit only 500 bits of information per second. And the eye comprises only one of the several sensory faculties of man feeding information to the brain simultaneously. The brain is still a far more remarkable intellectual mechanism than a computer, ingenious as are these most advanced machines of man. Whether man will or can improve further these "thinking" machines to where they will equate man's intellectual capacity is doubtful. Judgement, analysis, imagination, intuition, compassion and other features of the human intellect appear impossible to program fully into a computer. Computers, it would seem, are destined to remain the slaves of men.

More disturbing, however, is that man will use computers as he has his other technology to dominate his fellow man. And because of the possibilities of error in programming coupled with the mechanical (absence of judgement) operation of the computer the accidental injury and destruction of mankind has been increased. The chance of such judgement-less precipitation of nuclear warfare (now largely computerized) cannot be discounted. On a lesser scale the computerization of private information on individuals degrades their dignity and reduces human freedom creating a further source of unwanted oppression.

But man may already have adequate intelligence to emancipate himself from the devastating effect of his dominance instinct. And the key to his salvation may be the accumulating knowledge of himself, the universe and his rightful place in it that is being developed by his present intellect. In the words of the visionary Jacob Bronowski "knowledge is our destiny."

A small segment of mankind presently possesses a knowledge of man's rightful role in life and in the universe. This minority of the human race fully appreciates that man can no longer give free reign to his dominance instinct in the face of his ever increasing command of the fundamental energy of the universe without precipitating grave injury and damage on humanity. But alas, it is sadly not the ruling elite. The great problem of the day is how to inculcate the vast majority of mankind with this knowledge and understanding so that human relations may be placed on a rational basis.

The first obstacle to this goal is the psuedo-knowledge that conditions the minds of men. It prevents mankind from understanding and knowing itself and its rightful place in the universal scheme of things. And in many instances it merely serves to rationalize the manifestation of the dominance instinct.

Religion has played a vital role in the history of man. It provided him with a rationalization of his being at a time when his intellectual growth outpaced the accumulation of knowledge for a true comprehension of himself. Equally important religion established a moral code designed to control the grossest expression of the dominance instinct. The former has now been superseded by the accumulated knowledge developed by science and technology of the past hundred years or so. The latter, while it doubtless ameliorated the aggression and greed of man, has failed to bring under control his dominance instinct. Failure in both respects is no doubt attributable to the fact that religion is based upon a spurious knowledge and understanding of man.

Religious beliefs now block man's correct perception of himself and prevent the rational ordering of human relations. Nothing is so froth with emotionalism as religion. Any questioning of man's "faith" evokes an irrational response. The mere existence of another belief is resented as it places in question and doubt the veracity of one's "faith". The stubborn refusal of the Hindu to acknowledge Islam as the true belief drove the Muslims to fits of irrational and murderous behavior in India. Religion, most of which has lapsed into religiosity today, poses a tremendous obstacle to a reordering of life on a rational basis.

The Neo-Christianity of Nicolas Berdeyav, Pierre Teilhard de Chardin and even Arnold Toynbee merely compounds the problem. Chardin, a Jesuit priest and eminent geologist, tries desperately to reconcile the findings of science (that is, evolution) with his religion. But the coining of terms like the Omega Point add nothing to the true understanding of man. The vacillation of Toynbee, in this connection, is interesting. While advocating a return to a *Respublica Christiana* as the salvation of man in his earlier writings Toynbee tends to doubt his own widsom in his latter days. In *Mankind and Mother Earth* he writes:

> . . . On the other hand, it would have been a purposeless and unnecessary and supremely wicked act if a god had created the tiger to prey upon the lamb and had created the human being to slay the tiger and had created the bacillus and the virus to maintain its species by killing human beings en masse.

Thus, at first glance, the progression of life looks evil—evil objectively, even if we discard the belief that this evil has been deliberately created by a god who, if he has done his work deliberately, must be more wicked than any human being has ever yet had the power to be. However, this first judgement on the consequences of the progression of life testifies that, besides the evil in the biosphere, there is a conscience in the biosphere which condemns and abhors what is evil.

The concept of good and evil is an oblique way of dealing with man's dilemma. It permeates the Judeo-Christian religions. Its origin can be traced to Zoroasterism which equated good with the truth and evil with the lie. It was an early attempt to derive some recognition of man's true nature at a time when the knowledge of man's evolution was yet unknown. But good and evil are moral terms that have no meaning in evolution. Evolution is only concerned with the survival of the fittest. And what is or has been good for survival has now turned out to be "evil" for rational human relations. But calling the manifestation of the dominance instinct evil beclouds the true perception of its nature. Man is hardly evil living out his biologic heritage. Giving full vent to his dominance instinct, however, is now inimical to his survival. Recognizing that and bringing the instinct under control is the only way to man's deliverance.

The philosophical thinking of man has been equally ineffective in helping him out of his plight. Most philosophies simply drown in their own semantics and fail completely to give man a better conception of his true nature. Kant's categorical imperative, Hegel's dialectic, Nietzsche's superman, Berkeley's negation of matter, to note only a few, have added little to the understanding of man. Philosophical thinking must be predicated on the most advanced accumulation of knowledge to cope realistically with man's problems.

Then there are the host of spurious beliefs that befuddle the minds of men like astrology, scientology, the numerous cults and mysticisms. These too must be jettisoned on the way to the true perception of man's role on earth.

Western man, who now dominates the world, shall have to disabuse himself of the notion that he is a thing apart from the rest of life on earth. For some time he was aware that his biology differed little if at all from other animals. Modern biology now shows that man is the product of accidental genetic mutation like the rest of life on this planet. The Hindus and Buddhists, who outnumber Christians, do not consider man apart from animals and are not plagued with this obfuscation. But their religious and philosophical doctrines of the transmigration of the soul (among humans and animals without differentiation) and nirvana too are spurious knowledge and must be superseded by the more advanced knowledge of the day.

Jacques Monod, who was awarded the Nobel Prize in 1965 for his work on the replication of life, deplores the stubborn adherence of man to this false knowledge of himself. "We would like to think ourselves" he writes in his book *Chance and Necessity* "necessary, inevitable, ordained from all eternity. All religions, all philosophies, and even a part of science testify to the unswerving, heroic effort of mankind desperately denying its own contingency".

There are some who question whether science has the ultimate answer. Frequently science is challenged for not being able to provide an answer beyond the Big Bang. The conclusion then drawn is that since science does not have the answer the "cause" of the Big Bang is a supernatural force, a God. Aside from the spurious nature of such reasoning an intellectual exercise of this genre is mostly irrelevant. To know what caused the Big Bang, interesting as it would be, would add little or no knowledge that would affect the salvation of man on earth. Knowledge of the universe and its origin (assuming the Big Bang theory proves out) gives man all the understanding he needs of the fundamental forces that effect his life. He must work out his reformation within that context.

On the other hand to revere science, to make of it another religion, is equally irrational. Science is not a thing to worship. It is an intellectual process for the acquisition of knowledge by man of the universe in which he exists. Moreover, it is not omnipotent, for the advancement of knowledge frequently supercedes or renders obsolete former scientific truths. But science is the only means through which man can acquire the necessary perception of himself and the universe to enable him to reorder his life and live in affinity and cooperation with his fellow man.

But is man, any man, really capable of a rational life. Rational behavior would be predicated on cooperation and affinity—not dominance and hostility—and should embrace a fair and equitable distribution of the wealth derived from man's technology. The problem of defining a fair and equitable distribution of this wealth immediately poses an obstacle to cooperation and affinity. It would not seem that egalitarianism is the solution. Creative persons, particularly in the technological sense, should be specially reward-ed as their efforts benefit the non-creative. Moreover, historical evidence appears to support the conclusion that without incentives (or compulsion) a society's technological innovation and productivity of wealth declines. Egalitarianism might, therefore, result in the equal distribution of poverty. It is noteworthy, in this connection, that the communist nations have not been able to establish the Marxist doctrine "From each according to his abilities, to each according to his needs". On the other hand, it is conceivable that mankind could achieve a mental conditioning that would accept egalitarian-ism coupled with a social responsibility whereby everyone would produce according to his ability. But scanning the human horizon past and present one can only view such possibility with disbelief.

Yet the struggle over the surplus product of his technology has been the primary cause of man's despair and unhappiness. The greed of the ruling elite throughout history has normally been carried to such extremes where the dominated majority was deprived of the fruits of its labor to the point of malnutrition and starvation. Even those who shared more fairly in the distribution reacted with resentment, envy and hate toward the wealthy. The rich in turn lived in fear of the mass of men who envied them their wealth. The imperial Roman was haunted by the fear that every slave was a potential enemy within. Murder, robbery, thievery and other crimes resulted from this struggle over wealth. And when the maldistribution of wealth became intolerable to the dominated majority a revolution would erupt with internecine warfare leaving much bad blood on the pages of the history of man's inhumanity to man.

An argument can be made not without merit that permitting maximum competitiveness in economic affairs provides the necessary incentives for greatest technological development and productivity which elevates everybody's distributive share of the prosperity of a society even though such system results in great disparities in wealth. In essense that has been the economic system of mankind generally throughout history. Western civilization has glorified the system to near religious dimensions. Unfortunately, it has also brought great dissatisfaction and despair to mankind. Various attempts have been and are being made to ameliorate its more inequitable aspects but the struggle over wealth continues. At this time there is a vicious conflict between the corporations, organized labor and the bureaucrats for a greater share of the national product. The socialist societies eliminated the first two groups but only at the price of making the bureaucrats all powerful. They now appropriate to themselves a disproportionate share of the wealth not through ownership of factors of production but through control of the fruit of their production.

Others contend that the struggle over wealth will cease once adequate economic growth is achieved so that there will be plenty for all. That, of course, is not possible until man has emancipated himself from the dominance instinct. Human greed knows no bounds! A person in the grip of the dominance instinct can never be satisfied with his share of the wealth. In America a family of four is considered below the poverty level (as of 1979) if it's income is less than $6700. That is 50 times the income or more of two-thirds of mankind living in Asia, Africa and Latin America!

Yet this conflict over the distribution of wealth is eclipsed by the struggle among nations to dominate each other and the world. This poses the greater danger to the demise of humanity. But here too attempts to date to ameliorate, let alone eliminate, the danger of one sector of mankind unleashing the awesome energy of man's burgeoning technological innovation for destructive purposes against another sector have been unsuccessful. The League of Nations and the United Nations have been largely failures in this respect. This danger to the survival of mankind too depends upon man's emancipation from his dominance instinct.

As man then approaches the 21st century what are his prospects for survival. Since there seems to be no quick and effective way to free man of the dominance instinct and no way to curb his technological innovation it would appear that man is, at the moment, programmed for destruction. The only way to salvation lies in the accumulation and widespread dissemination of a true knowledge and understanding of man and his place in the universe that alone can liberate humanity from the destructive grip of the dominance instinct programmed by nature into his genes in bygone eras of the evolution of life on earth.

Index

Abelard and Heloise, 361–62
Abgarus the Arab, 160, 162
Abu Bakr, 295
Acquinas, Thomas, 395
Adler, Mortimer, 114
Adornment, 394–5; cosmetics, 395; foot binding, 394–95, 600; hair dyes, 394; jewelry, 395; perfumes, 395; pompadour, 394; sexual stimulation, 395; wigs, 394
Aeschylus, 445, 449, 505
Agriculture, 63, 92–99, 104, 207, 466, 473–75, 537, 541, 553, 560, 602; Americas, 93; Catal Huyuk, 92, 466–67; China, 92, 581, 583, 605, 609; cotton/sugar cane, 93, 495, 530, 542; domesticated animals, 92, 93–102, 466, 467, 469, 475; Egypt, 92, 93, 466; Harrappa, 92; irrigation, 92, 466, 468, 474, 475; horsepower, 94, 99, 100; Jarmo, 92, 466; Jericho, 92, 468; plow, 99; rice, 93, 324, 581, 605; slaves/serfs, 102, 103, 107, 504, 506, 518, 554, 553–54, 584; Sumeria, 92, 466; wheat/barley, 92, 324, 466, 467, 469, 473, 581
Ajunta and Ellora, 379, 408, 553, 554
Akkadians, 472
Akbar, 71, 296, 409, 559–60
Akhenaton, 288, 439, 478, 492
Albuquerque, Alfonso de, 562
Alcium, 360
Alexander I, Tzar, 308–9
Alexander the Great, 93, 97, 98, 101, 158, 160, 166, 167, 208, 365, 404, 480, 500, 507–10, 511, 514, 516, 525, 545, 548
Alexius, Comnenus, 299
Al-Mansur, Caliph, 146
Alpha centauri, 27, 93
Al Sufi, 14
Ambrose, 359

Americans (USA), North European colonials, 285, 537, 610; architecture, 374, 377; English speaking peoples, 167, 532, 539; cuisine, 338; entertainment, 456, 460–2; foxtrot, 436; industrialization, 189, 530, 537; leadership of West, 285, 539–40; literature, 442; nuclear holocaust, 620; overconsumption of wealth, 621; sports, 457–60; superpower, 225, 235, 312; Vietnam, 314, 320, 539, 621
Amethyst Incident (1949), 257
Androcles and the Lion, 455
Andromeda, 13
Anthony, Marc, 162–3, 480, 514, 518
Anti-Romanism, 358–9, 405, 419, 420, 430, 521, 531, 532
Antipather of Thessalnico, 119
Anyang, Shang capital, 86, 386, 581
Arabs, history, 293–96, 480, 481, 493, 524–5; architecture, 378–80; calligraphy, 413; cuisine, 323, 343; dance, 430; music, 428; painting, 410, 417; prayer rug, 417
    Arab numerals, 18, 146; jehad, 280, 292–98, 417; Koran, 344, 350, 378, 384, 413, 438; Omayyad/Abbasid split, 295; Persianization, 295, 344, 428; shia/sunni schism, 238, 295; technology, 293–94, 469
Arbogast, Frankish general, 516
Archimedes, 202–3
Architecture, 369–87, 472; arch, 373–75, 495; Catal Huyuk, 370; cave temples, 379–81, 386; Greek columns, 373–75; Gothic, 376–78, 406, 419; Hagia Sophia, 375, 378; Hindu temple, 381–82, 555; Kailasa, 380, 555; Macchu Picchu, 387; mastabas, 371–72; modern, 374, 377–78; mosque, 378–81; Mughal, 382–85; pendatives, 375; pagodas, 382, 386; Pantheon, 375; Parthenon, 373–